FLORIDA STATE
UNIVERSITY LIBRARIES

MAR 26 1999

TALLAHASSEE, FLORIDA

Provincial Lives
Middle-class Experience in the Antebellum Middle West

Provincial Lives tells the story of the development of a regional middle class in the antebellum Middle West. It traces the efforts of waves of Americans to transfer their social structures, behavior, and values to the West and construct a distinctive regional middle-class culture on the urban frontier. Intertwining local, regional, and national history, as well as social, immigration, gender, and urban history, the author examines how a succession of settlers from "good" society – farmers and entrepreneurs, followed by capitalists, professionals, and "genteel" men and women from the urban East – interacted with, accommodated, and compromised with those already there to construct a middle-class society and culture. The author explores key phases in regional social development through a series of remarkably rich portraits of antebellum local and regional social life. A New England family who organized a regional support system stretching between St. Louis and the upper Mississippi river valley between 1810 and 1840; the men who established order among the predominantly male society of the urban frontier by creating a male subculture in Keokuk, Iowa, in the 1840s; the "gentlemen" and "genteel" women who struggled to introduce and cultivate the culture of gentility in towns across the region; and the lawyers and urban boosters who formed regional business, professional, and social networks in the 1850s each contributed to this story of regional social development. *Provincial Lives* explores social change through the lived experience of the actors themselves as they employed their understandings of self, gender, class, and culture to construct social order and contribute to the development of a western urban middle class while still remaining members of a national society and playing a role in shaping the emergence of middle-class culture across the United States.

Timothy R. Mahoney received his doctorate in history from the University of Chicago. He has won the Throne-Aldrich Award of the State Historical Society of Iowa and has received the Beveridge Grant of the American Historical Association, the National Endowment for the Humanities Fellowship, and the Mayers Fellowship of the Huntington Library. He is currently an Associate Professor of History at the University of Nebraska in Lincoln.

Provincial Lives

Middle-class Experience in the Antebellum Middle West

TIMOTHY R. MAHONEY

CAMBRIDGE
UNIVERSITY PRESS

PUBLISHED BY THE PRESS SYNDICATE OF THE UNIVERSITY OF CAMBRIDGE
The Pitt Building, Trumpington Street, Cambridge, United Kingdom

CAMBRIDGE UNIVERSITY PRESS
The Edinburgh Building, Cambridge CB2 2RU, UK   http://www.cup.cam.ac.uk
40 West 20th Street, New York, NY 10011-4211, USA   http://www.cup.org

© Timothy R. Mahoney 1999

This book is in copyright. Subject to statutory exception
and to the provisions of relevant collective licensing agreements,
no reproduction of any part may take place without
the written permission of Cambridge University Press.

First published 1999

Printed in the United States of America

Typeset in Ehrhardt 10/12 pt, in QuarkXPress™ [BB]

A catalog record for this book is available from the British Library

Library of Congress Cataloging-in-Publication Data

Mahoney, Timothy R., 1953–
Provincial lives: middle-class experience in the antebellum Middle West/
Timothy R. Mahoney.
p.   cm.
Includes bibliographical references and index.
ISBN 0-521-64092-X
1. Middle class – Middle West – History – 19th century.   2. Middle
West – Social conditions – 19th century.   3. Middle West – Social life
and customs – 19th century.   I. Title.
HT690.U6M34   1999
305.5′5′097709034 – dc21   98-35800
                                                                CIP

ISBN 0 521 64092 X hardback

Contents

List of illustrations		*page* vii
Acknowledgments		ix
	Introduction	1
1	The structure of provincial society: Native American, French, and American interaction in the upper Mississippi river valley	13
2	Family migration and social development on a "near" frontier	31
	The Hempsteads and Gratiots of St. Louis, 1804–1820	32
	The Hempsteads and Gratiots on a "near" frontier, 1820–1840	39
3	"A common band of brotherhood": Migration, male subcultures, the booster ethos, and the origins of the urban middle class	62
	Migration systems and the structuring of urban society	64
	Keokuk, Iowa: Vigilantism and the booster network	72
	Male subcultures and the booster ethos	83
4	The gentility system in the West	113
	Recognizing gentility	115
	Structuring gentility	120
	Housekeeping and genteel space	129
	The genteel set	134
	Delineating gentility	148
	Genteel family culture	155
5	"Brethren of the bar": Professional culture among lawyers and the regional process of elite aggregation	168
	Fathers of the bar	169

v

Contents

	Circuit riding and the social geography of law	178
	At the state supreme court	190
	"Brethren of the bar"	197
6	Boosters and railroad men: Constructing a regional society	213
	The spatial dynamics of regional society	213
	From lawyers to boosters to railroad men	217
	Convention culture	239
	Railroad society: Excursions, festivals, and jubilees	245
	Epilogue	257
	Appendices	263
	Notes	269
	Selected bibliography	321
	Index	325

Illustrations

1	Upper Mississippi river valley.	12
2	Public announcement of Henry Gratiot's death, Galena, 14 May 1836.	59
3	An 1846 handbill issued by David W. Kilbourne.	74
4	"Squire" or "Garret" Davis, "Lee" McGavic, and members of "The Twenties" dancing set, Keokuk, Iowa, 1854.	102
5	The Cosmopolitan Society program.	105
6	A yellow handbill, c. 1866.	107
7	A yellow handbill, 9 July 1866.	108
8	Mary Hempstead Kenney Lisa, "Aunt Manuel," c. 1868.	160
9	Mrs. Susan Hempstead Gratiot, c. 1847–1850.	161
10	Circuit court districts, 1841–1845.	179
11	Circuit court districts, 1846–1852.	180
12	Lawyers' crossovers between circuits in the 1830s.	186
13	Lawyers' crossovers between circuits in the 1840s.	187
14	Circuit convergences in fall 1841 circuit court schedules.	188
15	A "circular letter."	221
16	A "skeleton map" of the Peoria and Oquawka railroad, 1852.	238

Acknowledgments

Though for most authors writing a book seems to be a solitary endeavor, many people along the way have contributed their time, support, and help in contributing to this book. I thank the Research Council of the University of Nebraska – Lincoln for a Summer Research Fellowship in 1990. The National Endowment for the Humanities provided an academic year's residence at the Newberry Library in Chicago in 1991–1992. There I found myself among a real community of stimulating and rigorous scholars who in various ways – reading manuscripts, discussing ideas, organizing seminars, and providing collegial support – provided the impetus to push forward with this large project. Though, in the end, many of the leads I was pursuing in my research at the Newberry did not make it into the final book, in sharpening my questions and pushing me to think more about the practice of social history, the year at the Newberry propelled me into research and writing from which this book emerged. I also thank those who were in regular attendance at the Chicago Urban History Seminar in 1991–1992. Among the many scholars with whom I had the pleasure to talk and interact at seminars, presentations, colloquiums, or weekly meetings were Jean H. Baker, Kathleen Conzen, Michael Ebner, Laura Edwards, Michael Grossberg, James Grossman, John Hudson, Robert Scarakowski, Anthony Orum, Rima Schultz, and Richard White. I also thank Dympna Callaghan, Beth Newman, and Susan Rosa for support and colleagiality. I thank the Director of Research in 1991–1992, Richard Brown. The University of Nebraska – Lincoln provided me further time to focus on early research and writing with a Faculty Development Leave in the spring of 1993. The Huntington Library, San Marino, California, provided me with a fellowship from May through July 1996. Finally, I thank the Department of History at the University of Nebraska – Lincoln for continued support in producing the manuscript and the maps.

In the course of this project I have visited many historical societies, institutions, archives, and respositories in fourteen states from Maine to California. Whether my

Acknowledgments

stay was short or extended, in every case they were unfailingly helpful and generous with their time. I thank the staffs of the State Historical Society of Iowa, Iowa City, and the State Historical Society of Iowa – Des Moines, the State Historical Society of Wisconsin, the State Historical Library of Illinois, the Missouri Historical Society, the Nebraska Historical Society, the Minnesota Historical Society, the Colorado Historical Society, the Massachusetts Historical Society, the Maine State Archives, the New York Historical Society, the Chicago Historical Society, the American History Center, Austin, Texas, and the Library of Congress. Particular thanks go to Mary Bennett, Curator of Photographs, and Marvin Bergman, Editor of the *Annals of Iowa*, at the Iowa State Historical Society, Iowa City, who were always willing either to talk or help me pursue some minor point on my brief stops there between Nebraska and Chicago. I also thank the members of the staff of the the Washburn-Norlands Humanities Center in Livermore, Maine, who accommodated me during my two visits there in 1993 and 1995. In particular, Billie Gammon, the Director, and Norma Boothby, Librarian, facilitated my work at Norlands, the Washburn family homestead. Subsequent Directors Dorothy Zug and Judith E. Bielecki continued the tradition of generous support and encouragement for those interested in using the rich Washburn collections. I also thank the staffs of the the New York Public Library, Princeton University Libraries, the Huntington Library, the Newberry Library, the Putnam Museum, Davenport, Iowa, the Galena, Illinois, Public Library, and Love Library at the University of Nebraska. I also thank Edward K. Johnstone II, President of the Keokuk (Iowa) Savings Bank and Trust, who responded generously to my request to view the originals of the Caleb Forbes Davis Collection.

I thank those scholars who have read and commented on parts of the manuscript in its various earlier formats. These include the members of the Nineteenth Century Studies Group at the University of Nebraska – Lincoln, particularly, Benjamin Rader, Kenneth Winkle, and Dane Kennedy, as well as my colleagues James Rawley and Stephen E. Kalish. I also thank R. Douglas Hurt, Diane Lindstrom, Howard Chudacoff, Bruce Levine, Thomas Mackey, and David Goldfield for comments or discussions at professional conferences, and Frank Smith, the Executive Editor, and the manuscript readers at Cambridge University Press for support and encouragement.

Introduction

In *River Towns in the Great West*, I told the story of the rise and fall of a regional urban system across the upper Mississippi river valley during the middle of the nineteenth century.[1] American settlers and entrepreneurs, in search of land and economic opportunity, transferred the forces of capitalism across the West, reordering economic arrangements and stimulating urban development. St. Louis emerged as the entrepôt of a dynamic system of interconnected river towns and villages that served as the exchange points for a burgeoning regional market economy stretching across Missouri, Illinois, Iowa, and north into Wisconsin and Minnesota. This system was structured by the interaction between settlers and entrepreneurs, the technology of the steamboat, regional topography, and the environment. Within three decades, however, the extent and carrying capacity of the steamboat, which was the driving force of urban development across the region, reached a point of diminishing returns. In the mid-1850s, the railroads responded by penetrating the system from the east to the west and north of Chicago, where the impact of transportation inefficiencies bore heaviest on local economic development. Within a few years, the railroads triggered external and scale economies that caused the rapid centralization of regional market and industrial activity at Chicago and, to a lesser extent, and somewhat later, at St. Louis. By 1860, the rise of these metropolises, together with continued westward migration and development, undermined and restructured the discursive regional urban system of the Great West.

As important as the story I sought to tell was the complex manner in which I told it. Integrating the histories of systems, groups, towns, and individuals, unfolding across the long, middle, and short term, I provided the broadest possible historical explanation of the process of the development and decline of a regional urban system. From this perspective, the history of any community, town, group, or individual is shaped by the nature and timing of its interaction with the system. Likewise, the structure and dynamics of the system were shaped by the integration of many local or individual events into regional processes. Therefore, national, regional, and local history are intertwined together to create a complex understanding of economic and social change. This structuralist approach to history provides not only a "truly local history" which explores both what is specific and unique, as well as general, typical, or universal about the history of any town, place, or group at any time,[2] but also an integrated history of many and diverse systems which aspires to a "total" history.

River Towns in the Great West focused on explaining the economic–geographic dynamics which created and transformed a regional urban system across the antebellum Middle West. This study examines the development of urban society across the same system during the same time period. My purpose is twofold. On the one hand, I present a framework for the integration of local, regional, and national history. On the other hand, this study, like its predecessor, explores the definition and nature of regional history, and its interaction with broader national narratives and processes as they moved from the East, through the Middle West, and into the West. The framework for such a integrated analysis is to examine the dynamics of economic development from a social perspective. In this study I focus on the same individuals as social, rather than economic beings, operating alone or within families or groups within broader local and regional social systems, while pursuing opportunity, mobility, order, reproduction, satisfaction, or happiness.[3] From this perspective, individuals and groups act within and, therefore, both shape and are shaped by, the dynamics of both local and regional social development. The history of any region, community, social group, family, or individual is structured by the timing and nature of its interaction with the broader dynamics of the larger social system in which it exists. Local or regional society, therefore, is built up or layered by the arrival of different groups, each with their own cultures and agendas, affecting the nature or structure of that society. At any moment, however, regional or local social development was constantly being contoured and altered by the response of locals, whether through resistance, acceptance, or accommodation, to waves of newcomers. Such interactions could change individual action and behavior, define new groups, alter social alignments and coalitions, and restructure local society. Thus, living and acting both locally and regionally, townspeople mediated between parochial and more generalized values and connected themselves to the dynamics of a process of regional social development which they both affected and were affected by. Individual stories or biographies, local and community histories, and the dynamics of regional development thus continually interact with and explain each other, providing the historian the opportunity both to explain change and transformation on any level and to place or fuse any story or stories together into a regional social history.

At the center of this structuralist history of the development of urban society across the upper Mississippi river valley during the antebellum period lies the complex story of the emergence of a distinctive regional middle class. Waves of immigrants arriving in the West between 1800 and the 1850s from different regional social systems and cultures, as well as residents already living in their own social

Introduction

frameworks and cultures in the West, contributed to this social history. Over time, three groups, in particular, played key roles in constructing and defining the regional middle class. Early pioneers and settlers who considered themselves members of "good society" laid the foundation. Some of these people, as well as subsequent settlers – especially entrepreneurs, merchants, and professionals – driven by self-interest and a desire for social mobility, intertwined good society with collective booster activity in towns in the 1830s and 1840s – even if this meant participating in vigilante violence and the predominant male subcultures – and framed the structure. Finally, these groups, along with still later newcomers arriving directly from towns and cities in the East, employed a regional version of the cultural system of gentility to demarcate and define class lines, and provided the finishing touches. At each stage, these groups grafted their predominant values to this social and cultural work-in-progress. Members of "good society" provided the moral imperatives of evangelical Christianity. The boosters fused individual self-interest to collective action and helped construct community. Those who cultivated the male subcultures in the 1840s stifled social instability and a tendency to violence with the glue of fraternity and solidarity. Finally, gentility provided a coherent style and code of behavior which clarifed group identity.

Each of these contributions were made in the course of social experiences within specific social contexts. Initially, during the nascent period of urban development across the upper Mississippi river valley, pioneer villages and towns were but distant outposts of American society in the East. The early settlers from "good society" there, isolated from their home cultures and societies, shared a common frontier culture – fragmented, disorderly, and highly mobile in character – with the indigenous peoples and the French, French–Canadian, and mixed-blood residents of the region. Through accommodations and compromises, they were able, at least for a while, to coexist amid an ever-shifting geopolitical context across Illinois and Iowa. The increasing immigration of Americans after 1815, however, quickly shifted the forces of accommodation in their favor. Demographic power combined with more aggressive governmental policy to remove the Indians, to provide the framework in which settlers sought to recreate the society and cultures from which they had come across the region. In doing so, they developed strategies and established social outposts which would provide a template for both subsequent American and Native–American interactions and frontier social development in the trans-Mississippi West.

Initially, in the late 1810s and early 1820s, broad spaces and insufficient transportation isolated the mix of adventurers, entrepreneurs, and settlers at frontier outposts across the region from the main currents of American life. As individuals, groups, and then waves of settlers swept across whole counties claiming land and filling up towns in a few years, they quickly transmitted the mores, values, and behavioral traits of various regional cultures in the East into the valley. In some towns, this cultural transference took place through the collective logic of extensive family networks, operating as migration systems. Some of these families had connections with the French families from St. Louis, but most of them came from the

East, with the intent of transferring their predominantly rural or village values of "good" society and culture to the West.

As the broad migration streams building across the region encountered a developing regional marketplace operating through the dynamics of a nascent urban system, however, more individuals broke free from rural, family-based migration chains, and migrated within more diverse mixed streams of people directly to and among towns and cities across the region. Within this interurban "entrepreneurial" migration system, men, seeking short-term opportunities or making a tour of the country, were a significant majority.[4] At mining camps, steamboat ports, wood stations, and small villages along the river in the 1820s and 1830s, a predominantly male "proletariat" clustered to compete for local trade or resources, and to gain enough wealth to move on. Though usually ignored in the urban history of the West, these young men from diverse origins pushed the indigenous peoples aside and, amid danger and social disorder, laid the foundations of regional urban society. Common economic goals structured rudimentary cooperative networks. The need for common defense, whether against Native Americans or, a decade later, gangs, desperadoes, or Mormons, provided a further sense of commonality. Yet given the mixed society, in terms of both socioeconomic status and regional origins, in which individuals and groups with different values and attitudes routinely clashed, a fragile social order was forged mostly by cultivating male subcultures. Within these male subcultures, individuals eased competitive pressures and the tendency toward violence through collective modes of behavior and practices which employed sarcasm, dissimulation, and indirection to cultivate solidarity within town. They also engaged in aggressive border management strategies which involved vigilante action against outsiders. In doing so, they established the rudimentary framework of the booster ethos and town society. This distinctive urban subculture which developed across the upper Mississippi urban frontier would serve as a social and cultural framework in which those migrating further west "learned" how to construct urban society. Hence, the practices and behaviors within the urban male subcultures on the urban frontier were transferred into the even more discursive, predominantly male process of urban development which extended across the trans-Mississippi and Mountain West in the 1850s through 1870s and beyond.

It was out of and upon this roughly formed urban society, pieced together from persisters from two or three frontier subcultures, that subsequent settlers in the 1840s and 1850s would construct a more stratified, hierarchical, and institutional society more directly integrated with society in the East. Entrepreneurs, merchants, and professionals, whether immigrants or residents who rose up through local society, increasingly conflated their self-interest with that of the town. With the capital they acquired through surviving intense economic competition, successful merchants and entrepreneurs became boosters. To stabilize their social status, and also to avert violence and disorder, they even more aggressively directed the values of middle-class culture toward self-discipline and social control. In addition to transferring west the values and modes of behavior associated with evangelical Christianity, republican law and order, and market capitalism which they shared

Introduction

with other boosters and members of "good society," they began to employ, amid the relatively classless and disorderly western society, the cultural system of "gentility." They did this to secure their social position and social order in general through material display, mannered behavior, and moral admonition. Whether manifested by the establishment of genteel churches, institutions, associations, and clubs, or by delimiting and demarcating genteel sets, circles, or groups through material consumption and display, scripted behavior and etiquette, and intensified gender roles, gentility structured local society, reframed local politics, and firmly affixed public life to the booster ethos. In doing so, genteel people laid claim to elite status in local societies across the region. Securing their local social standing through persistence, economic achievement, and social differentiation, they began in the late 1840s and early 1850s to associate with others like them within the larger network of relations, or "trans-local communities" in regional society, and created a regional social group or class whose attitudes and actions transcended local concerns. The deepening of these interurban patterns or webs of social interaction set the framework for the development of a more integrated regional social process which, just before and after the Civil War, dramatically rearranged social power and altered the intraregional relationship among town societies.[5]

The members of these emerging urban middle-class enclaves played a central role in building a regional society across the upper Mississippi river valley and the Middle West. This made them, in the absence of a wealthy industrial or aristocratic elite, the brokers of regional society in the 1850s, and the conduits through which that system would be transferred further west in the 1860s and 1870s. In the towns of the Great West the middle class transferred a cultural and social system which middle-class people had only just formulated in the older towns across New York and Ohio and tested its ability to shape social order in the West (which they saw as western extensions of the "North") and in the whole of the United States. Small enclaves of "middle-class" people, using the towns of early Middle West as testing grounds for a cultural system, thus made those towns, as one historian argues, the embodiment of republican ideology in the 1850s.[6] If they could replace parochial localized versions of this social system with a more accessible generalized model, middle-class gentility could be transferred and reproduced endlessly from town to town no matter the local context. If this could be done, a new scale of social diffusion occurring at the national level would give the middle class broader hegemonic power and enable it to control and shape the mainstream of American society.

But no sooner had the middle-class elites of many towns and cities across the Middle West achieved social control, than new economic forces began to rearrange the structure of the regional system and undermine the power of those away from the center of regional economic–urban development.[7] The economic geography of railroads reshaped the structure and dynamics of the regional economy. By generating external and scale economies, larger firms, centrally located, gained control of markets, triggering intensive centralization and metropolitan development. Across the hinterland new towns on railroad lines rearranged the urban network, while settlement shifted toward the interior and away from the rivers. Unilateral and dependent city–hinterland interactions replaced egalitarian ones. The rise of the metropolis thus reordered and integrated social power across the system and elevated metropolitan society into the arbitrator of regional life and local societies across the system.

This process of regional integration lacked the power, however, to integrate and align all reality in its path according to its dynamics and directives. Divergent local and regional events and processes, and regressive or counteracting trends, evolved apace with or flowed out of the systemic forces of integration and development. In the interstices of the system, contrary tendencies manifested in failure, displacement, disintegration, enervation, decline, or stagnation are as much a part of the story of regional social systemic development as centralization and social development. For example, while migration chains drew diverse people into a common process, such chains also served to reinforce diversity and loyalty to kin, ethnic, local, or "tribal" identities. Nor could economic integration of diverse people into a regional market economy and the rise of an urban middle-class culture control the countervailing forces of individualism, capital mobility, economic specialization and differentiation, and social atomization. Likewise, a diminution accompanied by a resurgence of localism inevitably followed periods of regional integration. While centralization and systemic integration establish social control and homogenization, they also engender resentment and feelings of rejection that can lead to parochial or provincial retrenchment, antipathy, apathy, and exhaustion.

Just as systemic development drew everyone into larger networks, so too it shattered the cohesive worlds of local life in the mid-nineteenth century. Increasingly, life in a world of systems was lived not in overlapping and reinforcing local communities and social groups, but in a segmented web of different groups, defined locally, regionally, and nationally. Cultivating a sense of place became a matter of what aspect of one's life one chose to emphasize: One lived no longer entirely in any one place, but in several places at once, each defined by different criteria. Local society, nested in regional and national societies which it interacted with in countless ways, and localism, based on common experiences, on the belief of local autonomy, and on the belief that local society mirrored the structure of the larger society, eroded, leaving in its wake scores of fractured communities seeking, in the shadow of the metropolis, to reformulate their self-images and find new ways to interact with the new systems that ran their lives. Thus no sooner does one find order and a coherent process of social structuration, than it begins to unravel and disintegrate into several divergent processes which divide, separate, and rearrange various subgroups and individuals with varying interests, loyalties, and agendas.

Though ultimately metropolitan society and the social forces of centralization, integration, and control did prevail and two different regional societies were able to evolve and develop, the contrary forces unleashed by the application of each cultural and social system or implementation of mercantile and then industrial capitalism undermined the strength and cohesiveness of that development. The result was that the first "Great West" in the antebellum Middle West was a multicentered, loosely

Introduction

defined social network, undermined by diversity, racked by internal tensions, and pulled apart by centrifugal tendencies. What might have been a distinctive social and cultural region was, as a result, weakened, leaving it vulnerable to new forces of systemic organization and development which swept across the region and the nation in the years just before, during, and after the Civil War.

The general story of the transformation of one regional social system which is supplanted by another is, therefore, but one line of narrative emphasis following one theme or story line among the many stories in which each entity or process exists and operates. Alternating selectively between the aggregate of development, transformation, and superimposition, and individual, group, and local stories of action, experience, and adjustment, each of which run according to their own dynamics and follow their own concerns and narrative plots, highlights the complexity of the development of a system. This account will, therefore, selectively focus on different parts of different case studies in which the data in each case study provides the deepest insight into social developments that many individuals and groups in many towns or cities in the system, at roughly the same time, were experiencing. Following apparent shifts in focus among the historical actors from regional to local concerns and back in response to the forces pulsing through the region, this history will also shift its focus periodically, from regional to local to individual analysis. Intensive experiential histories of particularly representative families or individuals, for whom extensive records and evidence have survived, will tie together local and regional, individual and group, in roughly a chronological framework, through the antebellum period. Through the perspective of selected individuals, based on contemporary letters or journals, memoirs or autobiographies, records, and genealogies, the shifting patterns of social change and the complex interplay between individual experience, social change, and community structure, and how each shaped or were shaped by the other, will be explored. Like weaving a tapestry, many individual narratives are taken up for a time, then set aside, only to be picked up at a later point. Each intertwines with broader aggregate analysis and generalization, to tell the story of the development of a distinctive and influential culture in American life at mid-century: that of provincial small-town elites in the Middle West between 1800 and 1860. It was a culture which would later send its children into the highest echelons of national power in the East and the heights of corporate hierarchy and culture in the metropolis, as well as across the trans-Mississippi West, to invade, settle, organize, and integrate a new region into the national system which their parents had played a large part in constructing.

Methodologically, the intellectual assumptions and concerns of this work continue where *River Towns in the Great West* left off. Empirically based structuralism argues that the nature and meaning of social, economic, political, or cultural behavior, action, order, and organization at any time are real and empirically observable and are imbedded in and shaped by the structures of slow-to-change economic, social, political or cultural systems, and that as these systems change, the nature and meaning of social relationships and order changes as well. This perspective, when employed in history, seeks through contextualization based in systems or network analysis to provide the broadest possible explanation of the actions, behavior, and development of any individual, group, town, or society on any level of activity. A structuralist argues, however, that even as these systems change, deeper cognitive and cultural unities persist which tie the experiences of people in different subsequent systems together and provide historical continuity. Whether examining the deep underlying characteristics that manifested themselves in human geographical patterns and shaped all behavior through several economic systems across the region, or exploring various aspects of the rise and fall of a system, and the similar experiences of individual towns, groups, or persons within those systems, analysis is always rooted in "harder empirical reality."[8] Though occasional forays which try to discern the social and cultural meaning of a discourse or language may seem sympathetic to the poststructuralist analysis of deconstruction, discourse remains fastened to actions and intentions which are rooted in the precise historical context of real people who lived their lives in an empircally comprehensible past.

My deeper intellectual and methodological purpose lies in asserting the helpful nature of this structuralist empirical approach in enabling social scientists to deal analytically with complex reality. A basic premise of systems analysis is that the distinctive course of events in any one place or unit are explained not by their similarity or representativeness among others like it during the same period, within the same or a similar system, but by the interaction between that place and the system in which it existed. One explains the course of local events not by articulating the stages of local development and showing that they follow an internal linear process of events found in other cases, but by showing how local and regional events intersected at that place and time, as demonstrated, whether directly or circumstantially by the concurrence of the two.[9] Intellectually, such an approach is externalist and contextual, rather than internalist, a distinction made in debates on the formation of personality, the development of ideas in intellectual history, or historical explanation.[10] From the systemic urban historical approach, each place is defined by an amalgamation of its internal characteristics and processes and outside forces that affect the town by varying degrees depending on the degree of interaction and the power of the outside force. Each place, like each person or case, is, therefore, both similar and typical, but nevertheless unique. Unique not just because the people were different, but because the timing, degree, and intensity of the interaction between that town or group and others, as well as the places it interacted with, are specific to that time and place. The ability to discern what is typical and what is unique about any place in its time and place context is one of the things historians contribute to social science and the central goal of local and regional history.

Such a systemic approach enhances an historian's ability to move from local to regional or national analysis, or from individual to group to aggregate behavior. Individual cases can be more precisely understood, and their relationship to other cases clarified, by understanding how each was imbedded in its own web of interactions with the system and outside reality. Whether a case is representative or typical of a set of other places need concern historians less and less. By situating local or individual analysis within a densely woven analysis of the systemic context in which it exists, and delineating the way it interacted with other units and individuals within the system, one can explain what about that individual or society was unique and different, and also comparable to other cases. At the same time one can also do what historians are meant to do, explain events in a specific time and place context. Developing such densely woven explanations lies at the heart of the local history and should be the ambition, as well, of the urban history. Perhaps because the general patterns are understood, what makes places similar to each other interests fewer and fewer scholars. Accounts of general social processes or developments generally told quite well by case studies are rooted in the sampling assumptions and concerns for scientific objectivity and representativeness of a generation ago. Historians now seek to touch the reality of life and explore, discover, and explain how people experienced, responded to, and contributed to the forces of change, in all their nuance and complexity. If this is understood, as much as the sources permit, what makes that place representative of others, as well as unique, should be apparent, and any effective case study achieving this goal can serve as an example for historians of other places, towns, or cities.

The value and purpose of such a systemic approach are increasingly appreciated by urban and economic historians, for whom the dynamics of systems, whether of production, transport, communication, and marketing, are central concerns. Among social historians, however, efforts to understand how social systems were structured, operated, and changed, from both internal dynamics of human life and external forces like economic change, remain much less developed. The analysis of social systems continues primarily by intensive local case studies of one society at one town, community, or neighborhood.[11] Absorbing the dictums of the new local history, their value lies in the discerning the complexity and nuance of the local world they are able to discern and explain. The models employed reflect social complexity, describing grids, matrices, spheres, and architecture of society, often giving the reader a remarkable experiential sense of being alive at that time and in that place. Yet most microhistorical studies that explore the complexity of society and social change in one place leave it to the reader to connect these accounts to broader systemic or aggregate reality.[12] In such studies one encounters gender, class, social, and cultural systems and assumes somehow that they are "distributed," "diffused," "transferred," "extended," or "reproduced" from one place to another. It is often assumed that their character, structure, and ideology were internally generated, evolving from natural development or growth over time. External force arguments that view social change as caused by urbanization, industrialization, or immigration are generally stated but left unexamined. It is assumed that the character of the system is universal and the structures of local, regional, or national societies are parallel and analogous.

As a result individual cases are generally studied in isolation from each other. What is rarely addressed is how the development of a social system in one place interacts with the development of another social system in other locations at the same time. We know little how various local societies affect each other, how social systems are transferred over time and across space, and whether such interactions, between different local societies at different phases of development as shaped by their interaction with the system, alters and changes the general social structure across the system as a whole. In short, we never imagine that among all the local stories of social change is a process of regional social development that parallels regional economic and urban system development, because our methods ignore the interactions between. In addition, we ignore those who lived and acted within this realm, outside the confines of local society to which they remain a transient, unconnected, historical blur. We do not even have a vocabulary to describe the myriad of interactions and relationships that make up the dynamics of this regional process of social development. This work explores this regional social realm between local and national society.[13]

Yet all these structuralist ambitions are focused primarily in telling a story involving thousands of people, in numerous towns and cities, across the middle of the United States in the middle of the nineteenth century. Though the construction of models and the analysis of group behavior with an eye toward their contribution to broader dynamics, patterns, or structures may seem to leave the people out, in fact developing a broader contextual understanding of the general patterns and dynamics of social change deepens one's sense of the story line of countless individuals' lives. So too, such dynamics, patterns, and trends remain the aggregate result of thousands of individual actions made in response to general developments. General forces do not have a life of their own and should not be personified with that power. For all the social–scientific analysis, the story remains a plot with a cast of thousands, most of whom have left only traces or clues of their actions and behavior in aggregate records serially compared or tracked, and fewer of whom have left diaries, notebooks, letters, account books, and memoirs.

Structuralist social–scientific methods use the same sources as those writing biographies or linear narratives. The rules of evidence are more strict: Social scientists demand that data correlate, often statistically, rather than merely associate, thus significantly narrowing the range between action and circumstance in providing circumstantial evidence and thus explaining an argument. Social scientists require several layers of evidence to make a case or demonstrate a point. They tend to argue that events are not as linear, further complexifying their reading of evidence. Nor do they allow the use of general evidence to construct composite portraits. For historians, the precise time and place context of events or activities matters. To a structuralist historian, and most social scientists, a steadfast rule is that a diary, letter, or account book must come from the exact place at the exact time being studied, or its value declines proportionally to its distance in time or place from the time and place of the study. Finally, social scientists eschew the imaginative realm of recreating plausible and factional episodes. If the record is silent, we can speculate over the silence, and present plausible circumstantial scenarios, but we cannot write a narrative or story in a way that gives the unaware reader the impression that this account is based on evidence.[14] Yet, we still tell stories. This, then, is an analytic narrative –

Introduction

in which plot or narrative lies rooted in an understanding of process, not in the literary conventions of the storyteller. It tells the story of a group of people who founded the towns of the antebellum Middle West and sought to make those towns the center of their lives and then, when they realized that the assumptions by which they achieved their goals no longer mattered within a rapidly changing regional urban and economic system, began to create a new kind of provincial life in the hinterlands of the new metropolises.

Figure 1. Upper Mississippi river valley.

1

The structure of provincial society: Native American, French, and American interaction in the upper Mississippi river valley

The origins of the urban middle-class American society that developed across the Middle West during the antebellum period lie in the efforts of French entrepreneurs of St. Louis to acquire wealth from the vast hinterland north and west of St. Louis. For a generation before the War of 1812, members of the leading families of St. Louis had traded for fur pelts with the Indians across the upper Mississippi and Missouri rivers, and mined lead from both Missouri and northern Illinois and southwestern Michigan territory. Operating as a family business, they transferred the values and dynamics of St. Louis society to both mixed-blood and endogamous social outposts across a "near frontier."[1] In doing so, they established the regional economic and social foundations upon which subsequent settlers and entrepreneurs would build outposts of capitalist middle-class society. The pattern of these initial economic and social forays across the adjacent region was shaped by the interplay between topography, the geography of resources, and the residential patterns and social dynamics of the Native American and mixed-blood societies they encountered across the upper Mississippi River, and prefigured the patterns and dynamics of subsequent societies and cultures across the same region. Therefore, examining the nature of these initial systems can deepen our understanding of some of the dynamics and pressures which shaped subsequent regional urban society in the 1830s through 1860s.

In spite of the great river which traversed the Middle West, each of the social systems which developed across it were centered to the east around the Great Lakes. Those who lived across the upper Mississippi river valley occupied frontiers, or hinterlands, which were always threatened, controlled by, or drawn into dependent relationships with social, economic, and cultural centers to the east, south, southeast, or even the north. The forces of structure, order, and centrality which sought to order various regional social systems across the valley would continually struggle against a general tendency toward provincialization or peripheralization into a backwater. As a result, most of the societies that formed across the region would have a highly mobile, unstable, and discursive quality.

When the periphery of American society, made up of French and American traders, settlers, entrepreneurs, and military personnel, moved across the upper Mississippi river valley between 1780 and 1810, for example, they found themselves, consciously or unwittingly, moving onto already deeply contested ground. Long occupied by two other societies, the region north of the Illinois River and across the Mississippi river valley had become, in the course of the shifting geopolitics of both New France and Native American tribes and villages, an insecure, in-between area. This was due primarily to its location west of the "pays d'en haut," a system of contacts, negotiations, and accommodations across the Great Lakes region which the French- and Algonquin-speaking peoples had formed in response to first the power of the Iroquois and then the British. By the late seventeenth century the eastern edge of the valley had become a vast "refugee center," a mixed and confused world of refugees from fractured tribes who had fled west from Iroquois hegemony and gathered around major French trading posts. The Sauk and Fox, two tribes which remained intact, migrated west, occupying central Wisconsin south of Green Bay. There, like other residents, however, they remained wedged between the Iroquois "hammer" on the east and the Sioux "anvil" to the west.[2] Both the French and Indian residents of the region lived remote from the centers of activity or geopolitical power within their societies and thus reacted to outside forces of change.

Though peace between the Iroquois and French reduced the pressure from the east and enabled these refugee centers to coalesce into "village blocs," the migrations of several tribes to the west continued to destabilize the geopolitics of the western periphery of the Great Lakes region.[3] Pressured from the north by Chippewas, on the west by Sioux, on the south and southeast by the Illinois Confederacy, and involved in continual war, the Sauk and Fox moved southwest across the upper Mississippi. Meanwhile continued warfare with the French over the fur trade, which extended east to Detroit, nearly replaced the whole of the tribe with captured warriors from other Algonquin tribes. By 1764 the Fox occupied villages around the lead mines at Dubuque and at the Rock River, while the Sauk established a large village on the Des Moines River above its confluence with the Mississippi in southeastern Iowa.[4] Yet they remained caught between enemies, the Illinois on the east, the Kaskaskias on the south, the Osages, Missouri, and Pawnees on the west,[5] and the Sioux on the north and west. Ironically, their move toward the river only made them more vulnerable to Sioux aggression, which increased around 1800. The great river, along which the Sauk and Fox located a number of summer villages and crossed their territory, was, simultaneously, a central artery, a border, a route to alliance and trade, and a path to war.[6]

As the British and then, after 1783, the Americans defeated one Algonquin tribe after another, refugees fleeing west were absorbed into the Sauk and Fox tribes, increasing their numbers while undermining their stability. Unprotected by treaty obligations and feeling duped by the treaty of 1804 in which they gave away most of their lands between the Rock River and the Wisconsin River to the Americans, the Sauk and Fox became two of the most steadfastly anti-American tribes. As Americans moved north, acquiring land from the Kaskaskias, erecting forts, and encouraging settlement, the geopolitical position of the Sauk and Fox became even more tenuous.[7] Though their main villages remained in the Rock River country, most of the Sauk and Fox yielded to American pressure and moved to points on the Missouri River. Discontented with the lack of trading opportunities around their new home, however, they soon returned to their old villages. Unable to make peace around 1810 with either the Sioux, their traditional enemies to the north and west, or the Americans, whom they held in disdain, they were reluctantly pushed or drawn into an alliance during the War of 1812 with the British, who, of course, were unable to help them. Meanwhile, American encroachment into the Lead Region between 1816 and 1820 further narrowed Sauk and Fox hunting grounds and pushed them west and north, where they confronted and quickly went to war against the Sioux, Omaha, and Oto tribes.[8]

The French, who had, for a generation or more, served as a mediating, ordering, and integrating force in the valley, were also, by 1810 or so, being differentiated by economic and social forces and thus increasingly less able to stabilize and order the discursive, volatile social geography of the valley. The French population in the valley came initially from a common French Canadian cultural hearth, and through trade, intermarriage, language, and custom had established regional social and economic "dominion" over various native tribes. The geopolitical shifts from French to British (1763), to Spanish (1783), and back to American control of Louisiana (1804), as well as the northward drift of the fur trade after 1800, and the American–Sauk and Fox treaty of 1804 worked to differentiate various roles and structures in the fur trade.[9] In the 1770s, French merchants and traders in vigorous towns like Chartres, Fort Kaskaskia, Prairie du Rocher, Cahokia, and St. Genevieve found themselves without imperial services, cut off from north and south, and peripheralized within the regional fur trade which was coming increasingly under British control.[10] As their trade contracted to their immediate hinterlands, and local economic life reverted to local self-sufficiency, more aggressive members of this society reconnected themselves to the regional trading network by moving to St. Louis, beyond American control, with the intention of joining St. Louis merchants in making the town the center of the regional fur trade with the Indians.[11] Their success is evident in the record of Auguste Chouteau, a prominent St. Louis trader whose trade with the Sauk and Fox averaged $60,000 a year by the early 1800s.[12]

But as the trade drifted north, more French traders and voyagers, who in more prosperous times had settled in and around the French towns and at forts and posts across the "pays d'en haut," followed the fur trade in that direction. In the 1770s and 1780s the numbers of resident French voyagers around the Sauk village above the mouth of the Rock River, at trading towns recently established at Peoria and especially at Prairie du Chien, which the Indians ceded to the British in 1781, and at smaller "jackknife" posts at Chicago, Kankakee, and Milwaukee, were increasing. A number of French residents of Prairie du Chien, at a later date, were immigrants from the American Bottom in Illinois.[13] As this migration continued, more of these French residents were drawn under the umbrella of Anglo–French influence centered at Montreal, Detroit, and Mackinac.[14]

As the economic system began to divide between those who traded out of St. Louis and those who settled among the Indians, French society was also separating into two subcultures differentiated not only by residence vis-à-vis the northward shifting fur trade and the frontier that divided American and Indian spheres of influence across the region, but also by blood. A steady stream of émigrés from France arrived in the center of the valley after 1790, and intermarried with the merchants and traders in towns in French Illinois, Missouri, and at St. Louis, while maintaining, via New Orleans, more direct social and cultural connections to France and Switzerland than to Montreal. As more residents of the French villages intermarried, their European blood descendants increasingly became distinguished from the mixed-blood offspring of the French Canadian traders, couriers du bois, and voyagers who had spread out from the village core to participate in the fur trade across the "pays d'en haut," and intermarried with Indians during the eighteenth and early nineteenth centuries.[15] In particular, St. Louis traders who had routinely intermarried with the native populations while maintaining their French marriages to white women retrenched toward more endogamous relations by 1810. French society in the region was, therefore, gradually dividing between an endogamous St. Louis base and a more mixed-blood northern base. The latter would be drawn toward a British sphere of influence and out of the main currents of regional history. The former would intertwine with American social and political agendas and thus play a central role in restructuring regional society after 1815 and establishing the framework upon which American society would develop.

In large part, this ethnic and economic bifurcation of French society shadowed and was affected by both the deepening geopolitical predicament of the Sauk and Fox tribes and the growing influence of Americans. As the Sauk and Fox retreated before American encroachment and migrated north in pursuit of trade, many voyagers simply followed their traditional trading partners. Tied by marriage and mixed-blood offspring and relations to the Native Americans, French Canadians and mixed-blood people came increasingly under Indian influence and supported their policies. Their movements also brought them under the sphere of the British and French Canadian traders out of Detroit and Montreal. By 1805, the population of mixed French and Indian people, numbering about 2,000 in Illinois and southern Wisconsin, and as many as 10,000 across the rest of Michigan territory, was centered at Prairie du Chien, Peoria, around the Fox village near the confluence of the Rock and Mississippi rivers, and in settlements or outposts along the rivers across northern Illinois and southern Wisconsin.[16]

The relentless migration of Americans from the south, however, further complicated the geopolitical position of the mixed-blood residents of "Chickago," Peoria, and the southern fringe of the fur trade country. As more French and Americans traded with the Indians around 1800, they employed mixed-blood people as translators, informers, and agents. Moreover, as American administrative power spread north under the mantel of the Territory of Illinois, many mixed-blood people became, unwittingly, citizens of the United States and began to assume that they were new Americans. During the War of 1812, mixed-blood loyalties, especially in the southern areas of the region, began to shift to the American side. The Native Americans, aware of this, increasingly assumed that Frenchmen, including those with mixed parentage, who traded with St. Louis were on the American side.[17]

Paradoxically, the Americans, though they hired mixed-blood men as intermediaries, generally assumed that the mixed-blood people, even those who had worked for them and lived in Prairie du Chien, Peoria, and Chicago, were politically pro-British and pro-Indian. They also believed that a mixed-blood presence, by maintaining contacts with the British, prevented Americans from drawing the Indians into a dependent trading relationship. An alien, invisible group, the mixed-blood population became pawns in a geopolitical struggle. Living in an in-between realm within an increasingly black and white world, they were forced to assimilate into one side or the other, or disappear.[18]

The French society of the valley was centered, of course, in the French families who founded St. Louis, in particular the Lacledes and the Chouteaus, into which newcomers from French Illinois, Gabriel Cerré and Charles Gratiot (pron. "Grash-it"), soon intermarried. Cerré's children married into the Chouteau, Lamy, and Soulard families. Gratiot, on the other hand, married Victoire Chouteau, the eldest daughter of Pierre Laclede, founder of the city, and his consort Madame Marie Thereze Bourgeois Chouteau, and then allied himself in the fur trading business with Madame Chouteau's sons by a previous marriage to Rene Auguste Chouteau, Pierre Chouteau and Auguste Chouteau.[19] Though both Pierre and Auguste Chouteau took Osage wives with whom they had mixed-blood children, as did two of Pierre Chouteau's sons by his second wife Brigitte Saucier, Cyprien and Frederick, who both worked for the Chouteau–Sarpy Fur Company, they seem to have been the last of their clan to do so.[20] In time, Pierre and Auguste Chouteau legitimized their marriages only to French wives. Pierre Chouteau's marriage to his second wife Brigitte Saucier connected him, through the marriages of her sisters, back to the important merchants William Morrison and Pierre Menard of Kaskaskia, Illinois.[21]

The children of Charles Gratiot and Victoire Chouteau married into the Labbadie, Cabanné, Maclot, Perdeauville, and Billon families, and also back again into the Chouteau family (a daughter Emille married her first cousin, Pierre "Cadet" Chouteau, son of her mother's brother and his first wife Pelagie Kiesereau). Another son, Henry Gratiot, married Susan Hempstead, daughter of a Yankee lawyer, Stephen Hempstead.[22] Her brothers had married French women, the sister of one of whom married Paul L. Chouteau, son of Pierre Chouteau and thus a cousin of Susan Hempstead Gratiot's husband, Henry Gratiot. For Paul L. Chouteau, this allied him back to the St. Vrains, the de la Beaumes, and de Launiers. In two generations, the same families, the Chouteaus, Gratiots, Labbadies, Maclots, and Bertholds, intermarried with cousins at least six times. In one instance, two children of Pelagie Chouteau and her husband Sylvestre Labbadie married first cousins, children of her siblings Pierre and Victoire Chouteau.[23] Such endogamy interwove the French clans, complicating local genealogy (to the delight of genealogists and frustration of family historians, one of whom, Thomas Scharf, remarked that "all the other [French] residents (or at least two-thirds of them in 1804) were connected with one another in pretty much the same way") and constructed a distinctive, closed society. In fact it became one of the most "tribal" societies in the valley, at the top of which Madame Thereze Bourgeois Chouteau, matriarch of St. Louis, reigned until her death in 1814.[24]

Moving out from this developing vortex of regional society, St. Louis merchants would set out to establish the framework of a new regional trading system. Their actions reoriented the lives of all other French, French Canadian, and mixed-blood residents of the valley in relation to St. Louis. As St. Louis merchants set out across the region to establish or extend trading networks, they interacted with other French residents across the region and demarcated indelible lines of interaction and differentiation, which would shape regional social developments for a generation. Some responded by migrating to St. Louis. Others participated, along with the Indians, in trade with St. Louis, allowing market relations to penetrate their lives and drawing them into dependent relations with St. Louis's merchant families. Still others sought to evade or compete against St. Louis merchants. Finally, the St. Louis French, through their trading interactions with Indians, would help shape American Indian policy. First they acted as intermediaries between the Americans and the Indians, and then as transmitters and facilitators of American economic and social goals and agendas. Early on, the common birthright and language that the St. Louis French shared with French Canadians and mixed-blood people, plus their long previous associations with the Indians, mollified, at least for a while, the Indians' suspicion that the St. Louis French had come under American influence after 1804. This enabled a few of the St. Louis French to continue through about 1820 to serve a similar liaison role between the Indians and mixed-blood people and the Americans, as the mixed-blood people had served between them and the Indians. Ironically, however, the St. Louis French, by extending market activity, transforming Indian life, and intermarrying with American settlers, would also serve as the conduits through which Americans would implement their more aggressive policies. By tracing the emergence of these various strategies, one can observe the dynamic origins of the economic and social structures of an American regional society.

While many French merchants in other French towns and villages across Illinois and Missouri, like the Menards of Kaskaskia, were drawn into St. Louis and married into St. Louis society, others joined the efforts of St. Louis merchants to trade across the region or established trading relations with them. The first and only French Canadian in the upper valley who regularly traded and developed a relationship with St. Louis merchants was Julien Dubuque, who in the 1780s established an outpost on the site where Dubuque, Iowa, would be settled.[25] Louis Honoré Tesson, who acquired a grant of land near the later site of Montrose, Iowa, also engaged in trade with St. Louis merchants, and planted an apple orchard with "trees carried from St. Charles Missouri on the back of a mule" which later settlers in Lee County in the 1820s and 1830s would encounter and marvel at, but he remained alone in the wilderness before selling his land in 1803.[26] Likewise, a man "named Du Bois" who lived just opposite Dubuque, Iowa, on the river bank south of the village of Dunleith, Illinois, about 1810, was there only briefly.[27]

Dubuque, a Canadian, deftly navigated the developing rift between St. Louis French and French Canadian and mixed-blood, pro-British interests. By remaining neutral, he managed to interact with both the Indians and mixed-blood people (he apparently had an Indian or mixed-blood wife) while remaining independent enough from the St. Louis French and Americans to trade with them without accepting their political agenda. Since 1788 Dubuque had gradually opened the "Spanish mines" and shipped fur pelts and lead semi-annually to Auguste Chouteau of St. Louis, a merchant who had extensive connections with the nearby Sauk and Fox.[28] When St. Louis merchants sought to enter the mining business directly, in 1804 Dubuque sold Chouteau a half-interest in the mines. But neither this sale nor the arrival of Chouteau's nephew, Pierre "Cadet" Chouteau, Jr. (with his wife Emilie), at the mines in 1810 seems to have altered Dubuque's neutrality and turned his multiracial operations into an outpost of St. Louis.[29] Dubuque thus maintained a peaceful relationship with both sides, while also employing mixed-blood people and French Canadians.[30]

In part, Dubuque maintained a middle course by being evasive about his affairs, which Zebulon Pike in September 1805[31] encountered during a fruitless fact-gathering visit to the mines. While trading with the French of St. Louis, Dubuque received recruits to prospect for lead from the mix of Winnebagoes, Mesquakies, and Sauk and Fox who moved across the area. From his village of some forty to fifty Indians and a few mixed-blood and French Canadian traders, Dubuque sent out forays as far as the Apple River in Illinois, and north and south along the west side of the Mississippi, covering nearly the entire Lead Region. Once they discovered lead, Dubuque either allowed Indians to work the mines, if they wanted to, or hired French Canadians and mixed-blood residents probably from Prairie du Chien, where he maintained a residence, to work the mines.[32]

That Dubuque's personality sustained this fragile French–Native American social order is evident, however, in its immediate collapse after his death in 1810. Pierre Chouteau, Jr., of St. Louis, who took over direction of the mines, was unable to sustain the production of lead. Chouteau's apparent loss of control, which involved greater difficulties in acquiring access or cooperation from the Sauk and Fox, seems to suggest that Chouteau himself was increasingly perceived as pro-American in the course of heightening tensions between the British-supported Indians and the Americans who were encroaching northward into the valley just to the south (Fort Madison had been established in 1808, Fort Mason near the site of Hannibal in 1812).[33]

This perception was, of course, supported by the nearby efforts of the St. Louis French to join the Americans to try to penetrate and gain control of the French Canadian and mixed-blood trading center at Prairie du Chien. During the same years that Americans were establishing forts to the south, traders from both St. Louis and Fort Madison ventured north to trade with the Indians at Prairie du Chien, and at the Fever River in the Lead Region.[34] Dubuque's death in 1810 had encouraged the Indians to establish a stronger presence in the Lead Region. When Nicholas Boilvin, an agent for the United States government, traversed the Lead Region in 1810, he noted that Sauk and Fox to the east and Iowas to the west of the river had completely "abandoned the chase" and taken over the mining of lead and traded as much as 400,000 pounds of it with French Canadians at Prairie du Chien. For Boilvin, writing in 1811, this provided an opportunity for the Americans to either purchase or take over the trading village at which several hundred Indians arrived and departed every year. It also enabled the Americans to get rid of the village's Canadian and mixed-blood population, containing some thirty-two families with another sixty nearby families, composed of "men [who] are generally French Canadians, who have mostly married Indian wives; [with] perhaps not more than twelve white females . . . in the settlement." To Boilvin, in the heated context of 1811, such residents were "great dangers" and stood in the way of drawing the Indians into dependent relations with the Americans. If the Americans could, therefore, purchase or take Prairie du Chien, build a fort, and put a trading factory with St. Louis connections in Prairie du Chien, Boilvin argued, market forces would routinize this shift among the Indians to mine and trade lead rather than furs. Though this might deepen their dependency on Americans, he also thought it might make them farmers and facilitate their assimilation into American society. In any case, it would, he argued, compel the mixed-blood residents, who were interested primarily in the fur trade, to retreat to the north.[35]

These immediate opportunities were thwarted, however, by the Indians' political alliance with the British against the Americans in the War of 1812. In 1812, the Sauk and Fox, and their temporary allies the Kickapoos, Potawatomis, Winnebagoes, and Osages, launched a series of assaults from the north to push back American encroachments and, indirectly, St. Louis French incursions on a line running from the St. Charles District west of St. Louis to Fort Madison to the Dubuque mines to Prairie du Chien, back down to Peoria and northeast to Chicago. In doing so, they demarcated a line of division across the region, striking against St. Louis French, Americans, and mixed-blood people alike, all of whom they associated with American power at St. Louis.

Initially their attacks centered primarily on the few Americans residing in the north. At Prairie du Chien resident Americans as well as French Canadians were "terrorized" by the Indians and in May 1812 the agent Boilvin was forced to return to St. Louis for several years. Though the Indians were determined to "revenge themselves against the Americans," they remained unclear whether they would "go to war again[st] the French people or not." By mid-year, Pierre Chouteau, Jr., was forced from the Dubuque mines by Indian harassment.[36] To the east John Kinzie, a French Canadian trader at Chicago, came under increasing suspicion as a "spy" and was forced to shut his post in midsummer. Another agent, Thomas Forsythe, Kinzie's half-brother,[37] was accused by the Native Americans of allying with the

Provincial society

Americans, and was told "to go down to St. Louis," in spite of his reply that he was "not acquainted with a single individual in St. Louis country." Likewise Antoine LeClaire, Sr., a French Canadian trader working for the Americans, found it necessary to disguise his association with them, and found the Sauks unwilling to talk about their country, fearful that he would "pilot the Americans to their villages." Meanwhile, on the Mississippi, a series of shooting incidents the summer before between Americans and both the Sauk and Fox and French traders had made it more difficult for Maurice Blondeau, a mixed-blood man appointed by the Americans as agent to the Indians at Fort Madison, to maintain amicable relations. When in September, the Sauk and Fox launched an assault on Peoria and destroyed the village, its mixed-blood population of some forty people, including Antoine LeClaire, Sr., and his son, Antoine Jr., suffered the brunt of the assault.[38] As the Indians attempted to draw a line to try to halt American encroachment, the mixed-blood people living near the Americans were suddenly caught on the wrong side.

Or, perhaps more accurately, along an imprecise line, or frontier, drawn between the dominant opposing societies. This line traversed Illinois territory roughly from "Chicago" to Peoria to Rock Island and down the Mississippi. Topographically, the line skirted the Rock River valley and crossed the Mississippi at the upper rapids. In later systems, forts, trading posts, towns and cities were settled along the line, and steamboat routes, roads, and eventually railroad lines would pass along this corridor (see Chapter 6). In 1812, while the Indians from the north attacked settlements along the line, most of which were inhabited by mixed-blood people and French Canadians, Ninian Edwards, Territorial Governor of Illinois, commissioned Captain Thomas Craig to go up to Peoria, which was located on the line, to arrest "certain persons," mixed-blood people and French Canadians, "who were there for the purpose of assisting the savages in murdering the frontier settlers." From Craig's "Indian-hating" perspective, the chief culprit was Thomas Forsythe and the mixed-blood "citizens" of Peoria over whom he had influence. Even though Forsythe had been allegedly attacked by the Indians, Craig was convinced that he was in collusion with the Indians because he was not afraid or concerned, but was "sulky and obstinate" "g[iving] rise to the strongest suspicion of his not being a friend," and, after being taken a prisoner, he refused to stay overnight on the boat in the river, for the sake of security, but camped on shore, always preferring the "Indian side for their camping ground." The mixed-blood residents were assumed to be enemies and reportedly "were abus[ed]" by Craig while en route to St. Louis.[39]

A series of petitions to the Governor of Illinois failed to clarify the mixed-blood people's anomalous position and placate American suspicions. Retreating to St. Louis the mixed-blood Peorians hired Edward Hempstead (brother to Stephen), prominent Yankee lawyer in St. Louis, to represent them in filing petitions of redress to the State of Illinois. Hempstead, the first American lawyer to break into St. Louis society, would, as we will see in Chapter 2, play a significant role in fusing American and French society in St. Louis. The mixed-blood petitioners felt, no doubt, that an association with Hempstead would demonstrate their loyalty. They portrayed themselves as residents "for many years" who were among those "white people residing west of [the] Detroit River" who, as loyal citizens of the United States, "kn[ew] full well the assistance we could render to our country in giving information of the movements of the Indians." The French and mixed-blood residents of Peoria, therefore, sought restitution for the willful destruction of their property and the wounding of their self-esteem. Particularly galling to them was that having successfully maintained their strategic position among the Indians under Thomas Forsythe, they should be attacked by a "military force of [our] own countrymen, who, under the most absurd pretexts, rob[bed] them of property, burn[ed] their houses, and insult[ed] their persons," a fate unacceptable to citizens of the country who have "hazarded every thing in its defence."[40]

Among the Peoria petitioners of 1812 was Antoine LeClaire, Jr. The second of two sons of Antoine Sr., a native of Montreal, and his wife, the daughter of a Potawatomi chief, who resided at St. Joseph, a "jackknife" trading post since 1792, LeClaire was born in 1797. LeClaire followed his father in his trading activities to Milwaukee in 1800. There, among several other mixed-blood traders, the elder LeClaire operated a trading post supplied out of Detroit. In 1809 he and his family moved to Peoria, where their activities came under American influence, in particular that of Thomas Forsythe, the Indian agent who Thomas Craig was sent north to arrest. After the Peoria debacle, they went south with Forsythe to St. Louis, and afterward were employed by Forsythe, who later headed the Indian department at Portage des Sioux, Missouri. After the death of his father in 1821, Antoine Jr. returned to Illinois and located among the Sauks at the Rock River village of Saukenauk and later nearby at Fort Armstrong and was an interpreter at the treaty which ceded land along the west bank of the Mississippi in Iowa to the Americans. For his services LeClaire received a large grant at the site of Davenport, Iowa.[41]

Though neither Antoine Jr. nor Antoine Sr.'s role in the Peoria affair is clear, it is notable that Elihu B. Washburne, an early American settler in Galena, lawyer, member of Congress, and statesman, who later played a central role in the construction of middle-class American society in the region, was unable, as an historian in 1885, completely to exonerate LeClaire. Remarked Washburne: "Among their numbers [Peoria residents in 1812]" was "Antoine LeClaire, a Canadian half-breed who was the first settler at the point where Davenport, Iowa, now stands. . . . Whatever he might have been in 1812, during his long residence in Davenport he was ever regarded as a most excellent, honorable, and liberal man."[42] In 1838 contemporary land speculator and lawyer Henry S. Austin, from Montrose, Iowa, was equally equivocal, noting, when they had appointed LeClaire a member of a commission to investigate the validity of land claims in the Half Breed Tract in southeastern Iowa (see Chapter 3), "Antoine LeClaire is one of them [the commissioners] and although he is part Indian (Potawatomi I believe) we have confidence in him as a man of integrity, fair judgement and . . . business capacity." As such not very subtle and condescending disclaimers show, LeClaire was considered the exception. Other mixed-blood people who would later try to cross the line into American society would be required to endure similar suspicion and doubt about their character and past loyalty, even after providing considerable service to the Americans.[43]

Meanwhile, to the north, the British retook Prairie du Chien in July 1814, and with Sauk and Fox support defeated an American relief force from St. Louis, in which both Edward and Stephen Hempstead were members, at Rock River in August 1814 (see Chapter 2). In response, most of the remaining Americans in the area retreated to the south. For a year, the Indians, with British support, were able to completely control the region around it, including the Lead Region. Nevertheless, the favorable outcome of the war for the Americans suddenly shifted the Indians' relationship with the Americans. With the British out of the way, the Americans could now proceed to undertake a more aggressive strategy to control the native tribes in the region. In 1816 Richard Graham envisioned the establishment of a fort, trading post, or agency at Prairie du Chien as part of a strategy to bring the native peoples under American control. He reported that the Foxes were "concentrating" around the mines with the "intention of working them." He suggested that the Americans continue their strategy of trading for lead because such trade increased the Indians' incentives to mine lead, which, by giving "them an idea of the value of fixed property, out of which a taste of agriculture and raising stock would grow," would civilize them and bring them within the American sphere.[44]

This recommendation was part of a broader American initiative in 1816 of establishing forts and connected trading posts along the upper river to trade with the Indians and opening the region to American settlement, a pervasive strategy conflating hegemonic geopolitical, capitalist, and social goals to support the expansion of American life into the region. Founded in 1816, Fort Crawford at Prairie du Chien and Fort Armstrong on Rock Island, rather than forming a clear military demarcation between American and Indian on an east–west line running across the river south of the Lead Region, cut deep into Indian territory on a north–south line along the river and established trading and military outposts. By carving new spheres of control and circumscribing the main Indian populations that remained at Saukenuk, up the Rock River; in a village along the Mississippi directly north of the Rock River and across from Rock Island; around Prairie du Chien; and at a village near the lead mines at Dubuque under American surveillance, the forts emboldened settlers to establish themselves within the midst of the Native Americans. This outpost system created "islands" of American society amid Indian society, resulting in sometimes surprisingly close interaction between two groups that in certain locales approached being a bicultural society.[45]

In this broader American policy the French Canadians and mixed-blood people were placed in an even more precarious position. In 1816, American officials expressed a desire to clear the French Canadians and mixed-blood people entirely from Prairie du Chien, though those people did not seem to care who ruled over them. When the Americans began arriving that summer, first in a trading expedition to set up a factory, and then a military mission to establish Fort Crawford, "they treated all the inhabitants as squatters and aggressors ... and disloyal intruders ...

to be driven out at will." Dividing their perception of French Canadians between loyal and disloyal people, the American government proceeded to rehire or continue appointing only French Canadians and mixed-bloods who had proved their loyalty as go-betweens with the Indians. By 1816, French trader Nicholas Boilvin was back as agent at Prairie du Chien, a position he held until 1827. Maurice Blondeau, a mixed-blood man who had been agent before the war at Fort Madison, was appointed agent at the Rock River settlement, evidence of the continuing American policy of using Canadian and mixed-blood traders as intermediaries.

Nevertheless, American officials increasingly hired their own or St. Louis French, some with associations to the American Fur Company, to serve as agents and traders. Richard Graham, a Virginian, was stationed at Fort Clark at Peoria, and another American, George Davenport, an English trader for the American Fur Company, was licensed to establish a post at Fort Armstrong on Rock Island. Pierre Menard, of Kaskaskia, the father-in-law of Auguste Chouteau, was hired as an interpreter, his strong connections to the St. Louis French and the American Fur Company suggesting the increasing influence of St. Louis merchants in this strategy. Meanwhile John W. Johnson, a trader working for the U.S. government, was appointed a factor at Prairie du Chien in 1815 and proceeded north in 1816.[46] Though the placement of these various traders did not yet constitute a system, the forts and posts were clearly meant to routinize interaction with the Native Americans. The regular movements of civilian and military personnel from fort to fort, and the regular supply run from St. Louis, touching at each fort, formed the basis of a supply network within the developing regional economy that persisted, as a distinct subsystem, into the early 1850s.[47]

Moreover, the systemic activities of John W. Johnson, government factor at Prairie du Chien, and George Davenport, Sr., trader for the American Fur Company on Rock Island, made it clear that this fort and trading post system was meant to encircle and economically penetrate the Lead Region. Johnson arrived with supplies and several other American men before the military officials arrived in May 1816 to begin construction of Fort Crawford. Johnson was a shrewd choice for an agent. An experienced trader who before the war had been at Fort Madison and several times had been across the Lead Region, he was married to a Sauk woman, a tribe with whom he had dealt before. Though resisted by local traders including representatives of the American Fur Company, and facing competition from British traders who relied on lingering good will with the Indians to maintain relations, Johnson established trading relations with the Sauk, Fox, Winnebago, Menominee, Iowa, Sioux, and even the Kickapoo and Potawatomi. Johnson also sold to a number of mixed-blood or French traders at Prairie du Chien who traded across the region, including A. P. Vanmeter, François Bouthillier, and Jesse Shull. In return for his cache of St. Louis goods, he traded primarily in lead, either directly from the Indians or through traveling middle men like Van Meter or Shull, thus bringing the region into his orbit of trade and achieving the government objective in establishing relations with the Indians by using only French Canadians or mixed-blood people who had proved themselves as loyal intermediaries.[48]

Provincial society

The arrival of the U.S. military in June 1816 confirmed for mixed-blood and French Canadian residents who remained loyal to the British the direction of the American policy. The residents of Prairie du Chien, including people of "French extraction having no mixed-blood" and mixed-blood people who had "Indian [or mixed-blood] wives from many different tribes," found themselves treated arbitrarily and were considered traitors by military officials. They moved some residents off their lands for military use. Others had their shops confiscated. They arrested and incarcerated others, and either fined them or exiled them from the town. Most came under harsh restrictions. Such harassment encouraged many to head north, a result that worked in tandem with the retreat of British trade into Canada to leave Prairie du Chien populated by a mélange of loyal French Canadians and mixed-blood people, a small group of Americans, including trader James H. Lockwood and St. Louisan Stephen Hempstead, and at least two black slaves.[49]

To the south, George Davenport of the American Fur Company traded without government interference. In 1814 he entered the upper valley and traded with the Indians in the region by following their seasonal movements both west of the river and across the Lead Region. In 1816, Davenport set up a temporary post near the mouth of the Fever River to trade with the Indians. Though later in 1816 he retreated to Rock Island and opened a trading post within the newly constructed Fort Armstrong, Davenport maintained the Fever River post for at least two seasons. During that time he integrated the post into a circuit that he traveled between his central post on Rock Island and temporary posts across east central and northeastern Iowa and northwestern Illinois to trade with the Sauk Indians. In both 1817 and 1818 the Lead Region was a seasonal stop, making Davenport, a British immigrant, the first white man to gain the trust and trade of the Indians since Pierre Chouteau, Jr.'s expulsion six years before.[50]

Wherever these traders made contact with the local Indian tribes, the economic and social lives of the tribes were fundamentally transformed. As Indians shifted from mixed hunting and farming to trading furs, they acquired more American goods, which made some aspects of tribal life more efficient. Such trade and the changes in production and consumption it caused, however, soon made Indians more reliant on Americans or trading-post blacksmiths, gunsmiths, and traders. In addition, as Indians reduced food production, placing more emphasis on hunting or mining, they required more foodstuffs from the trading posts. Trading posts quickly emerged as service and supply centers for the local tribes. Inevitably, here, as at so many places further east, alcohol arrived with foodstuffs and supplies, altering individual and group behavior and further undermining the fragile unity of local tribes. In time, Indians clustered around the more important posts – so long as the American population was not too large. Meanwhile transient traders were encouraged to establish more permanent posts. As traders and Indians became enmeshed in increasingly dependent relations, the Indians became more amenable to land sales and annuities, all of which continued to serve the purposes of American policy.[51]

Soon after traders like George Davenport arrived, others more interested in tak-

25

ing over Indian activities and ousting them from their territory than in trading quickly followed. As early as 1816, another American entrepreneur planned to open mines in the district, but instead of trading with the Indians, he intended to use "chiefly *Frenchmen* [his emphasis], natives of that region, whose manners and habits will be less likely to give offence to the Indians, than those of any other description of people in the western country." About 1818, St. Louis entrepreneur Col. John Smith arrived in the region and sought to wrest the mines away from the Indians, but failed.[52] Another named John Shaw was more successful, visiting the mines and taking away lead to trade at Prairie du Chien. Others who sought an ingress were chased away or killed.[53]

The following year, however, after Davenport had succeeded in shipping lead south to St. Louis, several independent traders entered the region encouraged by Davenport's success. Residents of Prairie du Chien, they had done business with John W. Johnson at the government factory there in 1816, and were aware of the wealth of lead in the region by their trade with the Indians.[54] Jesse W. Shull, formerly of the Hudson Bay Company, initiated trade near the Indian mines at the site of Dubuque. Later that year, he arrived, under protection of the American government, at the Fever River and built a post at the site of Galena. He was soon followed by a Frenchman, François Bouthillier, a "roving" trader from Prairie du Chien, who had followed the Indians across the region since 1812. Likewise, A. P. Vanmeter arrived at the Fever River to trade with the Indians. That same summer, Dr. Samuel Muir, a trader from further south on the river stocked with goods from Davenport's post on Rock Island, joined them and settled nearby. Amos Farrar, another American trader, arrived about the same time with goods from a French trader located in Fort Armstrong who got his goods from Canada, not St. Louis. Arriving with their Indian wives and settling among the hundreds of Sauk and Foxes, Mesquakies, and "their brethren," the Winnebagoes, who lived along the Fever river valley, these men lived in what became a local remnant enclave of the "middle ground." American military and financial support from Prairie du Chien, Fort Armstrong, and St. Louis foreshadowed the establishment of Americanized "islands" or "outposts" which drew new lines of interaction across the social geography of the region.[55]

The following year a Kentuckian, Col. James Johnson, arrived wanting not to trade with the Indians, but to smelt lead mined by the Indians and to ship it south. That summer, D. G. Bates, who had visited the mines as early as 1819, also arrived to engage in the smelting of lead. With this new desire to more systematically extract lead from the vicinity also came a deeper interest in establishing an outpost of American society in the Fever river valley. The arrival of Thomas January in late 1821 with his American wife initiated this new phase. Other Americans who brought their wives and children with them and built cabins near the river around soon followed him to "January's Point." Though in 1822 Col. Johnson and D. L. Ward, also of Kentucky, arrived with a large contingent of male workers, including African American slaves, to start a large-scale smelting establishment, the Moses Meeker party of some forty people, which arrived from Ohio in 1823, included some women: Mrs. Abigail Harris and her daughters Selinda, Lucinda, and Electa Harris, Mrs. Susan Harris Smith, Mrs. Mary Meeker, and Elizabeth Harris Hunt.[56]

Among the arrivals at the small settlement by the end of the next year were Henry and John Gratiot, sons of Charles Gratiot. Henry had married Susan Hempstead of St. Louis. In December 1824 they joined some 400 or 500 settlers, mostly men, who inhabited the several cabins and scores of shacks spread across the valley and hills that made up the "January Point" settlement. In the winter they "established a trading station and a store," and also a third smelter a mile to the northwest of the village on a site later occupied by William Hempstead of St. Louis. Therefore, although through early 1825 an American settlement of about eight to ten cabins and numerous wooden shacks and tents stretching a mile along the river bank huddled on the later site of Galena, some settlers, in search of lead and farm land, moved up out of the river valley onto the high ground north and east of the city. In 1824 both the Harrises and the Meekers established farms on the high ground east of the Fever River settlement. Others moved several miles east to an old Indian mine on the Apple River, later controlled by Frenchmen La Baum and St. Vrain. That same year Jesse Shull moved north up the Fever River into Michigan territory to a mine at New Diggings. In 1826, the Gratiots followed the Indians to a new mine about twenty miles north of the Fever River settlement. When the next year Shull moved further north onto a high ridge near the mine, joining the Vanmeter brothers immediately to the west, and P. A. Lorimer, a bit further west, as well as William S. Hamilton, who was a few miles to the east, they established the boundaries of a scattered series of sites, each consisting of several cabins, containing the few families of the founders and workers.[57]

A central component of this burgeoning American society was a core of French settlers tied not to Prairie du Chien, but to society in St. Louis. They arrived singly but had extensive contacts with each other. J. G. Soulard, son of Terese Cerré and Antoine Soulard of St. Louis, passed through the area and met Col. Johnson in 1821. By that time he was already married to Elizabeth Hunt, daughter of Thomas Hunt of St. Louis. Likewise, the miner and Indian agent Charles de St. Vrain was related to Jacques Ceran St. Vrain, one of the early prominent merchants at St. Louis.[58] So, too, P. A. Lorimer, the son of Peter de Lorimier, early trader on the Missouri who had come to French Illinois from Quebec with Pierre Menard and later "one of the founders of Dubuque, Iowa," was part of the St. Louis French society, as his later connections to the Gratiots and Hempsteads would show.[59]

The December 1824 arrival of Henry Gratiot and John "Bugnion" Gratiot, his younger brother, signaled a new phase in the transference of St. Louis society to the frontier.[60] As sons of Charles Gratiot and Victoire Chouteau, Henry and John Gratiot were related to most of the French families of St. Louis. They came, therefore, with the benefits of longstanding trade and financial relationships, extensive experience with the Indians, as well as considerable economic resources. This was evident both in the heavily capitalized nature of their mining and smelting operations, as well as in the request by the Winnebagoes in 1825 that Henry Gratiot be appointed agent to the tribe.

Provincial lives

Had the Gratiot enterprise on the Fever River been entirely a French operation, however, its history may have simply paralleled that of other trading and economic ventures undertaken by members of the St. Louis French elite up the Missouri or Mississippi or across the Santa Fe trail. It may have transformed the economics of tribal life through continual interaction at outposts, but left tribal social structure intact, in spite of occasional intermarriage between French employees and indigenous tribes, as well as disease. The marriage of Henry Gratiot with Susan Hempstead in 1813 in St. Louis, however, fused the discursive outpost frontier policy of the French with the more assertive economic and social goals and strategies of New Englanders and other Americans who had come west to achieve wealth and social mobility by transforming economic outposts into social and cultural beachheads of American society. The arrival of Susan Hempstead Gratiot, daughter of Stephen Hempstead, Sr., and sister of Edward Hempstead, in June 1826 directly connected the society of the Fever River district to the assertive regional family system of the Hempstead clan which for twenty-two years had been moving west seeking opportunity and social mobility within American society.

Their efforts to rely on each other and provide familial support struggled against the demands of the smelting business and interests of the diverse population that lived in or were migrating through the area. For several years between 1824 and about 1828, the society into which they moved consisted of five racial or ethnic groups. The nature of social interactions among these people, therefore, was in large part shaped by the relative balance in the numbers of people from the different groups living in the area. Initially, as we have seen, the population of Americans, French from St. Louis, French Canadians, and mixed-bloods numbered about 500 in and around Galena. A number of African American slaves accompanied them. By one account, there were 151 miners and almost as many black slaves (though it is unclear how many slaves they counted as miners) at the end of 1825.[61] Though Henry and John Gratiot arrived with "hardy and trusty" French Canadians rather than slaves, when Susan Hempstead Gratiot arrived in Galena in May 1826, two house slaves whom she would later free after a long period of service to the family accompanied her. Though both the Gratiots and the Hempsteads "abhorred" slavery, Henry continued to hold slaves as farm workers and house servants. This biracial population, with a very high male to female ratio, found itself, in 1826, amid about 2,000 Sauk and Fox Indians in the vicinity of Galena, with perhaps as many Winnebagoes, Mesquakies, and Menominees to the north and east.[62] Finally, interspersed among these people were at least several score mixed-blood people, many of them mixed-blood women who had married early French traders.[63]

During the year or two when the Americans, French, and French Canadians were present in fewer numbers, they seemed to defer to Indian activity and the two peoples lived together in a relatively "peaceable" manner. As their numbers increased to almost 500 by the end of 1826, with a hundred located in about fifteen cabins around the site of Galena, the Native Americans found themselves quickly drawn into increasingly dependent relations, the men hunting for food while the women and older men supplied lead for the smelters. The platting of the town of Galena in

1826 accelerated the process that pushed the resident Indians from the proximity of the American settlers in the Fever river valley, by establishing an urban foundation upon which American society, or the Gratiot–Hempstead subculture of it, could be constructed. When thousands of Americans rushed into Galena in 1827, and transformed it into a rudely built town of some 200 buildings almost overnight, the Indian presence retreated to small enclaves north of town, where they settled around various densely populated mining camps, and, in greater numbers and concentration, about twenty to thirty miles farther north of Galena.[64]

Although Galena, at this early date, quickly became an outpost of "civilization" and, in the tradition of forts and trading posts before it, separated itself from the "barbarism" in its hinterland, the scattered location of lead mines across the region pushed a clear line between the two farther north into Galena's hinterland. That line for several years was along "the Ridge" two miles north of Shullsburg (Wisconsin), about twenty miles north of Galena. Americans and some French and French Canadians settled in large camps and outposts consisting mostly of tents and dugouts scattered wherever lead was found across the district. While Galena's population became increasingly American and early settlers established themselves at the center of a set of relations upon which a local society would develop, the population retained a more mixed element, with a stronger St. Louis French and French Canadian component. In these camps French, Americans, mixed-blood people, and Native Americans initially lived and continued to live for several years, if not with, then certainly close to, each other. Eventually, however, those successful Americans within each of these settlements, drawing social and economic support from Galena, gradually displaced the Native Americans, and then the mixed-blood people and French Canadians, and carved out small social enclaves into which they could transfer the social structure, organization, and values of American society and push the frontier between "civilization" and "savagery" further north.[65]

As American settlers arrived and contributed to the structural development of an American society on the frontier, the dynamics of interaction among the various peoples across the frontier changed. Initially that process involved individuals or small groups of people, representing, at the point of their interaction, larger populations scattered extensively across the region. Their goals were to achieve some kind of mutual accommodation or coexistence within the context of their common interest in the fur or lead trade. Different social groups interacted and occasionally mixed with each other, while still maintaining their autonomy and viability within what has been called a common male-dominated "frontier culture" or a "mixed cultural world," characterized by the interaction between fiercely independent hunters and warriors who "depended on force and protestation to settle arguments," used similar techniques and technology, wore similar clothing, and indulged in hard liquor and brawling. When they interacted with others, defended their honor, fought, forged alliances by intermarriage, and made treaties, they did so through their kin group or clan, the primary "social nexus" of their lives, with the common goal of maintaining some kind of balanced interaction among groups and preventing one group or another from prevailing.[66]

Provincial lives

The arrival of more Americans shattered this balance and the common culture it supported. Both more numerous and better organized, the Americans emerged as a dominant force, and needed to negotiate less to maintain a balance that their presence undermined. The Native Americans and French Canadians across the region became increasingly subordinate to the American agenda. As a result, in the years just before and after 1827, an extensively settled, fragile, highly mobile, bi- or multicultural society was supplanted by a much more organized and homogenous society.

2

Family migration and social development on a "near" frontier

Between 1800 and 1840 streams of Americans moving west and north across the upper Mississippi river valley encountered a loosely organized society of Native Americans, French Canadians, mixed-blood people, French from St. Louis, and small groups of American traders, military personnel, and settlers living in a fragile multicultural "common frontier culture" on the edge of the "middle ground."[1] Migrating from the Upland south and then New England and the Middle Atlantic states and driven by a search for land and opportunity, American settlers moved across the region, sweeping away the demographic balance that sustained the common frontier culture and society. In its place they sought to establish outposts of American society and culture in which they would compete with different groups from different regions for hegemony and social control.

That this surge of American migration occurred just as the forces of the industrial revolution and market capitalism were sweeping across the West, triggering urban development and centralizing trade and production, transformed the dynamics and character of the transference of the social order and cultures of the predominant migration streams to the region. Market forces penetrated, undermined, and transformed not only the rural household and village economies which early settlers has established across the West before 1820, but also the lives of those who were still migrating west. Though many immigrants moved west seeking to preserve their traditional values, most, cut free from the strictures of community and family to fend for themselves as free agents within a rapidly changing, volatile marketplace, responded much like people in the East to the differentiating forces of market capitalism and industrialization. In the face of unforeseen challenges, each major immigrant group turned their traditional values – in the case of New Englanders, Calvinist values of self-discipline, hard work, stoicism, and frugality, which pervaded village life – more aggressively toward individualism and self-mastery.[2] Those who traveled alone viewed migration as an individualist endeavor and sought aggressively to transfer their values of discipline and order to the villages, towns, and cities to which they moved. Those who moved west within family systems, whether "patrimonial" – seeking to transfer landed wealth in rural migration streams – or "entrepreneurial" – following economic opportunity – sought to transfer traditional New England village culture more in a piece. In migrant families parents still sought to integrate the actions of each individual toward some common family strategy or goal rather than to encourage each member to pursue goals based on his or her own self-interest. But such family systems would also feel the impact of the individualistic impulses of market capitalism penetrating traditional family order and refocusing each family member's efforts to achieve individual success rather than the fulfillment of the broader social and cultural agendas of the family. Articulating the slowly changing logic and dynamics of such family systems, and the interweaving of individual stories and family stories – each with their own dynamics, timing, range, and possible outcomes – as family members migrated west, indicates the important role family support played in transferring and establishing outposts of urban society in the West. In these initial transferences of eastern society and culture to the urban West, and through their initial interactions with western society and culture, newcomers from New England, the Middle Atlantic, and even the South would gradually construct the foundations of a specific regional version of a broader middle-class culture within the towns and cities of the Great West.[3]

From the perspective of migratory family systems, the story of the isolated frontier family or individual, cut free from social support systems back home and fending for themselves in a hostile and undeveloped social environment, is given a more systemic explanation. At urban outposts such as Galena, Illinois, established in 1827 and connected by steamboat to the capital flows and migration streams that emanated from the regional center of American–French life around St. Louis, settlers transferred "American" enterprise, values, social order, and institutions to the urban frontier. Two groups, the French of St. Louis and New Englanders, and within these groups, two families in particular, aggressively pursued this American agenda. The Gratiots and the Hempsteads both arrived in the Lead Region in the 1820s within the context of well-established family migration and social systems. The Gratiots had been in the West for forty years, while the Hempsteads had been there for twenty years.[4] The marriage of Henry Gratiot and Susan Hempstead in St. Louis, Missouri, in 1813 fused two vigorous family systems and, through them, the social and cultural traditions, values, and goals that each had transferred to the Mississippi river valley. When Henry and Susan Gratiot migrated to Fever River in 1826, therefore, they brought with them the combined support mechanisms of both French St. Louis and the Hempstead family, giving them considerable influence as social catalysts and leaders in navigating the turbulent social conditions and laying the foundations of "good" society.

The Hempsteads and Gratiots of St. Louis, 1804–1820

On 13 January 1830 Stephen Hempstead, Sr., the seventy-six-year-old patriarch of the Hempstead family of St. Louis, consoled his daughter Susan in her "recluse situation" on the upper Mississippi frontier and promised her material, social, and spiritual support. Such letters to family members who, by 1830, were "so scattered about our country" that their "circumstances" were "but little known" to him had become for Hempstead, who was too infirm to travel, the only means he had left to maintain the lines of moral and spiritual support which defined the family. His patriarchal power weakened by deaths and out-migration, Hempstead's primary expectation was to sustain the dynamics of a migratory family system which had been moving west for twenty-six years and to contribute to the material survival and moral maintenance of each new branch of the family and thus to the transference of his Old Presbyterian and New England small-town cultural values and beliefs to the West. Through such efforts he and his family would help lay the foundations of good society on the frontier.[5]

The first step in this process was to migrate to the West. Stephen Hempstead, fourth son of the indefatigable diarist Joshua Hempstead and a direct descendant of the founder of New London, Connecticut, was born in 1754.[6] As a Revolutionary War veteran, he had been present at the reading of the Declaration in New York City,[7] and later, as a farmer, experienced Timothy Dwight's Great Awakening. He witnessed many of his neighbors head west into New York to "Connecticutize" America.[8] Hempstead, therefore, naturally related individual experience to the forces of history. So when his sons began to reach manhood, and felt the pressures of emigration that were pressing against all New England towns in the 1790s,[9] Hempstead must not have been surprised when they set their sites on the Far West. His oldest son, Edward, migrated to St. Charles, Missouri, in 1804 and opened a law office. He quickly rose in his profession, moved to St. Louis, and entered politics. Having established a successful beachhead, and succeeding in relating with the French society of St. Louis, Edward invited his younger brothers Stephen in 1808 and Charles and Thomas in 1809 to "join fortunes with him."[10] Migrating by way of Shawneetown, Charles entered Edward's law office and soon established a practice in St. Genevieve, while Thomas entered the Indian trade in which French merchants were so extensively involved.[11] They soon reinforced their professional good fortune within the dominant French communities in St. Charles, St. Louis, and St. Genevieve, by intermarrying with French society. Edward married Clarrissa DuBriel, the daughter of a prominent and wealthy French merchant in St. Louis, while Stephen Jr. married Marie Louise Lefebre of Cahokia at Portage des Sioux, thus establishing a connection to some old Cahokia families, in particular, a branch of the Gratiots, a prominent St. Louis family.[12]

Encouraged by his son's good fortune and desirous of helping his other children, but also aware of his diminished patriarchal role over his dispersed family, Stephen Hempstead wanted to reconstitute the "western branch" of his family and reclaim his status. Thus when Edward was touched by his "filial affections" and offered to bring his father and the rest of the family west, they responded positively.[13] In April and May 1811, the family and a large group traveled by way of the Ohio and, after staying for a while with family members in St. Louis while looking for a suitable plot of land, settled on "some new land . . . Edward gave [him]" five miles northwest of

St. Louis in St. Ferdinand township, at the later site of Bellefontaine Cemetery.[14] At this farm located on a high ridge overlooking an extensive river bottom to the north and northeast, Stephen Hempstead, Sr., as a slave-holding farmer, sought to reestablish the Hempstead family system and his patriarchal authority over it across the hinterlands of St. Louis.

Following the lead of his sons who intermarried into good French society of St. Louis, Stephen encouraged, or at least did not prohibit his daughters, Susan, age fifteen, and Mary, a widow at age twenty-nine, to socialize with their brother's French relations and friends. By November 1812 Stephen Sr. reported to a relative in Connecticut that the "probability" was that Susan, the youngest daughter, would be married in a "couple of months." "The young man that pays his address to her is . . . Henry Gratiot about 23 years of age of a French family of the first grade in St. Louis." As for economics, Gratiot possessed an "exceeding [sic] good" farm five or six miles from town, which had "been settled a long time" and contained fine "orcharding," and he owned a "negro woman and five or six negro men and boys" as well. So, too, Stephen Hempstead judged him to be a fine man: "he speaks good English . . . bears a very good character and promises to make a kind and good companion to a woman." Initially, Hempstead, regretting that this would leave him and his wife with only two children around the house and concerned about his daughter's youth (she was only sixteen), was uneasy with the match. Again, his son Edward played a lead role in family affairs, and understanding French laws and social customs, remarked that "we should do wrong to not permit this union to take place." Taking this advice, Stephen Hempstead and his wife Mary consented and blessed the union, "hop[ing] and trust[ing] that [Susan] will be contented and happy in her important undertaking" and that her "bring up [sic] in the world and the prudent use she has made of it will enable her to perform her duty in life to the full expectations of her husband, and friends."[15] For the Hempsteads, the wedding, a Presbyterian service, which took place at Edward's house in St. Louis before a small gathering of the Hempsteads and members of the French elite, expanded their family system, while further intertwining it with those of the French elite of St. Louis.

For Stephen Hempstead, as for many American settlers, an alliance with the French served several social and cultural purposes. First, the French presence served both as a go-between and a buffer between themselves and the mixed-blood and Native American people across the frontier. By facilitating communication, the French presence allowed the Americans to drive a small wedge of amicable interaction between themselves and the Indians, and thus enabled them to carry out their plans. Likewise, the ability of the French to sustain good relations with the Indians, and their support of American interests, alleviated qualms some settlers may have had in taking Indian land, and enabled more conscientious Americans to view themselves as the rightful European–American heirs to the region. Though the Europeanness of the French may have initially caused some ambivalence among the first Americans in the region, it was usually counteracted by the Americans' appreciation of their apparent sanctioning of the American agenda.[16]

So, too, the ability of many French, particularly in St. Louis to maintain racial solidarity, gentility, or "suavity and politeness" was taken by Americans as evidence that one did not have to degenerate socially and culturally on the frontier.[17] Travelers across the region were routinely amazed when they encountered what they called French "gentility" on the frontier. Visitor after visitor to St. Louis, for example, was astonished by the elegant style in which Pierre Chouteau, founder of St. Louis, lived.[18] Likewise, people back east (expecting to encounter backwoodsmen and hunters) were amazed to find such "gentlemanliness" among those who had spent their lives among the Indians. Later, in 1836, when an older Henry Gratiot visited Washington, D.C., people in the fashionable circles, responding much like Stephen Hempstead, "were amazed to find a man who had spent nearly his whole life on the frontier, and with the Indians, the highest type of gentleman, who, with his French vivacity and cordial manner, attached himself to all with whom he met."[19] Fearing social chaos and disorder, and aware of the head start the French had achieved in establishing a "civilized" or "settled" society in the West, many Americans, observing the French ability socially to prevail in frontier conditions, and their social and economic power in fostering social and economic development, saw the French as a means to facilitate and accelerate their personal and social agendas. French society in the West became both a model as well as a concrete structure in place, which was similar enough to the gentility system from the East to fuse their activities to it. The relaxed, simple, rustic, yet elegant French provincial style, as reflected in their manners, customs, life style, and architecture – all of which would affect Susan Gratiot – served as a model for frontier gentility across the West.[20]

Though, at times, it seems that the French were a "host" to the American parasite, it is more accurate to characterize the relationship as symbiotic. Each partner in the relationship benefited. Marriage into a French family gave an immediate boost to the economic and social standing of New Englanders like Stephen, Edward, and Susan Hempstead by opening up to them the resources of an ordered, well-off, closed society. For the French, intermarriage with the Americans maintained their presence and power and would facilitate their gradual acculturation into American society, which the Gratiots strongly supported. Though, in time, the French tradition would linger only as a nostalgic legacy and gradually become absorbed into middle-class urban society that arrived with determination and established the agenda of social development for a generation or more after 1835, it gave to that gentility a certain provincial, yet worldly tone that differentiated it from gentility in the East.

Fortified by their alliance with French society, Stephen Hempstead and his wife pursued their goal of strengthening their family around St. Louis. Stephen Hempstead, Sr., sought to make his new farm the center of a network of Hempstead residences spread across St. Louis County in which he and his wife would maintain regular contacts with their children and their families. Though his farm would never replace the old Hempstead house in New London, it would provide the members of the dispersed "western branch" of the Hempstead clan with a moral center, a revived emotional and cultural hearth to which they would, in time, be drawn, thus counteracting the centrifugal forces that had continued to pull or propel them in different directions. Mary Keeney, their widowed daughter, and William, their youngest son, lived at home. Thomas, when he was not upriver on a trading expedition, maintained a store on the Bellefontaine road which ran in front of the estate. Stephen lived at St. Charles, fifteen miles to the northwest. Susan was now at the Henry Gratiot estate five miles south on what later would become King's Highway. Stephen and Mary feared that when Henry and Susan took up "housekeeping" at the Gratiot estate located five miles away from his house, as well as five miles out of St. Louis amid "strangers" that "live near to there," their daughter would be very lonely and without support in assuming her duties as the "head of a family" at so young an age,[21] so he and his wife pledged to maintain close contacts.[22] There, Susan was equidistant, about five miles from her brothers Edward and Charles, who resided in St. Louis, and her parents' farm. At each place, the Hempsteads made contact with relations, neighbors, and friends who lived nearby, deepening their presence in the discursive urban and rural French community which centered at St. Louis but, given the French proclivity to reside on country estates, spread across St. Louis and St. Charles counties.

Within this network of related households, Stephen Hempstead, Sr., and his children sought to transfer the corporate family relationships and values that the family's serial chain migration from Connecticut to Missouri since 1804 had undermined. The Hempstead farm also became the center of a corporate network of family household economies that through barter, communal labor, sharing of resources, and specialization supported each household unit while also increasing the capital of the family as a whole. One can discern this reemerging patriarchal or "patrimonial" (though it was also clearly an "entrepreneurial") family system through a network analysis (drawn from Stephen's diary and family letters) of the pattern, frequency, and dynamics of the exchange of favors, services, goods, labor, and even slaves among Stephen Hempstead and his seven children across the area between 1813 and his wife's death in September 1820.

On a very mundane level, the various "branches" of the Hempstead family provided for each other the things that all farmers generally exchanged among themselves and their neighbors in a barter economy: plants and seeds to improve the products of fields or gardens; the bounty of each other's harvests; the purchase, sharing, breeding, and tending of each other's horses and livestock; the exchange of information about farming and gardening; household goods, furniture, and supplies; occasional help in heavy or communal tasks; and sometimes even the exchange of laborers and slaves.[23] His son-in-law Henry Gratiot, who Stephen Sr. came to call "Harry," for example, provided Stephen with seeds, plants, and tree graftings from his orchard, as well as tools, machinery, whetstones to sharpen his tools, a yoke of oxen to help his plowing, and a wheat fan.[24] Occasionally Stephen Sr. would reciprocate with produce from his farm,[25] but overall, Stephen's children could help him better than he could help them because their farms were more established than his "plantation."[26]

To compensate, Stephen provided material and logistical advice and support when his children needed it. He looked after his children's houses or their stores[27] when they were away, picked up and delivered loads of goods and items,[28] and supplied them with fresh horses when needed. Stephen and Edward, accepting local French practice, occasionally exchanged slaves, sent them to each other's places to help with heavy work such as construction, butchering, harvesting, mowing, milling wheat, cutting wood, or raising a barn, or even sold them.[29] Once Stephen Sr. sent his slaves "John and Steve" to help his sons Thomas or Edward. Several times, Edward simply gave his father slaves, such as when he "sent out a . . . Negro woman, about 38 year's old named Lucy and three children" to stay at Stephen Sr.'s farm. Another time Charles sent out a "black girl" to help his mother.[30] When Edward died in 1817, Stephen distributed his estate, sending Thomas three slaves while keeping two for himself, selling some others immediately, and then, a few months later, selling two male slaves to a "man from the Red River" for $1250.[31]

Perhaps more important than the material support that circulated within this family network, however, was the social, emotional, and medical support, which was provided primarily by the women of the family. Stephen Sr.'s diary records a regular routine of visiting which took place between the parents' and children's houses. Within the weekly or monthly cycle of visits, annual holiday get-togethers acquired special symbolic significance. Stephen Sr. assessed family deference to the patriarch by recording his children's presence or absence at traditional Hempstead family dinners on Christmas, July Fourth, and on special public or family occasions such as weddings or funerals. On 13 April 1815, for example, a "day . . . set apart by the President of the U. S. as a day of Thanksgiving in the U.S. for the return of peace to our country," it was Stephen's desire to have "all my children in this country with me this day" at a midday dinner. Another milestone was Christmas dinner, 1819, when "by the blessing of God," the family all dined at the patriarchal home for the last time before Mrs. Hempstead died and several children moved away. Conversely, occasions such as the Christmas dinner of 1816 at Susan and Henry Gratiot's estate, or the solitary Christmas of 1817 after Edward's death when Stephen brooded alone at home while his wife visited the children, signaled shifts in the power structure or losses in the family.[32]

Between these grand occasions, Stephen and Mary's relationship with each of their children varied with each child's age, marital status, family history, and distance from home. For example, within their network of family relations, the interaction between the Hempsteads and Susan, whom Stephen in his patriarchal way called "Daughter Gratiot," and Henry (or "Harry" or "Son Gratiot") became, given their proximity and the obvious affection they held for each other, the central and most frequently traveled artery of family society. From their marriage in January 1813 until Mary Hempstead's death in September 1820, Susan and Henry rarely went more than a month without getting together with her parents, either by "stopping" at the "plantation" or having them visit at the Gratiot estate. They visited, on average, ten times a year. These usually involved Sunday visits, but they also visited each other during the week and sometimes "stop[ped] the night."[33] Likewise, when

Thomas and Stephen Jr. married and established households, Stephen and Mary occasionally visited.[34]

In part, the access that Susan's marriage to Henry Gratiot gave Stephen and his wife to the Gratiot and Chouteau relations motivated this relationship, though Susan and her mother and father were clearly very close and shared a keen interest in matters of the Presbyterian church. Later, Susan would become the first Hempstead child to join the church Stephen helped found in St. Louis.[35] This interaction overtook the connection to French society which Stephen and Mary had initially acquired through his eldest son's Edward's marriage to Clarissa DuBreuil in 1808. When in 1818 Mary Hempstead and Susan Hempstead took a spa vacation together near the Gratiot estate, and were joined just before July Fourth by Susan's mother-in-law "old Madame Gratiot" (Victoire Chouteau Gratiot), the relationship deepened. Soon afterward they attended a grand dinner with several other "Gentlemen and Ladys [sic] from St. Louis" society.[36] That the Hempsteads had penetrated this small circle is evident in the remark made by Susan's sister-in-law, Adele Perdeauville Gratiot, after marrying Henry's brother John: "I . . . knew but few beyond the circle of my husband's relations. My mother-in-law [Victoire Chouteau Gratiot] was highly respected and accomplished and I was among the frequent visitors to her house. I became acquainted with some remarkable persons of these early times." Among them were "Edward Hempstead, first delegate in Congress from Missouri Territory and brother of Charles S. Hempstead, of Galena."[37]

The bonds established by parental social relations were no doubt deepened as Stephen and Mary provided support as each of their adult children began to have their own families. Between 1813 and her death in 1820, Mary Lewis Hempstead was present and helped her daughters or daughters-in-law in giving birth on a dozen occasions. As often as not, however, the happiness and satisfaction that Mary Hempstead received from aiding her daughters with the births of their children and adding to the size of the family was, in the primitive health conditions of the frontier, short-lived. During their years at Bellefontaine plantation, Mary and Stephen helplessly watched eight grandchildren, six of them less than two years old whom Mary had helped birth, succumb to the fever prevalent in the Mississippi valley.[38] So, too, illness for adults was a constant presence and danger and "Mother Mary" continually traveled to nurse her children, or welcomed them under the parental roof whenever they needed nursing.[39]

It was Edward's death that had the greatest impact on the family. In August 1817, he died of "a fitt [sic] of apoplex" which resulted from a fall from a horse, at age thirty-seven; the funeral became a central event in Hempstead family history. All the family gathered at Edward's home in St. Louis, and the day after, "all the Brothers and Sisters in the Vicinity," including Charles, who traveled overnight from St. Genevieve and "arrived this morning in time for the funiral [sic] of his brother," as well as a "very numerous collection of people of evry [sic] discription [sic] whose faces were uniformly wet with the tear of sorrow for there [sic] departed friend," marched in procession five miles to the plantation. There, as Stephen Sr.

described it, they were met by "Nieghbors [sic] in the county" who had "collected at my house" to commit to the grave "the remains of a beloved son, brother, and friend." Edward's wife Clarissa was "broke down with grief for the death of her husband" and the family seemed stunned by the "great loss" of Edward's death. The following Christmas, Stephen, alone on Christmas for the first time since coming to Missouri, ruminated on Edward's "seat" which was empty and the fact that he was "no more." Yet he took solace that Edward was "sleeping in the silent grave in my grave yard" beside his two children (an infant son and a stillborn child), and various nephews and nieces.[40]

For Stephen, the death of his wife was even more momentous. After failing to help her daughter Mary's husband, the old Spanish trader Manuel Lisa, who died of fever on 11 August 1820, "Mother Mary" nursed her widowed daughter back from the brink of death, only to be struck, in her husband's words, "with an afflicting stroke of divine providence" upon returning home in the last week of August. Ever more intensive care and medicine could do nothing to halt the advance of Mary's fever and she succumbed on 9 September, after an impressive Christian deathbed scene with her daughter Susan Hempstead Gratiot and Stephen Sr., her husband of forty-three years, by her side (Mary and Sarah were confined to their sickbeds in St. Louis and unable to be there).[41]

For the Hempsteads, funerals, as much as weddings or births, provided the emotional links in the chain of family experiences and memory that deepened family self-identity, shaped family culture, situated them within the community, and transformed the Hempsteads into Missourians and westerners. Each time Stephen stood at the "grave ground" or "the family buriing [sic] ground" "with the congregation of the dead of my family" which by 1831 included "my beloved wife and son, eight grand children of different ages, two sons-in-law, Manual Lisa and Elijah Beebe, [and] my only brother William and wife," he further consecrated the "hallowed ground" and transformed Bellefontaine plantation into the Hempstead family homestead.[42] Inevitably, however, the very prevalence of death on this fateful ground began to influence the logic of the family system. Surviving family members (Charles, William, and Susan) were increasingly motivated to vacate the murderous ground of Missouri and seek healthier climates to the north.[43]

Thus, through their intensive interactions across St. Louis and its adjacent hinterland, the Hempstead clan, between their arrival in 1804 and Mary's death in September 1820, and then somewhat less so later, under Stephen Sr.'s waning patriarchal presence through his death in 1831, was able to reorganize the semblance of a corporate family system, which provided economic, social, emotional, and cultural support, giving to each of its members who cared to participate advantages that improved their circumstances and enhanced and sustained their lives.

The Hempsteads and Gratiots on a "near" frontier, 1820–1840

Edward's death in 1817, Mary Hempstead's death in 1820, Stephen Sr.'s decision to give up farming and close his plantation for a few years, and the death of Charles's wife in 1823 weakened the core of the Hempstead family system. These disasters befell the Hempsteads just as intensified market forces reflected in an expansion of the trading activity of the St. Louis mercantile elite drew younger members of the family away from St. Louis. As family members sought to act for themselves, the family system again began to unravel and became more diffused and difficult to maintain. Nevertheless, though his power was undermined and he was increasingly isolated in St. Louis, Stephen Sr. and the remaining members of the family tried to provide material, social, cultural, and spiritual support for their kin who migrated to the upper Mississippi river valley. In doing so, the Hempsteads and Gratiots extended their family system across a "near" frontier and transformed it into a regional social system upon which a regional urban society would develop.

Though as early as 1815, Hempstead sons were drawn into trading expeditions up the Missouri and Mississippi rivers, it was only after 1820 that an entrepreneurial logic overtook the predominant patrimonial logic of the family system. In 1815 Thomas went on a two-week trading expedition up to Fort Clark, Kansas, and Stephen Jr. joined a military force on an expedition to survey the Arkansas Territory.[44] Stephen Jr., who had been upriver as far as Prairie du Chien possibly as early as 1809, joined, with his brother Edward, the military expedition led by Zachary Taylor in 1814 to relieve captured Americans there. The expedition got only as far as the Rock River in August 1814, where a combined force of Sauk and Fox and the British repulsed them. In May 1816, Stephen followed his deepening interest in the frontier and joined John W. Johnson's expedition as a contractor to go to Prairie du Chien in Michigan Territory to establish a trading factory. Later in the summer he brought his family there, making the Hempsteads one of the first American families at that northern latitude and placing them in the center of the emerging American policy of playing off loyal versus disloyal mixed-blood or French people while infiltrating Indian country, routinizing American–Indian interactions, and ultimately encircling the Lead Region in northwestern Illinois. During his stay there through October 1817, Stephen left a daughter and later a son to be educated by the Hempsteads at St. Louis and exchanged goods with his father at least once, thus initiating a regional support strategy into which other siblings would tap. In the spring of 1817 after briefly returning to St. Louis, he joined Major Stephen H. Long on his expedition to St. Peter's as a French interpreter and stopped again in Prairie du Chien on his way. After returning to St. Louis in October 1817 to spend the winter there, he made what was an increasingly routine trading voyage up to Prairie du Chien the following June, but then returned and later moved out to Portage des Sioux, Missouri, to go into merchandising.[45]

The Hempsteads continued to make occasional trips to the upper valley in the late 1810s, but it was not until reports of the first lead strikes in the Fever River district swept south, and American immigrants like the Meekers or Harrises from Cincinnati headed north, that another Hempstead, with the rest of St. Louis society, turned his head in that direction. In February 1822 Sarah Hempstead Beebe's husband Elijah Beebe, having followed the lead of his brother-in-law Stephen Hempstead, Jr., returned from a winter trip to bring the garrison at Prairie du

Chien a "drove of beef cattle and hogs." After returning, he set out again and spent the spring and summer trading at Prairie du Chien before returning in July. Given the growing American interest in the Fever River District, he probably joined a group from Prairie du Chien who made a tour of observation across the Lead District that summer. Beebe's entrepreneurial ambitions were cut short, however, and left for his brothers or brothers-in-law to assume when on 16 August 1822, a month after returning, he was struck down with a fever and died eight days later, leaving Sarah a widow with five children.[46] Other family members would take up the effort.

Meanwhile, the Missouri hinterland also attracted the Hempsteads' attention. In August 1819, Mary Hempstead Lisa accompanied her husband Manual Lisa on an expedition to spend the winter "at the trading station above the mouth of the Nebraska river" where she met many "old trappers, traders, and hunters." They stayed until April 1820.[47] Thomas Hempstead, no doubt with references from his brother Stephen Jr., helped supply Stephen H. Long's Yellow Stone expedition of 1820. In late 1821 or early 1822 he himself apparently went on an expedition up the Missouri River, returning in March. He then spent the next winter of 1822–23 "up the Missouri river," and after returning in January 1823 set out again in May, on a two-month expedition up to Council Bluffs. Meanwhile his younger brother William had established himself as a merchant at Wood's trading station in Kansas in 1820 and then, in late 1822, moved to Council Bluffs, where he joined his brother and spent the winter. After a brief visit to St. Louis in January 1823, he returned to the bluffs for most of the year.[48]

Eventually, even those members of the family securely residing around the core would feel the pressures of entrepreneurial promise. Henry and Susan Gratiot responded to these pressures by moving from the Gratiot estate to a site on the Merrimac River to mine and process salt in 1822. Relieved from family duties after her mother's death, and her father's subsequent decision to move into St. Louis, Susan no longer felt she needed to stay nearby, even though she was moving only another several miles to the southwest.[49] Such a response was the norm among the Gratiots.

Trade was a Gratiot family tradition; their famous father Charles, who had died only five years before, began trading at the post at Fort Mackinaw in the 1770s, and then, after 1774 at Cahokia, and finally, after the Revolution, in St. Louis.[50] Perhaps to investigate opportunities within the St. Louis trading network John Gratiot went on a far-ranging expedition to the Santa Fe country from which he did not return until late 1824.

When the family matriarch, Madame Victoire Chouteau Gratiot, died on 15 June 1825 at the age of sixty-one, the Gratiot brothers' last restraint against their leaving St. Louis was removed. But by that time, the trading business had changed significantly. Rather than simply establishing an outpost among the Native Americans who worked the mines or acquired the resources of the region, American settlers, with deeper capital, sought to enter mining and smelting themselves and transform the Lead Region into an extension – connected after 1823 to St. Louis by steamboats –

of the American economy and society. For the Gratiots, the decision to relocate to the Lead Region was perhaps another chapter in the family's trading tradition. For Susan Hempstead and her siblings who would later follow her, the decision to move to the Lead Region was another stage in the family's ongoing process of migrating west and, as settlers, transferring "good" society to an outpost of American life on a "near" frontier.

Months before their mother's death, John, Henry, and Paul Gratiot had followed the tide to Fever River and entered the mining business. In October 1824 the three brothers traveled in a "two-horse wagon" with three French Canadian guides to the lead mines at Galena.[51] There they settled among others already engaged in smelting, including Moses Meeker, and began a smelting operation. Following the Hempstead family agenda, the Gratiots planned to bring their families north "as soon as they could prepare a suitable shelter for them." In January 1826, Henry returned to St. Louis "to visit his family and buy materials" which he hoped to have shipped north as soon as possible so that he could "build them a comfortable house" and return to St. Louis later in the year to transport them to Fever River.[52]

Susan Hempstead Gratiot, following the lead of her sister Mary Lisa, who had gone up the Missouri to spend a winter in Nebraska a few years before, agreed to this plan in January 1826 and waited for her husband's return. In April, however, Susan became "very impatient" at the delays and without her husband's "knowledge or consent" and "in spite of friend's advice" not to go alone, set out with her "five children, two negro slaves, and a few household goods enough to establish their new home." In recalling her daring trip by flatboat, which in going against the current of the largest spring floods in years, lasted six weeks, what impressed Susan Hempstead Gratiot was the profusion of settlements already along the river.[53] In her litany of stops, Susan Hempstead Gratiot bridged her advance from civilization toward the frontier: "There were quite a number of stopping points on the river – Portage des Sioux, Grafton, Hamburg, Clarksville, Louisiana, Fort Edwards, foot of the lower rapids [now Keokuk], Oquawka, a little below present day Burlington, Phelps Landing or Yellow Banks, Fort Armstrong, on Rock Island under the charge of Mr. Davenport"[54] – though the residents of most of these places, such as Samuel Muir at the lower rapids, Isaac Campbell at the site of Nauvoo, and William Phelps at Fort Edwards, remained part of the French and mixed cultural world she eventually sought to transform.[55]

Upon his wife's arrival in Galena, Henry Gratiot quickly finished their cabin on Bench Street, and another cabin for their slaves, the fourth and fifth cabins in the town. Their immediate neighbors were Dr. Vanmeter and Josetta (or Jansette), his Indian wife. By the time John's wife, Adele P. Gratiot, arrived, the Gratiots had built another cabin which, among the "few scattered log cabins" in Galena, she was "put in possession of."[56]

Before having a chance to settle down to life in outpost Galena, the Gratiot brothers, finding Galena's environs already denuded of trees (requiring Henry's trip south for wood in January 1826), began looking farther afield for opportunities. In 1826 they took advantage of the traditional trust with which the Indians regarded them and were informed by their neighbor "Jansette, a Dubuque [woman] who married the physician Van Meter," of "the secret of the mines."[57] About the same time Jesse Shull had also been told of the mines on the prairie north of Galena by some Winnebagoes who fired an arrow in the direction of the mines and told him to follow, which he did. Being American, however, they soon drove him off. Again the Gratiots drew on their cultural and ethnic ties with the mixed-blood people among the Winnebagoes and smaller local tribes. With the help of a "friendly half-breed Winnebago woman" named Catherine Mayotte, who was "very popular with her tribe," they negotiated rights to survey the land and settle near the mines.[58]

By early summer the Gratiot brothers had laid out "Gratiot's Survey" (today on a rural site south of Shullsburg, Wisconsin). There "cabins, store-houses, and furnaces" as well as "houses for their families, domestics, and workmen" "appeared simultaneously." Though one account notes that the Gratiot families did not move to the settlement until 1827, Adele P. was there by late summer 1826 and Stephen Hempstead, Sr., was clearly under the impression that his daughter was there as early as 14 July 1826, for he addressed a letter to her at "Gratiot's Grove." In any case, we can place Susan Hempstead Gratiot there as early as the summer of 1826, for she addressed her first surviving letter from "Gratiot's Grove" in December 1826 and wrote as if she had been there some months. The settlement soon became a mélange of people. Besides the Gratiots and other associated French families, scores of American families arrived. Some sixty French Canadians and Indians were also hired to work the mines and smelting works, as well as a group of settlers from the ill-fated Selkirk settlement on the North Red River, who after moving to Galena had contracted to work for the Gratiot brothers and moved to the Grove in 1826.[59]

Susan Hempstead Gratiot's extensive correspondence with her father and sisters in St. Louis traces the deepening and more pervasive efforts of members of the family to transfer their social ways and values to the frontier and transform an economic outpost into an extension of New England village society once removed and filtered through life around St. Louis. Her father's and sisters' concern for Susan's isolation, loneliness, and exposure to a population of rough men from diverse origins – each of which gradually improved during the year – exhibit their clear interest in establishing good society on the frontier.

For the first year or two, Susan's difficulties were almost entirely shaped by her husband's business operations. By the time she arrived in Gratiot's Grove in spring 1826 in the company of her husband Henry and her brother-in-law John, they had already gone into the smelting business at Gratiot's Grove. In place of the decent cabin in Galena, all Henry could offer was a small wooden shack next to the smelting establishment. For a few months, Henry and Susan and their children essentially "camp[ed] out" at the Grove.[60] But as the establishment attracted miners from the entire district north of Galena, Gratiot expanded the operation to include a store which furnished "tools and provisions to hundreds of miners."[61] As the number of log smelting furnaces grew to nine, the store moved into a small cabin that they had built in early 1826, and then was enlarged in the fall of 1826. The store also served as an "ordinary" which Susan Gratiot, the only woman in the place, apparently agreed to run. By October, Adele P. reported that Susan greeted many visitors, "strangers as well as friends," and "offered [them] a pallet and a meal under [the] shade of [the] green boughs" of the large oak trees which gave the Grove its name.[62]

Her experience as the only woman among scores of men ended in late spring when her sister-in-law Adele came to spend the summer. Though they remained but two among the handful of women in the district, her father optimistically expressed his hope that "society is becoming more agreeable [there] on account of more females living in the neighborhood."[63] Unfortunately, the presence of other women turned out to be only temporary. In late autumn, Adele P. Gratiot returned, for health reasons, to spend the winter in New Orleans, leaving Susan again alone.[64] When Susan fell ill after the birth of a daughter in November, suffering from a "pleurisy," her isolation was again almost complete. "I have been sick five weeks and but seen one female – that is Mrs. Henry," remarking that "[had] I thought that I should have went through what I have I should have said no – without one of my sisters [or] without a female friend." Only an insensitive "Dutch Doctor," a young nephew, a niece, a servant, and an "old Indian woman" were there to help her.[65] The following February she again noted that "our . . . small and humble . . . house or cabin is continuley [sic] filled with men," preventing her from writing a coherent letter or establishing a private domestic regime.[66] As late as 1830 her father still responded to her comments by commiserating with her in her "recluse situation," "cumbered [sic] with a mother's care and thronged with a rude set of people of almost every nation."[67]

Initially just a settlement of a few "cabins or houses" clustered "within a stone's throw from each other," on the prairie surrounded by rolling hills near a grove of old oak trees, Gratiot's Grove grew quickly, placing the Gratiot cabin at the center of an ever larger population.[68] Though it is unclear just how large the settlement became that first year (Elihu Washburne argues it expanded to include 1,500 people, though in 1829, Caleb Atwater reported only twenty families), it was large enough in February for Susan Hempstead to call it "our city."[69] In May 1827, Adele P. Gratiot, upon returning from St. Louis, reported that "from the slope of the hill, you could see as far as the eye could reach, miners' shanties, and windlasses in activity."[70] Through the summer Susan Gratiot remained "surrounded by diggers" and was, under the strain, "sick of the sound of mineral and lead prospect[ing]" and the traffic of "four horse teams" which made "regular trips [from the inn] to town every other day, [so heavy] was the demand to transport the lead smelted day and night."[71] Only in August 1827 did Henry Gratiot finish building a "comfortable house" at the Grove where they could have some privacy and properly receive family and friends.[72]

For Susan Hempstead Gratiot the trials and "privations" of this isolation were exacerbated, ironically, by her husband's success.[73] The more successful his crudely built smelting establishment became, the more he had to travel through the region to draw in business. He also opened his own mines and later a mill, requiring him to spend more time in the mines and traveling around the Lead Region. In the winter, Susan worried, "think[ing] of the hardships" that Henry was so often "exposed to

. . . going and coming to the mill."[74] In other cases, he also seems to have maintained, during his travels, the family's social contacts with his brothers-in-law Charles and William in Galena, brother Paul, who was in Mineral Point between 1829 and 1832, and friends and family in St. Louis and back east.[75]

Henry's absences from home were a routine and frustrating part of Susan's life. During early 1826, for example, her sister-in-law Adele reported that Susan was left "most of the time alone, with her young family."[76] Later that year, Henry spent "more than half the time out to the diggings" and in November and December was absent continually for several weeks during which time Susan gave birth to daughter Adele, and then became ill, driving her almost "crazy."[77] Indian affairs and a short trip to St. Louis kept Henry away again in the summer of 1827.[78] Henry's participation in the Prairie du Chien treaty conference in August 1829 and his subsequent service as agent to the Winnebagoes in 1830 made his absences even more frequent.[79] In February 1831, Henry returned from an eight-day trip, then went to Galena for several days, then spent another week to go to Rock River, leaving him at home only four days that month.[80] In early 1832 Henry was again on a trip to St. Louis with his brother John when the Black Hawk war began, compelling him, as subagent, to return. No sooner had he secured the safety of his family than his presence was needed among the Indians for more than half the time between mid-April and mid-June 1832.[81] Though after the war he "settle[d] down to enjoy life," bought a farm outside Gratiot's Grove, and commenced building a "comfortable house," his varied business interests and duties as a liaison between the government and the Indians still kept him away.[82] When Theodore Rodolf visited Gratiot's Grove in April 1834, Henry Gratiot was not there, but "in the woods on the Peckatonica River," trying to arrange to ship wood via local rivers to a new flour mill he was building near the town of Gratiot.[83] In October 1835, Susan again regretted that because of his duties as Indian agent "Henry will be compelled to go to St. Louis . . . and then to Washington" to negotiate with the government.[84]

Susan Gratiot responded to her isolation, which made the "Grove lonesom [sic] and dull,"[85] by trying to construct a circle of local relations and friends upon whom she could rely for help in trying to establish a settled society. Susan found solace and support in other family members and close friends with similar values who lived in Gratiot's Grove, nearby Galena, and elsewhere in the Lead District. Her "family circle" at the Grove, however, included not only those who lived in the Lead Region, but also siblings or relatives from "down below" in St. Louis who came north to stay for extended periods. Therefore, although she resided on an isolated frontier, Susan also lived, through the intermeshing of local support, the arrival and departure of siblings and relations, and the exchange of letters, newspapers, and the shipments of goods, within a wider regional family and social support network. The overlapping concentric circles of these local and regional "sets of relations" formed Susan Gratiot's social maintenance system. They also formed the social architecture through which she would gradually transfer the family, religious, and cultural values and customs of her New England Presbyterian upbringing and her husband's

French "gentility" to the frontier and establish social hegemony amid the diverse world of Native American, mixed-blood, and other ethnic people.

Locally, the core of her family circle at Gratiot's Grove consisted of her brother-in-law John Gratiot (Susan called him "Bugnion") and, more important, his wife, Adele, who moved there in May 1827, first living with Susan and Henry, and then as neighbors through 1833. In Susan's letters Adele is a constant point of reference. Often when Adele was left alone by her own husband, such as in mid-1827, or again in the spring of 1832, she would move in with Susan "till her husband's return."[86] This local circle would be continually augmented by siblings who visited Susan or stayed at the Grove for extended periods. Susan Gratiot, after a visit to St. Louis, convinced her sister, Mrs. Sarah Beebe, "to stop the year" with her at the Grove, which she did in May 1827. When they returned to St. Louis in September, however, Sarah chose to stay the winter in St. Louis and delayed returning until May 1828. After that she remained at Gratiot's Grove through April 1829, supporting Susan with "sisterly love."[87] She was preceded by a nephew, Christopher, who had gone up to the Grove in December 1826, as well as another nephew, Albert, who started a business and served in the Winnebago war. After a visit to St. Louis in June and early July 1828, however, he returned to Galena, sold his business, and indulged in drink, much to his father's chagrin. Nieces Polly, who was in Gratiot's Grove throughout 1827, and Mary, Stephen Jr.'s daughter, who arrived in November, also made the trip.[88]

In the end, however, "Sister Sarah" shared Susan's experiences and needed more support than she could give. In July 1827 she recounted how they were all driven into Galena because of the Winnebago uprising and were unable to return to their house for a month.[89] A month later panic again swept the region, forcing Sarah, Susan, and all their children to join a steamboat exodus all the way back to St. Louis, which led to Sarah's decision to remain the winter and board with brother Charles.[90] Sarah's reluctance to return encouraged Mary Hempstead Lisa to make her first trip to Gratiot's Grove the following winter.[91] A year later, Sarah did return to Gratiot's Grove, but she still complained to her father about the spiritual deprivation of her life there.[92]

In response to Susan's pleas for aid, members of the immediate family banded together to help and continued to do so for nearly two and a half years, sustaining, indirectly, the Hempstead – Gratiot social agenda. But the network, reliant on the willingness of siblings to subsume their lives for a family strategy, was not seamless, and breaks could and did occur. When in April 1829, "Sister Sarah" returned to St. Louis, as apparently had the nieces, nephews, and cousins, Susan's family circle again narrowed to herself and Adele. That spring when her brother William visited her he found her "quite alone and lonesome."[93] She was left alone the following winter too, her father comforting her in her "lonely situation far from relatives and friends."[94] When, during the winter of 1830–1831 Adele made an extended winter visit back to St. Louis, even that support was lost.[95] The arrival in November 1833 of Susan's niece Mary, daughter of "Sister Beebe" (who had been up before in 1828 and early 1829 with her mother) and who stayed until spring 1835, along with her husband, Mortimer Kennett, ended this period of isolation, however. Her sister-in-law Eliza was at the Grove during the spring of 1834.[96] Her sister-in-law Adele returned in April 1834. Around the same time arrived a nephew, Edward L. Hempstead, thirty-five-year-old son of brother Joseph, who five years before had married a woman seventeen years older than him, but he proved to be a "great affliction," rarely seeing a "sober day."[97] Sister Sarah made another visit up to the Grove in early 1835, returning to St. Louis in June.[98]

All during this period Susan continued to have children at two- to three-year intervals. Arriving at the Grove with her five children – Charles (b. 1814), Edward (b. 1817), Susan (b. 1819), Mary, (b. 1821), and Henry (b. 1825) – the births of Adele in November 1826, William in May 1829 (who died in August 1832), Stephen Hempstead in November 1831, and Eliza in February 1834 increased the family. At age thirty-seven the last, her "eleventh" pregnancy (including her first stillborn, and probably a miscarriage), she remarked, "has left me weaker than the first."[99] Though Susan again turned to the broader family network for support, it was, however, not so regular or flexible that family members could time their arrivals and departures with the timing of Susan's births. No siblings or relatives were with her when Adele was born. Likewise, Susan gave birth to William a month after Sarah and her daughters had returned to St. Louis in April 1829. Her niece Mary was, however, with Susan when Eliza was born in 1834.

Besides encouraging Hempstead siblings to come to the Grove to help her, Susan also relied, in the other direction, on the family circle of brothers and sisters in and around St. Louis to take her children out of Gratiot's Grove as they reached schooling age and give them a proper education. Henry and Susan Gratiot's oldest son Charles, age thirteen, was sent south as early as July 1826 to go to school and board at his Uncle Charles's house. In February 1827, under the guidance of Stephen Hempstead, Sr., Charles was learning "the commandments, the creed, and the Lord's prayer."[100] After a visit to Gratiot's Grove for the summer, they permanently sent him south to be taken care of like an "adopted son" by her brother Charles Hempstead, up to whom she left the decision whether to board him at a school nearby or to have him stay with him and go to the "best school" in St. Louis. He apparently chose a different course, for Charles was sent to a school in St. Genevieve and later to another in Belleville. So, too, Susan sent Edward, age ten, "to board with" her sister Mary Lisa in July 1827, as she was unable to "see [her] children in such a place as this, my heart tells me that you will assist me in getting them away."[101]

Susan also sent her daughters away to be educated. Susan was placed in the convent at Florrissant near St. Louis at age eight in May 1827 and stayed there until 1833 or 1834. It is unclear whether Mary went to the same convent, but she was in St. Louis most of the winter of 1827–1828 with her Aunt Beebe.[102] As the number of children to be educated increased, Henry and Susan thought of sending them closer to home to Galena. Deciding against this strategy, however, they instead leased their house to two teachers in the summer of 1834, who turned it into a school where the local children, including their own Susan, Mary, Henry and Adele, would be educated. But this plan, by compelling them to board the "girles [sic]" with a neighbor, and forcing the rest of them into a single room, did not survive the winter. In June 1835, Susan went back to the established policy, and put "dear little" Adele, at age nine, with her sister Susan on a steamboat to St. Louis. By year's end, Susan contemplated sending Mary, age fourteen, to better schools in St. Louis as well.[103]

The children returned during Christmas and occasionally during the summers, but remained in St. Louis through the completion of their schooling. Meanwhile they were socialized away from the corrupting influence of the frontier among their Hempstead relations, especially "good aunt" Sarah, Uncle William (who occasionally stayed for long period in St. Louis), other "old aunts" and uncles, and their venerable grandfather, who doted on them when they visited.[104] Charles and then Edward went on to school in Belleville, Illinois, where they sent their cousins, and were socialized within the Hempstead social network of St. Louis for several years, not returning to Gratiot's Grove until 1833. Charles, after a long visit in late 1833, moved to Dubuque to work with Peter Lorimer and board with his family in 1834. Later his younger brother Henry would marry Lorimer's daughter, Adele.[105] Edward returned to Galena in 1834 and went into business with his uncle William Hempstead. After visiting the Grove for Christmas 1835, he went to work several months "with the men" in the mines and occasionally traveled on business, sometimes in lieu of his absent father, to Mineral Point and Platteville.[106]

Overall, the timing of the arrival and departure of Susan's siblings and relations with the major life course events in Susan's family – births, sending children off to school, children leaving home for work or marriage, deaths – indicates the logic of a dynamic regional family support network at work (see Table 1). A correlation of the number of relatives or siblings at Gratiot's Grove at any time, with Susan's household size according to the number of children present or absent, indicates an effort to maintain a certain level of support around her. From 1827 through early 1829, several relations provided help. When, in the spring of 1829 some of these siblings and relatives returned to St. Louis to get on with their own lives and attend to their own affairs, only one relative was at the Grove most of the period between 1829 and 1832. This dearth of outside support occurred just after the births of two children, which increased the number of children in the household to four or five (depending on whether her daughter Susan was at home), making the household the largest it had ever been. The arrival of Stephen later in the year would increase the family size to six children at home, with the two eldest away. Perhaps this pressure explains Susan's daughter Mary's delayed departure to boarding school. Being eleven, her presence was needed to help her mother in the absence of sibling aid. Though the timing is circumstantial, one is struck that Susan Gratiot's most desperate epistolary complaints occurred during the period when all support seemed to vanish. In the late winter of 1830–1831, which became known across much of the region as the "Winter of the Big Snow," one of the most severe of the century, when Henry was so busy and always away, and Adele had left for St. Louis, taking only her youngest with her, Susan had to take care of, besides her own four or five, five or six of Adele's children.[107] To make matters worse, her servant, "old Mary," was worn

Table 1. *The balance between children and the extended family support system in household of Henry and Susan Gratiot, Gratiot's Grove, Wisconsin, 1827–1835*

Year	1827	1828	1829	1830	1831	1833	1834	1835
Children in household	3	2–3	4–5	4–5	5–6	4–5	5–6	4
Other children					4–5			
Siblings or relatives	5	4	1	1	0	3	2–3	3
Children over Relatives	−2	−1 to −2	3–4	3–4	9–11	1–2	2–4	1

Source: Adele Gratiot Washburne Collection, Washburn-Norlands Humanities Center, Livermore, Maine.

out and Susan was forced to "give up" on her. As she watched her support system from family, friends, and servants collapse, and all the cares of the household settle upon her and her eleven-year-old daughter, even Susan Gratiot's impressive Christian patience was sorely tried, as evidenced by her weary and somewhat testy remark: "I have been here all winter half crazy with my teeth and ten children for you know that I am not confined to mine only," making it "really . . . too hard now."[108]

Apparently in response to the increased size of their family, Susan and her husband would begin another round of sending their children to St. Louis to be educated. Other relatives also began, again, to come up and stay at the Grove in 1833. Therefore, although there were notable breaks in this network, the family, in general, sought to provide Susan Hempstead Gratiot with a steady stream of family members who would help her endure the privations of the frontier and her husband's absences, and manage her duties of caring and providing for a large family while still operating the business tasks that devolved upon her.

Increasingly, the decisions of Susan's brothers and brothers-in-law played a significant role in shaping Susan's local support network. John Gratiot, tiring of the uncertainty of mining, decided to dissolve his partnership with Henry Gratiot in 1833. He went into farming, buying a farm at "the Cupulo [sic]" just outside Galena to which they moved in September that year.[109] This move shifted John and Adele into the small circle of society that centered around Susan's brothers Charles and William, both of whom had recently moved to Galena, which would later form the core of middle-class society there. From Susan's perspective, however, this placed Adele within a more extensive circle which extended between Gratiot's Grove and Galena, leaving her "lonesom" (though she still routinely visited her, being only fifteen miles away).[110] When in 1841, John suffered financial reverses from which he was unable to recover, he and Adele moved back to Missouri to live at the Gratiot family estate and retreated into a more distant network in Susan's social life, one maintained primarily by letters and through less frequent visits back and forth.[111]

Provincial lives

By moving to a location further afield within the Lead Region, Adele joined Susan's brothers William and Charles as part of an extralocal family network that established itself around Susan Gratiot across the district. Her brother William had first moved to Galena in 1827 to go into merchandising, and became a central person in the exchange network between St. Louis and Galena, or between Stephen Sr. and Susan. Though her brother Charles, a lawyer, was in Galena and Prairie du Chien as early as August 1828, and moved to Galena in June 1829, he still spent much of his time in St. Louis and back east and did not become a permanent resident of Galena until 1832.[112] Consequently, he played a role similar to William's, and only after 1834, when William moved back south for four years, did Charles become the center of Susan's local support network.

William made his first trip to the mines on 8 March 1827 "to obtain some knowledge of the country" "with a view of establishing myself this summer." For several years William's employment, first as a clerk, then as a partner, with the firm of George Collier & Co. of St. Louis, a branch of which shipped lead from St. Louis to the East, had turned his interests in that direction. On returning south, he arranged with Collier to purchase a stock of goods and returned north with his sisters and their families on 13 May 1827. William established himself in Galena in a store that traded lead under the name of "Collier and Powell."[113] In July 1827 he took in Sarah Beebe at his boarding house in Galena during the height of the Winnebago scare. In spite of the "disadvantage" caused by the Indian troubles, he was "doing well" by year's end. His business and regular travels south, however, meant that William was an infrequent presence in Susan's life. In June 1829 he visited Gratiot's Grove, but remarked it was only "the second time since I come up [sic]."[114] On other occasions, William would often come up for a visit with her husband Henry, when the latter had been in Galena on business or when returning via Galena from a business trip. William became and would remain a stronger presence in Galena through 1834. That year, he returned to St. Louis where he remained until 1838, when he came back to Galena.[115]

Charles, who moved to Galena in June 1829 to open a law practice, after eleven years in the law at St. Louis, was often present up at the Grove, though court business as U.S. Attorney at Prairie du Chien and travel east kept him away from September 1829 through the summer of 1830, and again in the spring of 1831.[116] These two fraternal connections were most continuous in 1831 through 1834, just as the arrivals of family members from the south stopped. When William moved south in 1834, another relative came north. And when William returned to Galena in 1838, and then Adele moved away in 1841, both William and Charles would become her primary contacts in Galena society, providing more close-by residences where nephews and nieces could stay when in Galena, while cultivating the creation of a small group of people who circulated, socially, between the two places. Interestingly, Susan never mentioned her brother-in-law Paul, who was apparently at Mineral Point, Wisconsin, between 1829 and 1832 before he returned to St. Louis to take up residence at the old Gratiot farmstead outside St. Louis.[117]

While members of the Hempstead family arrived for extended stays at Galena or

Gratiot's Grove, or moved back and forth between the Grove, Galena, and St. Louis, the local family network within the Lead Region was but an extension or outpost within a regional family network centered at Stephen Hempstead, Sr.'s Bellefontaine plantation, outside St. Louis. Along the lines of this network, family members traveled a regular circuit between St. Louis and the Lead Region, visiting each other and exchanging labor, goods, information, and support.

For a number of years all family members encouraged the family patriarch, Stephen Hempstead, Sr., to make a visit to Galena and Gratiot's Grove. As early as August 1827, Stephen was "contemplat[ing] . . . making a short visit . . . if the little steamboat can have water enough to go and come from Fever River over the rapids as is expected . . . in September" but later gave up on the idea when Henry thought it best to wait until spring "when the water is up." By May 1828, when there was the opportunity to accompany back north Sarah Beebe, her two daughters Mary and Sarah, and Mary Gratiot, however, a decline in Stephen's health, as well as a revival in his St. Louis Presbyterian church, prevented him from going. Prodded by a letter from William inviting him to visit, and with "all my children in town pressing me very much to go," Hempstead resisted and was unable to "accept my son's invitation." "Tell Susan," he told her sister Sarah, "I shall never go to Fever River to see her" and that from now on, "she must come and see me." A year later he still encouraged Susan to come south to visit him.[118]

Susan or Henry, as if to emphasize that they lived on a "near" frontier not far removed from the home they had left behind, made regular trips back and forth between Gratiot's Grove and St. Louis, the first as early as 1827. In April 1827, a year after she had left, Susan journeyed ten days by keel boat from Fever River to St. Louis to visit her father and siblings. During her five-week stay, she visited each of her siblings, dined at her father's regularly, and prepared, with "Sisters" Beebe and Lisa, to return in May with Sarah, her oldest child, brother William, and a stock of goods and supplies. On 2 September 1827, Susan Gratiot, fleeing the Indian threat at Fever River, again arrived in St. Louis with her children, Sister Sarah, and nearly 100 other refugees. For two weeks the family all stayed in Stephen's farm house. Though Stephen was glad to see them, he had to admit that crowding all his children and grandchildren into a small house "require[d] all the patience I am possessed of to bear with the noise and crying." Perhaps aware of their imposition, Susan and Sarah and their children went to visit brother Stephen before returning to St. Louis to catch a boat going north on 6 October. Meanwhile Susan, a member of the Presbyterian church organized by her father, took advantage of her presence in St. Louis to have her ten-month-old daughter Adele baptized. Disappointed that her father was unable to come north in May 1828, Susan and Henry, this time without the children, arrived again in St. Louis after a five-day journey on 7 July 1828 to visit Susan's father. Susan and Henry spent a quiet two weeks attending prayer meetings and visiting relations in St. Louis and St. Charles, but when the seasonal fever began to make its appearance among the neighbors, they chose to return north on 21 July.[119]

Susan was unable to visit St. Louis again until the spring of 1830. Her desire to

Provincial lives

do so intensified when her sister Mary's twenty-two-year-old only son Christopher, for whom the family had such high hopes, died of fever on 3 July 1829, making Susan want to "fly to join" her in the spring of 1830. On 4 May she arrived with three of her children in time for her father's seventy-sixth birthday. The next day Susan attended the wedding of her niece Mary Lewis, oldest daughter of Stephen Jr., and Peter Lorimer of Dubuque, Iowa, at St. Charles, and was present as well at the large wedding dinner given by Stephen Sr., in lieu of his son Stephen's, the bride's father's, absence in the East, the next day at Bellefontaine plantation. There, Susan met her brother Joseph for the first time in twenty years. Joseph, the oldest son of Stephen Sr., had, unlike the other Hempstead children, remained in Connecticut and only just recently immigrated to Missouri. She then returned to his new farm on the Missouri Bottoms and stayed there a week or two, before returning to St. Louis to stay with her increasingly frail father and nurse two of her children who had come down with fever. When the children were better, Susan rushed north, taking leave of her father, as it turned out, for the very last time before his death in October 1831.[120] After her father's death, trips became infrequent, her next being in the summer of 1834 and then again in the spring and summer of 1836, the latter trip made after her husband Henry's death in April 1836.[121]

Between her infrequent annual trips to the south, Susan relied on others to maintain contacts with her father and siblings for her. Traveling in the other direction John visited St. Louis in February 1827, April 1834, and at Christmas 1835.[122] Henry made the trip in August 1827, July 1828, February 1830, April 1831 (which included his last visit to Stephen Hempstead), and again in spring 1832. In the spring of 1836 he intended returning from the east via St. Louis.[123] It was William whose regular buying trips to St. Louis made him the most frequent go-between, carrying family mail and newspapers (which by 1830 they received regularly), sacks of goods, dry goods, and furniture, and bringing family and social news in far more detail than any letter could provide. William traveled to St. Louis in April and September 1827, January, March, and September 1828, April and August 1829, April 1830, March 1831 (which was his last visit to his father), summer 1833, December 1834, and again in spring and fall 1835.[124] When it was not William, then it was Charles, who, before going east in the fall of 1829 and 1830 and then returning permanently to Galena in 1833, visited Galena and the Grove in August 1828, April and July through August 1829, and August 1830.[125] When family members were not available to carry the family's letters, friends, neighbors, acquaintances, or even strangers stepped in.[126]

The constant movement of such intercessors, who could relay all the news by word of mouth, was a routine backdrop to the family's correspondence. The desire to "tell all the news" in a letter was often coopted by the knowledge that a brother or sister would soon be leaving to visit either St. Louis or Gratiot's Grove. For example, when Sarah Beebe wrote her sister Susan she often left it to Charles to give Susan the news because "he will tell you more than I can write." Likewise, when her father knew William was about to return to Galena, he simply noted: "I have nothing to write you more than William can inform you."[127] In addition, letters back and forth often included those written to Stephen Hempstead, Sr., by other brothers and sisters who were "so scattered about our country," which he then sent, either entirely or in "extracts," to Susan for her perusal.[128]

This family and social network of contacts, which mirrored the economic channels being carved across the region by the steamboat between St. Louis, the entrepôt, and Galena, the outpost, since 1823, provided the family on the frontier and in St. Louis with a steady stream of information and emotional and social support. As early as 1827, Charles S. Hempstead noted that news from Fever River reached someone in the St. Louis network "weekly," and from them news was disseminated quickly among the siblings there; a frequency that, as the time to travel from the Fever River dropped from ten to five days, was shortened to less than a week by late 1829.

These channels were also the conduits by which the family in St. Louis provided material support to Gratiot's Grove, transferring capital and goods and a material culture. Besides mail, family members and friends on the circuit carried supplies, household goods and furnishings, and other pieces of home that connected those "up" at the Grove to those "down" or "below" in St. Louis.[129] Among the many furnishings shipped over the years were a cupboard, a clothes press, a hand-me-down cradle from Mrs. McKnight sent from Stephen Hempstead to Susan in 1827, Charles's trunk for school, a portrait of Susan Gratiot's mother, a "miniature portrait" of Stephen Hempstead, Sr., and a "good high post bedsted [sic]." Other household goods or clothing sent north included presents to local Indians from Stephen Hempstead, a pair of white shoes from Aunt Sarah, a bundle of clothes for Adele, "two pieces of Russia sheating, a dozen good dinner knives and forkes [sic], and a piece of dark twilled bombazett for winter dresses for the girles [sic]." Farm equipment and supplies also went north along the route: two cultivators, a few good hoes, two old chains, a good carriage and harness, a bag of blue grass seed, a bag of garden seeds – as heavy as the courier "would take" (from which Susan planted an "excellent garden" in the summer of 1827) – a "full jar" of pepper seeds, and a few rose bushes. But the most frequent articles of supply were foodstuffs, including "three dozen chickens," "a coop with geese, guinea hens, and ducks," some livestock, a barrel of dried apples, sugar, molasses, rice, Irish potatoes, and some summer lard.[130]

Though the Gratiots lived on the frontier, far from family and relatives, the regional support network that Susan Gratiot established with her family, mirroring the structural development of a regional society, kept them in constant contact with the center. Centered at the estate of Stephen Hempstead, Sr., and extending between two local nuclei – one at the Grove and the other at Galena – this network, at times, was seamless and relatively closed. Whenever someone moved to a new location – whether to Dubuque, Davenport, Peoria, or further west – others in the network quickly knew and extended the benefits of the social and cultural network to them.[131]

Likewise, whenever any outsider penetrated the network, the tensile structure of this closed regional family system stretching from St. Louis to the Wisconsin frontier was apparent. When, for example, Theodore Rodolf, a German-American, arrived in St. Louis in 1834 with letters to John Gratiot,[132] the whole of Gratiot–Hempstead society across the valley was open to him. Not only did "friends of Mr. Gratiot" and Charles and William Hempstead in Galena, as well as Susan Gratiot, in her husband's absence, "hospitably receive and entertain" him, but he also met Susan's daughters, Susan and Adele, "afterwards the wife of E[lihu] B. Washburne." Rodolf also visited Adele Gratiot at her residence "which her husband had built for her" outside Galena and for several months he and his family were drawn into the Gratiot social circle that moved between Galena town houses and the country "farm." When Henry Gratiot – Rodolf's primary local sponsor – died, however, the door which opened the family system to him was shut and he was unable to sustain the connection.[133]

The Hempsteads and Gratiots, therefore, did not view themselves locally as establishing a new society, cut off and isolated from a society they had left, as was the experience of many American settlers from the East elsewhere in the West. Rather, they were simply extending the values, traditions, agendas, and material culture of an established society already in place in and around St. Louis, up to Gratiot's Grove and Galena. The establishment of a settlement in the Lead Region, which coincided with or just preceded the general American advance into the region, signaled a new stage in their regional social strategy. From their nearby base in St. Louis, they were able to carve out a social beachhead amid the diversity, chaos, and atomization of frontier society and sustain that outpost through far more intensive social contacts and regular material supply than that available to other settlers. As a result, they gained a deeper footing more quickly and set the agenda for a developing local society, which was an extension of St. Louis society on a "near" frontier.[134]

Having established a solid local family beachhead of good society, Susan and her family at Gratiot's Grove were able to play a significant role in structuring a broader social network, made up of enclaves, or "circles" of friends, neighbors, and newcomers who generally shared Susan Gratiot's values and became part of a small group of more "polished persons" at Gratiot's Grove and Galena in the late 1820s through mid-1840s. In the small cluster of cabins at the Grove, Susan's "neighbors" included seven wives of earlier lead miners and merchants, and two French women, one with St. Louis connections.[135] Both Susan Hempstead Gratiot and her sister-in-law Adele Gratiot noted their presence at the first Fourth of July celebration in Galena in 1827.[136] In each case, these women friends were wives of prominent early settlers and friends of Henry Gratiot. Further afield from her inner circle, Susan referred to early settlers, friends of her husband, and prominent men who she knew and who knew her, but increasingly fails to mention their wives, suggesting more formal acquaintance relationships.[137] In the course of a few years, Susan Gratiot had also established connections socially and through marriage with "good" families at small outposts at Benton, Hazel Green, Hamilton's Fort (later Wiota), and nearby Shullsburg, as well as over in Dubuque, all in Wisconsin Territory. These family and neighborhood networks were, from the start, nested within the large regional networks of family interaction stretching between St. Louis and the Lead Region.[138]

Susan consolidated her network of "good" society by selectively interacting with and then gradually marginalizing other ethnic and racial groups amid the diverse frontier population. She mentions a group of Swiss settlers who, under the leadership of Lord Selkirk, had attempted to establish a settlement at the North Red River, but retreated south to Gratiot's Grove in the first year the Gratiots were there. Adele Gratiot noted the arrival of the same group from Fort Snelling in 1826, naming the Rendesbachers (sic), Chetlains, Longets, and Bricklers, among others.[139] The fact that Lord Selkirk was "intimately acquainted" with Auguste Chouteau and had stayed with him at his house in St. Louis accounts, indirectly, for their decision to seek help from Chouteau's nephews.[140] Among the Swiss settlers[141] was Peter Rindisbacher and his family, who moved to Gratiot's Grove and hired themselves out to work for Henry and Susan Gratiot. They first wintered at the smelter and then, in the spring of 1827, built a house at the Grove and went into farming. Rindischbacher soon became known for his talent as a miniaturist and painted portraits of many of the settlers of Gratiot Grove (none of which seem to have survived). In 1829, Rindischbacher traveled south to St. Louis, where he stayed at Sarah Beebe's house and did a miniature of Stephen Hempstead, Sr., which Charles brought up to the Grove for Susan that fall. Rindischbacher was also apparently on the boat with Charles Hempstead, who traveled north to meet a delegation at Prairie du Chien before settling in Galena to practice law.[142] Later that year, however, Rindisbacher decided to return to St. Louis permanently.

Susan and those within her society were much less accommodating to the predominantly male French and American population around them, choosing, generally, to insulate themselves from rather than interact with that society. Though the house was "continuley [sic] filled with men," and public events were attended by a crowd of "miners with uncut hair, red flannel shirts, and heavy boots drawn over their pants," in great number, "all eager to dance and enjoy themselves to the worth of their money,"[143] Susan never mentioned any by name. She admitted that during the week, "you would think them decent to be about" and capable of behaving like "gentlemen";[144] on Sundays, however, "the town was full of drunken men," and the hotels and boarding houses incredibly noisy and rowdy. It was among this "roughest and hardest class of men, miners and adventurers" that everyday life was carried out.[145] Once, this culture even enveloped her family. In February 1831, after a birthday party for John Gratiot, Peter A. Lorimer and William S. Hamilton drew most of the men of the "village" of Galena into a series of midwinter "frolics," which involved, amid fighting and gaiety, dousing opponents in flour, feathers, or printer's ink, followed by considerable roughhousing and drinking. So intoxicated was Henry that "brother William" and Peter Lorimer had to help him find his way home. Two years later, William concurred with Susan's assessment of local society, calling it "debased." Later in 1840, Susan's future son-in-law Elihu Washburne agreed, disparaging Galena as a "horrid rough place," a "place of refuge for all the knaves in the U.S.," occupied by a "poor miserable set."[146]

Overall, Susan Gratiot tightened her social circle around her, and distanced herself from this male society, which in developing its specific values, behaviors, and

Provincial lives

attitudes would emerge as a subculture (see Chapter 3). That she did so is evident in her increasingly impersonal, even categorical references to them, in which she hardly bothered to distinguish between French and Americans. In some ways, this trend was demographic, and there was little Susan or Henry could do about it. As the numbers of Americans in the region continued to increase rapidly to as many as 4,000 or 5,000 by mid-1827, the presence of the mixed-blood people and French Canadians continued to decline.[147] Early on the Gratiots regularly interacted with both mixed-blood people and Indians. Henry Gratiot employed Oliver Emmel, a Frenchman who was married to a Winnebago woman and later was the first settler at the site of Madison, Wisconsin, and Catherine Mayotte, the mixed-blood sister of Winnebago chief White Crow, who in 1827 made a pact with and later sold her land to the Gratiots. By 1827, however, the presence of mixed-blood people among the workers at the smelting works was already less apparent. Mayotte seems to have remained in the area through about 1834. Nevertheless, the presence of mixed-blood people in the Gratiot social circle steadily declined between 1827 and 1834.[148]

By the early 1830s, the various enclaves of the Hempstead and Gratiot family were coalescing into a regional family system, which supported each of its many extended branches across the region. Stephen's death in 1831 established Charles, William, and Mary at St. Louis, and Susan and her husband at the Grove, as the arbitrators of regional family culture. Though the burgeoning market and better times allowed each unit to operate more independently, the various families remained integrated within a region-wide support system that, in its operations, helps explains their vitality and success.

Even as they achieved their goals, established their families, and supported the development of local society, the definition of what constituted "good" society was rapidly changing. In both Galena and Dubuque, new arrivals aspired to be members of a "genteel" middle-class urban culture that was developing around the country and migrating west. These new "genteel" middle-class settlers demanded a greater degree of social order, the rule of law, civic order, a stronger institutional framework, and greater social influence through religious moral suasion. They also cultivated a higher level of material display, polite behavior, and high culture. For them, the social "others" were not Indians, most of whom were gone, but the rowdy element that worked and lived in the mining camps and made life in Galena rough and dangerous.[149]

Charles Hempstead's arrival in Galena permanently in 1833, and William Hempstead's return in 1838, established this genteel social agenda at the center of the Hempstead family agenda. Through social influence, spiritual awakening, and institutional development, they sought, like so many other settlers by 1835, to establish a genteel middle-class society on the urban frontier (see Chapter 4). Susan, though not very impressed, did, nevertheless, consent to let her children seek opportunity and social mobility among those who pursued genteel agendas in Galena and Dubuque. Her son Charles moved to Dubuque to work for and live with her niece's husband Peter Lorimer in 1834. Henry followed a few years later. Her son Edward moved into Galena in 1834 to work for his Uncle William and later, in 1839, a family friend, George Campbell.[150]

Though the advance of the gentility system across the West, following the currents of American migration and social development, must have seemed inevitable to Susan Hempstead, so long as she and Henry remained at the Grove, they seemed disdainful of and uninterested in these new social developments. Given her husband's and his family's "special relationship" with the Indians and mixed-blood people, that it had to happen at the cost of their residence and existence within the region must have seemed ironic, if not disconcerting. From his first contacts with the Winnebagoes through his service as their subagent, Henry Gratiot and his family had managed to maintain a semblance of friendship – in spite of war, relocation, and growing dependency on government annuities. This indicates the degree to which Henry Gratiot navigated against the tide, and the ambivalence, anger, even shock that he, his family, and perhaps some of his people felt over the seemingly unstoppable course of events.

Called, like all French traders, a "Chouteau" by the Indians, and thus differentiated from the "Big Knives" or white men who craved Indian land in the Lead Region and encroached on it without respecting Indian rights, Henry and Susan Gratiot maintained a relationship with Catharine Mayotte between 1827 and 1835. So, too, it was the Winnebago Prophet who remained Gratiot's friend, and if he "came as a 'Chouteau' . . . welcome[d] him to his village; but if he came as a white man he must consider him, like all whites, an enemy."[151] In the winter of 1826–1827, the Gratiots maintained regular contact with their Indian neighbors, including a woman who doctored Susan, and with whom they exchanged gifts and information.[152] When the following summer the Winnebagoes went to war against the Americans, they warned the Gratiots of the danger.[153] Nevertheless, Henry Gratiot mustered with the American forces in 1827 and built a stockade at Gratiot's Grove (named Fort Gratiot) while they sent the women and children south to Galena and then St. Louis.[154] In the following years, ever more bands of Winnebagoes departed – though some lingered in the area to continue to trade with the Americans[155] – compelling Henry, as subagent in 1830, to travel further into Wisconsin to work out the payments of annuities.

During the Black Hawk war, while Henry Gratiot sought to maintain order and negotiate with the Winnebagoes and thus foster peace, he worked for both sides. When pushed, however, as in negotiations with the Indians to secure the release of American prisoners, he aligned with American interests. With the deterioration of relations after the Black Hawk war and the continued settlement of the region, Indians and mixed-blood people residing in or near the Grove and around Galena and Dubuque had, by 1833, all but vanished, being reduced to a "few poor and straggling Winnebagoes who lingered in the country."[156]

An annuity issue brought "four chiefs" from the Indians who still lived on the Rock River to Gratiot's Grove to meet with Henry Gratiot in the fall of 1835. As Susan reported, they informed Gratiot that the payments of annuities, "by some bad management," had been completely stopped, and that the "Indains [sic] on Rock River . . . are allmost [sic] starved and naked." Though it was unclear whether the chiefs would accompany him, Henry decided to go to St. Louis to acquire the necessary signatures on the documents to start the payment of the annuities from General Atkinson, and then expected to go on to Washington to clear up the matter in early 1836.[157] By that time few, if any, of the Winnebagoes were located near his residence. Within a year, as government policy shifted toward their removal, Susan wondered if Henry would receive another appointment and remarked that if he changed the way he managed Indian affairs "he [might] not los[e] by it."[158]

By this time, now that the real contest over control of the land was over, Henry and Susan's relationship with the Winnebagoes became poignant and nostalgic, based on traditions and values established while the small remnant of the "middle ground" which had developed across the area in the 1810s and 1820s still prevailed. In the early 1830s, bands of Winnebagoes came "every autumn" to visit their friends "the Chouteaus" and camped under the pine trees by the Gratiots' new house.[159] After Henry Gratiot's death and for many years these bands continued to come to visit Susan at Gratiot's Grove. When she later moved into Galena, bands of Winnebagoes continued to visit her "almost annually" and continued to visit Henry Gratiot's daughter – Adele Gratiot Washburne – "up to 1860" at her home in Galena "to pay a tribute of respect and affection to the memory of her father." Always welcomed with hospitality, they often remained at the Washburne residence "for several days, sleeping on the floor of her parlor" and always departed "satisfied and with best wishes for the happiness and well being of the daughter of their best friend and all her family."[160]

The Gratiot–Hempstead family was, locally and regionally, both an intermediary between the whites and Indians and a conduit through which "civilization," increasingly defined after 1830 by the middle-class cultural system of "gentility," would be transferred to this "near frontier." To some extent, the Gratiots focused on the former dynamic, while the Hempsteads established the latter. Susan and Henry Gratiot, by intertwining the two agendas, would feel intensely the tension and irony between them, trying to sustain the former strategy, while resisting the latter. Nevertheless, backed as they were by the social agenda of thousands of settlers, the capitalist marketplace, and the federal government, the Hempsteads' strategy prevailed because they flowed with, rather than against, the general currents of change.

Henry Gratiot was compelled to turn in the direction of the current. For him, this meant coming full circle by quitting and returning to the life that he had enjoyed as a young man in St. Louis. He gave up his agency, "closed up his mining and smelting business," and retired in 1834 at the age of forty-five to enjoy family life as a respectable, though restless, gentleman farmer. Henry purchased a section of land, leading Susan to exclaim that finally "the soil is ours."[161] Within a year he had built "a comfortable house" outside Gratiot's Grove, which Susan hoped would be "a fixed home for the remainder of our days."[162] From this vantage point, Susan could interact with the network of her relations in Galena, Dubuque, and across the

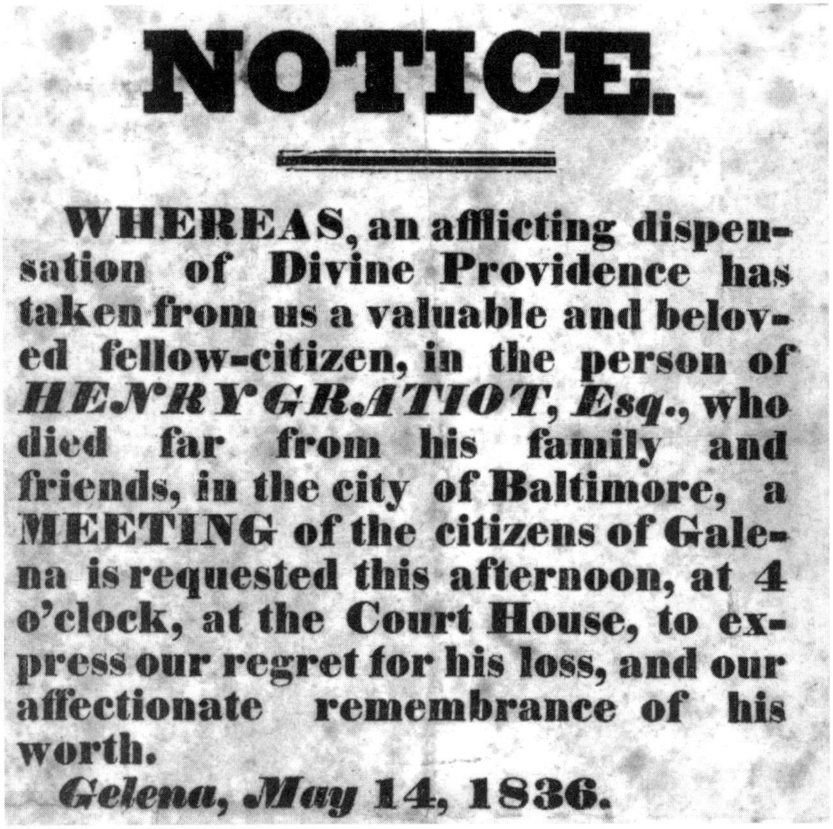

NOTICE.

WHEREAS, an afflicting dispensation of Divine Providence has taken from us a valuable and beloved fellow-citizen, in the person of *HENRY GRATIOT, Esq.*, who died far from his family and friends, in the city of Baltimore, a **MEETING** of the citizens of Galena is requested this afternoon, at 4 o'clock, at the Court House, to express our regret for his loss, and our affectionate remembrance of his worth.

Galena, May **14, 1836.**

Figure 2. Public announcement of Henry Gratiot's death, Galena, 14 May 1836. (Courtesy of Washburn-Norlands Humanities Center)

region, and observe from a distance, while continuing to disdain the force of urban development that drew regional social development toward the cities.

Susan's hopes of a quiet, secure future in the country were dashed on 27 April 1836, when Henry Gratiot, while on a trip to Washington to visit his brother Charles, chief engineer of the United States Army, died in Baltimore of a severe cold at the age of forty-seven. The citizens of Galena felt so strongly the loss of this "valuable and beloved" citizen that a public meeting was called to express regret at his death (see Fig. 2). Charles Hempstead lamented the death of yet another family relation and, perhaps ruminating back to the death of his wife, his third child, his father and mother, his several brothers-in-law, and his many nephews and nieces, remarked soon afterward to his brother William: "In our large and extended family connexion [sic] it would appear that we are never clear from sickness – or death."[163] Susan's estate was turned over to her brother and confidant William, to whom she assented without resistance. Being a widow brought Susan "new cares and anxieties" and she felt deeply "the want of him who was my guide, my counciler [sic], my all." But to William she wrote, "you my dear brother was his choice when he left me and his last wish when dying. My own heart would have led me to you without the sacred request of my much lamented Henry," and thus "to you I come with my problems."[164] Maintaining the house, managing the mines, farming the land, raising and educating the children overwhelmed Susan.

Within a year, the Hempstead family system – now structured by the sibling relationships among Charles, Susan, Mary, Sarah, and William – moved in to provide support. Susan's son Charles returned home to help on the farm. Her brother Charles visited more often.[165] Sarah came up to visit Susan for an extended stay.[166] William, in financial trouble after his company failed during the crash of 1837, moved back to Galena to take up the management of the Gratiot family mines near Gratiot's Grove and Shullsburg, which made him a constant presence at the Grove.[167] Sister Mary, called "Aunt Manuel," continued to live in St. Louis and planned to visit Susan; Susan hoped to go to St. Louis during the same period. Finally, in the fall of 1839, with brothers William and Charles and five of her children already in Galena, Susan decided to close the old place at "the Grove" for the winter and move in with William, establishing a seasonal pattern of city and country living which she would maintain for the rest of her life. By moving into Galena, Susan Hempstead Gratiot would partially leave behind her past life at Gratiot's Grove where, five years later, she still keenly felt "her lamented Henry's absence" and thought about his "silent tomb" so far away in the Catholic cemetery in Baltimore, and would situate herself, and especially her children, at the center of a small society of people who tried to form an enclave of genteel middle-class society.[168] One of the key figures in Galena's developing enclave of gentility of 1840 was, of course, her brother, the lawyer, booster, and later railroad man, Charles S. Hempstead. In 1840, she let her daughter Adele move permanently to Galena to live with her Uncle Charles.

Susan could hardly have missed the irony that as she and her daughter Adele moved from a log cabin, to a French-style stone farm house, to the townhouses of her brothers William and Charles, and finally to the Greek Revival house which her future son-in-law Elihu Washburne would later build for her daughter Adele, the family's old "friends," the Winnebagoes, moved during the same period between 1827 and 1860 from a seat at the table in her log cabin at Gratiot's Grove to a place on the parlor floor in her daughter Adele's Greek Revival house in Galena. Both journeys traveled along the same social and cultural line of structural transformation, though in opposite directions. By allowing her daughter Adele to move to Galena, Susan enabled her to meet and marry Elihu B. Washburne, and thus attach her family strategy to the even more aggressive strategy of a New England family, which, through Elihu Washburne's career, traveled its own cultural and social journey from a Maine farmhouse, to a townhouse and the Greek Revival house in Galena, to ever more elaborate and genteel houses in Livermore, Maine, Washington, D.C., at the American Legation in Paris, and finally on Dearborn Street in Chicago in the 1880s.

Family on a "near" frontier

The Native Americans and the French and Americans were two different groups of people, on two different social historical trajectories. Their different experiences trace the unraveling of a common frontier culture, which briefly held them together, and its supplanting by a more organized American social agenda, which in drawing power and strength from established French society and intertwining with the forces of economic and urban development would drive the Native Americans and all but a few mixed-blood people from the field and place middle-class Americans at center stage in the social development of the region. Before they could establish themselves and implement their social agendas, however, which we will study in Chapter 4, "good" or "genteel" settlers would have to confront and either reform or circumvent the rough, predominantly male population on the urban frontier.

3

"A common band of brotherhood": Migration, male subcultures, the booster ethos, and the origins of the urban middle class

Susan Hempstead Gratiot, the daughter of a man who "possessed all [the] elements of the best type of the New England character," strove to live a good, balanced, orderly life by practicing industriousness, perseverance, and humility within a patriarchal Christian society.[1] Supported by her family, she joined other "gentlemen" and "ladies" she encountered, and transferred "good society" – defined by the values of New England village life – to a predominantly rural frontier within the hinterland of Galena, Illinois, in the 1820s and 1830s. As Susan and, especially, her brothers were drawn into Galena or Dubuque, however, they encountered increased social and economic competition, amid a migratory "proletariat" of disorderly men who formed a majority of the local population.[2] Compelled to work even harder to establish social control, they aggressively applied their values of morality, self-control, and hard work to achieve personal and public success. In private, they sought individual fulfillment through self-mastery and establishing distinctive, gendered family values and practices. In public, members of good society fused the self-interest and the cooperative values of the booster ethos into a distinctive regional variation of middle-class "gentility" in the 1840s.[3]

Though the French of St. Louis had used the word "genteel" for a generation, in the 1830s and 1840s the term increasingly referred to the material and moral construction of a provincial "middle-class" "way of life." The local character of this cultural system was shaped by the economic and social context of the West. The volatile, proletariat population of the frontier compelled members of good society to work more aggressively to establish social control. Without formal means of doing so, they turned to "personal governance" and self-discipline by intensively practicing and adhering to the code of "gentility." That they were, by circumstances, compelled to pursue genteel social agendas on their own, and essentially in public, only heightened the self-consciousness of their genteel behavior. Whether driven by anxiety, insecurity, or feelings of isolation, exposure, and alienation, those who practiced "gentility" did so to fix their identity, intensify social meaning, and construct social order through encouraging others to emulate them.[4] Within this volatile world, they struggled in the 1840s and 1850s to invent and learn the rules, adopt and implement "genteel" practices and behaviors, and live as "respectable," even "beautiful," middle-class gentlemen and ladies.[5]

Given the disorderly, predominately male population of the urban frontier, many members of good society understood that social control would not come simply from imposing "gentility" on local society. Some "good" settlers isolated themselves from frontier society and did their best while biding their time for more settlers from "good society" to arrive to give them support. Others argued that social control would come through creating institutions and social and economic frameworks for "genteel" values which others would recognize as an achievement and seek to emulate to achieve social mobility. This strategy usually involved forming an informal network of entrepreneurs who cooperated with each other to develop and promote the town economy. They encouraged individuals to join collective efforts by aligning their self-interest with that of the town, thus initiating the discourse and behavior out of which the booster ethos would emerge. If to carry out this agenda, they needed to enforce law and order through aggressive posse or vigilante action against an internal or external ruffian element, they did so. Yet most, recognizing the risks of violence to town social order, sought instead to penetrate the ruffian element and try to draw specific individuals within it into their cooperative network. They did this by participating in male subcultures, in which men, through social bonding; ironic and sarcastic practices, behavior, and rituals; and collective recreation, cultivated fraternity and provided an outlet to vent and diffuse social tension and avert violence and disorder. Rather than avoiding or evading ruffianism, these settlers, many of whom were genteel, penetrated the disorder of frontier society. Ironically, though this did demarcate class lines more clearly, it also pulled the values of the male subcultures into the middle ground of the booster ethos, and gave to western middle-class gentility – long after gender ratios had equalized – a stronger masculine or fraternal, as well as public, cast, distinctive from the more feminized, domestic, and privatized version of middle-class ideology which predominated in the antebellum urban East. Eventually, by the late 1850s, a middle-class elite would consolidate their social position by further structuring the booster system, developing a web of voluntary associations and fraternal societies, professionalizing work culture, and constructing a life-style based on the more formalized system of behavior, etiquette, social interaction, consumption, and language of Victorian "gentility."[6]

This chapter explores the fluid dynamics of this intricate process of social development across the antebellum urban West, through the experience of one distinctive, richly documented, town – Keokuk, Iowa. First I will set Keokuk's larger regional context within the migration streams crisscrossing the West. Then I will examine the initial experiences of the early settlers and residents and then follow the development of a distinctive male subculture which would characterize the middle ground of urban life across the Midwest and later the trans-Mississippi West for a generation or more. Finally, I will note the emergence of "gentlemen" – boosters who self-consciously erected the scaffolding of an urban middle class in the late 1840s. In doing so, they would reconfigure themselves and create a distinctive provincial middle-class urban society and culture.

Migration systems and the structuring of urban society

In any town or city, intense competition amid rapid economic development drew together people from different migration systems and regions who – although they shared economic goals – had different social values and agendas. A town's location and the timing of its founding and development determined the nature of the people who arrived, sought to carry out their social strategies, or left any town or city. As local society was built up, layer by layer, with each new arriving group, arriving within different migration systems, the process of local economic development continued to differentiate successful from the unsuccessful, persisters from transients, and professionals, entrepreneurs, and middle-class residents from farmers, workers, or laborers. Market forces atomized social action and behavior and increased diversity. As individuals and groups intensified their efforts to achieve social control, many more were thwarted in their efforts than succeeded, and social conflict increased. Nevertheless, as the marketplace supported the emergence of a class system, that system would draw its capital from different migration streams emanating from different regions, and, by necessity, become more generalized, accessible, and adaptable to a range of social groups' interests and goals. Social homogeneity and traditional folk or corporate social frameworks were gradually circumscribed to social enclaves, which formed a demographic patchwork across the rural districts. In the 1830s and 1840s the towns and cities of the Great West became the nodal points of intersection and differentiation at which settlers from various groups and subcultures would construct a new regional society.[7]

At Keokuk, Iowa, the survival of a remarkable collection of autobiographies gathered together by an antiquarian historian a century ago allows us to analyze the complex sequence of such a layering or "sedimentation" process at any one place, and then to analyze who the people were, what they sought to achieve, and how the different groups interacted to achieve their goals, all the while as other groups arrived and departed according to the shifting functional interactions between the town economy and society and regional systems in which it existed.

Collected by Caleb Forbes Davis between 1883 and 1895 from surviving men who had been in Keokuk in the early 1840s, the thirty-six autobiographies, though a small sample, represent a cross-section of the population of Keokuk around 1850.[8] In birth cohorts, age at migration, region of origin, the sample parallels Keokuk's 1850 population overall. They were born mostly in the 1810s and 1820s, making them, on average, about age thirty upon arrival in Keokuk. The autobiographers represented a diverse mix of southerners and those from the mid-Atlantic states and eastern Midwest. In the 1850 census, 24 percent of Keokuk residents were southerners, 52 percent were from the north, and the rest, 24 percent, were English, German, and Irish immigrants. Among the native-born population alone, however, 30 percent were southern and 70 percent were northerners, and of that total 60 percent were from the mid-Atlantic states and Ohio, percentages which roughly parallel the native-born makeup of the sample of autobiographers. Among the autobiographers, two-thirds came from the North, most of these from Ohio and New York; while among the southerners, Virginians were dominant.

On a general level, these local patterns – given Keokuk's location – fit the more broadly understood migration patterns across the region. After 1800, three major American migration streams surged across the Great West. Whether described as "columns," "tides," "streams," or "extensions," each of these migrations represented a "migration system" with a specific logic and dynamic that drove the course of social change in every county or town through which it moved.[9] Pushing westward from three primary "cultural hearths," or core societies, in the East, the location, direction, and dynamics of these migration streams, and their intertwining and mixing across the western landscape, established the familiar broad parameters of the peopling of the region. Emanating from three central cores, Virginia and Kentucky, southern and southwestern Pennsylvania and western and central New York, and New England, migrants headed west, at first before 1800, a few at a time, into east central and northeastern Ohio and the plateau of Kentucky. By the 1810s, migrants at the front of these developing chains of migration had pushed west down the Ohio and settled on the American Bottom in Illinois, across from St. Louis. Simultaneously more densely connected migration chains pushed north across the Ohio River into southern and southwestern Ohio, and southern Indiana and southeastern Illinois up to the edges of the prairies. A decade later this Kentucky–Virginia flow trickled, then poured into the Missouri river valley, and, in later years, pushed north to the Iowa border. Another tributary of this stream turned north and east and settled the fringes of the prairies in south central Illinois and up the Illinois river valley.

To the north, Pennsylvanians, moving west across Ohio and Indiana, spread north along the river, reaching, in the 1830s, the outpost of Galena, having some impact at almost every point in between. Meanwhile, the lead mines above Galena and at Dubuque had also become the focal point of local migration. By the late 1820s thousands of Missourians and southern Illinoisans made the annual migration north to dig lead in the summer and return south in winter, giving them the name "Suckers," on account of their movements following those of a local fish.[10] A more permanent migration flow from the Ohio river valley and St. Louis had also entered the area around 1830. So, too, waves of English, Welsh, and then Irish immigrants established Galena and Dubuque as entrepôts in a migration system which operated for more than thirty years between mining regions in Great Britain, St. Louis, and its immediate hinterland in Missouri and the Lead Region. As Pennsylvanians and some Virginians filtered north, they encountered and interspersed with these groups. By the mid-1830s and 1840s waves of New Englanders crossed into Illinois by way of the lakes and spread across the region. Some of them moved south into Rock Island, Adams, Sangamon, and Madison counties, and even farther south to St. Louis and across the urban system, but most, in general, moved westward into Iowa and northwestward into the upper Middle West by the late 1840s, adding another cultural dimension to the region's population base.[11]

The result of these great population movements was to lay down three broad bands or cultural "zones" in which settlers from one eastern region dominated.[12] Across the southern part of the valley settlers from Virginia, Maryland, and Kentucky made up most local populations. To the north, New Englanders formed the majority across Wisconsin, the northern tier of Iowa, and northeastern Illinois.[13] In between, across south central Indiana, Illinois, and Iowa the majority of settlers came from the "Midland" area (Pennsylvania, New York, and Ohio).[14] Within several counties in the Military Tract of Illinois and into southeastern Iowa, where Keokuk is located, the migration streams of "Virginia Extended" and "Pennsylvania Extended" mixed.[15] To the west of the river this mixing was limited by the Missouri Compromise, which legislated the boundary between Missouri and the unorganized territory to the north as a boundary between slavery and free labor. A bit further north and along the rivers, settlers from the Middle Atlantic states mixed equally with New Englanders.

At Keokuk, the autobiographers' arrival dates roughly parallel the general frequency of immigration into the region and eastern Iowa as noted above. Migration to Keokuk increased between 1829 and 1835, reached a higher level in the mid-1840s, and peaked during the mid-1850s boom, only to end abruptly with the crash of 1857. The peak years of in-migration were 1846 and 1856, the former at the top of a steady surge of immigration through the 1840s; the latter, a sudden surge amid an uneven and unsteady flow of migrants into Keokuk during the 1850s, which peaked with the boom of 1856 and then ended with the collapse of the local economy in 1857. In any year, the influx of immigrants into the town included settlers from each of the major migration streams.

Individual-level data, however, allow us to get a better sense of the distinctive frequencies and flow of each major migration stream (see Table 2). The New York stream established itself the earliest and remained the most continuous among various streams entering Keokuk throughout the period. Ohio followed the New York pattern, but at a ten-year delay and continued with less intensity but greater staying power through 1856. A few Pennsylvanians arrived in Keokuk very early and others arrived again in a cluster in the late forties, but this migration flow failed to develop as much as the flow from Ohio and New York in the 1850s. The second most continuous track was that of the Virginians, most of whom arrived in the late forties and mid-fifties, closely paralleling the periodicity of migration streams from the North. The rest of the upland south migration provided support for the dominant Virginian flow in the mid- to late forties.

In general, the timing of such migration flows, as variable as they were, peaking, collectively, in the mid-thirties, mid-forties, and mid-fifties, suggests that Keokuk was most directly connected with primary migration streams out of New York and Ohio that were intertwined with a less continuous secondary migration stream trickling out of Pennsylvania throughout the period. This general northern migra-

Table 2. Place of birth/migration stream analysis: Keokuk, Iowa, 1831–1856

Year	1831–1837	1838	1839	1840	1841	1842	1843	1844	1845	1846	1847	1848	1849	1850	1851	1852	1855	1856
Conn.																X		
N.Y.	XX				X					X	X			X	XXX			XX
Pa.	X					X			X				X					X
Ohio			X	X												X	X	XX
Ind.							X					X						65
Md.								X		X	X							XX
Va.										X	X		X					
Ky.																		

X indicates the arrival of an autobiographer from that state in Keokuk in year indicated.
Source: Caleb Forbes Davis Collection, Iowa State Historical Society, Iowa City, Iowa.

tion stream was briefly overwhelmed by a major migration flow from the upland South in the 1840s, which then abated and intermingled with it only in the mid-1850s. Therefore, as different groups of northerners and southerners, migrating from their cultural hearths at different times, and under different conditions, arrived in varying numbers at Keokuk, they intertwined different aspects of their respective social and cultural systems from which they came with varying degrees of determination, and wove, thread by thread, the distinctive patterns of Keokuk society.

While each of these streams early on remained predominantly patrimonial, transferring wealth through land within the logic of family systems, the majority population in any area, transferring its social mores and culture, would shape local society and the course of local social development. In the 1830s, however, as market capitalism and the impact of the industrial revolution swept across the region, triggering urban development, transport innovation, and the centralization of trade and production, the logic of patrimonial inheritance, rural households, and village economies, and the societies they supported, were undermined. As more farmers made critical locational and production decisions based on market criteria, their world view became increasingly individualistic and "entrepreneurial." That this was occurring simultaneously with the development of an urban system drew many farmers and migrants into the accelerating economic and geographic forces of urban development. Within a decade an intraurban or "entrepreneurial" migration system emerged out of the patrimonial migration system.[16] As towns and cities became the nodal points that generated economic growth and development, they also became the points of interaction at which immigrants emerging out of the patrimonial migration system, and those moving within and through the entrepreneurial intraurban migration system, met, interacted, and forged, through accommodation and compromise, the framework of a new regional urban society.[17]

If one divides migration strategies among those in the sample between those who moved in from the nearby regional hinterland or system years after having migrated to the West (regional in-migration), and those who migrated directly from outside the system to the city of Keokuk (direct extraregional migration), the divergence of "patrimonial" migration streams into a two-tiered migration system entering Keokuk becomes apparent. For example, the earliest immigrants, not surprisingly, came from the trading post system. So, too, immigrants who took up farming upon arriving in the West, and then moved into the city, did so predominantly in the late 1840s, when urban opportunities were expanding. During the same period the number of merchants moving from regional trade and merchandising positions to Keokuk was on the rise, indicating the development of an urban migration system increasingly divergent from the deeper patterns of rural migration across the region. Imbedded within this system were also men with craft skills looking for work as coopers, plasterers, and carpenters. In the late 1840s more merchants within the urban migration system came from outside the region directly to Keokuk. Among professionals, those coming from outside the system predominated, especially in the 1850s. Thus, through the forties and fifties, a regional and rural-based migration system was supplanted by a system in which merchants and especially professionals came to Keokuk directly from outside the region, no matter whether the migration stream came out of New York, Ohio, or Virginia. In each migration stream, those who arrived in the 1850s were much more likely to come to Keokuk directly as a result of professional and mercantile decisions to locate there. In doing so they were tracing the structures and flows of an increasingly dense and interconnected national urban migration system, mirroring the interconnections between the regional urban system and, by 1855, the national system centered at New York. It is noteworthy that during the same period when Keokuk entrepreneurs sought to bypass St. Louis and Chicago and establish direct connections with New York City, a sample of immigrants to the Gate City indicates increased migration from there.

As different people from different regional migration streams navigated the shifting structural patterns of migration from trading post system or hinterland to town and town to city, from intraurban migration among merchants or skilled tradesmen within a regional system to merchants and professionals directly migrating to Keokuk from outside the region, the time spent in making the decision to move to Keokuk decreased. While those moving in from the trading post system often spent fourteen years, and farmers worked in the region ten years before moving into Keokuk, merchants and skilled tradesmen, moving more and more from town to town within the region, traveled around for five or six years before deciding to move there. In contrast, those coming directly to Keokuk from outside the region usually did so in less than a month, though a longer decision-making period often preceded the actual move. Thus, while a two-tiered migration system was supplanted by two separate systems, not only did the structure of migration patterns change, but so too did the speed of movement from place to place within those migration streams, and thus, implicitly, the nature of the decision-making process which immigrants undertook to determine why and when to move into or migrate directly to Keokuk. With the acceleration of the process, the transference of cultures along the various migration tracks occurred more quickly, reducing the possible eroding or homogenizing impact of experiences intervening between departure from one's birthplace and arrival in Keokuk. This resulted, as we will see, in perhaps more, rather than fewer, self-conscious regional attitudes being carried west in the 1850s than in the 1830s.

This increased speed of migration placed a premium on making a careful decision, a more rational calculation rather than a folk response. As immigrants intersected with shifting structural patterns of migration and were drawn into an increasingly urban migration network, they also broke free from the family and community context in which decisions were made within rural migration chains and acted increasingly as self-interested individuals trying, through rational analysis, to maximize economic gain and accelerate their social agendas (see Table 3).

Individual stories of immigration to Keokuk indicate that those migrants who had come from out of the trading post and military fort network which preceded urban development were the slowest to make the move. In contrast to these relatively carefully made decisions to move into Keokuk, those who moved into town

Provincial lives

Table 3. *Migration patterns into Keokuk, Iowa, 1820–1856*

Type of migration	Number	Years before in-migration
Regional immigration		
Trading post to urban	3	14
Rural to urban	4	10.5
Urban merchant	9	6.2
Urban skilled trade	4	5.5
Urban professional	1	1
Total	21	7.9
Direct extraregional		
Urban merchant	5	0
Urban professional	8	0
Total	13	0

Source: Caleb Forbes Davis Collection, Keokuk Savings Bank and Trust Co., Keokuk, Iowa.

from the country did not articulate any clear reasons for their actions. That they were mostly from the upland South and moved into Keokuk only after farming for about ten years in the local hinterland of Lee County shows a deep commitment to rural life, which they only gradually gave up as entrepreneurial opportunities appeared elsewhere within the system or nearby towns. Rural southerners, though continuing to follow the lead of others and imbedding individual decisions within group and family strategies, were gradually drawn away by the lure of opportunity in other economic endeavors, which, after 1845, centered more and more in the developing towns of the region. In doing so, they drew the values, practices, and behaviors of rural life into the towns and cities to which they migrated.

Unlike farmers who lived in the region and locally observed the changing economy and methodically inched toward a decision to move into town, most merchants and professionals moved quickly from town to town, searching for the optimum market conditions in which they could sell relatively low-priced goods to consumption-starved settlers for very high prices or find a practice where there were few competitors, but high demand. Every merchant or professional seemed to know of someone who had "hit it" in such a "first rush" of merchandising or professional practice and earned profits sufficient to allow them to fend off competitors for years to come. The difficulty was hitting such a first rush. They did not automatically take place in just any recently founded town. Nor did they necessarily happen if a town had all the correct prerequisites: good location, good transport service, mercantile connections, a rapidly filling back country, and a burgeoning local demand for goods in return for produce. For a town to experience such a rush, its merchants needed to be not just in the right place at the right time, they also needed to be adequately funded, in the right line of trade, and possess sufficient merchandising skills.[18]

Given the range of factors that had to come together to set a merchandising rush in motion, many merchants simply sought to locate in places that satisfied a number of criteria and then hoped for the best conditions in which to try to establish a niche in the local market. This was not a decision which could be lightly or easily made. Those who had been in the region for years, as a result, often made the most deliberate decisions to move to a town. Those who were in the West for a decade or more, in merchandising or trade at another place, very often spoke of their decision to move there in the most matter-of-fact manner, as if they had mulled over their decision for a long time and were at ease with it. During restless moving from place to place, driven by repeated failure and disappointment, rational strategies for finding a successful location unraveled. As some merchants lost faith that any rational strategy would pan out, they simply began moving from place to place trying randomly to find a successful venture. In time, individual rational analyses reverted to the time-honored strategy of letting others persuade or even cajole one to move to a town, or letting "fate," accidents, or, in two cases, a driving inner faith or a fortune teller lead one to Keokuk.

Often the most rational migrants ended up the most confused and let chance or fate decide for them. Merchants coming from outside the region sought to avoid such agonizing, time-consuming decisions by getting guidance from friends, relatives, and other merchants to pinpoint their destination and move directly to Keokuk.[19] While selectively shopping around the regional system, interurban migrants, having decided to move in a certain direction, often needed only one final piece of information to steer them to their destination. Unable to make their own decision completely, they relied on hearsay, word of mouth, and, perhaps most important, the rhetoric of boosterism which spread information about a town through the regional system. Such rhetoric provided the necessary data which many needed to calculate rationally the prospects of a town.[20]

Along the contours of this rapidly emerging intraregional, interurban professional migration system, middle-class professionals acted on their own behalf, as individuals, and sought support less from family members than from the members of the established profession or class of which they viewed themselves as members or prospective members. Within this interurban migration system, moving at faster speed, from city to city, a more precise job search or placement system had supplanted the family strategies undertaken by early settlers within the rural chains of migration, and the trial and error methods of early merchants and tradesmen moving toward Keokuk. Now individuals with references, letters of introduction, professional connections, and shared values assessed a range of variables and made quick locational decisions. Many merchants and professional men who moved to Keokuk in the 1850s pinpointed Keokuk, moved there, and established themselves in a small enclave or outpost of a larger social system. For those in each migration system, Keokuk represented opportunity. To settlers emerging from the rural chains of migration, Keokuk provided social mobility and contact with an economy and culture connected to the broader region and nation. For those who came in the 1850s Keokuk was a "field of opportunity" within the regional and national system. This difference in cohort experience would play a critical role in differentiating how members of these different groups would respond to the transformative changes of the late 1850s.

As the structures and dynamics of intersecting migration streams or systems changed, the values, expectations, and behavior of various groups who arrived and the nature of their interaction with residents continually shifted. At the interface between these two systems emerged distinctive local enclaves of a regional class culture. This fusion of several different subcultures in the 1830s and early 1840s involved people from both the rural and urban migration streams but increasingly, by 1850, involved middle-class urban people moving through the urban migration system. Drawn together by the forces of regional urbanization, diverse people located at the nodal points of the system and, in spite of cultural differences and different migration experiences, contributed to forming a new local society.

Keokuk, Iowa: Vigilantism and the booster network

Among western towns in the late 1830s and early 1840s, few developed on such contested ground as Keokuk, Iowa. Located at the southeast tip of Iowa just above where the Des Moines River meets the Mississippi River at the foot of the lower rapids, Keokuk was situated at or near the vortex of a series of economic, social, and cultural convergences between North and South, East and West; between "civilization" and "barbarism," and the core and the periphery; and between local investment and outsider speculation, and economic and social reality and booster expectation. Keokuk was a "border town" on the "Middle Border," inhabited by members of "border society" and surrounded by "border ruffians," and was known invariably as the "worst place on the river" and a "den" of "murderers, thieves, . . . and desperadoes."[21] One immigrant stopped in Keokuk to find "nothing but a string of log cabins under the bluff, occupied by Indians, half-breeds, traders, and groggery keepers," in front of which "half a dozen drunken squaws parad[ed] up and down the bank of the river, yelling and hooting like mad."[22]

As a trading post in the 1820s the site of the town was a point of contact and intersection between American and mixed-blood and Native American societies. When, in 1825, the federal government granted a large tract of land in southeastern Iowa, called the Half Breed Tract, which included the site of Keokuk, to the few hundred mixed-blood descendants of the traders who had aided American endeavors on the frontier since the late eighteenth century, the native and mixed-blood presence in its vicinity increased. By 1832 American settlers from each of the major migrant streams intersected and moved across the region, encroaching and squatting on tract lands. After Congress transferred to the mixed-blood residents the right to sell the land in 1834, they also bought lands from and settled among the few mixed-blood settlers who occupied the district.

In the 1830s waves of American squatters, land speculators, entrepreneurs, opportunists, land sharks, and criminals shifting their attention away from the Lead District in northwestern Illinois flooded the district in search of gain. That Keokuk and Lee County were located directly in a "zone" where migration streams from the upland South, Middle Atlantic states, and New England intersected, at a time when migration from the patrimonial system, while intertwining with in-migration from the declining fort and post system, mixed with entrepreneurial intraurban migration, only added to the social and cultural diversity of the local population and intensified disputes over land claims into social and cultural struggles for hegemony. Among the most significant entrants into the field was, for example, the New York Land Company which, through its agents David W. Kilbourne and Henry Austin, both of whom were "gentlemen" from New York, and, initially, Isaac Galland, a former "border ruffian" originally from Pennsylvania, began in 1836 and 1837 to purchase many of the "blanket claims" which squatters and mixed-blood people held on their plots and thus gain legal control of large tracts of land. Placing its agents at the settlements of Montrose, Fort Madison, and Keokuk, where Galland purchased land, laid out a town plat, and began to sell town lots to the mixed population of a few hundred men who had squatted at the site of the old trading post "Rat Row," where they engaged in the "lightering" of freight over the rapids, the New York Land Company set in motion the dynamics of urban development in the area.

In each case, however, that development would be carried out in the context of the larger legal and political confrontation over control of the Half Breed Tract which would embroil Lee County for years. The New York Land Company's effort to purchase large tracts of the Half Breed lands in 1837 were met with violent opposition by the few hundred settlers, squatters, ruffians, and mixed-blood people who had occupied and claimed rights to the land. When the territorial legislature supported the settlers by allowing them to claim and hold a plot until they settled all legal issues, the New York Company retaliated by getting the District Court to grant a consent decree of partition of the land to 101 persons, including both mixed-blood settlers and those who had purchased directly from mixed-blood owners, which rewrote the deeds on the land in "the tract" to facilitate its purchase and sale, on 8 May 1841. Many other claimants sued on the basis of insufficient notice of judicial proceedings and were countersued by the New York Company, entangling both sides in a complex litigation that would continue for fifteen years.[23]

In response, the settlers coalesced and hardened into a solid legal and social bulwark against the company, carving a fault line, "half and half," between the Settlers or Anti-Decree men, as the "outs," and the Decree men, the New York Land Company, Hugh T. Reid, and most newcomers, as the "ins," down the center of the rural and urban society within the region.[24] The Anti-Decree settlers, who were predominantly from the South, organized, in the tradition of rural populist resistance, as a "law unto themselves" across the Half Breed Tract and routinely threatened with bodily harm any agents who came out into the tract. In response to especially aggressive efforts by the company to establish control over their lands in 1840–1841, 1843, 1844, 1846–1847, 1849, and again in 1852, and 1853, settlers' mobs, or "committees," formed and marched into town to halt the company's efforts.[25] Urban vigilante committees and, once, even a "Decree mob" formed as a counter-response, resulting in a series of armed confrontations which degenerated into a "half-breed war."[26] Amid sporadic outbreaks of violence, the "half-breed war" was fought primarily by

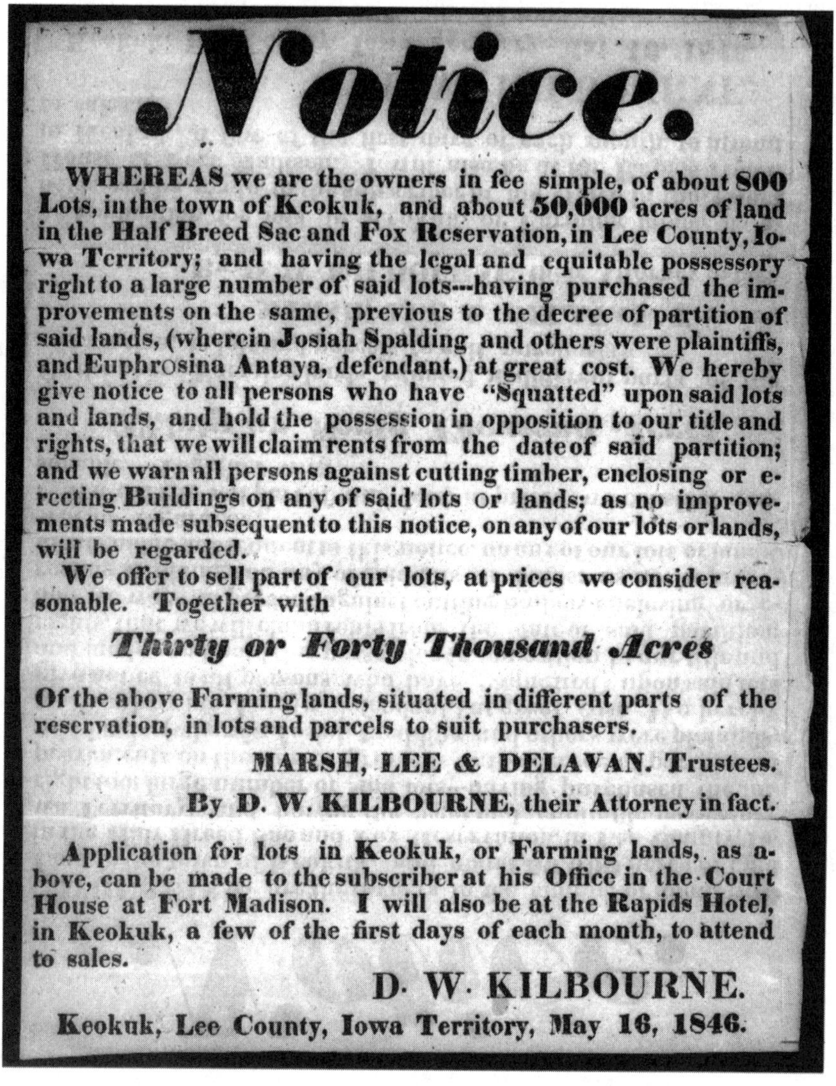

Notice.

WHEREAS we are the owners in fee simple, of about 800 Lots, in the town of Keokuk, and about 50,000 acres of land in the Half Breed Sac and Fox Reservation, in Lee County, Iowa Territory; and having the legal and equitable possessory right to a large number of said lots---having purchased the improvements on the same, previous to the decree of partition of said lands, (wherein Josiah Spalding and others were plaintiffs, and Euphrosina Antaya, defendant,) at great cost. We hereby give notice to all persons who have "Squatted" upon said lots and lands, and hold the possession in opposition to our title and rights, that we will claim rents from the date of said partition; and we warn all persons against cutting timber, enclosing or erecting Buildings on any of said lots or lands; as no improvements made subsequent to this notice, on any of our lots or lands, will be regarded.

We offer to sell part of our lots, at prices we consider reasonable. Together with

Thirty or Forty Thousand Acres

Of the above Farming lands, situated in different parts of the reservation, in lots and parcels to suit purchasers.

MARSH, LEE & DELAVAN. Trustees.

By D. W. KILBOURNE, their Attorney in fact.

Application for lots in Keokuk, or Farming lands, as above, can be made to the subscriber at his Office in the Court House at Fort Madison. I will also be at the Rapids Hotel, in Keokuk, a few of the first days of each month, to attend to sales.

D. W. KILBOURNE.

Keokuk, Lee County, Iowa Territory, May 16, 1846.

Figure 3. An 1846 handbill issued by David W. Kilbourne. (Reproduced by permission of The Huntington Library, San Marino, California)

each side posting handbills or broadsides on trees, posts, and buildings that either warned "squatters" off the land or threatened "Decree" men from the New York Land Company and their supporters from Keokuk to stay off the tract (see Fig. 3).[27] In time, so deep did the rift between Keokuk and its hinterland become that crossing out into the tract, the county,[28] or even farther out into the "Hairy Nation" of Davis County[29] became, for townsmen, a dramatic act fraught with political significance. The tract, in one local historian's eyes, became a kind a "small Ireland" set against the Decree men who analogously played the role of England.[30] It was upon this contested ground, divided by law, politics, and class, that those who arrived in Keokuk, following the sequence of the gradual shift in migration system from patrimonial to entrepreneurial to intraurban, carved out a town plat from the layering of contested land claims, and then gradually, by asserting law and order, established an economic nodal point upon which "good" society could develop.

When David Wells Kilbourne and Henry Austin arrived to establish the New York Company's presence in Montrose, Iowa, just north of Keokuk in 1837, they and fifty or so "genteel" settlers quickly found themselves involved in a "war" against a "gang of ruffians" over the rights to the land and town site.[31] Similarly, when Isaac Galland platted the town of Keokuk, he had to maneuver between the few legitimate settlers involved in the freighting business and the rest of the population, made up, as Hawkins Taylor recalled, of "the worst class of men that could be found, murderers and gamblers and thieves of every class," some of whom belonged to Murrell's clan, others to Price's and other gangs.[32] Around these hardcore criminal gangs, Taylor and others recalled other "ruffians," "hard cases," "black legs," "cutthroats," "wild cat males," and "river rats,"[33] as well as other "wild" or "rough set[s]" of men who, though "honest" and "not quarrelsome," were an annoyance to their more orderly neighbors. Such men, in the "southern fashion," generally rode into the nearest town on Saturday nights to drink, roustabout, "have a good time," and "test the manhood" of "neighborhood bullies" in "rough and tumble" brawls or organized fights. Taylor had encountered this society when he passed through Galena in 1832, which he considered the "most wicked" place in all the West, a veritable "sodom," full of "idle" miners, with few "reputable families" and even fewer reputable women, most of the women there being of the "worst of the worst class."[34] Susan Hempstead Gratiot had called such men a "curious medley" from "border society" at the 4 July 1827 celebration in Galena.[35] In 1839, A. Brown, traveling through Galena, could see "nothing going on [there] but gambling and drinking." Elihu Washburne a year later still found Galena's population a "poor miserable set of people" and the town a "horrid rough place," a "refuge for all the knaves in the United States" and "one of the greatest places for drinking and gambling in the whole West."[36]

Every genteel or polite settler in the late 1830s responded to social chaos by trying, in one way or another, to establish a border or boundary between themselves and the social "other" of the "border society" which emerged out of the common frontier culture. In their various responses, they would gradually find the common ground of more recognizable network or community around which they could articulate clear boundaries and within which they could cultivate their own social ways and ethos. Those who arrived with sufficient support from clans and family groups or religious organizations could, like the Gratiots and Hempsteads, or Horatio Newhall, another early settler in Galena, cultivate their own family or group social order. They did this by trying to isolate themselves from the rougher society of the town, and live aloof from it while waiting for more of their kind to arrive to allow them to extend the boundaries of their family cultures across a broader local community. Most settlers, however, could not isolate themselves in this way. Rather they undertook a two-pronged strategy against the forces of social disorder. Some settlers formed a network of entrepreneurs who clustered together "on the ground" around Keokuk's economic nodal point, to carve out a realm or space in which they could cultivate both individualism and cooperation under the rubric of the booster ethos. Others worked parallel with this structuring strategy to demarcate the lines of this network or community, by defining its edge through the vigilant policing of both internal and external boundaries between the legitimate activities among those in the booster ethos and the criminal activities of "ruffians" or outsiders. Toward this end, vigilante activity pulled together the community against a common foe and thus delineated its boundary by both cultivating a collective self-awareness within the community and clearly defining the nature of the "other." The symbiotic intertwining of these two boundary-maintaining social strategies, which resulted, in this fluid circumstance, in the interaction of "respectable gentlemen" and "rowdies" or "wharf rats" across the just emerging structures of local social order is evident in the activities of Laban Fleak of Keokuk.[37]

Laban Fleak, a thirty-two-year-old New Yorker, migrated to Keokuk in March 1840 after unsuccessfully trying to start mercantile businesses in two towns in central Missouri. Fleak had known about Keokuk for almost two years, having visited there on business. In his earlier trip to Keokuk, Major Taylor, General Jesse B. Browne (a Kentuckian), and Mrs. Gaines, the widow of a John Gaines (from New York), who had arrived in 1837 and opened a store house and tavern, all gave Fleak a hard sell he could not forget. Subsequently, a merchant in St. Francisville, Missouri, referred Fleak to two "honest, reliable" men, John Hillis and Valencourt Vanorsdal, both of whom quickly recognized the functional role Keokuk played in the steamboat system and entered the business of lightering boats over the lower rapids. Through "his very good friend" Gen. Jesse Browne, Fleak was also connected with Henry J. Campbell, a land agent and, since his arrival in 1838, prominent Democratic politician.[38]

Recognizing Keokuk's need for a grocery, Fleak arrived with five wagons of supplies to find the residents of the town, who lived in a few cabins in Rat Row along the wharf, in a "starving condition." Fleak opened his grocery, the first in town, in an old log building on the levee in front of the house he had purchased from Henry J. Campbell, and the next day Mrs. Gaines and Taylor were among his first grateful customers. Fleak "had not been there but two or three days" when he and Mr. McCall, based on this reference, "made the acquaintance" of John Hillis. They quickly entered into a partnership with him to build a store house and a hotel, which they opened a year later "above Rat Row" as the Rapids Hotel. When the river opened that spring, Fleak purchased a lightering boat and put his previous contact, Major Taylor, in charge of operating it in competition against John Hillis and Val Vanorsdal, and Dan Hine, a St. Louisan who had moved to Keokuk a few years before. Fleak enhanced his connections when, in summer 1840, he bought the new house Isaac Galland had built south of the wharf and opened it as the Keokuk

House, the first hotel in Keokuk. Galland, as noted, had recently made Keokuk "his headquarters" for dubious land sales from the Half Breed Tract, for which the New York Company sued him. Meanwhile, Fleak put a counter across the barroom of the hotel, and started a grocery for the convenience of river men. Located at the center of the wharf, Fleak's establishment and hotel became the central gathering place of Keokuk, "crowded to its utmost capacity" for most of the following season. Consequently, few newcomers and none of the older settlers failed to make Fleak's acquaintance.

Among those who joined Fleak in Keokuk that spring was Abraham Chittenden, a merchant from Warsaw, Illinois. He purchased a small log building which Mrs. Gaines had built earlier in the year and moved a stock of goods into it. Later that fall William McGavic, his partner, arrived and enlarged their stock, thus getting most of the town's trade. Major Ross B. Hughes from Maryland also arrived in 1840 and became Isaac Galland's secretary and sales agent for lands in the Half Breed Tract. From this position he would establish himself as Keokuk's official booster, and begin to articulate modestly a booster rhetoric. The town's first doctor, Dr. Birdsall, arrived the same summer.[39]

Clustered near the wharf, competing against each other, but also recognizing the need for cooperation to foster town prosperity, these first settlers forged the initial economic and social bonds out of which both a male subculture and the booster ethos would evolve. Yet in doing so, Fleak, who had been warned, and the rest of the new settlers challenged the several gangs of ruffians who had made Keokuk their "headquarters." Hawkins Taylor recalled that the Murrell and Price gangs controlled Baxter Gillock, the local sheriff, and voted their own people into office. Without law and order, Keokuk had become a "den" at which gang members and desperadoes from throughout the county converged on Saturday nights to drink and brawl. Less than a week after opening his store, Fleak was challenged by William Price, leader of the Price gang, who declared to Fleak that he was the "king" of the country. When Fleak stood up to Price and refused to serve him, he quickly gained the attention of the New York Company and its supporters in Lee County who were interested in rooting out the criminal ruffian element. Hawkins Taylor had recently been elected county sheriff, moved to Fort Madison, and, desirous of quelling the disorder in Keokuk, "found out who in Keokuk [he] could rely upon" and "entered into a compact" with Fleak, Val Vanorsdal, Col. Hillis, and others "to rid the place" of the gangs. With their aid, he formed a posse and set out with writs against the ruffians. By spring he had "seven of the worst desperadoes in jail."[40]

Fleak, on the basis of his public stand against "King" Bill Price, and his aid to Sheriff Taylor, had been appointed Justice of the Peace for Keokuk in the fall of 1840. In his year in office Fleak surrounded himself with a group of "his men" who he deputized to work as his officers to enforce the law. J. P. Mitchell, Charley Moore, Harvey Loomis, and Val Vanorsdal were the most active among his deputies. Mitchell gained fame for taking in a member of Price's gang, on a charge of theft, just days after Fleak took office. When Fleak served a warrant and convicted the man to time in Fort Madison, he became the first Justice of the Peace to stand up to

Provincial lives

the Price gang. A few years later, after arresting and incarcerating others in the gang, Fleak served a warrant on Price for theft and sent him for several months to the prison at Fort Madison to await trial. Though Price got off as a result of the efforts of his wife to bribe witnesses, his incarceration along with the confinement of several other members of the gang essentially broke it up. Fleak's success in breaking up the gang, putting some of its members in jail, and encouraging the others to vacate the region emboldened him, in lieu of an organized police force, to provide a broader umbrella of protection and justice for the town.[41]

Meanwhile, as the half-breed war heated up in the spring of 1841 and moved toward the litigation which would result in the 8 May decree, Isaac Galland broke off relations with the New York Company and moved into Keokuk. David W. Kilbourne, recognizing the difficulty of Galland's presence in Keokuk, sued Galland and made connections with Taylor and Fleak, both of whom, as Decree men, became the men in Keokuk Kilbourne "could rely upon."[42] Under Kilbourne's direction, the New York Company established agents, "made friends," and, in alignment with Fleak's agenda and with his participation, supported the formation of a Vigilante Committee among some of the more legitimate settlers in town – including Val Vanorsdal and John Hillis – and also alleged ruffians William Clark and Charley Moore. For five years, the Vigilante Committee waged a periodic "war" against gangs and defended the town against recurrent Settlers' mobs and encroachment by Mormons, to whom Galland had begun selling tract land in 1840. As often happened among the disparate groups who joined in vigilante activity, as the committee prevailed over different outside adversaries, local support and social cohesion increased. In time, the Vigilante Committee thus held back the Settlers and their supporters, and isolated Galland.[43]

Fleak, Moore, and others had established a highly active and effective Vigilante Committee to police the town and maintain peace and order. Usually they apprehended suspected criminals and, with no regard for due process, dealt out quick justice before warning them out of town. In 1841 they ran an African-American man out of town. A year later they captured a horse thief who tried to steal two of Lyman E. Johnson's horses, took him to an island in the river, tied him to a tree, whipped him with hickory swatches until he bled, and then warned him to get out of town.[44] In another case a man caught stealing from a local steamboat captain on the river was dropped at Keokuk and turned over to the Committee, which dispensed swift punishment: beating and expulsion in a small boat onto the river. The next year, when a gang of thieves harassed the town, Henry J. Campbell joined Fleak in pursuing them, although Fleak was by then only the postmaster.

As often happens during such management strategies along an unclear boundary, the members of this committee and their adversaries held similar values, and thus could use both violence and the law to pursue their respective agendas. The Vigilante Committee was, for example, aware of the extralegal nature of their actions. They also knew that the "ruffians" understood the law and would, if the chance appeared, use it to file charges against them and have them indicted. In the spring of 1842, while still Justice of the Peace, Fleak was charged with inciting a lynch mob when he placed handbills around town offering a $100 reward to those who apprehended and had convicted "in the Court of his Honor Judge Lynch" those responsible for a series of thefts (one of which was perpetrated on Fleak). Incited by these posters, a mob formed, led by a newcomer from Mississippi, which captured a black man and whipped him until he identified the culprits and got the stolen goods returned. Later, in the spring of 1844, when someone attempted to steal the payroll for the U.S. Military at Fort Madison from Fleak "many of the citizens" turned out to comb the area in search of the criminal. After apprehending him and turning him over to the courts, they pursued his partner, who, it was rumored, had been taken in by Dr. Isaac Galland, an Anti-Decree man. "When the citizens heard that the Doctor protected him, they went in a body to his house to request him to turn the man out and let him leave town as he promised to do." Galland became "greatly excited" and confronted "the mob," armed with a pistol and a knife, threatening "to kill any man who attempted to enter his house." Though tense words were exchanged, the crowd dispersed. Incensed, the doctor gathered witnesses and had the new local sheriff serve warrants on "twenty to thirty of Keokuk's best citizens" for conspiracy to commit a lynching. Defended by Lewis Reeves, and supported by "his friends" in the court and jury, they threw out Fleak's case and dropped the charges. Fleak, after laying low for a brief stint in Missouri, returned to Keokuk to continue actively to defend the town against all criminals through 1846, when more legitimate police authority replaced the Vigilante Committee, though it reappeared as late as 1852 in response to threats from the Settlers.

On another occasion in 1846, when newcomer James Daughtery took up residence in a vacant house on right of possession, rather than based on the Decree – and thus unwittingly appeared to side with the Settlers and represented a breach in the Decree men's defense of Keokuk – a group of ruffians from the Decree party, headed by Dan Hine and Charley Moore, "got on a tare [drunken spree] in a saloon" down the street and formed a mob which moved en masse toward Daughtery's house. While the mob pelted the house with rocks and broke the windows, Daughtery escaped out the back door and came around to the front corner of the house. From there he fired his shotgun into the crowd, killing a younger brother of Jessie Huff, for which he was indicted and tried, but acquitted on the basis of self-defense. In another case, in Montrose, a mob, led again by Charley Moore and Dan Hine, pursued and captured a man who had allegedly committed a murder and brought him back to town to face vigilante justice, until the sheriff stopped them.

The Vigilante Committee could rise to meet any challenge, no matter how pervasive, because as the challenge increased, so too did local support and participation. When, for example, a wave of thefts hit the town and nearby hinterland – all allegedly by the Mormons – Fleak, Dr. Millard, Vanorsdal, and Moore called a public meeting to organize a strategy to rid the county of Mormons. When Fleak's name appeared on a "hit list" of the Danite Gang, the committee around him became more vigilant. Joe and Bill Clark joined the others in providing protection for Fleak. After Joseph Smith, leader of the Mormons, was murdered, the residents of Nauvoo fortified themselves against the impending assault of the non-Mormon residents, while at the same time continuing with (alleged) petty thievery and harassment throughout the region. In response to a Mormon attempt to ship some firearms to Keokuk a few days before a major battle between the Mormons and militia in Illinois, Fleak "called on Dan Hine, Bill Clark," Charley Moore, A. W. Griffith, and the rest of his "assistants" on the committee to prepare to block the delivery of the guns. Posting themselves strategically near the wharf, the committee lay in waiting. When they reached Main Street, Moore and Clark stepped out into the street, stopped them, ejected the drivers, turned the teams around, and brought them back to the wharf. Soon thereafter, when several Mormons, "armed to the teeth," arrived to retrieve the shipment, General Browne and Moore joined Fleak, Hine, and Clark to repulse them in a considerable "fray" in which several serious blows were struck but no one was seriously hurt. As the Mormons retreated empty-handed, "the whole town . . . turned out in hot pursuit" and engaged them in a brief altercation on the edge of town, in which one Mormon was wounded before they escaped to Nauvoo.[45]

From barroom brawls to personal retaliation, mob activity, and quasi-militia action, such actions among individuals in the booster network or the whole town served the purposes of genteel people and ruffians alike, clarifying, structuring, and delimiting the nature of the local social order. For the former, like Laban Fleak, collective action involving men from different classes and cultures provided an outlet for one's leadership and enabled one to articulate and consolidate one's social position. It also reinforced their desire to articulate and gain support for town policies which supported the development of the nascent booster ethos, because there were strong parallels in cooperation and action among townsmen in defending the town against desperadoes or competing economically against another town. Genteel boosters associated with men like Charley Moore, a huge, friendly, but violent man, because they needed his strength and power to maintain order. In providing support, they could exonerate such men for their brawling, drinking, carousing, and other habits of the "meanest sort." They could also accept them as a member of a network of settlers pursuing a common goal without fear that associating with them would lower one's own status. Finally, for men like Charley Moore and Adam Hine, such active interaction with those in the merchant and professional classes provided a "chance to enter into the activities of the leaders," and thus, by clarifying their own status, served as a stepping stone to social mobility.

For both groups, efforts against "outsiders" bound together all participants and subsumed individual self-interest to mutual agendas which defined the community. Memorable collective experiences of townspeople directed against "outsiders" had, to some extent, the effect of actual war, forging solidarity and fraternal bonds that facilitated collective economic and social action. Vigilante action and mob or crowd violence was imbedded in the ongoing process of social development. In fighting against outsiders, they were not fighting to create a society, but defending and, in so doing, defining and delimiting the boundaries of a community they were in the process of creating. Vigilantism did not precede the creation of a legal and political system, but was intertwined with and supported its development.[46]

"A common band of brotherhood"

As more of the Vigilante Committee's supporters were elected to office – Bill Clark became the first mayor of Keokuk, Hawkins Taylor, Marshall and later mayor, William Patterson and John Graham, later mayors – a framework for peaceable town development was established. While establishing law and order and the public space of their community through vigilante action, this small group of settlers, which included both gentlemen and ruffians, clustered around an economic nodal point centered at Keokuk which, by 1840, had reached a sufficient level of specialization to function as a local economy. Within this framework, merchants and entrepreneurs could increasingly work, if still somewhat reluctantly, not only out of self-interest but also for the general good of the town. Aware that individual achievement was contingent on town growth, members felt compelled to stimulate local growth by encouraging and helping newcomers. By cultivating the values of the burgeoning booster ethos, each newcomer, grateful to those who welcomed him into town society and provided critical support, reciprocated by taking part in an interdependent set of activities to attract people to town, do the same for them as others had done, and draw them into the economic community defined by the town's booster network.

Through the early 1850s, almost every immigrant encountered this developing network, and were either given an ingress to or closed from the inner workings of the community. Immigrants or travelers to Keokuk in the early 1840s were certain to encounter Ross B. Hughes. Whether prospective immigrants came to Keokuk to look around before deciding, or moved directly there and needed a temporary place to stay, they were sure to find a room at Laban Fleak's Keokuk House or later John Hillis's Rapids Hotel. For local real estate needs, each newcomer soon met Mrs. Gaines or John Hillis. If one wanted to risk the uncertain titles and purchase land in the Half Breed Tract, Ross B. Hughes, Isaac Galland's assistant, was the man to see. One could get initial supplies at Fleak's grocery, but serious buying was done at Chittenden's and McGavic's. Later, if one went into farming, one would sell produce to Chittenden and McGavic in exchange for credit for merchandise. The only blacksmith shop in town in spring of 1841 was Charley Moore's.

Each newcomer was greeted by a member of the booster network with three questions: "Whar did you come from?" "What did you run away for?" and "How much money have you got?" In Keokuk, as elsewhere, social adherence to migration streams and a proclivity to cooperate and associate most freely with residents from one's cultural region or ethnic group shows that acquiring "the freedom of the town" was contingent on who you were and who you knew.[47] Though the town was divided among northerners and southerners throughout the period, it was the northerners who were most prevalent in cooperating in the booster network. From Fleak's entrance when only one southerner was involved in the network, to E. R. Ford's when several had become involved, southern participation was continually less than 20 percent of those involved, less than their share of the town's population. While there might have been a tendency among the northerners to seek aid from someone from one's home state, settlers from the Middle West and the Mid-Atlantic and New England states interacted without any apparent preference for people from their home states (see Table 4).

Provincial lives

Table 4. *Initial contacts by birthplace of five newcomers to Keokuk, Iowa, 1840–1847*

	New England	N.Y.	Pa.	Ohio	Ind.	Ill.	Ky.	Md.	Germany
Laban Fleak (Ohio)		3	2	1	1			1	1
A. Brown (New York)	1	2	3	4	1			1	1
E. Dietz (Illinois)	1	2		3				1	
E. Ford (New York)	1	2		2			1	1	1

Source: Caleb Forbes Davis Collection, Keokuk Savings Bank and Trust Co., Keokuk, Iowa.

A. Brown's experiences in Keokuk in spring 1841 give us a fleeting, but rare image of the members of this local booster "network" springing into action to help a newcomer. Brown, a merchant, had traveled around the region working on steamboats for some years before opening a hotel in nearby Hamburg, Illinois. At Hamburg, he met Ross B. Hughes, who regularly stopped there to visit relatives in western Illinois. In the winter of 1840–1841 Hughes intensified his pressure on Brown, urging him to come to Keokuk. Finally, on 1 March 1841, Brown relented and went up to have a look, stopping at the Keokuk House. The next day he met Hughes, who took Brown over to show him the only log house available in town, which Hughes knew about because he boarded with Mrs. Gaines, the owner of the building. After some hesitation because of the high rent charged, Brown agreed to rent the place from Mrs. Gaines, but only providing he took possession of the house on 1 April, which he did, after some legal complications with John Hillis.[48] Soon afterward, with the help of Hillis, Abraham Chittenden, and William McGavic, Brown managed to acquire a liquor license and open a tavern, "A. Brown's Entertainment," which soon prospered as a local meeting place and became a regular stopover for steamboat captains and river men, its reputation spreading as far east as Ohio and Pennsylvania. Among those Brown met in the early forties were Adam Hine, who with his brother Dan was in the lightering business; Charley Moore, who had also arrived that spring; Bill Dierdorff; and others who later became involved in the local Vigilante Committee.

Subsequent newcomers to Keokuk in the 1840s encountered the mutualistic dynamics of this network. Edward Dietz, who arrived from Illinois in November 1844, first met Charley Moore, the blacksmith, who found him a room at Mother Meeker's. While there, Dietz got a position as a clerk for Ross B. Hughes. Hughes found him a place to board at Dr. John Olive's. In the next few weeks Dietz made acquaintances with L. B. Fleak, Henry J. Campbell, Adam and Dan Hine, Bill Clark, and Val Vanorsdal. Later he clerked for J. P. Reed and Arthur Bridgeman, newcomers from Virginia and Massachusetts, respectively.[49]

"A common band of brotherhood"

A. W. Griffith entered the same network even more directly in 1845. He bought a store next to Harry Fulton's place from Isaac Galland. His neighbors were Ross B. Hughes and Charles Ivins. Ivins owned a hotel which had become a center of boarding house society and Griffith was quickly drawn into it, befriending, again, the now familiar veterans of the network – the Hines brothers, Charley Moore, Bill Clark, and Val Vanorsdal, Henry J. Campbell, L. B. Fleak, Dr. Birdsall, and Lyman E. Johnson. It was only a matter of time before he broadened his circle to include other members of the core members of the network – William Coleman, John Brooks, William McGavic, and J. P. Mitchell – and some newcomers, in particular, Silas Heaight, agent for the Keokuk Packet company, a wharf boat operator, and for a time a distiller and manager of a storage house, and steamboat captain J. C. Ainsworth.[50]

The "network" was still operating efficiently in December 1846 when E. R. Ford, a physician, arrived with the ubiquitous Ross B. Hughes at his side. They had met on the steamboat and in a conversation the indefatigable Hughes convinced Ford to stop at Keokuk to have a look around. During a tour he and Hughes met Hawkins Taylor, now a resident, who also took the opportunity to ply Ford with "pertinent" information. By day's end, Ford had decided to stay, informing hotel keeper William Coleman of his decision. Coleman jumped into action to make sure that "through his instrumentality" Ford met the "leading physicians" of Keokuk, in particular, a very popular and convivial member of the drinking set, Dr. Justin Millard, who willingly took Ford in as an assistant and later formed a partnership with him. In an open, easy, and "off-handed [sic]" manner, Ford soon entered the inner circle of "Early Settlers of '40 or '41," as they referred to themselves by 1846. Among those Ford specifically mentions as notable friends were John Brooks, A. Brown, Henry J. Campbell, Laban B. Fleak, John P. Reed, Val Vanorsdal, Captain J. C. Ainsworth, and Silas Heaight.[51]

It was Caleb F. Davis, however, who gives us perhaps the most detailed look at the dynamics of this cooperative system after his arrival in Keokuk on 1 March 1849. Davis arrived in Keokuk with his cousin John P. Reed and immediately started as a clerk in Reed's and Arthur Bridgeman's store, where he joined another clerk, Edward Dietz, who had arrived in 1844. The first friend Davis made was Bill Clark, an "intimate friend" of Mr. Reed's, to whom Reed introduced him that afternoon. That evening Reed and Clark invited Davis to come along with them to visit "the billiard room and saloon kept by Kinney Said in the upstairs" of the frame building opposite the store. "Here I met . . . Henry J. Campbell, Charley Moore, Colonel Hillis, Ad Hine and others" in that group. Later in the same milieu he met other members of the early settlers' cohort and quickly became one of them.[52]

Male subcultures and the booster ethos

As this network of merchants, entrepreneurs, and professionals cooperating for the good of the town coalesced, some of its members began to employ the ideological force of boosterism, which sought to subsume self-interest into cooperative public efforts to draw more people into the network and the town and thus stimulate and promote town development. Those who ascribed to the booster ethos wanted to succeed in a town where legal and civic order had been established, invest in the local economy, and "identify [their] fortunes with those of the place and grow up with a place" equal to their goals and ambitions.[53] By integrating their self-interest to the collective interests of the local economy, and acting within a network of men who acted for the common good of the town, they would gradually seek by defining the structure and ideology of the booster ethos to prosper, persist at a higher level than most subsequent newcomers, and establish themselves as the ruling economic, political, and social elite who could impose social order on town life.

The reality, however, was that the booster ethos only gradually emerged as the driving force of economic and social development in the urban West.[54] Often more an effect than a cause of growth, the ethos flourished when town or city economic prosperity fulfilled boosterist predictions and expectations, empowering its practitioners and advocates to establish a unified economic policy. But because boosters could just as easily be repudiated by unfulfilled economic expectations, they were compelled, during periods of initial development, to proceed cautiously, set realistic goals, and rein in their rhetoric out of fear of losing their claim to social hegemony when raised expectations were disappointed. The social ordering power of the booster ethos was, therefore, contingent on, indeed, dependent on, the town social order and economic prosperity. Dependent on volatile forces it could not control, the booster ethos was, among other social ordering mechanisms of the time, an unstable force, able to lose its organizing power as quickly as it had been once able to articulate and establish order on the urban frontier.

Members of booster networks and genteel people were aware of the volatility of boosterism and, rather than engaging in unrestrained "wind work,"[55] used it cautiously and in a controlled way by muting its language and restraining its use according to local economic conditions. Consequently, boosters often viewed their work primarily in terms of managing a town's reputation across the region. Hearsay, word of mouth, or printed reports could spread a town's reputation across the migration system and vary widely from hyperbole to derision, exaggeration to understatement. Within a few years of each other, for example, various immigrants to Keokuk heard the town described as the future "large commercial center" of Iowa or "the worst place on the river."[56] Most townspeople understood, however, that it was the latter reputation that prevailed, and boosters tried to use that awareness to instill in locals an awareness of the need for reputation management. Once, when a vigilante committee meted out swift justice to an outsider, Dr. Galland gave them a stern lecture "telling them what a bad reputation the place was having abroad from such outrages, and appealing to their better nature to . . . help build up a town in which it would be a pride and pleasure to live."[57] The example of Alton, Illinois, which after the Lovejoy riots of 1837 had become a target of "unqualified, undiscriminating condemnation,"[58] was always nearby. A decade after the riot, a correspondent visiting the town still reported that he was in "that much despised and abused city."[59] Altonians could do little, however, to counter this image and the adverse impact it had on migration and town development. Within any town, however, reality and a sense of responsibility tempered most hyperbole, while self-interest and the need to establish goals and create incentives blunted excessive negative criticism. As locals aligned the boosterist ethos of the town with actual economic performance, however, they also narrowed its range and power in affecting social order.

Rather than articulating some grand speculative theory, one is surprised, for example, to find Horatio Newhall, an activist booster of Galena, quipping insecurely to his nephew, who had joined him in town in November 1832, that "our village appears better than he had anticipated. He has not yet seen a man dirked or an eye gouged." Only with the growth of the town would Newhall's rhetoric expand.[60] Later, as noted, Ross B. Hughes, Keokuk's unofficial booster, advertised the town by "always keeping in the strict line of the facts" and speaking in a "concise form and epigrammatic style" to E. R. Ford in 1846. Instead of trying to overwhelm prospective settlers with rhetoric, he wore them down with modest arguments based on theories and evidence and capped it off with a tour of the site. Furthermore, he was surprisingly blunt about the current condition and prospects of Keokuk. When Hughes tried to convince A. Brown to come to Keokuk, he admitted that the town did "not look very inviting to a stranger." Likewise, when he tried to woo E. R. Ford, he insisted Ford talk to others, to assure Ford that his opinions were widely held. Finally, aware that he had little but expectations really to sell, he simply presented it as a challenge, arguing that if settlers took the risk it would ultimately pay off. He challenged A. Brown by appealing to his origins, remarking that "if you will come you are just Yankee enough to make a fortune there in ten years." When pushing Ford, he used his own experience as a reference, citing four satisfied years in residence and challenging him "to form his own conclusions and see if I am not right and that this is the place you will select." Later, amid intensifying booster rhetoric, William Worth Belknap had "reconciled" himself to living in Keokuk, "this poor specimen of what we denominate here a 'one horse town.'" Those who articulated the booster ethos were aware of the risks to prospective newcomers and did not want to build up a place too much, out of fear that premature disappointment would cause the hasty departures of disappointed settlers.[61]

Many settlers who lacked the numbers to establish local enclaves or outposts of "good society" and were without family support were, in the course of their business and economic activities, compelled to accept living among the members of "border society" and try to operate as best they could. Though vigilante action had established a certain limit to community order, creating an "us" versus "them" dichotomy, the "us" was broadly enough circumscribed, as we have seen, to include both "genteel" settlers who participated in the booster ethos as well as disorderly "ruffians." Unable to use the booster ethos to create a line of difference within this defined community, many genteel settlers, by necessity, therefore, felt that to establish genteel order, they had to be more accommodating and interact on the common ground that they shared with members of this prevailing social "other." Horatio Newhall of Galena felt himself "thrown into a society where all are more or less strangers to each other – where each man looks out for himself and cares not a fig for his neighbors" and decided to interact with the element as best he could. Likewise, Junius Hall considered Alton a "land of strangers" and sensed little social cohesion.[62] Others, like William Worth Belknap, at Keokuk, noted that western towns were rife with "adventurers and seekers of fortune. . . . 'Every man for himself' is the motto which adorns the banner of each one of us." He despaired that all efforts to establish social order based on cooperative behavior were doomed to failure.[63]

Wherever "border society" predominated, the ruffians simply played and fought as hard as they worked. In Susan Gratiot's view, men who when sober during the week seemed able to "behave like gentlemen" on Sundays were "among the roughest and hardest class of men." Yet many "genteel" settlers – entrepreneurs, merchants, and professionals – found themselves doing business and socializing with these men, the land agents, speculators, gamblers, drinkers, river men, counterfeiters, horse thieves of the "meanest" sort, and members of the "wild frontier tribe, who lived in the woods and on the rivers."[64] Initially, they were satisfied with simply making themselves part of a group of people who worked together for the benefit of the town.

So long as the central border management activities in town focused on an outside "other," those who lived in town had to develop strategies which sought to maintain social peace and equilibrium somewhere between the extremes of violence at the boundary and social isolation or avoidance. Those who viewed themselves as genteel felt initially that they had little choice but to try to live within such an unformed society and cultivate associations with the ruffian element. For some, this meant merely tolerating the "other" and through indirection seeming to support them to get them to cooperate with the agendas of the booster network. Horatio Newhall articulated this strategy by observing that in a western town one "may choose . . . [one's] associates, but he must be complacent, and apparently interested in the welfare of the meanest men."[65] Where the ruffians were threatening – but not sufficiently so to warrant internal vigilante action – complacency and evasive coexistence evolved into more aggressive attempts to reform society, either by drawing this internal "other" toward them into the booster ethos through persuasion, comradery, and association or by infiltrating this internal "border" society and reforming the ruffian element from within.

The booster ethos was generally unable to reduce the tendency to disorder and violence for most settlers struggling to establish themselves within "border society." It satisfied people, eased social pressures, and established order only when, over time, the town proved an economic and social success. Such volatility compelled settlers to find indirect means that worked on individuals' behavior within the network to ease or release the pressures that caused disorder and violence and create a broader common ground with wider latitude between what they defined as "good" and "bad" society. Such tactics, by giving the booster ethos and the gentility system – both of which in time they would use to delimit their group or class within town society – time to evolve, would operate symbiotically with it as an agent of social structure.

"A common band of brotherhood"

But how, other than satisfying material, social, and physical needs and wants, does one inculcate social order through negative processes that defuse or vent social pressures? How does one satisfy and thus reduce social and competitive pressure, without really doing so? E. Anthony Rotundo has suggested that in such highly competitive venues and social circumstances, men, aware of the fragility of the urban social order and of the negative consequences of violence within the boundaries of the community, were compelled to pursue coexistence, accommodation, and compromise, and "maintain a judicious balance between cooperation and competition ... by channeling their individualistic and aggressive impulses in a way that would not tear the social fabric apart."[66] This can be achieved by developing modes of behavior which either toughen up individuals, making them less sensitive to social pressures, or make them better able to handle social pressures in which they live, such as learning to vent those pressures. In other ways, such social behavior also cultivates values of mutuality, voluntarism, and fraternity which by breaking down social isolation eased competitive pressures. In these gendered social realms, men from different classes, regions, and circumstances came together within a realm of shared masculine values – a zone or "sphere" of interaction encompassing both respectable and unrespectable society, in a kind of male demimonde, situated between and embracing both ruffian criminality and gentility – to pursue collective social goals.[67]

Urban and social historians have argued that across the antebellum urban North men in both the working and the middle classes, the two dominant social groups that emerged in response to the industrial revolution and rapid urbanization, responded in class-specific ways to create and cultivate new class cultures. In the large city and metropolis, middle-class "gentlemen" cultivated gentility and responded to the call of evangelical Christianity to draw social lines between themselves and their working-class brethren. Working people in larger cities responded to the dislocation, downward mobility, and pressure from judgmental middle-class social control concomitant with urbanization by developing more aggressive and distinctive "sporting-male cultures" or "bachelor subcultures" in which they cultivated and indulged in aggressive, uninhibited, liberating, and even violent recreational behavior and sexual activity which were at odds with accepted behavior in female-dominated middle-class mainstream culture to socially and emotionally empower themselves.[68] By flaunting the norms of self-control and self-discipline that were changing the lives of men who aspired to, or considered themselves, middle-class, they enhanced self-esteem, articulated self-identity, fended off loneliness, and eased or vented social frustration.[69]

In the highly developed, differentiated societies of the urban East, male subcultures formed in alignment with the general tendency and social dynamic resulting from the industrial revolution and urbanization by differentiating and separating themselves from a social other to articulate class identity amid rapid social change. As oppositional constructions from mainstream culture, they did cultivate male values that were at odds with the dominant culture, and were truly subcultures. In the

Provincial lives

boom towns of the Great West, a preponderance of young unmarried men from different social groups and subcultures, in highly volatile and competitive economies, far from patriarchal power and control, without a legal or political system, living in crowded, rudimentary housing, where the boundaries of community were widely drawn, and thus the differences between public and private, genteel and ruffian life and agendas blurred, the interaction among men had to cultivate homogenization and accommodation rather than separation. Given the high level of tension, anxiety, and frustration caused by social interaction, the potential for social conflict or war was too great – and the consequences of such violence to the prospects of the town too damaging – to allow men to work out their differences too frequently through direct action. Social order was too fragile to tolerate volatile means of boundary management which differentiated and separated one group from another.

Though, in the West, these male cultures were not, for several years, subcultures at all, but the predominant culture in town, their divergence from mainstream values gave them from the beginning an oppositional, subcultural characteristic and meaning similar to urban male subcultures back east. The predominance of these male subcultures necessitated that they work centripetally to draw men from diverse backgrounds together and thus facilitate social interaction and encourage compromise and accommodation within a diverse community, rather than sharpen lines of difference. They became a force or agent which settlers employed symbiotically along with the emergent booster ethos, but before the gentility system was in place, to establish a semblance of social order upon which their social, economic, and cultural goals depended.

In some ways, male subcultures ease social pressures and prevented confrontation just by keeping open the channels of interaction and communication among individuals and social groups within a town. By maintaining contacts, socially diverse, upwardly and downwardly mobile, married and single men were better able to compromise socially and accommodate each other. Their common experiences as young men founding a town and establishing an outpost of society, rather than ethnicity, place of origin, or the side they took in the half-breed war, forged social bonds and solidarity. This was almost exclusively a society of young, primarily unmarried men. In 1840, more than a third of the 250 men in town participated in the booster ethos. Though just a year or two before the male–female ratio had been about 9:1 in 1840, it had improved to 7:3. The average age among these men at time of arrival was twenty-seven. Though almost all were eventually to marry, 60 percent were unmarried for a year or more after their arrival. This society did not exclude married men, however. Indeed, some of its central characters, like Coleman, Fleak, and Hughes, had married before they arrived in Keokuk. They were family men, but being hotel operators and tavern keepers, they were inevitably drawn into the male subculture.

The primary way that men sought more aggressively to obfuscate social borders and elide rather than simply ignore or coexist with social diversity was by cultivating a range of dissimulating and indirect social behaviors. Nicknames, practical jokes, verbal jousting, collective conviviality, and frolics, to "mock" or "spoof" institutions and events, among which one "mock" institution, the yellow handbill meeting – a mock town meeting – was apparently unique to Keokuk, Iowa (see Figs. 6 and 7 below), all employed indirection, sarcasm, irony, and humor – all practices which crossed class lines – to help vent social tensions and thus defuse or avert the real danger that the "plain talk," insult, and bravado characteristic of everyday discourse and interaction among men, as well as efforts to establish law and order, would escalate into confrontation, internal violence, mob action, or even social "war." Through such behavior, many male residents of western towns and cities in the 1840s cultivated an open masculine value system which, in cutting across class lines and regional differences, enabled both "ruffians" and "gentlemen" to participate, compete, and cooperate within a fraternal booster ethos for the welfare of the town. But by facilitating the acculturation of newcomers to the booster ethos, and lubricating social interaction within predominantly all-male societies, male subcultures also created social distinctions and differences which formed the scaffolding or frame upon which urban public culture and social order would be constructed in the 1850s and 1860s.[70]

Places like Kenney Said's, A. Brown's Entertainment, J. H. Wise's, John Brooks's, Cyrus Harper's, Harry Fulton's, Charles Ivins's, saloons and the "old time barrooms of the hotels" were the principal places of resort for "amusement and refreshment" and patronized by the larger portion of the male inhabitants of the town.[71] These establishments, called "box traps," "whiskey shops," "wet grocer[ies]," or "deadfalls," were most often mere log cabins, shacks, and shanties on Rat Row which served liquor to the "wharf rats."[72] A. Brown described his "Entertainment," an old shanty on the wharf which, during high water, stood right at water's edge, in some detail: "My room for business was about ten by twenty feet constructed at the one end of the main hued [sic] log house by posts set in the ground and weathered boards with oak shakes four feet long and roofed with the same two feet long and floored with split logs. I fixed up some shelves at the back end where I displaid [sic] my stock in trade . . . with a single plank for a counter."[73] J. H. Wise simply added an upper room to a log house and opened it as a tavern in 1840.

With each year, however, the venue of this society improved somewhat. In 1841 Laban Fleak purchased the weathered clapboarded frame house, the first in town, built by Isaac Galland, and established a small hotel and barroom. That same year, in 1841, the Rapids Hotel, a "commodious" two-story stone building with clapboarded partitions and walls, opened for business. It contained two public rooms, in which, under William Coleman's influence in 1842, a barroom was placed opposite to the very first parlor in Keokuk.[74] By the fifties the town was full of places like Kinney Said's rooms in the second floor of a wooden false-front store, with a stove, billiard table, and simple counter as the only features.[75] Only with the opening of William Holliday's saloon next to the new Pressel House hotel in the mid-fifties did Keokuk acquire a "fashionable and elegant" Victorian saloon.[76]

Unlike Galena, Quincy, or St. Louis, where the area of town which catered to the male recreational subculture was, because of topography or the size of the town, physically separated from the business and residential areas of town, all of Keokuk's venues for male recreation and play were but a stone's throw from the wharf, the marketplace, places of work, and residences.[77] Abe Chittenden and William McGavic lived in "apartments" just above their store and just next to a whiskey shop.[78] Adam and Dan Hine lived in a house boat on the wharf where they kept their boat store saloon. L. B. Fleak lived just next to his first establishment, and then, after moving into the Keokuk House, resided above his store and barroom, which he combined. Justice of the Peace Joseph Clark lived and worked in an office in Rat Row next to a saloon, the proximity of which hastened his intoxicated downfall.[79] When A. W. Griffith described his neighbors, he thought nothing of the fact that within fifty yards of his small house were two whiskey shops. In front of one, which served as a popular boarding house, proprietors Charles Ivins and his son continually played the fiddle "to draw in trade," providing a musical background to the life of the area.[80]

Some business people simply merged the two functions in their establishments. Isaac R. Campbell and John Gaines, who, in 1837, ran the only forwarding and storage house in town, kept a tavern at the south end of their establishment. A tailor by the name of Aikman kept an informal meeting place in the back of his store. Likewise, Christian Garber, a merchant on Main Street, kept a large supply of fine "cognac and brandy," which everyone in town seemed to know about, at the back of his store. William Coleman lived where he worked, in the Rapids Hotel, which a number of single men, the most important among them being Bill Clark, the first mayor, used as a boarding house.

It was within these taverns, bars, and grog shops that the bonds of male recreational society were established. At one's regular place, one could meet, at all hours, friends and associates and gradually become part of their group. At the most informal level individuals met, joined in the usual barroom activities, and confronted each other. Through such interaction each individual established his niche in local male society. Isaac Campbell and John Gaines's establishment was, as early as 1837, a hangout for "Bill Price, Alexander Hood and the half a dozen other desperadoes" in Price's gang, all of whom, including John Gaines, when encountered by Hawkins Taylor, were in the "set" who played cards in the "office" and were routinely "pretty drunk." Charley Moore, as we have seen, held court at A. Brown's, where at least twice he came to the rescue of members of his set who got into trouble with strangers.[81] Moore also patronized Laban Fleak's, and also William Coleman's Rapids Hotel, where he and Bill Clark once got into a "general free fight" with some river men. Adam Hine was also a regular of A. Brown's "Entertainment." Later, both moved to Kinney Said's. Joe Clark, a judge, literally held court sometimes with Lyman E. Johnson at the "dive" in Mother Jordan's Rat Row establishment, described by one as "sort of a boarding house." His brother Bill Clark made William Coleman's Rapids Hotel his home away from home, but he too drifted to Kinney Said's later in the decade.[82] Clark was drawn into a group which included "Captain" or "General" Jesse B. Browne and his friends, Dr. O'Hara, Hugh Campbell, and Dan Hine, who regularly congregated at the Rapids Hotel "to concoct and perform their exploits." In addition, the Rapids Hotel was where David W. Kilbourne stopped when he was in town from Montrose.[83]

"A common band of brotherhood"

There individuals situated themselves among the regulars and formed themselves into groups or sets which, in time, and at more public events would assume an informal fraternal structure. One such group A. Brown described as making the back of Aikmen's tailor shop their headquarters. This "set of men" would frequently visit Aikman's "dressed in long evenings [coats] and brew tea and other hot drinks on the stove in back and tell stories, sing old-fashioned songs, and make speeches to suit themselves." This group, whose particular members are unknown, called these meetings "holding jollifications," appropriately named, thought Brown, for "if men ever enjoyed themselves I thought they did."[84] Often individual taverns or bars would become informal clubhouses or meeting places for specific groups whose members often wore special clothes to their meetings. Some of these informal sets or groups cut across and intersected some more formal enclaves, sets, or structures that gradually evolved in the public realms of law, politics, government, education, and medicine. At such gatherings men became known for their dress, how they drank, their ability to tell stories, and their personal traits and habits. As they became better known to each other, and provided support and comradery for each individual was drawn into "a common band of brotherhood."[85]

The intensity possible in the male bonding at the core of the male subculture is reflected in the development of an elaborate culture of nicknames among those traced above and others in town. In this culture, "nearly every man of any prominence" was "signified," indeed, defined, and became "known" by a nickname that was "more appropriate" to that individual's character "than [his] real [name]." Such "pet names," "titles," "sobriquets," or "aliases," which each person in the group secretly knew, were the rule among members of the fraternity and were generally considered "harmless and appropriate,"[86] though Hawkins Taylor admitted that many were "not so pleasant to repeat."[87] Nicknames were (and still are) most common among boys, and shared only among those within the innermost circle of a group of friends or brothers, conferring or confirming status or membership and defining the boundaries of inclusion within or exclusion from the group.[88] The distribution of nicknames among Keokuk's male population demarcated the boundaries of the male subculture. Keeping most nicknames private, if not secret, cultivated fraternity and mutuality. They were used only among those who shared them or knew the inside joke or incident upon which they were based, and were usually not even used to address the possessor of the name – except in the cases of the relatively few men who acquired public nicknames. The fact that nicknames were rarely mentioned in letters or newspapers and generally held secret among the members of the subculture across which the use of names extended created an elusive, oppositional element, which worked, much like in fraternal associations, to inculcate loyalty and fraternity among its members.[89] The use and distribution of nicknames among Keokuk's male population thus defined and maintained the boundaries and articulated some degree of hierarchical order among members of the male subculture.

Similarly, nicknames could be seen not only as evidence of the need to define a group, cultivate solidarity, and thus establish status in an unclear social context, but also as a way to reduce stress and tension in an impersonal and frustrating society, fraught with risk, tensions, and conflict, by prolonging the fraternal collegiality of "boy culture."[90] Correlating the timing of nickname assignment and their distribution on one side or another of major social or political issues indicates the mediating role played by nicknames in response to political or social conflict. Discerning the meaning of nicknames by relating specific names to the characteristics or actions of specific individuals further shows how, through dissimulation and irony, nicknames worked to mollify or vent social friction and thus promoted the emergence and diffusion of the booster ethos in town society and politics.

A number of autobiographers revealed the nicknames of twenty-eight men (and one woman, the wife of one of the members) in town during the 1840s, thus defining the "core" of the local male subculture. In a later memoir, Colonel J. M. Reid, a lawyer and antiquarian, identified the nicknames of seventeen more men who were mentioned by various autobiographers as key members of the male subculture and booster ethos, but whose nicknames they did not give. He then listed the nicknames of fifty-two additional men, most of whom arrived later and were not mentioned by any of the autobiographers. Finally, another memoirist mentioned the nickname of a second woman, bringing the total to a remarkable 106 nicknames, designating forty-five men and two women within the subculture described by the autobiographers and another fifty-two people, for a total of ninety-nine people (several people had two or three nicknames). Determining the timing of the assigning of these nicknames and interpreting their meaning regarding the character and behavior of specific individuals within the booster ethos specifically traces the emergence of the male subculture and the development of a town society.[91]

Though one or two members of the frontier culture had acquired nicknames from the Indians (suggesting a possible influence on the origins of the local practice) and another from his mother,[92] the first reference to any American settler assigning a nickname or title was in March 1840, when Laban Fleak, in confronting Bill Price of the Price gang, who announced himself to Fleak at his store as "king of the country," called him "King William," a sarcastic title which stuck from then on. Laban Fleak mentions, as early as 1842, a number of "alias" names of those around him, but it is unclear if they were given these names then or later. Fleak, on the other hand, was referred to as "Squire" as early as 1842. Hawkins Taylor revealed that Adam Hine, a Pennsylvanian who arrived in 1841, was "mainly the giver" of these names (though Lewis R. Reeves, General Browne, and others also assigned some nicknames to their associates).[93] It is also apparent, from Fleak's memoir, that John Hillis got his name before his departure from Keokuk in 1843. So, too, Lyman E. Johnson acquired his alias before he left town in 1849. In fact, of the forty-five men whose nicknames are known from the autobiographies, more than a third were given to those who arrived in 1840, 1841, and 1842, or between Adam Hine's arrival and John Hillis's departure, a period coinciding with the initial burst of mercantile activity at Keokuk. Therefore they assigned most nicknames in the early 1840s just as the Decree and Anti-Decree fault line threatened to divide town society and undermine the operations of the fledgling booster ethos.

"A common band of brotherhood"

Adam Hine arrived to join his brother in 1841 when he was twenty and opened a boat tavern on the river catering to river men. Through his brother Dan Hine, he became a "regular" at A. Brown's "Entertainment" and the Rapids Hotel. There he entered the overlapping circles of friends and colleagues around Brown, Fleak, Bill Clark, Lyman E. Johnson, and others and quickly became an insider within the town's "booster" network. It was within these groups, numbering some twenty people around Fleak and about thirteen around Brown, that Adam Hine assigned the highest percentage of nicknames, indicating the key role that these men played in the forming the social core of the male subculture. Hine's nickname, "Government" Hine, evokes the central role he played in this male subculture.

That this small group began to give nicknames as a way to set themselves against, while maintaining relations with, the Galland faction and the Anti-Decree men during the crisis of 1841–1842, in general, is further suggested by the nature of the earliest names known. Among the people who both were mentioned by Laban Fleak (who was also dubbed "Pompey" Fleak) and acquired a nickname in the early forties, ten were in the Fleak coterie, which stood behind Fleak as Justice of the Peace in 1841 and Hawkins Taylor as sheriff as members of the Vigilante Committee for law and order and the rights of the New York Land Company. Most of these names ("Devil Creek" Bill Clark, "Citizen" A. Brown, "Cockeyed" or "Brooksie" John Brooks, "Penny" Price, "Sweet William" Coleman (also "Uncle Billy"), "Aunt Nancy" Coleman, "Peg Leg" or "Dot and Go 1" Silas Heaight, "Government" Adam Hine, "Geemes" or "Old Jums" J. H. Wise, and "General" or "Tall Cedar of Lebanon" Jesse B. Browne) were positive, descriptive, and supportive of equal status. Five of the six somewhat more negative, sarcastic, or ironic names from this period ("Doubleheads" John Hillis, "Heels" Lyman E. Johnson, "King" William Price, "Colonel" A. C. Dodge, "Bucket No. 2" Henry J. Campbell, and "Split Log" Colonel Mitchell) were among men within the opposition. Nicknames, whether near the core or in opposition, thus evaluated individuals and articulated social status from the perspective of those within the Decree faction.

The nicknames noted by J. M. Reid trace a similar social topography in town. On the side of the Decree were "Wharf Rat" Daniel Hine, "Flitterfoot" Valencourt Vanorsdal, and the "Native Chieftain" David W. Kilbourne, while (General) Hugh T. Reid, who with the aid of lawyers "Off Ox of Democracy" Jonathan C. Hall, "Garry" Lewis R. Reeves, and later, "Wapsi" or "Great Wapsi" Hugh W. Sample, was appropriately called "The Red Fox," as he maneuvered between the two. Most of these were playful, evaluative, or endearing names. Against them, supporting Isaac Galland or the Anti-Decree forces, stood "Colonel" or "General" Augustus C. Dodge, "Little Duff" or "Warrior" Dan Dierdorff, "R.B." Ross B. Hughes, "Alderman" James Mackley, "Ghost of Buster" Daniel F. Miller, "Jurisprudence" Joseph W. Clark, and Mrs. Gaines, who was sarcastically dubbed "The Mayor."[94]

The prevalence of names among those at the center of the conflict which threatened to destroy the town's booster ethos suggests the general role names played in allowing men to negotiate across lines or boundaries of opposition to get things done by bringing all participants down to a relatively equal level in town society. On a more subtle level, the evaluative pattern of names hints at how they helped to articulate and demarcate social status among townsmen. In general, from the perspective of Adam Hine and those who supported the Decree, names among themselves were evaluative, descriptive, even diminutive and endearing, while those given to men in the opposition, or whom they had noted as ruffians, tended to be more ironic, sarcastic, and critical or "not so pleasant to repeat."[95]

Among the most common, even ubiquitous titles which men used were "honorifics" earned by military or government service, or professional achievement. The use of honorific titles was on the increase in the 1840s, reflecting the proliferation of militia companies and government offices, the rise of professions, as well as a pervasive status anxiety among middle-class men. Among the two "Generals" and two "Colonels" in Keokuk, three were southerners, though they all earned their titles in the North, suggesting, perhaps, that southerners traditionally employed honorific names more often. So, too, familial nicknames that were either descriptive or simply expressions of endearment also seem to have been more prevalent among southerners. Four of the seven men in Keokuk with the title "Uncle" or "Cousin," for example, were from Virginia, each of them described as having a friendly or avuncular style which gained them the affection of their "brothers."[96]

Diminutive nicknames, on the other hand, seem to have had no regional origin, nor were they particularly familial. A number of men in town were called "little," either in reference to their age or size or simply as an endearment.[97] Nor does the nickname "Old," of which there were nine cases, seem to have a southern source or a familial connotation, evoking a comfortable, collegial personal quality which made it seem as if the person, though he could still be quite young, had been there forever as a trusted or familiar associate. It is also intriguing to note, however, that some men whom they nicknamed "old," such as "Old Timber" James Woods, were considered by their fellows as "sui generis," or eccentric, and, thus, as a source of amusement to all, men who "defined" – as a kind of mascot – the structure and quality of the local male subculture. Most of these names predominated among those within "good society" and thus the town Decree faction.

Most nicknames were assigned during social interactions among men from diverse backgrounds in a frontier town. Intriguingly, three-quarters of the rest of the men who had nicknames were from the mid-Atlantic region. Significantly, Adam Hine, who assigned the nicknames, and Silas Heaight, who organized yellow handbill meetings, and thus together helped construct the center stage of this male subculture, were both mediating, compromising Pennsylvanians. Most nicknames which those in the fraternity acquired were taken from the slang language used in the military, politics, the legal profession, and in saloons or gambling halls. Descriptive names drawn from slang language were more vulgar and caustic and thus much more ironic, interested as much in exposing or commenting on a character trait, action, or point of view as in establishing one's status within or endearing one to the group.

While the use of slang vulgarizes, however, it also complexifies, acquiring subtly different meanings in various contexts. Slang nicknames assumed a more complex semantic structure, able to serve the purposes of the various people who used them while they interacted in different circumstances and episodes with those persons. Nicknames could often censure and ridicule actions, question a man's ethics, honesty, or character, castigate him for the order of his priorities, or simply mock or torment him, while, in the spirit of friendship, still exonerate him or support or encourage him.

On the simplest level some nicknames that were "not so nice to repeat" unkindly or sarcastically called attention to a physical characteristic or character flaw. The oldest of such names, belonging to "Big Neck" William Phelps, derived from his Indian name ("che che pe ne quah"), and, indeed, a surviving portrait of Phelps shows that he did have an enormous neck. "Cockeyed" Brooks or "Brooksie" was walleyed and was often the butt of jokes played on him by his customers.[98] Silas Heaight, on the other hand, had broken his leg when a barrel fell on it in a distillery he operated before he came to Keokuk. For his distinctive limp, "the boys" accorded him the sobriquet "Peg Leg" or "Dot and Go 1" (the noise a person with a limp makes when walking across a wooden floor), both common contemporary slang words for a man with a bad or wooden leg. So, too, General Browne's nickname, "Tall Cedar of Lebanon," obviously referred to his height of six feet, seven inches.

Some descriptive names, however, could begin to slip into sarcastic commentary on a person's character, not just a physical trait for which they were not responsible. The name "Sweet" which William Coleman got may have simply referred to his "tender-hearted innocence" and his poignant unhappiness in living in a rough place like Keokuk. But according to the word's meaning as "gullible, easily deceived," it also probably referred to the ease in which "Devil Creek" Bill Clark and others could play elaborate practical jokes on him, without him ever being aware of the perpetrators.[99] Similarly, the name "Double Heads," which was a two-headed false coin usually the "property of a gutter sharper or con man," cast serious aspersions on John Hillis's honesty in his real estate deals,[100] and Dr. Sherman's as well as T. B. Thurman's name, "Chips," reproved them for their excessive gambling.[101]

Honorific titles could acquire a similar mocking, sarcastic quality reproaching the bearer of the title for falling short of the stature implicit in one's title or deflating him for his pretentious claims, which could explain the pervasiveness of such names in the subculture. One of Laban Fleak's titles, "Squire," could have been either just a shortened form or a send-up of the official title he held as Justice of the Peace in the early 1840s. Calling Fleak "Squire" was also a way to satirize his self-importance, snobbery, and dandyism manifested in his "great circumspection in dress and deportment," all of which clashed with his fun-loving, practical-joke-playing sense of humor, as well as his contradictory proclivity to ignore the law and participate in the town's Vigilante Committee actions against horse thieves, criminals, desperadoes, and Mormons.[102]

Likewise, "General" Jesse B. Browne's title spoke less to his military record in the Iowa militia during the Missouri border war of 1838 than to the notoriety he acquired for leading his troops to Keosauqua where they indulged in a two-day "grand drunk" or "bender" before they and the enemy met and negotiated a peace without firing a shot. Other men with the title "General" acquired it not from military service, but from serving, if only for a year or two, as the territorial or state attorney general.[103] Similarly, "Citizen" Brown, whose name evokes a revolutionary salutation, acquired it because of his stubborn nonpartisanship in a Democratic town with a vocal Whig minority. As Brown remarked, "I was as much a Democrat as I was a Whig, I voted for whom I thought was best." One suspects, however, that Brown's bipartisanship was most appreciated in his often extraordinary efforts to make sure that the town was well supplied with liquor every election day, no matter who won.[104] Similarly, "Government" Hine may have been the man who, in assigning nicknames, scripted the subculture, but his quick temper, which involved him in a number of fistfights and run-ins with the law, hints at the more obscure meaning of his name – "a government man" being one of many slang expressions for a convict. In contrast, the sarcasm in naming the town's two doctors "Peril" and "Terror" is clear.

In a similar vein, Mrs. Gaines was a "coarse and hard" widow, known for her bilingual swearing and oft-repeated boast that "she would shoot anyone who molested her." Her boarding house and saloon on the wharf became the headquarters of a number of ruffians. The men of the town, "pretend[ing]" to be "afraid of" her, elevated Gaines to a "position of arbitrator" in their numerous disputes and allowed her to generally "manag[e] the affairs of the town"; she was dubbed "Mother" Gaines or "the Mayor."[105] Equally sarcastic was the expropriation of Indian names and titles as nicknames, including "Black Hawk," "Chief of the Blackfeet," "Native Chieftain," and "Warrior," which, by "playing Indian," enabled the men of the subculture to mock the social and political order.[106]

Nicknames cut deep, commenting on some character fault or personal failing, or more precisely on a moment of embarrassment that forever "named" one in front of one's colleagues. To deflect the directness of comment, slang expressions with obscure or multiple meanings were often used. "Heels" (Lyman E. Johnson's name) meant in the slang of the period that he was either heavily armed, a political sycophant who was always at one's candidate's heels, or a heavy drinker – a "heel" being the liquor at the bottom of a glass. Likewise, at subculture dances, Johnson was laughed at openly for (as a versifier described him) "light are his movements and heavy his heel." The most memorable story by which he became known in town was the time when while trying a case against Mrs. Gaines in Judge Clark's courtroom, she lost her temper and pulled a gun, in response to which Johnson "took to his heels." That, for a lawyer, one's behavior in court could assign one's nickname is evidenced by Lewis R. Reeves's case. Once he prosecuted a ruffian leader of the Settlers' named Garry Lewis in such a long, drawn-out trial that his friends believed that he was becoming the defendant and began to call Reeves "Garry."[107]

Similarly, other misadventures or stories embarrassed and thus marked individuals for life. Every time someone called Mr. Turner "Tight Squeeze," they reminded him of the time he went to a dance and became so excited to be dancing with a woman that when he thanked her and tried to express his romantic interest in her he "squeezed" her so hard that he broke one of her ribs, for which he was arrested and fined for assault. So, too, the name "Hold Him Shores" reminded everyone of the time when "Devil Creek" Bill Clark spurred Mr. Shores's horse and sent it running and Shores, unable to control it but unwilling to let go, held on for dear life and was dragged all through town, everyone exhorting him to "hold him, Shores!"[108]

When vulgarisms were used for nicknames, they lost the indirection of sarcasm and could, through thinly veiled double entendre, become insulting, censorious, and even cruel. "Split Log" Mitchell could have gotten his name from a tall and lanky physique (his height is unknown) but the term was also close to vulgarisms that meant either the group "dunce" or penis. The word "Jum(m)" – as in "Old Jums" – had a similar meaning.[109] Such a vulgar reference suggests a deeper meaning behind this and other nicknames, referencing them to eighteenth-century folk culture in which the word "prank" was a vulgarism for penis, and referred to the crude practice among opposing combatants (or "pranksters") to gesture to, grab, or shake their genitals to display their prowess (displaying their "prankes") and taunt or unnerve their opponents.[110] A similar vulgar double entendre emanates from several nicknames we know existed in Keokuk, but whose possessors, interestingly, were censored by the autobiographers (though, in two cases, not by J. M. Reid). "Saddle bags" was probably a reference to an ample backside.[111] "Sheeps Quarters" was an expression of contempt. "Taller Treats," Dr. Thomas Sullivan's name, referred to his drunkenness. "Flitterfoot," Val Vanorsdal's name, may have been an expression of political contempt, a comment on his tendency to drink too heavily, or on being a silly coxcomb, but its root later became a slang word (still heard) for a gay man (a "flit").[112] More direct is the name "Two Backs" – "doing the beast with two backs" – being a common slang term in the nineteenth century (and sometimes also still heard today as a Shakespearean reference) for sexual intercourse. Such names hint at the vulgar, ribald "blackguarding" side to nickname culture. In a more civil context, such repartee among "blackguards" (a word which by 1840 meant a scoundrel, ruffian, or excessive swearer) was manifested by a kind of verbal jousting through which individuals could release tension by creating an aura of vulgar boyish comradery amid intense conflict and competition.[113]

Nicknames could, therefore, be considered as the signifying consequences or marks left on men during their interactions with other men which established both their membership and their status in the social hierarchy. They ranged from descriptive and endearing names or titles emerging from male bonding to more obscure or ambiguous names that used slang, sarcasm, and indirection to sustain dissimulating behavior. When nicknames became more blunt, vulgar, and insulting their use became analogous to male verbal jousting involving bravado, braggadocio, and blackguarding, and an occasional duel (of which there were only two recorded in Keokuk), which emerged from greater tensions and more intense confrontations. Either way, such names lubricated social interaction by allowing men, in daily interactions, to say things and express emotions not otherwise able to be said or expressed. Semantically layered names allowed people, within different subcultures, to respond in various ways depending on the circumstances, and thus say something about someone that they were unable to say clearly to their face (though some more blunt nicknames were apparently never used directly to one's face). In one instance one might take the positive meaning of the name, in the next the negative, the name mediating both encounters and defusing tension by allowing one to insult without damage, criticize without reprisal, or compliment or support without becoming maudlin. This maintained a certain level of emotional balance, coolness, or detachment.[114] Finally, indirect nicknames excluded outsiders from the group, because in not understanding the inside jokes, references, or even histories implicit in such names, they could not know their meaning and give meaning to the interactions among members of the group. Covering the stores, places, and streets in town and also places in the surrounding county with a slang lexicon of nicknames, like in Keokuk and down in Quincy, Illinois, further served this purpose.[115]

When the motives imbedded in nicknames suffused language and discourse, they conflated with the male practice of verbal jousting. Verbal jousting, as a combative discourse, most often involved, on some level, a question of someone's status, character, and honor. Though sometimes, when such jousting intertwined with more extensive mockery or roughhousing, it began to approach the imbedded point of more elaborate practical jokes and organized oppositional cultural activity, in which someone or a group sought to comment indirectly on the character trait or action of another through action rather than discourse.

Once when "Captain," "General," or "Tall Cedar of Lebanon" Jesse B. Browne, a six-foot-seven-inch Kentuckian who strutted "with gentlemanly deportment" around town with a "hickory cane" and had become famous in town for the "grand drunk" which he indulged in with his troops during the border war with Missouri in 1838, entered a saloon to find all chairs taken and no one willing to offer him a seat, he took what he (but no one else) knew to be an empty powderkeg and threw it, swearing, into the fire. Everyone in the place "ran for his dear life" into the street for safety. When no explosion occurred, however, the patrons cautiously reentered the tavern to find the "General" sitting comfortably "in front of the fire" drinking old bourbon. "In his Chesterfield style [he] invited them all to drink with him, never once alluding to the keg or the stampede it had caused . . . and from that time . . . he never failed having the most comfortable chair in the room . . . offered him whenever he went in."[116]

In another instance, Daniel S. Lee, "scion" of the "first families of Virginia" (F.F.V.s) arrived in town, intending to settle there. Finding out there was a dance of "The Twenties," a subculture group which had been organized as a "dancing set" at a local hotel, he got an invitation. When he arrived dressed in a "Chesterfieldian style," "the boys" mocked him by parting their hair in the middle, buttoning up their coats to their chins, and walking around talking "with all possible dignity" in an affected Virginian accent. Lee, oblivious to the impression he made, ensconced himself in the best hotel in town, and, being "too-too" to engage in any business or "sordid employment" "devoted most of his time to the ladies, dress, and politics" and collecting minerals. When he decided to ship his mineral collection of geodes back to Virginia, some pranksters, tired of his tales of aristocratic lineage in Virginia, stole the geodes and replaced them with local bricks, which the General forgot to check before opening the boxes in a grand lecture and presentation before his "scientific" friends back home, who were amused and unable to repress laughing when they saw bricks instead of geodes. To send him packing, a group of "wild boys" gave him a spoof banquet, and even had the Governor Stephen Hempstead come down and grant Lee an "entirely honorary title" in the state militia, which Lee, entirely unaware of the joke, thought was very important and later proudly proclaimed to friends back home, but which was "insignificant" and "not . . . sought after nor cared for by anyone else."[117]

More specific practical jokes or pranks played by members of this fraternity of friends with nicknames served a similar role, although in their more direct approach and thus apparent meaning, in a more risky, even dangerous manner. Rather than using sarcasm and wit, practical jokes were meant, as they still are today by those who still play them, to expose, embarrass, or show up someone whose behavior or character the perpetrator wanted to comment on.[118] A number of members of this inner group of society in Keokuk were serious players of practical jokes. Reid noted that "Devil Creek" Bill Clark, Old Rouser, General Browne, "Wharf Rat" Daniel Hine, James Mackley, Charley Moore, "Cockeyed" Brooks, Lyman E. Johnson, and "Bucket" Campbell, the very core of the booster ethos network established in 1840 to 1841, "were always getting up jokes or playing pranks" on various townsmen, strangers, and travelers, and "delighted in laughing at their calamities and mocked [them] when their fear came." Dr. Justin Millard was another serious practical joker, there being, in the early forties, "scarcely a piece of harmless mischief afloat that could not be traced to Dr. Millard as its originator in his sly way of bringing about a good joke on some of his friends."

In the autobiographies and memoirs from the early forties there are a number of examples of such jokes. These tricks and jokes ranged from doctoring the liquor in a bottle before someone drank it, to turning furniture over or setting it in other rooms of a hotel to infuriate the landlord, dousing men or pouring water into their pockets on freezing winter days, sabotaging harnesses and ropes on carriages, springing a bear free from a stockade and chasing it around town (until it chased them), trapping a wild animal inside a tavern to empty it out, to simply pulling a person's leg, sometimes Indians', but mostly travelers', by performing a spoof. Such jokes eased tensions by releasing an animus built up by disagreement or competition, by getting something off one's chest, or by exposing the truth of someone's behavior. Practical jokes could also be carried out simply to have fun or to be cruel.[119]

One intriguing practical joke, carried out directly across the fault line which divided town society, involved, unexpectedly, cross-dressing. A "lady" who arrived at William Coleman's Rapids Hotel on a spring evening in the early 1840s was discovered with a man in her room by Coleman, who had been informed by Bill Clark. When Coleman barged into the room, "he discovered a young lawyer . . . holding the lady on his lap with his arms around her neck." Startled, the lawyer ran for dear life ahead of Bill Clark, who chased him the length of Rat Row. Coleman, meanwhile, angrily ordered the woman to leave the hotel, but quickly discovered that "she was of the male persuasion and one of his boarders." In this joke, Clark and the perpetrators played the joke not only on Coleman, but on the lawyer, who had a reputation in town for being "very fond of the society of a certain class of ladies," luring him to the room with a false note from Isaac Galland's female assistant and then having one of the perpetrators, dressed as a woman, entrap him in a compromising position that he could not explain away. The lawyer, apparently unaware of the joke, soon left town in disgrace.[120] Coleman and his wife were outraged and embarrassed by the whole matter and concerned about the reputation of their establishment, a necessary concern in a town where houses of assignation were so close by.

Another practical joker in town was Dr. Justin Millard, "the leading and no doubt ablest medical man of the city." Millard was apparently behind an elaborate joke which turned Laban Fleak's attempt at a practical joke back against him. When a farmer who had moved onto Millard's farm asked Fleak to marry him to a woman in the neighborhood, Fleak agreed, but when told by the man that he was unable to pay him – which Fleak knew to be a lie – he jokingly "replied to him that if he would let him sleep with his intended the first night after their marriage, that would be satisfactory pay, which the bachelor agreed to at once." The following night at the wedding, when the groom got up to leave, following Fleak out the door, Fleak inquired where he was going. The groom told Fleak that he intended to fulfill his side of the bargain and informed him that his wife was willing, indeed flattered, to sleep with him for services rendered. In spite of Fleak's protest that his remark had been just a joke, the groom persisted and remarked that he would get his wife or nothing for payment. In the persistence of the man, Fleak soon recognized that they were playing back the joke on him, and laughed embarrassingly, along with the entire bridal party, who now stood at the door, laughing as they observed Fleak's embarrassment. Caught with having made a ribald joke, Fleak stood exposed and, by laughter and rumor, was chastened for it because "it got circulated through the town and in three days, there was not a man, woman, or child in Keokuk that had not heard of it."[121]

Among those men from different regions and classes in the group, nicknames, practical jokes, and verbal jousting served the purposes of social order, situating individuals, articulating mores, and creating, on an individual level, the experiential commonality out of which more formal expressions of social structuring emerged. Practical jokes built upon the sarcastic equalizing rhetoric of the core of this group by testing, controlling, and chiding its members, while blowing off steam and commenting indirectly on social reality in primarily harmless ways. As such each of these practices sought to cultivate dissimulation and indirection, which fostered the creation, among friends, of a recreational and convivial culture situated between ruffianism and gentility.

As early as 1840 informal personal relationships structured more public (although still primarily informal) social circles or sets in which individuals acted as members of groups. The chief organizers of a series of "cotillions" at the Keokuk House were the "young gentlemen" of the town, Val Vanorsdal, William McGavic, A. Chittenden, Mr. King, and M. McCall, all friends of Fleak's. It was a weekly occurrence for the sisters of Adam and Dan Hine and some of their friends "to go to Fleak's store about 9 o'clock P. M. and invite him to a supper and cotillion party at his own house." A. Brown during the same period opened his house to much the same crowd, to which most of married and unmarried men and women in town came.[122]

So, too, "Mother" Meeker routinely opened her house for parties or celebrations of one sort or another in the early 1840s. Her parties grew so in size that members of the fraternity formed themselves into committees. "Devil Creek" Bill Clark, Val Vanorsdal, Charley Moore, and Dan Hine were "standing floor managers." Citizen Brown, Cockeyed Brooks, Squire Fleak, and Harry Fulton made up the "standing committee on invitation." "Heels" Lyman E. Johnson, Ross B. Hughes, Cyrus Harper, and "Chips" Sherman were on the "standing committee on refreshments." Again, in the winter of 1846, the same company showed up intact at the grand Masquerade Ball in honor of Iowa's entrance into the Union. Dan Hine and Dan Dierdorff arrived dressed as military officers, Lyman E. Johnson and A. W. Griffith as Quakers, Split Log Mitchell as a hemp grower from Missouri, and Dr. Birdsall as a drunken sailor – a role he played "to perfection." Ross B. Hughes, Val Vanorsdal, and most of the rest of the subculture also attended.[123] About the same time, Harry Fulton served as the "Generalissimo" of Ross B. Hughes's second wedding party which lasted nearly all night, a party which marked the last time the entire group met intact.[124]

As the numbers involved increased, and the social aspirations among many in the subculture began to rise, some "gentlemen" began to organize more formal parties and balls to separate themselves from more informal parties and cotillions. Though rooted in the male subculture, more genteel people in town society, as their numbers increased and they gained confidence, began to sharpen the porous boundary which they always envisioned between them and the more ungentlemanly "ruffians" within the male subculture. Situated on this emerging boundary between the male subculture and the gentility system, balls and parties quickly became highly charged exercises in social gatekeeping. To control attendance and screen those present, genteel managers replaced the earlier informality of subculture affairs with more formal arrangements including published invitations, admission tickets, and dress codes. From the few surviving published invitations, we know that Daniel Hine, a ruffian member of the subculture, was still one of eight managers at a Settler's Ball outside Keokuk on 28 January 1848. The Keokuk Thespian Ball two years later at the Thespian Hall in Keokuk also had eight managers, but men who increasingly viewed themselves as "gentlemen" were in the majority. By the time Caleb Davis arrived in 1849, the spirit of these initial dancing parties survived in a more genteel set of ten couples called "The Twenties" who danced every two weeks during the winter of 1850–51 at the Keokuk House. Among the men only Lee McGavic and William Patterson were connected to the initial social group, McGavic's older brother William having been one of the main "gentlemen" at the Keokuk House at Fleak's cotillions in 1840–1841 (see Fig. 4). The Military Ball given by "the Keokuk Guards" on 4 July 1854 was run by two committees. Among the members of the invitation committee were Caleb Davis and John A. Graham, both of whom

Figure 4. "Lee" McGavic (*second from left*), "Squire" or "Garret" Davis (*second from right*), and members of "The Twenties" dancing set, Keokuk, Iowa, 1854. (Courtesy of Keokuk Savings Bank and Trust Co., Keokuk, Iowa)

emerged as gentlemen out of the subculture. On the other hand, Dan Hine and Harry Fulton, two old members of the subculture, and Thomas Swanick, a gentleman, were among the floor managers.[125] As elite "genteel" culture acquired more adherents within town society, they could begin to screen out and exclude members of the subculture. Not surprisingly, as those who were still in the subculture encountered this newly drawn border, they became increasingly frustrated at being socially coopted and excluded.

As these pressures from the gentility system intensified – with its more organized system of parties, balls, and banquets ruled by ever more elaborate etiquette and rules – and spread through society and professional and public life, members of the subculture responded by increasingly indulging in behavior specifically to offend that culture. Initially this manifested itself in holding more rowdy, tongue-in-cheek dinners and parties to which increasingly only men were invited. They soon went further by organizing sarcastic, spoof "oppositional" events. Rather than merely being more raucous versions of genteel events, such "oppositional" occasions went beyond mere sarcasm. They took place in an absurd realm in which the etiquette, procedures, and assumptions of real events or organizations in society were turned topsy-turvy. "Spoof" or "masquerade" balls, mock banquets or celebrations, the "lobby" among politicians, and "mock tribunals" which emerged out of debating societies among lawyers represented the real world in reverse, providing for the participants liminal experiences that intensified the venting functions of dissimulation and sarcasm at the center of the male subculture. To operate these balls, parties, and dinners, members organized themselves (much like legislators did in the "lobby") into a profusion of tongue-in-cheek "committees," in which the participants performed sometimes practical, sometimes absurd duties.[126] In the autobiographies one can trace the membership of various informal and formal committees throughout the forties. Not surprisingly, those who were active in the oppositional "committee culture" were the very same men who gave each other nicknames and traded practical jokes.

On the surface some of these convivial parties or banquets were just more raucous than genteel events. The "oyster and champagne" "high carnival" which the local lawyers gave Milton D. Browning in his cell after he was thrown into jail for contempt of court, or the "jolly" and splendid banquet given to Hugh W. Sample "by his friends" after Sample had refused a challenge to a duel by a Virginian gentleman, or the spoof banquet given in "honor" of General Lee were among an increasing number of "levees," "roasts," or "Barmecide feasts."[127]

Sometimes the oppositional agenda of such mock parties and dinners led to organized sporting contests or team hunting competitions or spilled onto the streets in general, yet harmless, "horse play" or roughhousing behavior by large groups of men throughout the town.[128] In Keokuk, only a few instances were recorded of a party or fight spilling out onto the streets in which a crowd of men "went on a tare," "spree," or "bender." One time a large group of men, led by Devil Creek (Bill Clark), Bucket (Henry Campbell), and Wharf Rat (Dan Hine), joined in a "terrific chorus" of "unearthly war whoops" to scare a group of travelers and then all went off on a "revelry," roaming the streets drinking and screaming. In another case, Bill Clark, the night he was elected first mayor of Keokuk, mimicked Tammany Hall proceedings and dressed up as a "big injin" (sic); joined by a large group of supporters who dressed as "braves," they all marched single file through the town huzzahing Clark's victory. Such events were similar to town "frolics" that broke out elsewhere. At Galena, Illinois, in 1831, for example, groups or "teams" of men challenged each other for control of the town and commenced dousing each other in flour, feathers, and finally, in one case, printer's ink, the team that prevailed "taking the whole village."[129] Similarly, "grand frollicks" often accompanied the conclusion of a day of horse racing in nearby Lee County.[130] Such spontaneous outbursts of fun seemed a natural outgrowth of verbal jousting, practical joking, and general male comradery. More organized teams in sports or hunting seemed to reflect a deeper need for satisfying competitive needs or pressures. Such contests, frolics, and general "fun" among townsmen fostered comradery and thus solidified the fraternal bonds that sustained the male subculture.

When suffused with sarcasm, such events could become elaborate oppositional events which mocked the local social order by creating a topsy-turvy world. At the late date of 1858, the tone and style of such events in the earlier subculture still emerge in an intriguing invitation to an Annual Festival, organized by a group called the "Cosmopolitan Society" on 15 January 1858 (see Fig. 5). Using the biting sarcastic and ironic language of the male subculture (several references to specific members of the male subculture are in the text) the invitation upbraids the social

Cosmopolitan Society.

Will hold their First Annual Festival at the WESTERN HOTEL on FRIDAY EVENING, JAN. 15th, 1858. All who have no *patrician proclivities*,

"Propped by a rotten Peer or two,"

or are in any way hazy upon the subject of—GENEALOGY—are invited to be present. No one belonging to any of the annexed Associations will be eligible to admittance:

Whose Fathers *fit* in the Revolution.
Whose Fathers defended Washington in 1814.
No member of the Saint Andrew's Society.
No member of the Sons of Rip Van Wynkle.
No member of the Haddock Club.
No member of the West End Club.
No member of the Sons of Africa.
No one who boasts of Plymouth Rock,

"The Yankee Blarney Stone."

No one who claims descent from "Daniel Boone," *John Randolph*, Fred or the Black Douglas.

No one who was ever snipe-shooting on the *Eastern Shore of Maryland*, or held the bag for any snipe operation

"In our own Green Prairie Land."

FUGLEMAN'S SWINETTE BAND is engaged for the occasion.

A. BASTARD, Esq., of Point-no-Point, has kindly volunteered to sing a number of new and popular Songs, including

"Whar did you come from."

"Music, moonshine, love and cider."

"Topsey deah, your brow am clouded."

"Is your maternal progenitor advised of your absence."

Mr. U. GREEN PLEBEAN will recite Coleridge's celebrated poem of the "Ancient Raftsman," Thomas Hood's "Lost Heir," and the best part of "Miss Killmansegg and her precious Leg.

A number of powerful Speakers are expected *down on a Raft*, and many distinguished "*Strangers*" are looked for, "*in a horn.*"

A collection will be taken up, which, in connection with the proceeds of the Festival, will be applied towards the erection of a "Foundlings Home" in Hoop-Pole Ward, city of Keokuk, and it is hoped that all *Charitable Young Men* will come right down with the "*Spondoolicks.*"

E. PLURIBUS UNUM.

Figure 5. The Cosmopolitan Society program. (Courtesy of Keokuk Savings Bank and Trust Co., Keokuk, Iowa)

pretensions of emerging local elite by articulating, in a mock, sarcastic, reversed image, the socially demarcating agenda of more formal genteel occasions. By spoofing elite social groups to which residents from New England, the Middle Colonies, and Virginia attributed membership, and then including Irish, blacks, and illegitimate progeny, and then covering it all with a sarcastic mockery of elite philanthropic efforts under the canopy of the motto of Union, the "society" creates a negative image world in which the hierarchical matrix of regional, class, gender, and race identities which structured Keokuk society were literally elided by music, liquor, capital, and sarcasm. Though the author of this very funny invitation is unknown, the title of the first song proposed to be sung, "Whar did you come from," is exactly the first question which E. R. Ford reported everyone who entered Keokuk was first asked by some member of the subculture. So, too, the person who named the second ward of Keokuk the "hoop-pole" ward (hoop poles for barrels were "currency" accepted for payment at his store) was none other than Ross B. Hughes, Galland's secretary and the town booster in an earlier day.[131] Such oppositional groups, filtered through the dynamics of the booster ethos, reflected frustrations of some members of the subculture of others who gradually differentiated themselves as "genteel," "polite," and "successful" men who sought to reform and order society from common working people who eschewed social agendas. The development or formalization of such events reflected a sharpening of class lines, and the desire or efforts of some members of the subculture to begin to separate enclaves or pockets of genteel society from out of the male subculture.

By the early 1850s the internal lines of Keokuk society hardened and became more demarcated, and a greater diversity of voluntary and fraternal associations provided venues in which individuals could enhance or gain social mobility and status.[132] Even as this occurred, the various kinds of behavior central to Keokuk's active male subculture – heavy drinking, nicknames, verbal jousting, swearing, practical jokes, oppositional parties and balls, team and group frolics and competitions – all carried out to relieve tensions and vent competitive pressure by connecting individuals to a common brotherhood converged in Keokuk's "unique" public institution, which developed in 1844 precisely along the fault lines over the Decree which threatened the order of the booster ethos and male subculture and became, through continued Half Breed fights and frictions over strategies to take within the booster ethos, an institutional mainstay of town life through the mid-fifties, and continued as a town tradition until the late 1870s – the yellow handbill meeting. Though J. M. Reid described these meetings as "free and easy citizen meetings . . . something like a third house [a lobby] or mock legislature" in which "any citizen could be attacked" and all were expected to take such criticisms "good humordly" (sic),[133] such formal mock institutions were affected by rather than affected the male subculture. Both "moot" or "mock trials" among lawyers and the mock legislatures or the "lobby" among legislators emerged as those who entered the professions combined their new procedures – whether court, debating societies, or sessions of the legislature – with the "horse play" and sarcasm of the male subculture.[134]

Caleb F. Davis perceptively noted that "Silas Heaight . . . was the getter up and moving spirit" of such meetings. "They were the escape pipe to the effervescing cussedness of the early settlers; as necessary for the time as the blow-off pipe to a steam engine. They were necessarily periodically [sic] and frequent, for in the early settlement of the country the congregation of all classes of humanity, upon a new soil, rank with vegitation [sic], course [sic] diet, and poor whiskey, the accumulation of bile was rapid and required frequent throwing off. Heaight was the exculpatis [sic] to furnish the remedy." Heaight was described in classic male subcultural fashion as "a man with a rough exterior and expression, yet with a heart as tender as that of a woman." We are told that "he could weep with the mourners at a Methodist revival [which he did in 1855], play faro and poker, dance all night in Rat Row, hold high carnival with convivial spirits in Barlow's saloon, or make a 'ten strike' at Galt's bowling alley, and in each and every instance, 'hold his own, like a man.'" Agent for the Keokuk Packet Company, Heaight, a native Pennsylvanian who had spent some time in New York, was a constant presence on the wharf and up and down Main Street and became deeply entrenched in the male subculture of the town after his arrival in 1840. Perhaps sensing that nicknames, practical jokes, raucous parties, and general "fun" were too discursive to ease the building tensions simmering just beneath the surface of this urban male subculture, Heaight sought to draw together and concentrate the palliative of parody, humor, sarcasm, and irony by organizing more structured spoof meetings to discuss political issues.

Defining the underlying point of nicknames, practical jokes, verbal jousting, blackguarding, and the entire male subculture, Heaight expected that at these meetings, "each and every person would 'pitch into' every other one, and anyone so sensitive that they could not stand a little lying or abuse had better be at home resting quietly in the bosom of his family." These meetings were usually announced by handbills printed on yellow paper (see Figs. 6 and 7) which called upon "the people of the town or county to come out and listen to discussions between noted speakers on controversial subjects" or, as Hawkins Taylor recalled, "any question [they] chose to speak on," often ranging across "twenty different subjects, none having any connection with any other."[135]

The first such meeting was launched in secrecy just before the elections and after the issuing of the Decree partition in the spring of 1844. "No one [initially] knew where these posters originated, or who wrote or printed them, or posted them." The first handbills of the early forties were of "large size" – Taylor described them as "immense"[136] – "full of capital head lines and impressed the idea of an immense organization behind the movement." The notices invited the voters of Lee County in highly sarcastic language to come to a special meeting to discuss the Decree, Settlers' Rights, and the County Seat question, issues which divided the town and county in the current campaign for county offices. Announced to be among the speakers were A. B. Chittenden (a merchant and "Chesterfield gentleman"), Dan Dierdorff (a well-known ruffian), Squire Van Fossen (a politician), Solomon Spann (another gentleman), and others, all of whom (except Van Fossen) in the past had never been known to give a speech, or even speak out or express an opinion on the issues dividing the town. To anyone who knew these men, the announcement of a

YELLOW HAND-BILL!

COME ONE! COME ALL!

The War is over, the President is to be Impeached,
—AND—
The Whiskey Ring has been Broken up!

RAILROADS  & STEAMBOATS
RUNNING OPPOSITION!

CITY COUNCIL GONE CRAZY!
To clear the wharf of Obstructions and Nuisances!

CITIZENS, COME TO THE
COURT HOUSE !
This Evening!
And see what is to be done at an old fashioned "YELLOW HAND BILL MEETING!!!"

S. HEAIGHT.

Figure 6. A yellow handbill, c. 1866. (Courtesy of Keokuk Savings Bank and Trust Co., Keokuk, Iowa)

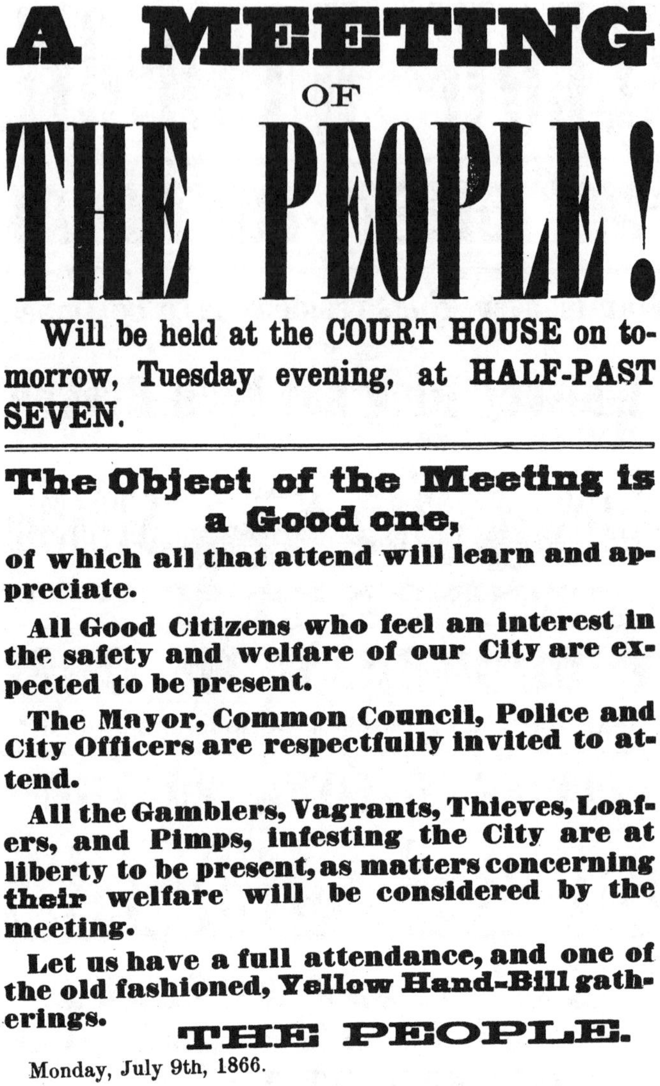

Provincial lives

A MEETING
OF
THE PEOPLE!

Will be held at the COURT HOUSE on to-morrow, Tuesday evening, at HALF-PAST SEVEN.

The Object of the Meeting is a Good one,
of which all that attend will learn and appreciate.

All Good Citizens who feel an interest in the safety and welfare of our City are expected to be present.

The Mayor, Common Council, Police and City Officers are respectfully invited to attend.

All the Gamblers, Vagrants, Thieves, Loafers, and Pimps, infesting the City are at liberty to be present, as matters concerning their welfare will be considered by the meeting.

Let us have a full attendance, and one of the old fashioned, Yellow Hand-Bill gatherings. **THE PEOPLE.**

Monday, July 9th, 1866.

Figure 7. A yellow handbill, 9 July 1866. (Courtesy of Keokuk Savings Bank and Trust Co., Keokuk, Iowa)

meeting at which they were to speak seemed absurd and the signs created a furor throughout town and on "the Tract." That the notices were unsigned added to the agitation of the townspeople and Settlers who were nearly at war with each other over the Decree.

In spite of the notices, however, no yellow handbill meeting actually took place in

"A common band of brotherhood"

May 1844. Indeed, for Silas Heaight, the "fun" was in pulling off an elaborate practical joke – from secretly posting the handbills, to organizing the fake meeting they had no intention of holding, to drumming up excitement in anticipation of the meeting, to, finally, observing the response of the hundreds of people gathered for the meeting when it became apparent to them that there was no meeting and that they had been hoaxed. Among the named speakers the initial response of only one man is known. As Hawkins Taylor later told it, one of the "named speakers" was Solomon Spann, "a man of dignified deportment and elegant leisure" who became "mad enough to fight the man who issued the handbills." He "smothered his wrath however, put on a ruffled shirt [usually the mark of a Kentucky gentleman],[137] and with a large gold-headed cane and a roll of documents under his arm, procured of 'Government' Adam Hine [the meaning of carrying the papers is unclear] and spent the day visiting the drinking houses followed by a large crowd, all of whom he treated, but paid nothing."

As this classic convivial ritual gained momentum and crowds gathered, Heaight conspicuously sent "outriders" into the country who later returned to announce that a large crowd "a thousand strong" of angry settlers had gathered and were marching toward town. To fan the growing excitement and sense of expectation, later in the afternoon Heaight dashed around town in his hack in all directions conveying the latest news. "He would drive out to the end of Main Street, and return to the Levee at full speed" and report to the crowd that "The Settlers were entering the town on Main Street in full force." Just at the peak moment of excitement, however, with a crowd of townspeople gathered by the wharf expecting to be confronted by an agitated mob marching down Main Street toward the river, Heaight "disappeared," leaving the crowd in town at first expectant, then impatient, then befuddled, and finally aware that they had been "sadly hoaxed" too. By the time that Heaight quietly reappeared at a drinking place later that evening, most of the crowd, and several of the announced speakers, who had dispersed into the barrooms and had been drinking for several hours, welcomed him warmly, "enjoying the joke" and "talking over" all aspects of "the farce" and how he had pulled it off. Such was not the case with Dan Dierdorff. He confronted Heaight "as the 'getter up' of the handbill and at once prepared for a fight." When Heaight, wanting no part of a fight, took to his heels, limping as usual, Dierdorff followed and a feigned foot race down Main Street in the manner of a town "frolic" ensued. It ended when Heaight found refuge at Widow Gaines's "corner" at the foot of Main where his "friends interfered and prevented trouble" amid the general merriment and fun of the spectacle.[138]

The language of two later handbills from July 1866 reflects the emergence of the full-blown sarcastic wit evidenced in the 1858 "Cosmopolitan Society" invitation blending with the populist rhetoric of antiwar Democrats during the war (see Fig. 5, above). Such extraordinary sarcastic verbal jousting manifests an effort to apply the primary "raison d'être" of the male subculture to the new more rigid class and cultural structures of a rapidly changing society. In the early 1840s and 1850s, the very effort to organize meetings at which men were expected to blow off steam in much the same way they had been doing so in the male subculture testifies to the desire, in a rough town like Keokuk, to maintain social order. By the mid-1840s and 1850s, the meetings, perhaps in response to a perceived demand, actually took place and developed into unscripted verbal jousting bouts between speakers and the audience. The meetings were organized like town meetings, but with roles and rules of such meetings or civic procedures, relaxed or reversed. As such, yellow handbill meetings became a kind of "oppositional culture," not unlike more raucous spoof militia or burlesque street parades, charivaris, "rough music," or mardi gras festivities in other cities of the time.[139]

Nevertheless, as the increasingly structured and oppositional nature of such meetings indicates, the informal, fraternal style and language of the male subculture of the 1840s was, under migration pressure, institutional formalization, and new cultural influences, losing its mediating ability. The participants in the male subculture had managed to prevent violence (with some exceptions) from undermining social development by restraining themselves or venting tensions through interaction which valued fraternity and comradery over self-interest. Even those genteel members of the subculture who were always covertly interested in contributing to the gentility system subsumed their agenda into a common subculture, biding their time until conditions would be more propitious for achieving their social goals. As more genteel people arrived and set themselves apart, the need to dissemble declined. Therefore, two social systems, or two visions of social order, existed simultaneously within the early urban settlements of the West, a genteel social order and a common frontier male subculture. During the 1840s the former penetrated and intertwined itself with the latter, moving through it like an undercurrent, awaiting the convergence of demographic and economic forces that would allow it to emerge and join those genteel settlers who had remained aloof from the male subculture.

The increasing practice of defining members of the male subculture as "gentlemen" reflects in the 1850s the degree to which the genteel men within the male subculture gradually eschewed the strategy of dissimulation and egalitarian mutuality and began asserting their genteel values – albeit still fraternally – by establishing social lines around themselves. By the early fifties, these lines were increasingly articulated by professional or economic achievement. Almost anyone who had acquired wealth or status within Keokuk's male subculture was described as a "gentleman." Among the twenty richest men in town in 1850, half had been active members of the male subculture from the early forties and had conferred upon them gentlemanly status. Hugh T. Reid, the richest man in town in 1850, was a man of "influence."[140] Lyman E. Johnson, a "fair lawyer," acquired gentlemanly status by marrying a "most estimable lady." John Graham was a Virginian gentleman and "mayor for three successive terms." Abraham Chittenden was "esteemed by all who knew him, and when among the ladies was a perfect Chesterfield [gentleman]."[141] His partners William and Lee McGavic were, in A. W. Griffith's words, "noble hearted spirits, honest, just, and charitable, and as true friends as ever lived on this green earth."[142] William Leighton and John P. Reed were also considered "gentleman" in local society. Time even softened the image of the "old war horse" Isaac Galland, who "did not love the world nor the world him." According to one he had "many redeeming qualities, he could be a rowdy and lead a mob, could swear like a pirate and . . . drank to excess, yet when he chose to be so amongst gentlemen in society he was courtly and elegant."[143]

Though wealth, occupation, and time could elevate one above the egalitarian subculture – or show one's gentlemanly qualities – and make one "esteemed," "prominent," "a man of influence," what really made one a gentleman was, within the gentility system, the quality of one's character. Those without wealth or status, as well as those with faults, if they possessed sincerity, "nobility," and honesty, virtues highly regarded among the members of the male subculture, could still be gentlemen. Ross B. Hughes was a "genial whole-souled man, . . . true and noble in his nature."[144] A. W. Griffith remarked that it was true Bill Clark "had some faults," but he was "noble hearted," "charitable," and a "friend as true as the needle to the north pole." Later, Verplanck Van Antwerp recalled his rough-edged friend Dan Hine, a noted roughhouser, by contrasting him to the duplicitous untrustworthy men of a later time: "How unlike that true hearted, gallant spirit, Dan Hine, who would rather have cut off his arm than to have betrayed a friend! There was a man for you, that was a man! . . . and yet how little was he generally appreciated by the brutal crowd!" Valencourt Vanorsdal, who stood closer to gentlemanly status, was, in Griffith's similar effusive language of manly comradery, "the noblest work of God, an honest man and a friend as true as steel."[145] Silas Heaight was "the embodiment of the trait of off handed generosity" which guided male relations in the 1840s.[146] Others who were active among the subculture were also increasingly referred to as "gentlemen."[147]

Even morally suspect southerners could be covered by the diffusion of gentility. Bill Clark, his cousin John P. Reed, Ross B. Hughes, Caleb F. Davis, George Smythe, and John A. Graham all were drawn into the male subculture, absorbed its style, and learned to behave much like their colleagues from the North, and were described as others within the culture were. Another southerner, Christian Garber, was also described as "born a gentleman and still inherits that virtue; though frequently rough when addressing his male friends he was as polite as a French dancing master when addressing the ladies; was liberal almost to a fault, when charity was really needed," and remained "a confirmed jolly old bachelor from his youth to the present day."[148] Even the notorious General Jesse B. Browne, though a true southern gentleman in the "Chesterfield" manner and when intoxicated "one of the meanest drunk men to be found anywhere," was "during his sober moments . . . a polished gentleman and detested anything savouring of drunkenness."[149] Such "gentlemen" drank, interacted with the male subculture, played practical jokes, and had nicknames; only as they matured and married did they abandon such behavior. What mattered more than impeccable morals and proper behavior was honesty, integrity, and a willingness to treat everyone openly and equally. Indiscretions and occasional mistakes could not obscure the goodness of one's heart. Forgiveness, an understanding of human foibles, and even compassion guided such gentlemen's code of behavior. They and many of their cohorts would leave the male subculture behind and help construct a new social class based on gentility.

Provincial lives

When public life was still an "open field" to all entrepreneurs and settlers, the central focus of the members of male subcultures in the 1840s was, as historian Robert Wiebe has suggested, to "reorganiz[e] the interior" structure of a relatively classless society. Male subcultures on the urban frontier supplanted patriarchal hierarchy with a fraternal-based social order. This laid the framework for the development of a genteel middle-class, "fraternal democracy" which rose out of the society and culture of the antebellum urban Middle West to shape the character of national public life in the Gilded Age.[150]

4

The gentility system in the West

Genteel society in the West was established both by settlers who arrived before 1840 and lived with the urban male subcultures while waiting for a more stable social context to develop and by newcomers, especially merchants and professionals, who arrived within the intraurban migration system after 1840 intent on bringing their more aggressive versions of gentility to the West. The convergence of these groups in the late forties and early fifties at urban centers throughout the region gave genteel people sufficient numbers to form "sets" and family-based "enclaves" of "good" society to supplant the male subculture as the prevailing social ideology of local and regional urban society.[1]

The genteel people who arrived earlier were deeply affected by their experiences rising out of, encountering, or evading the male subcultures of the urban West. Encountering the egalitarian social order of the West, they sought to develop gentility by simply suffusing the capacious structures and fluid dynamics of the urban male subcultures with genteel values, standards, and behavior. The western gentility system they implemented, therefore, may, initially, at least, have had a more fraternal, masculine cast to it, if only because much of the focus of class formation during the 1840s was carried out in a public realm, depriving genteel women of the proper venue to articulate their moral and genteel values.[2] Gentility in the West was also based on somewhat more broadly defined standards and behaviors able to accommodate genteel people from a range of social and regional traditions, ranging from "aristocrats" from the upland South to "simple" people from New England villages. As subsequent immigrants arrived and found that they were unable to shape unilaterally the values and mores of gentility, they accepted a broader range of variation in practice and behavior.

The booster ethos that sprouted up between the cracks of diverse social traditions in the early West formed the framework for the development of gentility. In such a system, people were strong enough to assert social control, but their actions were construed broadly enough that both residents and subsequent newcomers felt little pressure to struggle for social power or to defend their regional identities. In such a segmented social realm, individuals were able to express their class ideology or regional identity privately or publicly, as the situation warranted. The institutional structure and polity that emerged became a neutral, common meeting ground upon which people with different views and attitudes could interpret specific procedures and arrangements to their own liking. The result was a diverse social kaleidoscope of individuals with shared class values, mediating each in his or her own way between his or her private realms of family and kin culture, and the relatively capacious public structures of class, culture, and community. This created a far more complex society than might at first seem apparent.

The construction of gentility and its gradual emergence as the dominant social ideology of the urban Middle West occurred during the 1840s and 1850s on three fronts. Individuals migrating west, or having come west earlier and bided their time, began, after 1840, to act and behave more aggressively as gentlemen and genteel women. In doing so, they differentiated themselves from others based on their shared values and created venues for people to interact and come together as a set or group. Through such initial networking the first public manifestations of gentility began to appear. Meanwhile, gentlemen and genteel women formed partnerships, institutions, and societies to advance their social agendas.

While establishing gentility in public, entrepreneurs and professionals also cultivated private familial subcultures in which, by raising families and cultivating domesticity, they reproduced the class and forwarded its agenda. Cultivating a specific and unique familial subculture which, experience by experience, bound members into a collective memory and consciousness, involving the distinctive fusion of different personalities, values, ideas, styles, and goals that intertwined with the more general social ideology of class was, for the emotionalized child-centered bourgeois family, a primary task of private life.[3] Within this more private realm, fostering an interior private life, with its own narrative, separate from public narratives, was expected. The family became an intimate realm, an inner sanctum, screened from the public view and protected from the public realm of politics, work, rituals, and institutional life. The domestic circle formed a world apart where one could find all the satisfaction, happiness, and fulfillment in life that one would ever want or need.[4] As a member of a class one acted out social agendas and strategies like all other families of one's group. By such action one established, first through action and behavior which others could emulate and then as a group by forming institutions that developed strategies to interject one's mores and values into public agendas, the foundation of social order.[5]

Everyone followed this trajectory of class formation from individual experience through one's family and social life. The diverse ways that individuals and families contributed, in their own way, to establishing the gentility system as the predominant social system across the antebellum urban West are apparent in the intertwined experiences of hundreds of genteel families across the Great West – three of whom, the Washburnes of Galena, the Langworthys of Dubuque, and the Brownings of

Gentility in the West

Quincy, provide deeper experiential insight into the process of the construction and diffusion of gentility.

Recognizing gentility

As the urban migration system emerged and the towns and cities of the West were connected to eastern cities, more professionals, business people, and other middle-class people migrated directly into the West. In general, strong family migration systems transferred social values, attitudes, behavior, and practice more directly to the West. Those who arrived as individuals within a migration system had to pursue individual, entrepreneurial strategies to establish a local business or practice. In time, both groups would interact and together begin constructing middle-class society.

Immigrants within coherent, well-organized family migration systems had fewer concerns about establishing themselves within the volatile social order of the urban West. For Solon Langworthy of Dubuque, as for the Hempsteads and Gratiots of Galena, migration involved following the dynamics of a family system and arriving at a known destination to contribute to a family-based outpost of gentility. With three older brothers, for example, Solon Langworthy simply followed the paths they had broken. Settling with his family, in the spring of 1821, on land near Diamond Grove (just south of Jacksonville, Illinois), a location selected by his brother James L. Langworthy, "who after a thorough examination of a large portion of Illinois made choice of this point for the settlement of our family," Solon, with his father, brothers, and sisters helped establish a successful farm which provided for the family by mixing collective or corporate activity, a degree of self-sufficiency, and market farming until 1831. Langworthy's father continued to support the family by practicing medicine, which he had learned at Yale College.[6]

One by one, however, the older sons were drawn away from subsistence and small profit farming. First, James departed for St. Louis where in 1822 he opened one of the first steam flouring mills in Missouri, the proceeds of which he remitted to the family, along with a regular stream of supplies he sent from St. Louis. In May 1824, James "was induced from the reports of the new lead mines in the northwest to lay his fortune in that direction," and arrived at Galena when there were "but a few white men and . . . a small trading post for Indians at the place," serving again, as he did at Diamond Grove, as the adventurer "for the family." Within three years James had formed a partnership with Orrin Smith, later a brother-in-law, and engaged successfully in mining above Galena. His success enticed his next youngest brothers to come north and seek their fortunes as well. Lucius and Edward, "being curious to see the country," "obtained [their] father's consent to go to the mines" and in May 1827, "with stout hearts," accompanied by their sisters Mary Ann and Maria, who were "pale with sorrow," left home with a fully stocked wagon. Solon accompanied them to Quincy where they found "one log cabin occupied by John Wood Esq., [later] Governor of Illinois," and luckily encountered only the second steamboat which had ascended the river. Solon then returned alone across the prairies to the family homestead, though only thirteen, to take over the operation of the farm.[7]

Provincial lives

Lucius and Edward followed their brother James in successfully engaging in mining, smelting, and keeping a store at Buncombe, Wisconsin. They, too, followed James, who in 1830 under Indian guidance, "cross[ed] the Mississippi[,] . . . explore[d] the country between the Maquoteka and Turkey rivers" in eastern Iowa,[8] and made a claim to mine lead on the site of Dubuque. Though evicted by military forces who pushed them off Indian land and then by the Black Hawk war, they resettled their claim in 1833 and thus laid the foundation of the Langworthy fortune and their subsequent social hegemony in Dubuque, Iowa.[9] In 1831, Stephen Langworthy sold his Diamond Grove farm near Jacksonville and resettled near St. Charles, Missouri, freeing Solon "to seek employment elsewhere." After a stint with the U.S. Rangers, Solon joined his brothers in early 1834 at Dubuque and was hired to "draw rails, build fence [sic], and break more than forty acres of bottom land where the city of Dubuque now stands," apparently the first tract of land plowed in Iowa.[10] The decision of all four brothers to pool their resources and form a partnership in 1836, "James L. Langworthy and Brothers," which operated as miners, smelters, land agents, merchants, railroad investors, and bankers and stayed in business until James Langworthy retired in 1862, enabled them by the early fifties to become the richest men in town, paying together about one-twelfth of the town's taxes.[11] The Langworthys were thus able to exert almost oligarchical social and economic influence over the booster ethos and the life of the town.

In contrast, most immigrants who arrived alone, even if they considered themselves "gentlemen," had to concentrate initially on establishing a business or practice before concerning themselves with establishing gentility. Orville Hickman Browning, a Kentucky lawyer who arrived in Quincy, Illinois, in 1831, for example, migrated alone, following the rural or urban migration streams of Kentuckians into Illinois. Browning arrived "almost penniless" in Quincy, with a letter of introduction in hand attesting to his "amiable character" and "fine requirements."[12] Through this letter he befriended John Wood, the New York-born founder of the village, whom the Langworthys had met on their journey north in 1821, and Archibald Williams, another Kentuckian and one of the few lawyers in town.[13] Browning threw himself into civic affairs, participating in town meetings, volunteering for the Black Hawk war, and joining in local politics. In legal affairs he helped organize the local bar, which included only a few members, but which, as early as 1832, endorsed local, state, and national political candidates and sent a delegation to ride the rigorous Sixth Circuit which stretched north to Galena.[14] In 1836 Browning was elected as state senator from Adams County to the Illinois legislature, extending his circle of connections and setting the stage to fulfill his ambitions first at Vandalia and then, from 1837 through 1840, at Springfield. Absent from Quincy so often during these years, he formed, in 1837, a partnership with Nemehiah Bushnell, a Connecticut-born Yale graduate who had recently arrived in Quincy to help him carry on his legal practice.[15] Within a decade, Browning had established himself as one of the more prosperous, widely connected, and prominent lawyers in town.

Browning's Kentucky-bred "genteel" social mores, values, and behavior shaped the structure of his professional and social relationships. He grew up in a "gentle," landowning, upwardly mobile family, "related by blood and marriage to clan after clan of Kentuckians who helped to form the newer West," in Cynthiana, Kentucky, in Harrison County, about forty miles north of Lexington.[16] Browning was socialized on the borderline between the rural and urban gentry, midway between the hardscrabble rural life of his friend Abraham Lincoln in Hardin County and the refined elegance of Lincoln's wife Mary Todd in Lexington,[17] where urban petit-bourgeois manners and attitudes intertwined with those of "aristocrats," "blue bloods," or "gentry," whose "refined sense of honor" and style defined upward mobility and social achievement in the region.[18] His father, like other landowning gentry residing outside Kentucky towns, not only owned a plantation with one slave but also invested in and operated a manufacturing establishment and was involved in mercantile activity as well.[19]

What differentiated Browning from the aristocrats was his "moral sensitivity" and belief in strict standards of conduct, rooted in "old school" Presbyterianism which he encountered during his education at a small genteel academy just south of Cincinnati.[20] Browning was a model "Christian Gentleman," a variation of the Kentucky "gentleman of the old school" enabling him to interact easily with moral gentlemen from New England. He possessed good looks, a "self-assured personality," a "grave," "sober," and even riveting speaking style, as well a "polished manner" which sometimes manifested itself in a somewhat "dandyesque" interest in clothes, interior decoration, and gardening, a love of socializing with women, and a haughty, standoffish manner.[21]

Gustave Koerner, a German-American lawyer in Edwardsville, Illinois, and friend of Browning's since 1842, described Browning in "Chesterfieldian" terms[22] as "of an imposing stature, a really handsome man, with speaking darkish eyes, and in dress most exquisitely dandy. He always wore a dress-coat of peculiar cut – Prince Albert fashion [an oversized coat with thin lapels, double-breasted with six rows of buttons buttoned to within a few inches of the neck] – with an outside pocket, from which the ends of a white or light yellow handkerchief dangled out.[23] What made him particularly conspicuous was his ruffled shirt and large cuffs [a Kentucky mannerism of the 1820s],[24] then hardly ever seen. He was not only a good debater, but at times could rise to oratory. . . . I came into very pleasant relations with him, but I should have liked him better if he had been a little less conscious of his own superiority."[25]

Nevertheless, Browning's style was manifested in his lifelong friendship with his law partner Nemehiah Bushnell. Sharing a "cultural refinement," "moral sensitivity," fine intelligence, and superb conversational skills, Bushnell and Browning established what seemed the perfect partnership.[26] "Join[ing] issues instinctively," and having career interests that dovetailed, Browning and Bushnell's partnership was the "ideal [of] strength and harmony" which lasted for thirty-seven years. "During all that time there was never a harsh word, or an unkind thought or feeling between us," Browning wrote upon Bushnell's death in 1874. "He was very dear to me. I loved him as a brother."[27] On the strength of this relationship, Browning established himself as a central figure in the town's professional culture and thus stood prepared to play a central role in the construction of gentility in Quincy.

Elihu Benjamin Washburne headed west in the spring of 1840, a New England moral gentleman imbued with the social and cultural values – including constructions of self, gender, family, class, and community – from both rural, even frontier, Maine, and the urban professional gentility of Harvard and Boston. These were more aggressive, individualistic formations of the traditional values of self-discipline, stoicism, frugality, hard work, stern independence, and economic self-sufficiency[28] that served as the basis of Congregationalism and the New England way. Cut free from communal values by the industrial revolution, New Englanders turned aggressively toward self-mastery and social reproduction through revivalism and reform to maintain social order.[29] Washburne's belief that law was a "distinctive [masculine] endeavor" in which one applied a strong ethical code based on responsibility, morality, and honor to the active work of litigation and politics only inflamed his passion to change himself and the society around him.[30] Washburne was convinced that only migration would give him the opportunities he craved to achieve his professional, social, and cultural aspirations and validate his manhood and social status. Though the expanding economy would, in time, provide the free or "broad" field that the egalitarian individualism of the 1830s promised to every man,[31] the legal profession remained too "crowded" in the East.[32] Washburne, who loved his home, felt that people in New England towns remained too "cursed aristocratic," hierarchical, and stagnant, and tended to "hold a prejudice against" young men, "pulling [them] back by the coat tails" rather than encouraging them to achieve success.[33] Accordingly, Washburne decided to leave New England and "pursue his destiny" – "Westward Ho!" – in the "wide, wide world," a decision he never regretted.[34] The imprint of the social and cultural values of the "hearth" from which he left, shaped – within the context of a family system, a chain migration, and cultural extension to the West – his strategy and actions and his contribution to western society once he settled there.[35]

In traveling west in the spring of 1840, Elihu Washburne moved within three intertwined migration systems. On one level he migrated as a New Englander, a son of Maine, following thousands of his peers to the West. He also migrated within a nascent family migration system, following his brother Cadwallader, the second of four sons who eventually would emigrate to the West to achieve mobility and then send what capital they could back to their patriarchal home in Livermore, Maine. Finally, he traveled as a professionally educated, urbane "gentleman" within the emerging "entrepreneurial" migration system connecting eastern cities with the urban frontier. Though Washburne understood the dynamics of these systems, he viewed himself as a single New England gentleman and lawyer, who intended to settle in a town in eastern Iowa, hang out his shingle, and begin to climb the ladder of life on his own.

The system most operative in Washburne's progress west was the professional code of behavior and ethics established among middle-class gentlemen. The central premise of this code, shared by all gentlemen of integrity, who were honest, temperate, and moderate, and through hard work and self-discipline had succeeded in life as men of action, was egalitarian reciprocity. Gentlemen treated each other as equals in an open and magnanimous manner, and reciprocated all favors or actions to sustain and enhance each other's honor and self-esteem. Through egalitarian interaction, men socially supported each other, sustained their control of society and public life, and contributed to the construction of middle-class social order. As a Maine country boy, Washburne gave this code a simple, colloquial style, but, he knew, at age twenty-four, what he was about and what he wanted in life.[36] He also knew that men who eschewed these values were rowdies of a lower social station, to be abided by and interacted with only so much as to achieve the purpose at hand, but not to be treated as social equals.

For Washburne, migration to the West was a matter of correctly and effectively navigating within the system of behavior shared among gentlemen. The letter of introduction tucked in his pocket, written by a prominent lawyer for whom Washburne clerked, stating that Washburne had become a "member of [his] family" and was a young man with "most perfectly correct" "moral habits," "highly respectable" "talents," and a "zeal in pursuing his professional studies too ardent and unintermitting for his strength to support,"[37] as well as a few other letters to gentlemen in Cincinnati, would blaze Washburne's trail among western gentlemen. As Washburne traveled, he assessed every gentleman he met, and if he found them useful, Washburne exacted information or letters of introduction from them, to further his progress west. In Cincinnati, his letters brought him the "civility" and "polite attention" of one "gentleman," another modest "true gentleman" who also happened to be a "good Whig," a pair of "first rate fellows," and finally, a "fair old chap."[38] Each of these men, once they approved of Washburne, reciprocated the letters to them, by giving Washburne "eight [to] ten strong letters to men in different parts of the [Iowa] territory," thus giving him a range of choices of towns to settle in.[39]

Washburne then went to Rock Island, Illinois, where his brother Cadwallader had settled a few years before. From there, he expected to go to Iowa. At Rock Island he found "Caddy" teaching school and "quite a man among them." Cadwallader and his friends advised Elihu to locate in Galena, Illinois, "the best place in the whole West," rather than cross the river into Iowa Territory. They encouraged Washburne to go there because Galena had a surplus of Democratic lawyers and needed more Whig lawyers, and suggested that the only Whig lawyer in town, Thomas Drummond, a native of Maine, might be willing to form a partnership with Washburne. It was on the strength of this expectation that Washburne chose Galena.[40]

Arriving on 1 April 1840 he walked through "knee-deep" mud to look among "the log and frame buildings all huddled together" for Thomas Drummond. Drummond, though a fellow Whig and "Maine boy," was not interested in taking on a partner and in fact discouraged Washburne from settling there. Feeling as if he had been brushed off, as well as misinformed about the prospects for a law career in Galena, the stubborn Washburne, who always tenaciously rose to meet a challenge, determined at once to settle in Galena "on my own hook, hit or miss."[41] He then looked up Horace H. Houghton, editor of the Whig paper, a "man of great good sense" who told him to "ask no questions of any of them, but sit . . . right down and mind [his] own business," an approach he guaranteed Washburne "would insure him success." Then Houghton, acting as a mentor within the booster ethos, "took hold" of Washburne, helped him find "a good office in a good part of town" which he rented from Horatio Newhall, and offered to room with him in "one of the best private boarding houses in town." Thus Washburne, by relying on a key member of the booster network, by the end of his second day in Galena had everything suited "to a T" and was "very respectably situated."[42]

Structuring gentility

Settled within a new town, most immigrants recognized that before any real public social order emerged in a society dominated by the male subculture, genteel families were havens of social order. Thus, each immigrant, whether, like Langworthy, in one's own family system, or single, like Washburne and Browning, set it as their goal to pursue such families, attach oneself to them, and, through connections within their enclave, meet and marry a genteel woman and start a genteel family of one's own. In their efforts each man was compelled to assess the social geography of the town in which he lived, and act accordingly. In the settled realm of Langworthy culture, one needed simply to go out and bring a wife into one's genteel culture. For most men like Washburne and Browning, however, establishing gentility often involved locating it first. Often, if one was able to distinguish gentlemen from ruffians in one's professional culture, one could establish connections through which one gained entrance into a genteel social enclave. There one might find an appropriate spouse and marry into gentility. If such connections evaded one, however, a gentleman could marry a woman interested in gentility, and together, as man and wife, a couple could seek entrance to genteel society.

To Elihu Washburne, Galena society was divided into good, civil, and polite gentlemen from different regions and all sorts of unprincipled men, ruffians, or rowdies. Washburne preferred to associate only with the former and set out, after delineating the lines of social interaction in Galena in the spring of 1840, to do so. Washburne arrived just as members of genteel society in Galena who had isolated themselves and bided their time while the male subculture was predominant were beginning to join those genteel people who had chosen to interact with the subculture to fuse their different strategies into a common social class agenda. As a lawyer, Washburne would feel the pull of the male subculture, but the alignment of his personal agenda with those of genteel people in town drew him toward them and into the strong currents of the fusion they were carrying out through the Episcopalian and Presbyterian churches and within the booster ethos. In law, politics, on Main Street, and at church, Washburne would meet those who were directly or indirectly connected with one of the strongest and most cohesive family systems and genteel "set" operating in the West – the Hempstead–Gratiot clan – and unrelentingly, on several fronts, seek entrance.

Washburne made his first step toward this goal by establishing a business relationship with Horatio Newhall, which quickly grew into friendship.[43] Through Newhall, Washburne gained introductions to several genteel people.[44] Since his arrival in 1827, Newhall had associated with William Hempstead, J. H. Lockwood, and D. B. Morehouse, both socially and as a member of the local volunteer militia.[45] More important, as a member of the Presbyterian church, Newhall knew and associated with Susan Hempstead Gratiot, plus several other prominent genteel men in early Galena society.[46] Through Newhall, Washburne, no doubt, became aware of and set his sights on entering the small enclave of "respectable" or "cultured" society which, since 1830, was centered in the households of William and Charles S. Hempstead and Susan Hempstead Gratiot, who lived seasonally within one of her brother's households and out on her estate at Gratiot's Grove, Wisconsin,[47] as well as those of Major T. B. Farnsworth, Moses Meeker, Ezekial Lockwood, John and Nicholas Dowling, and Aratus Kent.[48]

In the weeks after his arrival, Washburne strategically sought to gain entrance into the Hempstead–Gratiot "set" or "circle" in town society, in his choice of a professional mentor. Differentiating the members of the local bar between good and mediocre lawyers, Whigs and Democrats, New Englanders and southerners, but especially between gentlemen and ruffians, Washburne honed in on one man. Prominent among those who Washburne approved of was Charles S. Hempstead, who, in spite of being a Democrat, was a New Englander, and "one of the crack lawyers of the place," "an old lawyer of good ability and good standing" and "a very fine clever man." Thomas Drummond, the lawyer who rebuffed him a few weeks before, he now judged to be a "tolerable good lawyer, and a man of decent talents and great industry, [a] Whig." Among others who drew his appreciation were A. L Holmes, "a young man about a year from New Hampshire" who appeared "to be a pretty clever fellow." The rest of the lawyers in town, whom overall he considered a "decent set of fellows," nevertheless fell short of his moral and legal standards.[49] Among the few acceptable lawyers he found himself able to ally with, therefore, Drummond was already out of the picture, Holmes was too young, Newhall and Wyeth good friends – among the eight Harvard or Yale graduates he associated with[50] – but not lawyers. This left Charles S. Hempstead as his apparent choice.

Meanwhile, Washburne continued to navigate along the boundary which divided gentlemen from the male subculture. Recognizing that as a young single man in a highly competitive profession, he had to socialize with the members of the local bar, with whom he spent considerable time while on the circuit or "a tour,"[51] Washburne chose to equivocate. In his "windy," colloquial style, Washburne called himself one of the "western boys" and a "good fellow" who was a "crack stump speaker" at political camp meetings (which he believed privately to be "moonshine"), but which he went to primarily "as a matter of policy" to make his name "known" and "obtain all [his] business." Aware of the more convivial aspects of behavior on the circuit, Washburne deftly navigated on the line between the two by deigning to play at being a "hail fellow, well met with Tom, Dick, and Harry," but, as a temperance man who neither smoked nor played cards,[52] only "so far as I can without participating in their vices."[53]

At home, he drew a sharper line, making it clear that rather than dissembling and interacting with this culture, he wanted nothing to do with the "fellows," "drunkards," and "blackguards" of the male subculture,[54] who often caroused just outside his office windows. Washburne disparaged Galena as "one of the greatest places for drinking and gambling in the whole West. There are, I should judge, forty grog shops and gambling houses in town, and all on the Main Street, and all kept open on the Sabbath." "[Yet] I have not yet been into the first 'hell' in town. I avoid them as I would the pestilence that walketh at noonday. I was told by many fellows that if I settled here, in order to succeed, I should have to take my glass of liquor and game of cards, and be a hail fellow. I told them if my success was to depend on that I was bound not to succeed. But there is no greater mistake in the world. A steady and moral man is respected here as much as at the East."[55] Washburne intended to go about his business, keeping the male subculture at home and on the circuit at a distance by attending only genteel social occasions and pursuing a connection with professional, social, and familial networks of like-minded people, genteel, moral New Englanders.[56]

Washburne pursued this strategy by becoming actively engaged in politics, attending whatever genteel social occasions were held, and attending the Episcopal church "because it was the best in town."[57] There Washburne befriended Nathan and Henry Corwith, Frederick Stahl, H. H. Gear, E. D. Kittoe, James Carter, John and Sherwell S. Lorraine, John Turney, Artemus L. Holmes, Madison Y. Johnson, and Frederick E. Bergman.[58]

Professionally, Washburne tried a few cases with Hempstead and they grew to know each other better. Through this effort, Washburne received, six weeks later, the professional offer for which he had been working. "Charles S. Hempstead, Esq., the oldest and most respected lawyer in northern Illinois, standing in need of someone to assist him a little in business, [asked] me if I would give up my office and come in with him and assist him, and do my business in his office." Such an arrangement, in Washburne's view, connected him with "one of the best kind of men, a good lawyer, with a large library," and took him "out of the way of politics, the bane of lawyers." Washburne was aware of the breakthrough nature of this offer. "I shall stand in the way of becoming acquainted with a great many business men here. I consider the offer to be quite a compliment."[59]

This move shifted the trajectory of Washburne's professional and social progress in town. Until his connection with Charles Hempstead, Washburne had been balancing deepening relationships with the professional fraternity among lawyers and the Whig party, and primarily a "social" connection with the Episcopal church. Hempstead was, at forty-six, one the oldest members of the local bar and provided the twenty-four-year-old Washburne with not only mentoring, but through his connections, the opportunity for rapid professional advancement. He also provided Washburne with an introduction into the "genteel" life of the Gratiot–Hempstead subculture. That, as a moderate Democrat, Hempstead would be no help in Washburne's political future[60] mattered little. In fact Washburne probably saw his connection with Hempstead either as a way out of politics or as an expression of a more disinterested, nonpartisan gentlemanly style he sought to cultivate.

Nevertheless, through Hempstead, Washburne was given an ingress into the genteel subculture of one of Galena's most distinguished families. By mid-August, Hempstead invited Washburne to board at his house and live with his family, rather than sleep in a room next to the office. Hempstead had just finished the construction of a small brick Greek Revival house directly above and behind the wharf where he had his office near Bench and Magazine streets. William Hempstead, his wife Sarah, and their two children lived close by. Within earshot of the wharf, lower Bench Street had developed into a small neighborhood where several elite families of the town resided. Among their neighbors were Henry and Nathan Corwith, who, during this period, became friends of both Washburne and the Hempsteads.[61] From the moment he moved up to Bench Street, Washburne was impressed. "Mr. Hempstead lives in a fine style"[62] and as "the most charming of men," made his house "the seat of the most refined and generous hospitality. Strangers from distant cities who found themselves guests . . . in our then remote town, were equally surprised and delighted at the elegance and grace with which they were entertained." Washburne remarked, "I have never, in my life, lived in such style."[63] Though he sometimes found it difficult to enter very effectively into this "gay, lively, fashionable, and intelligent" society because a "defective hip" prevented him from dancing, he still got out enough to "see all that was going on," to meet others in society, and to find a wife.[64]

In entering this genteel circle, Washburne also found himself in the midst of one of the town's most fervent religious families, and thus in one of the New England families at the front line in forging a new middle-class ideology through a fusion of Christianity, capitalism, and gentility in Galena. Years before the arrival of Aratus Kent in Galena in 1829 as a representative of the Home Missionary Society with the task of founding a Presbyterian church in Galena, the Gratiots and Hempsteads had defined "good society" in spiritual terms. For them, politeness and gentility became expressions of sincerity, morality, and piety. For traditional Presbyterians, like patriarch Stephen Hempstead, the hardships of frontier life, so "far from relatives and friends," had been compounded by one's distance from a "church and the ordinances of God's house" which joins the fellow worshippers in a "Christian fellowship."[65] The Gratiots and others felt this lack deeply and Susan Gratiot joined five other settlers as the first members of the church which Kent founded on 23 October 1831. Soon after, Horatio Newhall joined the church. The following spring Kent left Galena "to visit New York and New England," and although his itinerary is not known, the fact that he returned a changed man suggests that he must have been exposed to the wave of revivals sweeping across the towns of New York and inland New England after Charles Finney's Great Revival which began in the Presbyterian church of Rochester in 1830–1831. Kent returned in December 1832 with "a wife, a young man by the name of Hall, and a young lady by the name of Pierce, all come out for the purpose of devoting their lives to do as much good as possible."[66]

While his assistants opened a Sabbath school, Mr. Kent concentrated on preaching and holding communion. The members of the church were astonished by Kent's new fervor. In January 1833 Kent held a communion, "for the second time in Galena" and "there were several persons admitted to the church by letters from other churches, and four new members were received, among the latter Mrs. Newhall" (who at the time was eight months' pregnant with the Newhalls' first child). Another new member was Daniel Wann, a lawyer friend of Charles Hempstead. Kent, employing Finney's Rochester tactics, began to preach more intensively on "Sunday forenoon and evening and also Wednesday evening" as well as holding separate weekly prayer meetings for men and women. Having "just come warm from the midst of numerous revivals" back East, Kent particularly focused on "female prayer meetings" and exhorted them particularly to influence others to increase church membership. Mr. Kent was sure that "there are signs of a revival which cannot be mistaken" as evidenced from the crowds that overflowed the meeting house at the weekly preaching, and intended to have another "communion" in the spring. Horatio Newhall, an early member of the church and contributor for the first building, was surprised by the Kents' vigor, remarking that they were probably "a little too zealous" for this "longitude" and "actually astonish the poor natives of Galena."[67] Nevertheless, by November 1833 the "shower of divine grace" had reached Gratiot's Grove, according to Susan Gratiot. The revival continued for several more months, so much so that Susan Gratiot remarked to her sister, "you will find a great change here." After subsiding, it began again in 1836 and 1837, and was periodically reinvigorated by further revivals in 1840, 1841, 1842, and finally, 1844.[68]

Susan Hempstead Gratiot sought to convert her brothers and to marry her sons to a religious woman who would do the same. When her son Edward married Ellen Hager in Terre Haute, Indiana, in 1846, Susan expressed her views on the role of Christian women in marriage: "I trust and hope that she once had a deep and sincere regard for religion, that it may return to her with double force and make her more lovely as a married woman and be the happy means of converting Edward. They have had time for due reflection and I feel as if it was all for the best and as we both have known when once married and settled the tumult of imagination will naturally subside and be succeeded by an endearment that affects the heart in a more equal[,] more sensible and tender manner."[69] So, too, she prayed for the conversion of her brothers, William and Charles, as well as that of her other children. Charles S. Hempstead's conversion, at age forty-seven, finally occurred in a "feast of never ending love" on 5 January 1841 during the revival of that year. Overcome with feelings of happiness, his sister "did not dare breathe hard for fear of losing those happy feelings we have when we feel as if we were hallowed by the presence of departed spirits." Under the influence of this power, her son Hempstead admitted that he too was "bound to be a Presbyterian." William Hempstead joined the church more like an "old Saint than a new Christian" during the Great Revival of late 1844.[70] Thus when Elihu Washburne arrived in Galena, he encountered, first in Horatio Newhall, and then in Charles and William Hempstead and Susan Hempstead Gratiot and her children, the full force of a religious and social transformation sweeping through urban America.[71]

In establishing their social position, middle-class people increasingly distinguished themselves from others not only by their profession and occupations, but also by their morality and gentility. Middle-class men portrayed themselves increasingly as moral gentlemen even as their wives, through religious conversions, asserted a new role as the primary source of morality and purity within the household. It was almost inevitable, therefore, that Elihu B. Washburne, a professional, college-educated, moralistic man from New England, seeking to achieve professional advancement and establish himself as a middle-class gentleman, should have met a clan, a family, and, in particular, a mentor, all of whom in the winter of 1841 were in the throes of an evangelical revival. It would have a fateful effect in his choice of a spouse, a choice which, by combining the various cultural and social forces then at work in town, would make his an almost archetypal "genteel" marriage in the region's social history.

In 1840 the twenty-four-year-old Washburne had proclaimed his love of freedom and independence from a marital connection as "single blessedness"[72] and expressed no interest in getting married until he was fully established. Yet like other "genteel" men, he understood the social necessity of marriage. Marriage grounded one's public efforts to the moral, private, domestic influence of a middle-class woman, who, like other middle-class women, sought to define the moral imperatives of bourgeois identity. By providing one with a domestic life, marriage provided a counterbalance to the trials and tribulations of public life and gave one a chance at personal happiness. Like another gentleman who left behind the male subculture and the public milieu among other men for marriage, Washburne understood that "life [was] not life until you marry ... in one state, a man's life is a waste, in the other it is a garden." With such thoughts, no doubt, in mind, Washburne intensively scrutinized the town's women.[73] In general, he felt that the "handsome" "young ladies" or "intelligent, accomplished and beautiful" "girls" of Galena, who were "from almost every part of the country," were prettier than the "old maids" or the "too cursed aristocratic" women back East.[74]

Not surprisingly, he would meet such a woman within the Hempstead–Gratiot circle, though when he first met her she was still just a girl. Upon entering the Hempstead household, Washburne met Charles's nieces who stayed there seasonally with their mother, Charles's sister Susan Hempstead Gratiot, Susan Gratiot, age twenty-one, and Adele Gratiot, age fourteen. In a much later reflection, Washburne noted that he first met Adele when one day in 1840 she stopped by the office and called him to dinner.[75] As a man of twenty-five he seems to have been initially more aware of Susan. She married Thomas Chiles on New Year's Day, 1841, an occasion which seemed overshadowed by the end of a festive season and her brother Charles's conversion the same week.[76]

If Washburne's interest in Susan was ever romantic, he did not express it. While Adele went off to study in 1841–1843 at the Menard Academy in Kaskaskia, Illinois, to complete her French education begun in St. Louis at the Visitation convent, thus postponing any courting Washburne may have had in mind, Washburne uncomfortably extricated himself from an engagement to an "aristocratic" eastern woman. He wished his brother to "keep the matter to *yourself entirely*, as it is a matter of no public interest and could not possibly do you any good to make it known."[77] Gradually, Washburne was drawn into the private realm of the Gratiot family. His highly emotional response upon hearing of Susan's sudden death, a few days shy of her third wedding anniversary, attests to this. Reaching out to Susan Hempstead Gratiot, whose "heart" was "bursting," and who would still refer to Susan's deathbed soliloquy a year later,[78] Washburne, with uncharacteristic passion, wrote: "To know Susan was to love her – the beauty and honor of her character – the kindness of her disposition – the benevolence of her feelings bound her with 'hooks of steel' to all who knew her. The news of her death coming upon me so suddenly and unexpectedly has almost unmanned me.... I can only offer to you, in your bereavement and to dear child, Adele and the rest of the family the warmest sympathies of a heart deeply penetrated with sorrow." Intriguingly, as if fate had touched the family, Susan's husband died soon afterward and their orphaned son, Will, would die eighteen years later at the battle of Shiloh.[79]

In September 1844 after returning from an extended trip to Baltimore, Philadelphia, and Washington, D.C., Washburne stopped at Gratiot's Grove. When he came down with a severe chill after arriving on Saturday, the Gratiots invited him to stay the weekend until he recovered. Washburne was drawn further into the family emotionally, and got an extraordinary lesson in family dynamics during the next two months,[80] when the family closed ranks to respond to yet another disaster in November 1844. On 11 October 1844 Uncle William's wife, Sarah Bouton, gave birth to a boy, whom they named Charles Smith Hempstead, after Uncle Charles. The birth weakened both the child and mother, however. Sarah died of a postnatal infection three weeks later on 7 November 1844. William, inconsolable, took the "sweet little babe" to his namesake's Uncle Charles's house to be nursed back to health, but the baby succumbed on 25 November. Unable to care for his children, William broke up his household. Years before, when his brother Charles's first wife had died in 1823, he had sent his two sons, Edward and Charles, to be raised by "Aunt Manuel" (Mary Lisa) until he chose to marry again. No doubt, at Charles's suggestion, William chose to do the same. He sent his daughter Mary Lisa to St. Louis to be adopted and cared for by her namesake Sister Mary Lisa. For Mary Lisa, this was the third time a sibling would call on her to "mother" the "motherless" children of the Hempstead family, a task she performed "tenderly" yet "strictly."[81] William kept his son George and daughter Augusta in Galena, sending them to his brother-in-law Edgar Bouton's home. Stunned by grief, and suffering from consumption (which would eventually kill him a decade later), William turned to his sister Susan. She led him spiritually toward a conversion experience at the end of 1844, after which he dedicated his life to service to the church.[82]

One can only surmise Adele's emotional response to these misfortunes. Nevertheless, it seems hardly surprising that after two such great disappointments, Adele, in her mother's words, was "more like an old settled woman than the girl of eighteen." "She is a great comfort to me." "But," as Susan noted, "I shall not have her for long." Sometime in the midst of this highly emotionalized family culture before 14 December Washburne and Adele became engaged, a step Washburne took "without consultation with anyone." By Christmas Susan had become aware that "our friend E.B.W." had "made his sentiments known and thinks he must have her to share his all in all with him." Of course, Susan could say or do nothing and expressed no direct opinion on the matter. "It seems that I saw more in her heart in one hour's conversation with her after she had accepted his proposal and more to admire than I ever saw in all her life."[83] Her daughters were responsible for their own marital decisions. Susan could hardly question a man with a promising legal and political career ahead of him, sponsored by her brother Charles and, in many ways, not unlike her brothers and father.

When the engagement became known, Adele and Washburne were presented to town society in 1845 at a New Year's "cotillion party." In a letter to his brother Cadwallader, Elihu remarked that "she is a noble little girl and I know you must like her for everybody does." In March, Adele went off to St. Louis to consult with her French relatives and assemble her trousseau from Paris, but was back at Gratiot's Grove by June and hard at work, sewing in preparation for the wedding.[84] Washburne apparently made a brief visit to St. Louis in May, no doubt to be introduced around to the Chouteaus, Gratiots, Lisas, Hempsteads, and others, though no record remains of this ritualized entrance of a fiancé into closed, genteel St. Louis French society.[85]

The wedding was a major event in Susan Gratiot's life, to be held at her house at the Grove. She gathered friends and cousins around her for weeks before to help her and Adele prepare for the event and, in a frenzy of sewing, for the "housekeeping" to follow. Besides some cousins and relations who came up from St. Louis to help Adele's preparations, they invited "but very few outside of the connection." Cadwallader, Elihu's younger brother who had, in March 1842, moved to Mineral Point, Wisconsin, brought some Gratiot relatives down to the Grove, then went to Galena to round up Elihu and return with him and the Hempstead brothers and their families the Wednesday night before the wedding.[86] The couple was married in a Presbyterian service on 31 July 1845. Though Washburne and his young wife of eighteen proceeded to set up housekeeping immediately after the marriage, their wedding and their married life for years afterward remained firmly placed within the Hempstead–Gratiot family system.

In contrast to Elihu Washburne, a regular "hail fellow," Orville Browning, who had settled in Quincy in 1831 and, as a politician and lawyer, had established himself as a central figure in the construction of gentility in town, was an aloof, formal man who was "not easy to know." Browning, therefore, would establish his social position in town primarily through and among his friends and colleagues in the law and fellow Kentuckians with whom he had "day-to-day associations in the country courts." Such interaction at work "broke down some of the barriers of his reserved nature" and through "common experiences . . . provided [him with] the basis for amicability."[87] Among Browning's friends were Archibald Williams and J. H. Ralston. A closer friend was Henry Asbury, who arrived at Quincy, Illinois, in 1832 and entered Browning's law office to read law in 1834. In 1837 Asbury was admitted to the Quincy bar and became Browning and Nehemiah Bushnell's associate, though he spent most of his time as Justice of the Peace of the County Court, an office he was elected to in 1836 and retained through 1850; in 1849 he was made Register of the Quincy Land Office.[88] When on 31 May 1855 Asbury ended his association with Browning and Bushnell to enter a partnership with Abraham Jonas, a prominent Jewish lawyer in Quincy, their friendship seemed to cool for a while, but afterward resumed its course.[89] While serving as justice, Asbury gained prominence as the author of *Asbury's Justice*, a "little" legal self-help book which was "extensively circulated" in the 1850s and made Quincy a center of Kentucky jurisprudence in the West.[90]

Bushnell and Asbury were Browning's oldest and closest associates. Browning's other friends included Calvin Warren, a New Yorker and a graduate of Transylvania University in Lexington, and thus connected to Kentucky, who arrived in Quincy in 1836 and became a partner to J. H. Ralston, one of the earliest Kentucky lawyers, along with Williams and Browning, to have arrived in town. Almeron Wheat, another New Yorker, came over to Quincy from Springfield in 1839 and joined the "select array" of men who gained Browning's confidence, though Wheat, Warren, and Ralston were on the fringe of Browning's inner circle.[91] James Singleton, a Virginian who had been a lawyer in Schulyer County before moving to Quincy in 1852 and a regular associate on the circuit, later joined this group.[92] Though five of seven members of this circle were from the South or had experience there, two were from Pennsylvania. Jackson Grimshaw, a Pennsylvanian lawyer who for many years was a lawyer in Pike County and also an associate from his circuit contacts, moved to Quincy in 1857.[93] Among Browning's closest friends in the mid-1850s, however, was a newcomer, John Cox, a Pennsylvania lawyer eleven years younger than Browning, who became his protégé.[94]

It was among these friends that Browning began, as a single man, to cultivate his aspirations to genteel status. When, like other "gentlemen," he chose to marry, he sought to draw his friends into the effort. In choosing a wife he was as selective as he was in choosing his associates and friends. In the years before he had employed his sister and friends to tap the Kentucky connection and find him a suitable woman from the Lexington area who would be willing to marry him and come out to Quincy. The woman he found was Eliza Caldwell, from a "good family" in Richmond, Kentucky, a town about twenty-five miles south of Lexington.[95] Caldwell's brother David was described by Henry Asbury as "as fine a specimen of an educated southern gentleman as I ever knew – handsome, courteous, and refined, . . . and rich in southern sentiments" which viewed slavery as a curse on his class.[96] Eliza had gone to one of the famous "young ladies'" academies in Lexington and was an accomplished "hostess" who had mastered all the social graces and could, in Browning's mind, create, in his private life, the refined life of central Kentucky.[97] They were married in Richmond, Kentucky, on 25 February 1836 and moved back to Quincy where they started housekeeping in a log cabin in the center of the town.[98]

Gentility in the West

Housekeeping and genteel space

Housekeeping, in the coded language of genteel people, was more than simply living together in a house. To the new middle class, a house provided both a man and a woman duties and responsibilities that solidified their marital roles in a way that a boarding house or hotel could not.[99] For the married man it generated an incentive to work, reflected on his manliness, and provided a private realm away from the cares of public life. For his wife, taking care of the house fulfilled her role as wife and mother as increasingly prescribed by the cult of domesticity and true womanhood. It also required, now that one lived as an embodiment of the values of one's social class, that as a couple, in possession of a proper venue for socializing, they would enter the intricate rhythms of social interaction and become bound by the procedures, rules, and customs of genteel society.[100]

After Browning finished his term as state senator, during which time he and Eliza lived in a hotel, he and his wife began planning to build a house in the Greek Revival style at Seventh and Hampshire streets, just two blocks east of the town square. They did this apparently in anticipation of the expansion of the family, because in 1842, the year Browning began to plan the house, Eliza was pregnant. That it was seven years before Eliza conceived in a social class that expected children within a year of marriage (the Brownings' friend Mary Todd Lincoln had her first child "nine months less three days" after her November 1842 marriage) shows inability rather than volition on their part. When in April 1843 Eliza almost died in giving birth to a stillborn baby, and after that was unable to have children, their eight-year-old marriage, rather than unraveling, became even more intensely domestic and private, perhaps focusing their energies on establishing a model domestic regime in the Kentucky manner.[101] This led to much unhappiness when they were apart, which Browning expressed when on a trip to Kentucky in the summer of 1844.[102]

The house built in the Greek Revival style in 1844 at an estimated cost of $30,000 became the center of their social circle for a dozen years.[103] They built such a house, standing on low hill northeast of the town square overlooking a working-class neighborhood and the ramshackle outskirts of town built across lower ground to the northeast, to make a statement. To one observer, the Brownings' house, being "larger than any other building in town and topped only by church steeples" indicated his social leanings as part of the town's "apish aristocracy."[104] Only Governor John Wood, who had built a wooden Greek Revival house above Germantown several blocks to the southeast at Twelfth and State streets in 1835, lived in similar style. As a result it became something of a stage for the display of gentility and came to acquire a symbolic presence to Quincy residents. A year later, Browning's partner built a similar "summer house" a block to the east. About the same time Judge Leavitt built an even more pretentious house at Vermont and Eighth streets, a block south and east of the Browning mansion. For nearly a decade this small cluster of Greek Revival houses stood out for their size and pretension among the one- and two-story wooden and brick houses of Quincy.[105] John Cox and James W. Singleton, two of Browning's closest friends, chose to build country houses rather than houses in town. Cox built an estate about a mile north of Browning's house on the road north out of town, while Singleton built a true country estate several miles northeast of town on a beautiful plateau near Ellington, naming it, as was the custom in Virginia, Boscobel.[106]

So close to the center of town, such houses became showpieces of gentility in the late forties. One Quincy resident in November 1848 reported that the town had fireworks, a parade, and a "grand illumination" to celebrate Zachary Taylor's election to the presidency, and focused not on the business blocks as Laban Fleak did in Keokuk, but on describing Browning's and Bushnell's homes. The "Bushnells' place looked beautiful [with] over 150 lamps of varying colors . . . in the trees and a transparency" across the front of "his summer house"; the "Brownings' house and garden [were] also elegantly lighted up."[107]

In 1845, up in Galena, Elihu and Adele Washburne, without apparently taking a wedding trip, also took up "housekeeping" in the finished part of a small Greek Revival house that Elihu was having built on the high ground across the river amid open fields on the corner of Lafayette and Third Streets. Surrounded by a picket fence, the austere red brick house stands two stories tall, one room across and three rooms deep. A Greek-style pediment supported by four Ionic columns encases the entire façade, with its characteristic simple door casings and three windows across on the first and second floors. On the first floor, two parlors, one behind the other, were located to the right, while stairs went straight ahead up to the second floor. In each parlor was a marble fireplace from the East. Sliding doors sided by columns separated the two rooms. Though we do not know what the furniture looked like, we do know that Washburne had budgeted $400 to furnish the house and that the furniture had arrived "in very good order" earlier in the month.[108] When finished, this small, but stylish house would become, for Washburne and Adele, as she described, "our own sweet home." There they set up house with a French accent (Adele signed some of her letters "adieu ma cher ami votre petite femme" and later she taught her husband French and insisted that French be spoken in the house) and threw themselves into their respective social roles as genteel husband and wife in their neighborhood of Galena which they styled, as early as September 1845 (with obvious reference to Washington, D.C.) "Lafayette Square." That winter, the two "settled down" to "fill our cup of happiness" in their "little dining room" where, one evening, Washburne contentedly sat "before a little fire, . . . by the side of his little wife, with a little banjo."[109]

The house, the first New England-style Greek Revival house in Galena, standing on open ground east of the river facing the town, made quite an impression. In the few years before some of his merchant and lawyer friends, particularly Joseph P. Hoge and Frederick Stahl, had built small brick houses across the river in the Greek Revival style, but the Hoge house was a low-set Ohio River-style house, and the Stahl one a town house crowded onto a city lot. Another merchant and fellow Presbyterian, Artemus M. Haines, had built a larger wood house in the Federal or Greek Revival style on High Street the year before. Yet no other house had the "country house" pretensions of Washburne's compact Greek Revival house at "Lafayette Square."[110] Perhaps Washburne's inspiration to build such a house came from his father's recent decision in 1843 to pull down the original family house in Livermore, Maine, in which Elihu had grown up, and replace it with a simple Greek Revival farm house.[111] However, since Adele played an influential role in establishing the family culture throughout the marriage, perhaps she influenced his decision to build a Greek Revival house in a country setting. Adele had grown up in a capacious country house in the French style built by her father just outside Gratiot's Grove in 1834.[112] As early as 1835 Adele had been sent, like her brothers and sisters before her, to St. Louis and had certainly visited several Federal or Greek Revival houses built, in the "French manner," on open suburban lots on the edge of St. Louis by her Chouteau relatives. No doubt Adele visited, as all the Gratiot children did, her aunt's sister-in-law, "Mother Berthold," who lived in splendor in one of the first brick houses in St. Louis, a Federal-style mansion which her husband built in 1831 at Fifth and Pine streets.[113] Likewise, Adele's aunt, Madame Chouteau, who guided her education in St. Louis, lived in an elegant Federal-style house at First and Washington and Adele's mother's sister, "Aunt Manuel," lived in a fine house at Third and Myrtle streets throughout the 1830s and 1840s.[114] A relative, Henri Chouteau, built an even more pretentious Greek Revival house in 1830 with a full Greek pediment and four Corinthian columns across the front on a hill above Chouteau's Pond and the town.[115] Adele, known for her elegance and taste, may very well have urged her new husband to express his, or her, social aspirations, by boldly building a New England version of these Federal-style houses, similar to those of the urban gentry in the East, in their "remote town."[116]

The impulse to display gentility motivated the Langworthy brothers who lived in Dubuque one by one to abandon the fine houses that they had built on the plain to the north of town in the 1830s and 1840s and build more magnificent, stylish mansions up on Third Street on and behind the bluff just above the town. In 1849 James Langworthy built a large Greek Revival house, with a broad double-level portico, at the corner of James and Langworthy streets and called it "Ridgemont."[117] That same year Solon Langworthy, who had only moved to Dubuque from Peru, Iowa, a town north of the city, in 1848, built a similar Greek Revival house with a "plantation" portico on a hill facing town at Third and Locust. Lucius Hart Langworthy soon followed by building a Greek Revival mansion at Hill Street just south of Third, while in 1854 Edward built an unusual octagonal house with a tower in the new Italianate style just across from Solon's house at the corner of Third and Alpine.[118] That year marked the completion nearby on Alta Vista Street at the bluff of James Marsh's magnificent Italianate mansion, with a tower and solarium, though Harriet Langworthy, his wife for whom he had built the house, died before it was completed. Until the late 1860s when a street railway was built up to the bluff, only others within the family circle built there.[119] Later Sol Turck, who married a Langworthy daughter, built an Italianate house nearby. Clustered within sight of each other and standing like country estates, connected to but separate from the town below, the Langworthy houses on the hill or on "Langworthy bluff"[120] expressed the material, ideological, political, and spiritual faith and vision of a stable, ordered Victorian world resulting from the fusion of capitalism, republicanism, Christianity, and gentility.[121]

Provincial lives

For many middle-class people in the urban West in the 1840s this "borderlands" intertwining of city and country, material and spiritual, simplicity and gentility was embodied in the suburban villa or house with views of a city or river valley below as cultivated on the bluffs above Cincinnati. There, in the early 1840s, many residents moved and built suburban villas on large estates or farms that, in their distance from the city, were as much rural as suburban.[122] In 1843, a Cincinnati traveler to Galena aesthetically expressed this when, climbing the bluffs above the city, he admired the picturesque view: "Standing on one of the many hills that surround the city, and looking down on the busy and populous streets on the one side, divided as they were from the opposite by the beautiful little river one sees the hum of commerce on the one hand and all the rural quiet on the other."[123] Solon Langworthy and his bride Julia Patterson honeymooned in 1840 at such a suburban house in Cincinnati, owned by a relative, Samuel Smith, where they "spent a month or more visiting friends in the country," an arrangement that so impressed Langworthy that he spoke of it twenty years later.[124] When, in 1848, he purchased a large tract of land above Dubuque and proceeded to build a suburban estate similar to that he had seen in Cincinnati, Solon Langworthy was expressing a "borderlands" sensibility which was felt by many others from Alton to St. Paul who chose to live on bluffs above the cityscape and the river below. Langworthy's impressive Greek Revival villa, surrounded by farms and open fields to the west, a herd lot, orchards, a large outer garden, a front garden surrounded by a gate, a greenhouse, and a vast front lawn shaded by several great old trees, in front of which ran the road from town out to the nearby Cooler valley mines, all situated on the bluffs with remarkable views of Dubuque, stood at the center of his "borderlands" cosmos.

Though we do not know how the Langworthys furnished their houses in the 1850s, we can infer it from details about the interiors of Solon's brothers' houses, if simpler, tending toward the interior decor of the new house of Richard Bonson, who, in summer 1860, by purchasing "another new carpet for the parlor chamber" and a "new black sofa," seems to have joined the "parlor culture" of genteel society in Dubuque.[125] James Langworthy's parlor set the tone for the rest of town society. Fully furnished with rugs and carpets and "rose and cherry wood" "carved furniture" purchased in New York and shipped via New Orleans, it was, in 1849, a model of High Victorian style.[126] When the politician and lawyer Lincoln Clark took up residence nearby on "Langworthy bluff" in Dubuque in 1853, he furnished his parlor with a "dark red . . . parlor carpet . . . with most distinctive flowers in the center," a Rosewood parlor suite, with a settee instead of a divan, "marble ornaments," and cornices and curtains for the windows.[127] We also know that each parlor later had elaborate gasolier chandeliers, the first in Dubuque, which were first illuminated in the houses of Solon, Edward, and Lucius Langworthy from Solon's rosine gas works, the technology for which he purchased in Brooklyn in September 1858.[128] Later, James Marsh, who married Harriet Langworthy, built his house near to other Langworthy houses and increased the level of decorative detail. His house contained eight Carrara marble mantlepieces, a walnut staircase, and elaborate woodwork carved throughout by a craftsman from Switzerland. The furnishings included French windows and mirrors, bronze chandeliers, a double front door of carved walnut, and an ornately carved parlor set.[129]

Such furnishings may have been influenced by the hotel parlor style introduced to the West at the Planters Hotel in St. Louis in the 1840s, and then taken up by the elite of St. Louis, and then gradually diffused northward via the American House Hotel (built mid-1840s, burned down 1851) and Desoto House Hotel (1854–55) in Galena, the LeClaire House in Davenport (1853), the Quincy House in Quincy (1841), and the Julien House in Dubuque.[130] Elihu B. Washburne had seen the Planters in 1840 when it was under construction and was deeply impressed.[131] A year later, Washburne "stayed for a few nights" there, which no doubt influenced his choice of decor when he later built his own house.[132] Later, in 1850, Peter Lorimer of Dubuque (a former business partner of Adele's brother Charles and brother-in-law of her brother Henry), who was connected to St. Louis society, was similarly influenced when he built a "fine, brick" house and furnished his parlor with furniture and carpets bought in St. Louis.[133] So, too, Orville Browning and his wife were impressed by the Planters Hotel. Whenever they went on excursions to St. Louis, they stopped, met friends, or dined there.[134] The inventory of the parlor of a St. Louis house owned by William Glasgow, Jr., in the mid-1850s gives us an idea of the general style. Glasgow's parlor contained a Wilton carpet, six rosewood chairs, two small square ottomans, a large satin lounge sofa and pillow, a mahogany rocking chair, a rosewood marble table, and a door mat. The artwork included two marine oil paintings, two Renaissance portrait paintings, a marble statue on a pedestal, two bracketed candelabra with four lights, two mantle candelabra with three lights, and two ambrotypes.[135]

The Langworthys, however, as natives of Watertown, New York, and Solon Langworthy, in particular, having taken two business trips to New York City in the previous two years, may in fact have been influenced by hotel parlors they encountered there. It is intriguing to note that during each of their later trips to New York City, Langworthy and his wife made a point of stopping (perhaps at the suggestion of prominent Dubuque citizen George W. Jones, U.S. Senator from Iowa, who stayed there in June 1858, or even Langworthy's neighbor, Lincoln Clark, who had stayed there the year before) at the famous St. Nicholas Hotel on Broadway.[136] The renowned Ladies Parlor, which contained fine carpets, draperies, furniture, and a grand piano from the 1853 Crystal Palace Exposition (which the Langworthys may have attended), was almost considered a "must-see" in New York, and exposed the Langworthys and, through them, Dubuque society, to the epitome of High Victorian parlor style.[137]

Elsewhere in the house, it was at the dining room table, near the parlor, that Julia "took her place" and set table for formal occasions with the "blue and white" china from the 1851 International Exposition in London which her husband had purchased for her. The blue and white pattern, reflecting Julia's simple southern taste (she was from Maryland), carried into the color scheme of the other rooms of the house. This choice simply reflected her self-definition against that of the other Langworthy women, for whom each of their husbands had purchased similar sets of china, in different colors. The borders of each set of china were painted with each wife's name: Valeria, burgundy on white; Julia, blue on white; Agnes, gold on white; and Pauline, white on gold. One can surmise that these distinctive color motifs ran through each of the Langworthy wives' dining room and parlor.[138] Upstairs each child had separate rooms, as, apparently, did Solon and Julia, since he refers to "her room" during his wife's convalescence in the spring of 1860.[139]

The genteel set

Building genteel houses provided middle-class people the proper venues in which to transform their enclaves into a social class. Local genteel society was, for Browning, Washburne, and Langworthy, an ordered group of people who, whether connected to families or aligned with others because of shared or agreed upon social and moral values, attitudes, and rules of behavior, lived together in harmony, as free and equal individuals, to foster social reproduction, promote and maintain order and harmony, and to support and validate public authority.[140] In the public realm, those who cared about and participated in public affairs advocated and articulated the booster ethos and then, through investment, running for political office, founding churches, academies, clubs, and societies, and staging and attending public and civic events, turned it into a booster system, differentiated themselves from those who did not. In the private social realm, such people constructed enclaves of genteel life and sought friends who would validate, support, and sustain self-esteem, family name and honor, and social values, mores, and strategies of socialization and social reproduction. Intermarriage and partnerships were one way of achieving this. Constructing a system of social action and behavior that demonstrated the "gentility" and "urbanity" was another. Though this system could have taken a number of forms, the social vacuum in which they acted elicited exaggeration. The result was a more visual and elaborate aristocratic style – influenced perhaps by steamboat architecture, French gentility of St. Louis, or Southern "aristocratic" immigrants – and a heightened urgency in establishing intricate customs and etiquette. In their efforts to differentiate themselves from others, genteel westerners defined themselves by practicing the intricacies of the "system of calls," or the elaborate etiquette of dinners, suppers, teas, balls, and parties in ways that, at times, seem at odds with piety and morality.[141] The web of such social interactions among certain people in the parlors and dining rooms of the new houses in the elite neighborhoods of town defined, or at least sketched out, the social geography of gentility in a western town.

Amid the "mixed" or "mongrel" society of the urban West, this was often a frustratingly slow and halting process. The failure to find enough people who shared one's goals and values or who understood the rules and procedures by which genteel people such as oneself aspired to live, or who were willing or able (given the considerable effort and money involved to be "genteel") to play the "social game" often led to disappointment, loss of nerve, apathy, withdrawal, or self-imposed isolation.

Unlike the gentry of the eighteenth century or in the South in the 1820s through 1860s, who were validated by the public display of this sensibility and the honor it sustained, the northern bourgeoisie of the 1840s cared less about whether someone appreciated or recognized one's character than how one's private life reflected it. One could turn inward, privatize one's life, enjoy one's genteel existence in a very small circle, and continue with a meaningful life while living in town and waiting for the numbers of genteel people to increase. Public satisfaction from the acknowledgment or display of gentility was not easily forthcoming in a western town.

At the center of the social procedures which genteel people cultivated was a scrupulously held notion of equality of each man and woman. This idea was deeply imbedded in the republicanized American gentility system and, when honor was at stake, could be the source of social friction.[142] To maintain harmony among social equals (those given entrance to the genteel circle and worthy of giving and receiving respect) one had to host as well as be hosted, and to give as well as receive with magnanimity, openness, and generosity. David Davis, a gentleman associate of Browning's, who was born in Maryland and had immigrated to the new town of Bloomington, Illinois, known, like Browning, for his gentlemanly style, articulated this code of behavior to his son George: "always be truthful and honorable ... scorn a mean action. Treat everybody well and respectfully – always be a gentleman – consider your self the equal of all and as superior to none. This makes the true gentleman."[143] In the intricate social procedures of gentility, therefore, one was looking not just to differentiate between genteel people and others, but also for those who understood this code of reciprocity and acted accordingly, giving to both families involved the social and individual self-esteem and support required to be friends and to be happy. To the Chesterfield gentleman friendship implied affection, even love (routinely expressed as brotherly love) built upon affinities, shared experiences, and interests, but also involved mutual understanding and recognition and providing support by fair, honest, and reciprocal treatment at all times.[144]

The first step in establishing a genteel set was to situate oneself in the networks in local society in which genteel people circulated. Ironically, Elihu Washburne's continual absences, and his and his wife's intensely private life when at home, made it difficult for them to participate actively in constructing local genteel society in Galena. Elihu and Adele, relied, therefore, on the set of relations and friends in which they had circulated when they were single to situate themselves as a married couple. With few exceptions, Washburne's friends came from four networks or circles to which he had attached himself as a single man – the local bar, the Hempstead–Gratiot set, the Whig party, and the Episcopal church. His marriage to Adele intertwined these circles with the broader realm of Hempstead–Gratiot relations in Galena, Gratiot's Grove, Dubuque, and St. Louis and brought him into the Presbyterian church and, with his move to the east side of the river, a new set of neighbors, though in 1845 he and Adele were among the few people who lived there. Located just across the bridge to lower Main Street, where Elihu had his office, and lower Bench Street, where he had lived as a single man, both venues remained central in his social interactions with townspeople. Finally, Washburne's interest in civic

Provincial lives

affairs, first as a citizen and supporter of the booster system,[145] and then as a representative, brought him into contact with a broader city- and county-wide population, some of whom became friends.

Washburne made his first friends the day he arrived. Horace H. Houghton, the editor who gave him advice and helped him get settled, became a friend for life. So, too, did D. C. Wyeth, a doctor.[146] Thomas Drummond, who rebuffed Washburne his first day in town, later joined him and Charles Hempstead in fending off Democratic lawyers before he became a judge and later a friend and coinvestor in the Galena and Chicago Union R.R.[147] Susan Gratiot mentioned Mrs. Drummond in her correspondence.[148] It was during his first weeks in town that Washburne also established connections with Horatio Newhall, the family doctor, and A. L. Holmes, a lawyer who later was also a neighbor.[149]

Once settled Washburne made friends naturally, both around the wharf, in the Whig party, and at church. Among those who had businesses on the wharf who maintained a friendship with Washburne over the years were H. F. McCloskey,[150] George[151] and Benjamin H. Campbell (both Virginians),[152] Orrin Smith,[153] John and Sherwell S. Lorraine,[154] and S. W. McMaster,[155] all merchants; Nathan and Henry Corwith,[156] merchants and bankers (and all financial supporters of the Galena and Chicago Union R.R.),[157] and Peter Stemler, proprietor of a coffee house just up from the wharf and across from Washburne's law offices in the Peck Building at the foot of Main and the wharf.[158] Benjamin H. Campbell and Orrin Smith were not just working neighbors, they were also "active friends" in the Whig party.[159] In addition, B. H. Campbell's clerk in the mid-1840s, Joseph Russell Jones, would prosper as a merchant and build a house across the river next to the Washburnes' and become one of their closest family friends.[160] Nearby, in the new brick block on the east side of Main north of Warren Street, directly accessible by stairs to the Bench Street neighborhood, were the stores of A. H. Davis,[161] an acquaintance, and Frederick Stahl,[162] good friend and perhaps Washburne's clothier, for whom Elihu wrote a letter of introduction as early as 1840 when he went on a buying trip to Boston. When he went shopping with Mrs. Charles Hempstead, however, they went to Lucius S. Felt's[163] near the American House Hotel and Doctor Newhall's store.

While living in Hempstead's house, Washburne's neighbors included both Corwiths[164] and Thomas Foster, a lawyer (all who boarded at Mrs. Eddowes, a close friend of Susan Gratiot and Sarah Beebe – who also boarded there when she was in town).[165] Nearby, Joseph Russell Jones and the Lorraine brothers boarded at Mrs. Moulton's. Benjamin Campbell boarded there for a few years before building a house nearby. Just above them on Prospect Street were the houses of George Campbell and Edward Beebe,[166] in whose house William Hempstead boarded.[167] Daniel Smith Harris and Frederick Stahl lived on Bench Street south of Spring Street on the south side of town.[168] Though Thomas Foster, a boarder at Mrs. Eddowes's during the winter of 1844–1845, remarked that "we are the most quiet set in town – hardly a word escapes our lips at the table," the members of this neighborhood interacted and gradually developed into a lively, cohesive social set in Galena society. Among their numbers were Joseph Hoge, John Lorraine, and Nicholas Stahl, who, after marrying Sarah Beck of St. Louis, returned to Galena and began boarding in Benjamin Campbell's house.[169] That Washburne was part of the group is evident from Foster's announcement from the "matrimonial world" in January 1845 that "Washburne is engaged to Miss Gratiot."

Other marriages followed among the people within this set. Besides Washburne marrying Charles Hempstead's niece, Joseph Russell Jones married B. H. Campbell's sister, and Sherwell S. Lorraine married Mrs. Moulton's daughter, Marcia.[170] The Moultons and Campbells later became very good friends with a new lawyer in town, Madison Y. Johnson and his wife. In 1844 Johnson was listed as a member of the Odd Fellows lodge.[171] When Washburne married and shifted to the Presbyterian church, he not only joined his mother-in-law and wife, but also Horatio Newhall, George Campbell, Thomas Foster, and, after 1841, Charles S. Hempstead, the latter of whom joined Aratus Kent and the Washburnes, Gratiots, and Hempsteads in breaking away from First Presbyterian church and forming the South Presbyterian church about 1847.[172]

Except for his friendship with Horatio Newhall, who lived on North Bench Street, all of the people Washburne mentioned as friends or acquaintances were from the south side of town, working near the wharf and living just above it. It was this group of people who ranked among the wealthiest merchants, professionals, and entrepreneurs in Galena, associated as they were more directly with the regional trade (ten of the richest men in town were Washburne's friends from this neighborhood).[173] It is not surprising, therefore, that when Washburne decided to build a house he followed a pattern of movement begun by other members of his social set. As early as September 1844 Henry Corwith and Thomas Foster began to move across the river by buying plots "on the east side" "fronting the river," a move that threw the town, we are told, "into a ferment . . . of speculation." The next spring Washburne followed suit and purchased a lot and began to build just across the Spring Street bridge facing the wharf. There he was joined later by Joseph Russell Jones, who located there in November 1853, and Nelson Stillman, who built a large house on Bouthillier Street in 1858, both south-siders who simply moved across the bridge.[174]

When Elihu Washburne married Adele Gratiot he fused her and her mother's social relations to his, to complete what would form the basic social architecture of his life in Galena.[175] At the center of these relations were, of course, Adele's uncles Charles and William and her siblings Edward, Charles,[176] Susan (who died in 1844), Stephen, and Eliza (who died in 1854), and Elihu's brother Cadwallader and his wife Martha.[177] So, too, Adele's mother's friends at Gratiot's Grove, Shullsburg, Mineral Point, Wisconsin,[178] and Dubuque,[179] and also her "numerous [social] connexions" in Galena, shaped her social world.[180] Among her oldest friends was Mrs. D. B. Morehouse, and she got "all the Galena news by our friend Mrs. Campbell."[181] Indeed, Susan knew both Mrs. B. and Mrs. George Campbell, with whose husband her son Edward entered a commercial partnership in the spring of 1840.[182] Otherwise Susan mentioned Mrs. Baker, Mrs. Eddowes, and other "Galena friends."[183] On 4 January 1854, Susan reported that Mrs. Stillman "had the long

Provincial lives

talked of dinner party for her mother and it was a party of old ladies – Mrs. Woodward, Lisa, Eddowes, Porter, Hoge" and herself along with Olivia Jones, all of whom she had met at a lecture earlier that winter where they all predicted that Mr. Washburne was "to be the greatest man in Illinois."[184]

Adele and Elihu's friends were often of interest to Mrs. Gratiot. At her brother Charles's house she had met and become friends with the Drummonds, and paid some attention to their daughter Delia, who was a friend of Mrs. Frederick Stahl, and reported their actions to her daughter. She also kept an eye on Meeker Harris, one of the Harris brothers, and on Nicholas Stahl,[185] as well as on Mrs. Stillman, the prominent socialite daughter of a friend. Mrs. Stillman's six-hour dinner was of considerable interest to Adele. Susan also took great interest in some of the Washburnes' friends, particularly those in their "own . . . neighborhood connexion."[186] Of chief interest were Joseph Russell Jones and others who lived "on the east side"[187] (in a simpler house which preceded the elaborate Italianate house, the Belvedere, which he had built in 1857), which led Mrs. Gratiot to call the south Bench Street neighborhood and downtown "the other side."[188] The Washburnes established solid social relations with the Drummonds, Harrises, Stahls, B. and G. Campbells, the Stillmans, and Joneses, all of whom were south-siders, even if they did not live on the same side of the river.

By establishing a genteel home and then connecting themselves to a group of people who, economically, could build suitable "genteel" houses, the Washburnes and their connections within the set or neighborhood were increasingly able to act like genteel people elsewhere. Before the construction of adequate houses, gentility existed only in an occasional party or ball at the best hotel in town. Style in dress and comportment, as well as education and social etiquette, set one apart from the male subculture. Such displays of gentility were, however, infrequent and isolated. On 22 February 1827, for example, the "Bachelors" of Galena gave the first annual Washington's Birthday ball, but had to go searching through the "diggings" to invite all the "ladies" they could find. A year later Horatio Newhall reported on a series of balls, the last of which, again on Washington's birthday, was better attended with "ninety gentlemen and sixty . . . elegantly dressed . . . ladies." Those in attendance at the Cottage House comported themselves with a "propriety and decorum" which Newhall remarked was "scarcely to be expected," imagining himself to be in "some eastern city" rather than on the frontier; yet it was still an isolated event, not yet a part of a culture. By 1837 a New Year's ball seems to have become a more regular feature of society at Galena, "concentrating the youth and beauty and fashion of Galena, Dubuque and Mineral Point."[189] In such events, as in 1841, when Laban Fleak and his colleagues in Keokuk had an "elite" ball and charged an admission to control the door, all involved were aware of the fragile nature of this temporary social boundary. Such balls and parties at hotels, or even organized dancing clubs, such as "The Twenties," in Keokuk, in 1850–1851, were the mainstay of fledgling genteel culture, amid the male subculture, through the late 1840s.

With the construction of separate genteel houses, parlors went from being public rooms in hotels to formal rooms in private houses. Increasingly decorated in an eastern style, such venues now gave those who owned them the opportunity to invite guests to their house, for dinners, teas, or parties. As more couples built houses and furnished their houses with carpets and furniture from St. Louis or the East,[190] they could begin to socialize within a private realm, connected by status, social prestige, style, and proper etiquette and behavior.

That this privatized genteel culture, a true sign of urbanity, evolved in Galena in the mid-forties is apparent in a progression of observations about genteel socializing during the period. In the early 1840s, only Charles S. Hempstead, John Turney, the Soulards, the Stillmans, and a few others had suitable dining rooms or parlors to entertain in style and elegance. Charles Hempstead's son, Charles Wilt Hempstead, later recalled the elaborate wallpaper in various rooms and the sense of awe upon gaining a peek into the "best parlor used only for formal parties," which was a "model of elegance."[191] Horatio Newhall noted that during the winter of 1840–1841, scarcely a night passed, "but someone gives a party" (though by contrasting these parties with those pursuing "higher objects," Newhall suggests that they were of the male subculture). That same winter, Washburne, noted the "gay, lively, fashionable, and intelligent" society which he "did not go into much" because dancing was "order of the day," though he did attend a ball in Bellevue, Iowa.[192] Joseph Russell Jones, who worked across the street in B. H. Campbell's store and lived next to Washburne, noted that he did not have much of a social life either: "I very seldom leave the store evenings except to go up to Mr. Campbell's house. He has a very fine wife and a beautiful little girl," though Jones did find time to go to "several dancing parties during the past winter."[193]

Edward Hempstead, Charles's son and Adele Washburne's cousin, reported in March 1843 on a winter in Galena of "soirees, balls, and sleigh rides," which some locals connected to eastern society tried to introduce into town amid the apparently prevalent "sighs and vows, nonsense and morality, [and] revivals." "Mrs. Judge Stone gave the first soiree, of course, after the most improved and latest Washington style, that is, entering the room at precisely eight, conversation until nine and tongue and coffee and promenading until eleven. [Then] came plates and a spreading of handkerchiefs, with politeness diversified by the gentlemen waiting on their fair ones as 'Miss will you have this or will you have that' then the answer 'No sir, I am very well helped.' . . . after eleven came dancing until two. Mrs. Farnsworth, Mrs. Soulard [connected to the St. Louis French circle] and Mrs. Stillman came next in parties."[194]

After a dull season in which revivals seem to have quashed social life, society revived during the winter of 1844–1845. Thomas Foster reported a very "gay winter" in Galena, coyly noting how it was "a sad contrast with last winter, balls, dancing parties, . . . 'donation parties' and other gay amusements instead of the house of prayer and the closet." As in every year, society relied in 1844 on newcomers to enliven its style and sustain its elegance. That year it was Mrs. Nicholas Stahl, a new arrival from St. Louis who, Foster noted, "made a valuable addition to our society" during the season. A highlight of the season was Elihu and Adele's coming out as an engaged couple at a "great" New Year's "cotillion party." The following winter,

1845–1846, Adele G. Washburne reported that many things were again going on "in the line of parties" and that "suppers have been the order of the day and night both." Moreover, the Grand Fireman's Ball, which A. L. Norris called "tremendous," pushed elegance to new heights. "All ladies and maidservants are to be dressed in red jackets and the men in red woolen shirts" with tailcoats. Adele reported on it as a very "rich scene" and though Adele was "unable to attend" because she was pregnant, her friend from St. Louis, Bazier, apparently dazzled those in attendance with her refined "beauty" and stunning "red waist and black velvet trimmings, silver lace, cords, tassels, and stars." The following season, Adele, again sick, reported that another active season in which "private parties are the rage" was taking place in Galena.[195]

That such "society" was becoming more segmented is suggested by the diary of Benjamin Felt, brother of Lucius, who, as a single man who boarded at the American House, had, like young Washburne and Russell Jones, hardly any social life. That year he reported four public dances or parties and attended only three: an 11 January dance at the American House, a "Bachelors" ball there on 1 February, and a dance at the courthouse on 3 May. In the new season, he attended a party at the American House on 20 December. He did not go to any private parties. Felt's experience shows how exclusive "the round of parties" had already become. Felt attended no dinners, except Thanksgiving dinner at his brother's. The rest of his social life revolved around occasionally visiting the ladies' Sewing Society and making a call or two to A. M. Haines or Mrs. Corwith. That the sewing society evenings took place at the homes of various members of the South Presbyterian church suggests that these were church-sponsored events and that Felt was a guest in that capacity and was not, at other times, usually on south-siders' invitation lists. One member even called her event an "open house," suggesting how much the inner circle of genteel socializing had withdrawn from public view.[196]

By January 1854, when Susan Gratiot reported to Adele and Elihu that the "neighborhood connexion[s]" were "still treating each other with dinners and tea parties and the dancing folks are improving this their time in sleigh rides, surprise parties, and oyster suppers," society had become a separate private world.[197] The fact that that winter the town elite divided between those who gave "dancing parties" and those who gave "sitting parties" (at which no liquor was served) encouraged Joseph Russell Jones to give both kinds. The latter was attended by Charles S. Hempstead and wife and Mary Kennett (of St. Louis) and Nicholas Stahl. Though Susan Gratiot commended Jones for his diplomacy, his efforts reflected the depth of the struggle between secular gentility and Christian propriety.[198] In Galena this culture and the nature of social interaction within it is unrecorded. Meanwhile, the Washburnes, given Adele's illnesses and Elihu's absences, only rarely ventured out into society. The first time Adele reported that she was "entertaining the neighbors," or had had "Mr. and Mrs. Corwith to tea" was not until after 1860.[199] For us to understand the genteel social experience further we must venture elsewhere in the urban system.

The dynamics and extent of Orville Browning's strategy to define the genteel set in Quincy was, like the Washburnes', also constricted[200] by his seasonal legal and political activities that took Browning away for, on average, half of every year between 1850 and 1856. He was in town only in mid-June through early July, all of August, and November into mid-December. Whatever social life he and his wife would establish in Quincy had to fit within this grueling "work year" cycle.[201]

The most immediate impact was to narrow the extent of the Brownings' social circle. Browning, though a public figure since 1836, known to all in a town of from 6,000 to 14,000 between 1848 and 1856, and quite often "the Lion of the day" at picnics, political assemblies, public rallies, and meetings, recorded in his diary between 1850 and 1856 only between fifty and eighty people within his small genteel circle, that is, those with whom they socialized (defined as having tea, dinner, supper, going to a party with, recreating with, attending a wedding or funeral for, or helping a friend with a personal problem). From 1852 to 1854 Browning mentions socializing with only about fifty residents of Quincy per year. Though in 1855 and 1856 the number of people he mentions jumps to eighty and then to over 100, perhaps an effect of the arrival of the railroad, the size of his circle, as a percentage of town population, continued to decline. During any year within this five-year period, the Brownings socialized with less than one person among every hundred of his fellow townspeople for whom he worked so hard.

Within this small group even Browning's closest relationships with "friends" are, by any standard, discursive and occasional. It is intriguing to note that among the fifty to 100 people mentioned by Browning each year only six couples or individuals in 1852, 1853, and 1855, and about ten in 1854 and 1856, socialized with the Brownings three or more times during the year. Moreover, only four couples, families, or individuals in Quincy stayed within this select group for five consecutive years: Mr. and Mrs. Henry Asbury, Mr. and Mrs. Nehemiah Bushnell, Mr. and Mrs. John Cox, and Alex and Miss Pearson, relatives from Kentucky. Among these friends, Browning mentioned John P. Cox and his wife most frequently, making them intimate friends. Browning mentioned them more than twice as many times as the Asburys or Bushnells.[202]

The rhythm and pattern of genteel socializing with both friends and acquaintances indicates that Orville and Eliza Browning and other genteel people held to their beliefs and sought to cultivate social interaction according to the rules of genteel reciprocity and social etiquette. Those rules, outside larger cities where published manuals helped participants learn etiquette and how properly to act and play the game, were picked up from mentors or by observation, learned as best as one could. In a town like Quincy, the primary currency of social exchange was the "system" of calls, teas, dinners, suppers, parties, and entertainment events. Social calls were the first steps, usually made in mid-evening or mid-afternoon, and were an opportunity, without much obligation, to introduce oneself, catch up on news, or continue a relationship. Such social occasions were often reserved for certain days of the week, and were preferred by unmarried people or people not yet housekeeping. If, at the level of calls, a connection was not wanted, either the person who made the invitation or the other person did not reciprocate or follow it up, thus ending the matter. If someone wanted a relationship, a call could lead to an invitation for tea. Teas were somewhat more formal small parties involving a group of "invited" guests in late afternoon. Invitations, though required, could be impromptu, and reciprocity, while required, could be more relaxed as well, sometimes extended for six months or a year before satisfied. Tea, which in smaller towns, where calls could be infrequent, seemed to have subsumed the social purposes of the "system of calls," allowed old friends to catch up or to resuscitate a waning relationship, but also enabled one to "visit" with new people and contemplate initiating new relationships.[203]

A tea or a call could be a prelude to dinner or a party invitation and perhaps the beginnings of friendship. Dinner, which in Quincy in 1852 meant a substantial, more formal (especially in winter) midday or early afternoon meal, held most often that year on Monday or Thursday (each town had its own hours and days for calling or other occasions)[204] was a more significant, personal social affair. An invitation expressed a desire to become acquainted, to get to know someone, or to continue and deepen a friendship or relationship – with the exception, perhaps, of the occasional obligatory invitation of one's minister to Sunday dinner. Parties were more general and created fewer obligations. In all of this, one was expected to keep track of one's social debits and credits and act accordingly. Acceptance of any invitation, according to etiquette books, put one under the obligation to reciprocate with a similar invitation to one's house within a "reasonable time." For any couple, "housekeeping" was, therefore, a prerequisite for participation. Because these circles were small, and based on couples socializing, however, out-of-towners and single persons were welcome and excused from the obligations of reciprocity. The time it took to reciprocate was taken as an indicator of enthusiasm for the friendship or relationship.[205] Likewise, the frequency of invitations and reciprocated social occasions needed to remain balanced, to support equality among couples. The constructed nature of this etiquette was highlighted by the fact that infrequent, special, or unusual events or emergencies – illnesses, scandals, marital discord, accidents, crimes, or deaths – which demanded personal intervention to help a friend or associate lay outside the logistics of the "system." Over five years, Orville Browning involved himself in a full range of these events of real life.

One can discern the use of such rules of etiquette, and trace the Brownings' standing and nature of their relationships with other couples in their genteel circle in the ebb and flow of calls, teas, dinners, and parties during the early 1850s. Gone as he often was, Browning, whenever he returned to Quincy, usually threw himself intensively into a three-tiered social strategy: catching up and providing and receiving support for his friends, seeking out and cultivating new relationships, and ending or redefining other relationships. In 1853, for example, her husband's tight and hectic schedule in the spring compelled Mrs. Browning to take matters into her own hands and schedule social occasions whenever they could be fit in. Having spent most of 1852 out of town, Browning had not seen many of his friends since brief breaks in his schedule in November and August 1852. Consequently, every other day in the late winter and spring when the Brownings were home, they had someone to tea or dinner or had tea or dinner at someone's house. In particular, they arranged dinners with their closest friends. The teas that spring that the Brownings gave were almost exclusively for newcomers in town. In general, by mid-June the Brownings had given teas for fourteen different couples, of whom only two guests, being single, were not required to respond. In the other direction, the Brownings had the energy and time to accept only three invitations to tea. In their social calculation of such things, by midyear, therefore, the Brownings needed to have two couples over for tea and another over for dinner, while they could expect from at least seven couples invitations to tea or dinner (dinners could reciprocate for a tea, but not a tea for dinner unless the person was a very close friend or some extenuating circumstance explained the inequity).[206]

Whether or not the Brownings or others were adept or fully informed about such things, the pattern of their social life in July and August makes it apparent that they sought to operate within local genteel society according to the rules of reciprocity. Upon settling at home, the Brownings had their annual summer party, this time for about 200 people, in honor of the daughter of an acquaintance[207] and former townsman who now made occasional trips to town. Such parties, which, in 1853, only the Brownings and a few others could give, allowed them to return obligations they really did not want to continue, while not creating new obligations, though it may have prompted those who owed returns to the Brownings to reciprocate. The party also initiated a few new relationships.[208] For the rest of the summer the Brownings allowed others to reciprocate their well-known "hospitality." In six grueling weeks, all but two couples had reciprocated. The fact that all had responded within six months (apparently the local time limit for reciprocity involving teas), satisfied and no doubt encouraged the Brownings that, even in a rough western town, those who accepted their hospitality were, perhaps, beginning to learn the rules of genteel etiquette.[209]

The Brownings, at year's end, had nearly balanced their social obligations. On each level of social interaction, whether sustaining friendships, cultivating new members of society, or excluding others and clarifying membership of the group, the rules of reciprocity applied. Though the Brownings did befriend people and become emotionally attached to them, they appreciated their friends precisely because of the intensity with which they played the social game. Sometimes, however, when emotions became involved and two couples who took a real liking to each other temporarily ignored the rules of reciprocity, uneven resources could create an imbalance and lead to awkwardness which could imperil the relationship. Between 1852 and 1855, for example, the Brownings' friendship with the Coxes followed this scenario. Having begun on a reciprocal basis, the Brownings then took over the relationship and built up a considerable debt to the Coxes, which awkwardly forced them to withdraw from the friendship until the Coxes, realizing their predicament, tried to reciprocate and equalize the balance. Whenever the balance moved toward one couple or the other from that point on, the couple with a credit waited for the indebted couple to reciprocate before continuing the relationship. Eventually, the imbalance in resources and interest in sustaining the reciprocal nature of the relationship put a stress on it that the relationship could not sustain, leading to an obvious cooling off (see Table 5).[210]

Such circumstantial evidence of efforts to maintain a balance in social exchanges even among good friends indicates that the Brownings and those with whom they socialized operated according to the rules of genteel etiquette. Among those at the core of the circle or set, such socializing was carried on in a balanced, reciprocal manner – though not without effort – from year to year. For many newcomers, however, socializing with people like the Brownings, given the degree to which they apparently kept score (though how they did this is not known), was clearly demanding. Their famous "hospitality" required reciprocity, putting those who accepted it in debt to them. Those unwilling to meet their demanding social standards were likely to find their relationship with them stillborn. From the Brownings' perspective, therefore, the edges of the set they defined were characterized by more uncertain behavior and less awareness of the arithmetic of social intercourse. For those at the center, social identity and position was secure. As one moved toward the edges, the borders of gentility fluctuated back and forth, and one's awareness of the meaning of behavior became very sensitive indicators of one's genteel status.

Rather than situating themselves at the center of their circle, the Brownings spent considerable social time managing its boundaries by interacting or attempting to interact with newcomers, or people yet unacculturated to the gentility system. In this border area social actions and responses could bring abrupt outcomes. Indifference to an invitation by a couple ended any further effort by the party who sent the invitation. Not to return a call, if only by leaving one's card, to decline a tea or supper, or, worse, to accept one and then not show up, likewise ended a social exchange. Those who were invited to a Browning tea and declined are rarely recorded in the diary thereafter. Genteel people had little patience for weak excuses. Take, for example, a friend of Sarah Davis's, the wife of David Davis, a friend and associate of Browning's who curtly told Sarah of her effort to befriend two newcomers to her town of Bloomington: "I called and invited the young ladies [the Misses Kellogg] to tea. . . . When the tea time came I got an apology, one of them being slightly ill – thus began and ended my acquaintance with the Misses Kellog."[211]

One needed to do more than reciprocate to become friends with the Brownings and gain entrance into their circle; one needed to act with gentility. The Brownings' brief dalliance with the Judge Peter Lott[212] and his wife ended when the Lotts, perhaps too impressed by the Brownings, were overeager and disregarded the proper intervals expected before one reciprocated in inviting them to their place. When Browning went to the Lotts against his wife's advice – she did not go – and realized the occasion was a party "given for his servant girl who got married," Browning, unamused by this rowdy, sarcastic event worthy of the male subculture, paid his respects, "did not stay long," and then cut them off.[213] Similarly, when compelled to socialize with merchants in the booster ethos, such as the Godfreys or the Bulls, relationships waned when the Brownings realized that these individuals, with their big new gaudy houses out on Maine Street, were not quite genteel enough for them.

Table 5. *The balance sheet of social debts and credits between the O. H. Brownings and J. Coxes, Quincy, Illinois, 1853–1857 (advantage in favor of Brownings (+B) or Coxes (+C))*

Date	Occasion	Teas/calls	Dinners/suppers
10 February 1853	Dinner at C		+1C
17 June 1853	Tea at B	+1B	
19 August 1853	Tea at C	Even	
20 August 1853	Breakfast at B		Even
6 September 1853	Dined/tea B	+1B	+1B
18 November 1853	Tea at C	Even	
29 January 1854	Supper at B		+2B
7 February 1854	Tea at C	+1C	
28 February 1854	Tea at B	Even	
3 March 1854	Dined at C		+1B
11 April 1854	Supper at C		Even
15 April 1854	Dined at B		+1B
31 May 1854	Dined/tea B	+1B	+2B
16 June 1854	Tea at B	+2B	
30 June 1854	Supper at C		+1B
21 July 1854	Diner at B		+2B
31 July 1854	Tea at B		+3B
10 August 1854	Party at C		
27 December 1854	Call to C	+2B	
29 December 1854	Dined at B		+3B
9 February 1855	Supper at C		+2B
15 February 1855	Supper at B		+3B
12 March 1855	Call to C	+1B	
6 February 1856	Supper at B		+4B
17 June 1856	Dined at C		+3B
5 July 1856	Tea at C	Even	
14 August 1856	Tea at B	+1B	
15 August 1856	Party at C		
22 August 1856	Breakfast at B		+4B
26 October 1856	Call to C	Even	
4 December 1856	Supper at C		+3B
9 December 1856	Supper at C		+2B
16 April 1857	Supper at C		+1B
29 June 1857	Call to C	+1C	
4 July 1857	Dined at C		Even
12 August 1857	Tea at C	+2C	
11 September 1857	Tea at B	+1C	

Note: Parties are not included in calculation of debts. Calls to the Coxes are considered events hosted by the Coxes even though the Brownings made the effort to call. Dinners with Mr. Browning and Mr. Cox only are not included.

Source: Theodore C. Pease and James G. Randall, eds., *Diary of Orville Hickman Browning*, vol. 1: *1850–1864* (Springfield: Illinois State Historical Society, 1925).

For these and other infractions, many social interactions and dalliances came to nothing. Only those who understood the dynamics of maintaining a properly balanced social relationship and had the resources could sustain a relationship with the Brownings. Such daunting standards, no doubt, helps explain the narrowness of their social circle.[214]

Along the edges of their narrow circle, the Brownings also helped in socializing single and young married people into genteel society. Several times the childless Brownings invited a single woman to board with them, become part of their family, and then be introduced into society. The Brownings also sponsored single men and women and introduced them into society with an eye to matchmaking, by inviting groups of single people to tea, to picnics, or even to "spend the day" at their house.[215] The expectation that married people should provide chaperone service for single people, especially women, allowed Browning the apparent freedom to escort both single and married women other than his wife to social occasions, concerts, lectures, banquets, or even to recreate publicly with them, without, apparently, drawing any suspicion of impropriety.[216] On almost every occasion, however, another woman friend or acquaintance was always present, the exception being his attendance at a "feminist" lecture with a local teacher, Miss Dora Howells. Yet because this lecture violated what Browning called "female decorum and delicacy" and was, therefore, "extremely unpleasant" to "admit of any enjoyment," one suspects that he took Miss Howells because he refused or was embarrassed to take his wife, and because Miss Howells was an educated woman friend whose opinion he sought.[217]

The single men whom the Brownings knew were, of course, allowed to socialize more independently, but still came under the scrutiny of genteel chaperonage. Jackson Grimshaw, a Pennsylvania lawyer who had settled in Pike County in 1843, over the years on the circuit developed cordial relations with Browning. After a brief stint in Springfield where he became friends with Ozias Hatch, Grimshaw moved into Quincy, established a partnership with Browning's friend Archibald Williams, and then joined Williams and Browning in the Quincy contingent, regularly riding the circuit and attending the state supreme court in Springfield and then at Chicago. He had gained some political renown as one of the leaders in the 1856 Bloomington convention that founded the Illinois Republican party, for which they rewarded him with the nomination for Congress in 1858 (he lost).[218] Grimshaw's dozen letters from Quincy to his Springfield friend Ozias Hatch between 1858 and 1860, combined with sporadic references in Browning's diary, enable us to discern how Grimshaw navigated as an unmarried man in his mid-thirties along the edges of genteel society.

By any standard his arrival in town with longstanding references and friendships quickly drew him in as a regular in the Brownings' circle. After two teas with the Brownings in the fall, and joining them for a holiday dinner at the Asburys' two days before Christmas, Grimshaw's socializing narrowed. For Grimshaw, work came first, and he reported in April 1858 that due to being "very busy" he had "only paid a few visits of ceremony" and that, overall, the town that winter had not been "socially, very gay." He then added that "there is to be a party tomorrow night at the

Brownings', to which, of course, I must go," suggesting that he did not enjoy parties there, even though his presence confirmed his proximity to the inner circle. Nevertheless, obligation compelled him to attend.[219]

Grimshaw preferred subscription parties, similar to Bachelor's Balls, which were held at the main hotel in town, and to which they charged admission. Such parties involved a larger contingent of single people but also still included many married couples. Grimshaw and the "invitation" committee, besides including friends, sent out 350 invitations; 175 attended. "We asked all the married people and [especially] all the clever ones we knew. A good many married ladies came, in fact about half the party was married." Some people unsure who was giving the party R.S.V.P'd to the "chairman of the committee." Others, uncertain what kind of event they were invited to, made what Grimshaw called "'party' call[s]" at the hotel that evening (a practice in which one paid a call at the hotel parlor in expectation that there would be a party). Grimshaw and his closest friends paid for most of it and, as a "compliment to our married friends," paid their admission, thus enabling Grimshaw and his bachelor friends to reciprocate, in a more democratic manner, on their social debts as well as express their further desire to be included in the genteel circles of town society.[220]

Of course, the Brownings were included on the invitation list and attended this unusual party, which seemed securely rooted in the tradition of the Bachelor's Balls and hotel and boarding house parties of the 1820s through 1840s[221] within the male subculture,[222] as well as William Worth Belknap's elegant party for his married friends in Keokuk in 1852.[223] Orville Browning remarked that at the "party by Grimshaw and others at the American House" they had a "pleasant evening."[224] Grimshaw concurred, noting that "we had a nice dance and everyone enjoyed themselves."[225]

After a trip to New York, where he became affianced to a certain "Miss C," Grimshaw entered the heated political campaign of 1858 as a candidate for Congress and campaigned occasionally with Browning from September through November, only to lose by 2,000 votes.[226] He then resumed his social routines:

I took tea at the Asbury's a few nights ago on Miss A's birthday.[227] She has two cats a yellow one she calls Hatch [after Grimshaw's friend Ozias Hatch] on account of its amiability and a black one after me, "Grim" because she says if it is not petted all the time it gets cross. Our town is very dull and but little amusement except occasionally a little party of ladies at whist. Tonight a large party at Joel Rice's and of course no dancing. I am going with Miss W. and will do my best to enjoy it.[228]

Not surprisingly, Grimshaw and his companion met the Brownings, who attended this Friday evening party by going there "in an omnibus and return[ing] the same way at 1 o' clock."[229] A week later the Brownings went over to the Asburys' for Christmas dinner while Grimshaw headed off to the court in Springfield.[230] Even single people found genteel social circles very small.

In his absence, Archibald Williams, his partner, wrote Ozias Hatch with his interpretation of the practice of New Year's calling in Quincy, and Quincy society in general. Williams was a widower, his wife having died suddenly four years before,[231] and Browning found time for dinner with him once a year since then. The last time Williams was mentioned by Browning was when he attended a dinner with him at Norman Judd's in Chicago on 16 July 1858.[232] In any case, Williams's single life had drifted into the border area where gentility and the male subculture merged:

> It was kind of you to try to amuse me for I needed it I assure you. I was never in so terrible a state in my life. The reaction of a month's dissipation I did not find agreeable. New Year's day was terribly stupid to me. I was alone and besides had only about fifty visitors. I needed a hundred at least to make it worthwhile being very agreeable. I could not find one among them to whet my wit upon and considered them all intolerably shallow! When I was qualified for more healthy reflection I remembered that maniacs are wont to consider everybody crazy but themselves.
>
> The "Quincy Guards" had the annual Ball last Friday. It was to commemorate the 8th so I felt duty bound to remain until that date. I came home at four o'clock Saturday night. I entertained a card party until our Sunday consciences got up an alarm. Yesterday I went to our new church with a most beautiful little widow whose eyes an artist once said "glorious to inspiration – they are black as night, probably in mourning for the murders they have committed . . . beware!"[233]

As a single man, Williams navigated along the boundaries of genteel society. Aware that those boundaries were shifting and becoming less traversable, he was, therefore, especially sensitive to any enumeration of his social standing.

Delineating gentility

Williams's assessment of his social position based on the number and quality of his visitors on New Year's Day indicates the degree to which this social ritual, in moving west, had acquired the function of an annual gate-keeping exercise that genteel elite society used to screen newcomers to town or single people who wanted to present themselves to society. When the practice of New Year's Day calling reemerged in New York City in the early nineteenth century (though its origins go back to Dutch New Amsterdam), it developed as a special winter occasion within the more intricate and intimate dynamics of the private "system of calls" to enable more friends and the ever-growing number of acquaintances, newcomers, and strangers in the city to pay their respects.[234] Initially, ladies who were securely established in local "society" opened their parlors to the gentlemen of the city, friends, acquaintances, and newcomers alike, who made very brief calls to express their New Year's greetings, partake of refreshments and sweets offered by the hostess, and depart without leaving their cards, so as not to create a social obligation. By the late 1820s, however, apparently in response to New Year's Day open houses being overrun by more and more diverse people from every social rank, these traditional open houses were narrowed to include only friends and acquaintances. Elite women did this by sending invitations to call at their house to only certain men in society.[235] They hoped that this would make the day more friendly and personal, and thus more relaxed, while making it more exclusive.

It was in its more public form as a reception or open house that the custom arrived in the West. Recorded in St. Louis just before 1800, in which "on New Year's day, there was a stampede" of residents wanting to rush to "the oldest members of the community to offer his or her good wishes" in response to which the head of families might reconcile or exonerate some "discord arisen during the past year," the practice diffused across the urban system following migrants from New England and the Middle Atlantic states, as well as the ability of locals, given the size of population, to introduce everyone to each other within the confines of private social occasions.[236] Stephen Hempstead, after moving into St. Louis after his wife's death in 1820, usually spent New Year's Day at Presbyterian prayer meetings, but on New Year's Day, 1827, involved himself in the apparently routine practice of both Yankee and French St. Louis. He spent "most of the day making calls on friends," though the following year he returned to prayer meetings.[237] In ensuing years the practice gradually became a ritual of local society. By 1847, Edward Bates, a Yankee lawyer who recently had arrived in St. Louis from the hinterland, was aware of the custom, though he chose that year not to "venture out." The following year he recorded his own "calling" activity, but it still seemed a novelty: "It is the fashion here for females to stay at house on this day to receive company and the males to spend the day making visits – short calls, to exchange congratulations and pass mutual compliments. I believe it is not usual to have any regular dining. Refreshments are set out in every house, in many places, in great variety, and costly profusion. My visit to Mrs. Cabanné was highly interesting. She received me with marks of deep emotion – a mingled expression of pleasure and solemnity."[238]

It was in 1847 that the practice apparently made its first appearance upriver at Galena. That the custom had not yet reached Galena seem apparent in Susan Gratiot's concern the year before on sending her twelve-year-old daughter Eliza to boarding school in St. Louis that she would be "not accustomed to the way they spend New Year's" there. In 1847, Adele Washburne, though ill and unable to take part, noted that "we had a glorious time . . . sleighs and private parties are the rage," and the Washburnes received "thirty calls" at their new house.[239] Two years later, New Year's Day calling in Quincy appears to have become an annual event. George Berrian reported to his brother about the "sleigh loads of 'gents'" covered against the cold by "handsome robes" riding in very "ornamental sleighs" ranging from "a Jumper" to a "Swan Neck" "with four horses attached and plenty of bells around their necks" going from house to house. Later in the evening, after calling hours were over, many "females" joined the "males" for sleigh rides, the mix of jingling bells and "squalling" voices resonating through the town into the night.[240] Two years later, the Galena newspaper reported that "New Year's Day passed off very agreeably in this city. . . . The houses of our hospitable citizens were open for 'calls' and their tables groaned," being "abundantly covered with every possible luxury." In the gendered ritual of the day "ladies, of course, were all at home" receiving numerous guests, mostly male, "with their gracious smiles." The awkwardness of the practice was apparent in the description of "young men busy saying the prettiest and funniest things they could think of" and some uncertainty about behavior.

In Galena that year the big question was whether or not to greet the women of the household with a kiss, as was the practice back East; in one house a caller who tried it received a box on the ears. The depth of the tradition, referring back to the practice in St. Louis and the East, was suggested by the presence of "old gentlemen" who, "as they went their annual rounds, grew young again and cracked jokes which they had got up when they were boys and had said every New Year's Day since."[241]

Orville Browning limited his calling to friends. He had first "appropriated" New Year's Day "to calling on my friends" while on the circuit in Springfield, Illinois, in 1853. In the following years he described calling as early as 10 a.m., often continuing until 8 p.m.[242]

A few years later, George Sargent of Davenport, Iowa, after building a large mansion above the town in the late 1850s, held enormous "open houses" for the citizens of the town on New Year's Day, encouraging townsmen not usually within his social circle to cross his threshold and pay their respects.[243] In Dubuque, practice of New Year's calling at Solon Langworthy's house in Dubuque involved, as is evident from those who signed their names in his book, a similar mix of friends and strangers. On New Year's Day, 1861, ninety-seven people, including six members of the related Langworthy families, signed the book. Of those who signed the book "to our beloved friend," only three were female, one of them Solon's daughter. Of the only sixteen men who can be positively identified in the census the year before, the average age was twenty-eight, more than half were married, and all were merchants or professionals. However, among the others on the list many were newcomers to Dubuque, visitors or relatives from out of town, but few, if any, were established members of town elite, or at least, as we will see, that part of the elite who socialized within the aloof Langworthy circle.[244] Though the event seemed restricted to members of the professional classes, the presence of young, married men and those just starting out indicates that, in Dubuque, "calling" on New Year's remained a relatively open event, in which those not usually within a genteel enclave introduced themselves to one of the prominent families in town and got a rare look at life behind the increasingly dense thicket of social rules and customs that separated the elite from other townspeople. The fact that two of the people who signed the book included their nicknames suggests that on such a day a small element of the male subculture of the town was allowed to cross thresholds which had, for some time, been closed to them.

For some an enumeration of one's callers was a barometer of one's social standing or the vitality of local society. As noted, Adele Washburne thought that "thirty calls" constituted a "glorious time." Williams, on the other hand, seemed disgusted at receiving only fifty calls, even though the Langworthys of Dubuque received 100.[245] George W. Kilbourne of Keokuk, however, clearly interpreted New Year's Day, 1860, as a sign of social apathy: "There was but very little calling. The largest number of calls at any one house I heard of was 32. [Keokuk] is too dull and dead to even have a good time on New Year's Day." This impression seemed to continue a Keokuk trend that Charles Mason had recorded the year before when he chose to make "no calls" and reported that "not as many have been made as usual."[246] Nevertheless, given the uncertainty of controlling the arithmetic of calling at New Year's, many people seem not to have cared and chose to call or not call as their spirits moved them, suggesting, perhaps, that such public calling either had served its purpose and no longer seemed necessary in a town in which the population was not growing or was simply retreating within the more privatized system of calls. Richard Bonson of Dubuque, not a very social man, only once chose to go calling on New Year's Day, and then, in 1859, went with four of his best friends and called at five other friends' houses.[247] He, like Stephen Hempstead, preferred religious occasions on New Year's.

A similar reticence characterized the Washburnes' and Gratiots' views of calling. What turned out to be Susan Hempstead's last New Year's Day was further confused by religious concerns. Because New Year's fell on a Sunday that year, the day was spent at church. Then the New School churches declared 2 January a day of "fast and prayer," pushing visiting off to the third, which, of course, "rather changed the day." Susan spent Tuesday with her sister-in-law Eliza Hempstead, to keep her company in Charles's absence in the East. They received a few calls, and those they did were "mostly within the family" and "immediate neighborhood," and though they had to replace the coffee boiler twice, they spent the day "quietly in the back parlor" mostly keeping to themselves. Two years later, while in Washington, D.C., Elihu did not engage in extensive calling, being "modest" and "did not travel . . . about much," though his brothers Israel and Cal went "out calling to a pretty high extent this morning." Washburne did, nevertheless, make what turned out to be a memorable social call on Col. Thomas Hart Benton, with whom he exchanged stories about the Hempsteads of St. Louis.[248]

When westerners went east, as a result, they were impressed by the more elaborate New Year's Day there. The first New Year's that Charles Mason spent in Washington, in 1856, he started the day by paying his "respects to the President and all the Heads of the Departments" and afterward "received many calls" himself. Mason thought calling "a very pleasant and useful custom" and speculated in his diary whether the custom "was introduced into this country by the low Dutch whose practice it was to wipe out old scores and open new books something after the manner of the Old Jewish jubilee," but even he was "glad when the day is ended."[249] Edward Bates of St. Louis, who had gone calling in 1848 but chose not to go out again in that city, had a similar reaction upon his arrival in Washington five years later. As a member of Lincoln's cabinet in Washington, however, he felt obliged, and scornfully noted the prevalence of the custom there (which remained "very brilliant" there until well after 1880), remarking that it was worth seeing the "gawdy show" for once. Upon arriving home he found crowds of callers at the gate, though "less perhaps at my house than any other," and from 1 to 5 o'clock endured a "constant stream" though the Bateses "prudently resolved to give no refreshments . . . in fear of the repetition of former disorders." And so, he remarked sarcastically, "the day was very quietly and *respectably* spent."[250]

Though the doors to genteel society remained ajar on New Year's, they were, in most western towns, being left less widely open by the late 1850s. New Year's calling still afforded male strangers or acquaintances a chance to present themselves or pay their respects to the social elite without the proper credentials, letters of introduction, or invitations that were normally required to gain their attention and provided the elite a chance to meet newcomers without incurring a social obligation. In a series of visits it was hoped one would make a range of contacts, and possibly initiate a social connection by getting an invitation to make a more serious call, the first step into the exclusive system of calls. That the elite themselves were giving up on this practice, however, indicates that they saw nothing gained in people trying to enter society in this way. In addition, such open houses offered fewer social prospects to newcomers because, in such small towns, those who had any social potential were sure to come to their attention during the cycle of calls, exchanges of cards, invitations, and social occasions during the year. Those who had managed to evade the local social system did not their warrant attention.

Intriguingly, while the practice of New Year's calling was narrowing, the extensive use of letters of introduction, which served the similar purpose of introducing people into local society, was also in decline. The rules and expectations regarding such letters, dating to the eighteenth century, remained generally unchanged through 1850s. Letters of recommendation gave the recipient an introduction to the bearer of the letter and thus, with it, a request that the recipient respond accordingly and do whatever he could do for him. A letter was a kind of transference or extension of one man's honor or reputation, on behalf of another, to a third party. How the exchange actually worked, and what was exchanged or done, depended on the status of the writer, the character and intentions of the bearer, and the status and relationship of the recipient to the writer of the letter. In general, the more important the status, and the closer the friendship between writer and recipient, the more directly would the transference work in the bearer's interest. As the status of the writer, or his relation to the recipient, declined, or became more distant, what the recipient was expected to do or could do for the bearer also declined. So, too, what the recipient provided depended on what the bearer wished. If he had arrived to settle and live in a place, obligations were far different than if he were simply visiting or on his way to somewhere else. If one was in transit, such letters could facilitate the acquisition of new letters, to different people, and thus represent a reciprocal extension of one's initial sponsorship.[251]

"Strong letters of recommendation," such as those that Theodore Rodolf had from friends of people in St. Louis to members of French society of St. Louis, gained one immediate social access. Once inside the family network he no longer needed letters, because within families, spoken, not written words counted. Subsequently, Rodolf had to employ only a single letter he had from the widow of Alexander Hamilton to be received by William S. Hamilton in southern Wisconsin, who in turn wrote him a letter for Major John Sheldon in Mineral Point, thus extending the leverage of his initial letters several times over.[252] Similarly, when Elihu Washburne arrived in Cincinnati with letters from a Boston editor to his friends there, they gave Washburne all courtesies and exchanged his letters to them for letters to their contacts in Iowa.[253] When R. B. Ogden headed west with direct letters to gentlemen in Cincinnati in 1841, he was able to acquire direct letters from the recipients in Cincinnati to Ralph P. Lowe in Muscatine and Henry W. Starr and James M. Grimes in Burlington and went to both places for advice on where to settle and to acquire letters to others in Iowa. The next year, he finally acquired letters to a personal reference in Keokuk, in Iowa City, before migrating there.[254]

More general letters to recipients who were mere acquaintances or even strangers carried less weight. General "dear sir" letters were even weaker in obligating any potential recipient to respond. Among these more general letters, however, letters from representatives or senators in Washington carried the most weight. H. W. Leffingwell, on arriving in St. Louis, presented such a letter to George Y. McGunnegle and "that gentleman treated Mr. Leffingwell with much kindness and procured him a position as a clerk" in a friend's office.[255] William Worth Belknap carried similar general letters to people in Keokuk, and they provided aid. On the other hand, it was the very general nature of Elihu Washburne's letters written by a Boston lawyer to open recipients in Galena that may have affected his initial chilly reception from Thomas Drummond, though the letter itself, describing Washburne as a "clerk in my office and a member of my family" thus enabling him to "speak of him with confidence," was quite strong.[256]

Edward Bates of St. Louis routinely rebuffed politely callers who did not have proper letters of introduction. One interesting case indicates some of the intricacy of the etiquette of presenting letters. Charles Gibson arrived in St. Louis "friendless and unknown" with only a "general letter of introduction." The first night at the hotel he met Edward Bates, "by accident" "at the dinner table of the hotel" but apparently chose not to introduce himself. The next day, he stopped by Bates's office and offered him his "general" letter "which that gentleman refused to read, saying that he had observed him at the table the day before." Gibson responded that "he had observed Mr. Bates at the table without knowing who he was" implying that no offense was intended. They got to talking and Bates "expressed a desire to take up with him on his own hook," thus initiating, by breaking the rules, a friendship that lasted twenty-five years.[257] In another case, Bates simply questioned the veracity of the former law partner of William Seward, who introduced himself as such, remarking he "said he had a letter of introduction to me from Mr. Seward, but, being separated from his trunk in traveling, could not now produce the letter," an excuse Bates did not buy, resulting in a reserved conversation.[258] However weak some letters were, they were still better than none. If one had no letters, of course, one would risk rebuff, as Stephen Douglas found out.[259] Similarly, if one allowed the chain of letters to break by failing to present it, or not getting a letter from the recipient, one wasted a letter's potential leverage. So concerned were contemporaries about making letters of introduction work for them that if they chose not to use a letter, or did not get to the town in which they had intended settling, they might send a letter to the person to whom the letter was addressed and still ask for references to others in the region based on the letter.[260]

Once established in a local society, however, one began to screen and draw as well as extend and broaden the boundaries of one's local social enclave by means of receiving and writing letters of introduction oneself. As Washburne had counted on others to broaden his acquaintance, so, too, he aided his new friends in expanding theirs. When his friend Frederick Stahl went to Boston, Washburne gave him a letter to his brother: "This letter is handed to you by Mr. Frederick Stahl, one of the finest merchants of our place.... You will find Stahl just 'O.K.' and I know that it will be a pleasure to you to extend all those little civilities to him which are so agreeable to strangers."[261] The arithmetic of letters did not necessarily have to be one for one, however. Sometimes one could give a friend several letters to one place. This is what Henry Austin did when he sent his friend David W. Kilbourne to do business in Burlington in December 1837, giving him letters to five prominent members of the territorial government whom he knew.[262] On the other hand, one could send only a few letters with several people hoping a less than one-to-one ratio would suffice to introduce all to one person. In 1841 Elihu Washburne remarked in a letter to his brother that "eight to ten of the Galena merchants slope for Boston on the first of January and I shall give some of them letters to you by that means you can become acquainted with the whole... should you be at home."[263]

However complex the system of letters of introduction was, its practice apparently became more generic, more impersonal, and thus less socially obligating on the recipient during the period. Increasingly, personal references, in direct letters between recipient and someone in a place to which the person in question was moving, appeared as an alternative. Such references involved a request by one party to receive or expect a visit from a friend or acquaintance and a request to offer them hospitality, though final discretion was usually left to the addressee. In the other direction, one could write and request that someone visit a friend or acquaintance who had already arrived in one's town, but again, the decision to do so remained that of the person requested. Either way, they facilitated and controlled the introduction between themselves and strangers to local society by behind-the-scenes correspondence, rather than by the writing and presentation of a more public letter of introduction. This reflected an uncertainty about how the letter might be employed or perhaps was seen as a less formal and officious way of communicating with a friend or member of the family. After all, if a member of the family presented oneself, no letters were needed. Doors were generally open to all family and relations, despite their credentials and how much they were or were not acquainted with each other.

The declining usage of letters of introduction among members of genteel enclaves across the region reflected a decline in the number of people who sought entrance to increasingly settled enclaves, a dynamic that no doubt also began to erode the purpose of New Year's calling. Moreover, as these local enclaves became more settled, clearly defined, and interconnected by intraregional social contacts, a member of any enclave could increasingly travel among enclaves within a society of known people rarely leaving the web of family connections, friendships, or business or professional acquaintances, and thus only infrequently find him or herself in need of a reference to acquire access to the hospitality offered by those in other social enclaves. This reflects the more settled, sharply defined, segmented structure of genteel society across the urban West by the middle 1850s.

Gentility in the West

It was within private houses, enclaves, neighborhoods, circles, and family and social networks that middle-class westerners established their status and fulfilled their ambitions. These public characteristics and cultural manifestations of the genteel culture they employed to establish their status are apparent and can be generally traced in their diffusion, establishment, and development at towns and cities across the region. The nature and quality of this culture and the personal lives which members of the elite constructed, lived, and experienced is more difficult to discern.[264]

Genteel family culture

Cultivating a private world within the family enclave, distinctive and meaningful to its members, was a central premise of middle-class family culture. At the core of these private realms was, of course, the intimacy of marriage and the domestic family life which marriage anchored. The significant events of life that demarcated the evolution of this familial culture were commemorated by oneself and one's spouse and family members. Birthdays and anniversaries of the significant events of family life – arriving in the West, the day one met, one's wedding, or honeymoon, the births of one's children, or, tragically, their deaths, momentous private milestones marking successes or failures, memorable parties, social occasions, and holidays – filled the pages of a family's history. As the years passed, one commemorated these events more intensely and self-consciously, deepening family identity and anchoring one to something continuous, enduring, and entirely one's own, in an increasingly transient and alienating society, which, in the West, had shallow roots. To self-consciously construct a family "history" in such new towns, ancestral family portraits, heirlooms, and mementos were brought west and hung, used, and displayed alongside new paintings, photos, furniture, and curiosities. Western residents kept diaries and journals, assembled scrapbooks, collected and displayed artifacts, mementoes, or souvenirs – even to the point of weaving the hair of departed relatives into a hair wreath – wrote memoirs and autobiographies, and built and maintained the tombs of one's departed loved one's often nearby on the grounds as memorials to one's eternal family members. Middle-class people displayed these mementoes in the parlor or library within one's house or, better yet, in the family or patriarchal homestead (if it was nearby or one's father still lived there), gradually transforming each home into a museum of family history (the Washburne family, much later, actually built a separate library and family museum in Livermore, Maine).

Within a month or two of his marriage, Elihu Washburne resumed his seasonal practice of riding the circuit and was off to Mineral Point, Wisconsin. During the early years of their marriage, before Washburne was elected to Congress, he rode part of the circuit in March and October and went to Springfield to try cases in the state district or supreme courts in winter and summer.[265] Washburne's departure in early December 1847 to Springfield initiated a new strategy, requiring him to be away for even longer periods of time. That year he stayed in Springfield for a month attending the state constitutional convention and continued on to Washington, D.C., where he remained until late summer 1848. They broke this separation when Adele traveled east to Maine to spend the summer. Washburne was unable to join her for long in Maine, because he had to rush back home to Galena on business in September and stayed there until Adele rejoined him. In November he returned to Washington and stayed until late summer 1849 to do business, politic, and attend Zachary Taylor's inauguration.[266] In the intervening years, such extended absences from late fall to summer continued with regularity as Washburne's legal practice and political activities broadened. During the first five years of marriage Elihu Washburne was generally away from home about five months of the year. When he was elected to Congress in November 1852 he went to Washington until March 1853, briefly visited home, and then returned. From then on, Washburne's absences, through the mid-1850s, increased to almost ten months per year, a situation that they found necessary to break by more regular two- or three-month-long visits to Washington by Adele and the family. Nevertheless, they still lived half of each year apart.[267]

Though, initially, they seemed to have handled their time apart in stride, Elihu Washburne's increasingly extended absences became a source of unhappiness between them. In Adele's few letters through the middle fifties, Washburne's absence was a constant theme. In her early letters Adele recounted her efforts to keep busy and make progress in domestic life and assured Elihu "that you are frequently the theme of my thoughts" and expressed, given the novelty of his traveling, considerable interest in her husband's work and travel experiences. Later, however, after hearing nothing, she was short of money and deferentially requested: "if you can spare a few dimes I should not object to them." Another time, Adele had to admit to her brother-in-law, in whom she sometimes confided her frustrations, that her husband failed to tell her where he was going, and only instructed her to be ready to leave when he returned. When he was at Washington in 1847, she tersely remarked to Elihu: "I feel very anxious to hear from you. I have not heard a word from you since you left St. Louis. At Washington I presume you have so much to occupy your time and thoughts that you scarcely have time to bestow a wandering thought on your little one in Wisconsin," begging him, almost, to write her more often. As if to literally seal the point, she attached a sticker to seal the envelope which read: "Home is not home without thee." About the same time Adele again told her brother, "Elihu must take me to Main[e] soon" or "I will commence to show some of my French temper," saying of Washburne's continual excuse of land sales business, "hang the land sales until I make my visit," arguing that her view was "very rational" and acknowledging that she was, in her outspokenness, "an exception to the general rule of wives."[268]

When Washburne's election to Congress extended his absences, Adele's patience grew even thinner, compelling him to bring her and the family east. Elihu, on his part, balanced "tremendous homesick [sic]" with his desire to "make a few dimes" which would make him "better satisfied." Upon his election to Congress in November 1852 and his necessary residence in Washington for most of the year, which he initially sought to do without bringing his wife, the issue became more urgent and a matter of great concern.[269] What Elihu failed to say in his letters some of his friends implied through their constant reporting on Adele. One friend chidingly reminded Washburne that although "your family . . . all seem to be doing first rate," they still face "dissolution" by the "loss of the head."[270] Charles S. Hempstead, a bit later, reported to Washburne that his wife was "unwell" but was "getting along and recovering." The next day, however, a friend exhorted Washburne "to make no unnecessary delays in Springfield."[271]

As it turned out this solicitous prodding by older men, both of them members of the Presbyterian church and mentors, heralded the beginnings of Adele's health problems that, for the rest of her childbearing years, would impair her ability, even with the latitude of a "circuit court widow," to effectively carry out the duties of a genteel middle-class wife according to the cult of domesticity. Adele, in mid-December, was already about four months' pregnant. For a while Horatio Newhall, the family doctor, and Washburne tried to care for her, but this apparently was not possible. By late January, "as soon as she was smart enough," the doctor turned her over to the care of her mother, who transported her out to Gratiot's Grove and for almost three months "nursed Adele like an infant very often carrying her from her bed to her lounge first one thing and then another." Though he apparently kept hard at work in Galena, Elihu made weekly visits, except when weather prevented him and was on call as her due date approached. When, in mid-April, a month premature, Adele went into labor, Elihu, accompanied by William Hempstead, rushed out to the Grove to find Adele attended by Doctor Newhall, within a hour of giving birth to their first son.

Washburne bluntly reported the events of the day to his brother: "The sufferings of Adele for the last four months resulted in the birth of a fine boy on Monday last. Its birth was premature, but still it was a perfect child and we had great hopes of raising it. We were, however, doomed to disappointment. About dark last night it died. We are all in much grief. It was hard indeed for its mother, who had suffered so much, to be so soon called upon to yield up her first born. But she has done it with the calm resignation of a Christian and submitted to the dispensation of Divine Providence with that humility that belongs to her gentle spirit. I am happy to say she is doing well and we trust she will be soon restored to health."[272] Susan Gratiot's recounting of the same events to her sister is instructive: "the dear little boy," a "perfect little miniature" "so bright" with "fine black eyes" was from the first fatally weak. "At first the Doctor thought he might live," but "within ten hours the seeds of dissolution" set in and though Adele "had set her heart upon it and could not give it up" as she watched her baby suffer "she could only say the will of God be done and not mine."[273] Adele absorbed the blow with compassion and resignation: "He was a delicate little flower and lived but two days and a half – even that was too long for the suffering he endured while here on earth, although we thought it hard to give him up. But God knew what was best and we tried not to murmur." Adele remained weak the rest of the year, while Elihu stayed close to home. After a visit to the Grove in November, Adele returned to Galena, only to fall again "dangerously ill" in early December. Susan moved to Galena for the winter while Elihu "took leave" again for Springfield, in spite of his wife being bedridden and, in her words, "subject to the most racking pains . . . endured . . . [by] humankind." "Bitterly disappointed" in missing Christmas and New Year's, alone without husband or brother-in-law, Adele was able only to sit up in bed and still unable to walk on 7 January. The Washburnes never mentioned the disastrous events of 1846 again in subsequent letters, memoirs, or autobiographies; in fact, the death of their first child is rarely mentioned in biographical data. While Elihu worked in Springfield, Adele, at age nineteen, gained wisdom, remarking that "sickness has made quite a philosopher of me and I am determined to take the world as it comes and goes . . . [even if] it goes against the grain sometimes."[274]

Their personal trials of 1846 deepened their attachment to each other, binding them with "hooks of steel," and fortified their determination to establish a moral genteel middle-class family in a small western town. Within the larger family system, the death of their first-born and Adele's subsequent serious illness delayed the couple's emergence as a separate nuclear family out from under the influence of Adele's mother. Though not really a problem, there was some initial awkwardness between Susan (to Elihu, "Mrs. Gratiot" or "Col. Gratiot"s wife") and Elihu (called by Susan "E.B.W.," "Mr. Washburn," or (in quotes) "Elihu").[275] In the next several years Adele's continuing weakness compelled her mother to continue as her daughter's primary caregiver. The next winter, Adele traveled out to the Grove, feeling "my duty to be at home with ma just now," and stayed there, and at Mineral Point, for several weeks. Susan was again at the house in Galena for two or three weeks in June 1848 and again for an extended period before and after Adele's first successful birth in May 1849.[276] When, in late summer of 1850 after a holiday at Lake Pepin, Adele visited her mother at her new, smaller house in Shullsburg, Wisconsin, Susan remarked that Adele "looked badly" and "has not been well since she came back." Later, "E.B." telegraphed Susan "to go in [to Galena]" because "he was going away and Adele [was] not well."[277]

Over the years, whenever Adele was ill, she went to her mother or her mother came to her. When her daughter's life geographically followed her husband's career, Susan followed where she was needed. In 1854 Susan apparently made her first trip back east since she had traveled to Baltimore to visit her husband Henry Gratiot's tomb eighteen years before. She spent the winter with Adele (who was pregnant again) and Elihu in Washington, and in the spring apparently accompanied Adele on a short visit to see relatives in the Green Point section of Brooklyn and in Philadelphia before returning to Washington to attend to the birth of William Pitt Washburne, the couple's third son, on 24 April 1854.[278] They stayed in Washington until mid-May, when Adele, the children, and her mother returned, via St. Louis, to Galena, reaching there on 1 June.

The marriage of Elihu and Adele fused two self-conscious and distinctive family subcultures. Each of these would, over the years, seek influence over their life. The proximity of Adele's mother, siblings, uncles, and other relatives placed the new family, for several years, primarily within the sphere of the Gratiot–Hempstead clan. Elihu, an amateur historian intrigued by the French society in the valley, did not really have any difficulty with this. "Everything connected with Adele's family and history was of interest to him and a source of pride." The Gratiots and Hempstead family histories represented social progress and paralleled national history in a way that he hoped his own career and family history would.[279] For Washburne, both families also were agents of his accelerated social mobility.

The extended Hempstead family support system was fortified in November 1851 when Uncle William Hempstead, a widower for eight years, built a new house on Bench Street, reconstituted his family, and invited his sister Mary Lisa to move to Galena to take over the household. After the house was "newly furnished" it was officially "opened" on Thanksgiving Day 1851 with Mary Lisa, or "Aunt Manuel," as the "Lady of the Manor." The arrangement not only reunited a broken family "for the first time in nearly ten years" and provided Aunt Manuel with an enlarged family role, but also provided Susan with a ready place to stay in Galena, thus allowing her to be closer to Adele (see Fig. 8).[280]

The Washburne family, except for Cadwallader, who lived in Mineral Point and occasionally served as Adele's confidant and whom they visited occasionally, was a more distant presence in the young couple's life. Nevertheless, through his trips to Maine, Elihu remained deeply connected to his family and saw himself throughout his life as a "son of Maine" living in the Great West.[281] Therefore, he sought, as quickly as possible, to introduce his new wife to the society of rural Maine and the Washburne family culture at Livermore in the early years of their marriage. As part of his effort to establish a Washburne counterbalance to Gratiot influence, Washburne had no intention of leaving his life in Maine behind. As early as December of 1842, he made an extended trip back to Hallowell and the family estate of Israel Washburne at Elm Hill, an old farm house, on a hill top in North Livermore to visit family and friends.[282] In summer 1848 he presented his wife Adele to his father and brothers, who later dubbed her "The French lady." Again, he mentioned the idea of Adele traveling to Maine in July 1850, and planned another trip there in December 1851. When Washburne was in Congress, he placed Maine in a broader circuit which he and his wife traveled routinely. Adele spent considerable time "in the snows of Maine" during the winter of 1853–1854. He tried to "slip down to Maine for a few days to see the old people" in early 1855 but could not find the time amid the crush of congressional business.[283]

Whatever imbalance existed in the relative influence of the family cultures on the Washburne–Gratiot marriage, it abruptly ended the day after the Washburne family's return trip from Washington to Galena on 2 June 1854. Arriving in Galena via Freeport, to which point they took the train from the East, Susan, Adele, the new baby, and young boys, were all well, if predictably tired, when they arrived at "Lafayette Square." Susan spent the night and set out for Shullsburg, Wisconsin, the following morning. While en route and only about ten miles from home, she was struck with an attack of cholera and carried to a nearby inn and put to bed. She died within ten hours at the age of fifty-seven (see Fig. 9).[284] Adele, with a new baby boy and two young children to care for, was now without her primary means of support

Figure 8. Mary Hempstead Kenney Lisa, "Aunt Manuel," c. 1868. (Courtesy of the Library of Congress, Prints and Photograph Division)

and, stunned, fell into a deep grieving that persisted for months. Elihu, upon hearing the news, tried to console his wife by finding "consolation and a comfort . . . that I can realize the influence of her spirit and her example in you. And how poignantly do I feel my own short comings."[285] As if in reaction to the death of his sister Susan, Adele's Uncle William, after returning from a winter in New Orleans in 1853–1854 where he had sought relief from his chronic consumption, finally succumbed only eighteen days later and died in Galena on 20 June.[286] Months later, when it seemed Adele was over the worst, yet another blow hit the family. On 6 November, Adele's twenty-year-old sister Eliza, who had, over the years, come to replace her dear departed sister Susan, but who also suffered from consumption, succumbed to the

Gentility in the West

Figure 9. Mrs. Susan Hempstead Gratiot, c. 1847–1850. (Negative no. X3 27168, State Historical Society of Wisconsin, Madison)

same epidemic. At this point Adele drops out of the family correspondence for nearly two years.[287]

The depth of Adele Washburne's grief at losing her mother, her uncle, and her sister within six months of each other can only be surmised from letters to her from her husband. For Elihu, away from his wife in her time of need, the end of the year found him reclusively staying at home in his living quarters in Washington, "studying French," feeling "homesick and uneasy," "disgusted with public life," and yearning to be "quietly settled down," undisturbed by the "trouble and vexation" of politics. The year 1854 has been "to us . . . a sad year, and its recollections will sadden our memories for our whole lives."[288] Upon receiving a letter from his "dear little wife" he intoned and consoled her: "its desponding tone and mournful spirit quite unmanned me and the long night gave but little sleep to my eyes. . . . We indeed have been greatly afflicted and can never cease to mourn a mother who was but a little less than the angels, and a dear sister who combined all the qualities both of head and heart that beautify and elevate human nature. But we should bow with submission to the will of him who overruleth all things for good. His ways are the ways of wisdom, though they may be past finding out to us poor weak mortals," and he concluded, "to one so much devoted to my home, as I am, the sacrifice of being so long away from home is almost too much to bear." He promised, when he arrived at home in the spring, that he "would take the care off [sic]" his wife and let her have a good rest. "I can stay at home and look after the children," which if Elihu did, could be taken, in its contravention to the prevailing family ideology of the time, as indicative of the disorientation the two felt from their loss.[289]

But if Elihu did help, he did not do it for long, for in mid-May 1855, almost unannounced, Elihu, without his wife and family, rushed to New York City, spent a night in the fashionable St. Nicholas Hotel on Broadway and Spring streets, and got on a boat with three other congressmen – his travel companions – to join a "big crowd" "of fashionable people" bound for Europe. Though he was a member of the Committee on Manufactures in Congress, officially served as a representative of the State of Illinois at the Paris Industrial Exposition, and, with a future position in mind, sought to gain acquaintance of European courts, to which he had been given letters of introduction, Washburne's main interest seems to have been travel itself. For seven weeks, Washburne and his companions made an intensive Grand Tour of England, France, Switzerland, and Italy.[290]

Elihu Washburne in July 1855 dissimulated not very convincingly to his lonely wife that "this sightseeing is hard business" and justified his extravagant trip by describing it as a "trial trip" which he was making in anticipation of them all, including Uncle Charles and Aunt Eliza, touring Europe some day, because, as he noted, increasingly expressing the genteel assumptions of the day that a grand tour was necessary to be really educated, "everybody that can, should come to Europe." Meanwhile he described the "singular beauty of the English countryside," "the grandeur of this magnificent tribute to the greatest of all men" (which he wrote on seeing Napoleon's tomb in Paris at Les Invalides), the "splendor and magnificence" of the court of Versailles ("worth a dozen trips to Europe alone"), the "awful sublimity" of the French Alps, and the "splendors of Rome."[291] It is unclear what Adele thought of this, though she must have been pleased by her husband's admiration of France as well as his decision, upon returning to Washington, to eschew the boarding house routine and establish himself and his brother in a large elegant house fitted with "all the modern conveniences" – gas, water, a furnace – and with two parlors that he decorated with carpets, elegant furniture, and "his paintings and statuary" which he purchased in Europe, all of which was staffed by several servants, including "his Frenchman" (either a cook or butler), in anticipation of her coming to join him in the spring. Apparently, his trip to Europe dramatically elevated Washburne's definition of gentility.²⁹² Elihu and Adele Washburne stood on the threshold of a larger stage than the one they had built at "Lafayette Square" in dear "old Galena."

Across the river, Solon Langworthy, as Christian gentleman, entrepreneur, capitalist, elite businessman, mine operator, farmer, country squire, friend, brother, father, and husband, in his daily routines from house to town to mine, lived in an equally rich, though more spiritual and parochial, Victorian cosmos. A member of the "Congregational society" and active contributor to the construction of a new church, Solon Langworthy was deeply influenced by the evangelical revival sweeping across the urban West in the wake of the crash of 1857 and the failed crops and "hard times" of 1858.²⁹³ Influenced by Rev. John C. Holbrook, the same minister who encouraged Lincoln Clark to move to Dubuque, Langworthy shifted his priorities from the materialism of gentility to demand more of himself theologically. Pleading guilty to Holbrook's charge that "men who devote the principal part of their time" to trying to attain "riches or honor" were "too apt to overlook the more important concern of tilting themselves for eternity," Langworthy bemoaned his single-minded devotion to "business pursuits, the multiplicity of which had almost consumed in me the desire for nobler existence" and so "entwined itself around him like an anaconda" "that he had almost lost sight of himself." Rejecting the materialism and vanities of Lord Chesterfield (whom he mentioned by name) Langworthy vowed instead "to do and live like" Christ and to intensify his "resistance to vice." He would strive for "perfection" by doing "good to others" and making sacrifices "for the good of . . . fellow men," and focus his energies on cheerfully "secur[ing] the comforts of life for my wife and the support and education of [my] five children."²⁹⁴

From this evangelical perspective one's relationship with Christ was mediated through one's relationships with one's wife, family, kin, the members of one's church, the residents of one's town, region, nation, and world, and the dynamic forces of nature, as expressed in human reproduction, the cycle of the seasons, the fertility of the soil, and the laws of the cosmos through which God "in his wisdom" worked his mysterious plan. Solon took joy in devoting some of his time to farming for "farmers . . . of all the men in the world . . . should be most happy." "It is pleasant to plant as in it we see that reproduction is a never failing principle of the creator and we may apply it to our own immortality and redemption."²⁹⁵ By tracking the weather, following the rise and fall and the opening and closing of the river, noting planting time, weeding periods, harvest times, and changes in vegetation from season to season and year to year, commenting on natural phenomena, such as storms, eclipses, comets, the movement of the stars, and, closer to home, the health and mortality of his neighbors and friends, and wife and children, Langworthy observed the workings of God and the harmony toward which all creation tended.²⁹⁶ He believed real wealth lay in "mother earth" and that the "earthly goods" gained from mercantile and financial returns were speculative and "unsatisfying."²⁹⁷ Personal wealth depended, therefore, on the vitality of the town economy, which in turn, was based on the wealth of natural resources and the soil that, as elements of nature, were created by God.

Provincial lives

From the lookout atop his house Langworthy took in all around him, from the stars to weather, the flow of the Mississippi River, and the appearance of the rolling landscape stretching east toward Galena, northeast toward the distant Blue Mounds of Wisconsin, and west across the mines and farms that stretched toward the horizon along the road leading to the village of Center Grove. In October he took the appearance of the Donata comet, which was "distinctly visible on the western horizon, its appearance very brilliant and quite large with a less brilliant tail of exceeding great length pointing to the north," as a cosmic omen. The following spring he tracked the near record rise of the Mississippi River and sought to discern whatever impact it had on local health, farming, and business. Langworthy touched the dynamics of the cosmos by tending his gardens, fields, and orchards that surrounded his bluff-top estate. Gardening and farming were for the Solon Langworthys a family endeavor which brought them into contact with the creative forces of nature and the cyclical rhythms of the seasons, an accurate understanding of which he gained by recording their progress in his journal. Season after season he recorded new gardening experiences or strategies, the timing of the growing seasons, bountiful harvests, disappointments, and the incidents of the weather. His wife Julia, his son Forrest, and his daughters, ages six and sixteen in 1859, all took pleasure in gardening, managing the planting of the front and side gardens, and making the cycles of the garden part of their lives. When a bountiful spring followed the barren year of 1858, he and his wife were "delighted with [their] success" and took it as a sign of spiritual satisfaction.[298]

Langworthy, like any country squire or farmer, understood that nature could also take away what it gave, and gardening often succeeded by sheer luck, as occurred in both 1859 and 1860. For him storms and poor weather, like the extended rains of 1858 or the tornado that swept a path of massive destruction from Des Moines to the south of Dubuque on 2 June 1860, might be harbingers of more ominous natural phenomena. Storms in particular seemed to usher in unhealthy conditions, by changing the atmosphere or, "according with the old saying," releasing the diseases of diphtheria, scarlet fever, typhoid, cholera, and other bilious fevers which lurked in the garden or earth.[299]

When, for example, a month after the great storm of June 1860, Solon Langworthy and his family went to the country town of Monticello for a Fourth of July picnic, oration, dance, and visit to some friends, Langworthy expressed concern that the daughter of one of his friends was laid low with "fever and a sore throat" and was relieved when they returned home apparently "all well." A week later, however, the cosmos turned against him and his family. On 14 July, contagion theories had little to do with Solon's ominous explication of the sudden death of his six-year-old daughter at two in the morning: "It was on that Independence day . . . [that] a poisonous vapor from the earth or some strange vine from out [of] the ground entwined its circles around my dear one's neck and day by day its coils compressed above her heaving snowy breast until its poisonous fangs by stealth . . . diffused itself from head to feet and plucked the rose from off the cheek of our dear Lois . . . and the ruthless hand of death was laid on her."[300]

Even amid such a stunning blow, nature helped vent his grief. While she lived, the garden had manifested Lois's joy and happiness. Upon her death, it became a reliquary and a memorial: "she only lived to see the seventh summer flowers which by her mother often she stood and helped her with a knife or wood to till the ones she loved and with her tiny hands withdraw the weeds to pull. 'Oh ma ma dear' she oft would say while round the walks she skipped away" or ran to the gate to greet her father when he arrived home. As if to prolong his agony, the weather remained dry, hardly wetting the ground "leaving dear Lois' foot prints still visible in the garden walks and the flowers planted by her seem[ing] to droop their heads in mourning her whose constant care over them was remarkable."

Within a week the Langworthys turned their grief from Lois "who slept . . . silent . . . in the bosom of the earth" in the garden family plot, and directed their concern to Forrest, who, like many other children, was struck with the diphtheria that in mid-August swept through the town and rose up onto Langworthy bluff. Constant care, a change of doctors, and, so Langworthy believed, his son's pious ways enabled him to survive the epidemic which claimed five or six children a day in Dubuque throughout the month. Just to the east of Center Grove, a village two miles west of the Langworthy estate, where Richard Bonson and his English relations lived, the epidemic took the daughters of three of Bonson's friends.[301]

Contemplation on the family plot where his daughter who he imagined laying and looking skyward seemed for months, even years, to haunt Langworthy, tending him toward spiritualism and otherworldly ruminations. The death of their youngest daughter had followed another of his wife's reproductive misfortunes earlier that year. In mid-February Julia's fifth pregnancy ended in a "premature confinement" and a stillborn child. With filiopietistic reverence he undertook "the sorrowful task" of putting "the infant of my darling wife by the side of our two boys who are sleeping on the spot chosen by my father for . . . [the] family resting place." "James, who is always ready to perform real acts of kindness went with me and we placed the dear little one near his two brothers, Solon and Forrest [they named a subsequent son Forrest as well] in that silent spot where in 1848 we entered our beloved father." In much the same way that Stephen Hempstead twenty-nine years before felt that he and his family consecrated the ground at Bellefontaine outside St. Louis, Solon Langworthy considered this "silent spot" in Iowa where he buried his children and father as "hallowed ground."[302]

By such tragic events, Langworthy's idealized, universalized view of natural and social harmony, represented by balanced natural and family order in which everyone carried out one's prescribed roles, was made into the real, specific history of his family at this place. Likewise, the interior of the Langworthy house was "consecrated" or "marked" for Solon by the happy or sad events that occurred in its various rooms over the last decade. It was at the front gate that Lois used to greet him every workday until 14 July 1860. Lois consecrated the marble mantlepiece in the parlor when she fell and cut her head against it in February 1860, the day before her mother went into her tragic premature confinement, which took Julia, whom they described as simple, "inspiring and selfless," away from her "regular place" "around the family fireside and at the table." It was also in the parlor that the family circle gathered each evening for family prayers that their son Forrest presided over, before his harrowing brush with death. These somber family experiences of 1860 shadowed the family's subsequent "parlor culture," though in "family sociables" that fall, or at a party on 12 January 1861, family and friends "sang, danced, played old treasured games and then went into the kitchen afterwards for a cup of coffee," or callers on New Year's Day 1861 and 1862 signed Langworthy's book, drank punch, and ate sweets oblivious to the room's private meaning.[303]

In most of Solon Langworthy's relationships, society and family were synonymous. In 1859, he still lived, as he did when he was a boy, as one sibling among the "four Langworthy brothers" and viewed his life through his experiences with his brothers and sisters and the family as a whole. James, the oldest, was a central influence, always caring deeply and acting selflessly to help his younger brother. He had supported the family in southern Illinois, and on his visits home, "would one by one take us in his arms and press us to his noble generous heart." Thirty years later, James, now sixty years old, was still "always ready to perform real acts of kindness." Solon, who was forty-six, marveled at his "remarkable energy and endurance," whether in visiting on New Year's Day, getting up and going out to the mines every morning at seven, or in his "kind hearted[ness]" in loading a wagon with goods and traveling with a friend in twenty-degree-below-zero cold to go "in search of the suffering poor of Dubuque [to] supply . . . their wants." Solon said less about Lucius H., with whom he socialized occasionally, and was most closely connected in business and the booster ethos with Lucius. Edward, the third brother, was mentioned least by Solon, though he was involved in most family business affairs.[304]

His brothers' vigor and longevity stood in contrast to his sisters', all but one of whom were gone. His oldest sister Eliza had died many years before in St. Charles, Missouri. Laura, the fourth oldest child, followed by younger sisters Lucretia and Harriet (Mrs. James M. Marsh), all passed away in Dubuque. Sarah Maria, who had married Daniel Smith Harris, a steamboat operator in Galena in 1835, died in Havana, Cuba, in 1850.[305] In December 1858, Solon ruminated on these sad stories as he visited his last surviving sister, Mary Ann Smith, who was sick and confined to her room. Mary Ann was married to Orrin Smith, a steamboat owner from Galena whom he first met and did business with in 1836.[306] As it turned out, Solon's prayers for his sister's health, whose "tender and gentle care" was so "required" by her "beautiful little daughters," were answered. She recovered, and through her "culture and rare goodness of heart," and her and her husband's expansive "hospitality in their luxurious home in Galena" in which they entertained "thousands of guests" over the years, continued to play a central role in Langworthy family culture up to her death in 1881.[307]

This inner core of Langworthy family society was completed by the wives of the four Langworthy brothers. The closest to Solon and his wife Julia was Agnes, James's wife. An energetic Scottish woman, fifteen years younger than James, whom she met and married in Galena only six weeks before Solon and Julia's wedding, it was Agnes who during Julia Langworthy's near-fatal confinement that resulted in a stillbirth in February 1860 showed her "kind and tender heart" by staying with her sister-in-law and helping to run the motherless family for nearly three weeks.[308] Lucius's second wife, Valeria, was from Maryland and with her distinctive "southern charm and sweetness" projected a different tone onto Lucius's scholarly, genteel household, making it occasionally the center of great family gatherings. Pauline, Edward's wife, played a less important role in Solon's affairs; though being "rigorously opposed to all appearance of ostentation" and described as "plain in dress, direct in thought," we are told she "exerted a gentle influence on those around her," "her virtue shining most brightly around the fireplace of her house." Her muted style added charm and simplicity to her husband's fanciful Italianate-style octagon house.[309]

The self-enclosed collective social dynamics of the Langworthy style were honed by years of corporate family behavior under the influence of its patriarch, Dr. Stephen Langworthy. Whenever any of the sons were married, it was a family event and the brother and their wives formed a "wedding party" to accompany the new couple to this fraternal society. Likewise, Langworthy social life included informal gatherings or "family sociables," which often took on greater importance when relations from out of town were present, occasional "visits," local outings, and even extended family trips, such as one to the Illinois State Fair in September 1860.[310] These events seem to have roughly alternated among different sets of brothers, as did the gatherings at the houses of the "Langworthy family on the hill" in which only rarely did all the brothers and their wives manage to congregate at the same time and place.[311] Such family social occasions reinforced family culture and maintained its distinctiveness from the society around them. By 1860, locally, regionally, and even nationally, Langworthy culture had constructed a private familial network separate from the impersonal public world evolving around Solon and his family. Perhaps implicitly, Langworthy knew that the familial network that he had constructed, rooted in a cohesive image of the town and the cosmos as two interlocking parallel worlds, was, even as he now traveled within it by the railroad, being transformed by regional and national economic, social, and political forces which would, in time, transform him, his family, and everyone in his enclave of genteel society, into members of an increasingly provincial elite.

Elihu and Adele Washburne, Solon and Julia Langworthy, and Orville and Eliza Browning all struggled to balance contradictory forces to create a genteel lifestyle in the urban West of the 1850s. They sought personal meaning and authenticity through their belief in God, their cultivation of private family life, and their loyalty to clan, friends, neighborhood, and town. Yet their need for social identity and validation through social mobility compelled them to live genteel provincial lives. This agenda both drew them centripetally home while pushing them centrifugally out into a broader regional and national system. Ironically, their regional activities would undermine the very domesticity, localism, and "romantic" sensibility they cultivated at home.

5

"Brethren of the bar": Professional culture among lawyers and the regional process of elite aggregation

The task of establishing oneself and constructing an outpost of genteel society was predominantly a local enterprise. For both early settlers from "good society" and subsequent "genteel" newcomers, social mobility proceeded from establishing oneself economically amid intense local competition to situating oneself, given the timing of one's efforts, within a dynamic process of local social development. Some early settlers tried to avoid the male subcultures which dominated the society of the urban frontier entirely. Others chose to dissemble and accommodate themselves to or interact with them only as much as was necessary. Whatever strategy "good" settlers took, however, as more of their kind arrived, they began to form booster networks, define their own social sets and circles, and establish genteel clubs, associations, and institutions that demarcated and differentiated urban social space between public and private and genteel and "rowdy" spheres of activity. Through aggressive articulation of their social values and vigilant border management, middle-class genteel people cultivated solidarity and established themselves as social elites who defined the booster ethos and directed and shaped local society. All the while they remained confident, given their belief in "parallelism," that social mobility achieved locally translated into elevated status within American society as a whole.

Elevated local status, by involving them in wider business, professional, and social interactions with other genteel people across the region and nation, provided an increasing number of opportunities to test their egalitarian parallelist assumptions. Regional business and professional activity, social visits to friends and family across the urban system, and more extensive travel increased social status at home but also made one more aware that local status was validated by others with genteel status across the region. Though they were attached to their personal and corporate realms, whether that of their family, the "way of the town," the booster ethos, the fraternity of the male subculture, the local version of gentility, or the collective experience of local history, local elites increasingly understood that their local world was situated in, and to a certain extent dependent on, its interaction with the larger system stretching across the region and nation.[1] Compelled, in the late 1840s and early 1850s, to follow business, professional practice, or politics to the entrepôt or metropolis, or to circuit or state jurisdictions, many boosters began to construct a broader regional context around their local lives. By "coming out" or going "abroad" they validated and gave deeper meaning to their local status. They also contributed to constructing a regional space – defined by interactions, friendships, associations, and institutions – in which, paralleling what they had done locally, they could cultivate regional social solidarity through shared values, assumptions, and social practice and behavior. As they were drawn into a regional process of elite aggregation, they helped construct a regional society.

This chapter explores the dynamics of the social process of elite aggregation through the well-documented local and regional professional practices of lawyers – most of whom considered themselves middle-class gentlemen. Lawyers and politicians forwarded their careers by broadening their professional activities to circuit, district, state, or even federal jurisdictions or levels of government. There they found themselves acting within a regional realm defined and demarcated by broader parameters and dynamics and more general values which encompassed, subsumed, and coopted local society. Inevitably, therefore, lawyers, perhaps more than others, would intersect with regional forces and begin to feel, as litigators, boosters, businessmen, and gentlemen, the countervailing forces which pulled them toward broader regional venues. To some extent, regional experiences reinforced local loyalties. They would also destabilize and subtly transform one's locally based social status and identity.

Fathers of the bar

In business, law, and, as we will see, the booster ethos, local activity and policy was inevitably connected to the dynamics of the regional system. Members of the legal profession played a central role in the effort of town boosters to establish law and order, construct networks of commonality, and demarcate social structures and class lines. For lawyers like Orville Browning and Elihu Washburne, for example, achieving social and professional status were intertwined endeavors. At each step of the process their professional behavior and interactions, developed alongside, intersected with, or paralleled the structural development of the local booster ethos, the male subculture, and genteel society. Therefore, the history of the construction of local, circuit, and regional bars is, on one level, the history of the development of a regional power and social elite. In lieu of social evidence, examining the formation of the occupational culture of the bar provides us with insight into the intricate dynamics of the process of regional social development.

In the uncertain context of a western town, whatever social and civic status "gentlemen" like Orville Browning, Elihu Washburne, and Solon Langworthy had achieved by the 1850s was firmly rooted in a foundation of professional or business achievement and support from members of local and regional social and professional networks within the booster ethos. Lawyers, particularly, had been active "structuring" agents in the development of the booster ethos and local society. In migrating west, they had brought aggressive entrepreneurial values and a strong sense that professional achievement was validated and defined by a solid position within a local bar. Believing in "parallelism," they assumed such new local positions were the equivalent of the status of lawyers in towns and cities across the region. Hence, local achievement gave them official access to the circuit, state, and federal courts, success which could open doors to political offices and appointments. From migrating west to finding a position, building a local practice, establishing a position within the legal culture of the local bar, riding the circuit to broaden one's caseload and skills, and traveling to the state supreme court or federal courts, the professional, political, and social activities and strategies of lawyers, recorded in letters, memoirs, and documents, responded to and reflected, and thus provide evidence of, the dynamics of a regional process of elite aggregation that shadowed the pattern and dynamics of urban and metropolitan development in the 1840s and 1850s.

It was the new, relatively more open and flexible branches of the legal profession, in which status was determined by merit, ability, and hard work, not connections and family – the prerequisite for entrance into the almost closed oligarchy or patriarchy of the legal profession in towns and cities in the East – that drew lawyers west to establish local practices.[2] Practicing law there was, therefore, more competitive and "entrepreneurial" than in the East. Western lawyers initially acquired cases and built practices as free agents within a free market across a broader field in which a changing supply of practitioners sought shares of a continually expanding demand for litigation. In comparison to the traditional and hierarchical profession in the East, the law in the West remained open to any young lawyer who showed initiative and ability. Elihu Washburne, for example, considered the legal profession in New England too "crowded," "damned aristocratic," hierarchical, and "prejudice[d] against young men" by "pulling them back by the coat tail" rather than spurring them on to success.[3] Consequently, it failed to give him a sufficiently "broad field" for his professional ambition.[4] William Worth Belknap concurred, remarking that the East "is no place for a professional man to practice, and a young lawyer commencing [t]here without money would starve outright. 'Westward the march of Empire takes its way' – westward should every young man take his way."[5] J. Y. Scammon, however, noted in 1835 that because of the nature of litigation in the West and the prospects for Chicago to grow into a large city, he did not think "there is much choice for professional men between [the East and the West]. If one can get into a good practice here and sustain himself in a place like Chicago he will eventually do better, or at least, as well, as he can in the East, the large cities excepted."[6]

While law in the West provided more opportunity, it also required much more entrepreneurship than in the established bars of the East. Henry Hitchcock of St. Louis saw a direct connection between local business and litigation, arguing that to be successful a lawyer must go "where there is the most business"; where, "if you deserve it," you will be assured of "your share in time."[7] One assessed western towns, quite bluntly, by an equation of opportunity in which one gaged the prospective demand for legal services and the prospects for remuneration with the competition one faced as determined by the number of lawyers already there. The impact of this strong "entrepreneurial" impulse on migration is evident in both the close correlation between economic development and migration patterns and lawyers' increasingly systematic methods in deciding where to settle. Intense discussion and research at home, "tours of observation" around the region before concluding to settle in a particular place, and consultations with lawyers and professionals already in the West to scrutinize the prospects for developing a paying practice at various towns across the region reflects the highly competitive dynamics at the center of every local bar.

Most lawyers who came west no doubt were told, for instance, that General Land Offices at Quincy, Illinois, after 1830[8] and Dubuque and Burlington after 1838 promised a steady source of litigation.[9] By 1836, Keokuk and Fort Madison were considered "a great field of legal controversy, owing to the legislation of the Half Breed land titles."[10] Burlington's status as the capital of Iowa Territory from 1838 to 1846 (an advantage which after 1839 belonged to Springfield, Illinois, as well) further enhanced its attractiveness to lawyers. Elihu Washburne in 1840 viewed Galena as "the best point . . . north of St. Louis for doing foreign collections"[11] because the people "were a litigious set" and, as a result, there was "considerable litigation."[12] R. H. McClellan agreed, explaining that Galena was attractive because "after 1830 . . . [it] was the only town in the West in which there was any considerable amount of money of any kind, and the only town where gold and silver,"[13] mostly "English sovereigns," exchanged at roughly their "real value." This fact "induced many eminent lawyers from all parts of the country to come [there] and open up offices."[14]

Not surprisingly, lawyers migrated into the upper Mississippi valley alongside miners, merchants, and entrepreneurs who located at Galena, Prairie du Chien, Mineral Point, and then, after the Black Hawk Purchase of 1832, Dubuque. Several of the first lawyers in Galena had been in the West and were drawn by the pull of economic opportunity in the Lead Region. George Wallace Jones, Augustus C. Dodge, Thomas S. Wilson, and Stephen Hempstead, for example, all followed family migration streams from the southern part of the valley to Galena or the Lead District, and later relocated in one of the river towns of Iowa.[15] Charles Hempstead, of St. Genevieve and St. Louis, followed the same migration stream.[16] Administrative directives and appointments overlaid each of these migration systems and further determined lawyers' movements. Richard M. Young and Thomas Ford were both established at Quincy in the mid-thirties, and then appointed to work in Galena.[17] Similarly, the division of western Wisconsin territory into Iowa Territory in July 1838 with Burlington as its capital drew lawyers practicing in southwestern Wisconsin and northwestern Illinois. Among them were David Irvin, who moved from Belmont, Wisconsin Territory, to take up his duties as District Judge in Burlington in 1837 (taking his friend Charles Mason with him), Augustus C. Dodge, whom Van Buren appointed Register of the U.S. Land Office at Burlington in 1838, and George Wallace Jones, who chose to live in Dubuque as territorial representative in 1835.[18]

Other lawyers arrived in the West as representatives of land companies and large capitalists. James Grant, soon after arriving at Chicago in 1834, represented an "eastern capitalist" in the sale of 7000 acres of land at the terminus of the Illinois and Michigan canal.[19] At Fort Madison, David W. Kilbourne, as we have seen, arrived in 1836, and Henry Austin and Josiah Aiken in 1837 as lawyers for the New York Land Company, the trustees of which were Messrs. Marsh, Lee, and Delavan, with the assignment to secure claims to as many of the Half Breed titles as possible. When, in 1852, Charles Mason purchased most of the deeds of the New York Land Company, he went to Keokuk to go into the land business.[20] In 1839 Charles A. Savage arrived in Quincy, Illinois, as agent and lawyer for the Munn Land Company. Cadwallader Washburne, the brother of Elihu, moved to Mineral Point, Wisconsin, and formed a partnership with Cyrus Woodman, and his firm became, in 1846, the agent for the "New England Land Company" and made enormous profits in the purchase and sale of pine lands.[21]

Many of these moves were the result of careful entrepreneurial decision-making. In July and August 1836, for example, Charles Mason made "an excursion to the 'wild west,'" not only to "behold Mother Nature in her dishabille" but also to confirm his growing feeling that in the West "there [would be an] altogether more favorable field for my future exertions either professional or political." After traveling by way of Detroit and the lakes, Mason visited Fort Mackinaw, Green Bay, Milwaukee, Chicago, and southern Wisconsin and decided that he would reassemble his family, so "widely scattered" around the country, at Belmont "on the prairies of Wisconsin."[22] Similarly, James W. Grimes, who arrived at Burlington in the spring of 1836 after reading law in Peterboro, New Hampshire, visited Alton, Peoria, and Monmouth, Illinois, before his "attention was directed to Burlington, Iowa."[23] Daniel F. Miller came west after litigating in Pittsburgh for three years "to visit the Black Hawk Purchase or Iowa Territory," arriving in Keokuk on 15 April 1839. The roughness of the place so shocked him, however, that he went to Fort Madison, where he stayed for twenty years before returning to Keokuk.[24] James Grant, a native of North Carolina, moved to Davenport in 1838 for health reasons after a four-year stint in Chicago where, as one of town's first lawyers, he had acquired a large practice, served both as state's attorney for Cook County and prosecuting attorney for the Sixth Judicial District, and rode the circuit across all of northern Illinois, as well as making trips to the state supreme court in Vandalia.[25]

Many other newcomers came west directly out of law school or from reading law in a law office and followed the advice of mentors to pursue well-worn professional paths through connections and references. The "first lawyers" arriving at Quincy, Illinois, for example, had all just been admitted to the Kentucky bar. Archibald Williams and Orville Browning, arriving in 1829 and 1831, established a Kentucky connection that other young lawyers followed. Among them were Milton Browning, Orville Browning's brother, Henry Asbury, and Andrew Johnstone, a family friend of the Brownings'.[26] Calvin Warren arrived in Quincy via Transylvania University, where he received a law degree, and a law practice in Batavia, Ohio. When his partner's son migrated to Quincy in 1836, a town any graduate of Transylvania knew, Warren followed but, unable to find a position there, went up to Warsaw, where he practiced for two years before returning to Quincy.[27] New England immigrants who mixed with this Kentucky establishment at Quincy also came directly from their schooling or training in the East. Nehemiah Bushnell arrived right out of Yale Law School.[28] Charles B. Lawrence of Massachusetts had studied law in St. Louis and been admitted to the Missouri bar the year before he moved to Quincy.[29]

Ironically, however, in law as in business, the open venues of the West, while easy to enter, initially provided limited litigation. A few lawyers could, therefore, quickly satisfy all but the fastest growing town or city's legal needs. Thus the lawyers who arrived first quickly monopolized most local business, making it difficult for subsequent arrivals to break in. For a lawyer arriving in the West in the 1830s, finding a place where, in Elihu Washburne's words, one could "hit it" required precise locational strategies.[30] Choosing a location by the 1840s and 1850s became, therefore, a complex, multivariate decision-making process in which one weighed a number of factors and calculated a ratio between the number of lawyers in a town and the present or prospective amount of litigation.

Charles Gilman of Quincy gathered data in 1839 to answer one question: "Can I better myself . . . by going to . . . Rockford?" For Gilman an answer required having "as correct an idea of the state of business there as is *possible*, a round, *unvarnished* account of it. First – the business of the place and its growth and prospects; then the amount of business I could do and the *description* of the business, the number of terms of the circuit court a year, the number of entrees, whether clients would pay promptly, and the cost of living, by boarding in a *good* place, or by housekeeping."[31] For Junius Hall, in 1836, though Alton physically presented "no attractions," the fact that the local bar was uncrowded and the town was a fast-growing place with a "great deal of business" and had prospects of becoming "an important place" convinced him to stay.[32] Elihu B. Washburne's brother's logic, in declaring Galena, Illinois, "the best place in the whole West," was also impeccable: Galena was a thriving mining town with a considerable potential for extensive litigation, and though it had an established local bar, eight or nine of the lawyers were Democrats while only one was a Whig. In addition, the only Whig lawyer, Thomas Drummond, was, like Washburne, a native of Maine, and thus might be willing to form a partnership.[33] No matter that when Washburne arrived Drummond rebuffed him, and then he realized that his brother's logic was based on poor information. "Though there may be considerable litigation, there is no money to pay a lawyer," as "the territory is entirely drained of money" from land sales. Yet in spite of concluding that Galena was "not the place at this time for the practice of the law" Washburne stayed.[34]

William Worth Belknap first considered California, where "young lawyers . . . pay immense sums for office rent and board and still *live*," and "many of them are laying up money and all of them will in time succeed." Deciding he did not have the money to get there, however, Belknap followed the advice of George Wallace Jones, U.S. Senator from Iowa, who told him that "from all accounts the towns in the state are growing rapidly," and took a personal tour of inspection to Chicago, St. Louis, and several towns in Iowa. He returned to Washington, settled his affairs, and set out for his choice of Keokuk.

For Lincoln Clark, a Massachusetts-born lawyer who moved west after practicing law ten years in Tuscaloosa, Alabama, the calculus of opportunity at any place, determined by the size of the local bar and potential growth, was complicated by two significant factors. Being a middle-aged man, Clark worried that he could not break into an established bar because he would not be able to stand the hard work necessary to recoup his social position, and therefore looked for a place with a small local bar, and preferably one with a "vacancy" caused by the departure or death of an established lawyer. Clark also felt that, as a slaveholder, he would have political problems acquiring a practice in the North. With these concerns in mind, he set off on a preliminary tour of observation across the West in the summer of 1843, and followed it up with closer scrutiny in three further tours in 1846 and 1847 before choosing a place to settle.

With each trip, he fine-tuned his decision on the basis of more precise data. By 1846, he had honed in on Quincy, Burlington, and Dubuque, but concluded, after interviewing local lawyers, that "professional prospects" in Quincy and Burlington were "not very encouraging . . . [the] amount of business [was] considerable [but] brethren of the craft numerous." In Dubuque, he feared that business would not be sufficient, but remained interested enough to establish a correspondence with the Reverend Holbrook of the Congregational church to keep him up to date on professional prospects there. When in September, his sister exhorted Clark to settle in Chicago, though she conceded that he could more easily break into the Dubuque bar than the crowded Chicago bar – which she feared would take two or three frustrating years – that city seemed to gain an edge.[35] Subsequent news from his informant that a prominent Dubuque lawyer, James Crawford, had unexpectedly passed away, however, seemed to give the nod back to Dubuque.[36]

The following year Clark gradually edged toward an excruciating final decision, at each step consulting with his wife Julia. In a March trip to New York, he interviewed the poet William Cullen Bryant, who introduced him to his brother-in-law "Mr. Ogden," who "has been much in the West" and pressed him heavily with tales of the advantages of Chicago.[37] A month later Clark finally discounted any chance of returning to Massachusetts, fearing that having to start from the "bottom of the ladder" would reduce him to poverty.[38] Answers to queries to "several western men" that concluded "it was impossible for a southern man to go East or West," lost Chicago the ground that Ogden's booster treatment had gained it, leading Clark to conclude that in Chicago "I do not believe I could acquire the standing I have here (in Alabama) in five or ten years."[39] A trip to Chicago, in which he arrived on the opening day of the great Western River and Harbor Convention to find the city "in perfect tumult" and full of at least "one hundred lawyers" reinforced his conclusion that prospects there were "not encouraging."[40] After a trip east, Clark returned west in the fall to visit Dubuque one more time. Evident signs of economic growth and prosperity, a warm reception by Rev. Holbrook, who had continued to write him, and assurance from locals that local Democrats did not care about his southern proclivities and slaveholding experience relieved Clark. A long talk with the judge of the circuit court (probably James Grant of Davenport),[41] who told Clark that Dubuque was "a good place for a lawyer who will attend to his business" because "those [lawyers] here [were] of but little account" and Dubuque's legal business which is "small . . . will unquestionably much improve" also assured Clark of good professional prospects.[42] He was finally convinced that "he [could] succeed without delay and trials" better in Dubuque than in Chicago when he was informed that another prominent lawyer besides Crawford, both of whom had "obtained decidedly the leading business here" had "deceased within a year and none have come to fill their places, and one of these passed to the head of the bar in the space of eighteen months." Armed with this last detail Clark and his family, still apprehensive of making an "erroneous decision," determined on Dubuque and settled there later that month.[43]

Whether competing with other newcomers or seeking an ingress into a local bar, lawyers sought to acquire secure practices by monopolizing local litigation and limiting subsequent competition by controlling the membership of the local legal community. They did this by forming local bars. Members of the local bar exerted control by limiting new memberships to those who entered under the auspices or sponsorship of, or invitation from, members of the local bar who needed a partner as their practices expanded. The establishment of such procedures marked the initial stages, locally, of the process of professional networking and aggregation out of which a local, circuit, state, and regional legal and political elite evolved.

At each stage of this process, from choosing which applicants among the newcomers to sponsor or examine, to choosing whom to invite into partnerships or introduce to other lawyers one knew were looking for a partner or to the right people in local politics to get them a local appointment or involve them in local politics, to referring business to help their practice, members of the local bar served as gatekeepers before almost closed doors that presented "by invitation only" signs to newcomers. They acquired sponsorship while trying to gain admittance to the state or territorial bar to practice law. Lawyers who were admitted to the bar of another state – proven by a certificate, license or, a "diploma from the Supreme Court"[44] – had only to appear at a district or the state supreme court, present credentials, and take the oath, to be admitted to practice law in Illinois or Iowa. A new lawyer, however, was required to "satisfy . . . the court . . . that he possesses the requisite learning" by taking an exam and proving he was "of good moral character" before he could take the oath.[45] Therefore, at each stage of the process, the cooperation of local lawyers was necessary. Because the examination was administered and sponsored by local lawyers and judges, making oneself known locally was required before a local lawyer or judge would allow one to pass and to take "the attorney's oath"[46] and practice in the local, state, or territorial courts. When the supreme court was in session, applicants could appear directly before the court to be examined and, if admitted, be given a certificate of admission and sign the "roll of attorneys."[47] Later they appointed a regular examining board to screen new applicants.[48] In any case, those admitted at the local level in any year usually appeared at the supreme court later to be admitted formally.[49]

At each stage of this process, newcomers sought a sponsor, mentor, or "godfather" who was a member of the local or state bar to further one's career. As members of local bars struggled to make a living and wearied under constant requests for support from newcomers, they required better and more specific letters of introduction. The quality of one's portfolio increasingly influenced the outcome of one's search and determined the direction of one's migration and career. Lyman Trumbull, for example, arrived in Belleville, Illinois, in 1837 with letters to two prominent local lawyers and entered into a partnership with one of them, former governor John Reynolds, who became Trumbull's sponsor and mentor.[50] Similarly, Thomas Rogers, a New York lawyer who arrived in Burlington in 1835, was immediately accepted, started a practice, and entered the Dubuque bar on the recommendation of Augustus C. Dodge, who wrote a letter to George Wallace Jones of Dubuque for him.[51] In contrast, in March 1842, Platt Smith, after reading law by himself for four months "during the winter," applied to practice in Dubuque. Arriving "in old clothes [dressed] as a raftsman and [knowing] no one in the town" Smith applied to the judge, who was "not prepossessed in his favor" and "refused even to appoint a committee to examine him" "because he had not studied long enough," thus denying Smith admission to the bar. In response to this rebuff, Smith, on the advice and with the help of Ralph P. Lowe (who later helped William Worth Belknap), went to Muscatine, where Theodore Parvin, "struck by his frank and candid manner," took him in to "read law." A year later, "after much hesitation," a committee was appointed and reported favorably that the examination was satisfactory (Parvin called it "very good") and Smith was admitted to the bar. Parvin then offered Smith a partnership, but Smith refused, wanting instead to return "to practice where the examination had been refused him" in Dubuque.[52]

Stephen A. Douglas of Vermont was similarly slighted when he appeared before Edward Bates with no letters of introduction, a situation about which Douglas felt "great delicacy." When another lawyer also informed him that he had no position for him, Douglas left St. Louis, passed through Alton, and went on to Jacksonville. There Murray McConnell, an established lawyer, advised him to go to Pekin, Illinois, the same town up on the Illinois that two years later Levi Davis of Vandalia would advise David Davis of Maryland to go to (advice Davis took). Douglas set out for Pekin, but finding no boat until spring, gave up and went to teach school in Winchester, Illinois. There he managed to find a sponsor and read law and gained admittance to the Illinois bar in 1834. Douglas then moved back to Jacksonville, Illinois, and hung out his shingle. Later, in 1841, for political reasons, he moved to Quincy, and then, after becoming U.S. Senator, in 1852, to Chicago.[53]

John F. Dillon, a businessman in Davenport, acquired a sponsor by sitting in the court room listening to the trials and taking note of local lawyers whenever the circuit court was in session. Ebenezer Cook, one of the lawyers, noticed Dillon's interest and encouraged him to enter his law office to read law when he was old enough, which he did in 1850. His friend Austin Corbin made the motion at the circuit court in May 1852 to grant Dillon admission, an act which led Corbin to style himself Dillon's "godfather in the law."[54] Cook's brother John then invited Dillon into a partnership which lasted until his election as district court judge in 1858. Ironically, Austin Corbin, an established lawyer, had come to Davenport on the strength of a letter of introduction from Judge James Grant, who was holding court in Dubuque, to the young John F. Dillon.[55]

The tendency to form partnerships was motivated by a desire among lawyers to increase their practice in a competitive environment through both specialization and covering a broader range of cases. Lawyers who continued to ride the circuit in the 1840s or accepted a local or state appointment in the courts, government, or administration were especially in need of partners. At the same time, partnerships reflected a growing desire among lawyers to consolidate and control the membership of the local bar and thus indirectly the local market. The appearance of more partnerships thus narrowed opportunity for newcomers in the 1840s.[56] The need to have someone maintain one's business while serving a term in government or performing the duties of an office to which one was appointed led to the formation of most partnerships. This reason led to the partnership arrangements of Lyman Trumbull,[57] Orville Browning, who needed someone to cover his practice while away,[58] James Grimes, William W. Chapman,[59] and Henry W. Starr; Junius Hall and William Martin; and Ralph P. Lowe and William Worth Belknap. In one complicated case, the original partners of Rankin and Curtiss in Keokuk changed several times.[60] Similarly, the negotiations to enter a partnership, such as those between Junius Hall and William Martin of Alton,[61] could often be very complicated. Usually those partnerships succeeded in which the talents and interests of the partner dovetailed nicely, such as Browning and Bushnell in Quincy, or Starr and Grimes in Burlington,[62] in which one partner did court cases and the other outside litigation.[63] Young lawyers like Elihu Washburne, William Belknap, or Junius Hall in joining a partnership quickly found themselves with a more established practice and connections within the local bar. For Hall, the partnership provided "prospects . . . fairer than I could have anticipated so early." [64] For Belknap, entering a partnership brought him "suddenly from no business to a paying practice," with fifteen cases in the current court session. "Can any lawyer of six months' residence in a western town say more?"[65]

The tendency to form partnerships or search for new partners enabled the established members of the local bar to screen, select, and control the membership, and influence the politics, of the bar. At Quincy, Orville Browning and Archibald Williams shaped the careers of subsequent newcomers. In 1832, Browning took Henry Asbury, a Kentuckian, into his office to read law, sponsored him when he was admitted to the local bar in 1837, and made him an associate in his law office. That same year, Browning joined in a partnership with Nehemiah Bushnell soon after his arrival from Yale Law School. Archibald Williams, meanwhile, accepted Andrew Johnstone as a partner and later, after Johnstone moved to Virginia, became a partner with Abraham Jonas, a prominent Jewish lawyer. Likewise, J. H. Ralston offered a partnership to Calvin Warren, a New Yorker who had graduated from Transylva-

Provincial lives

nia University in 1837. Later, through his contacts with Browning, Williams, Bushnell, and Warren, James Singleton, who practiced in Schuyler County, Illinois, from 1837 to 1852, decided to move into Quincy. Jackson Grimshaw worked in Pike County and knew through contacts at the circuit court all the Quincy attorneys. Archibald Williams finally convinced him to move to Quincy in 1857 by offering him a partnership.[66] It was also Orville Browning who took in his brother Milton to read law with him in the mid-1830s, and then sponsored him on his arrival in Burlington, a place where Orville had done some legal business, in 1837.[67] Gradually, by establishing local practices, forming partnerships, and screening and controlling their membership, members of the local bars consolidated their power and established the foundation from which to expand their practices into a broader sphere.

Circuit riding and the social geography of law

For most lawyers, that meant practicing law across the circuit. The court system of the western states, borrowing from eastern practice, employed the circuit system and expected lawyers in frontier towns not only to provide a full range of legal services in the local courts but also to ride to the other circuits across the state to help frontier lawyers with more difficult cases or to simply to act as counsel where there were no lawyers. Just as lawyers from the established towns in the southern part of the valley rode north to provide legal services to towns in Illinois and Iowa in the 1820s and 1830s, the lawyers who later established themselves in the major towns of the West were expected to provide legal services to settlers across new counties within each town's sparsely settled hinterlands. Judge John D. Caton understood this symbiotic relationship between the legal profession and urban development. "With the growth of towns and cities" "resident lawyers of ability and learning" appeared "in every county seat at least" and thus "no assistance in the conduct of the most important cases" was required. From the 1820s to 1840s, however, "the few local lawyers who had settled in the county towns [and on the frontier] were generally newcomers, without experience and self-confidence, and both they and their clients depended largely on assistance from abroad, especially at the trials of causes. This state of things necessitated a class of itinerant lawyers whose ability and experience had secured to them reputations coextensive with their judicial circuits and, in many cases, throughout the state."[68] For lawyers who established a successful local practice, the circuit courts not only served as a venue of further opportunity, but would become a viaduct to a broader realm of professional practice and experience (see Figs. 10 and 11).[69]

The dynamics between town litigation and circuit courts are reflected in lawyers' variable interest in riding the circuit. When, before 1850, litigation was generally insufficient for more than a few lawyers in any town to acquire a remunerative practice, most lawyers viewed the circuit as a means to supplement their practices by adding to their case loads.[70] Newcomers especially relied on picking up extra cases from the circuit courts around them to break into the local monopoly by established

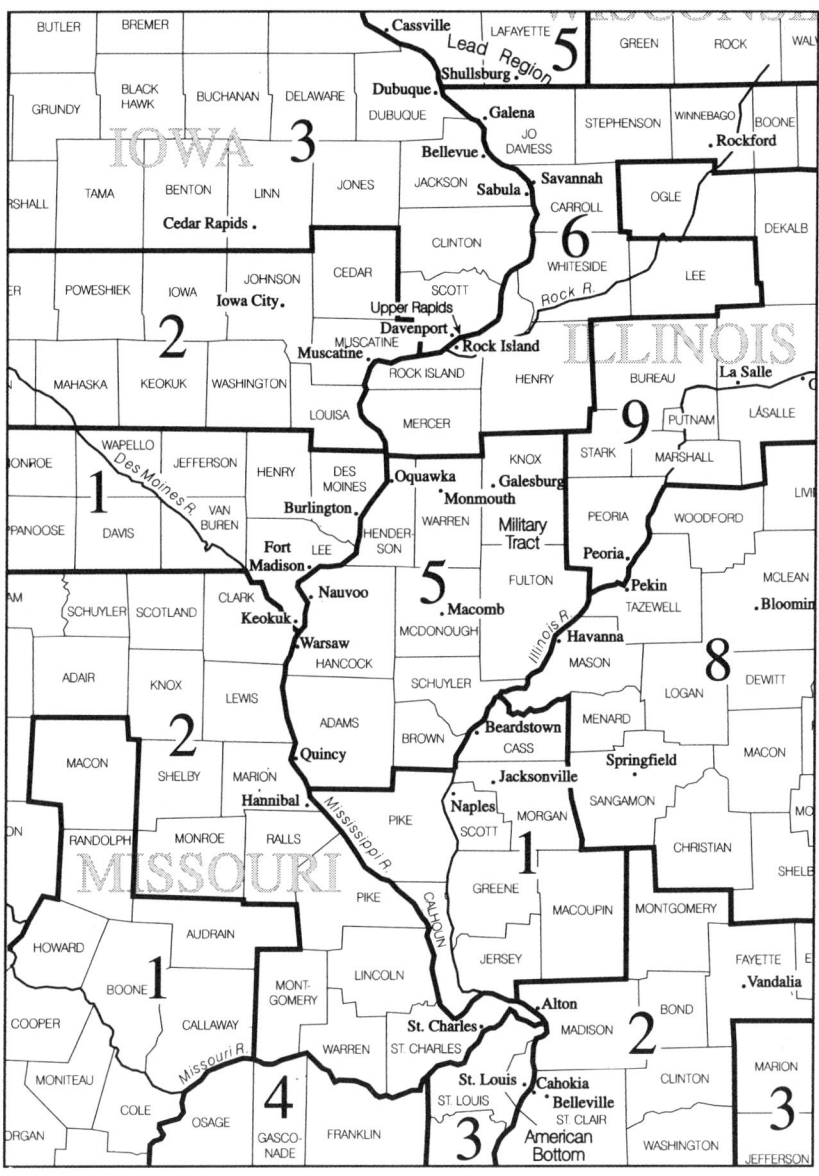

Figure 10. Circuit court districts, 1841–1845.

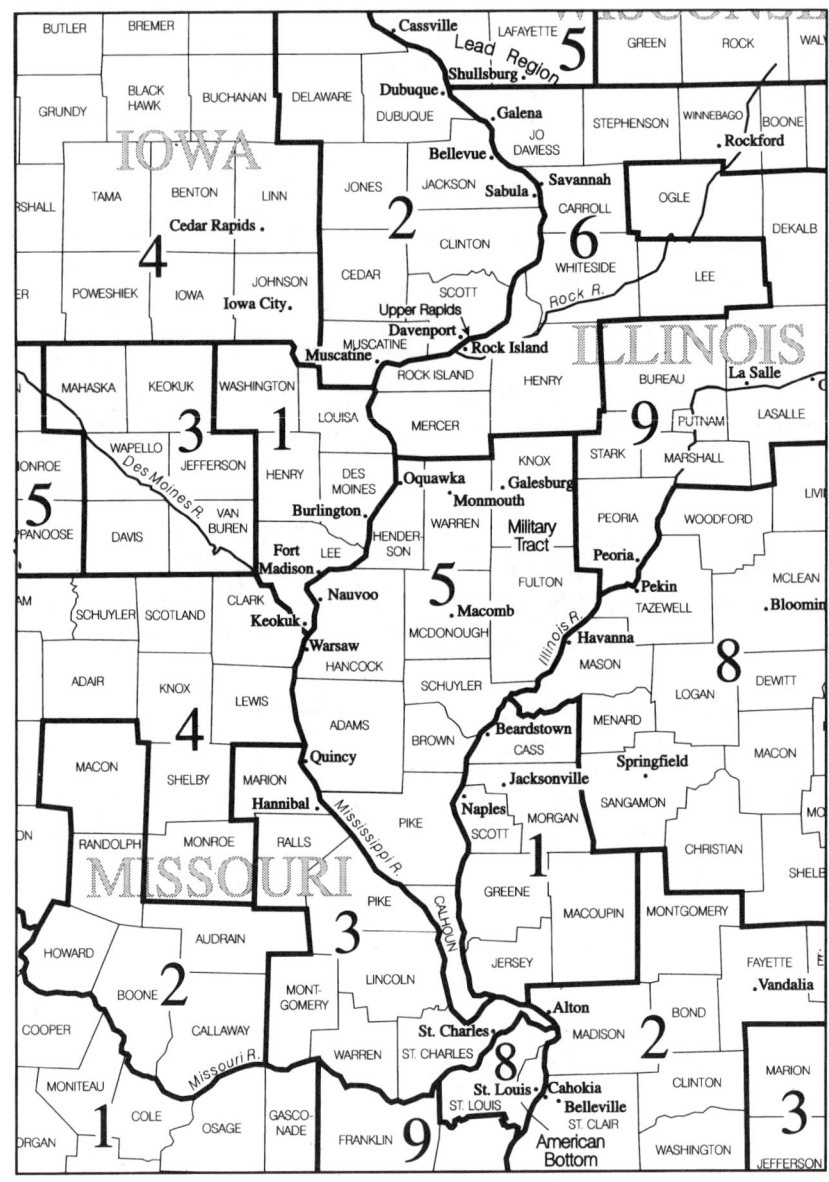

Figure 11. Circuit court districts, 1846–1852.

lawyers and to initiate or enlarge their practices. Riding the circuit became, therefore, for many lawyers and judges across the region a routine semiannual field of opportunity that structured one's spring and fall business.

As urban litigation increased and lawyers' practices were increasingly taken up by local cases, however, more lawyers concluded that circuit practice was an extravagant use of time away from the office and sought to curtail circuit-riding. Reflecting this urban preference, they arranged the circuit schedules to reduce the time and effort town lawyers invested in circuit practice, while maximizing their access to various sessions on the circuit, thus subtly affecting the structure and dynamics of networking among circuit lawyers. In some circuits, the first session of the circuit court started in its least populated county. Subsequent court sessions moved toward the largest town, where court sessions were scheduled about halfway through the circuit, and then went back out toward less populated areas to the end of the circuit. Such an arrangement allowed the lawyers from the major town – who, after all, were expected to provide services for those in less populated areas – a mid-circuit respite at home between visits to courts around the circuit. Generally, as the number of cases in the largest town's circuit court session increased, judges were compelled to start the session earlier and extend it later in the circuit schedule, thus causing it to run over the scheduled starting times for court sessions in the adjacent counties. In either case, these urban-centered schedules generally allowed most town lawyers to stay at home for three to four weeks while attending court sessions in adjacent counties only if required.

Though judges and clerks had to travel the entire circuit, lawyers seem to have followed only if case loads, special cases, or remuneration were sufficient to cover expense and the cost of an extended absence from home. Much romance surrounds the life of the circuit – particularly in the literature and "lore" (which is vast)[71] surrounding Abraham Lincoln's practice in the Eighth Circuit. Many lawyers, however, rode the circuit reluctantly, and viewed it as more of a nuisance or burden than a field of opportunity. James Grant gave up riding the enormous Sixth Circuit in Illinois in 1836 because "it interfered too much with his home business."[72] Elihu Washburne was never very enthusiastic about the circuit. When his case load declined in 1840, and he feared that the "heydey [sic] of his business was over" and that he would have to go "a begging,"[73] Washburne irresolutely "marked out a circuit in which to practice regularly hereafter, which will cost me much mental and physical labor."[74] His brother Cadwallader felt that his new practice was "not very pleasant, as we have to travel the circuit and put up with pretty hard fare sometimes."[75] Likewise, Junius Hall, at Alton, felt the court system was so packed that it gave one "hardly time to breathe" with no "respite" for any kind of leisure. Circuit-riding made Lincoln Clark of Dubuque lonely and "heartsick," and he routinely disparaged the "laborious service" of a "vagabondizing lawyer" before he decided it was "not worthy the attention of a lawyer who has any ability" and gave it up as unremunerative. Usually, as local business increased, more lawyers "tended to limit their practice to their own counties, occasionally traveling to a neighboring county for a particular case, but no longer attempting to cover the whole circuit."[76]

Provincial lives

Initially, when circuits often stretched across the entire state, lawyers and judges committed extended periods to visiting all the courts in the circuit. In the 1830s, when the Sixth Circuit included all of northern Illinois above Peoria, Judge James Grant and several Galena and Chicago lawyers made trips across the entire circuit.[77] The impracticality of such extended circuits, however, led to remapping the circuits in 1841 with an eye to allowing town lawyers to maximize attendance while minimizing effort and absences from home. Because the Fifth Circuit 1841 schedule essentially broke in half at Quincy, local lawyers could go out to the court sessions in the early and later weeks of the circuit schedule, while spending time at home between. Though Stephen Douglas, as circuit court judge in 1841, was obliged to travel the full Fifth Circuit, which began in Fulton County in April and continued through Lewiston, Rushville, Mount Sterling, Macomb, Oquawka, Monmouth, and Knoxville – which he felt were all "off the road"[78] – through May, Orville Browning and Archibald Williams only followed the circuit at its beginning and then went all the way out to Warren County.[79]

By 1850 increased litigation had necessitated pushing the Quincy court session toward the end of the circuit while court sessions opened in counties next to Adams County for more than a month, allowing Browning to go on forays out to different courts and return to Quincy in between, without having to ever stay very long on the circuit. Through 1853, Browning, regularly made forays out at the beginning and end of the circuit.[80] In 1852–1854, he made separate forays that were facilitated in river counties by access to the steamboat out and back to Hancock, Pike, Henderson, Brown, and Mercer counties, before winding up business with a circuit-ending session of the Adams County court. When a new schedule in 1853 doubled up sessions in certain counties, Browning now had to choose between forays to Henderson and Pike counties early in the circuit, and then Brown or Hancock, and Schuyler or his home court in Quincy through October.[81] In this way he could continue his practice in Quincy while attending to cases in nearby court sessions on the circuit. In 1854, choosing the easiest access by steamboat and good roads, he attended the courts in Henderson and Hancock to the north and then went back out to the courts in Schuyler and Pike to the east. In between he stopped to visit his brother (lawyer Milton D. Browning) in Burlington. Meanwhile, Browning skipped the court sessions in Brown, McDonough, and Schuyler counties. By traveling out to circuit courts, but not riding the circuit between them, Browning cut his time on the road from a potential of 110 days to only forty-five days. For Browning, Quincy was the center of a circuit or circle that he, like apparently many lawyers, traveled or "rode" by traversing the radii back and forth to each court rather than following its circumference, as the judge and some others did.[82]

In contrast, in the Sixth Circuit, the Galena court session opened and closed the circuit that made a similar circular progress from county to county moving away and then returning toward Galena. Given this schedule, Galena lawyers lacked the flexibility to go out to and return from different court sessions along the circuit and tended, therefore, to divide sharply between those willing to commit to riding the circuit and those who only attended sessions in adjacent counties. Elihu Washburne, one of the latter, never devoted much time to riding the circuit. In fall 1845 he stayed home and only visited the adjacent counties, probably Stephenson and Carroll counties. The following year, he remarked on having been out on the circuit, then coming home, and having to go back out again to the Carroll County court. He later admitted that he never attended the court in Lee County. In January 1851, starting his third year as circuit judge, Benjamin R. Sheldon (a Galena lawyer), complained about the broad extent of the Sixth Circuit, noting that "it . . . subjugate[d] me to much additional inconvenience and travel and deprive[s] me of the privilege of holding court *at home* and about home which you know is desirable on account of one's private affairs."[83]

Even in an extended circuit like the Eighth where several courts were too far away from the urban center to be reached by sorties, Lincoln and others sought to intersperse their time on the circuit with trips home (see Figs. 10 and 11). Between 1841 and 1849, Lincoln regularly road the circuit from Sangamon north to Livingston County and back via Christian, Coles, and Shelby counties for several weeks, then broke the circuit and returned to Springfield, and caught the Menard or Christian county courts afterward. When in 1850 Lincoln expanded his circuit-riding, it was a specific choice to do so. That year he rode the entire circuit. He traveled most of the circuit again in spring 1851, though he missed two sessions before rejoining the circuit at Urbana and following it to its end. Subsequently, Lincoln traveled the entire circuit in the fall of 1851, and in the spring and fall of 1852. During this period, Judge Davis, Lincoln, and a small coterie of lawyers, including Leonard Swett, "were the only lawyers" who "passed habitually over the circuit."[84] All but Lincoln seem to have been worn out by it. That Lincoln's commitment to ride the circuit was the exception among his legal brethren indicates that he did so for more than economic reasons. While Lincoln enjoyed himself, David Davis, the circuit judge after 1848, complained to his wife in August 1851, "The circuit must be lessened [by] a county or rearranged . . . or I shall quit."[85]

In Iowa, where sparser population and greater distances made riding the circuit for extended periods an even greater commitment, lawyers still sought to make forays whenever possible. In 1848, Lincoln Clark introduced himself to the circuit by making a series of forays out and back to Cascade, Delhi, Bellevue, and Dewitt. The following year Clark continued his foray strategy in the spring but extended his search for cases out to Linn and Jones counties in the fall. In 1855, Clark went out onto the Third Circuit again, but at Delhi continued west to Independence, and then went on an extended foray up to "the public lands" in Blackhawk, Butler, Floyd, and Mitchell counties before returning home.[86]

Within each circuit this coterie of "circuit riders" gained more attention and status. Defining who they were, and when one met them and entered circuit society, became, for memorists and eulogists, a stock-in-trade. Often, who these lawyers were was apparent at one's first meeting at the circuit court. Such appearances were critical moments, stepping stones in the widening of one's career and, in the process, through one's broadening contacts, of elite aggregation. In southern Illinois, Gustave Koerner recalled the beginnings of his circuit career, when he met

Judge Sidney Breese at Edwardsville in 1836 and he, Walter Scates, and Judge Breese proceeded to ride the new circuit for the first time.[87] At Galena, R. H. McClellan remembered that John Turney, William Smith, James M. Strode, and Benjamin Mills all made their first appearances at the October 1828 court. According to Elihu B. Washburne, Charles Hempstead, Thomas Drummond, Joseph P. Hoge, and Thompson Campbell were the most regular circuit-riders in the Sixth Circuit.[88] Down at Quincy, Orville H. Browning, Nehemiah Bushnell, Archibald Williams, Almeron Wheat, Calvin Warren, Henry Asbury, and J. H. Ralston (who became a circuit judge for a term),[89] regularly visited the circuit, where they all met Jackson Grimshaw and James W. Singleton of Pike County, and Ozias Hatch, clerk of the Pike County circuit court from 1841 through 1848.[90]

In Iowa, the first court in the Wisconsin Territory Third District was held in Farmington, in Van Buren County, which David Rorer, Charles Mason, Jonathan C. Hall, Phillip Veile, and Judge Irvin all attended. Later when Mason became the judge of the new First Judicial District, it was he, Gideon S. Bailey, Edward Johnstone, and J. C. Hall who rode the entire circuit. Hall, as we have already noted, was the most frequent circuit-rider among the lawyers of the First District, while James Woods was nearly as prevalent.[91] Theodore Parvin and Stephen Wichler visited the Dubuque Court with Judge James Grant for "twelve years."[92] Parvin as District Attorney was also present at Judge Williams's first court in Johnson County at the site of Iowa City in 1839.[93]

This core group would only gradually emerge from the larger group of lawyers who rode the circuit. Town lawyers who only visited certain courts formed a significant subset of the core. Likewise, other local lawyers would ride the circuit for a session or two, briefly joining the core group as it traveled the circuit, and return home. Again, the intensely studied Eighth Circuit provides some evidence of these dynamics. Lincoln, Edward D. Baker, John T. Stuart, and David B. Campbell formed the core group in the 1840s. In Sangamon County and the western part of the circuit, Stephen T. Logan would join the circuit. While "on the eastern part" of the circuit, Usher F. Linder and O. B. Ficklin would put in appearances. In between, any number of local lawyers would participate – Asahel Gridley of Bloomington, Lawrence Weldon and Clifton H. Moore of Clinton, and many other members of nascent local bars throughout the circuit.[94] According to David Davis, the circuit also attracted, from time to time, Stephen Douglas, James MacDougall, Cyrus Walker, Kirby Benedict, Asahel Gridley, T. Lyle Dickey,[95] and, after 1849, Leonard Swett of Bloomington. In 1850, as noted, David Davis as circuit judge, David B. Campbell as state's attorney, Leonard Swett, and Lincoln formed the core of the famous circuit riders about whom so much has been written.[96]

The records of cases tried at the state supreme courts between 1838 and 1850 by the lawyers who first appeared there before or in 1840 that indicate the "circuit lawyers" as those lawyers who tried cases from most of the counties in a circuit, as opposed to "town lawyers," that is, those who tried cases only from the county in which they lived, confirm the impressions of memoirs and letters. By 1840, it is apparent, therefore, that each circuit sent to Springfield, the new capital of Illinois, a small elite coterie of established circuit riders to practice at the state supreme court (see Appendices 1 and 2). Together the thirty-one lawyers from nine circuits who converged on the new state capital at Springfield in December 1839 would form the core cohort of lawyers and politicians who would control the profession in Illinois for a decade or more to come. In Iowa, an even tighter group of lawyers established a near monopoly over case loads at the supreme court (see Appendix 3).

Some lawyers sought out activity in a larger realm by extending their practices to nearby circuits. Both "town lawyers" and some circuit lawyers often sought to visit sessions in adjacent counties, whether those counties were part of their own circuit, in another circuit, or across state or territorial lines. Such a strategy reduced absences from home, while maximizing case loads, professional contacts, and remuneration. Location, cost, and the size of one's home practice were also key factors in determining one's ability or desire to visit nearby venues. Such lawyers who, instead of local business, searched for business in other circuits or venues were considered "visiting" or "foreign lawyers" who were "crossing over" or, in Lincoln Clark's words, "attending courts abroad."[97] In their efforts in venturing out, lawyers met their colleagues from other towns and circuits and initiated the regional process of professional networking out of which regional or state bars evolved.

Evidence of crossing over from letters, biographies, or memoirs indicates how extensive the practice was in the 1820s and 1830s and the role it played in regional aggregation (see Fig. 12). Among the forty-five specific references from the 1820s and 1830s, for example, extensive crossing over the river, especially around Keokuk and Burlington, and Galena and Dubuque, as well from Chicago and St. Louis, is apparent.[98] In the 1840s, increased local court case loads, combined with smaller circuits, caused a decline in the practice (see Fig. 13).[99] Except for the continuation of the practice near the frontier, where sparse population necessitated it, crossing-over was in decline everywhere except around Keokuk and Fort Madison, where the Half Breed Tract litigation drew lawyers from across the region.

In addition, convergences in court schedules in adjacent circuits provided lawyers in some towns more opportunities to cross over than in other towns. Lawyers in Quincy, Galena, Davenport, and Alton were adjacent to a choice of other circuits across the river, or to the north or south (see Fig. 14). Fall circuit courts opened, for example, on the fourth Monday of September in both Scott County and across the river in Rock Island County, Illinois, although the Iowa court was at the beginning of the circuit, and the Illinois session near the end. A week later, courts opened simultaneously at Carthage in Hancock County, Illinois, and Keokuk, in Lee County, Iowa. Likewise, throughout October courts in the Iowa Third and the Illinois Sixth occurred within a week of each other across the river, providing opportunities for those who wished to add to their case loads.[100] For those lawyers on the circuit willing to travel the extra miles, such convenient convergences maximized their time and effort and introduced them to the lawyers and judge of another circuit.

An analysis of cases from various circuits tried by lawyers at the Illinois state supreme court between 1835 and 1850 shows that some lawyers tried more cases

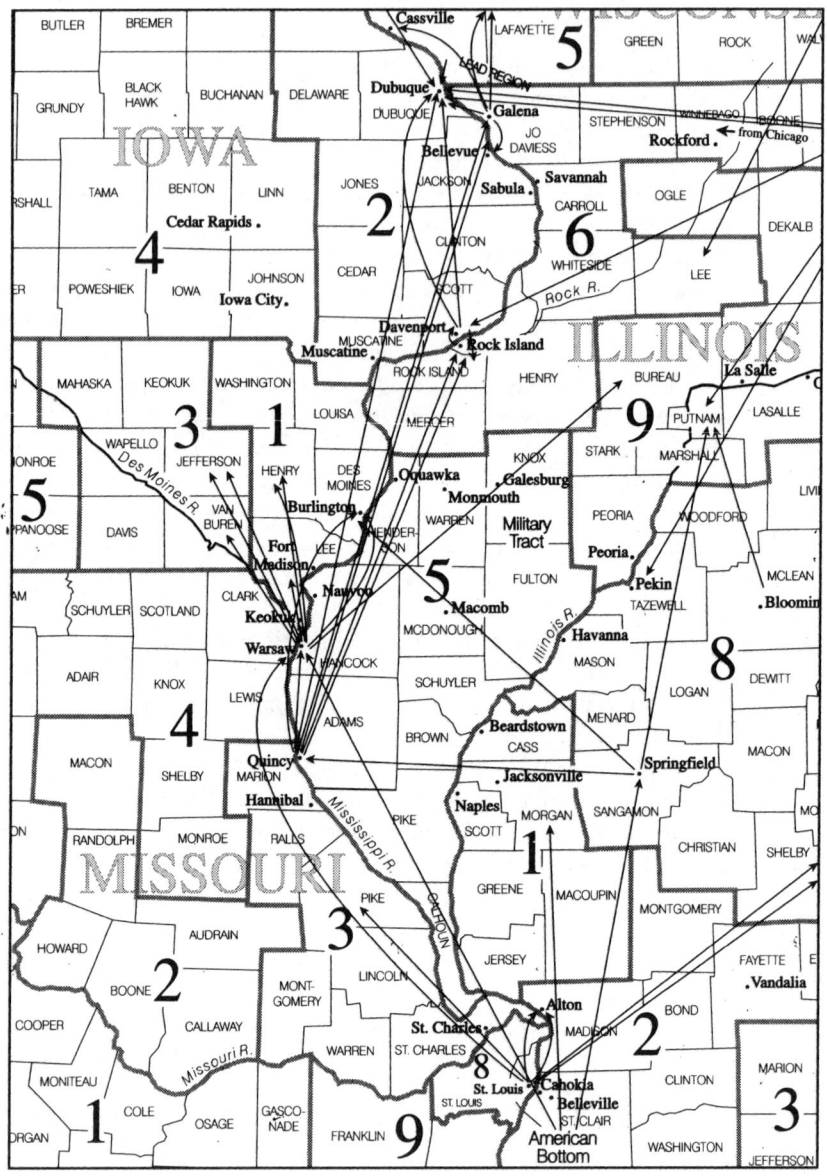

Figure 12. Lawyers' crossovers between circuits in the 1830s.

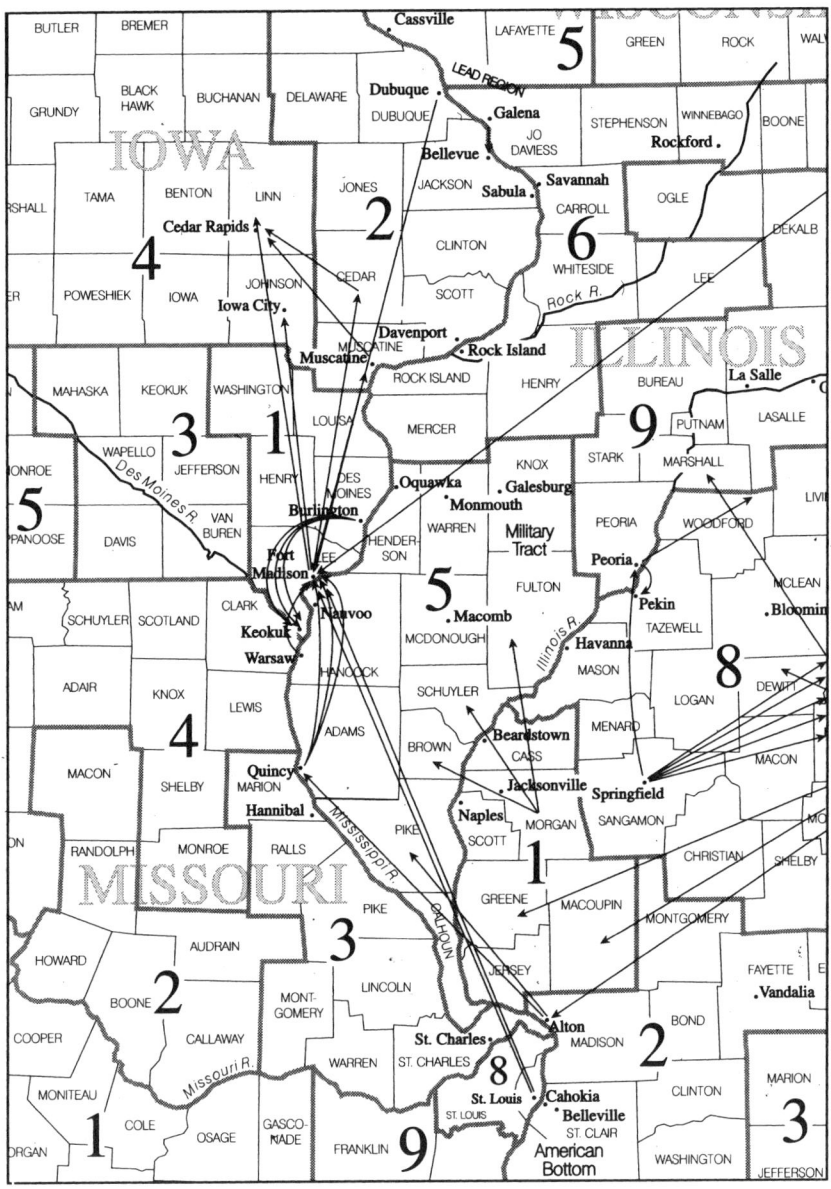

Figure 13. Lawyers' crossovers between circuits in the 1840s.

Provincial lives

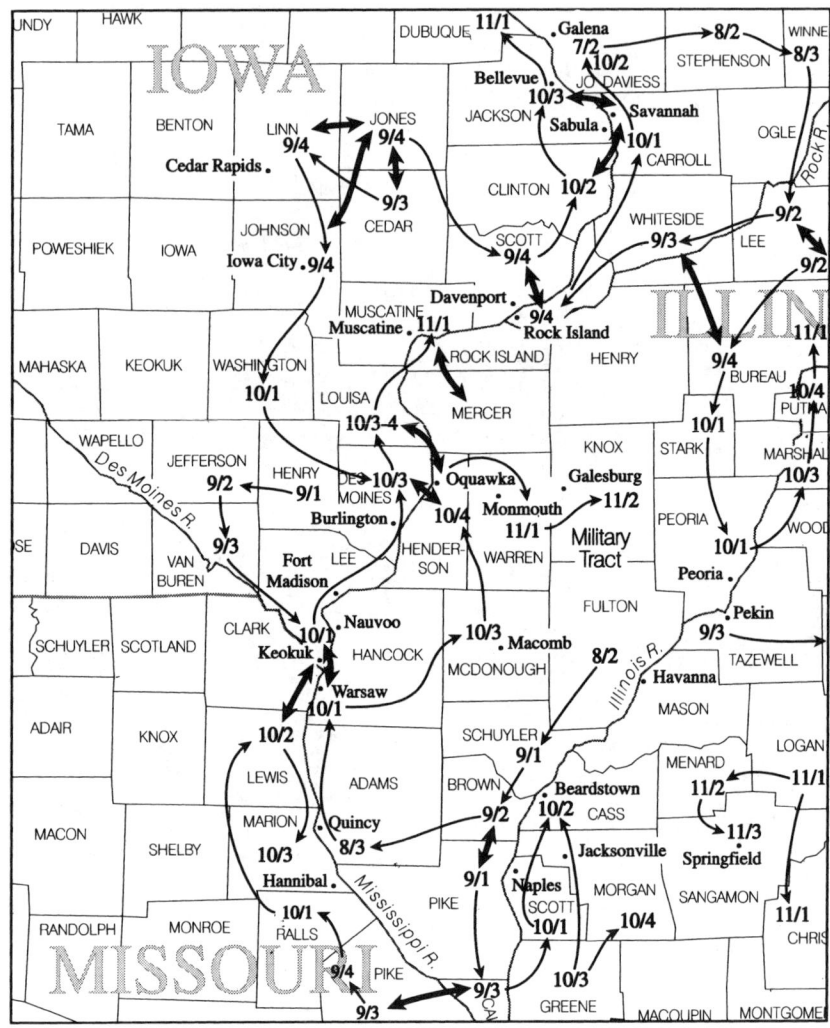

Figure 14. Circuit convergences in fall 1841 circuit court schedules.

than others from outside their circuit, and thus may have practiced in the circuit from which that case came (see Appendix 2). Though one could try a case from a circuit other than one's home circuit as part of a temporary partnership or correspondent arrangement with a lawyer from that circuit, cases from adjacent counties within the adjacent circuit probably indicate crossing-over. For example, among the 259 cases taken by lawyers from the First Circuit at the Supreme Court, 24 were from the Fifth Circuit, 21 from the adjacent Second Circuit, and 18 from the adjacent Eighth Circuit. Of these 63 cases, 39 were from counties bordering the First

Regional professional culture

Circuit – primarily, Adams, Brown, and Schuyler in the Fifth, Sangamon in the Eighth, and Montgomery and Madison in the Second Circuit. One lawyer in particular, James MacDougall, was active in both the Quincy and Alton courts. Similarly, half of the outside cases tried by lawyers from the Second Circuit were from the adjacent First and Third circuits. Orville Browning, Nehemiah Bushnell, and Archibald Williams from the Fifth Circuit also occasionally went over to the court session in Peoria County. J. Young Scammon, Giles Spring, and Justin Butterfield of Chicago continued their earlier practice of taking cases from the circuit courts in LaSalle, Putnam, Marshall, and Peoria counties between 1835 and 1850. Butterfield also maintained contacts with Galena and Freeport, suggesting that he continued to visit the circuit court session there as well. Meanwhile, Usher F. Linder of Coles County, in the Fourth Circuit, apparently made regular visits to the courts in the adjacent Eighth and somewhat farther afield in the First and Second circuits.[101]

A smaller case load and a smaller coterie of lawyers made the practice of "visiting" much less prevalent in early Iowa (see Appendix 3). Most of the lawyers who tried cases from the First Territorial District crossed over a few times to adjacent Louisa County, but only two ventured so far as Muscatine or Scott counties. Similarly, two Davenport lawyers crossed over from the Third District to hear cases in Cedar or Muscatine. After the division of Iowa into four circuits, crossing-over occurred predominantly between the older riverside circuits and the new interior ones. Jonathan C. Hall was the only lawyer from the First District regularly to cross over into the new Third District in Jefferson, Van Buren, and Keokuk counties to compete with the several lawyers who handled most of the cases there. In contrast, because there were only two lawyers in the new Fourth Circuit, most of the second circuit lawyers – including W. G. Woodward, Stephen Wichler, and John Cook – took on a couple of cases each between 1846 and 1850.

Each individual lawyer set his circuit within the context of the circuit geography around him, a decision that determined with whom he would network in the regional and state bar. Earlier on, when circuits were larger, crossing-over and therefore contact among lawyers from a wider territory was more common. The geography of the circuit itself provided contacts to a wider network. As circuits narrowed in size and case loads increased, however, those lawyers able to cross over and visit other circuits declined, therefore decreasing the number of contacts and narrowing the range of one's legal acquaintance. Judge Caton noted this ironic shift from wide-ranging lawyers to more circumscribed realms as the number of lawyers increased, remarking that circuit lawyers were "few at first, but with the increase in population and business their numbers increased, while their theaters of action became more circumscribed."[102] Though Joseph Gillespie of the Second Circuit did not like the narrowing of his circuit, he understood the pressures that were causing it: "I dislike, of course, to lose any of the counties in the circuit as it always affords one pleasure to meet old friends in them. But as the country increases in population and commerce, the suits become more numerous and complicated and it requires more time for examination and reflection to decide cases correctly."[103]

By the 1850s the work of "visiting lawyers" tended to only involve "special retainers and . . . important cases," and the number of lawyers visiting other circuits declined.[104] Whenever a court session was held in an adjacent county, those lawyers who were willing to travel thirty to forty miles would make the crossover. Thus, while crossing-over contacts and activity in the 1830s seemed to establish the foundation of a regional network, the more circumscribed activity of the 1840s concentrated legal practice back on the circuit, focusing the attention of ambitious local lawyers on establishing a local reputation and building case loads. In the 1840s the path to a broader network of skill and power was through the circuit courts. There one demonstrated knowledge, talent, and skill by practicing law. By increasing the numbers of cases one tried, one could acquire a special reputation as a "circuit rider," but most important, one dramatically increased the chances that any number of the cases one tried would be appealed to the state supreme court.

At the state supreme court

Rising out of these local and circuit legal fraternities, those lucky few from within the coterie of circuit riders who tried cases in which an appeal was made would be required to travel to the state supreme court. To do so was to travel not only the often great physical distance to the court, but also to step into the vortex of a regional process of elite aggregation, in which nearly everyone who had achieved some local prominence interacted, networked, and competed for cases and also for power and influence in a much more cutthroat, higher stakes venue. Not only did cases at the supreme court hold out the chance to make a contribution to establishing a law or legal principle, and thus enhancing one's reputation across the state, but they also presented the possibility of broadening one's practice, solidifying one's professional standing, and increasing one's political prospects and economic opportunities, all of which increased one's chance for an appointment to the higher echelons of justice in the state, nation, or territories. Traveling to the state capital or to the metropolis also allowed one to engage with the larger political issues of the day by observing state government and to hobnob – for political advantage or merely society – with the membership of both the house and senate, as well as the leaders of the state political parties. Through such contacts, one could establish a position within a broader state or regional political or social elite and thus draw on the resources of the region rather than just those of one's locality. By broadening one's relations and contacts, therefore, one enhanced the potential for further professional and economic opportunities upon which one's social mobility would, in time, depend.

The aggregating dynamics of the supreme court sessions and, indirectly, the structure and distribution of power within the regional professional, political, and social networks that developed around them varied with the frequency and timing of the court sessions. Balancing the practical need before 1840 simply to bring together enough cases in any one year to make a court session worthwhile and the republican desire – rooted in an anxiety about centralized power – to decentralize justice and bring it directly to the people – as embodied in the circuit system –

Regional professional culture

Illinois and Iowa during the 1840s gradually moved from a centralized supreme court system with one annual session at the state or territorial capital to a decentralized system in which they held several supreme court sessions each year across the state. In Illinois, the supreme court sessions moved, with the capital, to Springfield in 1839. For two years they held semiannual terms of court in July and December. When they reorganized the court in 1841, they expected the supreme court judges to ride the circuit. Thus summer terms were abandoned and the court was concentrated into one winter term often lasting several weeks from mid-December into early February. The judicial reform of 1848 again concentrated the judiciary in the hands of a few judges, but then dispersed the court sessions to Ottawa, Mount Vernon, and Springfield, a practice that continued through the Civil War. The scheduling of the Iowa supreme court followed a similar pattern, except that litigation was not sufficient to warrant two sessions a year during the territorial period. Therefore there was one term a year in 1846 and two in 1847. In 1848 Iowa, like Illinois, decentralized the sessions of the supreme court, holding sessions in a circuit that went from Burlington to Ottumwa, Iowa City, and Dubuque or Davenport at one-month intervals from May to July.

Between 1841 and 1848 the supreme court at Springfield drew in lawyers from across the state and region. The territorial supreme courts of Iowa at Burlington in 1838 through 1841 and at Iowa City from 1843 through 1846 were similarly centralized. The impact of the shifting patterns of court sessions is evident in the number of lawyers who attended the supreme court in both Illinois and Iowa between 1838 and 1850 (see Table 6). In Illinois, the sessions of December 1844 and 1846 attracted the most lawyers, with 1842, 1843, and 1845 close behind. With the dispersal of the courts to various venues through the year, the number of lawyers at Springfield declined, in 1848 by 20 percent, and by 1849 by another 10 percent, dropping, by 1850, to less than half the number of lawyers present in the peak year of 1846. A similar pattern is evident in Iowa, where more lawyers arrived at the centralized territorial supreme court in 1843, 1844, and 1845 than in any other year.[105] This concentration of lawyers was also reflected in the numbers of cases tried in each court session (see Table 6). Again, the peak years in Illinois were between 1841 and 1846, with December 1845 session being the busiest, followed by 1842, 1843, 1846, and 1844. In Iowa, not surprisingly, 1843, 1844, and 1845 were the years with the most crowded dockets.

Lawyers who appeared at the supreme court in 1845 and 1846 at Springfield and 1844 and 1845 at Burlington – the peak years of case loads and lawyers present – most intensely experienced the aggregating forces of centralization and forged a legal "power" elite which dominated the supreme court and state politics for a decade or more and would form the foundation of a regional middle class. Contemporaries were aware of the importance of these annual gatherings of lawyers in making connections, solidifying friendships, strengthening political connections, and gradually creating a power elite. From a local perspective, interaction with this regional elite enhanced one's social prestige, deepened one's support, and estab-

Provincial lives

Table 6. *Lawyers present and case loads at Illinois supreme court sessions, 1838–1850*

Supreme court session	Lawyers present	Cases
12/38 Vandalia	46	107
7/39 Springfield	30	54
12/39	51	131
6/40	65 (6)	158
12/40	63 (7)	172
7/41	28	73
12/41	55	202 (7)
12/42	75 (3)	264 (2)
12/43	70 (4)	251 (3)
12/44	79 (1)	234 (5)
12/45	66 (5)	261 (1)
12/46	79 (1)	242 (4)
12/47	56 (8)	143
12/48	54	166
6/49 Ottawa	25	75
11/49 Mt. Vernon	17	30
12/49 Springfield	44	197
6/50 Ottawa	55	176
11/50 Mt. Vernon	32	89
12/50 Springfield	36	222 (6)

Note: ( ) indicates rank.
Sources: J. Young Scammon, ed., *Reports of the Cases Argued in the Supreme Court of the State of Illinois*, vols. 1–4 (Chicago: Callaghan and Company, 1880); Charles Gilman, ed., *Reports of the Cases Argued and Determined in the Supreme Court of the State of Illinois*, vols. 5–10 (Chicago: E. B. Myers and Company, 1886); E. Peck, ed., *Reports of Cases Determined in the Supreme Court of the State of Illinois*, vols. 11 and 12 (Chicago: Callaghan and Company, 1881).

lished one socially and professionally within a new framework. Whether one went back to one's town or the circuit to practice law, began a political career, or received an appointment, the lawyers who attended court in these peak years became part of a regional legal fraternity associated with the state bar.

In law, one built a reputation through litigation. Case loads, therefore, provide evidence of a lawyer's legal proficiency plus his social, political, and professional connections and power. Ranking lawyers by their case loads in the peak years of state supreme court activity provides a barometer of their reputation and influence among lawyers from the different circuits. Intriguingly, by 1845 and 1846 Abraham Lincoln had parlayed his experience in getting cases at the Illinois supreme court during his partnership with Stephen T. Logan (which ended amicably the year before) to become the busiest lawyer there. He edged out his former, more experienced partner – known for his prodigious case loads – by a margin of thirty-four to

Regional professional culture

twenty-five cases. Lincoln, who made his first appearance in 1840, was one among several younger lawyers – including Onslow Peters, Justin Butterfield, Lyman Trumbull, James McDougall, Nehemiah Bushnell, Elihu N. Powell, and Elihu Washburne – who, between 1839 and 1843, overshadowed the cohort who, though the same age, had practiced for years at the court – Edward D. Baker, Murray McConnell, Archibald Williams, and Orville H. Browning – and acquired a significant percentage of the cases tried in 1845 and 1846. Lincoln and Logan together tried 10 percent of all the cases brought before the Illinois supreme court in 1845 and 1846. Together with the case loads of Onslow Peters, Justin Butterfield, and Lyman Trumbull, the five busiest lawyers tried 25 percent of all cases, though the busiest half of the lawyers present ended up trying only about half the cases brought before the court.

Lincoln and Logan gained their advantage not only through a vigorous practice in the Eighth Circuit – which Lincoln would continue with his next partner William Herndon with such success that during the fifties Lincoln and Herndon tried on average 20 percent of all the cases in the Sangamon county circuit court[106] – but also from their advantageous location in Springfield. This not only enabled them to take a lion's share of local cases coming up before the court, but also many cases from other circuits where they had established correspondent partners or knew lawyers who were unable or unwilling to come to Springfield to try a case themselves. Stephen T. Logan covered cases from the First, Second, Fifth, Sixth, and Ninth circuits (see Appendix 2). That 54 of the 103 cases Lincoln tried at the court between 1840 and 1846 were from outside the Eighth Circuit shows that he was also, according to one historian, "'a lawyer's lawyer' whose services were in great demand by the members of his profession."[107] He was especially active with cases from the Fourth Circuit, where he had a partnership with Ward Lamon Hill of Danville between 1852 and 1858 and tried fourteen cases for between 1840 and 1850.[108] Lincoln also covered cases for lawyers in Madison County, Jo Daviess County, and across the Seventh Circuit. Among those he took cases for during the 1840s were Archibald Williams, Orville Browning, Nehemiah Bushnell, Buckner S. Morris, William Martin, Onslow Peters, Elihu N. Powell, and Charles Ballance (a Peoria "town lawyer"), favors occasionally reciprocated when he asked local lawyers to continue cases he could no longer try at the circuit level.[109]

Lincoln and Logan's advantage is even more evident in view of the number of cases tried by lawyers from other circuits. Lincoln and Logan's practice skewed the degree to which the lawyers of the Eighth Circuit were represented at the court. Only one other Eighth Circuit lawyer, Lincoln's neighbor, J. C. Conkling, tried cases at the supreme court. Nevertheless these three lawyers tried more cases than any other three lawyers from any other circuit. Besides the impact of Lincoln's and Logan's practices, however, the traditional dominance of about thirty lawyers from the First, Second, Fifth, and Seventh circuits – each of whom tried from forty to fifty cases – clearly emerges (see Appendix 2). The limited role lawyers from the remote Third, Fourth, and Sixth circuits played in the supreme court indicates the degree to which distance affected case loads.[110]

193

Provincial lives

So dominant was this group's control that only about ten among the 113 lawyers who arrived at Springfield to try cases before the supreme court between 1840 and 1845 moved from riding the circuit to trying more than a handful of cases before the state's highest tribunal. As noted, Lincoln was the dominant figure among these newcomers. Also from the Eighth, Albert T. Bledsoe (a partner of Edward D. Baker),[111] J. C. Conkling (Lincoln's neighbor), and John T. Stuart (Lincoln's first law partner) broke into the elite group of supreme court lawyers in 1841 and 1843. From the Fifth Circuit came R. S. Blackwell, Julius Manning, and Andrew Johnstone, Browning's friend from Kentucky. Thompson Campbell arrived to try to increase the Sixth's limited role at the supreme court in 1841. Madison Y. Johnson and Elihu B. Washburne joined him in 1843. Meanwhile Halsey O. Merriman and Elihu N. Powell joined their legal brethren Purple and Peters from the Ninth Circuit.[112]

The smaller cohort of nineteen lawyers who appeared in the Iowa territorial supreme court sessions of 1844 and 1845 had a similar degree of control and success. Of them, the busiest lawyer, Jonathan C. Hall, future supreme court justice of Iowa, tried 10 percent of all cases. The five busiest lawyers tried over half of all the cases at the court. Among these – J. C. Hall, Ralph P. Lowe, Stephen Wichler, Serranus C. Hastings, and David Rorer – one would serve as U.S. District Attorney for Iowa, and three were elevated to the state supreme court. Only David Rorer never served in a public office. Overall, more than half of both the nineteen lawyers present in 1844 and 1845 and the lawyers of the bar of 1836, as calculated by Theodore S. Parvin, went on to hold an appointed or elective office.[113]

To arrive at the supreme court was, therefore, to step into another level of professional activity and to meet and practice law among men who operated on a state, regional, and even national level. Elihu Washburne clearly sensed this when, in December 1843, he walked into the supreme court library that was next to the court room in the new state capitol building and met Abraham Lincoln holding forth as he always did, "sitting in a cane-bottom chair leaning up against the partition, his feet on the round of the chair, and surrounded by many listeners" telling and trading stories with the other lawyers in the room.[114] Among them was Thompson Campbell, another Galenan who Washburne believed to be a "a man of very decided talent . . . but . . . a perfect drunkard and a gambler" as well as a "bully and a blackguard." He admired him nonetheless, because, like Benjamin Mills before him, Campbell had used his locally well-known conviviality and wit to gain a reputation amid greater competition in Springfield as "a brilliant man and a celebrated wit" and become a "strong personal friend" of Lincoln's, so much so that the two "were never so happy as when together and listening to the stories of each other" before a delighted audience of their legal brothers. Lincoln was such a fixture of the law library coterie that when he was absent for any reason, Washburne admitted that "there was a great void."[115]

The "set of fellows"[116] which gathered around Abraham Lincoln in the law library after the supreme court sessions in Springfield in the middle 1840s – and thus the structure of the Illinois legal fraternity – was a hierarchy of influence and power based on achievement, political action, and longevity. The fourteen lawyers who usually attended Lincoln's evening "levees" in the supreme court library in the statehouse, or the forty lawyers who were present at the supreme court in 1845 or 1846, had distinguished themselves by the number of their visits to Springfield, the number of cases they had tried and won in the supreme court, their record of political activity, and the number of political offices – and thus political influence – they had held.

Washburne, was, of course, both a late arrival and an infrequent visitor to this inner circle of men who gathered at the library. Though he recalled Thompson Campbell and Lincoln as a focal point there, his own limited experience at the court shaped his recollections. In fact, Lincoln and Campbell first met only in 1841, a year after Lincoln's first appearance at the court. They subsequently attended the court simultaneously in only three other years – 1843, 1845, and 1846 – which happened to be three of the only four years that Washburne had the time to attend the court. The record indicates that it is unlikely that these sixteen men were ever together in the supreme court library. That fourteen of the sixteen were present when Washburne first attended the court in December 1843 – O. B. Ficklin and Thomas Drummond being unaccounted for – attests to the impact of Washburne's first impression on his more general recollection (see Table 7). Lincoln, a newcomer himself, had attended the court four years in a row and would attend the court every year between 1840 and 1850 except 1847 and 1848, when he was in Congress in Washington. Norman Purple and James MacDougall were as frequent visitors to the court as Lincoln. Joseph Gillespie, Lyman Trumbull, Archibald Williams, and Orville Browning were, however, the journeymen among the lawyers of the supreme court bar, having been present every year from the arrival of the supreme court in Springfield in 1839 through 1850. Orville Browning began attending the court in Vandalia in 1835. His Quincy colleague, Archibald Williams, had first attended the supreme court in Vandalia in 1832, giving him seniority of the supreme court bar. For this record the members of the bar elected him chair of the informal precursor of the Illinois Bar Association, made up of lawyers in practice at the supreme court who occasionally met to attend to court matters and the legal profession and issue resolutions in honor of any member who passed away.[117]

By 1843, the structural reality of the law library coterie was that Lincoln, Purple, and MacDougall had emerged to join Browning, Williams, Trumbull, and Gillespie as the most frequent visitors to the state supreme court. Equally persistent through the mid-forties were John J. Hardin, Edward D. Baker,[118] and Stephen T. Logan. Likewise, Judges Stephen A. Douglas and James Shields were present every year through mid-decade.

Washburne recognized that not only shared professional status but also friendships made during their public service as representatives and senators in the Illinois state assembly in the late 1830s bonded this group of men together. Lincoln, of course, was elected to the state legislature in 1834 where he met Orlando B. Ficklin and Archibald Williams, the state senator from Quincy. In the next assembly, Lincoln met and became friends with Stephen A. Douglas, James Shields, John J.

Table 7. Network analysis of the law library coterie around Abraham Lincoln at the Illinois supreme court, 1839–1850

1839–1850	1839	1840	1841	1842	1843	1844	1845	1846	1847	1848	1849	1850		
A. Lincoln (W)[b]		X	X	X	X	X	X	X			X	X	9	93
I. N. Arnold (W)				X	X	X		X	X		X		6	
E. D. Baker (W)		X	X	X	X	X							6	
O. H. Browning (W)	X	X	X	X	X	X	X	X	X	X	X	X	12	95
T. Campbell (D)[c]	X		X	X	X	J							4	
S. A. Douglas (D)	X	X	J		J								6	
O. B. Ficklin (D)		X	X	X	X								3	
J. Gillespie (W)	X	X		X	X	X	X	X	X	X	X	X	12	57
J. J. Hardin (W)	X		X	X	X	X	X						7	
J. A. MacDougall (D)	X	X	X	X	X	X	X	X	X			X	9	74
N. H. Purple (W)		X	X	X	X	X	J	J	J				9	
J. Shields (D)	X	X	J	J	X	J	J						7	20
L. Trumbull (D)	X	X	X	X	X	X	X	X	X	J	J	X	12	78
E. B. Washburne (W)					X		X	X	X				4	
A. Williams (W)		X	X	X	X	X	X	X	X	X	X	X	11	74
Totals[d]	7	11	13	13	14	12	12	11	8	4	5	7		

[a] (X) in attendance; (J) judge.
[b] (W) Whig.
[c] (D) Democrat.
[d] Total includes Lincoln.

Sources: J. Young Scammon, ed., *Reports of the Cases Argued in the Supreme Court of the State of Illinois,* vols. 1–4 (Chicago: Callaghan and Company, 1879, 1880, 1886); Charles Gilman, ed., *Reports of the Cases Argued and Determined in the Supreme Court of the State of Illinois,* vols. 5–10 (Chicago: E. B. Myers and Company, 1886); Ebenezer Peck, ed., *Reports of Cases Determined in the Supreme Court of the State of Illinois,* vols. 11–12 (Chicago: Callaghan and Company, 1881).

Hardin, and Edward D. Baker in the legislature, and Orville H. Browning in the senate. It was at the legislative session of 1836–1837 in Vandalia that Usher F. Linder, as a member of the house, made twenty-seven friends, among whom were Lincoln, Douglas, Shields, Williams, Hardin, Browning, and Minshall.[119] Browning, Hardin, and Lincoln went on to become especially good friends and associates from 1836 to 1840, when they served together in the state assembly.[120] After 1840 Browning returned to Quincy, while Lincoln continued to serve as a legislator until 1842 and Baker until 1844 as a senator. The election of Lyman Trumbull, Joseph Gillespie, and Thomas Drummond to the state legislature in 1840 also drew each of them, the latter two as Whigs, into Lincoln and Hardin's group. Therefore, among the fifteen other members of the law library coterie whom Washburne encountered in December 1843, eleven had previously been to the statehouse – though only two continued to serve – and had met each other and become friends with the two longest serving members of the group, John J. Hardin and Abraham Lincoln. When Elihu Washburne walked into the law library in the state capitol building in December 1843, he was, therefore, stepping into the center of a legal and political fraternity whose members had aspired, quite literally, to define the legal profession in Illinois, forge a new political party across the state, and help run, as much as they could from a minority party role, the government of Illinois.

For most of these men the path to the supreme court and the statehouse had moved symbiotically along parallel or intertwined trajectories. Supported by the members of the local bar, their friends nominated them and they canvassed the town or county while practicing in the local or circuit courts. There, practice in the courts prepared them for appearances before the supreme court at Vandalia or Springfield, while election to office sent some to the statehouse. In the new state capitol building in Springfield, the legislature and supreme court sometimes sat concurrently in sessions across the hall from each other, and some members apparently moved back and forth between sitting in the house and preparing and presenting cases to the supreme court. For many lawyers, experience in the parallel world of politics from the local, district, to the state level further exposed them to the dynamic forces of regional aggregation.

"Brethren of the bar"

Whether in town, on the circuit, or at the supreme court, the social and cultural construction of the bar, situated between male subcultures, the booster ethos, and the gentility system, forged the connections, bonds, and shared values and attitudes through which a regional society formed. The transference of the structure, behavior, and values of the local bars to the county, circuit, and regional level played a central role in the process of diffusion, intersection, and combination – drawing elements from male subcultures, the booster ethos, and gentility – through which a fraternal, secular, professional middle-class society and culture would gain ascendancy across the antebellum Middle West.

At the local, circuit, and regional level, lawyers sharing a common educational background and intellectual and civic values sought to turn the occupational culture of the bar into a legal fraternity, and a subset of both the local male subculture and genteel society. One one level, collegiality was cultivated by the professional and personal self-consciousness of being a lawyer which lawyers were acculturated to during their education. For many law was a "distinctive [masculine] endeavor" which applied the rule of law and a gentlemanly, middle-class moral code based on responsibility and honor to order an immoral world. The competition among practitioners of the law was, therefore, muted by a spirit or culture of occupational comradery and affinity as fellow litigators and "gatekeepers against social disorder" combatting the world.[121] Stephen Hempstead, nephew of Susan Hempstead Gratiot, and Charles and William Hempstead, who became a lawyer in Dubuque, and later Governor of Iowa, though only twenty-one, expressed cogently this fusion of professional practice, morality, and social order:

I have commenced the study of a profession which requires the deep and profound reflection of the mind, an undivided attention and a firm unshaken determination to push forward and surmount every impediment. The law is a profession which . . . must lead a *man* to *honor* and renown [author's emphasis]. It is in my opinion one of the most noble of all professions for it teaches the first principles of nature and lays down rules of conduct, which must control the wickedness of mankind. In one word, it is the pedestal on which stands governments, kingdoms, and empires. When law is overturned, that moment does civil government cease to exist and then rages the violent and almost ungovernable spirit of mankind. Then must that inundation of violence and passion bear away upon its surface all the glorious relicks [sic] of peace, order, and happiness.

Under this view of the law, and with a deep reverence for its authority, I am determined to acquire a full and complete knowledge of it, in order that I may be fitted to act my part upon the theater of life, but how that part will be acted remains to be seen.

I have laid this down as a principle always to cast my eyes to the loftiest pinnacle [of] fame . . . for an individual who aspires to nothing, will eventually gain nothing.[122]

Though common professional values naturally bonded all lawyers, the processes of the socializing them into the fraternal ethos of the bar, with its distinctive practices, behavior, and rituals, occurred during each lawyer's work and daily interaction with other lawyers and judges in the courts and law offices of any town. Though the dynamics would vary from the town to the circuit to the state supreme court, because of different physical circumstances and the different types of practice and litigation, the transference or diffusion of analogous practices, procedures, behavior, and rituals from one level to the next by those who followed litigation from local to the state courts reflects the dynamics of a regional process of aggregation.

The central fact of physical proximity whether in town, on the circuit, or visiting the supreme court shaped bar culture. In town, each lawyer acted within a group of ten to thirty men who shared a set of professional standards, ethics, and values, as well as courthouses, offices, meeting places, and the demand of a limited clientele base. Continual interaction in one's daily work and social routines in the shared, yet segmented, public and semi-public spaces of the courthouse and its court rooms, law offices, and library or in the streets, boarding houses, or taverns inevitably cultivated familiarity with each other. Each individual established his identity, while scrutinizing one's colleagues based on their character, talent, and skill to determine their status, identifying friends or enemies, and maintaining among all the brothers of the bar an agreed-upon code of behavior and ethics.

The dynamics of the process of local structuration and socialization that occurred within this public space are evident in almost any lawyer's efforts to situate himself socially, professionally, and politically within the culture of the local bar. To maneuver and succeed in this world of men, where character and reputation affected one's business, required one to hone the skill of determining a man's character or "signifying" him, from observation, personal interaction, credentials, or reputation, and then to interact with that man accordingly, though still within the guidelines of genteel interaction. As Elihu B. Washburne, who possessed a talent for thumbnail sketches, once remarked, about someone that he "never knew a man who could so readily and accurately take the measure of another man," or as Joseph Gillespie said of Usher F. Linder, that "he could penetrate a character at a glance," was, in this male culture, a high compliment.[123] Lawyers' discourse, like that of most politicians during the 1830s and 1840s, was, as a result, full of thumbnail sketches of others in the profession, efforts to define oneself by defining others and to clarify one's own status and character (if only to oneself, or one's correspondent) by situating one's place in the local bar and male subculture. Such sketches were, of course, critical in the work lawyers did. Having an idea of one's legal opposition could shape the way one might try a case. In addition, character sketches, which identified a man among other men, were the raw material from which, through ironic renderings, nicknames were designated, though nicknames were not as prevalent among lawyers as they were among the "gentlemen" of male subculture as a whole (see Chapter 3).

Elihu Washburne scrutinized the Galena bar, in 1840, while sitting at his desk in a court room in the Galena courthouse waiting for a case to be called. He socially assessed the members of the bar by dividing male society into different subcultures of gentlemen and ruffians. Through character sketches of the other lawyers in town from the viewpoint of a "moral gentleman," Washburne fit each lawyer into the taxonomy of regional stereotypes, which influenced how he assessed their legal skills and politics. He did this not only to scope out the competition but also to identify a potential partner. Charles S. Hempstead, "one of the crack lawyers of the place," "an old lawyer [at age forty-four] of good ability and good standing" and "a very fine clever man," was at the top of Washburne's list. Thomas Drummond, the lawyer from Maine who had rebuffed him a few weeks before, Washburne styled a "tolerable good lawyer, and a man of decent talents and great industry, and [a] Whig," and Artemus L. Holmes, "a young man about a year from New Hampshire" appeared, in Washburne's eyes "to be a pretty clever fellow." These lawyers were, like himself, New England moral gentlemen and, except Hempstead, fellow Whigs.

The rest of Galena's lawyers apparently lived on the other side of a line separating New England moral gentlemen like himself from southern gentlemen, Democrats or "locofocos," or men who were not gentlemen, encompassing both country lawyers and ruffians who, as members of the male subculture, fell short of his moral, legal, and political standards. John Turney was "an old cock" and though "a good judge of law" was "an unprincipled man" and a "violent old loco." Joseph Pendleton Hoge, a Virginian, he considered "a good lawyer and man of genius and talent" but a "warm loco who gambles and drinks some . . . and an 'overbearing aristocrat,' . . . very apt to crowd." Thompson Campbell, an Irishman, was "a young man and great locofoco gun and candidate for legislature. A man of very decided talent, both natural and acquired, but horribly dissipated, a perfect drunkard, gambler, bully, and blackguard." Still others Washburne disparaged by demeaning their manhood, calling one a "weak sister" "about to abandon the law" and another "no lawyer at all and not much else." Perceiving these men as potential adversaries who were "determined to frighten and bully him out of the field," Washburne vowed that he was prepared to "stand up and defend myself at all hazards," telling his brother that if any of them tried to lay violent hands on him, he would "blow [their] liver out," for in such a place as Galena, he believed, there was "no other way." "A man must stand up for his own, or he is a gone case."[124]

Though Washburne, as young aggressor at the local bar, sought at this stage to differentiate himself from and defend himself against these gentlemen, and carry on with his own business, he gradually aligned his behavior with the more dissimulating style of the male subculture. Like all lawyers, politicians, and military men, he would gradually learn to be a little more indirect and pretend to be one of the boys, a brother in the law, and reluctantly admit that they were a "decent set of fellows." In behaving this way, Washburne situated himself as a lawyer within a subset, distinguished by their titles "Esquire" as "gentleman" within the male subculture. Though he tended to avoid the male subculture at home, and, indeed, his significations supported his desire to associate only with other moral New England gentlemen, he did admit playing the part of a "hail fellow well met" while on the circuit.[125]

The membership of the local bar, whether the Galena bar outlined by Washburne in 1840, the lawyers among the Keokuk male subculture of the 1840s and 1850s, the well-known local bar of Springfield, Illinois, during Lincoln's time, or the prominent bar of Burlington, Iowa, as described in memoirs, reminiscences, and autobiographies a generation later, was almost formulaically described as a taxonomy of professional men, described in much the same language, though in different combinations and with an eye for specific and unique character traits. To be a well-rounded and complete microcosm of regional or national culture, every local bar needed to have its full range of stereotypical figures. On one side were usually the New England moral gentlemen, imbued with the values of genteel urban middle-class culture. Among these were always a few more secular, convivial New England gentlemen, one or two of whom eventually reformed themselves. Opposite them was always a contingent of southern gentlemen or "aristocrats" who eschewed many middle-class values and attitudes. Interspersed with the southerners were often one or two country lawyers who were not really gentlemen. Between these two larger groups were a few men from the Middle Atlantic states or from southern Ohio, Indiana, or even northern Kentucky (especially if they were Whigs who eschewed slavery) who occupied the middle ground of the subculture, mediating between the two and playing, with the New England convivial gentlemen, a central role in the creation of a professional culture among the members of the bar (see Appendix 4 and Chapter 3).

Among these men, certain personality types and stock characters from regional "cultural hearths" in the East invariably played the same roles in city after city. The bar in every major town had (or felt it had to have) a full cast of types and related characters. Every bar had its great orator, political manager, judge, "hail fellow," impartial mediator, paragon of virtue, spiritual leader, and haughty aristocrat. Among such "gentlemen of the old school" were those from the First Families of Virginia, Kentucky gentlemen, and Knickerbockers. Among the more practical "old school" types were usually the local antiquarian, folklorist, collector, scholar, literary or artistic gentleman, confirmed bachelor, and connoisseur of food, wine, or liquor. Each bar also had its storytellers, pranksters, and practical jokers, as well as its tragic soul (perhaps a widower), its sad and unsuccessful man, irascible troublemaker, and its true eccentric or "sui generis" type whom they could not categorize. Finally, each bar had its heavy drinker, Lothario, or violent ruffian. The range of social types and characters within a local bar – which correlated with the number of nicknames – was a kind of barometer reflecting how much indirection and dissimulation they needed to vent social and professional tensions. The extent of a bar's cast of characters also paralleled the richness and vigor of the local convivial male subculture and the degree to which they needed it to maintain social order. Rather than a picturesque background, the culture of the bar provided the emotional, moral, and social support that gave meaning and direction to the actions of each of its members, defining them as brothers within a fraternity of professional gentlemen (see Appendix 4).

For the members of the bar who rode the circuit, these tendencies were intensified by the shared experience of traveling, eating, sleeping, and relaxing together. Circuit lawyers became "of necessity, more social and better acquainted with each other" than lawyers of a later day, and "their mutual hardships begot a brotherly attachment for each other akin to that which a soldier feels for his comrade."[126] The members of the core group of lawyers and judges gradually became friends and brothers in a fraternity based on "mutual acquaintance" and, finally, a "sort of a family to itself."[127] Elihu Washburne recognized the intensity of socialization as one of the "great features" of the annual meeting of the supreme court at Springfield in the 1840s. There "lawyers from every part of the State had to follow their cases for final adjudication, and they gathered from all the principal towns of the State. The occasion served as a reunion of a large number of the ablest men in the State . . . bringing them together . . . much closer than they ever have been since" and developing an intense sense of "esprit de corps."[128] Washburne noted that "coming from long distances and suffering great privations in their journeys, they usually remained a considerable time in attendance upon the court."[129] Often they would stay in Springfield to also attend the semi-annual term of the U.S. district court held in Springfield during the 1840s.

Provincial lives

Indeed, one's arrival, often "more dead than alive," and meeting, for the first time, eminent lawyers about which one had heard so much from other circuits were significant moments in the process of one's socialization into the court bar. When Washburne first met Gustave Koerner in Chicago 1852, "bespattered with mud," he seemed to be "tired out," having, in Koerner's eyes, a "rugged, uncouth" look, "blunt in his speech" and "rather unmannerly," but, nevertheless, "full of confidence and energy and hard sense."[130] In another meeting among peers with reputations that preceded them, "the courtly and polite" Orville Browning met the "unpolished and irreverent" John Wentworth of Chicago in Bloomington in 1856. Browning began politely, "I have never had the pleasure of meeting you, but I have heard much of you." In response to which Wentworth blurted out: "Damned much against me!" which Lincoln, who was nearby, thought a particularly "comical" comeback in such a ritualized exchange within the network.[131] In 1846, Elihu Washburne "stopped at the American, the crack [sic] house" in Springfield, exclaiming, "God save the crack!" because there he met "some of the best Whigs . . . you ever met anywhere," including Justin Butterfield of Chicago.[132] Orville Browning first met David Davis, and then roomed with him, in December 1850. Gustave Koerner met and also roomed with John D. Caton in the 1846–1847 session.[133] They and the other lawyers present no doubt met Joseph Gillespie, the eminent lawyer from the Second District, state representative until 1842 and state senator after 1846 who "night after night" told stories, particularly about his old friend the convivial Benjamin Mills of Galena, in the "hotels of Springfield."[134]

Every lawyer remembered when they first arrived at the supreme court. Isaac Arnold recalled that Thomas Drummond, David Davis, and Archibald Williams made the trip to Vandalia as early as 1836.[135] Usher F. Linder remembered meeting Justin Butterfield and Giles Spring of Chicago at the supreme court at Vandalia in 1836–1837.[136] Williams, John M. Palmer recalled, was "frequently on attendance at the Springfield courts" through the thirties and forties.[137] By 1837, Lincoln, Joseph Gillespie, and Lyman Trumbull made their appearances at the court. James A. MacDougall and J. Young Scammon appeared the next year. By 1839 Arnold noted that "among the leading practitioners in this Court, held in Springfield, were Logan, Lincoln, Baker, Trumbull, Butterfield, and Collins, Spring and Goodrich, Cowles and Krum, Davis, Hardin, Browning, and Archy Williams." By the June term of 1840, Isaac Arnold was in the "habit" of attending the court, and was later "proud to find my own humble name on the record among these great lawyers and advocates."[138] On 9 December 1841 Arnold "entered the bar of the Supreme Court" and "from that time until his retirement he was a conspicuous figure, and his name was familiar in all the courts of the State."[139] Elihu Washburne first attended court in December 1843 and recalled that he made the annual trip there from Galena for "many years," though his name appears on the court dockets only through 1848.[140] Washburne recalled that he "had known" Isaac Arnold "as a gentleman and a lawyer" and met him "frequently at sessions of the Supreme Court at Springfield and Ottawa."[141] Gustave Koerner remembered staying the entire winter of 1847–1848 in Springfield "assisting in holding the Supreme Court."[142]

Regional professional culture

While travel and lodging on the circuit and at the state supreme court may have taken away from the dynamics of the process of situating oneself among one's colleagues, extended periods together in uncomfortable circumstances may have made up for it. Every "cavalcade" of lawyers and judges who traveled the circuits across the region on their regularly appointed semiannual rounds from session to session experienced "mutual hardships" and "uncomfortable experiences." "Mud stories" of impassable roads or fording streams and rivers, stories of poor and crowded accommodations, sleeping in "omnibuses" – dormitories made up in the spare room of a tavern[143] – and tales of bizarre circumstances for holding court, whether out of doors or in rough "log house" courthouses, became among lawyers the raw material from which they forged the "lore of the circuit."[144] Such stories interspersed with tales of frontier hardship attested to the heroic effort made by early lawyers and judges to extend the rule of law and civilization into a new county and region. Riding the circuit – both in the kind of law practiced, as well as in the privations suffered – tested the activist's "manly" qualities accorded so much importance among lawyers. The hardships of primitive conditions, the "promiscuousness [sic]" of shared accommodations and conveyances (a constant refrain),[145] and the pressures of intense competition among friends or adversaries in procedures that required absolute impartiality – all away from the influence of settled society – simply intensified the social pressures out of which male subcultures in towns emerged.

Lawyers traveling to the supreme court experienced a similar test of endurance. Arnold and Washburne recalled the difficult trips to the court from their remote parts of the state. Elihu Washburne in a recollection shuddered "to think of those dreadful stage rides" more than 300 miles on "horrible" roads, "occupying usually three days and four nights, traveling incessantly," through dreadful cold and snowstorms across uninhabited prairies, on which the rider might lose his way.[146] Isaac Arnold, traveling south on roads to the east about the same time, recalled similar December trips by coach which took up to "five days and nights, dragging drearily through the mud and sleet" attended by "an amount of discomfort, vexation, and annoyance . . . sufficient to exhaust the patience of [even] the most amiable" traveler.[147]

Enduring and surviving such trips alone gave attendance at the supreme court an air of significance and excitement. Once at Springfield or Iowa City, one scrambled for accommodations, which were generally better than those on the circuit. Though Lyman Trumbull, Democratic Secretary of State during 1843, all but took up residence in the new state capitol building at Springfield, writing to his brother: "The court meets here and all the business I do is within the building. [Therefore] I make use of one of the committee rooms in the State House as a sleeping-room, so you see I almost live in the State House, and am the only person who sleeps in it,"[148] most lawyers sought nearby hotels or boarding houses or lodged with friends. Nevertheless, as on the circuits, living arrangements at the court involved, early on, considerable comradery. Through December 1854, Mrs. Eno's boarding house was Orville Browning's residence of choice. This was a popular house among lawyers from Quincy and central Illinois. In 1850 Browning shared a room with David Davis and

Provincial lives

R. S. Blackwell. In 1852 Browning and his Quincy colleagues, Archibald Williams, Charles B. Lawrence, and Col. Calvin Warren shared his room, while Jackson Grimshaw and John Wood also lived in the house. David Smith of Jacksonville, Joseph Gillespie of Edwardsville, as well as Charles Hodges and James and William Brown all took lodgings at Mrs. Eno's. The following year the same three were "in room" together again.

When, however, Mrs. Eno "quit housekeeping" sometime before December 1854 the disappointed Browning was forced "to stop" at the City Hotel. By the next year he was more prepared and arranged to stay at the American House. The American House, by this time, was losing the position it had held in the 1840s as Springfield's "genteel" headquarters for the male subculture that surrounded the statehouse and the courts. Opened in November 1838 by a Boston hotel manager, its size and lavish interior decor, which included one of the first men's and ladies' parlors in the West, caused a sensation. Being near the statehouse it quickly became the unofficial "tavern" for the legislators, government workers, and, when in town, supreme court lawyers and judges. The American House became, therefore, a hotel to stay in and perhaps to take tea, but was no longer the "crack house" of Springfield. Browning stayed there every year from 1856 to 1860, yet each time he stayed for shorter stays.[149]

Except for Springfield's elegant state capitol building, the venue of law, in town, on the circuit, and at the capital was basic and nondescript. The built environment of this shared public space was, as in almost every town, plain, functional, and unrefined. Most of the early courthouses of the 1830s were "shambling great log houses" often two stories tall, "with one floor devoted to offices and the other to court and jury rooms" located near the center of town or on the central square – if one existed – and indistinguishable from the other small log and clapboard one- and two-room structures that characterized the region. Old, more developed towns, such as Galena, Dubuque, Quincy, and Fort Madison, soon afterward replaced these with stone and brick structures built in a simple "cheap modification"[150] of the Greek Revival style with front porches, pediments, and pillars, with court rooms located left and right of a central hall.[151] Some courthouses were adorned with a bell tower or cupola.[152] Others like the "large brick building" called "The Veranda" in Keokuk,[153] or in Springfield after 1845, were business blocks indistinguishable from commercial buildings and hotels and "devoid of distinction."[154]

Lawyers' offices were in the wooden and then the simple brick structures that, in the mid- to late forties, were constructed in towns across the region. Elihu Washburne considered himself "respectively situated" in two rooms on the second floor of a "partly log" building on the wharf at Galena, "with three windows and whitewashed walls," "a franklin stove . . . a table and three chairs."[155] Later he relocated in a new brick building on the site, in rooms over a wholesale store, which a later visitor found "dingy," "ratty," and "dusty," furnished only with a "rickety table, a few common chairs, and several tiers of shelving on which are piled innumerable volumes of governmental publications."[156] Orville Browning started in the "east room of the old Land Office Hotel," a frame building on the square in Quincy, where

Henry Asbury joined him in 1834.[157] James Grimes installed himself and his "fifty dollars' worth of law books" in a log cabin near the wharf in Burlington in 1836,[158] while David Rorer occupied a small brick building he had built near Fourth Street in which he had a simple office with a "collection of old law books."[159] Similarly, Lincoln's law office was but a single room with "a small lounge or bed, a chair containing a buffalo robe, . . . a hard wooden bench, a feeble attempt at a bookcase, and a table which answered for a desk." A few years later, Lincoln had changed partners and moved into the second floor above the court rooms in a new brick building south of the statehouse, but had added only a "small desk," a few extra chairs, and a "few shelves [which] had been enclosed" to his surroundings, suggesting that while gentility was the principle at home, professional arrangements remained Spartan, dingy, and even "uncouth" through the 1850s.[160] These and all such offices of the time, when "overrun with clients,"[161] were places "where something was usually happening," where one of the partners, who was usually there, engaged in a continual discourse with the men of the town who liked to "drop in, to chat and read the news and hear the latest joke" or story.[162]

Whether in town, on the circuit, or in the capital, the commencement of court, or court day, brought a rush of intense work. Locally, law cases went on discursively, away from public view. Those who attended court tended to be directly involved or people who were interested in following the legal process itself by "court-watching," such as John Dillon, whose interest in attending the local courts led him to decide to read law. Whereas the supreme court was a venue mostly outside public view, the circuit courts were a kind of public stage upon which individuals established their careers and developed local reputations. The semi-annual court session was, for any town, "the great event of the season, which was looked forward to by all, and afterwards proved the source of general conversation."[163] To another "court week . . . ranked with the annual circus as one of the few entertainments possible in this new and distant region," around which farmers scheduled "semi-annual shopping visits" and did business, and politicians took to the stump.[164] During the first few busy days, during which the lawyers "were on exhibition and they knew it," they presented themselves to the local populace, making their "speeches as much to the people as to the magistrate."[165]

While town work or litigation at the supreme court tended to favor "digest" or "book" law, most judges and lawyers conceded that circuit practice favored those with common "good sense" and an "instinctive," "rudimentary" or "intellectual" understanding of the general principles of law,[166] rather than the "educated" learning of a "book lawyer" or "digest-lawyer."[167] This was reflected in an ability to state facts and make brief simple arguments,[168] a practical, instinctive style one judge would later call "the instinct of the concrete."[169] Others noted that the circuit "exerted the instincts of smarter men, of genius, nerve, and novelty,"[170] flexibility and quickness of response, "a rapidity of action," an ability to "think quickly and make no mistakes, and to act promptly to take advantage of the mistakes of the adversary."[171] Yet the range of men who were able successfully to practice this circuit "mode of practicing law," or "law on the wing,"[172] and rise to the top of their respective "circuit bars" indicates that no particular type succeeded over others. In any case, those who felt they lacked some of these "nuts and bolts" skills in law, could, after 1850, purchase a pocket-sized form book known colloquially as *Asbury's Justice*, written by Henry Asbury, clerk of the Adams County court, which went through three editions and was "very extensively circulated" among lawyers in the West.[173]

The nature of circuit law encouraged other lawyers to follow the circuit whether they had business or not. "Old Timber" James Woods, for example, traveled the First Circuit of Iowa with such regularity, simply because he "loved the excitement of the early courts" and enjoyed the opportunity to make acquaintances and do business, that he was often "as much expected as the presiding judge."[174] By following the cases, discussing law, legal procedures, and ideas, and socializing, lawyers like Woods or Leonard Swett[175] would give to the fringe of circuit activity the character of a kind of traveling apprenticeship in law, in which the lawyers, when out of court, formed "associations" as mentors and students, described by one observer as akin to those of "a debating society or a law school." "Whatever point of law, past or present, pending or probable, could be raised, they . . . discussed, dissected, worried, fought over it, until, whether convinced or not, all knew more than when they first commenced." By "struggling over these made-up issues of debate," participants not only displayed their "forensic ability" but also sharpened their legal skills and understanding.[176] Likewise, there was an element of such discourse and discussion around the supreme court. Much of the discussion in the law library was, of course, serious talk about legal and political matters. So, too, lawyers routinely crossed the hall to attend the legislature or informally participated in the legislative and political discourse in the lobby or even in the supreme court room, where they continued discussions or debates that began in the legislature. Sometimes lawyers would join the members of the legislature who tarried in the lobby after the last session of the season, to participate in the more serious mode of a mock legislature, which they styled "the Lobby" or the "Third House."[177]

Such discussions often led to apparently infrequent decisions to have a meeting of the county, circuit, or state bar. Some bars held meetings to elect officers or put on annual "bar suppers" or banquets, though it is unclear whether these organizations had any actual power such as controlling local membership, forming examination committees, sanctioning members, or requiring them to pay dues.[178] In several more serious meetings, county bars expressed their favor for judges or candidates for office or wrote memorials and obituaries for deceased members. The earliest reference to a county bar meeting is that of Coles County, in October 1840.[179] In December 1842, the members of the Galena bar tried, unsuccessfully, to have the circuit judge, Thomas C. Browne, removed from office. In November 1846, the members of the Des Moines County bar threw Charles Mason a "public dinner" to commemorate his term as district judge.[180] The bar was active in Sangamon County in 1846 and 1847.[181] In 1849, the bar of Adams County held a short meeting at the office of the clerk of the circuit court to commemorate the death of fellow member Charles Gilman of Quincy, supreme court reporter of Illinois, by passing a resolution by Judge Peter Lott; the bar also elected Orville H. Browning chairman and Charles B. Lawrence secretary.[182] In July 1854 the members of the Chicago bar held a similar meeting, with Grant Goodrich serving as chair, to commemorate their "brother" James F. Collins, who had died.[183] Later, the members of the bar in Springfield – including Lincoln, Stuart, and Logan – expanded their domain by writing a letter to support David Davis as judge of the Eighth Circuit in 1855.[184]

Lawyers needed to detach emotions and personal beliefs from the legal procedures and issues at hand and join other lawyers who were or were not their friends, as either members of a team jointly trying a case or adversaries. This, combined with the presence of numerous single men living in boarding houses, working in law offices, and encountering each other at the courthouse, public meetings, associations, clubs, social occasions, or the tavern or ordinary, proved fertile ground for the cultivation of convivial, as well as indirect and dissimulating behavior similar to that among their other townsmen in the male subculture (see Chapter 3). Even Stiles recognized the existence of this culture, remarking that unlike doctors and ministers, "who were comparatively isolated in their fellowship and professional action," lawyers worked in teams and, especially when traveling the circuit, "flocked together" and spent considerable time together. This "almost constant companionship naturally made them convives,"[185] among whom practical jokes, lively and theatrical conversation, mock trials, parties, and "indulg[ing] more freely" in the "flowing bowl" were routine.[186]

The circuit was, in the words of one observer, "the perfect school for storytelling" and for bringing out the "play-instinct" in men, in "amusements, pastimes, and practical jokes" all directed to "soften the asperities and quicken the sensibility of human nature."[187] Acting in the courtroom or in politics for one's "friends" and against one's "enemies" required impartiality and following procedures and protocol. Though aware of their personal affinities with and differences from other members of the bar, lawyers had to restrain personal feelings and impulses and political or social viewpoints and attitudes in pursuit of a higher goal. Judges and lawyers worked in a high-stakes, competitive, adversarial, and emotional process framed by strict technical procedure and the rule of law. Friends and adversaries were brought together as counsel for or against defendants or plaintiffs in cases one may or may not believe, before local, circuit, or state judges one considered either friend or foe. Lawyers needed a strong sense of duty and a sensibility for potential conflicts of interest to litigate with impartiality, equanimity, self-control, indirection, and assure the proper carrying out of the law. Judges were required to avoid personal bias in declaring both friends or adversaries in contempt and in maintaining order among gentlemen and rowdies, lawyers and litigants, defendants and plaintiffs. Not surprisingly, to ease tensions of competition and the need for impartiality and emotional control between friends and adversaries, to assuage wounded egos, and to encourage members not to take the practice of the law personally, it is not surprising that some "brethren of the bar" who in town were active members of the male subculture would apply the tonic of wit, sarcasm, irony, indirection, and dissembling to their conviviality.

In the towns, socializing among the legal fraternity was rooted in the larger male subculture. This was apparent in both Keokuk and Fort Madison. The latter in the late thirties and early forties "made large pretensions" of being "the leading town of the Territory," and, as a result, it became the home to a group of "twenty to thirty of the most fascinating, polished gentlemen . . . most of them Kentuckians, the others from Philadelphia," that were "ever known" by Hawkins Taylor of Keokuk. "Highly gifted" and "convivial," this set was headed by General Jesse B. Browne (the "Tall Cedar of Lebanon"), later of Keokuk, who would take "possession" of young men, few of whom would safely escape. Such was the case of several lawyers in town, but especially the lawyer Alfred Rich, a bright, "though naturally despondent" young man who arrived in Fort Madison. He was drawn into the glamour of the group and too often joined his new companions "in a night to kill time," hard living which ended in his premature death of consumption and drink in early spring 1842.[188]

Such drinking was, as James Woods remarked, the "practice of nearly all the lawyers of those days." Stiles himself admitted that lawyers "indulged more freely" than members of the other "learned" professions, but both noted that usually drinking was not really "debauched," "rarely abused," and only a few times done "to hurtful excess."[189] Newcomers accepted into the county bar were expected to "treat" the other members of the bar or undergo an "initiation."[190] John Dreschler threw a "blow-out" in Burlington before 1843 for the committee of lawyers who passed him to the bar – Milton D. Browning, Henry W. Starr, Jonathan C. Hall, James W. Grimes, and "the rest" of the local bar – in which "different liquors were mixed in a pail" to make "a pretty strong beverage"; all had to take a drink or the rest "would make them."[191] The centrality of drinking to this convivial culture is also suggested by the wild night of drinking about the same time in Fort Madison, during which George Dixon, Herman Blennerhassett, and another lawyer on their way back to their hotel wandered into a circus ring and marched "on and on" round and round in the circle until daybreak, when the hotel keeper saw them and sent them in the right direction.[192]

At the supreme court, conviviality was usually more genteel. Orville Browning remembered Judge Sidney Breese's New Year's Eve ball held in the ballroom of Springfield's American House Hotel in 1842, reported as a "splendid blow-out" attended, characteristically, by 300 to 400 gentlemen and only forty to fifty women. Browning was also probably present at a series of "levees" or evening entertainments through the years, among them James Semple's "brilliant party" in 1844 or James Shields's party in 1849.[193] By 1856 shorter visits and the gradual eliding of the male subculture into gentility shifted the venues of socializing from the hotels to the private homes of lawyers and politicians in town. The shortening of his stays compressed, by necessity, Browning's socializing into a frenzy of shorter private visits or calls rather than dinners or evenings at the houses of his "friends." Annual dinners or parties at the homes of several genteel friends – in particular, the Ridgelys, James Barrett, Ben Edwards, William Fondy, John T. Stuart, and Abraham Lincoln (where, Isaac Arnold recalled, Mrs. Lincoln kept everything "orderly and refined" and a "cordial and hearty" welcome "put every guest perfectly at ease")[194] – narrowed into calls or teas and "spending an hour or two" with his friends by the late 1850s.

Nevertheless, whether Browning stayed for over forty days or less than three weeks after 1857, he never recorded more than three or four social occasions to break the work and the evenings at the supreme court law library. Only occasionally would he note when socializing there spilled over into a dinner, party, or "levee" (a reception hosted by a local individual specifically for the lawyers visiting town). On 16 January 1850, for example, Browning dined with Thomas Drummond, Benjamin Bond, William Pope, Ninian Edwards, and R. S. Blackwell. On 13 January 1855, John Wood, Henry Asbury, Nehemiah Bushnell, and John Tillson – all Quincy men – "spent the evening at my room." On another occasion, some newcomers to the court dragged him out of bed, "made" him dress himself, and took him out to an "oyster and wine supper." And on yet another occasion, Browning attended a levee at Governor Bissell's house where a "great crowd" was present. Though Springfield was known for its "old fashioned, generous hospitality" most of the time, work and a few genteel social occasions filled Browning's time in what he described, on Christmas 1850, when there were "no festivities of any kind," a "dull town."[195]

On the circuit conviviality would gradually flow over the more serious business of the court. When the period of "all business" – with its spirited debates and controversies, was over, the convives among the circuit riders suffused these informal and sometimes more formalized debates and seminars with sarcasm, irony, and humor. John D. Caton noted that such conviviality and other amusements tended to occur on Tuesday or Wednesday nights after the main "pressure" of the first day or so of court was past.[196] Similarly, Leonard Swett recalled that Wednesday nights, more than other evenings, was the time for another convivial festivity that interacted, directly or indirectly, with the happenings of the court session. Often conviviality simply broke out as debate or discussion slid into the "long-indulged-in right of unhappy lawyers of 'going down to the tavern, swearing at the court' and taking other consolation."[197] Such spirited commentary or discussions directed at the court or another lawyer could easily cross the line – "in no spirit of ill-will, but to vent [one's] feelings" – into fictional "moot tribunals" or "moot courts" which were held occasionally for educational purposes by local lawyers to the debate over legal issues after hours. When suffused with irony, sarcasm, and conviviality such traditional "courts" were transformed into "mock trials"[198] which became a well-known secret part of circuit life.

Much like "oppositional" events such as the yellow handbill meetings at Keokuk, Iowa, the mock trial was a spoof or fiction of a real proceeding in which they turned all the rules upside down. At such gatherings, according to Caton, the judge and other members of the bar would gather and present "an indictment against some other member of the bar, accusing him of the most ridiculous of crimes." Lawyers would be appointed, or one would defend oneself in such a trial. In this topsy-turvy burlesque[199] or spoof, boisterousness and hilarity were no longer "a breach of decorum," rules of law and evidence were abandoned, and jury procedures were thrown to the wind as the members of the jury moved toward the "inevitable foregone conclusion" of a verdict of guilty which the judge punished by meting out penalties that were often "the most ludicrous and amusing of all the proceedings." In all of this, one must, as lawyer, jury, plaintiff, defendant, or judge, present and face the sarcasm and wit with coolness and indirection, rather than insult. Caton noted the rules which governed these occasions, as well as the entire male subcultural world of nicknames, practical jokes, pranks, frolics, and conviviality: "if the wit was keen, it was frequently deeply penetrating, but the subject of it must bear it good naturedly and console his irritated feelings with the reflection that he would get his revenge on some future occasion. To show irritation at hard rubs was the worst thing a man could do, but to turn them off in some witty way enhanced his popularity for the time." Henry C. Whitney noted that all of this was "desultory and evanescent" and occurred under a necessary cloak or "seal" of secrecy, and though he never recalled "anything wrong . . . said or done," it was, nevertheless, felt by the participants "atrocious to disclose the secrets of the . . . coterie." Apparently the participants so closely held the secrets of these courts – which heightened the aura of the spoof – much like they kept secret the proceedings of fraternal societies, that Whitney never recalled "ever" hearing anything "discussed there mentioned, or alluded to," in the "outside" world.[200]

The few examples we have of such mock trials, which Judge David Davis in the Eighth District called his "Ogmathorial Court,"[201] shows how much these secret events paralleled the scripts of other spoof occasions or entertainments like the yellow handbill meetings, or legislative "lobby" sessions (both of which spoofed debates),[202] convivial dinners, banquet "roasts," or farcical parades. The highly sarcastic, verbal jousting that characterized such "trials" is evident in the mock trial of a lawyer in one of Judge Caton's circuits:

Benedict, who had a fog horn of a voice, which he used most recklessly when excited, and who had been roaring to a jury at an evening session, was met when he came to the tavern, by the sheriff, with a bench warrant, on an indictment "for making loud and unusual noises in the night time," and soon court was organized and he was put upon his trial, and before midnight he was convicted and sentenced to repeat the offense in arguing a motion for a new trial, or to pay a heavy fine, upon the ground that two affirmatives would make a negative, or that the hair of the same dog would cure the bite. It is said that he fairly outdid himself in that effort, so that he aroused the whole town from their slumbers, and he came near being fined for overdoing it.

Sometimes these courts would less formally organize as a spoof debating society, which occasionally occurred in conjunction with a "court party"or "levee."[203] These events were usually orderly, but sometimes degenerated into a free-for-all, storytelling competitions, "barmecide feasts," "oyster suppers," champagne "high carnivals," or whiskey-induced (usually served from a pail or jug) "blow-outs."[204] At his levee, Judge Davis was well known for strictly controlling the door, warmly welcoming those they wanted to roast, while those he did not want to join he "fired" or "froze out" by fabricating some ruse at the door among the lawyers in the room, action which one historian characterized as "hazing newcomers callously."[205] At his court, Davis, we are told, would "gather his courtiers about him, and make of night of it, similar to the Knights of the Round Table, or the Pickwick Club."[206] Leonard Swett recalled that Davis was "paternal and patriarchal to all. If any of the lawyers got wild, the judge often made them stop it, and go to bed and sleep it off."[207] At other levees "editors, local statesmen, bankers, merchants, physicians, and farmers" were as welcome as the lawyers of the circuit.[208] At such occasions a highly sarcastic level of debating and verbal jousting carried the evening. At Keokuk, Hawkins Taylor noted that these events interacted closely with the emergence of yellow handbill meetings run by Silas Heaight primarily during the winter months.[209]

Occasionally, lawyers fused these events with the spoof dinners common in the male subculture. Once, for example, when Milton D. Browning of Burlington was jailed for contempt of court, the "members of the bar were so incensed" that they went to jail with Browning and, sending for oysters and champagne, "held high carnival and abided him until he was released" and then took the debate – in a Dickensian style – to the press, which continued it for days in a highly sarcastic style.[210] On other occasions, food and liquor would be followed by "euchre parties," rounds of poker, or by someone – such as Judge Young in Illinois – pulling out a fiddle and providing music for singing or dancing: At Davenport, John P. Cook was the "legal vocalist of the day."[211] Further afield, invitations to social occasions in the town or perhaps an excursion or frolic[212] to a nearby town filled out a lawyer's stay in a circuit court town, before packing up and heading onto the next session the following week or month.

Through such activities true friendships were born. Among these men, to speak of one's friends fraternally became ubiquitous. Usher F. Linder remarked on his friendship with Joseph Gillespie that they "were more like brothers than any two men who ever lived who were not brothers," and on his friendship with Judge Douglas that "I loved him with the love that Jonathan had for David – 'A love that passeth the love of woman.'"[213] So, too, James Singleton admitted that his "fond attachment" for Orville Browning "had ripened into fraternal attachment."[214]

On each level, the brothers of the bar, friends and adversaries alike, sought, in spite of political and personal differences, to present a united front. In town, on the circuit, or at the state supreme court, this cohort of lawyers, this "select array,"[215] a "class of lawyers" unparalleled in later times,[216] this "band of illustrious men,"[217] a "phalanx of worth and excellence," the "fathers of the bar,"[218] or the "old guard" of the legal fraternity,[219] individually and collectively forged the bonds of social class and furthered regional social development. The prominence of the local bar when conflated with the booster ethos was presented as evidence of the quality and degree of development and achievement of town, region, or state society. No matter how wracked by political factions, cliques, circles, or personal animosities, the Galena bar remained to Elihu B. Washburne "the ablest in the State." Likewise, the "prominence" of the Quincy bar in state affairs was "admitted by all."[220] Each member was free to use his association with the local or county bar to both enhance his credentials within the state, region, or nation and to advertise and "boost" his town.

Provincial lives

Through regular professional travel to county seats, the state capital, and the metropolis, lawyers became part of a regional network, fraternity, society, and culture. Ironically, it was their professional activities, involving the "way of the town" and the booster ethos, which took many lawyers into the regional system. There, they networked as intensively as they did at home, making friends and associates who they would meet several times or once a year, but with whom, given the circumstances, they developed intense professional associations and even new friendships. Lawyers, therefore, schooled in networking at the local level, transferred that skill to the regional level, and thus were among the most active in the professions of the urban West to establish regional contacts, friendships, and associations, from which a regional middle-class elite would emerge. They were also, therefore, among the first in their towns to encounter the elevating standards of social behavior, gentility, and status at the capital or metropolis, and would become among the first in each town to respond and alter their behavior accordingly. Being most intensely local, and creating, before others, stronger ties to regional activity, lawyers, more so and earlier than others, experienced the tug and pull between local loyalties and regional opportunities. Recognizing the need to follow opportunity wherever it was, "the brethren of the bar" would most intensely debate whether they should stay in a place which stopped growing as the forces of regional development shifted that opportunity elsewhere.

6

Boosters and railroad men: Constructing a regional society

The spatial dynamics of regional society

The structure and dynamics of local and regional social development – whether manifested in family systems, the diffusion of male subcultures, the construction of an enclave of gentility, or the emergence of a network of professionals who acted in a regional realm – was shaped by the interaction between transport technology and the topography and environment across the Great West.

In the 1820s and 1830s, the steamboat revolution, which had "annihilated" "time and space,"[1] transformed the upper Mississippi River north of St. Louis into a corridor of preferential access and accelerated returns that generated the development of a river-centric urban and economic system. In time, however, the steamboat system, limited by variable water flow and the upper and lower rapids at Keokuk and Davenport, and overwhelmed by freight and passenger traffic demands made upon it, stopped expanding. Seasonal variations in navigation from north to south across the system[2] placed significant limits on the expansion of the system to the north and west in the 1850s. As migration, settlement, and development continued west and north into Iowa and Minnesota, the returns of the system diminished and the willingness of locals to support its maintenance waned. Residents north of a line that runs roughly from Keokuk or Davenport, Iowa, through Peoria, Illinois, and across to Fort Wayne, Indiana, and Columbus, Ohio, were frustrated by the seasonal inefficiencies and costs of this "structural" reality. As diminishing returns set in and demands for efficiency and higher returns from an ever-growing population increased, a once revolutionary agent of change was perceived by 1850 as a problem to be overcome.

For most businessmen, merchants, and professionals these seasonal cycles, which affected the cost and access of transportation to the south and east, structured their lives.[3] Economic and social interaction across the region coincided with seasons of

Provincial lives

easy access and interaction, especially as one traveled north of Davenport where the stoppages during winter and spring "shut out [residents] from all intercourse with the world."[4] In this world, meetings, rallies, government activities, circuit courts, and the activities of the booster ethos as well as socializing, visits, travel, and excursions clustered between April and July and again in September and October. Whether on the road or receiving visitors in town, one could feel the pulses of a larger regional system in which one hoped to play a part more intensively during the late spring, early summer, and fall than at other times of the year. A yearning to feel the dynamics of a broader system, a social dynamic larger than one's locality, may explain the later obsession of going to conventions or on excursions and trips to the metropolis. Henry Hitchcock expressed what others felt: "I should always rather mingle in the crowds of a large city than be anywhere else [for] to *live* one must go back among men . . . busy striving, thinking men."[5] In the crowd of people from other towns and cities across the system, one could feel the currents of the road and the pulse of the larger social and economic system and the world at large.

Between these periods of action and excitement, town life and society would retreat into local routines and settle into a dullness in which "nothing of interest" happened, routinely reported by contemporaries in their correspondence. Those who experienced the greatest variations in seasonal access – inland towns in Illinois and Iowa, and towns north of the rapids such as Burlington, Muscatine, and Davenport, Iowa – felt the inadequacies of transport most urgently and saw in the railroad far more immediate benefits than those who lived further south in the valley nearer to St. Louis and had access to year-round transportation by stage and steamboat. Ironically, however, the residents of those towns, cut off for extended periods each year, probably had the most localized views of development, the fewest outside contacts, and thus the least ability to launch a regional strategy. In their isolated worlds, they cultivated localism, based on parallelist thinking, and thus would most dramatically experience the impact of the shift of systemic forces that occurred when the railroad broke through the cordon of space that surrounded them.

Wherever one was across the system, the time it still took to get from place to place, combined with uncertainty of schedules and the physical difficulty in doing so, assured that any event – whether a meeting, transaction, or exchange – had to be important enough to warrant the travel. Because transport was undependable, one could not place a specific cost on time. The value of a meeting, convention, or buying trip in the 1830s or 1840s lay in the event itself, despite how long it took to get there. Results measured efficiency or success, not time expended. When travel was even more difficult, and distances farther, as with the state supreme court sessions at Springfield, Illinois, in midwinter, this was even more the case. During these instances – when only lawyers, doctors, merchants, and itinerate professionals with important business were out traveling – harrowing encounters with poor roads resulting in perilous and time-consuming journeys were routine. Orville Browning recalled one ordeal across the Military Tract in western Illinois in 1852 that left him so sore he could "hardly move."[6] Elihu Washburne "shudder[ed]" to "think of those dreadful stage rides" across central Illinois on roads so bad that "the old saying 'that the passengers walked and carried fence rails' was very nearly verified."[7] Isaac Arnold had similar experiences "dragging drearily through the mud and sleet" for four days between Chicago and Springfield.[8] In spring 1838, Charles Mason and David Rorer, when caught in a thunderstorm west of Burlington, Iowa, walked their buggy, navigating only by "suppos[ing] [themselves] in the right way" where "the mud was the deepest."[9] Gustave Koerner and Lincoln Clark told similar tales of travel outside Chicago.[10]

Through the late thirties and forties, when they thought that no alternatives existed, such experiences were, in Charles Mason's words, "lightly regarded"[11] and thus generally taken in stride. In the late thirties as westerners who traveled east began to encounter the new railroad lines being constructed east of the Appalachians, they became increasingly aware of the differences in travel between West and East. Usually, trips to the East, lasting weeks and undertaken at considerable cost, were infrequent. Thus, when business or public life demanded, they combined trips with personal visits to one's family – often for the first time in decades – which still predominated. Charles Hempstead went east in 1829 and 1830. Henry Gratiot did the same in 1836, a trip from which he never returned. John Reynolds went east to serve his terms in Congress in 1834. Elihu Washburne went east on political business in 1842, 1843, 1844, 1847–1848, 1848–49, and regularly after that.[12] Thompson Campbell, Edward D. Baker, Abraham Lincoln, and others would follow them east in the forties. Lincoln Clark routinely traveled when he was in Congress and politics in the early fifties.

Most western middle-class men, traveling beyond their localities into another part of the country, so far from their new homes that their old home seemed like another world, were disoriented by a perception of skipped time, or being in another life, set free and unable to recognize that which was familiar yet different. Such occasional ruminations about their fractured lives caused by their move west suffused the consciousness of western middle-class people with a vague unhappiness or homesickness. The railroad promised in the late 1840s to connect the West to the East, to reattach westerners to their old lives in the East and the larger life of the nation and thus fuse the bifurcated sense of identity they felt and make them whole again.

In July 1836, Charles Mason, on his way west via New York City, articulated this disorientation, and over the years never seemed to have overcome it:

I seem to have been witnessing two entirely distinct and separate states of existence for some time past. My life here and my life elsewhere have little to connect them with each other. I exist in two worlds – I am two distinct and almost unconnected beings. So far as my existence here – the space which has elapsed since my last visit seems nothing. It appears to me that . . . I have been in a disturbed dream, with occasional moments of waking, and here I stand another Rip Van Winkle while years in their progress pass me at a leap and all their consequences are the magic creatives of a moment. The friends of my childhood are dear or scattered or so altered in feeling as not to be recognized as the same beings. Those early ties so tender and grateful which entwine young hearts have nearly all been severed by the touch of distance. . . . Every familiar object too that calls up some early association wakens a feeling of tender yet deep melancholy.

For Mason, deracinated and disoriented, the trip west was an effort to find a "quiet corner" where he could "reunite all the members of my father's family" who "at present . . . [were] so widely scattered in such a manner that we can never again be collected around the home of my youngest, my tenderest memories."[13]

Such feelings, though rarely so well articulated as they were by Mason, a contemplative, even gloomy man, were ubiquitous among western men and women. Seven years before, Charles Hempstead of Galena took a detour on his trip to Washington in late 1829 to visit, for the first time in twenty years, his Hempstead family relations in New England. However, he also traveled on his father's behalf, Stephen Hempstead, Sr., who, at age seventy-seven, was too infirm to travel. At Boston, Charles toured the Roxbury and Dorchester Heights where Stephen Sr. "was encamped" and endured "sufferings" as a Revolutionary soldier in 1775 and 1776. Hardly able to believe that he really stood where his father had served fifty years before, Charles gathered pieces of bushes from the "hallowed ground" for him. He then visited relatives "at the old place" in New London, Connecticut, who he found "much as [he] left [them] twenty years" before.[14] Horatio Newhall, after twenty-one years in the West, decided to make a long journey home to Massachusetts. He experienced a similar disorientation, but rather than musing on the passage of time over which little had changed, found everything changed, making it "all strange to me. I looked East, West, North, and South, all was altered, everything changed. . . . The ancient cemetery had a new fence around it . . . my father's tomb . . . [was] the only object I recollected of having seen before. I could not see my mother's house for large splendid edifices cut off the view." He thought it even stranger that he should have thought his relatives so changed, while they all thought he had not altered any and they "should have known [him] anywhere."[15] Even Elihu Washburne, who, only two years after emigrating west, journeyed back to Livermore, Maine, found that his parents and family lived in a different world. The town he left in 1839 seemed, to him, "as dead as the devil . . . going down every day," and everything, including society, seemed to have changed "most astonishingly."[16]

What increasingly struck western travelers in the late 1830s and early 1840s was the transformative power of the railroad that they encountered on their trips east. Horatio Newhall recorded his slow progress east in 1838 by counting days until, upon reaching Johnstown, Pennsylvania, he for the first time stepped onto a train to find time accelerated. From Harrisburg, he traveled by rail to Philadelphia, 105 miles away, in a mere ten hours – in some places reporting that the train traveled at "twenty to twenty-five miles per hour." A day later he made the quick eighty-mile trip to New York City, by steam and rail, in eight hours.

For Newhall, an impatient traveler, sitting in a steamboat "with nothing to do" and not much to look at for two weeks was a "terrible" experience, which put him into a kind of suspended animation, or as Elihu Washburne described it, a state "more dead than alive." The "eighteen and a half days on the road from Galena to New York," though a decent time, given the fact he stopped for six days in transit, seemed, to Newhall, a "journey of a lifetime." Now he arrived at places "the same night," covering hundreds of miles in a day. He experienced this sensation in reverse when, on his return, he reached the end of the line at Ypsilanti, Michigan, in spring 1838, and was thrown back into the reality of western travel, reduced again to slow "stages, wagons, and carts" on the "awful" roads around Chicago; he vowed that "if I lived through it that time I would never travel again." Breaking his promise in May 1846, Newhall got stuck again just west of Chicago and took "a whole night to go twelve miles to Chicago!"[17]

For westerners, the railroad promised to connect them to the East and allow them to go back and forth without severing family relations and friendships for decades or a lifetime. Westerners also were aware that as railroads were built across the East, the lack of railroads west of Chicago became more apparent, leaving the region a backwater outside the vortex of economic–geographic forces that transformed every kind of social, economic, political, or cultural arrangement in the nation. This awareness was particularly strong among those who, like Newhall, had traveled east and experienced the transformative power of the railroad.

In such a world, the dynamics of local society only occasionally and discursively interacted with the aggregating forces of a regional society. One acted primarily in a social realm of face-to-face interactions among known people within one's community and within social structures which one had helped construct. In this local society there was a correlation between personal character, individual behavior, social action, and social order. Status and self-identity were established and reinforced by living in an autonomous and self-defining local microcosm of regional and national society. The dynamics of regional and national economic and social systems lay outside local life. While the West remained beyond the national railroad system, this bifurcation between individual and aggregate, local and regional, and unit and system would continue.

From lawyers to boosters to railroad men

The railroad shattered these arrangements and transformed the nature of local and regional social interactions among middle-class people. Charles Mason – writing from New York in 1852 – marveled at how the railroad had reduced the trip from Chicago to New York to a mere two days and expected before the end of 1853 the trip would be reduced to thirty-six hours. Comparatively, he expected the railroad would reduce the journey from Chicago to Burlington from three days to less than forty-eight hours, and that "within the next two years it will be diminished to less than half of what it is at present." Mason felt "justified in being astonished" at all of this and pondered its "effect upon those who have traveled over this ground fifteen years ago."[18]

Such anticipation, combined with general expectations that the railroad would transform all intraregional and national economic and social relations, motivated lawyers, merchants, and entrepreneurs in disproportionate numbers to support local and regional railroad projects not only as stockholders but also as board members, directors, or even presidents of companies who supervised, financed, constructed, and operated the railroads.

Such work – which entailed making contacts with other towns or counties along a proposed line and acquiring capital and material both within and outside the region – naturally cultivated among these men a more integrated view of the urban, economic, and social systems. Regional thinking gradually eroded their parallelist notions that all local activity across a system was equal. These same men played active roles in organizing and carrying out the activities such as regional steamboat and railroad conventions, public railroad celebrations and excursions, and business trips to New York City or Washington, D.C., which came to define the emerging regional system. At each step of this process of elite aggregation lawyers, merchants, and politicians built upon their previous regional networking activities in their businesses and practices to create a regional social realm or system. Ironically, then, in building upon the structure and intensifying the networks of power they had already developed, lawyers and businesspeople oversaw the construction of a new regional system that would transform the nature of variable economic and social interactions and accelerate, through more intensive elite interaction and aggregation, the development of a new regional society in the 1850s.

Railroad "fever" or "mania" spread across the regional urban system from east to west, beginning in interior places or towns in the north that were unable to enjoy fully the advantages of the steamboat revolution. Long before practicable, residents of Springfield, Chicago, Jacksonville, and Galena in the 1830s initiated railroad fever within the region. In the 1840s the same towns plus Alton continued to be the centers of enthusiasm. As the range and efficiency of the steamboat system reached its limits and westerners became increasingly aware of the impact of the railroad in the East in the late forties and early fifties, railroad fever reached epidemic proportions. Davenport, a town that for a variety of economic–geographic reasons seemed most adversely affected by the obstruction of the lower rapids, was the first to respond. Quincy, Bloomington (Muscatine), and Galena soon followed. Dubuque and Burlington, followed finally by Keokuk, experienced recurrent waves of manias into the late fifties and early sixties. Meanwhile, because of a flood of eastern capital sweeping into the region seeking to extend eastern railroads farther west, Chicago became the center of railroad construction and of a new regional railroad network. St. Louis exerted similar, though less extensive, power across its hinterland. Each city, nevertheless, began to exert a systemic attraction on local railroad schemes across the region in the 1850s.

Following the practice in the East, urban boosters called the earliest railroad meetings in the West. Railroad meetings were held in Springfield or Jacksonville as early as 1831, then spread to Springfield,[19] Chicago,[20] and Grant County, in the Wisconsin territory, opposite from Dubuque, in 1837.[21] When interest revived, after the economic downturn of 1837, a meeting was scheduled for 28 November 1845 at Rockford to discuss plans for renewing the railroad project.[22] Often one or two members of the elite who had discussed the idea and thought something should be done about it generated the call for meetings. In April 1856 while traveling on a

Constructing a regional society

steamboat, Charles Mason was approached by Dan F. Miller, who "came on the packet at Fort Madison" to "express his wish to form a [railroad] company" to build a road from Fort Madison to Mount Pleasant, Iowa.[23] This led to a series of "interviews" or discussions with other members of the elite,[24] out of which came the call for a local railroad meeting. Meanwhile, incessant conversations with locals "talk[ing] up railroad matters" ensued, sometimes reaching a frenzy, described by one observer as a "great talk about railroades [sic]."[25]

Railroad fever reached Galena in late 1845. Elihu Washburne's mentor and friend Charles Hempstead kept the absent Washburne abreast of local initiatives. On 26 December they called for a meeting, but Hempstead feared "our citizens will not attend as they ought."[26] He underestimated the "fever" that was "coming on" among the people,[27] however, for it turned out to be a "large meeting" attended by a "numerous company" who discussed the prospects for Galena's involvement in the Galena and Chicago Union Railroad. From the meeting came an invitation to attend a convention at Rockford, Illinois, on 7 January. Twenty members present volunteered to go; Hempstead wished, amid the "railroad mania," that Washburne was home to be able to join them.[28]

Fifteen months later, the citizens of Dubuque followed with several local meetings to discuss their possible connection to the Galena and Chicago Union railroad. At a meeting held on 11 March 1847, Senator George Wallace Jones, who was a major force in railroad matters, "set forth the advantages to be derived from communication by railroad with the eastern cities as a means of conveying to market the surplus products of the West." The same month citizens held another meeting to discuss "the Oregon Railroad" – their version of a plan for a transcontinental railroad from Dubuque to the West. The following year, and for two years afterward, a number of meetings were held in town to propose and push forward railroads from Dubuque to Keokuk via Iowa City, and railroads to the West and Southwest.[29] Subsequent meetings were held in Dubuque, Iowa City, and Keokuk for the Dubuque and Keokuk Railroad.[30] Similarly, discussions and talk about railroads in Dubuque in the spring of 1853 culminated in a meeting on 16 May at which the Dubuque and Pacific Railroad was incorporated.[31]

The first railroad meetings in Davenport occurred in 1848. "Railroad fever" spread to Burlington that same year. It then crossed the river to Quincy in 1849 and 1850. In subsequent years, "railroad mania" – a kind of secular religious revival – would periodically sweep through these and other towns. At each meeting, the members present would formulate plans, charter and organize a company, and ask townspeople for support. Burlington's second round of railroad mania struck with a vengeance in the winter of 1851–1852. After a series of meetings in December, three meetings on 7, 15, and 17 January gave birth to the Burlington and Missouri River Railroad. Four years later more meetings would take place to continue to support the fledgling project that came to a vote by the townspeople on 7 April 1856.[32] Later in 1858, Charles Mason would personally organize several meetings to construct a local line to Fort Madison.[33]

When the fever finally spread to Keokuk, its residents alarmed by the head start

219

gained by Burlington, Davenport, and Dubuque in getting an eastern connection, it struck with a vengeance. Townspeople held a series of meetings in winter 1852. One sent a delegation to a convention in Fairfield, another to Washington, D.C. A year later Keokukians met and voted on appropriations for an eastern connection, but Keokuk's voters rejected the funding. Subsequent efforts at small local roads generated similar efforts. During the same summer, the citizens of Fort Madison met several times to organize the Port Byron Railroad which would provide a connection to the Burlington line and give them an eastern outlet. In 1854, 1857, and 1860 Keokuk would continue to seek a direct connection – by building across "the gap" – with the eastern lines, either through Carthage and Clayton behind Quincy,[34] or from Hamilton, just across the river, up to the Chicago, Burlington, and Quincy main line.[35] Later, Keokukians would seek other connections both east and west.[36]

These flare-ups of railroad "mania" – generated by a desire or need to connect isolated towns or cities to the larger system – responded to calls to action by local boosters who envisioned a new future for their town or city. Real enthusiasm – reflected in boisterous meetings, parades, "excitement," "great ado," "getting crazy," or constant talk and conversation – fed the often extravagant, exaggerated, euphoric, sometimes even ironic language that detailed grand plans in circular letters, resolutions, or memorials (most of which – like town plans – were "pipe dreams" that came to nothing).[37] Similar language, often used to the point of mockery, was a ubiquitous aspect of spirited "newspaper debates" between towns, such as the time a Galena editor mocked Dubuque's calculations for its future commerce by suggesting they call their new railroad the "Dubuque, Pacific, Japan and Shanghai Railroad."[38] Though one can view such language as enthusiasm or hyperbole or bombast, one can also discern a restrained touch of the ironic and sarcastic language that pervaded the male subculture and the local bar (see Fig. 15). Not surprisingly, lawyers, who were at the center of this regional booster culture, came to the fore. They were especially active in smaller urban centers where the realms of law, business, and politics remained intertwined with the male subculture and the booster ethos long after they were being segmented in the larger city or metropolis.[39]

At Jacksonville in 1837, for example, the town's "first lawyer," Murray McConnell, was the catalyst behind the movement to organize and build the first Northern Cross railroad from there to Springfield.[40] The first "incorporators" of the Chicago and Galena Union Railroad which the Illinois legislature in 1836 established were three Chicago lawyers: Theophilius C. Smith, Josiah C. Goodhue, and James H. Collins.[41] When the original scheme failed in the crash of 1837, it was revived in November 1845 by the prominent lawyer J. Young Scammon. Scammon and Isaac N. Arnold were among the Chicago delegates chosen for a convention at Rockford scheduled for 7 January 1846. Elihu B. Washburne had to be in Springfield that January and missed the meeting, but a colleague in town, A. L. Norris, reported on considerable "railroad mania" in Galena. Washburne's friend, Thomas Drummond, served as chair of the convention. In a meeting in Chicago in February, Drummond, along with Washburne and Charles S. Hempstead, were appointed directors of the

CIRCULAR LETTER.

SIR:

At a recent meeting of the citizens of Burlington, held for the purpose of adopting measures to secure the early construction of a continuous line of railroads from Lafayette through Peoria and Burlington to the Missouri river, the undersigned were instructed to invite a general co-operation of all those who are friendly to the measure. Believing you deeply interested in the construction of such a work, we take the liberty of addressing you on the subject; especially do we solicit your influence and efforts towards securing from Congress all the aid for this purpose which precedent or propriety will justify.

We believe the contemplated road is eminently entitled to general favor and encouragement. It passes through the heart of the most populous and wealthy portion of Iowa. It takes a central direction through Illinois and part of Indiana, in almost a direct line to Philadelphia. At Lafayette it will connect with public works already completed or in progress—thus furnishing an immediate outlet to the markets of the east. These will soon be found too circuitous, and will be superseded by a direct route, centrally through the eastern part of Indiana and Ohio to Wheeling and Pittsburgh, thus furnishing the most direct route between the centre of the agricultural region of the west, and all the great commercial cities of the Atlantic seaboard.

Passing midway between the Ohio river and the lakes it will meet with neither interruption nor competition from those great thoroughfares, and will penetrate a region most of which will for all facilities of transportation be solely dependent upon this railroad.

From Wheeling to Baltimore, and from Pittsburgh to Philadelphia, New York and Boston, the system of roads may be regarded as already complete. These are the only difficult and expensive portions of the whole work. From Peoria to Burlington the road is in progress of construction, and will be completed within two years. The remaining portions of the route pass through fertile and populous countries, highly favorable to the cheap construction of such works, and where their utility and consequent profit will be made evident by a glance.

But more than this—the road we conceive is destined to be a portion of a greater improvement which is to extend to Oregon and California. Such a work we regard as a fixed necessity. Its completion within the next ten years will only be in keeping with the march of events for the ten years which are past. The valley of the Platte—the Pass in the Rocky Mountains—the Salt Lake settlements, and the emigrant tracks beyond, all clearly indicate that the natural route for a road across the continent is in almost a direct line with the route above indicated from Philadelphia to the Missouri river.

The plan above indicated takes us to the extreme limit of State jurisdiction—the point where the United States have an unquestioned right to take up and prosecute the work to its termination at the Pacific Ocean, in Oregon, or till it reaches the confines of California. The completion of the road through the States secures the extension of the route beyond. While others debate, let us act. While they are amusing themselves and the country with ingenious schemes and cunning abstractions, we can carry into practical effect a plan by which the road will find itself completed half way across the continent.

With a suitable effort on our part, the first railroad that reaches the Missouri will be that above contemplated, and if so it will be the first that strikes the Pacific running through our own territory.

Very respectfully,

CHARLES MASON,　　　　HENRY W. STARR,
WM. F. COOLBAUGH,　　DAVID RORER,
LYMAN COOK,　　　　　JAMES W. GRIMES

Figure 15. A "circular letter." (Courtesy of the State Historical Society of Iowa – Des Moines)

railroad and given the specific task of raising funds for construction by the sale of stock to Galenans. Among the few locals who purchased stock and a year later contributed funds to support the initial surveying of the proposed route were Washburne, Hempstead, Drummond, and a large contingent of Washburne's and Hempstead's business and social associates. Washburne and Hempstead were particularly successful among their social circles on the wharf and around the Presbyterian church.[42] At Alton, William Martin and George T. M. Davis provided early support for the Alton and Springfield Railroad, incorporated in 1845.[43] In Springfield, Judge Treat, Stephen T. Logan, and Abraham Lincoln were railroad enthusiasts. At Belleville, Joseph Gillespie and Gustave Koerner were especially active in the efforts of the local elite to draw the railroad into town, as was Usher F. Linder in Coles County.[44]

At Quincy, early support for the rejuvenation of the Northern Cross Railroad received broad support from the local bar. James Singleton, Calvin Warren, and Isaac N. Morris purchased land from the original survey for the Northern Cross railroad. A year later, Isaac N. Morris, James Singleton, Calvin Warren, Nehemiah Bushnell, O. C. Skinner, and Henry Asbury were among the railroad's first thirteen "incorporators." Later Orville H. Browning, Almeron Wheat, Charles B. Lawrence, and Abraham Jonas supported the project and helped drum up railroad enthusiasm. When, after two years of campaigning they finally convinced the townspeople to support a bond issue, the stockholders held a meeting on 22 March 1851 and elected Nehemiah Bushnell, Browning's partner, president of the railroad and appointed his friend John Cox as secretary.[45] Under Bushnell's guidance, the railroad got financing from Detroit capitalists and pushed through construction to Galesburg by January 1856. That same year, James W. Singleton assumed the presidency of the Quincy and Toledo Railroad, later the Toledo, Wabash and Western, and then the Wabash System.[46] Meanwhile, down in St. Louis, the Massachusetts-born lawyer Thomas Allen assumed the presidency of the Pacific Railroad Company and supported the Hannibal and St. Joseph railroads, both of which were incorporated in 1851. The lawyer Edward Bates delivered the Fourth of July oration in 1851 to exhort the people of St. Louis to support the construction of the Pacific railroad.[47]

Lawyers also came to the fore in the railroad movement in Iowa river towns. At Davenport, in November 1850, the Rock Island and LaSalle Railroad was organized to connect Rock Island to the Illinois and Michigan canal at LaSalle. This meeting followed a larger meeting on the same issue a month before in Iowa City. Judge James Grant was elected president. When they reorganized the railroad as the Chicago and Rock Island Railroad in April 1851, Grant retained the presidency. Two years later, John and Ebenezer Cook, along with James Grant and Hiram Price, were among the "leading members" of the Mississippi and Missouri Railroad.[48] Meanwhile, at Dubuque, George Wallace Jones was instrumental in getting the Illinois Central to place its terminus across the river from Dubuque at Dunleith in 1851, where it arrived four years later. Jones and Platt Smith, John Dyer, Caleb Booth, and merchants Jesse P. Farley and Lucius H. Langworthy formed the Dubuque and Pacific Railroad in 1853.[49] Smith, serving first as counsel and then as vice president and president would be closely associated with the entire history of the Dubuque and Pacific Railroad.[50] Likewise, at Dubuque, the lawyer Frederick E. Bissell became president of the Dubuque, St. Peter's and St. Paul Railroad Company, when it was organized three years later.[51] Two years later when the Langworthy brothers – James, Edward, Lucius, and Solon – launched a competing railroad and incorporated the Dubuque and Western Railroad, they did so with the support of Lincoln Clark, a prominent lawyer and former representative who became the company's president for a year. He joined fellow lawyers Thomas S. Wilson, William J. Barney, and Henry Wiltse and also merchants Caleb Booth and William Rebman as directors of the road.[52]

At Burlington, Charles Mason, Henry W. Starr, David Rorer, James W. Grimes, and Johnathan C. Hall were among the attorneys who boosted all rail connections to the East and West. In early 1851, each of these men signed their name to a "circular letter" calling for a Burlington connection to a cross-Illinois railroad from Lafayette, Indiana, via Peoria (see Fig. 15, above).[53] When the Peoria and Oquawka Railroad was incorporated in 1851, Charles Mason assumed the presidency and tried to organize the construction of the railroad to Peoria and, later, the connection with the Chicago, Burlington, and Quincy system. In January 1851, James Grimes was elected a director of the railroad and went to work to acquire a land grant from the legislature.[54] Over in Peoria, lawyers Charles Ballance – later the mayor – and Onslow Peters were actively involved in establishing this connection around Chicago to the West.[55] Much later, in 1858, Charles Mason would actively try to push the development of a local road from Fort Madison to Burlington, as well as from Burlington to Keokuk.[56]

That December James Grimes articulated in a speech his vision for Burlington to be at the head of a railroad to connect the Mississippi with the Missouri and on to the Pacific Ocean.[57] A few weeks later, on 7 January 1852, Grimes reported that prospects for land grant legislation, based on Stephen Douglas's bill for the Illinois Central in 1850, seemed encouraging. On this expectation, forty-six men met in Burlington on 15 January to draw up the articles of incorporation for the Burlington and Missouri Railroad. Among the lawyers at the meeting were Charles Mason, David Rorer, Johnathan C. Hall, Thomas Newman, Henry W. Starr, and James Woods. Though Grimes, who was about to become Governor of Iowa, was apparently not at the meeting, the company appointed him two days later to go to Washington to work further for a railroad grant, a task he combined with his broader interests in the Peoria and Oquawka Railroad to seek capital in the hinterland to the east of town, and in the East, in February and March 1852.[58] In 1855, Jonathan C. Hall was elected president of the Burlington and Missouri River Railroad and managed with such skill that one of the first locomotives to enter town was named the "J. C. Hall."[59] In 1856 and 1857 Charles Mason supported the efforts to acquire a land grant for the road, in both Congress and the Iowa legislature.[60] In 1858, his longtime friend David Rorer became the solicitor for the railroad, a position he would retain for the rest of his career.[61]

Finally, at Keokuk, lawyers Hugh T. Reid, James Love, and Lyman E. Johnson were the first in town to show interest in the railroads by going to a convention at Fairfield in January 1852.[62] Hugh T. Reid worked to develop the Keokuk and Missouri Railroad, and after the Civil War became the president and superintendent of the Des River Valley Railroad between Keokuk and Des Moines.[63] He was joined in 1856 by Davis Wells Kilbourne, Colonel Samuel R. Curtiss, and Judge Thomas Claggett.[64] General Verplanck Van Antwerp, a lawyer who spent his career in politics, was, with Hugh T. Reid, one of the directors of the Keokuk and Minnesota Railroad. Meanwhile judge and legislator Edward Johnstone supported the local railroad financially, though it is unclear whether he served officially in any of the towns' railroad projects. Dan F. Miller, on the other hand, was associated with the Keokuk, Mount Pleasant, and Muscatine Railroad.[65]

Building a railroad into a successful and profitable operating line was a daunting organizational and logistical process in which no one, especially small-town lawyers, had much experience. Among the urban elite of the region, it was widely believed that all a town needed to do was to unify its people, organize the railroad company, raise funds locally, and then, with capital in hand, commence building the road. Yet as these lawyers-turned-railroad men quickly realized, local resources were woefully inadequate to meet the costs of railroad construction and operation. As a result, company officials and locals were compelled to cast a broader net in search of operating capital.

Besides seeking aid from townspeople, they sought funds from farmers and residents of towns along the proposed line[66] as well as from "outsiders." The sheer logistical and organizational challenge which "railroading" presented would gradually displace each participant's localist and parallelist world view. In accepting capital from outsiders, railroad men reluctantly let them have some say in company operations. As each aspect of railroading, from management to operation, became a regional enterprise guided by regional ideas and considerations, local people were compelled to contour or alter their ideas and begin to see local self-interest as distinct and separate from regional interests. The search for capital to build competing lines also made westerners, in general, more aware of how undercapitalized the western economy remained. "Going east" for governmental or capitalist support was, for railroad men, a moment of provincial self-discovery. At each stage, more and more company directors from across the region competed for funds at the centers of the developing regional and national financial systems. With each trip, meeting, sales pitch, or request – most of which were rebuffed, denied, or considered without a response – those men operating within this new system shed their parochial self-interests and parallelist booster ideology and received an education in the dynamics of the emerging regional and national systems.

The building of a railroad network in the 1850s corresponded – in iron and wood – to the construction of regional professional and corporate networks of power around the developing regional metropolises of Chicago and St. Louis in which many of these individuals would construct new careers. While pursuing corporate strategies, railroad men also had to get the required resolutions and charters

Constructing a regional society

for incorporation and gain public support for public resolutions and bond issues. This quickly drew them into the legal and governmental edifice which many of them had constructed in the previous decade and in which many of them already worked. The passage of the Illinois Central Act of 1850 supporting the railroads through land grants drew most companies toward the federal government for financial support. The approach of eastern railroads moving west further intertwined company agendas with the power networks of politics and the law. With the emergence of these new options, strategies for establishing and funding the operations of a railroad company became, in the 1850s, increasingly complex, directed simultaneously toward local, hinterland, regional, and national sources.

Adept in civil procedures involving the appeal of county and circuit cases to the state or even U.S. Supreme Court, and involved, as legislators, in framing legislation, submitting charters for approval or petitions for redress, and gaining support for each of these among the public, lawyers were, among the various actors, naturally called upon to sort through the myriad of legal, political, and financial procedures, maneuvers, and issues between local and national venues involved in launching a railroad company. As boosters, they were well acquainted with other circuit lawyers, and the regional coterie of lawyers and politicians who met at the state capital. Lawyers thus worked within a network of contacts, friends, and acquaintances in which they could find support for their efforts. Finally, because railroads, as legal entities, inevitably faced litigation, lawyers, as officers, litigants, and judges, began to handle ever more circuit and state supreme court cases involving the railroads – raising intractable conflict-of-interest issues. As the number of railroad-related cases increased in the 1850s, railroad law gradually emerged as a separate specialty within the law. Inevitably, western lawyers who became involved in the litigation of railroad companies found their subsequent professional legal careers structured by it. Railroad companies either became their clients or, if they hired them as counsel in the corporate legal departments in the 1860s and 1870s, their employers.

The procedures and strategies – or even processes – by which a local company was made a financial and material reality followed roughly the same scenario from town to town. Once they organized the company and "the papers [were] signed,"[67] the officers moved in three directions to fund the company and build a railroad. Initially their actions were personal, fraternal, and local. Funding usually began with nominal cash donations by one or two of the directors to fund a survey or have stocks and documents printed in preparation for a public sale of stock. After the Galena and Chicago Union was organized and directors were elected, Charles Hempstead and Henry Corwith, after coming up with $75 and $40, respectively, went around town acquiring "promises to pay" from thirty-five others varying from $2.50 to $30 each to "defray the expenses of preliminary surveys of a route or routes for a railroad from Chicago to Galena." Elihu B. Washburne added only five dollars to the total collected of $423.50.[68] After an initial informal collection, a closed subscription among a very small group of the elite would be "thrown up." At Davenport, Antoine LeClaire began the funding effort for the Mississippi and Missouri Railroad by subscribing $25,000 in stock.[69] When the Dubuque and Pacific was incorporated in May 1853, three of the directors, all businessmen, F. S. Jessup, J. P. Farley, and H. W Sanford, laid down $10,000, $10,000 and $4,000 each.[70] In St. Louis, James H. Lucas challenged two other capitalists in town to join him in combining to subscribe half of the $200,000 needed to get the Pacific Railroad under way in January 1850. Daniel Page and John O' Fallon accepted the challenge and then tossed a coin "for the honor of becoming the leading subscriber." O'Fallon won and contributed $33,400.[71]

With the books still closed, company officers would solicit private subscriptions more broadly among the members of the town elite. In 1853, when railroad enthusiasm was ablaze in Keokuk, a director of the Warsaw and Lafayette Railroad personally solicited private subscriptions of $1,000 to $1,500 from ten or so of his booster friends.[72] Several years later, when the townspeople expressed a need for a railroad from Carthage to Clayton, Illinois, which would give Keokuk the longed-for "eastern connection," James L. Estes, Charles Mason's agent, suggested they start the process by throwing up a subscription among ten or more of the town's leaders which would encourage the "citizens to go their last dollar" on it.[73] In the elite subscriptions in Galena in 1847 and 1848, fifty-two members of Galena's booster network purchased stock in the railroad.[74] The underwriting of the Northern Cross Railroad began with a private subscription in small amounts among Quincy's elite totaling about $10,000. This was apparently insufficient to "seed" the townspeople, for when company officers presented their case to the people and requested a public subscription in 1850, they were voted down.[75] In 1851, in Dubuque, when plans were afoot for the Dubuque and Western Railroad, "nearly all the capitalists of Dubuque subscribed liberally to the stock."[76]

Individual efforts by the members of the elite, in showing their confidence in the road, sought to encourage townspeople to subscribe stock themselves or vote for publicly funded stock subscriptions. Nevertheless, the original subscribers often remained as a private – though limited – reserve source of capital for the company. In Quincy, in 1853, when the company needed more to complete the railroad project, key members of the elite again stepped forward to offer another $35,000.[77] In 1857 when the Dubuque and Pacific Railroad was in desperate need of operating funds, Platt Smith – unable to get any publicly – personally contributed $5,000 in stock to the company and in a letter to Jesse P. Farley "put down" eleven other men in town – including Richard Bonson, who he was sure would "do the same" to come up with the $60,000 needed to help save the railroad and, indirectly, Dubuque.[78]

As private subscriptions ran their course, the company's books would be opened and stock offered to the public. In the view of those who believed that people who use a railroad must support it for it to be profitable, the public sale of stock was both financially and ideologically crucial to the success of the railroad. Thomas Drummond of the Galena and Chicago Union Railroad hoped that "every farmer along the projected line" would purchase at least one share of stock ($100).[79] By such reckoning, railroads could anticipate a funding level of approximately $100 for each household (about one-fifth of the population) in the towns and the townships along the line. The Galena and Chicago Union not only had more than fifty subscribers among Galena's elite, but also drew in subscribers from along the line and up to Grant County, Wisconsin.[80] The citizens of Scott County supported the Chicago and Rock Island Railroad with $75,000 in a subscription in the fall of 1850 and another $225,000 by the following March, which exceeded sales expectations by three times.[81] As local sales leveled off, company stock would be placed on the national market in New York City, where it would hopefully draw national and international investors. By 1860 the "List of Preferred Stockholders of the Dubuque and Pacific Railroad" included seventy-four men and one woman (the wife of a director). Among the stockholders, however, only about a dozen were local residents who held a mere 13 percent of the total stock valued at $1.4 million.[82]

Since most subscriptions were promises to pay, however, the money in the bank represented by subscriptions was, given the means of most residents, and the slowness of payments or nonpayments, often in question. James L. Estes inferred as much when he reported that the planned-for Pekin and Wabash Railroad which would give Keokuk a connection to the East had almost a million dollars in stock "taken in this road" but still was unable to predict "what the result will be."[83] In 1854, in spite of the Burlington and Missouri Railroad's considerable stock subscriptions, money from subscriptions for shares "trickled in slowly."[84] Charles Mason himself, as president of the Peoria and Oquawka Railroad, tried to deal with the problem of nonpayment of promised funds by having a form printed which tersely "hereby notified" each late subscriber or nonpayer "that there is now due from you . . . [an amount] upon your subscription of . . . dollars to the capital stock of said company" and that if they did not receive payment by a specified date "suit will be commenced against you."[85] They intended such notes to avert time-consuming litigation, such as that pursued by the Sangamon and Alton R.R. against three subscribers in default. Hiring first William Martin of Alton and then, in an appeal, Abraham Lincoln, the company won a judgment in its favor.[86]

Given the difficulties with public stock subscriptions, railroad companies concluded that a quicker way for them to acquire capital was to encourage people to authorize their county or city governments to issue bonds and purchase stocks from either the revenues from the sale of city or county bonds backed by city or county tax revenues or credit or in a direct exchange with the railroad company, which would accept the city bonds as an asset.[87] Resolutions passed at railroad meetings regularly led to a call for an election within two or three weeks, a short intense campaign by leaders and directors to convince the townspeople to support the railroad, followed by an often overwhelming vote in favor of authorizing the city or county government to issue bonds backed by city or county credit.

The residents of Dubuque were among the first and most enthusiastic followers of this strategy.[88] Beginning with a lopsided vote in favor of a bond issue to buy stock in 1852, the citizens of Dubuque, between 1851 and 1857, authorized the issuing of more than $1.6 million in city bonds while residents of the county committed another $400,000 in county bonds to support local railroads, thus making the city liable to pay interest for twenty years on the bonds that sold.[89] No other city came close to Dubuque's profligate opening of the city's coffers to railroad companies. The citizens of Davenport in 1853,[90] Burlington in 1854[91] and several times in Keokuk between 1851 and 1858 voted on average $250,000 in support of various railroad projects.[92] Across the river in Quincy, stock subscriptions voted in 1849, 1850, 1856, and 1857 totaled about $600,000.[93] Meanwhile, down at St. Louis, the city residents voted for a subscription of $500,000 to support the Ohio and Mississippi Railroad in 1851.[94]

Though seemingly excessive, such locally derived funding supported the localist strategy of "building the road from home means," that is, "by the people who are on the spot," which Platt Smith of Dubuque described as the "original plan" of the Dubuque and Pacific Railroad[95] and considered the only sure means of putting any road on a solid basis. The amount of local support depended, however, on both bond or stock sales. If they did not sell, funds to the railroad company would, like everything else, dry up. Nevertheless, by placing bonds into the bond market, funds were funneled from the city government to the company, thus reinforcing local control – though interest obligations to purchasers from the outside eroded some control. In contrast, the public sale of a corporation's stock created the possibility that an outside party would buy enough stock to gain control of a company's operations and thus increase the risk of losing local control.

Because most private and public stock subscriptions sold locally, however, were still inadequate to fund the construction and operation of a railroad line, this risk was ever present. Individual contributions from citizens in the midst of railroad fever barely scratched the surface in accumulating the capital necessary to construct and operate a railroad. With costs for construction estimated at around $6,000 a mile for the Davenport and Iowa City Railroad, $8,000 to $10,000 a mile for the Iowa Western Railroad (both very low estimates), and $15,000 to $25,000 a mile to build and equip, a railroad of even a hundred miles in distance would cost anywhere from $800,000 to $2.5 million.[96] Therefore both directors and local supporters were compelled by necessity to seek support elsewhere. They first went to the people living along the line to request county bond issues. Such a hinterland strategy, undertaken by the directors and members of the elite who supported them, to both sell company stock and encourage the people to vote stock subscriptions for the road, involved them in a range of self-interests and divergent opinions that made their plan a harder sell. And the farther from home they went, the more they encountered a diversity of interests working against the policy of the directors at the center or terminus.

First, the directors decided the general route of the proposed road. To do this, they hired either a survey team or rode out across the hinterland themselves. Once they decided upon the route, the directors and officers would send out "circular letters" announcing their intentions and soon afterward set out "along the line" to "stir up the people" (see Fig. 15). In each significant town this series of events, involving letters, petitions, resolutions, and votes to provide support and subscriptions of stock or land, which had occurred in the town where they organized the railroad, was replicated on a smaller scale. For many lawyers, these forays were akin to a political "canvass" or riding the circuit. Through personal appeals, the direc-

Constructing a regional society

tors and their supporters would make the intentions of the railroad company known, broaden its reputation, and hopefully deepen support for it.

A more public and efficient way of doing this was to call for a regional or hinterland general railroad meeting or convention at some place on or near the proposed line of the railroad.[97] Regional or local conventions which by 1850 had become regular events in the political movement to advocate the improvement of western rivers – at Rock Island in 1846, Davenport in September 1849,[98] and Burlington in October 1851[99] – were efficient because those who attended them were already disposed to more general plans and thus better able to integrate their interests to a regional strategy.[100] In moving from local meetings to a regional convention, members of town delegations followed the closely intertwined structure of the political system, from county seats to the state capital. Conventions in St. Louis in 1836,[101] Springfield in December 1845,[102] and Rockford in January 1846 launched the convention movement.

In anticipation nearby towns called local meetings to choose and pay for delegates to go to the convention. At Galena those present at a railroad meeting responded to the call and sent twenty delegates, including Charles Hempstead and Thomas Drummond, to the Rockford Convention on 7 January 1846. While on their way to the convention, the delegates, such as J. Young Scammon from Chicago, promoted the idea of the railroad to the people whom they met along the way. Some 319 delegates, all of whom had been chosen at local meetings, or caucuses, in counties and towns along the proposed line of the railroad, attended the convention at Rockford.[103] With Thomas Drummond of Galena serving as chair, the delegates voted to incorporate the Galena and Chicago Union Railroad, named directors, and called for a stock subscription. Elihu Washburne, meanwhile, learned with interest that the "meeting was very large and enthusiastic – some 800 being present" and expressed the sentiment that he "should like mighty well to see the thing go through, but do not expect it to at present."[104] The delegates also passed resolutions to send to Congress.

All conventions, like that held at Davenport in September 1849[105] and Burlington in October 1851,[106] provided opportunities for large contingents of different local bars and booster networks to meet each other. At Burlington in 1851, seventy-five merchants and lawyers from St. Louis met the most active fifteen to twenty-five members of the local bars, male subcultures, and booster ethos in Keokuk, Burlington, Fort Madison, and Dubuque. Those attending from Keokuk were the elite of the male subculture (see Chapter 3), county bar, and booster ethos, all of whom were shifting their attention to railroads. In attendance were Hawkins Taylor, Daniel Hine, Silas Heaight, Lyman Johnson, and Lewis Reeves, the core of the male subculture and the local bar, and more recent members Ralph P. Lowe, Thomas Claggett, Thomas B. Cuming, Hugh T. Reid, and Edward and George Kilbourne. The leaders of Burlington's booster ethos knew each of these prominent men: James W. Grimes, Augustus C. Dodge, Charles Mason, Milton Browning, L. D. Stockton, Henry W. Starr, David Rorer, and Jonathan C. Hall. Also present were prominent members of the state bar from Fort Madison, Judge Edward Johnstone and Dan F.

Miller, and Dubuque, Ben Samuels, Thomas S. Wilson, George Nightengale, and Stephen Hempstead. Samuel R. Curtiss, who in 1851 divided his time between St. Louis and Keokuk, was also present.[107]

Though called to discuss the obstructions of the rapids, most delegates at Burlington turned their attention to railroads and proposed the construction of the south-to-north Dubuque and Keokuk Railroad. A letter from the members of the committee appointed "to obtain statistics showing the value of the commerce of the Valley of the Upper Mississippi" indicates apparent differences between the Burlington and Dubuque delegates over building the road. The committee, made up of Henry W. Starr, Lacon D. Stockton, David Rorer, and Johnathan C. Hall of Burlington, all local advocates of the railroad who would be present at a meeting in December to establish the Burlington and Missouri Railroad, wrote a letter on 18 February 1852 to Thompson Campbell, representative from Galena, arguing that Dubuque already had a terminus and that "fairness and equity" as well as national interest should now favor a connection to Burlington. Campbell, aware that railroads spelled Galena's doom, would argue that the railroad would undermine support for river improvements and later in spring 1852 opposed a national bill to give public lands to the railroads.[108]

Another convention was called to incorporate the Dubuque and Keokuk Railroad later that month in February 1852 at Fairfield, Iowa.[109] As at the other conventions, the delegates present memorialized Congress – and in particular Senator George Jones – to pass a bill giving public lands (on the model of the Illinois Central bill) to support the south-to-north road. The residents of Keokuk, suddenly aware of the nature of the road and the town's important role in its development, sent a delegation of twenty residents to the convention. Among the delegates were other key members of the town's male subculture including General Hugh T. Reid, General Arthur Bridgeman, Guy Wells, Captain Love, Dan Hine, Bill Clark, Edward Kilbourne, Henry J. Campbell, Lyman E. Johnson, Abraham Chittenden, and General Van Antwerp,[110] of whom the lawyers Reid and Johnson, as well as Hine and Kilbourne, had been at Burlington several months before. The following October, a group of St. Louisans, at the North Missouri Railroad Convention at St. Charles, Missouri, a month before the Mississippi Valley Railroad Convention in St. Louis for which the Burlington Convention of October 1851 had made a regional call, pledged their support for "a North/South route along the Mississippi Valley."[111]

In most cases, such conventions were either impractical or, given the personal nature of connections among those "boosting" the railroad in different towns or cities, unnecessary. The directors of incorporated railroad companies generally set out again into the hinterland to sell the idea of the railroad to the people. On a basic level, Charles Mason and Judge Wightman of Keokuk in July 1858 went up the "Mississippi Bottom" to "see the people concerning the railroad" where they called on a number of people with the "purpose . . . to set in motion a project for a railroad from Fort Madison through Columbia City through Burlington." A month later Mason was out with Judge Wightman along the Skunk River to look at the railroad route.[112] Mason had himself once received a delegation from the Keokuk, Mount

Pleasant, and Muscatine Railroad at his residence above Keokuk, who requested a right of way across his lands to allow the railroad to follow a certain route. Mason accepted the request provided they "agree to allow any other railroad to connect with theirs on fair terms."[113]

Such individual actions and negotiations to gain support for a railroad were in keeping with Charles Mason and other lawyers' personal style of leadership, which they cultivated on the circuit and at the state bar. When, in early 1852, Mason was elected president of the Peoria and Oquawka Railroad, the goal of which was to build a line between Burlington and Peoria, he sent his colleague James Grimes on a trip to the east of Burlington and then to the East Coast to establish the line and drum up support for the road. On 27 January, Grimes reported that "circular letters" and petitions were in circulation "all along the road" and had stirred up residents in Knoxville, Galesburg, Oquawka, and Farmington to call meetings and "pass subscriptions" for the road. Meanwhile, Richard Morgan and other directors from Peoria had been elected and set out inspecting the eastern end of the proposed route for the road.[114]

In the fall of 1847 William B. Ogden and J. Young Scammon of Chicago traveled the proposed line of the Galena and Chicago Union railroad to solicit subscriptions and procured enough to begin construction.[115] At Alton, Charles Hunter reported in May 1850 that not only had Alton's citizens "taken" $50,000 in stock for the proposed Alton and Terre Haute road in May 1850, but that "the portion allotted to the counties along the route [had] also been made up."[116] Similarly, in the wake of the 15 January 1852 incorporation of the Burlington and Missouri Railroad several directors and supporters of the road went west into Des Moines, Henry, Jefferson, and Wapello counties campaigning for both individual support and county subscriptions in the same manner. The following year residents rewarded their efforts by providing funds through bond subscriptions of over $100,000 per county.[117]

In 1852, Orville Browning and his colleague Calvin Warren stumped the hinterland of Quincy to encourage locals to buy railroad bonds or issue bonds to buy stock. On 18 February they addressed the people of Brown County at the county courthouse in Mt. Sterling "in favor of subscriptions of stock to the rail road." "There were probably two hundred persons present, and I have no doubt that an impression highly favorable to the work was produced upon them," remarked Browning, though he doubted, given their "outward appearance," that they had much capital to give and seemed a bit sheepish in requesting $50,000. Nevertheless toward the end of the meeting a "resolution was offered and unanimously adopted requesting the county court to submit the proposition to the people."[118] Through similar persuasion the people of other nearby counties contributed similar amounts to the Northern Cross, later the Chicago Burlington and Quincy Railroad.[119]

It was on such forays into their immediate hinterlands – when requests for support went from rhetoric to money – that company directors first encountered the economic interests of other towns and counties. Different interests created suspicions and disagreements that began to undermine the unanimity of hinterland support for a railroad. Whether among power elites, directors and stockholders of a newly formed company, or townspeople from different places, such differences fueled by self-interest and intensified by higher stakes involving the very survival of one's town quickly led to acrimony, animosity, and disputes, which further eroded regional unity.

To avert this tendency and cultivate unity as they moved farther afield into the region, those directors with contacts in the legal fraternity of the circuit or state wrote letters to their colleagues along the line, or visited them in person, to try to convince them to join the leadership of the company or exert influence over local directors in the company. Through collegiality and personal influence they sought to cultivate a spirit of compromise and agreement between the directors and integrate various self-interests into a common interest for the sake of the road. Charles Mason corresponded with Onslow Peters and Charles Ballance of Peoria, both of whom he already knew, and sought from them advice and support on how to manage a particularly political director from Peoria. So, too, Charles Hempstead and Thomas Drummond corresponded with each other and with J. Young Scammon concerning the Galena and Chicago Union, and the latter wrote to the Langworthys in Dubuque.[120] Such correspondence, involving countless "railroad letters," which paralleled and fed off an almost continual regional discourse of "railroad talk" concerning the proposed routes and operations of the railroads – Mason in 1858 noted that that was all people talked about, as did Hempstead in 1845–1846 – had become a ubiquitous part of the working lives of these men by the 1850s.

The officers of a railroad, through railroad correspondence, did much of the work of reestablishing or making connections to solicit aid, calling for support through local meetings, sending petitions and resolutions to the state legislature or Congress, and advocating stock subscriptions and bond issues. To expedite their correspondence, they organized "committees of correspondence" and committees to investigate the route, gather information, or seek funding by memorializing the state legislature or one's representatives in Congress.

Despite such efforts, however, in the hinterland along the proposed line of a railroad the unanimity which most local booster ethoses cultivated was fractured by intraurban rivalries and clashes between conflicting self-interests. Railroad boosters routinely presented similar proposals, and raised similar expectations, among competing towns. Orville H. Browning admitted that when he traveled the circuit above Quincy, he told residents from different counties, along potentially different routes of the road, the same thing, no matter where the railroad, when built, would run.[121] Others did the same.[122] Yet local supporters regularly failed to recognize the difference between direct and indirect benefits that the railroad brought and thus questioned whether they should support a road that did not intend to go through their town.

Galenans, for example, doubted the intentions of the Illinois Central Railroad when, after the Illinois Central bill of 1850, the company's intention of making the Lead City its western terminus waned. Drummond and the people of Galena sought assurances from the Galena and Chicago Union Railroad that Galena would be the terminus, but the company was unresponsive. When the Illinois Central took over railroad construction, Galena was able to get even fewer assurances and its citizens lost interest in supporting the road.[123] All the while, the directors, in both Chicago and, after 1851, New York, lost patience with the constant petitions and threats from Galenans and pursued a course that would send the tracks through Galena and onto Dunleith, thus effectively taking the railhead function away from Galena.[124] In defense of Galena, Elihu Washburne argued that Galenans "pursued the only course that was practicable [because] the Central co[mpany] understood to run over us and through us" and then charged that the Illinois Central raised a chorus of "bitter and irreconcilable hostility" against Galena, to which they finally responded by supporting a railroad connection to Milwaukee.[125]

When, in late 1849, Stephen Douglas introduced the Illinois Central bill, Dubuque's senator in Washington, George Wallace Jones, asked Douglas to amend the bill to read that the Illinois Central would establish its terminus eighteen miles west of Galena at Dunleith, opposite Dubuque. Jones advocated making Dunleith the terminus on national grounds, seeing a benefit in connecting the Illinois Central to the Mississippi River, a great national public highway, rather than for "petty parochialist interests" of Dubuque. Edward D. Baker and later Thompson Campbell, along with many Galenans, saw this as a maneuver to entice the Illinois Central to bypass Galena and operate to the benefit of Dubuque. This suspicion, once planted in the minds of Galenans, further fostered their fear that the directors of the Galena and Chicago Union railroad would, upon merging with the Illinois Central, ignore Galena's interest and build the terminus at the Mississippi, which is, of course, what they eventually did in 1855. Based on these suspicions, a "jealousy and rivalry" carried forward by a "belligerent newspaper discussion" developed between Galena and Dubuque.

The proposed construction of the Dubuque and Keokuk Railroad from south to north across the state inflamed similar urban jealousies and set in motion intense intraurban rivalries. To river town residents, an interior railroad either challenged the urgency of clearing obstructions from the Mississippi or appeared irrelevant, since the best railroad connections were to be made directly to the East. Burlington's residents opposed the road because it maintained Keokuk's advantages, from which Burlington suffered; it undermined support for the improvement of the rapids; and it also threatened to divert support from getting an eastern connection. The committee from the 1852 Burlington Convention also charged that the railroad seemed to give undue advantages to Dubuque. One Dubuque observer noted in January 1852 that Davenport preferred the plan "because she will secure the main line," while the building of branch routes to Muscatine and Burlington itself would "mollify Burlington's opposition."[126] Thompson Campbell of Galena charged that Keokuk supported the railroad because the road would delay the improvement of the rapids and thus sustain Keokuk's position as a trans-shipping point to the north, forcing "every city, every town, and every hamlet from the Des Moines rapids to the falls of St. Anthony . . . to pay tribute to this town of Keokuck [sic]." Meanwhile, Lincoln Clark of Dubuque charged that Galenans opposed it because it undermined the river interest in general.[127]

Similar suspicions between interests from different towns along the line sabotaged the completion of the Peoria and Oquawka Railroad. The directors in Peoria, aware of their proximity to an eastern connection, turned a blind eye to the concerns and interests of the directors in Burlington. While Peoria supporters feared that Burlington would, at first chance, redirect their interests toward Chicago, Burlington supporters feared that the Peoria support necessary to build the road would evaporate when they could not secure an eastern connection. Accusations that Peoria's directors favored construction on the eastern side of the line deepened animosities among the directors as well as among residents from towns along the western part of the line. By this point, a call from a Galesburg resident for residents in "Burlington, Monmouth, Knoxville, and Galesburg . . . to harmonize their views with regard to their respective interests and . . . to unite as *one man* in building a line of railroad that shall be for their mutual benefit," Julius Manning's (of Knox County) concurrence that "we are one company and as such are interests are one," and Onslow Peters's commitment to "dwell together in unity" seemed to fall on deaf ears amid the constant squabbling.

Such acrimony, which led to Mason's resignation from the Peoria and Oquawka, was rooted in trying to build railroads without sufficient capital. Many concluded, as James Knox of Knox County did in a letter to Charles Mason, just before Mason abandoned his interests in the railroad: "We are too poor to keep up with the spirit and progress of the times," and though he hoped that Mason would be able to make some arrangement that would allow the company to build a part of the railroad, he feared that ultimately he would have to sell out its interests "entirely to outsiders" and have them finish the job.[128]

Many westerners had initially attempted to construct their "eastern connection" to the broader system in alignment with their localist views of their position within a regional urban system – that as a central place they generated economic dynamics and feedbacks that moved out from and returned to their center to generate local growth and development. They were forced east in search of funding, or as Onslow Peters of Peoria termed it, "material aid" from "individual capitalists," "by forming a connection with other railroad companies," or through land grants from the federal government. "Going east" "to enlist capitalists there"[129] became, in the early 1850s, an emerging structure in the business lives of most western railroad men. It was within this broader national structure, which superseded the regional system they had initially sought to reconstruct by means of railroads, that westerners' parochialist regional views would run headlong into and be "provincialized" by emerging metropolitan, eastern, and national perspectives.

The business or political trips to the East of Elihu Washburne of Galena, James Grimes and Charles Mason of Burlington, James Grant of Davenport, Richard Morgan of Peoria, Lucius H. Langworthy and Platt Smith of Dubuque, Nehemiah Bushnell and James Singleton of Quincy,[130] Hugh T. Reid, Hugh W. Sample, and David Wells Kilbourne of Keokuk,[131] among many others, trace the emerging structure of a national power network to which the West was attaching itself. Centered at Capitol Hill in Washington, D.C., and Wall Street and Broadway in New York City and to a lesser extent State Street in Boston and Lake and LaSalle streets in Chicago, the corridors of this network followed the main railroad lines from the West to the East, step by step, as they built the connections in the 1850s.

Forays into the national realm at New York or Washington, propelled by local self-interest, inevitably confronted "national interests" which cared little for the nuances of "purely local" competitions between towns and cities for "individual aggrandizement."[132] Those who went east hoping to convince capitalists and politicians from around the country to support their railroad plans often found that their plans were already being coopted or superseded by the national plans and interests of eastern railroad capitalists and politicians. Even George Wallace Jones, senator from Iowa, would find that eastern capitalists responded to efforts to sell Iowa railroads within a framework of local or regional plans by quickly turning the discussion around and suggesting how it was that the Iowa roads would fit into their plans for extending their roads to the West. While westerners viewed eastern roads as the "eastern connection" which would bring them prosperity by connecting them to the national railroad network, eastern capitalists such as Abel Corbin of New York saw it differently. "Your roads," he wrote to Senator Jones, were but *"mere extensions of Boston, New York, and Philadelphia roads,"*[133] and, therefore, capitalists in eastern metropolises would decide where to build them. For towns like Burlington and Davenport that lay in the path of eastern plans, such dictates were easy to live with, even if it risked the loss of local control. For towns like Galena, Dubuque, Alton, Quincy, or Keokuk, which, to easterners, seemed off the direct east-to-west railroad routes, such plans presented a challenge.

As happened in James Grimes's trip east in early 1852, trips into the national system often fused two strategies. One goal of these forays was purely economic: to find the capital to build their road. Another, following the lines of contact between constituencies and representatives, pushed for land grant legislation to support railroad construction across the state or region. Both strategies were formulated in the meetings and local conventions called to organize railroads and offer stock subscriptions. On the one hand, business travelers went east loaded with maps for demonstration and bonds and stocks for sale. On the other, they carried the ubiquitous resolutions from meetings or memorials to Congress from city councils or state legislatures requesting support for a bill to charter a corporation.

For example, a meeting organized at Sinipee, in Grant County in Wisconsin territory, by John R. Plumbe, Jr., in 1837 issued a memorial and resolutions requesting George Wallace Jones, their delegate to Congress, to request an appropriation from Congress to survey a route from Milwaukee to Sinipee to San Francisco for a transcontinental railroad, an appropriation that, despite the ridicule heaped on it, Jones was able to get.[134] A Dubuque meeting in late 1847 named Lincoln Clark chair of the Committee of Correspondence while they appointed Lucius Langworthy chairman of the Committee to Petition the State Legislature and the Congress.[135] Jones presented resolutions from the Iowa state legislature to Congress for the Dubuque and Keokuk Railroad on 24 January 1848. His colleague Augustus C. Dodge presented the first resolution from the Iowa legislature for an east-to-west road at the same time. In December Congress passed this resolution. A month later, on 20 January 1849, Jones again introduced a resolution to Congress for the Dubuque and Keokuk Road, a bill which passed in the Senate but failed in the House. Another effort in February 1851 again failed, leading to an outpouring of memorials from the residents of Burlington urging Senators Jones and Dodge to push for the bill again, as well as a call for an October convention.[136]

Meanwhile, Jones gained an amendment in Dubuque's favor to alter the land grant of the Illinois Central in 1850, which established the precedent of offering public lands for sale to support railroad development.[137] As railroad construction approached Iowa, and national support for transcontinental railroads across Iowa deepened, Jones and Dodge again took the resolutions to Congress in the winter of 1851–1852. This time, rather than offerring the Dubuque and Keokuk, Burlington and Missouri, and Mississippi and Missouri lines as separate bills, they combined three proposals into a single comprehensive proposal for a railroad system in Iowa, in hopes that by addressing more national interests between East and West, they could avert the charge of local favoritism and gain broader support. To urge on and aid their legislation, lawyers from Burlington, Dubuque, Davenport, as well as Keokuk – represented by James Grimes, Lincoln Clark, Judge James Grant, and Hugh W. Sample, respectively, memorials, maps, and documents in hand – all headed for Washington to lobby for support and "look after" their interests.[138]

On 17 January, even as they brought the issue to the floor of the Senate, the directors of the Burlington and Missouri Railroad got $500 in City of Burlington script from the city council to pay James Grimes's expenses to "go to Washington and work for a land grant for the road."[139] As a director of the Peoria and Oquawka Railroad, Grimes was also commissioned to stir up interest in the P & O along the line and try to get eastern support, as well as keep an eye on the efforts of "committees" from Dubuque and Keokuk to thwart the Dubuque and Keokuk Railroad bill. A week before, aware of Burlington's aggressive strategy, Keokuk's elite authorized Hugh W. Sample to go to Washington to look out for Keokuk's interests. The city council appropriated $500 "to bear" Sample's expenses and he set off on his desperate mission in mid-January. Edward Kilbourne believed that "Burlington was playing a strong game" and feared that since Jones "dared not oppose them" they just might – based on the great interest in a transcontinental railroad – kill both the river improvements and the Dubuque and Keokuk Railroad. If that happened he feared that "it will all be up with us and the question of supremacy settled."[140] Judge Grant of Davenport, meanwhile, arrived in Washington in late February and, by one account, was "storming and swearing about the railroad, Sundays and all other days." Representative Lincoln Clark, who had taken up his duties in Washington in November, and Lucius Hart Langworthy represented Dubuque.

Soon after Augustus C. Dodge presented a resolution before the Senate, placing the bill on the agenda for introduction, debate, and vote later in the spring, James Grimes left Burlington on his double mission. Perhaps in his possession was a copy of a petition that a committee of Burlington men – led by Charles Mason and David Rorer – had sent to Senator George Wallace Jones, to exhort Jones toward a more statewide view of the issue (assuming that Jones was for Dubuque and against every other town's interests). Arguing that "we are no more interested in this improvement than the people of Keokuk, Muscatine, Davenport, Dubuque or any other town on the river in this state," the committee noted a shift in public interest eastward in the construction of railroads and away from improvement of the rivers.[141] On the day the bill was presented to the Senate, Grimes arrived in Indianapolis to urge the Indiana state legislature to issue a memorial in support of a western connection to the proposed Peoria and Oquawka Railroad, and then continued to Cincinnati, where he acquired similar resolutions from the city council, as well as from the local congressmen.[142]

Upon his arrival in Washington in mid-February, Grimes took "a survey of the land" and did not like what he saw: Dodge and Henn (from Burlington) and Jones and Clark (Dubuque) were opposed to each other, and therefore disinclined to combine the two bills. As it turned out, the disagreement between Clark and Jones was both political and geopolitical. Clark, a newcomer, was convinced that instead of the Dubuque and Keokuk Railroad, railroads to the Northwest and West seemed more urgent. When he presented a bill to support a Northwest railroad on 28 February 1852, and later expressed support to Lucius Langworthy about a railroad due west from Dubuque, the wrath of Jones and his "men" in town and to the southwest rained down upon Clark, costing him all support in his district, except in Davenport and Burlington, where support for the east-to-west railroads remained strong.[143]

Amid such internal bickering, Grimes exhorted the Iowa men to come together to resist support for the east–west route from Stephen A. Douglas and Illinois representatives Thompson Campbell of Galena and William Richardson of Quincy. A 17 March banquet, given "to and in honor of the Iowa delegation" and attended by Clark, Jones, Dodge, Henn, and about fifty others, seemed a step in the right direction, but the event was awkward and icy, the Iowa senators having nothing to say. Nevertheless, in his misreading of Jones's position, which actually favored Dodge's plan to merge the two plans, Grimes identified the source that would temporarily draw the various Iowa forces together in the debate to come.[144] Jones had been informed of Thompson Campbell's "ungenerous" opposition to the Iowa grant a week before by Lucius H. Langworthy, a vigilant spokesperson of the booster ethos in Dubuque.[145] Aware of this impending opposition and the erosion of his support, Lincoln Clark of Dubuque readied himself to oppose Campbell whenever he prepared to speak in the House. Meanwhile, each politician received visits from representatives of various towns sent east to assure the unified passage of the now combined Iowa bill.

Grimes stayed in Washington to hear Augustus C. Dodge's great two-day speech in support of the bill on 3 and 4 March 1852, and then, while Senator Jones impatiently pushed the Senate to consider the bill for debate, which finally occurred on 17 March, left for Boston to discuss a possible connection between the Galena and Chicago Union Railroad and the Peoria and Oquawka; he later stopped in New Hampshire before returning to New York.[146] Charles Mason, following Col. Morgan, proceeded to Washington himself, arriving on 18 March, to attend the debates

Provincial lives

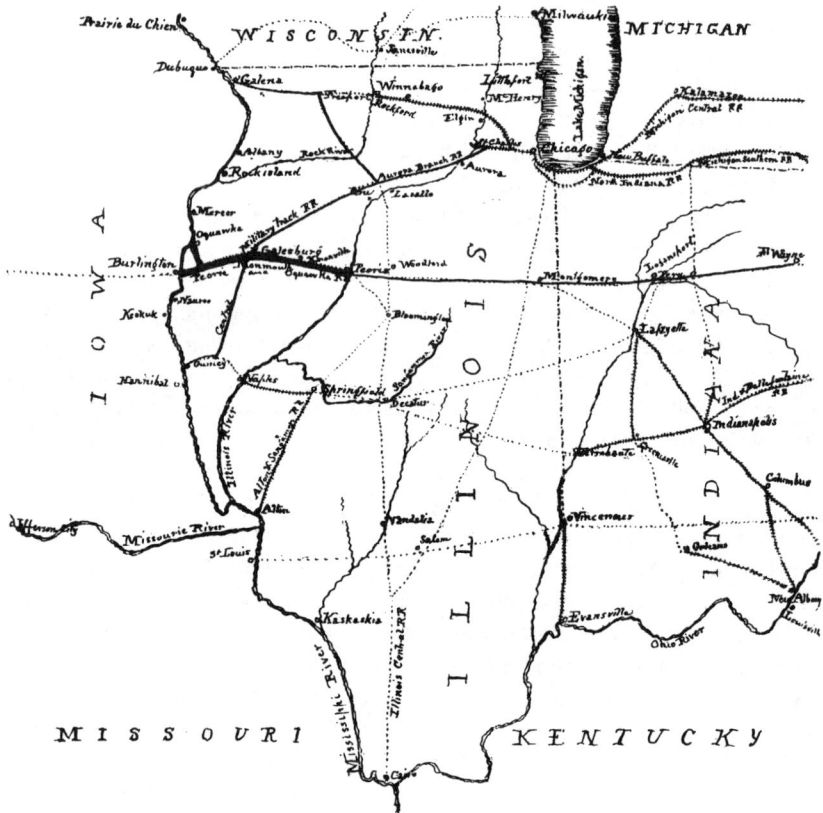

Figure 16. A "skeleton map" of the Peoria and Oquawka Railroad, 1852. (Courtesy of the State Historical Society of Iowa – Des Moines)

on the railroad issue.[147] Mason was surprised to find only tepid excitement about the bill and believed Morgan's report of the enthusiastic congressional support "a mere fiction." In spite of his pessimism, Mason, armed with his "skeleton map" of the railroad, plunged into the complexities of the politics of the issue which were quickly becoming intertwined with a larger debate concerning the relationship between the federal government and public lands (see Fig. 16). One evening he even went out to a reception with his friend Lincoln Clark.[148]

Nevertheless, having arrived during a lull in the bill's progress through either the Senate or the House, Mason followed Grimes to New York – where Judge Grant of Davenport had just been – and met some capitalists at the Astor Hotel. He then returned home while Grimes stopped in Detroit for discussions with a director of the Michigan Southern Railroad.[149] Both were back in Burlington by 29 April, the day that city's representative, Bernhart Henn, spoke before Congress on the Iowa land bill.[150] On 4 May the bill passed the Senate[151] and on 28 May Lincoln Clark and Thompson Campbell engaged in a memorable debate on the floor of the House.[152]

Again, however, evidence of internal squabbling between the Iowa men and the appearance of special advantages to the "local interests" of Iowa undermined the support for the bill in the House and it expired on the floor on 5 June 1852. To Jones and others this was bitterly disappointing, repudiating their serious effort in previous years to mollify opposition and coalesce local interests into a regional interest which they could integrate with national interests. Jones, taking the high road, articulated the need to address national interest when presenting bills to Congress and swore to Mason, "[A]s God is my judge I was and am personally as much a friend of Burlington and her interests in this and other particulars . . . as I am of Dubuque or any other place and would under similar circumstances serve one people or one place as much as the other."[153] Jones and his colleagues cultivated this regional and national approach, by following the integration of local interests into regional and national ones which had been occurring at series of larger regional or national transportation conventions. Lincoln Clark was less sanguine about "this hard blow to us," made especially hard as a similar bill for Missouri had passed. Attributing their failure to the smallness of the influence of the Iowa delegation, which made Iowa "not worth bargaining with," Lincoln Clark was convinced the result for him, due to his opposition to Jones, would be "adverse, . . . perhaps fatally so," and "composed" himself "to what may be meted out to me" while ruminating that in Washington "trials are the portions of life and history." His independence, characteristic of a relative newcomer, led to Clark's defeat in the August elections and his return to Dubuque at the end of the year.[154]

Convention culture

As local boosters among the elite in towns across the West pursued funding for their railroad projects – locally, then regionally, and finally through Congress – they navigated along the dynamics of a process of elite aggregation that would integrate their actions with an emerging regional and national power elite. In the mid-1840s through early 1850s, some local boosters, lawyers, legislators, politicians, and businesspeople sought support for their local interests by trying to unite them with broader regional and national issues and interests. At first their efforts concentrated on the western movement for river improvements. When this failed to achieve its goals, they sought, amid deepening sectionalism, to push for the route of a transcontinental railroad supported by federal land grants which would aid the building of local roads. Intertwined with and arising out of these efforts to pursue funding in Washington or New York and argue their cases, the convention movement developed and then waned.[155]

A merging of the political debates on western demands for river improvements, the location of the transcontinental railroad, and also the need for defenses in the West (in case the Oregon Question led to war with Great Britain) provided the energy which gave birth to the southern and western national convention movement, a phenomenon that would run its course through the urban West between 1845 and 1852. Arising from the enthusiasm generated from a series of meetings on the Oregon Question in Springfield, Illinois, a "great meeting" congregated on 10 June 1845 in that city.[156] The participants called for a "great Western Convention" in Memphis on 4 July.[157] When a quorum failed to appear at Memphis, the delegates met briefly, had a cordial discussion on general issues of importance, and called for a reconvening on 12 November.[158] On 13 November, the 600 delegates, including twenty-three Illinoisans,[159] thirty-seven Missourians,[160] and four Iowans – including Augustus C. Dodge and H. T. Reid[161] – initiated the political movement to seek funds for internal improvements in the West. When the progeny of that movement, the Rivers and Harbors Appropriation bill of 1846 that passed both the House and Senate, was vetoed by President Polk, a call went out for national River and Harbor Convention to be held in July the following year at Chicago.[162]

The Chicago River and Harbor Convention occurred at the vortex of a series of coalescing regional economic, political, and cultural forces in 1847. The thousands of easterners descending on Chicago, following the recent establishment of steamboat service along the lakes, placed the city at center stage and linked its future to the deepening economic forces surging west from New York across the upper Middle West. The convention was, as one historian notes, "a powerful symbol of change" not only representing "a decision about national public policy by westerners" for the first time, but also heralding the emergence of a northwestern entrepôt that had the power to control a vast hinterland.[163] Though the delegates gathered to discuss rivers and harbors, a "committee of the whole," which included the directors of most of railroads that would enter Chicago within a decade, met after the convention officially adjourned to discuss Chicago's prospects both as the future terminus of the Pacific road as well as the in-between point of a transcontinental railroad system from New York to San Francisco, thus helping to "spike [Asa] Whitney's Pacific railway plans."[164]

The failure of St. Louis to host the convention triggered its subsequent efforts to sustain the fusion of western and southern interests at its own convention in 1849, as well as its booster and economic efforts to match Chicago's every step as the terminus of the Pacific railroad. Though a large St. Louis delegation did travel north to attend the convention, including both Thomas Allen and A. B. Chambers of St. Louis – the only westerners who seem to have attended both the Memphis and the Chicago convention – and even supported the publication of its own report of the convention,[165] representation from across the Mississippi Valley was uneven. This was due to a reluctance both to subsume local interests to regional and national ones so quickly as well as to participate in what many perceived as a Whig forum. Among the 425 Illinois delegates at the convention, most were from the heavily Whig northern part of the state. Only ten delegates from Madison County and three each from Knox and Sangamon counties were present. David J. Baker was the primary representative from Madison County, and Abraham Lincoln, one of three delegates from Sangamon County.[166] Not surprisingly, heavily Democratic Iowa sent only a dozen delegates, the most prominent being Henry W. Starr and Judge George H. Williams from Burlington and George B. Sargent from Davenport, both towns with burgeoning railroad interests.[167] Elihu B. Washburne arrived early with a Galena delegation, in hopes of getting rooms at the Lake or Sherman houses, but both were "filled several days before." Washburne noted many easterners at the convention, as well as "one big Whig, Old Ab. Lincoln," repeating a nickname that only that day Washburne had heard Lisle Smith say.[168] Jesse B. Thomas and William B. Ogden were also at the convention, though not as delegates.[169]

Yet while many Illinois lawyers congregated at the convention and sustained their professional relations established at the bar and on the circuit, for most, such a "vast assembly" of strangers presented a rare opportunity to intermingle and establish a reputation in a "national" realm. The convention provided Lincoln, for instance, his first appearance before a national audience.[170] Elihu Washburne, who had made some contacts with the national Whig party as a delegate to the 1844 National Convention in Baltimore, could hardly afford to miss the opportunity to reacquaint himself with those he had met before and make new connections as well.[171]

For Edward Bates of St. Louis, the convention clearly represented a breakthrough into a national realm and established for him a national reputation which would shape his subsequent public career. After a pleasant trip up the Illinois River valley, along which he examined the proposed route of the Illinois and Michigan Canal, Bates arrived to find "every tavern crowded and every room and bed occupied, except only the one reserved at the Lake House, for my party, by previous arrangement." The next morning, Bates reported that:

after a great parade of marchings and processions, civic and military, the convention was organized in an immense circular pavilion supported in the center by a lofty flag staff. About 2000 delegates, some say 4000, from 18 states were in attendance, and among them a great many men of eminent rank in the nation, and distinguished for long and great public services.

Bates was unprepared for what followed:

It was with deep astonishment . . . I was chosen and instantly conducted to the platform to preside over the deliberations of this great assembly. . . . The Missouri delegation . . . urged my name and pushed my qualifications so strongly that a large majority of the committee agreed to the nomination and the convention, with but one dissenting voice, cordially ratified it.

Standing at the vortex of interaction between regional and national interests, Bates cleary felt its power.

The convention . . . is to me more full of public honor and private gratification than any passage of my life. . . . Certainly the conduct of the whole convention towards me, from the beginning, was marked by respectful kindness; but the closing scene was the crowning act of my life. My parting address was received by the vast multitude . . . [with] long – loud – hearty – universal applause. . . . The immense assembly – some 3 or 5000 – seemed absolutely mesmerized – their bodies, hearts, and minds subjected to my will, and answering to my every thought and sentiment with the speed and exactness of electricity. . . . I confess that my vanity has been flattered . . . in a manner and degree far beyond what I thought could ever reach me. I do believe that these three days at Chicago have given me a fairer reputation and a higher standing in the nation, than I could have hoped to attain by years of labor and anxiety in either House of Congress.

Flushed with his success, Bates set out with a party of "some 200 in number" of "very high talent and intelligence" on the steamboat *St. Louis* on one of the very first "grand excursions" to occur in the West "to take our pleasure" on the Lake. For several days they "made a tour" all the way to Mackinac Island before returning. Bates disembarked at Milwaukee and returned via Galena and the Mississippi to St. Louis.[172]

The "celebrated"[173] and "carefully planned" Chicago River and Harbor Convention had been organized to advocate internal trade and improvements of western harbors and rivers. Though the St. Louis convention report made effective arguments for the removal of the lower and upper rapids of the Mississippi at Keokuk and Davenport, focusing on Burlington, Iowa, to highlight the economic cost of the obstruction of the rapids on commerce and agriculture, the convention, in its exclusively northern delegations and strong support for the northern transcontinental railroad route, both marked a "new orientation for western aspirations" and permanently sectionalized the western convention movement.[174]

The debate over the routes of the Pacific Railroad combined with the railroad fever that swept across the urban West in 1849 to shift the central focus of the national convention movement from internal improvements to railroads. Thomas Hart Benton's introduction of a Pacific Railroad bill favoring a St. Louis to San Francisco route in the U.S. Senate in February 1849, followed by the incorporation of the Pacific Railroad from St. Louis to the western border of Missouri a month later, rekindled regional competition and sparked another round of conventions. In June a call for a national Railroad Convention to be held at St. Louis in October was made at a "mass meeting" in St. Louis. Thomas Allen, an incorporator of the new road and delegate at both the Memphis Convention of 1845 and the Chicago Convention of 1847, was in charge of publicity for the convention and distributed a "circular letter" nationwide.[175] Meanwhile, the legislature of Arkansas, to protect southern interests, called for a Pacific Railroad with Memphis as its terminus and the convening of another national convention in Memphis in November 1849.

Though the St. Louis convention convened to foster national unity, the call, coming so soon after the incorporation of the Pacific Road across Missouri, convinced many from the Illinois delegation that it would merely be a platform to make the case for St. Louis, serving as that city's answer to the Chicago River and Harbor Convention of 1847. A St. Louis delegation including the most prominent men of the booster ethos, including Edward Bates, James H. Lucas, John M. Krum, Luther M. Kennett, Thomas B. Allen, and John F. Darby, controlled the convention. Some 530 delegates from Missouri supported them, making up half the 1,056 present. To confront their influence about 350 Illinois lawyers, businesspeople, and railroad men, but few from the circuit bars across the state, made the trip to St. Louis. Yet so pervasive was the draw of the St. Louis convention across the state that a planned meeting of the board of directors of the Galena and Chicago Union Railroad scheduled for that week was canceled because "some of its members... expect to attend the St. Louis Convention."[176] Unlike at Chicago, however, a large delegation of seventy-five Iowans appeared for the proceedings in St. Louis. Among the disparate delegations from different counties in the state – Davenport sent no delegates, Dubuque sent only two – the core of booster ethos and male subculture of Keokuk again turned out. Among the Keokuk delegates were John A. Graham, Samuel R. Curtiss, David Wells Kilbourne, Verplanck Van Antwerp, Guy Wells, John W. Rankin, Lyman E. Johnson, William L. McGavic, Edward Kilbourne, Lewis R. Reeves, and L. H. Houghton. Theodore S. Parvin and Henry W. Starr were also there. The delegates appointed Stephen Douglas president, but, amid the brewing debate between the pro-Chicago and pro-St. Louis forces, he resigned. With either side unable to make their case strongly enough, they agreed, after an extended speech by Thomas Hart Benton, that the "Convention would avoid having any thing to do in the way of fixing upon a route or termini" and chose instead to urge Congress to pass a memorial with the resolution that "a grand trunk railroad with branches to St. Louis, Memphis, and Chicago would be... a central and national one."[177] To accommodate with the Memphis convention, which was mostly attended by southerners, fifty delegates at the St. Louis Convention – including two Illinoisans – were sent there, "to request said Convention's concurrence" with the resolutions of the St. Louis Convention.[178]

The convergence that facilitated the compromise resolutions passed by the two conventions within a month of each other in the fall of 1849 marked, ironically, the dying aspirations for a unified national effort to push for a single route to the Pacific. Subsequent conventions advocated their own sectional routes or proposed several routes that would allow both the north and south to acquire land grants and government support. In part, the passage of the Illinois Central bill, which provided for such a grant and thus enabled each railroad to draw from its own survey line, contributed to the sectionalization of the issue. Subsequent "national" conventions, like the one at Philadelphia in April 1850, which George Wallace Jones of Dubuque, Samuel R. Curtiss of St. Louis and Keokuk, and William B. Ogden of Chicago attended, were really sectional conventions.[179] Likewise, the conventions at New Orleans in January 1852, St. Louis in November 1852, Memphis (again) in June 1853, and Charleston in 1854 each advocated strictly sectional agendas and were attended only by delegates from either the North or South.[180]

The western convention movement drew its energy from the north-to-south patterns of trade and development that moved along the axis of the Mississippi River. The general east-to-west orientation of the developing railroad system, however, combined with deepening political fissures along sectional lines to undermine and then split the regional vision that supported the movement. In addition, the political force behind the movement, though at first bipartisan – John C. Calhoun, Thomas Hart Benton, and Stephen Douglas (all Democrats) supported western national conventions and the call for internal improvements – rose and fell ultimately with the ability of the Whig party to overcome sectional differences and launch effective national campaigns. By 1852, as the energy and organization of the party waned, resolutions from sectionalized national conventions lost whatever influence they had gained beyond resolutions coming from regional or local conventions. Therefore the means of acquiring land grants were channeled back along the lines of contact, interest, and influence between town elites, railroad companies, and their representatives in Congress.

Even so, the conventions had some impact on western political and social life. To make one's case for essentially local or sectional support for the railroads, one had to speak the language of "national interest." Whether in Congress or out, those Iowans who played a role in advocating or lobbying for legislation in 1852 (Augustus C. Dodge, George W. Jones, Hugh T. Reid, William H. Starr, George B. Sargent, Samuel R. Curtiss, and others) were more politically adept than local politicians and boosters, save for their crisscrossing of east-to-west and south-to-north schemes. Four years later, the same people, associated with reorganized companies, would repeat the process and push for the passage of a more extensive land grant for Iowa. By 1856, the completion of three railroads to the Mississippi, combined with construction west of the river, and a growing bipartisan, albeit sectional, consensus among northern Democrats and Republicans in support of using public land grants to fund the transcontinental railroad, broadened support for an Iowa land grant bill.

That spring, James Thorington of Davenport and George Wallace Jones of Dubuque presented railroad bills to the House of Representatives and the Senate, respectively, to grant to the state of Iowa four land grants for railroad construction from Burlington (the Burlington and Missouri Railroad, which had been subscribed for by the citizens only on 7 April 1856),[181] Davenport (the Mississippi and Missouri Railroad), Dubuque (the Dubuque and Pacific Railroad), and Lyons (the Cedar Rapids and Missouri Railroad) to points on the Missouri River. Charles Mason, having moved to Washington to take a position with the Patent Office a year before, was in Washington to argue for the legislation on behalf of Burlington, but having extensive land investments in Keokuk as well, was concerned about the Gate City's omission from the bill. After much less debate than in 1852, the bills passed the House and then, on 15 May 1856, passed the Senate. George Nightengale, a Dubuque lawyer, on hearing the news in Dubuque, wrote his friend Jones remarking that "we feel here in Dubuque that your untiring vigilance in our interests has made us what we are and what we expect to be," and as a result of Jones's efforts, "things look brighter for our beloved 'city of the mines,' every day add[ing] to our importance, wealth, and improvement."[182]

Meanwhile, James Grimes, now governor of Iowa, praised the bill and on 3 June 1856 called for a special session of the Iowa legislature to be held on 2 July to consider whether to grant the land from the state to the railroads and on what terms or conditions.[183] Sensing the realization of a three- or four-year campaign, railroad directors and boosters from each of the terminus cities descended on Iowa City. From Dubuque, Richard Bonson and Ben Samuels, state legislators since December 1854, arrived in Iowa City on 2 July. A delegation of supporters representing the Dubuque and Pacific Railroad, including Lucius Langworthy, James Burt, Shepard

Leffler, Charles VanDever, Lincoln Clark, and Platt Smith, soon followed.[184] On the third, after Bonson (a director of the railroad) opened the house, he had a "very agreeable" conference in Ben Samuels's room with the "friends of the railroad." In the intervening days, Bonson had a long talk with Governor James Grimes on railroad matters and heard, on consecutive evenings, talks in favor of the railroad by James Grant of Davenport and Ben Samuels and Shepard Leffler of Dubuque. Steven Hempstead and William Lovell arrived at Iowa City a week into the proceedings. After unexpected debate, and some disagreement with the Langworthys which resonated back to a deepening local dispute in Dubuque, on 11 July the bills passed both the House and the Senate, where William F. Coolbaugh, director of the Burlington and Missouri road, as well as Milton D. Browning, held seats from Burlington, and became law on 14 July 1856.[185]

The bills that passed the Iowa legislature, while providing each of the capital-poor companies vital support upon which they could draw to continue construction to the West, also included a qualification that, ironically, would put pressure on the railroads after the crash of 1857. The state granted lands acquired from the federal government to the four railroads with the stipulation that each company construct seventy-five miles of track by 1 December 1859, and thirty miles each year after that for the next five years, or the unsold land would revert to the state. In the palmy days of the summer of 1856, few gave such requirements any notice.

Railroad society: Excursions, festivals, and jubilees

By that same summer of 1856, the last connections in the much anticipated railroad network between East and West and between Chicago and its hinterland were rapidly falling into place. In the north, the Galena and Chicago had pushed west to Belvidere by 3 December 1851, Rockford by 2 August 1852, Freeport by 1 September 1853, and finally, after the Illinois Central took control over construction, reached Galena and Dunleith, across the river from Dubuque, on 30 October 1854.[186] From the south the Chicago, Alton and St. Louis Railroad reached Springfield by 9 September 1852, Bloomington by 15 October 1853, and by January 1854 connected with the Illinois Central at Bloomington and via the Chicago and Rock Island at LaSalle connected to Chicago. The direct line reached Chicago on 26 July 1854.[187] Meanwhile, the Chicago and Rock Island Railroad reached Rock Island from Chicago on 22 February 1854.[188] On 21 April 1856, the bridge over the Mississippi River between Rock Island and Davenport was opened, providing a direct contact between the west side of the river and Chicago and the East. To the south construction on the Peoria and Oquawka line from across the river at Burlington toward Galesburg reached the latter town on 17 March 1855. On 30 May 1855 the Chicago Burlington and Quincy reached Galesburg and made the connection with the Peoria and Oquawka Railroad, thus connecting Burlington to Chicago.[189] Meanwhile, from the south, construction on the Northern Cross Railroad progressed from Quincy to Avon, Illinois, by 1 January 1856, and on to its connection to Chicago at Galesburg by 24 June 1856.[190]

Wherever and whenever these connections occurred, travelers immediately, and irrevocably, boarded the cars and entered "railroad society." Well aware of the advantages of the railroads and having striven for years to get them, westerners were eager to enjoy their benefits. To honor those who had worked to secure rail connections and to celebrate, enjoy, and advertise their triumph and the future prospects of the road, town, region, and nation, almost every significant town and city to which a road was completed ritualistically marked this revolution in their lives, and consecrated its "wedding" to a "sister city" with a railroad excursion followed by a public celebration, often called a jubilee or festival.[191]

Railroad excursions and jubilees heralded a town or city's entrance into a new age, or its "rebirth," by inviting dignitaries and people from towns along the line to be present at the opening of a connection at the end of a line.[192] For many, festivals were civic and economic wedding ceremonies or christenings, properly followed by feasts, processions, and balls before the consummation in which individuals ritually surrendered a part of their individuality to join or fuse into a higher social state, to give of themselves for a higher purpose, or join in creating and giving birth to something new. Whatever each participant had been before he arrived at the celebration – an individual, local delegation, townsman, westerner, or easterner – by stepping onto the train, following the excursions, and partaking in the ritual, each walked across the threshold into a new era, a new realm, as a new person, in a new regional society.

To express this ritually and visually, imagery and metaphors of "unions," "weddings," and "nuptials," as well as references to the "fruits" resulting from this new intercourse, pervaded these events, drawing from an array of public and private occasions. By combining civic boosterism, public relations, advertising, political and interest group conventions, and religious revivals, festivals drew together a variety of practices and rituals from public and private, male and female spheres. In railroad excursions and festivals, practices and procedures were borrowed from steamboat excursions, political conventions or celebrations, formal balls, banquets, baptisms, christenings, weddings, holiday celebrations, as well as the fraternal rituals and behaviors of the male subculture. Varying in scale and duration, festivals involved various combinations of parades, bands, concerts, illuminations, town decorations, bonfires, cannon firings, fireworks, balls, "sumptuous" banquets, picnics, and political barbecues. These were preceded or followed by a free trip or excursion on a decorated train down and back along the line for large groups of residents from the two joined towns, towns along the way or nearby, plus guests – especially politicians and newspaper editors – from across the state, region, or even nation. In serving a wide range of specific local and regional economic and business purposes, for a variety of participants ranging from politicians to railroad men, investors, members of the elite and their families, and even strangers, festivals and excursions became extremely popular public events which, like special holidays or rituals, would be a milestone in the history of the town or city and often "one of the brightest days" in the lives of the older residents.[193]

Excursions and festivals or jubilees also became, because of the extensive mixing of people and ceremonial images and practices commemorating fusion and joining, fascinating events in which the members of various subcultures – male subcultures, politics, the bar and other professional cultures, civic life, and the gentility system – vied with each other for influence and control, while together finding their actions, behavior, and ideas being integrated into the dynamics of regional social development. For many, attending an excursion offered the first real opportunity to participate and act within the regional public realm. Although residents did not sometimes succeed in mixing, tending to stay in their circles and maintaining their localisms throughout the event, many experienced the potential of having one's modes of action and behavior and social strategies integrated into the more formal and categorical modes of behavior appropriate to the impersonal social realm of the region and metropolis. Such cultural interactions and fusions foreshadowed the convergence of various segmented subcultures – male, genteel, working-class, rural, and the booster ethos – which in the Gilded Age would gradually form into a new urban, commercial, public, and popular culture. In the 1850s, however, by attending a festival and excursion one celebrated not only the rebirth of one's town or city and the rejuvenation of one's social and economic aspirations at home, but also one's headlong entrance into a new economic and social realm and the integration and fusion, "for better or worse," of one's life and the life of one's town into it.[194]

Wherever and whenever a line approached or reached a major town, a railroad excursion was organized, usually quickly enough to allow the excursion train to be the first train to arrive into town. Such excursions usually involved the people from one or both of the two cities joined. Celebrations and festivals or promotional excursions were usually scheduled the following summer. These were larger in scale, more carefully planned, and thus more elaborate, and usually involved guests from across the region and the nation. The organization of some excursions could be quite simple, involving a day trip or overnight trip to the other end of the line to join a large group of people at the terminus town for a banquet and then return. Such events celebrated the efficiency and speed of the connection. More elaborate excursions added more diverse elements from public celebrations and rituals to the festivities at either end of the line. These included many more people, sometimes lasted for three to five days, and, like the railroad system, the regional urban and economic systems, and the metropolis, entailed more elaborate, even daunting, organization and logistics. By joining a grand excursion, therefore, one stepped into a more systematized realm of order and control.

Among the earliest railroad festivals and/or excursions in the West was the 1844 excursion from Springfield to Jacksonville upon completion of the Northern Cross Railroad.[195] In 1852 a group of St. Louisans took an excursion by steamboat and rail from St. Louis to Springfield to celebrate the opening of the Chicago, Alton and St. Louis Railroad.[196] Excursionists were on the move again to celebrate the completion of the Rock Island Railroad to LaSalle and Peru in March 1853. When the Chicago, Alton and St. Louis connection to the Rock Island, via the Illinois Central, at LaSalle from Springfield was in place, the mayor of Chicago invited the legislature to come to Chicago on an excursion on 17 February 1854. A week later another excursion ventured out to celebrate the opening of the line from Chicago to Rock Island. The great Rail and River Excursion of June 1854 followed this smaller excursion, sponsored by the Chicago and Rock Island Railroad Company. The Galena and Chicago Union railroad also held an excursion to the end of the line at Freeport later that summer. The Chicago and Burlington Railroad celebrated its connection to Burlington with an excursion on 30 May to 2 June 1855.[197] Later that summer the people of Dubuque threw a railroad festival to celebrate the arrival of the Illinois Central across the river from them on 18 July 1855. The greatest excursion of all, however, was the "Great Railway Celebration," involving an excursion from Baltimore to Cincinnati to St. Louis to celebrate the opening of the Ohio and Mississippi Railroad in June 1857.

The excursion from Springfield to Jacksonville in 1844 involved a relatively small party of sixty to eighty people. When the legislature of Illinois visited Chicago in 1854, some 225 people went along.[198] Between 250 and over 300 excursionists in six cars traveled down the line to Rock Island the following week.[199] About the same number made the excursions on the Burlington line and the Illinois Central to Dubuque in the summer of 1855. In 1852 about 400 St. Louisans made the trip to Springfield. The Great Excursion from Chicago to St. Paul the following June transported about 1,000 guests, in two trains with nine cars each and fifteen very crowded steamboats.[200] The Great Railway Celebration of 1857 included more than 2,000 guests whom they transported from Cincinnati to St. Louis in three trains over two days.[201]

Who the excursionists were depended on the invitation list, the timing of the planning, as well as the availability of space in the cars and in town. Small excursions such as the one from Chicago down to LaSalle, Illinois, in March 1853 seem to have been spontaneous, more of a "grand jollification" than an organized event.[202] The invitation to the legislators to come to Chicago in February 1854 arrived only a day before they left, so the affair was spontaneous and entirely male. In May 1855, the mayor of Burlington sent out invitations across the East only two weeks before, and then formed Reception, Entertainment, Refreshments, and Bonfire committees only a few days before the arrival of the excursionists – the mayor and common council of Chicago.[203] The return Burlington excursion to Chicago in June 1855 was spontaneous enough – though the mayor and other dignitaries were expected – for James Grimes to decide only at the last minute not to go.[204] At Dubuque, an Arrangements Committee among the booster ethos was formed in early 1855, followed by a Correspondence Committee, which sent letters of invitation "to many distinguished strangers from around the country."[205] Once the directors of the Chicago and Rock Island Railroad sent out the general invitation to attend the Great Excursion, letters were sent months in advance to editors, businessmen, statesmen, poets, and artists across the country. To control the numbers each respondent received a ticket. However, on the day of the excursion many people with a single ticket brought entire parties while other "interlopers," who John Munn wanted to purge from the party, simply joined the excursion without a ticket. Nevertheless, at the other end of the line, more than a hundred people were left behind, unable to fit on the boats available. A similar procedure resulted in comparable problems of overcrowding at the Great Railway Celebration of 1857, so much so that to avoid the crowd many excursionists departed the day before or the day after the scheduled excursion trains.[206]

Once settled, the new and "splendid" locomotives, all "gleaming and bright" often "gayley decorated," with "flags and evergreens"[207] shaped in "wreaths and garlands," as on the Rock Island excursion in February,[208] or with "flowers, flags, and streamers"[209] and "banners and boughs"[210] as on the Great Excursion that summer, set off down the line, to the cheers of the crowds and the booming of cannons. Because excursions were meant to advertise the efficiency of the railroad, they often moved at steady speed from one town to the next until the end of the line. To add to the celebratory atmosphere, bands routinely joined the excursionists on the train and played during the trip. On the Rock Island excursion, "additions to the company" were made at each station, and they were greeted at every town by cannonades of "field pieces."[211] By 1854, to maintain their schedule, the rail companies provided refreshments on board, which had been stored in picnic baskets in the baggage cars and were served as a kind of 1850s box lunch while en route, precluding the necessity of stopping for a banquet lunch at some place between. Through these actions, the cars, occupied by a crowd of people "in their best holiday attire" which gave them "the air and mark of distinction," began to acquire the character of a regional public space.[212]

The risky nature of intermediate stops was made apparent in the legislative excursion to Chicago in February 1854. Having to change trains, the legislators were given a "luxurious lunch" at which "the choicest liquors and wines were served in abundance." By the time entirely male delegation reboarded the connecting train, the excursion had turned into a rolling "jollification" or "convivial banquet" characteristic of the "lobby" – in which many of them had participated – with, as Gustave Koerner noted, "no end of story telling, singing, and playing of practical jokes." Later, when the party was marooned on a cold railroad platform for two hours waiting for a missed connection, the delegates and their guests passed the time by roughhousing and drinking liberally "from the life preserver[s] in [their] carpet bags." Koerner incitefully attributed the regression of this affair into a rolling male subcultural "frolic" at which fun rather than commemoration was the order of the day to the absence of the restraining impact of women guests and to the tendency among his American colleagues, when together, to "act like a parcel of school boys."[213] In any case, by the time they reached Chicago, cold and hungry, the reception committee, recognizing the state of the party, abbreviated the reception festivities and sent them off to the Tremont House hotel.

Two less rowdy interruptions slowed the progress of the Great Railway excursion from Cincinnati to St. Louis in June 1857. Around midday, the 800 hungry passengers on the second day's train arrived at the appointed stop for a planned banquet, but found instead that the excursionists of the day before had exhausted the local food supplies, leaving barely enough to serve 150. Several hundred men broke for the station, charging the banquet tables, leaving more than 500 men and 100 or more women to observe them from a distance and go hungry or eat from their own supplies. Later that afternoon, when a broken axle stopped the train for an hour, the uncomfortable crowd went for a "run in the woods" and then demanded that the dignitaries aboard – including Senator Stephen Douglas – who were riding in cars fixed up with cooling machines, sofas, and fine paintings, to come into the forest and deliver stump speeches. That this was an all-male interlude is evident when one speaker chose, in contrast to Douglas, to speak facing the cars, "in which most of the ladies were seated," resulting in a storm of protest from the men sitting in the woods, to which he remarked that "he never refused to face the ladies yet," a comment drowned out by the train whistle that sent the whole crowd rushing back to the train.[214]

This tension between conflating genteel and male subcultural practices and behavior would continue as a submotif in most excursions during the 1850s. The mixing of images and practices from politics, military life, fraternal associations, or the private domestic sphere manifested this tension. On one level, crowded accommodations that limited privacy, comfort, and propriety eroded genteel boundaries. Likewise, all-male formal banquets – because of sumptuous food and considerable drinking – tended to unravel into convivial banquets or "roasts," and the participants resisted the efforts of genteel people present to establish decorum and order. Even the balls that followed, though organized by women in local society or the wives of the guests who advocated gentility and thus primarily genteel events, were still heavily male and often lasted far into the night, well past a proper time to adjourn. So, too, the images of the women of Burlington presenting the mayor of Chicago with a bouquet of orange roses – "blossoms of the bride" – and the recitation of an extended sentimental poem in 1855,[215] or the enthusiastic women of LaSalle presenting to the perplexed directors of the railroad "a white flag to commemorate the occasion" seem at odds with military parades, cannonades, fireworks, and bonfires.[216]

Some participants eschewed excursions because of the crowds, discomfort, noise, public display, and frolicking male element. James Grimes, a temperance man, refused to go on the Burlington excursion to Chicago because he abhorred public dinners and dinner speeches and was certain that they would serve champagne at the all-male banquet with the certain result that "some of the guests and hosts would be drunk."[217] Gustave Koerner's wife wanted nothing to do with an invitation to the St. Louis excursion, because "she was no great friend of such revelries."[218] In the lottery for rooms on the steamboat during the Great Excursion, John Munn, noting the boisterous crowd and dreading having to fend for himself out on the deck, was relieved to be assigned to a small private cabin. The next morning he reported many "amusing" stories told of the discomforts endured during the night, happy he did not have one to tell.[219] Meanwhile, he fretted over some family he knew who were disgusted with the accommodations and complained loudly and bitterly to the organizers. Nor did John Kirk, a Presbyterian minister touring the West in search of a location, seem to appreciate all aspects of getting caught in Peru "in the midst of roaring cannons, bands of music playing, stump speaking, and *wine bubbling*, etc. . . . all part of a great celebration coming off."[220] Adele Gratiot Washburne, deep in grief over the death of her mother three days before, was no doubt indifferent to the arrival on 6 June 1854 of fifteen steamboats in the rain, carrying about 1,000 passengers on the Great Excursion to St. Paul, at the crowded wharf in Galena, literally just outside the windows of her house. On a more general level, Richard Yates, evidently tired of them, thought "excursions are pleasant to no one."[221]

Intersections between the genteel decorum of a public ceremony or ritual and the male subcultural conviviality of a political convention, bar meeting, or "frolic" continued throughout the public moments of the excursions. At Bloomington in February 1854 the "luxurious lunch" was served in a "sort of shanty"; the banquet for the 1852 Alton and Springfield excursion, "in the machine shops." The afternoon banquet at Rock Island in February 1854 was served right "in the depot."[222] At Dubuque, they held the "public dinner," like a picnic, outside in a grove on the bluff south of Dodge Street.[223] In Burlington, the banquet was set in the largest room in town in a commercial building, thus limiting the number present. The "evident favoritism" for recent arrivals rather than old settlers, and the private nature of the event that allowed few Burlingtonians to be involved, drew considerable complaint and was criticized with "deep bitterness and dissatisfaction."

After the women departed such banquets, the men stayed to give round after round of toasts, with as many as twenty "regular" toasts followed by any number of "volunteer" toasts, many of them going unheard beyond twenty feet because of the noise of "popping champagne bottles, laughing, talking, . . . moving of chairs," and a general lack of decorum (which at the Burlington banquet in Chicago the emcees tried to combat, "without availing anything").[224] The toasts and speeches, some a bit risqué, and full of wit and humor (which Koerner attributed to the fine champagne) were more appropriate for a "roast" than a genteel public banquet, and would continue, under a thickening cloud of cigar smoke, for hours until either fatigue set in, the emcee got up to leave, or the organizers expelled them from the room or hall so it could be cleared and rearranged for the ball, which usually did not start until nine or ten in the evening.[225] At this point the women would reemerge in their evening dress and dancing would commence until after one, sometimes as late as two.

Meanwhile in the crush of people, borders between public and private, individuals and their towns and the masses eroded. At Rock Island delegations from towns up and down the river were coalescing into a throng of thousands of people crushed together to line the streets, stand on roof tops, crowd doors, and lean from windows and balconies. Women waved their handkerchiefs to add to the banners, bunting, flags, streamers, garlands, and wreaths which covered windows, cornices, balconies, towers, and podiums. The people of Dubuque joined the excursionists of July 1855 at the wharf and walked in a great procession quite a distance to the bluff where they held the dinner. This made up for the Great Excursion boats of 1854 arriving in Dubuque in the midst of a thunderstorm, creating, for John Munn, "the curious appearance of a mass of human beings protected by umbrellas."[226] Before opening their houses to the many guests, most of them strangers, the people of Davenport and Rock Island put welcoming candles in the windows of every store, house, and

Provincial lives

public building, "illuminating" both sides of the river.[227] The people of Dubuque and Burlington in 1855, as well as the citizens of St. Louis in 1857, also opened their houses, providing "a spare bed" for the comfort of the excursionists.[228] Meanwhile, the national guard, military units and bands, fire brigades and hose companies, singing clubs, gymnastics clubs, and political clubs organized processions by day. The procession in St. Louis in 1857 lasted two hours.[229] At night, a torch procession and fireworks ended the Davenport celebration in the Rock Island excursion, while a great bonfire set atop the hills of Burlington on 30 May 1855 heralded the end of the day.[230] In contrast, the excursionists of 1857 arrived at East St. Louis at midnight and were greeted by hundreds of pine torches lining the tracks "for several hundred yards," cannons firing from across the bluffs, fireworks, and the wharf illuminated by "the glare of torches, Roman candles, Grecian fires, or other pyrotechnic devices."[231]

Amid all the celebration, rituals, and display, the central fact of these events was clear to any of the participants and was expressed, directly or indirectly, in almost every word spoken or written in connection with the celebrations. Everyone present knew that the railroad created a new regional network, a system, with new structures and dynamics of economic and social interaction that would, in many ways, transform the structure of the economy, society, and culture in which they lived.

Whoever did business within the network of relations that existed before the railroad system was in place, after 1856, could hardly resist the growing impact of Chicago and St. Louis on their hinterlands. Excursions announced, for those present, the entrance of the power of the regional metropolis and metropolitan culture and society into their lives. All those who visited Chicago and witnessed its development between 1853 and 1856 saw clearly the deepening vortex of a regional process of development, and its growing attraction, a thought Joseph Gillespie expressed awkwardly with the after-dinner comment at an excursion banquet, "the people here bored with a bigger auger."[232] Among the local boosters, gentlemen or ladies, politicians, lawyers, or public men who, on excursions, plugged themselves into the new network centered at Chicago, were a number of people we have traced through the construction of the regional system.[233]

Among those from the state bar who came to Chicago with the legislative excursion of 1853 were Joseph Gillespie, Ninian Edwards, ex-Governor John Reynolds, William Snyder, Judge John D. Caton, and Usher F. Linder. Linder chose the occasion to remark that he "had determined to become a citizen of Chicago" and made the announcement early so that other gentlemen of the bar "might hunt up other locations."[234] Also there was A. B. Chambers, editor of the *St. Louis Republican* who had been to all the conventions in the late forties. Henry W. Starr was among the members of the Burlington contingent who greeted the excursionists from Chicago on 30 May 1855 and then went to that city himself in June.[235] In the other direction, when Chicagoans came out to meet delegations from the terminus, most of the same men who had started the railroad companies were actively involved. Austin Corbin, a banker in Davenport, and Judge R. S. Wilson of Dubuque made it over to the Chicago to Rock Island excursion in February 1854.[236] James Grimes and David

Constructing a regional society

Wells Kilbourne greeted the excursionists at Burlington on 30 May 1855. The directors of the Dubuque and Pacific Railroad, as well as Ben Samuels, George Nightengale, William Barney, and T. S. Wilson of Dubuque were among the active participants in the Dubuque railroad festival in July 1855. In June 1857, Edward Bates, a decade after his triumph at the Chicago River and Harbor Convention, was among those who greeted the excursionists – including Stephen Douglas – at St. Louis. Douglas had also been an excursionist to Burlington in May 1855, as had Judge Thomas Drummond, formerly of Galena.[237]

Within days of the arrival of the road, professionals and businessmen boarded the train and entered the new system without hesitation. Lincoln got on the Illinois Central train at West Urbana, Illinois, for the first time on 26 October 1854, a few months after it opened. When the connection came through Bloomington in 1855, he quickly took that route, on 30 June 1855, to Chicago. In July 1856 Lincoln again took the train to Chicago, and then made a quick round trip to Galena on the Galena and Chicago Union Railroad to attend a meeting there on 22 July. Afterward he traveled mostly by rail.[238] In late May 1854, Adele Washburne, her mother, and children took the train all the way to the end of the line at Freeport on their return to Galena. Lincoln Clark had taken the very same line only the week before to Chicago. His wife Julia took the line to Galena as early as February 1855.[239] A year and a half later, on 28 and 29 November 1855, Elihu Washburne first made the trip between Galena and Washington entirely by rail, taking less than two days.[240] Orville H. Browning took the train to Galesburg the day after the train had arrived in Quincy. Two weeks later, he was "ready to take the cars" to Chicago and on 7 July 1856, took the overnight train to Chicago without so much as a comment, apart from the "cold" weather and closed, unheated cars.[241] By August he had made the connection via Galesburg with Burlington, replacing the steamboat route.[242]

Charles Mason traveled by rail from Chicago to Burlington for the first time on 13 July 1855 (a month after it opened) and thought the road "greatly improved." When he came down the line again in September, he thought it was a "pleasant road and unusually well conducted" and made the trip in a quick ten hours. By the following year, he hardly felt he needed to mention the trips between Chicago and Burlington, except that the travel time was down to nine hours.[243]

Such accelerated travel transformed every accustomed social and economic structure. The initial impact that everyone noted and commented on was the shorter amount of time it took to get to places. The greater regularity of arrivals and departures plus the time of trips drew fewer and fewer comments. Everywhere the railroad made connections, such arrangements became so routine within a few months that they hardly warranted a comment. The increased speed and regularity of travel had a marked and immediate effect on the nature of local and regional economic and social interactions and on the structure of the networks and systems based on transport by steamboat and stage. On the one hand, the increased speed and ease by which one could get to a place, do what one needed to do, and return home meant that one's absences from home were initially reduced. Increasingly, one "stopped" in a place, rather than stayed there. Such logistics initially weakened those structures based on slower travel while increasing one's presence and perhaps influence in local society. In addition, because one could travel to a place for a specific business task and return home the same day, business trips became much more intensive in their use of time. As meeting times narrowed, social and business interactions became briefer and more impersonal. In such impersonal meetings one aspired socially to make acquaintances rather than "friends" as understood in local society, the male subculture, or the society of the bar in the pre-railroad era.[244]

Contemporaries recorded these effects in letters and diaries. Before the railroad, Orville Browning tended to stay at the Illinois supreme court in Springfield for about forty days. Within two years, Browning stayed in town on average only about twenty days. This compression in his stay intensified his work schedule, leaving less time for collegial socializing. Rather than spend time with friends or associates, he more often traveled and worked. He also had less time to visit friends. The intensive aggregating nature of state supreme court sessions quickly disappeared after 1856. As Elihu B. Washburne noted about the early days – when he attended the Illinois supreme court – "the lawyers of that day were brought much closer together than they ever have been since, and the 'esprit de corps' was much more marked . . . [on account of] . . . remain[ing] a considerable time in attendance upon the court."[245]

The railroad dismantled social structures, large and small across the region. For example, the social networks that emerged out of circuit riding especially in those circuits – such as the Eighth Circuit – which covered great distances and required extensive travel by stage or buggy were also undermined by the railroad. Between 1854 and 1857, for example, the completion of the railroad system transformed the behavior of lawyers on the Eighth Circuit. The uninterrupted circuit riding which Lincoln practiced through 1853 was, in the new system, a thing of the past.[246] Indeed, from 1852 to 1855 alone, the impact of the railroad on Lincoln's circuit shows that the more he traveled by rail, the greater number of miles he traveled, in fewer days on the circuit. While increasing the miles he traveled between 1851 and 1857 from a few hundred to almost 2800 miles, the percentage Lincoln traveled by rail rose from none to almost all, and the days he spent on the circuit dropped from 130 to around 100.[247] On the local, circuit, and regional level, the new transit system allowed lawyers, businesspeople, merchants, and travelers to use their time more effectively than before by both spending more time at home and traveling greater distances when away. The desire to use time efficiently eliminated many opportunities during the extended days and nights spent together on the circuit or at the supreme court in Springfield to develop deep friendships among one's non-local colleagues. Though regional aggregation intensified interaction, it became increasingly impersonal.

The push for speed and efficiency increased the cost of everyone's time, compelling people to travel, work, socialize at an accelerated pace. Charles Mason, who took up residence for a few years in Washington, D.C., routinely made quick or "flying" trips on business between Washington and New York, and two or three times a year would return to Burlington and Keokuk. Within the first year he became accustomed, therefore, to quick visits, rushed meetings, quicker communications caused by the railroads. In August 1855, while en route through New York State to the West, he even arranged a meeting "of two or three minutes" on the platform of the station at Utica, New York, with Governor Seymour, who was summering there, while the cars briefly stopped. And though Mason admitted "nothing could of course be consummated in that short interview," Mason felt he had "made him some propositions which may result in something" and sped toward Chicago and the West satisfied.[248] Five years later, Lyman Trumbull, canvassing the state of Illinois, traveled at a frenetic pace, unable even to spare a moment to stop at home and visit his wife and family when he passed by.[249]

In these as in other examples, travelers inevitably passed through Chicago, the center of the new regional system. In this new larger, faster, more impersonal system, more people could be at a greater variety of places, over shorter and shorter time frames than before, thus undermining the structure of hinterland networks, while drawing them toward the metropolis. Across the hinterland, the chances that any significant group of men would be able to meet and interact in the routine course of their business on the circuit or at the state supreme court, for example, gradually declined. It became harder and harder for any group of people to congregate casually or in the course of their work in any one place. Locally, more people would be routinely away on business or socializing, while others continually faced the building pressure from the metropolis to migrate there. People from throughout the urban system found themselves increasingly compelled to travel to Chicago or St. Louis if they were looking for capital, work, or opportunity. There, as well as at New York, these hinterland urbanites encountered coalescing corporate and metropolitan power and in 1856 only just began to recognize that the structure and assumptions of the dispersed, multicentered, egalitarian regional and national genteel society in which they believed themselves to be living was being supplanted by a new regional, metropolitan-dominated social system.

For most boosters, the arrival of the railroad in the middle 1850s immediately transformed local life. As businesses opened, immigrants rushed in, land values skyrocketed, and infrastructural investment deepened, the possibilities unleashed by the railroad were exhilarating and promised a truly metropolitan future which would fulfill the wildest expectations of local growth and development. Charles Mason, who a year or two before praised the railroads, in 1855 pondered, somewhat more anxiously, the changes they had wrought: "How much the world has changed. ... The first time I was ever a mile from home I felt farther away than I do now when in Iowa. When I went to West Point, I felt like [I was] going to another world. Now we make the journey in a few hours and return in the same day. Now we can also come from Iowa in two days and make little account of the journey. The whole world seems a whirlpool, the circles of which grow narrower and swifter."[250] A member of St. Louis's elite put the question more directly:

Thus it is that the railroads and the iron horse have annihilated space and made neighbors of those who are hundreds of miles apart. These mighty changes are to be followed by mighty results. What are they to be? But be they what they may, I doubt whether the sum of human happiness will hereby be increased. All sudden changes are, to a certain extent, mischievous – until time has accommodated everything to the new order of things. But I am, nevertheless, for rational progress in all things and as there is no unmixed good in this world I am content to take the evil with the good.[251]

Such ambivalence, by two men who traveled the system and recognized the rising power of the metropolis, was, however, drowned out by "boomers" who heralded an unlimited future.

Epilogue

The society and culture which middle-class people established across the urban West in the 1850s was a fluid, changing work in progress, rooted in social assumptions, values, expectations, and goals which evolved locally or were brought from the East. These people sought to make each new town with a sufficient economic base into a microcosm of American society. Its members sought and expected to interact openly and equally with people from other towns and cities across the country. They had achieved this equality by initially integrating their local efforts to the broader assumptions and goals of the booster ethos, subsuming their agendas to those of the predominant male subcultures and then using their acquired economic capital to define and demarcate themselves as a middle-class social elite by ascribing to and practicing a western version of gentility. Their efforts, as we have seen, resulted in moments of clarity, stability, and meaning, rooted in historical experience, on an unstable economic and social foundation. Even as they endeavored to pursue local social agendas, the values imbedded in those agendas – self-interest, individualism, and social mobility – drew or pushed merchants, professionals, and entrepreneurs into a regional process of elite aggregation. For a few years in the middle 1850s, it seemed that such extensions of local life would only enhance, enrich, and deepen the local social context, and enable residents to imagine the "way of the town" as, indeed, a microcosm of the "wide, wide world," situating its inhabitants within a rich local society in which one could live a complete and fully satisfying life.

This social history ends, just as were the towns across the upper Mississippi river valley, which to some seemed the embodiment of American and especially republican social order, perched on the brink of achievement and fulfillment in a period of accelerating structural changes.[1] As middle-class residents continued to broaden, deepen, and integrate their control of local society, by trying to clarify and solidify the tentative, uncertain, and very self-conscious cultural system of gentility, they, the booster ethos, and the community and economy it circumscribed faced a wave of transformative change. Their encounter with these changes, and its consequences for their lives and the lives of the towns they lived in, and the broader society and culture of America just before, during, and after the Civil War, is the subject of a sequel to this history.

That history begins seamlessly where this history ends, seeking to unravel, explore, and explain complex social and cultural developments and transformations in Amercian society by interweaving individual, local, regional, and national histories. It begins, again, in these same towns in the boom of 1856 and 1857 when the arrival of the railroads began to accelerate the development of Chicago and St. Louis and rapidly transform the discursive regional economic, social, and cultural system of the Great West. The businessmen, merchants, and lawyers who, as we have seen, increasingly traveled across the region were initially exhilarated as they were drawn into the more centralized dynamics of a regional process of elite aggregation. As they pursued their own local dreams of progress, however, they increasingly recognized, more so than those who maintained localist values and assumptions rooted in local business and practice, that the dynamics and character of regional interaction within this new system represented new power relationships and interactions which challenged and threatened to undermine the assumptions, structures, and dynamics of the local economies and societies they had worked so long to construct and in which they lived.

As they were soon to discover, metropolitan development differentiated and redistributed regional economic functions, wealth, and status, and integrated diverse local concerns and actions into regional and national agendas. Consequently, the rise of the metropolis concentrated economic power and centralized decision-making into the hands of a few. A new metropolitan and corporate and professional elite exerted broader power and influence over others, both sharpening and skewing local and regional social orders while re-landscaping the terrain across which regional social interaction occurred. As this happened, the local agendas and plans of townspeople across the urban system would eventually be cut short, stall out, or simply end. This undermined both their status and that of the others in the local elite who both validated and supported them. In response, smaller town elites were forced to adjust their behavior and change their strategies to maintain and protect the regional status they had only just acquired. Rather than voluntarily interacting across the region, members of local elites who continued to seek upward mobility and success in their profession or activity increasingly felt compelled to follow the currents of business activity and opportunity toward the metropolis. As small-town elites followed these currents, they began to interact more intensively with or try to become part of a regional society at the apex of which stood members of the metropolitan elite. In response, metropolitan elites, besieged by more people seeking entrance to their circles, constructed barriers to entrance by assessing and screening applicants' credentials more rigorously and accepting fewer and refusing more over time. This both narrowed their membership while unilaterally exerting more influence across the hinterland.

By the late 1850s, as centripetal regional forces intensified with the completion of the rail system to the west of the Mississippi River, the erosion of the local assumptions of town and social status within the system, those within and outside of any town's booster ethos, were increasingly differentiated between local and regional interests. Locally, horizontal lines which separated "genteel" people and "elites" from "rowdies," workers, or immigrants were superimposed on by vertical lines that separated those within the elite "set" who were activists in the booster ethos and operated in a broader regional framework from those who, for whatever reason, did not. Many members of the local elite who were drawn into the regional process of "elite aggregation" became more regional in their values, perceptions, and attitudes. Their "parallelist" assumptions that supported the "way of the town" were, in the course of their interactions with centralized power at the metropolis or state capital, undermined.

Every individual or group confronted these bewildering countervailing social forces unleashed by the first tremors of the structural transformation of the regional and national economy rippling through the West. On the one hand, one was drawn inexorably toward the metropolis and felt its attractive force. On the other, one intensely felt metropolitan pressures bearing down on, undermining, transforming, and even eliminating the structures, values, assumptions of local society. Pulled between expectation, excitement, and euphoria, and disappointment, dread, and a foreboding sense of closure, residents across the region, as they discovered their provincial status in the larger system, became insecure, disoriented, and untethered. Given the range of possible responses to these pressures, it is not surprising that many clung to what was familiar and secure. Though credentials based on impersonal professional values and performance mattered more and more, many small-town boosters would continue to refer to and act upon local assumptions and procedures – as a defense against anomie and isolation – whenever they could in the regional or national realm.[2]

In these reactions of the middle and late 1850s lie the roots of the emergence of a distinctive small-town provincial middle class in the 1860s and beyond. Middle-class elites, securely in control of the booster ethos in the middle 1850s, would, based on localist and parallelist assumptions, construct a local world which, on a smaller scale, paralleled the larger structures and entities of the metropolis and the regional system. Rooted in organic, fraternal, and corporate bonds forged in the male subcultures and defined and demarcated by gentility, members of the social elite entwined themselves in a web of institutions, companies, associations, and mutual investments. Created among friends, siblings, and associates, as well as competitors, many of the institutions and associations within this booster network were paper companies – echoing the speculative "paper town" origins of so many places – funded on optimism and wishful thinking and secured by the real legal promises and commitments of taxpayers or subscribers who subscribed to the values of the booster ethos. Formed amid the fraternal culture of the booster ethos, this construct was unwittingly entangled in intractable conflicts of interest and faulty logic. When the crash of 1857 swept across the region, one town after another realized that there was, indeed, no capital supporting the legal obligations which put people into debt to corporations for years, even decades to come. The collapse of the structures of the local booster system deflated elite hopes and expectations of further social mobility to higher status in the urban system. That the Civil War broke out just as these towns were experiencing fracture and bifurcation came, to many, as a release from a local historical chapter, indeed, a whole "old settlers'" history, that had suddenly come to an end.

The cohort of middle-class men and women who dissembled their way through the predominant male subcultures, employed gentility to construct and solidify middle-class status, and established themselves as elites within the booster ethos responded to their transformations in regional power and their impact on local life in a variety of ways. Many among the elite, finding local horizons too restrictive, increasingly viewed themselves as part of a larger entity, called "the North," and sought opportunity elsewhere.[3] The well-worn paths to broader influence – the bar, politics, and business – were traveled by those who survived the crash of 1857 and led to Chicago, St. Louis, Springfield, New York, and Washington.

The outbreak of the Civil War sent more men and women into the national realm. Many who sought mobility through state or federal appointments in Chicago, Springfield, or Washington, doing all they could to gain benefit from the patronage many midwesterners considered their due during the Lincoln, and, later, Grant presidencies, left for good, starting new lives in those more cosmopolitan places.[4] Members of the regional bar and political community were appointed to posts in the territories, Latin America, and even Europe, drawing them further away from local concerns and into a new life. Others moved west to repeat the urban booster experience yet again. In time, many members of these small-town elites of the 1840s and 1850s had scattered from coast to coast and to Europe and Latin America. As each of these people took these paths, they encountered and became involved in the wave of gentility, materialism, extravagance, and even corruption which suffused the life of the upper middle class in the Gilded Age. With every mile they traveled to the metropolis or to a foreign post, they moved further from their relatively simple lives, based on modest ambitions and localist assumptions of their earlier years. The further they moved, the more they held those values in deeper esteem. With a powerful nostalgic sense of loss, sometimes felt only a few years after their departure from the "old town," they constructed romanticized images of a stable society they felt they were losing.

Meanwhile, in the older towns of the Middle West across the hinterland of Chicago, boom had deflated to stasis. Instead of major transformation, life in the 1870s and early 1880s was characterized by superficial change. Growth and development shifted to the metropolis and further west. One local function or activity after another had been coopted, integrated, and absorbed into the increasingly centralized regional urban system centered in Chicago. More and more local decisions were made by outside managers with few local interests or concerns. Increasingly, each town "became more readily identified as part of a network of places and relied increasingly on the network's existence for its life."[5]

The context in which gentility and social aspirations mattered and flourished retrenched to a common middle ground. New localist ideologies emphasized the benefits of smallness and stability of life in the "village," in contrast to and at the same time insulating the "village" from the evils and instabilities of city life. The booster ethos operated at a more modest level, self-consciously articulated reasonable plans for small places, and cultivated the very moral values which observers noted were lacking in the city. The booster "gentlemen" of the 1850s became the "old boys," even the "croakers" of the 1870s through 1890s who ruminated on a past quickly disappearing with the closing of a local kind of frontier.

Those few who chose to continue to live genteel lives in the provincial towns did so self-consciously, as part of a hinterland genteel society, now stretching from Chicago to Davenport and Burlington, to Omaha and Lincoln, to Denver, Colorado, and Sheridan, Wyoming, and even on to Portland and Seattle. At each place, they interacted with members of the railroad elites and corporation men and their families who lived in genteel enclaves throughout the railroad-defined urban system. Meanwhile, they undertook regional strategies to enter into or maintain some positions within regional society which they had had a taste of before and during the war. Drawing on social connections in the metropolis, visits there became a routine part of life. Whether to introduce oneself or one's children, with an eye to making a match, such efforts, on the uneven terrain of regional society, became increasingly fraught with anxiety and potential embarrassment. Besides the network of men who cultivated regional business, professional, and political contacts and involved themselves in a deepening culture of conventions and fairs, much of this social work was carried out by women. Rather than stay at home, middle-class and elite women were on the road collecting social credits and paying debts within regional society.

One could decide that no matter the costs, one was willing to play the "social game" as read about in national periodicals and try to integrate oneself into a regional or national elite from afar. One would summer in the right places, take trips or excursions to the required spots, and see the typical sites all with an eye to enhancing both local and regional status. Such contacts validated membership in a larger society and maintained a sense that one's town or city was still "in" the regional social world, not just an outside observer of it, even as that social world became a more impersonal and categorical realm of mostly strangers, which like the metropolis itself, one observed and experienced individually and privately but never really "lived" in.

When one came home, one sought to interact with those among local society who cared. But in doing so, one observed how the metropolis, as Oliver Wendell Holmes, Sr., put it, regularly "drained off" "their promising young author and rising lawyer and large capitalist" along with their "prettiest girls." For the residents of hinterland towns, the big city was the locus of "all their ambition" and "all their thin gliding or glory." "Society" and "experience" seemed increasingly "outside" one's environs. While the local newspaper reported the comings and goings of local society, they also reported who was in town from elsewhere.[6] Evidence of systemic forces and connections was eagerly sought and noted. At the railroad station, in nearby hotels, and in the taverns and clubs, all the domain of travelers and businessmen who inhabited an urban male subculture, the pulse of the metropolis drew attention. Whether involving travelers arriving or departing, news of events along the railroad line, tales of transients and migrants, or off the wire from Chicago or Denver, all were religiously reported as if they were extensions of local society and its concerns.[7]

Over time, railroads continued to integrate, coopt, and shape local economies and local power structures across the metropolitan hinterland, compelling more and more citizens to follow their directives and demands. With each further erosion of control, more residents in older towns ruminated nostalgically about an earlier, more vibrant stage of urban development in the 1840s and 1850s. These social and cultural forces would shape the emergence of a deeply nostalgic provincial small-town culture which, though it never quite slumbered as peacefully in "island" communities "living largely to themselves," as Robert Wiebe has suggested, did evolve slowly, beyond or on the periphery of the main currents of change, across the urban Middle West in the 1870s through 1890s.[8] Even as the region acquired its designation as "the Middle West," life within the region remained, as it began, peripheral and in-between in character. Eventually, economic and political forces, driven by regional economic restructuring or recession, would periodically pulse through the system and energize the people of these towns to support populism or to send their youth in waves to the West or to the city. There, imbued with a deep strain of nostalgia, they sought to reform the modernizing metropolis by fusing the rationality and science of the city with the evangelical Christianity of the country through Progressivism. In doing so, they would seek yet again to integrate local and regional life and contribute to the dynamics of national development.[9]

Appendix 1

Cases tried by lawyers from different circuits who first appeared at the state supreme court between 1832 and 1839 at the supreme court of Illinois between 1838 and 1850

Circuit	Cases from circuit	Outside	Total	Outside/Total
First	259	104	363	.29
Second	382	83	465	.18
Third	34	3	37	.08
Fourth	42	6	48	.13
Fifth	229	41	270	.15
Sixth	12	1	13	.08
Seventh	235	75	310	.24
Eighth	66	134	200	.67
Ninth	126	27	153	.18
Totals:	1385	474	1859	.25

Note: The 1832–1839 cohorts, that is, those lawyers who arrived at Supreme Court for first time in those years, were chosen as a control group. Their careers were then followed at the supreme court from 1838 to 1850.

Sources: J. Young Scammon, ed., *Reports of the Cases Argued in the Supreme Court of the State of Illinois*, vols. 1–4 (Chicago: Callaghan and Company, 1879, 1880, 1886); Charles Gilman, ed., *Reports of the Cases Argued and Determined in the Supreme Court of the State of Illinois*, vols. 5–10 (Chicago: E. B. Myers and Company, 1886); Ebenezer Peck, ed., *Reports of Cases Determined in the Supreme Court of the State of Illinois*, vols. 11 and 12 (Chicago: Callaghan and Company, 1881).

Appendix 2

Case distribution of prominent lawyers from circuits at the supreme court of Illinois, 1838–1850, and circuits from which outside cases came, 1832–39 cohorts

(Home circuit) Lawyer	1	2	3	4	5	6	7	8	9	Total
(1) Murray McConnell	59	2		6	3	1	4	1		76
(1) D. A. Smith	50	4	1		3					58
(1) William Thomas	42	4					1	1	1	47
(2) Lyman Trumbull	1	57	4	1		1		4	2	70
(2) Joseph Gillespie	1	51								52
(2) William Martin	1	45								46
(2) John M. Krum	2	29								31
(3) James Shields		21	3					7	1	32
(3) Walter B. Scates		1	14				1			16
(3) Henry Eddy			12					1		13
(4) Orlando B. Ficklin				17						17
(4) Usher F. Linder	1	1		11				1		14
(5) Orville H. Browning		1			75	2		4	3	85
(5) Archibald Williams	1				60	2		2	3	68
(5) Nehemiah Bushnell		1			46			4	3	54
(5) William Minshall	1				25		4	3		33
(7) J. Young Scammon		5				2	35	2	6	50
(7) Giles Spring						1	33	1	5	40
(7) Justin Butterfield		5				16	30	1	9	61
(7) Isaac N. Arnold							28		1	29
(8) Stephen T. Logan	14	11	3	3	13	9	4	40	10	107
(8) Edward D. Baker	6	1		3	6	9		11	2	38
(8) Jesse B. Thomas		9	1	1	4	6	7	7	4	39
(9) Onslow Peters		1			3	5	5		57	71
(9) Norman H. Purple					1	6	3	1	18	29

Sources: Scammon, ed., *Reports of the Cases Argued* . . . ; Gilman, ed., *Reports of the Cases Argued*; Peck, ed., *Reports of Cases Determined.*

Appendix 3

Circuit lawyers at Iowa supreme court, 1846–1850

First circuit	Cases/	Crossovers	Second circuit	Cases/	Crossovers
Jonathan C. Hall	77	5	William G. Woodward	26	6
David Rorer	44	0	Stephen Whichler	21	3
Henry W. Starr	20	0	John P. Cook	17	3
James W. Grimes	20	0	Stephen Hempstead	13	1
Milton D. Browning	23	0	Timothy Davis	13	1
Cyrus Walker	12	0	Ralph P. Lowe	8	3
William H. Starr	11	0	Serranus C. Hastings	7	2
Lewis R. Reeves	7	0	Ebenezer Cook	6	0
Hugh T. Reid	6	0	Thomas S. Wilson	15	0
Others	14	3	Others	26	4
Totals	234	8	Totals	152	23

Sources: William E. Miller, *Reports of Cases in Law and Equity Determined in the Supreme Court of Iowa,* vol. 1 (Chicago: T. H. Flood and Company, 1892); George Greene, ed., *Reports of Cases in Law and Equity Determined in the Supreme Court of the State of Iowa,* vol. 1 (Chicago: T. H. Flood and Company, 1892).

Appendix 4

The social construction of the Burlington, Iowa, bar in the 1840s and 1850s

New England moral gentlemen:

James W. Grimes,[a] New Hampshire, 1836; "profound," "imperturbable," "farseeing"; territorial legislature, 1838, 1843; Iowa state legislature, 1852; governor of Iowa, 1854–58; U.S. Senate, 1859–65.

Charles Mason, New York, 1837; a "moral" and "natural" "gentleman," "a democrat of the old school"; chief justice, Iowa Territory supreme court, 1838–46; State Commission of Code of Law, 1851; Half Breed Tract Commission.

Henry W. Starr,[a] Vermont, 1837; "fond playe[r] of practical jokes," "dressed in exquisite attire," "charming ... conversationalist."

James W. Woods,[a,b] Massachusetts, 1837; "highly convivial," "hard-rid[ing] drinker, story teller, practical joker, prankster, a good mixer, and an all around 'hail fellow well met,'" "old Bass" or "old Timber"; clerk of territorial supreme court, 1838–46; clerk of Iowa supreme court, First District, 1846–53.

Stephen Wichler,[a,b] [Muscatine], Vermont, 184– ; "a true eccentric," "strange behavior," "aristocratic in bearing and reserved," "loved to tell stories"; U.S. District Attorney for Iowa, 1849–53.

Chesterfield/ Pennsylvania gentlemen:

Verplanck Van Antwerp, New York, 1838; "prided himself on being a Knickerbocker," "aristocratic, dignified, with ... hauteur in his bearing," "the man with the boiled shirt and the starched collar"; receiver of Land Office, 1838–40 (to Keokuk, 1840), Iowa territorial legislature, 1840; commissioner, Des Moines River Improvement, 1851–53.

John Gear, New York, 1843; alderman, Burlington, Iowa 1852; mayor, 1863; Iowa

Appendices

legislature, 1871–77; governor of Iowa, 1877–87; U.S. House of Representatives, 1887–93; U.S. Senate, 1894–1901.

Theodore S. Parvin,[a] New Jersey, 1837; "a scholar and great collector of Iowa history"; territorial librarian, 1839; secretary of territorial council, 1840; clerk of U.S. district court, 1846–56; county judge, 1840–50; founder, Iowa State Historical Society.

Ralph P. Lowe,[a] [Muscatine], Ohio, 1838; "gentlest of men," "a reliable and abiding friend," "a believer in the common honesty of men"; First Iowa Constitutional Convention, 1844; governor of Iowa, 1858–60; Iowa supreme court, 1860–68.

Jonathan C. Hall,[b] [Mt. Pleasant], Ohio, 1839; "inattentive to little conventionalities of society and careless in dress," "convivial to a high degree," "fond of anecdotes, liked a good story, and could tell better ones than anyone else," "much sought out and courted in society"; Iowa supreme court, 1854–55; Iowa Constitutional Convention, 1857; Iowa state legislature, 1860.

W. W. Chapman, Virginia, 1835; to Oregon in 1847; U.S. District Attorney, Wisconsin Territory, 1836; U.S. House of Representatives, 1838–41; (to Ottumwa 1843), First Constitutional Convention, Iowa, 1844.

Southern gentlemen

David Rorer,[a,b] Virginia, 1836; "a great orator, full of virile qualities," "deep and sonorous voice," "perfectly 'sui generis' determined, self-willed, egotistical, and domineering."

David Irvin, Virginia, 1837; "a genuine 'high-toned' gentleman," "at all times ready to attend to any fun," "most profoundly impressed with the F.F.V.'s [first families of Virginia]."

Milton D. Browning,[a,b] Kentucky, 1837; "great honesty," "candor," "tall, dark-complexioned, grave appearing," "bore a likeness to Daniel Webster"; Iowa territorial legislature, 1840; Iowa state senate, 1846–48, 1852–54; U.S. District Attorney, 1867–71.

Augustus C. Dodge, Missouri, 1838; "though warm-hearted and approachable, was highly dignified and courtier-like in his bearing," "discountenanced the drink habit," "incorruptible statesman of the old school"; register of Land Office, Burlington, 1838; delegate, U.S. House of Representatives, 1841–46; U.S. Senate, 1846–55; Minister to Spain, 1855–59.

Lacon D. Stockton, Kentucky, 1839; "dignified in appearance," "amiable, decisive, and strong – all manly virtues," "among the noblest type of Kentuckians," "adapted himself to the West"; Prosecuting Attorney, First District in 1840s; Iowa supreme court, 1856–60.

Bernhart Henn, 1839; "a dominant character, strong literary taste, and force as a writer which made him dictatorial in politics," "a 'democrat of the old school'"; U.S. Land Office, 1839–48; U.S. House of Representatives, 1851–55.

Appendices

[a] Lawyers present and admitted to first term of the supreme court of Iowa Territory which was held at Burlington on 28 November 1838.

[b] Lawyers who made appearance at state supreme court of Iowa in 1845 or 1846.

Sources: Edward H. Stiles, *Recollections and Sketches of Notable Lawyers and Public Men of Iowa* (Des Moines: Homestead Publishing Co., 1916), 566–67, 59, 21, 19, 274, 294, 263, 260, 385, 285, 361–62, 245, 240–41, 265, 24, 275, 295, 89–91, 92, 296–97, 129; T. D. Eagal and R. H. Sylvester, *The Iowa State Almanac and Statistical Register for 1860* (Davenport: Luse, Lane and Hart, 1860); *Report of the First Annual Meeting of the Iowa State Bar Association* (Davenport: Egbert, Fidlar and Chambers, 1895), 42; Theodore S. Parvin, *Early Leaders in the Professions* (Iowa City: Iowa State Historical Society, 1894), 79; Theodore S. Parvin, "Glimpses of Early Iowa or Recollections of Territorial Times," *Pioneer Lawmakers Association of Iowa, Reunion of 1892* (Des Moines: G. H. Ragsdale, 1893), 30.

Notes

Introduction

1. Timothy R. Mahoney, *River Towns in the Great West: The Structure of Provincial Urbanization in the American Midwest, 1820–1870* (New York: Cambridge University Press, 1990).
2. Timothy R. Mahoney, "Down in Davenport: A Regional Perspective on Antebellum Urban Development," *Annals of Iowa* 50, no. 5 (Summer 1990): 451–74; Timothy R. Mahoney, "Down in Davenport, The Social Response of Antebellum Elites to Regional Urbanization," *Annals of Iowa* 50, no. 6 (Fall 1990), 593–622; Kathleen N. Conzen, "Community Studies, Urban History, and American Local History," in Michael Kammen, ed., *The Past Before Us* (Ithaca: Cornell University Press, 1980), 290.
3. D. W. Meinig, *The Shaping of America: A Geographical Perspective on 500 Years of History*, vol 2: *Continental America, 1800–1867* (New Haven: Yale University Press, 1993), 264–84.
4. Kathleen N. Conzen, "A Saga of Families," in Clyde A. Milner II, Carol A. O'Conner, and Martha A. Sandweiss, eds., *The Oxford History of the American West* (New York: Oxford University Press, 1994), 315–57.
5. Andrew R. L. Cayton and Peter S. Onuf, eds., *The Midwest and the Nation: Rethinking the History of an American Region* (Bloomington: Indiana University Press, 1990), 43–45, 50–58.
6. William L. Barney, *The Passage of the Republic* (Lexington: D. C. Heath, 1987), 182; D. W. Meinig, *The Shaping of America*, vol. 2: 273, 426.
7. Timothy R. Mahoney, "Perspective on Nature's Metropolis, A Book Forum," *Annals of Iowa* 51, no. 5 (Summer 1992): 490–500.
8. Kenneth Cmiel, "Poststructural Theory," in Mary K. Cayton, Elliot J. Gorn, and Peter W. Williams, eds., *Encyclopedia of American Social History*, vol. 1 (New York: Charles Scribner's Sons, 1993), 431.
9. Allan Pred, *Making Histories and Constructing Human Geographies* (Boulder: Westview Press, 1990), 41–48.

Notes

10. Peter Novick, *That Noble Dream: The "Objectivity Question" and the American Historical Profession* (New York: Cambridge University Press, 1988), 380–82.
11. Kenneth A. Scherzer, *The Unbounded Community: Neighborhood Life and Social Structure in New York City, 1830–1875* (Durham, North Carolina: Duke University Press, 1992); Jeffrey S. Adler, *Yankee Merchants and the Making of the Urban West* (New York: Cambridge University Press, 1991); Susan E. Gray, *The Yankee West: Community Life on the Michigan Frontier* (Chapel Hill: University of North Carolina Press, 1997); Kay J. Carr, *Belleville, Ottawa, and Galesburg: Community and Democracy on the Illinois Frontier* (Carbondale: Southern Illinois University Press, 1996).
12. Anthony F. C. Wallace, *Rockdale: The Growth of an American Village* (New York: Alfred A. Knopf, 1978); Laurel Thatcher Ulrich, *A Midwife's Tale: The Life of Martha Ballard Based on Her Diary, 1785–1812* (New York: Alfred A. Knopf, 1990); Mary P. Ryan, *Cradle of the Middle Class* (New York: Cambridge University Press, 1981); Stuart M. Blumin, *The Emergence of the Middle Class* (New York: Cambridge University Press, 1989).
13. Richard L. Bushman, *The Refinement of America: Persons, Houses, Cities* (New York: Alfred A. Knopf, 1992), 383–90; Stuart M. Blumin, *The Emergence of the Middle Class*, 298–310.
14. Simon Schama, *Dead Certainties (Unwarranted Speculations)* (New York: Alfred A. Knopf, 1991).

Chapter 1. Provincial society

1. John L. Brooke, *The Heart of the Commonwealth: Society and Political Culture in Worcester County, Massachusetts, 1713–1861* (New York: Cambridge University Press, 1989), 77, 80.
2. Richard White, *The Middle Ground: Indians, Empires, and Republics in the Great Lakes Region, 1650–1815* (New York: Cambridge University Press, 1990), x, 11.
3. Ibid., 145.
4. Anthony F. C. Wallace, "Prelude to Disaster: The Course of Indian-White Relations which Led to the Black Hawk War of 1832," in Ellen Whitney, ed. and comp., *The Black Hawk War, 1831–1832*, vol. 1, Collections of the Illinois State Historical Library, vol. 35 (Springfield: Illinois State Historical Society, 1970), 13.
5. Ibid.
6. Ibid., 11–12; Roger L. Nichols, *Black Hawk and the Warrior's Path* (Arlington Heights: Harlan Davidson, Inc., 1992), 4–9.
7. White, *The Middle Ground*, 511.
8. Wallace, "Prelude to Disaster," 24; Nichols, *Black Hawk*, 19.
9. Wallace, "Prelude to Disaster," 13–17.
10. Winstanley Briggs, "Le Pays des Illinois," *The William and Mary Quarterly* 67, no. 1 (1990): 55.
11. James Neal Primm, *Lion of the Valley: St. Louis, Missouri*, 2d ed. (Boulder: Pruett Publishing Company, 1990), 49–54; Tanis C. Thorne, *The Many Hands of My Relations: French and Indians on the Lower Missouri* (Columbia: University of Missouri Press, 1996), 127.
12. Wallace, "Prelude to Disaster," 17–18; Thorne, *The Many Hands of My Relations*, 88.
13. Jacqueline Peterson, "Many Roads to Red River: Metis Genesis in the Great Lakes Region, 1680–1815," in Jacqueline Peterson and Jennifer S. H. Brown, eds., *The New*

Peoples: Being and Becoming Metis in North America (Lincoln: University of Nebraska Press, 1985), 58, 60.

14. Milo M. Quaife, *Chicago and the Old Northwest, 1673–1835* (Chicago: University of Chicago Press, 1913), 128–29, 286–290; Clarence E. Carter, comp. and ed., *The Territorial Papers of the United States*, vol. XVI: *The Territory of Illinois, 1809–1814* (Washington: Government Printing Office, 1948), 154–55 (hereafter cited as *Territorial Papers*); Jacqueline Peterson, "Many Roads to Red River," 57–58, 60–61.
15. Jennifer S. H. Brown, "Diverging Identities: The Presbyterian Métis of St. Gabriel Street, Montreal," in Jacqueline Peterson and Jennifer S. H. Brown, eds., *The New Peoples*, 196–198; Thorne, *The Many Hands of My Relations*, 83–97; Thomas Ford, *A History of Illinois* (Chicago: S. C. Griggs and Co., 1854), 36.
16. Ford, *History of Illinois*, 36–37; *Territorial Papers*, vol. XVI, 155–56; Peterson, "Many Roads to Red River," 63.
17. *Territorial Papers*, vol. VII, 273.
18. R. David Edmunds, "'Unacquainted with the Laws of the Civilized World': American Attitudes towards the Metis Communities in the Old Northwest," in Peterson and Brown, eds., *The New Peoples*, 188–91; Thorne, *The Many Hands of My Relations*, 97.
19. Primm, *Lion of the Valley*, 49–55.
20. William E. Foley and C. David Rice, *The First Chouteaus, River Barons of Early St. Louis* (Urbana, Illinois: University of Illinois Press, 1983), 45; Thorne, *The Many Hands of My Relations*, 93–97, 162.
21. Foley and Rice, *The First Chouteaus*, 44.
22. Primm, *Lion of the Valley*, 85; Mary B. Cunningham and Jeanne C. Blythe, *The Founding Family of St. Louis* (St. Louis: Midwest Technical Publications, 1977); Paul Beckwith, *The Creoles of St. Louis* (St. Louis: Nixon-Jones Printing Co., 1893).
23. Cunningham and Blythe, *The Founding Family of St. Louis*. For the record the six intermarriages of cousins within this generation were: 1) Victoire Gratiot, daughter of Charles Gratiot and Victoire Chouteau, married Sylvestre Labbadie, Jr., son of Sylvestre Labbadie and Pelagie Chouteau, sister of Victoire Chouteau; 2) Emile Ann Gratiot, daughter of Charles Gratiot and Victoire Chouteau, married Pierre Cadet Chouteau, son of Pierre Chouteau, brother of Victoire Chouteau; 3) Sophie Labbadie, daughter of Sylvestre Labbadie and Pelagie Chouteau, married August Pierre Chouteau, son of Pierre Chouteau; 4) Julia Augusta Gratiot, daughter of Charles Jr., married Charles P. Chouteau, son of Pierre Cadet Chouteau; 5) Virginia E. Maclot, daughter of Marie Therese Gratiot, married Pierre A. Berthold, son of her cousin Pelagie Chouteau "Madame Berthold"; 6) Bernard F. Hempstead, son of Edward Hempstead, married Stephanie Pauline Gratiot, niece of Susan Hempstead.
24. Primm, *Lion of the Valley*, 49–55; Beckwith, *Creoles of St. Louis*; Cunningham and Blythe, *Founding Family of St. Louis;* Jay Gitlin, "'Avec bien du regret': The Americanization of Creole St. Louis," *Gateway Heritage* (Spring 1989), 3–11; Jay Gitlin, "The French in the Mississippi River Valley" (Ph.D. dissertation, Yale University, 1994); Foley and Rice, *The First Chouteaus*, 190.
25. Foley and Rice, *The First Chouteaus*, 174.
26. Nelson C. Roberts, ed., *The Story of Lee County, Iowa* (Chicago: S. J. Clarke Publishing Company, 1914), 104.
27. Reuben Gold Thwaites, ed., "Notes on Early Lead Mining in the Fever (or Galena) River Region," *Collections of the State Historical Society of Wisconsin*, vol. XIII (Madison: State Historical Society of Wisconsin, 1895), 280.

Notes

28. Ibid., 283.
29. Foley and Rice, *The First Chouteaus*, 174.
30. Ibid.; Thwaites, ed., "Notes on Early Lead Mining," 279–82.
31. Donald Jackson, ed., *The Journals of Zebulon Pike, with Related Letters and Related Documents*, vol. 1 (Norman: University of Oklahoma Press, 1966), 19–20.
32. Thwaites, ed., "Notes on Early Lead Mining," 280, 282–83.
33. *Territorial Papers*, vol. XVI, 156; Foley and Rice, *The First Chouteaus*, 174; John M. Faragher, *Daniel Boone: The Life and Legend of an American Pioneer* (New York: Henry Holt, 1992), 304–5.
34. Bruce E. Mahan, *Old Fort Crawford and the Frontier* (Iowa City: The State Historical Society of Iowa, 1926), 41–42
35. *Territorial Papers*, vol. XVI, 156; Peter L. Scanlan, *Prairie du Chien: French, British, American* (Menasha, Wisconsin: Banta Publishing Company, 1937), 172–73; Mahan, *Old Fort Crawford*, 52.
36. *Territorial Papers*, vol. XVI, 187–188; Faragher, *Daniel Boone*, 304–5; Scanlan, *Prairie du Chien*, 174; Nichols, *Black Hawk*, 42–47.
37. *Territorial Papers*, vol. XVI, 248; Elihu B. Washburne, ed., "The Edwards Papers, Being a Portion of the Collection of the Letters, Papers, and Manuscripts of Ninian Edwards," *Chicago Historical Society's Collection*, vol. 3 (Chicago: Fergus Printing Co., 1884), 80.
38. Washburne, "The Edwards Papers," 63–67; Jackson, ed., *The Journals of Zebulon Pike*, 20; *Territorial Papers*, vol. XVI, 250, 252.
39. Washburne, "The Edwards Papers," 68, 86, 90; *Territorial Papers*, vol. XVI, 311; White, *The Middle Ground*, 368–69, 384–96.
40. *Territorial Papers*, vol. XVI, 380–81.
41. Reuben G. Thwaites, ed., "Antoine LeClaire's Statement," in *Collections of the State Historical Society of Wisconsin* (Madison: State Historical Society of Wisconsin, 1888), 238–42; *Territorial Papers*, vol. XVI, 386, 253–55.
42. Washburne, ed., "The Edwards Papers," 68.
43. Richard White, *"It's Your Misfortune and None of My Own": A History of the American West* (Norman: University of Oklahoma Press, 1991), 47; Diary of Henry S. Austin, vol. 7, 2 January 1838, p. 38, Caleb Forbes Davis Collection, Iowa State Historical Society, Iowa City.
44. Mahan, *Old Fort Crawford*, 54–62; *Territorial Papers*, vol. XVI, 155–56; Thwaites, ed., "Notes on Early Lead Mining," 285; *Territorial Papers*, vol. XVII, 384–85, 388.
45. Ibid., 346; Nichols, *Black Hawk*, 64–65.
46. *Territorial Papers*, vol. XVII, 402; Scanlan, *Prairie du Chien*, 95–96, 176–80.
47. Timothy R. Mahoney, "Down in Davenport: A Regional Perspective on Antebellum Town Development," *Annals of Iowa* 50 (Summer 1990): 455.
48. Scanlan, *Prairie du Chien*, 95–97.
49. Ibid., 178–80, 124, 96–97; Dana O. Jensen, ed., "I at Home: Part III, by Stephen Hempstead Sr., the Diary of a Yankee Farmer in Missouri, 1817–1818," *Bulletin of the Missouri Historical Society* 14 (October 1957): 74.
50. Ibid.; Thwaites, "Notes on Early Lead Mining," 286.
51. Peter C. Mancall, *Valley of Opportunity: Economic Culture along the Upper Susquehanna, 1700–1800* (Ithaca: Cornell University Press, 1991), 54–64.
52. *Territorial Papers*, vol. XVII, 324–25; Thomas C. Scharf, *The History of St. Louis City and County*, vol. 1 (Philadelphia: McDonough & Company, 1883), 187.
53. Mahan, *Old Fort Crawford*, 194.

Notes

54. Scanlan, *Prairie du Chien*, 96; Thwaites, ed., "Notes on Early Lead Mining," 286–87.
55. *The History of Jo Daviess County, Illinois* (Chicago: H. F. Kett & Co., 1878), 233–37; Thwaites, ed., "Notes on Early Lead Mining," 287–88.
56. *History of Jo Daviess County*, 236–44; Horatio Newhall to Isaac Newhall, 1 March 1828, Horatio Newhall Papers, Illinois State Historical Library.
57. *History of Jo Daviess County*, 243, 244, 231, 236; Florence Gratiot Bale, "When the Gratiots Came to Galena," *Journal of the Illinois State Historical Society* 24, no. 4 (1932): 672, 673; "Mrs. Adele P. Gratiot's Narrative," *Report and Collections of the State Historical Society of Wisconsin for the Years 1883, 1884, 1885*, vol. X (Madison, 1888), 266.
58. *History of Jo Daviess County*, 236, 241; Beckwith, *Creoles of St. Louis*, 79; Primm, *Lion of the Valley*, 71, 85.
59. Beckwith, *Creoles of St. Louis*, 81.
60. Ibid., 96–97; "Adele P. Gratiot's Narrative," 261.
61. Thwaites, ed., "Notes on Early Lead Mining," 291; *History of Jo Daviess County*, 257.
62. "Adele P. Gratiot's Narrative," 265; Bale, "When the Gratiots Came to Galena," 674; *History of Jo Daviess County*, 243; Wallace, "Prelude to Disaster," 11–12.
63. *History of Jo Daviess County*, 234–37; "Adele P. Gratiot's Narrative," 267–69.
64. *History of Jo Daviess County*, 243, 247, 225. Mahan, *Old Fort Crawford*, 196; Reuben G. Thwaites, ed., "Prairie du Chien in 1827," in *Collections of the State Historical Society of Wisconsin*, vol. 11 (Madison: State Historical Society of Wisconsin, 1888), 365.
65. *History of Lafayette County, Wisconsin* (Chicago: Western Historical Company, 1881), 439, 437–38.
66. Wallace, "Prelude to Disaster," 11; Faragher, *Daniel Boone*, 19, 19–23.

Chapter 2. Family on a "near" frontier

1. Anthony F. C. Wallace, "Prelude to Disaster: The Course of Indian-White Relations Which Led to the Black Hawk War of 1832," in Ellen Whitney, comp. and ed., *The Black Hawk War, 1831–1832*, vol. 1, Collections of the Illinois State Historical Library, vol. 35 (Springfield: Illinois State Historical Society, 1970), 11; Richard White, *The Middle Ground* (New York: Cambridge University Press, 1991).
2. Jane C. Nylander, *Our Own Snug Fireside: Images of the New England Home, 1760–1780* (New Haven: Yale University Press, 1994), 7–8.
3. Kathleen N. Conzen, "A Saga of Families," in Clyde A. Milner II, Carol A. O'Conner, and Martha A. Sandweiss, eds., *The Oxford History of the American West* (New York: Oxford University Press, 1994), 315–57; Robert Abzug, *Cosmos Crumbling: American Reform and the Religious Imagination* (New York: Oxford University Press, 1994), 57–60.
4. *History of Lafayette County, Wisconsin* (Chicago: Western Historical Co., 1881), 437–439; "Mrs. Adele P. Gratiot's Narrative," *Report and Collections of the State Historical Society of Wisconsin for the Years 1883, 1884, 1885*, vol. 10 (Madison: State Historical Society of Wisconsin, 1888), 266–68; Florence G. Bale, "When the Gratiots Came to Galena," *Journal of the Illinois State Historical Society* 24, no. 4 (1932): 671–82.
5. Stephen Hempstead to Susan Hempstead Gratiot, 13 January 1830, Adele Gratiot Washburne Collection, Washburn-Norlands Humanities Center, Livermore, Maine (hereafter cited as AGW); Stephen Hempstead Diary, 3, 4 July 1831, Stephen Hempstead Collection, Missouri Historical Society (hereafter cited as SHC).
6. Richard D. Brown, *Knowledge Is Power: The Diffusion of Information in Early America, 1700–1865* (New York: Oxford University Press, 1989), 132–40; George Collier Hemp-

Notes

stead and William Hempstead Stahl, comps., *Stephen Hempstead and His Descendents: A Genealogy and Biography* (Galena, Illinois: Gazette, c. 1929), 9–14.

7. Stephen Hempstead Diary, 4 July 1831, SHC.
8. Brown, *Knowledge Is Power*, 138–39; Abzug, *Cosmos Crumbling: American Reform and the Religious Imagination*, 37.
9. Hempstead and Stahl, comps., *Stephen Hempstead and His Descendents*, 16–18.
10. *The History of Jo Daviess County* (Chicago: H. F. Kett and Co., 1878), 637– 38; Elihu B. Washburne, *Address of Honorable Elihu B. Washburne and Response of Governor Thomas Crittenden on the Occasion of the Presentation of a Portrait of Hon. Edward Hempstead to the State of Missouri* (Jefferson City: Tribune Printing Company, 1881), 9, 10; Charles Hempstead to Christopher H. Kenney, 1 December 1826, SHC.
11. *History of Jo Daviess County*, 638.
12. Dana O. Jensen, ed., "I at Home, by Stephen Hempstead, Sr., the Diary of a Yankee Farmer in Missouri, 1811–14," *Bulletin of the Missouri Historical Society* 13 (October 1956): 31, 33, 32 (hereafter cited as Part I).
13. *Address of Elihu B. Washburne*, 9.
14. Florence Gratiot Bale, "A Packet of Old Letters," *The Wisconsin Magazine of History* 11 (1927–28): 158; Dana O. Jensen, ed., Part I, 30, 31; "Memorandum of My Journey from New London Conn. to St. Louis," Letterbook, SH.
15. Stephen Hempstead to Elijiah Beebe, 29 November, 25 December 1812, AGW.
16. William Schieck, *The Half Blood: A Cultural Symbol in Nineteenth Century American Fiction* (Lexington: University of Kentucky Press, 1979), 2–3.
17. Thomas Ford, *A History of Illinois* (Chicago: S. C. Griggs and Co., 1854), 36.
18. John F. McDermott, "August Chouteau, First Citizen of Upper Louisiana," in John F. McDermott, ed., *Frenchmen and French Ways in the Mississippi Valley* (Urbana: University of Illinois Press, 1969), 11–13.
19. Elihu B. Washburne, "Col. Henry Gratiot – A Pioneer of Wisconsin," *Report and Collections of the State Historical Society of Wisconsin, for the Years 1883, 1884, 1885*, vol. 10 (Madison: The State Historical Society of Wisconsin, 1888), 257.
20. Thomas C. Scharf, *The History of St. Louis City and County*, vol. 1 (Philadelphia: McDonough and Company, 1883), 316; Theodore Rodolf, "Pioneering in the Wisconsin Lead Region," in Reuben G. Thwaites, ed., *Collections of the State Historical Society of Wisconsin*, vol. XV (Madison: The State Historical Society of Wisconsin, 1900), 351; Stephen Hempstead to Elijah Beebe, 29 November 1812, AGW; Stephen Hempstead to "Dear children," 25 December 1812, AGW; Scharf, *St. Louis City and County*, vol. 1: 313–14; John F. McDermott, "August Chouteau," 8–9; see Lawrence Lowic, *The Architectural Heritage of St. Louis, 1803–1891* (St. Louis, 1982), 22; Washburne, "Col. Henry Gratiot," 256; Susan Hempstead Gratiot to Henry Gratiot, 17 March 1836, AGW; Charles Hempstead to William Hempstead, 28 September 1835, Susan Gratiot to William Hempstead, 4 March 1836, William Hempstead Papers, Illinois State Historical Library.
21. Stephen Hempstead to Elijiah Beebe, 25 December 1812, AGW.
22. Jensen, ed., Part I, 32, 33; Stephen Hempstead, Sr., to Edward Hempstead, 23 January 1813, AGW; Frederic Palmer and Lillian Blankley Cogan, "The Hempstead House," *Antiques Magazine* 69 (February 1960): 179–85.
23. Conzen, "A Saga of Families," 315–57; for example, Jensen, ed., Part I, 36, 37, 42, 47; Dana O. Jensen, ed., "I at Home . . . 1815–1816," *Bulletin of the Missouri Historical Society* 13, no. 3 (April 1957): 294, 295, 299, 300 (hereafter cited as Part II); Dana O. Jensen,

ed., "I at Home . . . 1817–1818," *Bulletin of the Missouri Historical Society* 14 (October 1957): 60 (hereafter cited as Part III).

24. Jensen, ed., Part II, 292; Part I, 47; Part III, 84, 66, 63; Part II, 285, 295; Dana O. Jensen, ed., "I at Home . . . 1819," *Bulletin of the Missouri Historical Society* 14, no. 3 (April 1958): 274 (hereafter cited as Part IV); Part I, 39, 45, 49.
25. Dana O. Jensen, ed., "I at Home . . . 1820," *Bulletin of the Missouri Historical Society* 15, no. 1 (October 1958): 44 (hereafter cited as Part V); Part I, 42.
26. Ibid., Part II, 309.
27. Ibid., 301.
28. Ibid., Part I, 36, 40, 46, 52; Part II, 300.
29. Ibid., Part I, 52; Part II, 301, 290; Part I, 49, 33; Part II, 299; Part III, 68, 91; Part I, 40; Part III, 91.
30. Ibid., Part II, 296, 298; Part IV, 274, 285.
31. Ibid., Part III, 78, 79, 91.
32. Ibid., Part IV, 288; Part II, 291, 300, 317; Part III, 77.
33. Ibid., Part II, 294; Parts I-V.
34. Ibid., Part II, 289, 310, 311; Part III, 62, 65, 69, 70.
35. Ibid., Part II, 314.
36. Ibid., Part III, 88–89.
37. "Adele P. Gratiot's Narrative," 264–65.
38. Jensen, ed., Part I, 44, 45, 46; Part II, 287–89, 311–12; Part III, 66, 69; Part IV, 273, 278; Part V, 40; Part II, 309, 310, 312; Part III, 81; Part IV, 283, 284; ibid., "I at Home . . . 1823–1826," *Bulletin of the Missouri Historical Society* 22, no. 1 (October 1965): 75, 76–77 (hereafter cited as Part VII).
39. Ibid., Part VII, 75, 76–77; Part IV, 281–83, 284; Part V, 45, 46–48.
40. Ibid., Part III, 69–70, 77.
41. Ibid., Part V, 46–48.
42. Ibid., 48; Part III, 69; Diary of Stephen Hempstead, 3 July 1831; 5–8 December 1830, SHC.
43. Jensen, ed., Part III, 309; Part III, 74, 75, 86; Part IV, 280; Part V, 42; ibid., "I at Home . . . 1822," *Bulletin of the Missouri Historical Society* 15, no. 3 (April 1959): 225 (hereafter cited as Part VI).
44. Ibid., Part II, 295, 298.
45. Peter L. Scanlan, *Prairie du Chien: French, British, American* (Menasha, Wisconsin: Banta Publishing Co., 1937), 181, 96, 121; Jensen, ed., Part I, 51; Part II, 311, 315, 316; Part III, 73, 86.
46. Ibid., Part VI, 227, 231, 236, 239; *History of Jo Daviess County*, 238.
47. Stephen Hempstead to Lyman Draper, 23 April 1867, Lyman Draper Collection, State Historical Society of Wisconsin; Jensen, ed., Part V, 42.
48. Ibid., Part IV, 280; Part VI, 228, 242; Part VII, 63, 64, 68, 70.
49. Ibid., Part VI, 225.
50. Washburne, "Col. Henry Gratiot," 239–42; James Neal Primm, *Lion of the Valley, St. Louis, Missouri*, 2d ed. (Boulder: Pruett Publishing Company, 1990), 53–55; Tanis C. Thorne, *The Many Hands of My Relations, French and Indians on the Lower Missouri* (Columbia: University of Missouri Press, 1996), 85–90; Washburne, "Col. Henry Gratiot," 244.
51. "Adele P. Gratiot's Narrative," 265.
52. Bale, "When the Gratiots Came to Galena," 673.

Notes

53. Ibid., 673–74.
54. Susan Hempstead Gratiot, "Memoir," AGW.
55. "Isaac R. Campbell," Caleb Forbes Davis Collection, Keokuk Savings Bank and Trust Co., Keokuk, Iowa; A. T. Andreas, *Andreas' Historical Atlas of the State of Iowa* (Chicago: Andreas Atlas Company, 1875), 481.
56. "Adele P. Gratiot's Narrative," 266.
57. Susan Hempstead Gratiot, "Memoir," AGW.
58. Washburne, "Col. Henry Gratiot," 244–45; "Adele P. Gratiot's Narrative," 267.
59. Ibid., 267–68; Washburne, "Col. Henry Gratiot," 245–46; Stephen Hempstead to Susan Hempstead Gratiot, 14 July 1826; Susan Hempstead Gratiot to "My Dear Sister," 21 December 1826, AGW.
60. Susan Hempstead Gratiot, "Memoir," AGW.
61. Ibid.; "Adele P. Gratiot's Narrative," 268.
62. Stephen Hempstead to Susan Hempstead Gratiot, 15 October 1826, AGW; Washburne, "Col. Henry Gratiot," 247; Elihu B. Washburne, *Historical Sketch of Charles S. Hempstead to which Is Appended a Memoir of Edward Hempstead* (Galena: Gazette Book and Job Printing House, 1875), 18.
63. Stephen Hempstead to Susan Hempstead Gratiot, 14 July 1826, AGW.
64. "Adele P. Gratiot's Narrative," 268.
65. Susan Hempstead Gratiot to Stephen Hempstead, 21 December 1826, AGW.
66. Susan Hempstead Gratiot to Sarah Beebe, 16 February 1827, AGW.
67. Stephen Hempstead to Susan Hempstead Gratiot, 13 January 1830, AGW.
68. "Adele P. Gratiot's Narrative," 267–68; Susan Hempstead Gratiot, "Memoir," AGW.
69. Washburne, "Col. Henry Gratiot," 246, 248; Susan Hempstead Gratiot to Sarah Beebe, 16 February 1827, AGW; Washburne, "Sketch of Charles S. Hempstead," 18.
70. "Adele P. Gratiot's Narrative," 268.
71. Susan Hempstead Gratiot to Mary Lisa, 4 July 1827, AGW; Susan Hempstead Gratiot, "Memoir," AGW.
72. Sarah Beebe to Stephen Hempstead, 27 August 1827, AGW.
73. Susan Hempstead Gratiot, "Memoir," AGW; Stephen Hempstead to Susan Hempstead Gratiot, 15 October 1826, AGW.
74. Susan Hempstead Gratiot to "My Dear Sister," 21 December 1826, AGW; Susan Hempstead Gratiot to William Hempstead, 18 December 1834, in Bale, "A Packet of Old Letters," 160–63.
75. Mary B. Cunningham and Jeanne C. Blythe, *The Founding Family of St. Louis* (St. Louis: Midwest Technical Publications, 1977), 304, 306–7; Stephen Hempstead to Susan Hempstead Gratiot, 17 August 1827; Susan Hempstead Gratiot to Mary Lisa, 26 April 1830; Susan Hempstead Gratiot to Henry Gratiot, 17 March 1836, AGW.
76. "Adele P. Gratiot's Narrative," 268.
77. Susan Hempstead Gratiot to "my dear sister," 21 December 1826, AGW.
78. Stephen Hempstead to Susan Hempstead Gratiot, 17 August 1827, AGW; Stephen Hempstead Diary, 11, 17 August 1827, SHC.
79. "Adele P. Gratiot's Narrative," 270–73; Washburne, "Col. Henry Gratiot," 249–56; John Dowling to Peter Menard, 30 November 1829, Pierre Menard Papers, Illinois State Historical Library.
80. Susan Hempstead Gratiot to Sarah Beebe, 28 February 1831, AGW.
81. Milo M. Quaife, ed., "Journals and Reports of the Black Hawk War," *Mississippi Valley Historical Review* 12, no. 3 (1925–26): 392–409; "Adele P. Gratiot's Narrative," 271–73.

Notes

82. Washburne, "Col. Henry Gratiot," 257; Susan Hempstead Gratiot to William Hempstead, 30 June 1835, in Bale, "A Packet of Old Letters," 164.
83. Theodore Rodolf, "Pioneering in the Wisconsin Lead Region," *Collections of the State Historical Society of Wisconsin,* vol. 15 (Madison: The State Historical Society of Wisconsin, 1900), 344.
84. Susan Gratiot Hempstead to William Hempstead, 4 October 1835, in Bale, "A Packet of Old Letters," 164–65.
85. Susan Hempstead Gratiot to William Hempstead, 20 September 1833, in Bale, "A Packet of Old Letters," 161.
86. Susan Hempstead Gratiot to Mary Lisa, 4 July 1827, AGW.
87. Sarah Beebe to Stephen Hempstead, 10 August 1828, AGW; Stephen Hempstead Diary, 13 May, 2 September, 6 October 1827, 28 May 1828, 13 April 1829, SHC; Charles S. Hempstead, to C. H. Keeney, 25 May 1827; Stephen Hempstead, Sr., to C. H. Keeney, 28 May 1827, SHC.
88. Susan Hempstead Gratiot to Mary Lisa, 21 December 1826, AGW; Stephen Hempstead Diary, 27 June, 7 July 1828; Charles S. Hempstead, to C. H. Keeney, 25 May 1827; Stephen Hempstead, Sr., to C. H. Keeney, 28 May 1827, SHC; Stephen Hempstead to Sarah Beebe, 10 August 1827, AGW.
89. Sarah Beebe to Mary Lisa, 8 July 1827, AGW.
90. Stephen Hempstead Diary, 2 September, 6 October 1827; Charles Hempstead to C. H. Keeney, 2 November 1827, SHC.
91. Stephen Hempstead to Susan Hempstead Gratiot, 17 August 1827, AGW.
92. Sarah Beebe to Stephen Hempstead, 10 August 1828, AGW.
93. William Hempstead to Sarah Beebe, 14 June 1829, AGW.
94. Stephen Hempstead to Susan Hempstead Gratiot, 13 January 1830, AGW.
95. Susan Hempstead Gratiot to Sarah Beebe, 28 February 1831, AGW.
96. Susan Hempstead Gratiot to Sarah Beebe, 24 November 1833; Susan Hempstead Gratiot to "sister," 12 March 1834; Susan Hempstead Gratiot to William Hempstead, 30 June 1835, AGW.
97. Susan Hempstead Gratiot to Sarah Beebe, 6 April 1834, AGW.
98. Susan Hempstead Gratiot to William Hempstead, 30 June 1835, in Bale, "A Packet of Old Letters," 163.
99. Susan Hempstead Gratiot to Sarah Beebe, 6 April 1834, AGW.
100. Stephen Hempstead to Susan Hempstead Gratiot, 17 February 1827, AGW; Stephen Hempstead Diary, 30 July 1826, SHC.
101. Susan Hempstead Gratiot to Mary Lisa, 4 July 1827, AGW.
102. Susan Hempstead Gratiot to William Hempstead, 18 December 1834, in Bale, "A Packet of Old Letters," 162; Stephen Hempstead Diary, 12 May 1827, 28 May, 14 October 1828, SHC.
103. Susan Hempstead Gratiot to William Hempstead, 18 December 1834, in Bale, "A Packet of Old Letters," 162; Susan Hempstead Gratiot to William Hempstead, 30 June 1835; Susan Hempstead Gratiot to "sister," 25 December 1835, AGW.
104. Stephen Hempstead Diary, 29 June 1829, SHC; Jensen, ed., "I at Home . . . 1829–1831," *Bulletin of the Missouri Historical Society* 22, no. 4 (July 1966): 410–12 (hereafter cited as Part IX); Susan Hempstead Gratiot to Sarah Beebe, 24 November 1833, AGW.
105. Cunningham and Blythe, *Founding Family of St. Louis,* 310; Stephen Hempstead Diary, 11 November 1827, 14 October 1828, SHC; Stephen Hempstead to Mary Lisa, 2 June 1829, SHC.

Notes

106. Susan Hempstead Gratiot to Sarah Beebe, 6 April 1834; Susan Hempstead Gratiot to "sister," 25 December 1835; Susan Hempstead Gratiot to Henry Gratiot, 17 March 1836, AGW.
107. Susan Hempstead Gratiot to Sarah Beebe, 28 February 1831, AGW; Paul Beckwith, *Creoles of St. Louis* (St. Louis: Nixon-Jones Printing Co., 1893), 97–98; Stephen Hempstead Diary, January–February 1831, SHC.
108. Susan Hempstead Gratiot to Sarah Beebe, 28 February 1831, AGW.
109. Susan Hempstead Gratiot to William Hempstead, 20 September 1833, in Bale, "A Packet of Old Letters," 161; "Adele P. Gratiot's Narrative," 273; Rodolf, "Wisconsin Lead Region," 351, 354, 355; Beckwith, *Creoles of St. Louis,* 97.
110. Susan Hempstead Gratiot to William Hempstead, 20 September 1833, in Bale, "A Packet of Old Letters," 161.
111. "Adele P. Gratiot's Narrative," 275; Susan Hempstead Gratiot to Sarah Beebe, 5 January 1841, AGW.
112. Sarah Beebe to Mary Lisa, 8 July 1827; Stephen Hempstead Diary, 10 August, 1 September 1828, 29 June 1829, SHC; Charles Hempstead to C. H. Keeney, 13 December 1828, SHC; *History of Jo Daviess County,* 638; Charles S. Hempstead to Lyman C. Draper, 16 May 1867, Lyman Draper Collection, State Historical Society of Wisconsin; Susan Gratiot to Sarah Beebe, 12 March 1834, AGW.
113. Hempstead and Stahl, comps., *Stephen Hempstead and His Descendents,* 58– 60; William Hempstead to C. H. Keeney, 22 February, 6 March 1827; Charles Hempstead to C. H. Keeney, 27 April, 25, 28 May, 12 September, 2 November 1827, SHC.
114. Sarah Beebe to Mary Lisa, 8 July 1827; William Hempstead to Sarah Beebe, 14 June 1829, AGW.
115. Hempstead and Stahl, comps., *Stephen Hempstead and His Descendents,* 59; Susan Hempstead Gratiot to Sarah Beebe, 28 February 1831, AGW.
116. *History of Jo Daviess County,* 255, 638; Susan Hempstead Gratiot to Sarah Beebe, 24 November 1833; Susan Hempstead Gratiot to "sister and brother," 25 December 1835, AGW; Stephen Hempstead Diary, 10 September 1829, 28, 29 August 1830, 6 April 1831, SHC; Charles Hempstead to Stephen Hempstead, Sr., 19 January 1830, SHC.
117. Cunningham and Blythe, *The Founding Family of St. Louis,* 306–7; Beckwith, *Creoles of St. Louis,* 102–3.
118. Stephen Hempstead to Sarah Beebe, 10 August 1827; Stephen Hempstead to Susan Hempstead Gratiot, 17 August 1827; Sarah Beebe to Susan Hempstead Gratiot, 14 April 1829; Stephen Hempstead to Susan Hempstead Gratiot, 13 January 1830, AGW; Diary of Stephen Hempstead, 26, 27 May 1828, SHC.
119. Stephen Hempstead Diary, 7, 29 April, 9, 13 May, 2, 4, 18, 30 September, 6 October 1827, 7, 8, 10, 16, 19, 21 July 1828, SHC.
120. Stephen Hempstead Diary, 2, 3 July 1829, 4, 6, 7, 10, 13, 27, 30 May, 1–4 June 1830, SHC; Susan Hempstead Gratiot to Mary Lisa, 26 April 1830, AGW.
121. Susan Hempstead Gratiot to "sister," 12 March 1834, Susan Hempstead Gratiot to "sister and brother," 25 December 1835, Susan Hempstead Gratiot to Virginia Gratiot, 11 August 1836, AGW.
122. Susan Hempstead Gratiot to Sarah Beebe, 17 February 1827, AGW; Rodolf, "Wisconsin Lead Region," 338; Susan Hempstead Gratiot to "sister and brother," 25 December 1835, AGW.
123. Stephen Hempstead to Susan Hempstead Gratiot, 17 August 1827, Susan Hempstead Gratiot to Mary Lisa, 4 July 1827; Susan Hempstead Gratiot to Sarah Beebe, 28 Feb-

Notes

ruary 1831, AGW; "Adele P. Gratiot's Narrative," 271; Susan Hempstead Gratiot to Henry Gratiot, 17 March 1836, AGW; Stephen Hempstead Diary, 11, 17 August 1827, 7 July 1828, 7, 13 February 1830, 30 April 1831, SHC.

124. Susan Hempstead Gratiot to Mary Lisa, 26 April 1830, 4 July 1827; Sarah Beebe to Stephen Hempstead, 8 July 1827; Stephen Hempstead to Susan Hempstead Gratiot, 17 August 1827, 13 January 1830; Susan Hempstead Gratiot to William Hempstead, 30 June 1835, AGW; Stephen Hempstead Diary, 16 April 1827, 29 January, 31 March, 1 September 1828, 13 April, 27 August 1829, 12 April 1830, 24 March 1831, SHC; Susan Hempstead Gratiot to William Hempstead, 11 August 1833, 18 December 1834, 30 June, 4 October 1835, in Bale, "A Packet of Old Letters," 161, 162–63, 163–64, 164–65.

125. Sarah Beebe to Susan Hempstead Gratiot, 14 April 1820, AGW; Stephen Hempstead Diary, 10 August 1828, 16 April, 29 June 1829, 29 August 1830, SHC.

126. Stephen Hempstead to Susan Hempstead Gratiot, 15 October 1826, 17 February 1827; Stephen Hempstead to Sarah Beebe, 10 August 1827; Stephen Hempstead to Susan Hempstead Gratiot, 5 September 1829; Susan Hempstead Gratiot, to Mary Lisa, 26 April 1830; Susan Hempstead Gratiot to Sarah Beebe, 16 February 1827, AGW; Susan Hempstead Gratiot to William Hempstead, 18 December 1834, in Bale, "A Packet of Old Letters," 163.

127. Sarah Beebe to Susan Hempstead Gratiot, 14 April 1829; Stephen Hempstead to Susan Hempstead Gratiot, 5 September 1829, AGW.

128. Stephen Hempstead to Susan Hempstead Gratiot, 13 January 1830, AGW.

129. Charles Hempstead to C. H. Keeney, 29 August 1829, 25 May 1827, SHC; Susan Gratiot Hempstead to William Hempstead, 4 October 1835, in Bale, "A Packet of Old Letters," 164–65.

130. Susan Hempstead Gratiot to Mary Lisa, 4 July 1827; Stephen Hempstead to Susan Hempstead Gratiot, 17 February 1827; Sarah Beebe to Mary Lisa, 8 July 1827; Sarah Beebe to Stephen Hempstead, 27 August 1827; Sarah Beebe to Susan Hempstead Gratiot, 14 April 1829; Susan Hempstead Gratiot to Sarah Beebe, 28 February 1831; Susan Hempstead Gratiot to William Hempstead, 30 June 1835; Susan Hempstead Gratiot to Henry Gratiot, 17 March 1836, AGW; Susan Gratiot Hempstead to William Hempstead, 11 August 1833, in Bale, "A Packet of Old Letters," 161; Stephen Hempstead Diary, 13, 14 July 1826, 9 June 1829, SHC.

131. Beckwith, *The Creoles of St. Louis*, 81; *History of Lafayette County, Wisconsin*, 438; Foley and Rice, *The First Chouteaus*, 44–45; P. A. Lorimier to Pierre Menard, 16 April 1831, 17 January 1833, Pierre Menard Collection; Susan Hempstead Gratiot to Sarah Beebe, 6 April 1834, AGW.

132. Laurel Thatcher Ulrich, *A Midwife's Tale: The Life of Martha Ballard, Based on Her Diary, 1785–1812* (New York: Alfred E. Knopf, 1990), 75.

133. Rodolf, "Wisconsin Lead Region," 338–55.

134. John L. Brooke, *The Heart of the Commonwealth: Society and Political Culture in Worcester County, Massachusetts, 1713–1861* (New York: Cambridge University Press, 1989), 77, 80.

135. Washburne, "Col. Henry Gratiot," 248; "Adele P. Gratiot's Narrative," 266; Susan Hempstead Gratiot to "sister," 21 December 1826; Susan Hempstead Gratiot to Mary Lisa, 4 July 1827; Sarah Beebe to Stephen Hempstead, 27 August 1827; Sarah Beebe to Mary Lisa, 8 July 1827, AGW; Susan Gratiot Hempstead to William Hempstead, 18 December 1834, in Bale, "A Packet of Old Letters," 162.

Notes

136. "Adele P. Gratiot's Narrative," 266–67.
137. Susan Hempstead Gratiot, "Memoir," AGW; "Adele P. Gratiot's Narrative," 266.
138. Susan Hempstead Gratiot to William Hempstead, 18 December 1834, 30 June 1835, in Bale, "A Packet of Old Letters," 162–64; Susan Hempstead Gratiot to Mary Lisa, 4 July 1827, Sarah Beebe to Stephen Hempstead, 27 August 1827; Susan Hempstead Gratiot to Sarah Beebe, 28 February 1831, Sarah Beebe to Mary Lisa, 8 July 1827, AGW; Susan Gratiot Hempstead to William Hempstead, 4 October 1835, in Bale, "A Packet of Old Letters," 164–65; *History of Lafayette County, Wisconsin,* 449; Horatio Newhall Papers, Illinois State Historical Library.
139. Susan Hempstead Gratiot, "Memoir," AGW; "Adele P. Gratiot's Narrative," 267.
140. John Francis McDermott, "Auguste Chouteau, First Citizen of Upper Louisiana," in John Francis McDermott, ed., *Frenchmen and French Ways in the Mississippi Valley,* 13.
141. Susan Hempstead Gratiot to "sister," 21 December 1826, Stephen Hempstead to Susan Hempstead Gratiot, 5 September 1829, AGW.
142. Alvin M. Josephy, Jr., *The Artist Was a Young Man: The Life Story of Peter Rindisbacher* (Fort Worth: Amon Carter Museum, 1970), 47–63; Stephen Hempstead Diary, 4 June 1829; Jensen, ed., Part IX, 416.
143. Susan Hempstead Gratiot to Sarah Beebe, 16 February 1827, AGW; "Adele P. Gratiot's Narrative," 266; Susan Hempstead Gratiot, "Memoir," AGW.
144. Susan Hempstead Gratiot to Sarah Beebe, 16 February 1827, Susan Hempstead Gratiot, "Memoir," AGW; "Adele P. Gratiot's Narrative," 266.
145. Sarah Beebe to Mary Lisa, 8 July 1827, Susan Hempstead Gratiot to Mary Lisa, 4 July 1827, AGW; Rodolf, "Wisconsin Lead Region," 350.
146. Susan Hempstead Gratiot to Sarah Beebe, 28 February 1831, William Hempstead to Susan Hempstead Gratiot, 11 July 1829, AGW; Elihu B. Washburne to A. S. Washburne, 4 April 1840, Elihu B. Washburne Collection, Washburn-Norlands Humanities Center, Livermore, Maine.
147. Thwaites, ed., "Prairie du Chien in 1827," 365.
148. Quaife, ed., "Journals and Reports of the Black Hawk War," 393–95; Susan Gratiot Hempstead to William Hempstead, 30 June 1835, in Bale, "A Packet of Old Letters," 163–64.
149. Thomas H. Sheldon, "Narrative of Pioneer Wisconsin and Pike's Peak," *The Wisconsin Magazine of History* 12, no. 4 (June 1929): 414–15.
150. Susan Hempstead Gratiot to Sarah Beebe, 6 April 1834, 13 October 1839, AGW.
151. Washburne, "Col. Henry Gratiot," 253–54; "Adele P. Gratiot's Narrative," 269.
152. Susan Hempstead Gratiot to "sister," 21 December 1826, Stephen Hempstead to Susan Hempstead Gratiot, 17 February 1827, Sarah Beebe to Stephen Hempstead, 27 August 1827, AGW; John M. Faragher, *Daniel Boone: The Life and Legend of an American Pioneer* (New York: Henry Holt and Company, 1992), 300.
153. "Adele P. Gratiot's Narrative," 269.
154. *History of Lafayette County, Wisconsin,* 439–40, 658; "Adele P. Gratiot's Narrative," 269–70; Stephen Hempstead Diary, 2 September 1827, SHC.
155. Horatio Newhall to Isaac Newhall, March 1 1828, Horatio Newhall Papers.
156. Washburne, "Col. Henry Gratiot," 256, 258; Rodolf, "Wisconsin Lead Region," 356.
157. Susan Hempstead Gratiot to William Hempstead, 4 October 1835, in Bale, "A Packet of Old Letters," 164–65.
158. Susan Hempstead Gratiot to William Hempstead, 30 June 1835, in Bale, "A Packet of Old Letters," 164; Susan Hempstead Gratiot to "Sister and Brother," 25 December

Notes

 1835, AGW; Charles S. Hempstead to William Hempstead, 22 July 1835; Susan H. Gratiot to William Hempstead, 16 April 1836, William Hempstead Papers.
159. Bale, "A Packet of Old Letters," 154.
160. Washburne, "Col. Henry Gratiot," 258–59.
161. Ibid., 256; Susan Gratiot Hempstead to William Hempstead, 4 October 1835, in Bale, "A Packet of Old Letters," 164.
162. Susan Gratiot Hempstead to William Hempstead, 30 June, 4 October 1835, in Bale, "A Packet of Old Letters," 164–65; Elihu B. Washburne, "Col. Henry Gratiot," 256.
163. Washburne, "Col. Henry Gratiot," 257–58; Charles S. Hempstead to William Hempstead, 6 July 1836, Charles Hempstead Papers, Wisconsin State Historical Society.
164. Susan Hempstead Gratiot to William Hempstead, 6 February 1837, in Bale, "A Packet of Old Letters," 166.
165. Susan Gratiot to Mrs. Sarah Beebe, 5 January 1841, AGW.
166. Susan Hempstead Gratiot to Sarah Beebe, 13 October 1839, AGW.
167. Hempstead and Stahl, comps., *Stephen Hempstead and His Descendents*, 59.
168. Susan Hempstead Gratiot to Sarah Beebe, 13 October 1839, AGW; Joseph Schafer, "High Society in Pioneer Wisconsin," *The Wisconsin Magazine of History* 20, no. 4 (June 1937): 451–53.

Chapter 3. "A common band of brotherhood"

1. *Address of Hon. Elihu B. Washburne and Response of Governor Thomas Chrittenden on the Occasion of the Presentation of the Portrait of Hon. Edward Hempstead to the State of Missouri* (Jefferson City: Tribune Printing Co., 1881), 6.
2. Kathleen N. Conzen, "A Saga of Families," in Clyde A. Milner II, Carol O'Conner, and Martha A. Sandweiss, eds., *The Oxford History of the American West* (New York: Oxford University Press, 1994), 327–29.
3. Stuart Blumin, *The Emergence of the Middle Class: Social Experience in the American City, 1790–1900* (New York: Cambridge University Press, 1989), 4–11; Paul Johnson, *A Shopkeeper's Millennium: Society and Revivals in Rochester, New York, 1815–1837* (New York: Hill and Wang, 1978), 8.
4. Richard L. Bushman, *The Refinement of America: Persons, Houses, and Cities* (New York: Alfred A. Knopf, 1992), 402–9; Blumin, *The Emergence of the Middle Class*, 11.
5. Bushman, *The Refinement of America*, xi–xix; John F. Kasson, *Rudeness and Civility, Manners in Nineteenth-Century Urban America* (New York: Hill and Wang, 1990), 34, 59–69.
6. Blumin, *The Emergence of the Middle Class*, 11; John S. Gilekson, Jr., *Middle-Class Providence, 1820–1940* (Princeton: Princeton University Press, 1986), 3–11; Don H. Doyle, "The Social Functions of Voluntary Associations in a Nineteenth-Century American Town," *Social Science History* 1, no. 3 (Spring 1977): 333–55; Mary P. Ryan, *Cradle of the Middle Class: The Family in Oneida County, New York, 1790–1865* (New York: Cambridge University Press, 1981), 13–15; James Gilbert, *Perfect Cities: Chicago's Utopias of 1893* (Chicago: University of Chicago Press, 1991), 4–11.
7. Timothy R. Mahoney, *River Towns in the Great West: The Structure of Provincial Urbanization in the American Midwest, 1820–1870* (New York: Cambridge University Press, 1990), 16–54; Jacqueline A. Ferguson and Michael J. O'Brien, "General Patterns of Settlement and Growth in the Central Salt River Valley," in Michael J. O'Brien, ed., *Grassland, Forest, and Historical Settlement: An Analysis of Dynamics in Northeast Missouri*

Notes

(Lincoln: University of Nebraska Press, 1984), 157–191; John Mack Faragher, *Sugar Creek: Life on the Illinois Prairie* (New Haven: Yale University Press, 1986), 57–67.

8. Caleb Forbes Davis Collection, 9 volumes, Keokuk Savings Bank and Trust Company, Keokuk, Iowa; Microfilm copy at Iowa State Historical Society, Iowa City, Iowa (hereafter cited as CFD). The name in quotation marks indicates the autobiographer. Because many of the autobiographies do not have page numbers, no pages are noted throughout. In 1882 Davis began collecting over forty autobiographies and interspersing them with newspaper clippings, photographs, and other memorabilia. His initial method was straightforward. He wrote a letter to every member of the early society of Keokuk he could recall and knew were still alive. Davis asked each autobiographer simply to write as much or as little as they cared to about their early experiences in Keokuk. Respondents were apparently free to respond however they wished. "Autobiography of Hawkins Taylor," Western Illinois University, Macomb, Illinois, 36; "R. B. Ogden," CFD.

9. Robert Baird, *View of the Valley of the Mississippi; or, The Emigrant's and Traveller's Guide to the West* (Philadelphia: H. S. Tanner, 1832), 88–89; D. W. Meinig, *The Shaping of America: A Geographical Perspective on 500 Years of History*, vol. 2: *Continental America, 1800–1867* (New Haven: Yale University Press, 1993), 229–32, 264–84; Andrew R. L. Cayton and Peter S. Onuf, *The Midwest and the Nation: Rethinking the History of an American Region* (Bloomington: Indiana University Press, 1990), 25–30.

10. *The History of Jo Daviess County* (Chicago: H. F. Kett and Co., 1878), 247.

11. Jeffrey S. Adler, *Yankee Merchants and the Making of the Urban West: The Rise and Fall of Antebellum St. Louis* (New York: Cambridge University Press, 1991); Susan E. Gray, *The Yankee West: Community Life on the Michigan Frontier* (Chapel Hill: University of North Carolina Press, 1997).

12. John C. Hudson, "North American Origins of Middlewestern Frontier Populations," *Annals of the Association of American Geographers* 78, no. 3 (1988): 395–413.

13. Ibid., 401–7.

14. Ibid., 411–12; Frederick M. Wirt, "The Changing Social Bases of Regionalism: Peoples, Cultures, and Politics in Illinois," in Peter Nardulli, ed., *Diversity, Conflict, and State Politics: Regionalism in Illinois* (Urbana: University of Illinois Press, 1989), 31–60.

15. Meinig, *The Shaping of America*, vol. 2: 264–84.

16. Conzen, "A Saga of Families," 327–29; Richard White, *It's Your Misfortune and None of My Own: A New History of the American West* (Norman, Oklahoma: University of Oklahoma Press, 1991), 192–93.

17. Mahoney, *River Towns in the Great West*, 89–109.

18. John Beauchamp Jones (Luke Shortfield), *The Western Merchant: A Narrative* (Philadelphia: Grigg, Elliot and Co., 1849), 40–49, 62.

19. CFD.

20. See William Worth Belknap Papers, Princeton University Libraries (hereafter WWB).

21. "Laban B. Fleak," "R. B. Ogden," "J. H. Wescott," CFD; "Autobiography of Hawkins Taylor," Western Illinois University; Baird, *View of the Valley of the Mississippi*, 91.

22. Gaillard Hunt, *Israel, Elihu, and Cadwallader Washburn: A Chapter in American Biography* (1925; rpt., New York: Da Capo Press, 1969), 171.

23. "A. W. Griffith," CFD; B. L. Wick, "The Struggle for the Half-Breed Tract," *Annals of Iowa* 7, no. 1 (April 1905): 16–29; Virginia Wilcox Ivins, *Pen Pictures of Early Western Days* (n.p., 1905), 40–41.

24. J. M. Reid, *Sketches and Anecdotes of the Old Settlers* (Keokuk, Iowa: R. B. Ogden, 1876), 67.

Notes

25. David W. Kilbourne to Hiram Barney, 13 May, 5, 26 June, 21 August 1841, 11 May 1844, 3 March 1845, hint at some of the troubles with the Settlers. Hiram Barney Papers, The Huntington Library, San Marino, California. For a rare, brief, indirect reference to a Decree vs. Anti-Decree altercation see 26 April 1849, *Keokuk Telegraph and Weekly Dispatch*; *Letter of Charles Mason to Gen. A. C. Dodge in Regard to the Halfbreed Question* (Burlington; Chas. I. Baker, 1880), 11; James L. Estes to Charles Mason, 13 June, 6 September 1853, Charles Mason Papers, Iowa State Historical Library, Des Moines, Iowa; "A. W. Griffith," "David W. Kilbourne," CFD.
26. Hawkins Taylor, "Judge Mason and the Half-Breed Tract," *Iowa Historical Record* 2, no. 4 (October 1886): 354; "A W. Griffith," CFD; *Coy v. Mason*, 58 U.S. (17 Howard) 580 (1854).
27. On notices being posted, see Francis Scott Key to Hiram Barney, 13 May 1841; David W. Kilbourne, "Notice," 16 May 1846; David W. Kilbourne to Hiram Barney, 21 August 1841, 25 January 1842, Hiram Barney Papers.
28. D.W. Kilbourne to Hiram Barney, 11 May 1844, 3, 5 March 1845, Hiram Barney Papers.
29. Henry C. Ethell, *The Rise and Progress of Civilization in the Hairy Nation* (Bloomfield, Iowa: Republican Steam Print, 1883).
30. Taylor, "Judge Mason and the Half Breed Tract," 354.
31. "The Diary of Henry F. Austin," CFD; this account is corroborated in a remarkable letter, Harriet Rice Kilbourne to Mrs. A. Germain, 4 July 1838, Hiram Barney Papers.
32. "Autobiography of Hawkins Taylor," 37.
33. 9 March, 9, 13, 17 April 1838, "Diary of Henry Austin," CFD; Baird, *View of the Valley of the Mississippi*, 91; "David W. Kilbourne," CFD.
34. "Autobiography of Hawkins Taylor," 26–28, 16.
35. Susan Hempstead Gratiot, "Memoir," Adele Gratiot Washburne Collection, Washburn-Norlands Humanities Center, Livermore, Maine (hereafter cited as AGW).
36. "A. Brown," CFD; Elihu B. Washburne to A. S. Washburn, 4 April, 1 June 1840, Elihu B. Washburne Collection, Washburn-Norlands Humanities Center, Livermore, Maine (hereafter cited as EBW).
37. For a theoretical framework, see Kai T. Erikson, *Wayward Puritans: A Study in the Sociology of Deviance* (New York: John Wiley and Sons, 1966), 3–29.
38. "L. B. Fleak," "Hawkins Taylor," CFD.
39. "L. B. Fleak," CFD.
40. Ibid., "Autobiography of Hawkins Taylor," 27, 37; "Hawkins Taylor," CFD.
41. "L. B. Fleak," CFD.
42. Ibid; "Autobiography of Hawkins Taylor," 37.
43. "Hawkins Taylor," "L. B. Fleak," CFD.
44. "A. W. Griffith," CFD.
45. "L. B. Fleak," CFD; Reid, *Sketches and Anecdotes of the Old Settlers*, 64; "A. W. Griffith," "A. Brown," "Isaac Galland," CFD; Ivins, *Pen Pictures of Early Western Days*, 35–39.
46. Reid, *Sketches and Anecdotes of the Old Settlers*, 63–65; Patrick B. Nolan, *Vigilantes on the Middle Border: A Study of Self-Appointed Law Enforcement in the States of the Upper Mississippi from 1840 to 1880* (New York: Garland Publishing, 1987), 20; Erikson, *Wayward Puritans*, 3–29.
47. "E. R. Ford," CFD.
48. "A. Brown," CFD.
49. "Hawkins Taylor," "Edward Dietz," CFD.
50. "A. W. Griffith," "Hawkins Taylor," CFD.

Notes

51. "E. R. Ford," "A. W. Griffith," CFD.
52. "C. F. Davis," CFD.
53. Junius Hall to John Hall, 22 October 1842, Junius Hall Papers, New York Public Library.
54. Don H. Doyle, *The Social Order of a Frontier Community: Jacksonville, Illinois, 1825–1870* (Urbana: University of Illinois Press, 1978), 3, 5, 8–10, 9; Adler, *Yankee Merchants and the Making of the Urban West*, 8.
55. David W. Kilbourne to Hiram Barney, 25 January 1842, Hiram Barney Papers.
56. "J. H. Wescott," "R. B. Ogden," CFD; "Autobiography of Hawkins Taylor."
57. Ivins, *Pen Pictures of Early Western Days*, 39.
58. Junius Hall to John Hall, 5 January 1838, Junius Hall Papers.
59. Charles William Hunter to Zebina Eastman, 4 August 1847, Zebina Eastman Collection, Chicago Historical Society.
60. Horatio Newhall to Sarah Lewis Newhall, 17 November 1832, Horatio Newhall Papers, Illinois State Historical Library.
61. "E. R. Ford," "A. Brown," CFD; William Worth Belknap to Clara B. Wolcott, 17 March 1853, WWB.
62. Horatio Newhall to Isaac Newhall, 1 June 1832, Horatio Newhall Papers; Junius Hall to John Hall, 16 September 1836, Junius Hall Papers.
63. William Worth Belknap to Clara B. Wolcott, 17 March 1853, WWB.
64. Susan H. Gratiot to Mary Lisa, 4 July 1827, AGW; "Adele Gratiot's Narrative," 266; Theodore Rodolf, "Pioneering in the Wisconsin Lead Region," *Collections of the State Historical Society of Wisconsin*, vol. 15 (Madison: State Historical Society of Wisconsin, 1900), 350; Stephen Hempstead to Lyman Draper, 23 April 1867, Lyman Draper Collection, State Historical Society of Wisconsin.
65. Horatio Newhall to Isaac Newhall, 1 June 1832, Horatio Newhall Papers.
66. E. Anthony Rotundo, *American Manhood* (New York: Basic Books, 1993), 204, 196–205.
67. Karen V. Hansen, *A Very Social Time: Crafting Community in Antebellum New England* (Berkeley: University of California Press, 1994), 8–9; Rotundo, *American Manhood*, 199–205; Mark C. Carnes, *Secret Ritual and Manhood in Victorian America* (New Haven: Yale University Press, 1989), 11–14.
68. Timothy Gilfoyle, *City of Eros: New York City, Prostitution, and the Commercialization of Sex, 1790–1920* (New York: W. W. Norton and Co., Inc., 1992), 81, 92–116; George Chauncey, *Gay New York* (New York: Basic Books, 1994), 76–81.
69. Sean Wilentz, *Chants Democratic: New York City and the Rise of the American Working Class, 1788–1850* (New York: Oxford University Press, 1984), 300–301; Elliot J. Gorn, "'Good-Bye Boys, I Die a True American': Homicide, Nativism, and Working-Class Culture in Antebellum New York City," *Journal of American History* 74 (1987): 388–410; Michael Kaplan, "New York City Tavern Violence and the Creation of a Working-Class Identity," *Journal of the Early Republic* 15 (Winter 1995): 591–617; Amy Gilman Srebnick, *The Mysterious Death of Mary Rogers: Sex and Culture in Nineteenth-Century New York* (New York: Oxford University Press, 1995), 51–58.
70. Adler, *Yankee Merchants and the Making of the Urban West*, 64; Elliott West, *The Saloon on the Rocky Mountain Mining Frontier* (Lincoln: University of Nebraska Press, 1979), 4–11, 47.
71. "C. F. Davis," "A. W. Griffith," CFD.
72. "Hawkins Taylor," "A. Brown," "A. W. Griffith," "C. F. Davis," CFD.
73. "A. Brown," CFD.
74. "L. B. Fleak," CFD.

Notes

75. "C. F. Davis," "A. Brown," CFD.
76. "R. B. Ogden," CFD.
77. Rotundo, *American Manhood*, 200; Richard Wade, *The Urban Frontier* (Chicago: University of Chicago Press, 1959), 219–20; Mahoney, *River Towns in the Great West*, 255–56; Daniel Curtiss, *Western Portraiture, and Emigrants' Guide* (New York: J. H. Colton, 1852), 338.
78. "C. F. Davis," CFD; Ivins, *Pen Pictures of Early Western Days*, 51.
79. "A. W. Griffith," CFD.
80. Ibid.; Ivins, *Pen Pictures of Early Western Days*, 50.
81. "Hawkins Taylor," "A. Brown," "A. W. Griffith," CFD.
82. "A. Brown," "L. B. Fleak," "C. F. Davis," CFD.
83. Reid, *Sketches and Anecdotes*, 11, 157; "A. W. Griffith," "C. F. Davis," CFD; D. W. Kilbourne, "Notice," 16 May 1846, Hiram Barney Papers.
84. "A. Brown," CFD.
85. "A.W. Griffith," CFD.
86. Hawkins Taylor to Caleb F. Davis, 25 April 1886, "Adam Hine," "E. R. Ford," "C. F. Davis," "A. W. Griffith," "A. Brown," CFD; "T." [Hawkins Taylor], "Early Days in Keokuk," *Annals of Iowa* 8 (April 1870): 144.
87. "T" [Hawkins Taylor], "Early Days in Keokuk," 144.
88. Gary Alan Fine, *With the Boys: Little League Baseball and Preadolescent Culture* (Chicago: University of Chicago Press, 1987), 134–35; Theodore J. Holland, "The Many Faces of Nicknames," *Names* 38, no. 4 (December 1990): 255–72; James K. Skipper, "Nicknames, Coal Miners and Group Solidarity," *Names* 34, no. 2 (June 1986): 134–45; Theodore J. Holland, Jr., "The Nicknames of Steam-Era Railroaders: A Code-Mediated Adaptation," *Names* 38, no. 4 (December 1990): 295–304; Paul L. Leslie and James K. Skipper, Jr., "Toward a Theory of Nicknames: Case for Socio-Onomastics," *Names* 38, no. 4 (December 1990): 273–82; Thomas J. Gasque, "Looking Back to Beaver and the Head: Male College Nicknames in the 1950s," *Names* 42, no. 2 (June 1994): 121–32; Carl M. Becker, "'Tardy George' and 'Extra Billy': Nicknames in the Civil War," *Civil War History* 35, no. 4 (1989): 302–10; Richard D. Alford, *Naming and Identity: A Cross Cultural Study of Personal Naming Practices* (New Haven: Hraf Press, 1988), 81–85, 156–59; George Earlie Shankle, *American Nicknames: Their Origin and Significance* (New York: H. W. Wilson, 1937); Wilson Somerville, *The Tuesday Club of Annapolis as Cultural Performance, 1745–1756* (Athens: University of Georgia Press, 1996).
89. Reid, *Sketches and Anecdotes*, 123. Contemporary references to specific nicknames are very rare. See James L. Estes to Charles Mason, 17 January 1854, Charles Mason Papers, Iowa State Historical Library, Des Moines, Iowa; James F. Cox to Thomas B. Cuming, 12 December 1852, Thomas B. Cuming Papers, Nebraska Historical Society. Dan F. Miller acquired his name, "The Ghost of Buster," from a poem he wrote and published in the local paper; *Keokuk Weekly and Telegraphic Dispatch*, 8 June, 3 August 1848.
90. E. Anthony Rotundo, "Boy Culture: Middle-Class Boyhood in Nineteenth-Century America," in Mark C. Carnes and Clyde Griffen, eds., *Meanings for Manhood: Constructions of Masculinity in Victorian America* (Chicago: University of Chicago Press, 1990), 15–36.
91. Nicknames are mentioned in "A. W. Griffith," "E. R. Ford," "C. F. Davis," "L. B. Fleak," "A. Brown," and "Adam Hine," CFD; Reid, *Sketches and Anecdotes*, 11–13, 74, 78, 144, 162, 167, 170, 176; Ivins, *Pen Pictures of Early Western Days*, 17.
92. Reid, *Sketches and Anecdotes*, 162–63; "William Phelps," "D. W. Kilbourne," CFD.

Notes

93. "L. B. Fleak," Hawkins Taylor to Caleb F. Davis, 25 April 1886, CFD; Reid, *Sketches and Anecdotes*, 170, 173.
94. For many other nicknames, see Reid, *Sketches and Anecdotes*, 11–13, 74, 78–79; Ivins, *Pen Pictures of Early Western Days*, 17.
95. "E. R. Ford," "Caleb Forbes Davis," Hawkins Taylor to Caleb F. Davis, 25 April 1886, CFD; "T"[Hawkins Taylor], "Early Days in Keokuk," 144.
96. "L. B. Fleak," "Index," comment by Caleb F. Davis on James F. Cox, CFD.
97. "C. F. Davis," "E. R. Ford," CFD; Reid, *Sketches and Anecdotes*, 11–13.
98. Edward H. Stiles, *Recollections and Sketches of Notable Lawyers and Public Men of Early Iowa* (Des Moines: Homestead Publishing Co., 1916), 260–62; Hawkins Taylor to C. F. Davis, 25 April 1886, "L. B. Fleak," "William Phelps," CFD; Reid, *Sketches and Anecdotes*, 60.
99. "L. B. Fleak," "E. R. Ford," "C. F. Davis," "Hawkins Taylor," CFD; Reid, *Sketches and Anecdotes*, 124, 123, 11–13, 129; John S. Farmer and W. E. Henley, comps. and eds., *Slang and Its Analogues, Past and Present: A Dictionary, Historical and Comparative, of the Heterodox Speech of All Classes of Society*, vols. 1–7 (New York: Kraus Reprint Co., 1965), 7: 42; Eric Partridge, *A Dictionary of Slang and Unconventional English* (London: Routledge and Kegan Paul Ltd., 1949), 853.
100. "L. B. Fleak," CFD; Farmer and Henley, comps. and eds., *Slang and Its Analogues*, 2: 314.
101. Farmer and Henley, comps. and eds., *Slang and Its Analogues*, 2: 94–95.
102. "L. B. Fleak," Hawkins Taylor to C. F. Davis, 25 April 1886, CFD.
103. "L. B. Fleak," CFD; Usher F. Linder, *Reminiscences of the Early Bench and Bar of Illinois* (Chicago: Chicago Legal News Company, 1879), "James Turney," 376.
104. "A. Brown," CFD.
105. Hawkins Taylor to C. F. Davis, 25 April 1886, "A. Brown," "L. B. Fleak," CFD; Partridge, *Slang and Unconventional English*, 346.
106. Reid, *Sketches and Anecdotes*, 11–13.
107. Ibid., 74; "L. B. Fleak," "A. W. Griffith," CFD; Partridge, *Slang and Unconventional English*, 100; Farmer and Henley, comps. and eds., *Slang and Its Analogues*, 3: 296–97; Reid, *Sketches and Anecdotes*, 170.
108. "A. W. Griffith," "L. B. Fleak," CFD; Reid, *Sketches and Anecdotes*, 61, 138.
109. Partridge, *Slang and Unconventional English*, 812; Farmer and Henley, comps. and eds., *Slang and Its Analogues*, 4: 81.
110. John M. Faragher, *Daniel Boone: The Life and Legend of an American Pioneer* (New York: Henry Holt and Company, Inc., 1992), 196.
111. Farmer and Henley, comps. and eds., *Slang and Its Analogues*, 6: 91; Partridge, *Slang and Unconventional English*, 721.
112. Eric Partridge, *A Dictionary of the Underworld* (New York: Bonanza Books, 1949), 254, 615; Farmer and Henley, comps. and eds., *Slang and Its Analogues*, 7: 197–98; J. D. Salinger, *Catcher in the Rye* (New York: Little, Brown, and Company, Inc., 1951), 143.
113. Farmer and Henley, comps. and eds., *Slang and Its Analogues*, 7: 246; Partridge, *Slang and Unconventional English*, 921; Skipper, "Nicknames, Coal Miners and Group Solidarity," 134–45; Farmer and Henley, comps. and eds., *Slang and Its Analogues*, 1: 212–15.
114. Reid, *Sketches and Anecdotes*, 123.
115. "Early Quincy, 1822–1833," *Transactions of the Illinois State Historical Society* (Springfield, Illinois State Historical Society, 1916): 146, 155.

Notes

116. "J. C. Parrott," "L. B. Fleak," CFD; Hawkins Taylor, "General Jesse B. Brown," *Annals of Iowa* (July 1872): 196–206.
117. "C. F. Davis," CFD.
118. For a rare contemporary view of practical jokes, see the feature-length film, *Watch It* (1993), Dover One Films, Skouras Pictures Release, starring John Gallagher, Suzy Amis, and John Tenley.
119. Reid, *Sketches and Anecdotes,* 59–60; "L. B. Fleak," CFD.
120. " L. B. Fleak," CFD.
121. Ibid.
122. "L. B. Fleak," "A. Brown," CFD.
123. "A. W. Griffith," CFD.
124. "L. B. Fleak," CFD.
125. "Settlers' Ball," "Keokuk Thespian Ball," "Military Ball," "C. F. Davis," CFD.
126. Paul Angle, *"Here I Have Lived": A History of Lincoln's Springfield, 1821–1865* (Springfield, Illinois: The Abraham Lincoln Association, 1935), 106–7.
127. Stiles, *Recollections and Sketches,* 346; Caleb F. Davis, "Yaller Hand Bill Meetings," CFD; Leon Herbert Swett, comp. and ed., *A Memorial of Leonard Swett, Lawyer and Advocate* (Chicago, 1895), 18; Henry C. Whitney, *Life on the Circuit with Lincoln* (Boston: Estes and Lauriat, 1892), 181; Frederick Trevor Hill, *Lincoln, the Lawyer* (New York: The Century Club, 1913), 173.
128. Angle, *"Here I Have Lived,"* 106, 195.
129. "A. W. Griffith," "C. F. Davis," CFD; Reid, *Sketches and Anecdotes,* 61, 91, 157–58, 176; Susan Hempstead Gratiot to Sarah Beebe, 28 February 1831, AGW. "Frolicking" described a variety of group behavior related to having a good time, which had been, for a long time, part of rural life. See Faragher, *Daniel Boone,* 29, 64, 109; John Mack Faragher, *Sugar Creek: Life on the Illinois Prairie* (New Haven: Yale University Press, 1986), 135; Jones, *The Western Merchant,* 63; see also Jane C. Nylander, *Our Own Snug Fireside: Images of the New England Home, 1760–1860* (New Haven: Yale University Press, 1994), 225–28, 234.
130. "Autobiography of Hawkins Taylor," 26–27.
131. "E. R. Ford," CFD; Reid, *Sketches and Anecdotes,* 176. The "spondoolicks" or "spondulicks" in the Cosmopolitan Society program were "resources," capital, or money. Elliott West, *The Saloon on the Rocky Mountain Mining Frontier,* 77.
132. Don H. Doyle, "The Social Functions of Voluntary Associations in a Nineteenth-Century American Town," *Social Science History* 1, no. 3 (Spring 1977): 333–55.
133. Reid, *Sketches and Anecdotes,* 78.
134. A rare example of such a "lobby" is the one which developed at the same time over in Springfield, Illinois. Angle, *"Here I Have Lived,"* 106–8. The best known "mock tribunal" is, of course, the "Ogmathorial Court" which occurred during Abraham Lincoln's attendance in the Eighth Illinois Circuit between 1849 and 1851. Whitney, *Life on the Circuit with Lincoln,* 50.
135. Caleb Forbes Davis, "Yaller Hand Bill Meetings," CFD; Hawkins Taylor, "Letters from Absent Members," *Pioneer Lawmakers Association of Iowa, Reunions of 1886 and 1890* (Des Moines: G. H. Ragsdale, 1890), 131.
136. Ibid.; Taylor, "Early Recollections," CFD; "J. Haines," CFD; Jones, *The Western Merchant,* 46.
137. Taylor, "Early Recollections," CFD; Jean H. Baker, *Mary Todd Lincoln* (New York: W. W. Norton, 1987), 64; "Dr. Josiah Haines," CFD.

Notes

138. Taylor, "Early Recollections," CFD.
139. Susan G. Davis, *Parades and Power: Street Theatre in Nineteenth-Century Philadelphia* (Philadelphia: Temple University Press, 1986), 36, 73–111; "A. Brown," CFD; "Autobiography of Hawkins Taylor."
140. "A. Brown," CFD.
141. "L. B. Fleak," CFD.
142. "A. W. Griffith," CFD.
143. Ibid., "A. W. Griffith," "J. Haines," "J. M. Reid," "Dr. Isaac Galland," CFD; Diary of Charles Mason, 28 September 1858, Charles Mason Papers, Iowa State Historical Society, Des Moines, Iowa.
144. "E. R. Ford," CFD.
145. "A. W. Griffith," CFD; Verplanck Van Antwerp to Thomas B. Cuming, 7 November 1854, Thomas B. Cuming Papers.
146. "E. R. Ford," CFD.
147. "L. B. Fleak," "A. W. Griffith," CFD; William Worth Belknap to Clara Wolcott, 3 August 1852, WWB.
148. "L. B. Fleak," CFD.
149. Ibid., "J. C. Parrott," CFD.
150. Robert H. Wiebe, "Lincoln's Fraternal Democracy," in John L. Thomas, ed., *Abraham Lincoln and the American Political Tradition* (Amherst: University of Massachusetts Press, 1986), 12.

Chapter 4. Gentility in the West

1. Richard L. Bushman, *The Refinement of America: Persons, Houses, Cities* (New York: Alfred A. Knopf, 1992), 406–9.
2. Gender imbalance affected the nature of gentility in the West by giving it a more masculine tone. The predominance of male subcultures enhanced the cultural role of gentlemen in public. In addition, the delay in building proper houses delayed the ability of genteel women to establish moral domestic regimes. The impact of gender imbalance on the early social history of the urban West and its subsequent impact on western society is a theme historians have noted often, but only indirectly examined. For a recent critique, see Susan Lee Johnson, "'A Memory Sweet to Soldiers': The Significance of Gender," in Clyde A. Milner II, ed., *A New Significance: Re-envisioning the History of the American West* (New York: Oxford University Press, 1996), 255–78. Though it is apparent that gender imbalances moved toward equality within ten years of settlement in most towns and cities, research strategies and available sources – memoirs, papers, etc. – continue to affect our gendered perspective of the early urban frontier. This study is based on a data base of over 100 families in which the male household head was a member of the professional or mercantile middle class or a town booster at a town within the urban system. Letters or diaries of only a dozen of these men were located. Among their wives, only Susan Hempstead Gratiot's extensive papers have survived. Adele Gratiot Washburne and Eliza Browning have left eight and three letters, respectively. Few, if any, extant letters from the wives of other well-documented men have been found. Therefore, though men and women worked together to construct gentility in both public and private in the urban West, the sources, combined with a focus on the prevalence of male subcultures, gives this examination a gendered emphasis which explores only certain public aspects of antebellum middle-class experience.

Notes

3. Ann C. Rose, *Victorian America and the Civil War* (New York: Cambridge University Press, 1992), 145–46.
4. Karen Lystra, *Searching the Heart: Women, Men, and Romantic Love in Nineteenth-Century America* (New York: Oxford University Press, 1989), 28–55.
5. Karen V. Hansen, *A Very Social Time: Crafting Community in Antebellum New England* (Berkeley: University of California Press, 1994), 1–2, 7–11.
6. Diary of Solon Langworthy, 16 September 1860, Iowa State Historical Society, Iowa City, Iowa.
7. Ibid.
8. William Franklin Langworthy, comp., *The Langworthy Family: Some Descendants of Andrew and Rachel (Hubbard) Langworthy Who Were Married at Newport, Rhode Island, November 3 1658* (Hamilton, New York: William F. and Orthello J. Langworthy, 1940), 260.
9. Ibid., 260, 262, 265–66, 268–69.
10. Ibid., 259, 271.
11. Ibid., 262.
12. Theodore Calvin Pease and James G. Randall, eds., *Diary of Orville Hickman Browning*, vol. 1, *1850–1864*, Collections of the Illinois State Historical Library, vol. 20 (Springfield: Illinois State Historical Library, 1925), xi–xii; Maurice G. Baxter, *Orville H. Browning, Lincoln's Friend and Critic* (Bloomington: Indiana University Press, 1957), 4.
13. Thomas J. Brown, "The Age of Ambition in Quincy," *Journal of the Illinois State Historical Society* 75, no. 4 (Winter 1982): 245; David F. Wilcox, ed., *Quincy and Adams County: History and Representative Men*, 2 vols. (Chicago: Lewis Publishing Company, 1919), 1: 157–58.
14. *History of Adams County, Illinois* (Chicago: Murray, Williamson and Phelps, 1879), 413, 415.
15. Ibid., 413; Baxter, *Orville H. Browning*, 9.
16. Pease and Randall, eds., *Diary of Orville H. Browning*, 1: xi, xiii.
17. Jean H. Baker, *Mary Todd Lincoln: A Biography* (New York: W. W. Norton and Co., 1987), 53–73.
18. Ibid., 51, 64, 11, 6; "R. B. Ogden," C. F. Davis, "Yaller Hand Bill Meetings," Caleb Forbes Davis Collection, Keokuk Savings Bank and Trust Co., Keokuk, Iowa (hereafter cited as CFD).
19. Baxter, *Orville H. Browning*, 2.
20. Ibid., 70, 11–12, 60, 2–3.
21. Bushman, *The Refinement of America*, 415; Baxter, *Orville H. Browning*, 10–12; James W. Singleton, *Memorial Address on the Life and Character of Orville H. Browning* (Quincy: n.p., 1881), 12.
22. Baker, *Mary Todd Lincoln*, 43; Baxter, *Orville H. Browning*, 12, 51.
23. Gustave Koerner, *Memoirs of Gustave Koerner*, vol. 1: *1809–1896*, Thomas J. McCormack, ed. (Cedar Rapids, Iowa: The Torch Press, 1909), 479; Roy Meredith, *Mr. Lincoln's Cameraman, Matthew B. Brady* (New York: Dover Publications Inc., 1974), 60–61, shows Brady photos of Prince Edward in the style named after his father. James Gilbert, *Perfect Cities: Chicago's Utopias of 1893* (Chicago: University of Chicago Press, 1991), 136, 146. Gilbert notes that Chicago industrialist George Pullman continued to wear this style of jacket into the 1890s.
24. Baker, *Mary Todd Lincoln*, 64.
25. Koerner, *The Memoirs of Gustave Koerner*, 1: 479; Baxter, *Orville H. Browning*, 51.

Notes

26. Baxter, *Orville H. Browning*, 9–10.
27. Wilcox, ed., *Quincy and Adams County*, I: 159; Baxter, *Orville H. Browning*, 51.
28. Jane C. Nylander, *Our Own Snug Fireside: Images of the New England Home. 1760–1860* (New Haven: Yale University Press, 1994), 7–8; Alan Taylor, *William Cooper's Town: Power and Persuasion on the Frontier of the Early American Republic* (New York: Alfred A. Knopf, 1995), 92–93.
29. Robert Abzug, *Cosmos Crumbling: American Reform and the Religious Imagination* (New York: Oxford University Press, 1994), 57–60.
30. Michael Grossberg, "Institutionalizing Masculinity: The Law as a Masculine Profession," in Mark C. Carnes and Clyde Griffen, eds., *Meanings for Manhood: Constructions of Masculinity in Victorian America* (Chicago: University of Chicago Press, 1990), 133–51, 134.
31. Robert H. Wiebe, *The Opening of American Society* (New York: Alfred A. Knopf, 1984), 287–90.
32. Russell K. Nelson, "The Early Life and Congressional Career of Elihu B. Washburne" (Ph.D. dissertation, University of North Dakota, 1953), 14.
33. Elihu B. Washburne to Algernon S. Washburn, 17 May 1840, Algernon S. Washburn Papers, Minnesota Historical Society (hereafter cited as ASW); Elihu B. Washburne to C. C. Washburn, 23 December 1842, Elihu B. Washburne Papers, Washburn-Norlands Humanities Center, Livermore, Maine (hereafter cited as EBW).
34. Elihu B. Washburne to William Schouler, 1 April 1853, William Schouler Papers, Massachusetts Historical Society; *Dedicatory Exercises of the Washburn Memorial Library, Wednesday, August 5, 1885 at "The Norlands," Livermore, Maine . . .* , (Chicago: Fergus Printing Company, 1885), 32.
35. D. W. Meinig, *The Shaping of America: A Geographical Perspective on 500 Years of History*, vol. 2: *Continental America, 1800–1867* (New Haven: Yale University Press, 1993), 264–70.
36. Elihu Washburne to Algernon S. Washburn, 17 May 1840, ASW.
37. Hon. Samuel Shaw to Unknown, 29 November 1839, Washburn Papers, Massachusetts Historical Society, Boston, Massachusetts.
38. Elihu B. Washburne to A. S. Washburn, 15, 18 March 1840, EBW.
39. Elihu B. Washburne to A. S. Washburn, 15 March 1840, EBW.
40. Elihu B. Washburne to A. S. Washburn, 4 April 1840, EBW; Gaillard Hunt, *Israel, Elihu, and Cadwallader Washburn: A Chapter in American Biography* (1925; rpt., New York: Da Capo Press, 1969), 171.
41. Hunt, *Elihu Washburn*, 172; Elihu B. Washburne to A. S. Washburn, 4 April 1840, 27 October 1840, EBW.
42. Elihu B. Washburne to A. S. Washburn, 4 April 1840; Elihu B. Washburne to Adele G. Washburne, 1 April 1861, EBW.
43. Elihu B. Washburne to Adele G. Washburne, 1 April 1861, EBW.
44. Horatio Newhall to Hooper Warren, 2 November 1836; Horatio Newhall to Isaac Newhall, 29 April, 1 June 1832; Horatio Newhall to Sarah Lewis Newhall, 3 March 1833, Horatio Newhall Papers, Illinois State Historical Library, Springfield, Illinois (hereafter cited as HN)
45. *History of Jo Daviess County, Illinois* (Chicago: H. F. Kett and Co., 1878), 255.
46. Ellen Whitney, comp. and ed., *The Black Hawk War, 1831–1832*, vol. 1: *Illinois Volunteers*, Collections of the Illinois State Historical Library, vol. 35 (Springfield: Illinois State Historical Society, 1970), 499–500, 507–8.

Notes

47. Hunt, *Elihu Washburn*, 176.
48. Susan Hempstead Gratiot to Sarah Beebe, 28 February 1831; "Memoir of Susan Hempstead Gratiot"; Susan Hempstead Gratiot to Sarah Beebe, 27 August 1827, Adele Gratiot Washburne Collection, Washburn-Norlands Humanities Center, Livermore, Maine (hereafter cited as AGW); John Dowling to Peter Menard, 30 November 1829, Pierre Menard Papers, Illinois State Historical Library, Springfield, Illinois.
49. Elihu B. Washburne to A. S. Washburn, 20 May 1840, EBW.
50. Horatio Newhall to Isaac Newhall, 11 December 1840, HN.
51. Timothy R. Mahoney, "'A Common Band of Brotherhood'": The Booster Ethos, Male Subcultures, and the Origins of Urban Social Order in the Midwest of the 1840s," *Journal of Urban History* (forthcoming, 1999); Elihu B. Washburne to M. J. Washburn, 12 February 1841, EBW.
52. Nelson, "The Early Life and Congressional Career of Elihu B. Washburne," 14; Elihu B. Washburne to A. S. Washburn, 1 June 1840, EBW; Elihu B. Washburne to A. S. Washburn, 17 May 1840, ASW.
53. Elihu B. Washburne to M. J. Washburn, 12 February 1841, EBW.
54. Elihu B. Washburne to A. S. Washburn, 20 May 1840; Elihu B. Washburne to M. J. Washburn, 12 February 1841, EBW; Elihu Washburne to A. S. Washburn, 17 May 1840, 11 September 1842, ASW.
55. Elihu B. Washburne to A. S. Washburn, 1 June 1840, EBW.
56. Hunt, *Elihu Washburn*, 173.
57. Ibid.; Alice L. Bartel, ed., *Parish Register of Grace Church of Galena, Illinois*, 2 vols. (Wilmette, Illinois: Daughters of the American Revolution, 1964).
58. Ibid.
59. Elihu B. Washburne to A. S. Washburn, 26 July 1840, EBW.
60. Elihu B. Washburne to A. S. Washburn, 20 May 1840, 26 July 1840, EBW; "A Proposal That Charles Henry Ray Become a Candidate for State Senate," signed by local Democrats including Charles S. Hempstead, 23 January 1854, Charles Henry Ray Papers, The Huntington Library, San Marino, California.
61. *Galena Directory and Miner's Annual Register* (Galena: Green, Wilson and Co., 1847); Carl H. Johnson, Jr., *The Building of Galena: An Architectural Legacy* (Stevens Point, Wisconsin: Worzalla Publishing Company, 1977), 38, 42.
62. Elihu B. Washburne to A. S. Washburn, 14 August, 10 October 1840, EBW.
63. Elihu B. Washburne to A. S. Washburn, 10 October 1840, EBW; Hon. E. B. Washburne, *Historical Sketch of Charles S. Hempstead to Which Is Appended a Memoir of Edward Hempstead* (Galena: Gazette Book and Job Printing House, 1875), 20.
64. Elihu B. Washburne to A. S. Washburn, 23 December 1840; Elihu B. Washburne to M. J. Washburn, 12 February 1841, EBW.
65. Stephen Hempstead to Susan Hempstead Gratiot, 13 January 1830, AGW.
66. *History of Jo Daviess County*, 255–56; Paul E. Johnson, *A Shopkeeper's Millennium: Society and Revivals in Rochester, New York, 1815–1837* (New York: Hill and Wang, 1978), 95–109, 109; Horatio Newhall to Sarah Lewis Newhall, 3 March 1833, HN.
67. Horatio Newhall to Sarah Lewis Newhall, 16 February, 3 March 1833, HN; Johnson, *Shopkeeper's Millennium*, 100–101.
68. Susan Hempstead Gratiot to Sarah Beebe, 24 November 1833; 6 April 1834, AGW; "Aratus Kent" in "Sketches of Lives of Former Galenans," *Galena Weekly Advertiser*, 25 October 1870.
69. Susan Hempstead Gratiot to Sarah Beebe, 10 October 1846, AGW.

Notes

70. Susan Hempstead Gratiot to Sarah Beebe, 5 January 1841; Susan Hempstead Gratiot to Mary Lisa, 23 December 1844; Susan Hempstead Gratiot to Sarah Beebe, 17 March 1844, AGW.
71. Gilbert, *Perfect Cities*, 37–38.
72. Ibid.; Elihu B. Washburne to A. S. Washburn, 1 June 1840, EBW; Nelson, "The Early Life and Congressional Career of Elihu B. Washburne," 37–38.
73. James F. Cox to Thomas B. Cuming, 12 December 1852, Thomas B. Cuming Papers, Nebraska State Historical Society.
74. Elihu B. Washburne to A. S. Washburn, 1 June, 16 November, 4 April, 28 March 1841; Elihu B. Washburne to C. C. Washburn, 23 December 1842, EBW.
75. Elihu B. Washburne to Adele G. Washburne, 1 April 1861. EBW.
76. Elihu B. Washburne to A. S. Washburn, 23 December 1840, EBW; Susan Hempstead Gratiot to Sarah Beebe, 5 January 1841, AGW.
77. Elihu B. Washburne to A. S. Washburn, 30 November 1841, ASW.
78. Susan Hempstead Gratiot to Mary Lisa, 8 January, 23 December 1844, AGW.
79. Elihu B. Washburne to Susan Hempstead Gratiot, 1 January 1844, EBW; Paul Beckwith, *The Creoles of St. Louis* (St. Louis: Nixon-Jones Printing Co., 1893), 91; Mary B. Cunningham and Jeanne C. Blythe, *The Founding Family of St. Louis* (St. Louis: Midwest Technical Publications, 1977), 310, 321.
80. Adele Gratiot to Sarah Beebe, 7 September 1844, AGW.
81. Eliza Hempstead Cook, "Charles Wilt Hempstead," Hempstead Family Papers, Library of Congress; George Collier Hempstead and William Hempstead Stahl, comps., *Stephen Hempstead and His Descendents: A Genealogy and Biography* (Galena, Illinois: Gazette, c. 1929), 58–62.
82. Hempstead and Stahl, comps., *Stephen Hempstead and His Descendents*, 58–62; Susan Hempstead Gratiot to Mary Lisa, 23 December 1844, AGW.
83. Susan Hempstead Gratiot to Mary Lisa, 29 December 1844, AGW; Elihu Washburne to Cadwallader Washburn, 4 December 1844, Elihu B. Washburne Papers, State Historical Society of Wisconsin (hereafter cited as EBW, HSW).
84. Elihu B. Washburne to C. C. Washburn, 12 January 1845, EBW; Hunt, *Elihu Washburn*, 178–79; Susan Gratiot to "dear friend," 17 July 1845, AGW; Elihu B. Washburne to Cadwallader Washburn, 21 December 1844, EBW, HSW.
85. Elihu B. Washburne to Cadwallader Washburn, 10 April 1845, EBW, HSW; Elihu B. Washburne to C. C. Washburn, 27 April 1845, EBW.
86. Elihu B. Washburne to C. C. Washburn, 15 July 1845, EBW; C. C. Washburn to Israel Washburn, 7 August 1842, Cadwallader Washburn Collection, Washburn-Norlands Humanities Center, Livermore, Maine; Elihu B. Washburne to C. C. Washburn, 21 July 1845, EBW; Adele Gratiot to Cadwallader Washburne, 1 July 1845, AGW.
87. Baxter, *Orville H. Browning*, 54.
88. *History of Adams County, Illinois*, 412; Henry Asbury, *Reminiscences of Quincy, Illinois* (Quincy: D. Wilcox and Sons, 1882), 213; Henry S. Asbury Collection, Chicago Historical Society; Miscellaneous papers from Adams County Court, 1840–1850, Henry S. Asbury Papers, Illinois State Historical Library; Pease and Randall, eds., *Diary of Orville H. Browning*, 1: 77.
89. Pease and Randall, eds., *Diary of Orville H. Browning*, 1: 185, 57.
90. Henry S. Asbury, "Reminiscences," Henry S. Asbury Collection; Henry S. Asbury, *Advice Concerning the Duties of Justices of the Peace and Constables* (Quincy: C. M. Woods, Newton, Flagg, 1850); Henry S. Asbury, *Illinois Form Book; or, Advice Con-*

Notes

cerning *the Duties of the Justice of the Peace and Constables with Forms Required to Be Used in Discharge of their Respective Duties* (St. Louis: Edwards and Bushnell, 1856).

91. Wilcox, ed., *Quincy and Adams County*, 158, 159, 161; Baxter, *Orville H. Browning*, 54.
92. Wilcox, ed., *Quincy and Adams County*, 165.
93. *History of Adams County*, 413, 415.
94. Orville H. Browning to John Cox, 21 April 1866, Orville H. Browning Papers, Illinois State Historical Library.
95. Baxter, *Orville H. Browning*, 12–13.
96. David J. Caldwell to Henry Asbury, 17 May 1867, Henry Asbury Collection.
97. Baker, *Mary Todd Lincoln*, 37–45.
98. Baxter, *Orville H. Browning*, 12, 289.
99. Baker, *Mary Todd Lincoln*, 100–101; Laurel Thatcher Ulrich, *A Midwife's Tale: The Life of Martha Ballard, Based on Her Diary, 1785–1812* (New York: Alfred A. Knopf, 1990), 140–42.
100. Baxter, *Orville H. Browning*, 13.
101. Baker, *Mary Todd Lincoln*, 102; Baxter, *Orville H. Browning*, 52–53, 13.
102. Orville H. Browning to Eliza Browning, 24 July 1844, Ricks Collection, Illinois State Historical Library.
103. "Polly Sumner Chapter, Daughters of the American Revolution, Quincy, Illinois," in *Transactions of the Illinois State Historical Society for the Year 1915*, 164; Thomas J. Brown, "The Age of Ambition in Quincy," 249.
104. Baxter, *Orville H. Browning*, 70.
105. "Polly Sumner Chapter, Daughters of the American Revolution," 164.
106. Wilcox, ed., *Quincy and Adams County*, 165.
107. George Berrian to William Berrian, 25 November 1848, Daniel Weed Collection, Illinois State Historical Library.
108. Johnson, *The Building of Galena*, 43–44; Elihu B. Washburne to C. C. Washburn, 15 July 1845, EBW; Adele G. Washburne to Cadwallader Washburn, 21 September 1845; Elihu B. Washburne to C. C. Washburn, 14 December 1844, EBW, HSW.
109. Adele G. Washburne to Elihu B. Washburne, 7 December 1847, AGW; Hunt, *Elihu Washburn*, 179; Adele G. Washburne to "my dear lady," 18 January 1846, AGW; Elihu B. Washburne to Adele G. Washburne, 31 October 1845, Elihu B. Washburne Papers, Library of Congress (hereafter cited as EBW, LOC); Adele G. Washburne to Cadwallader Washburn, 21 September 1845; Elihu B. Washburne to Cadwallader Washburn, 2 October 1845; Adele G. Washburne to Cadwallader Washburn, 2 October 1845, EBW, HSW
110. Johnson, *The Building of Galena*, 35, 41, 42.
111. Hunt, *Elihu Washburn*, 2.
112. Elihu B. Washburne, "Col. Henry Gratiot – A Pioneer of Wisconsin," *Report and Collections of the State Historical Society of Wisconsin for the Years 1883, 1884, 1885*, vol. 10 (Madison: State Historical Society of Wisconsin, 1888), 256; Susan Hempstead Gratiot to Henry Gratiot, 17 March 1836, AGW.
113. Susan Hempstead Gratiot to "Dear sister and brother," 25 December 1835, AGW; Thomas C. Scharf, *History of St. Louis City and County* (Philadelphia: McDonough Publishing Co., 1883), 1:180–81; Lawrence Lowic, *The Architectural Heritage of St. Louis. 1803–1891* (St. Louis: Washington University Gallery of Art, 1982), 35; Susan Hempstead Gratiot to Sarah Beebe, 24 November 1833, AGW.
114. Hempstead and Stahl, comps., *Stephen Hempstead and His Descendents*, 22.

Notes

115. Hunt, *Elihu Washburn,* 178; Lowic, *Architectural Heritage of St. Louis,* 37–38; Dolores A. Kilgo, *Likeness and Landscape: Thomas M. Easterly and the Art of the Daguerreotype* (St. Louis: Missouri Historical Society Press, 1994), 197–98.
116. Washburne, "Charles S. Hempstead," 20.
117. Carl H. Johnson, Jr., *The Heritage of Dubuque: An Architectural View* (Dubuque: First National Bank of Dubuque, 1975), 18–19.
118. William Plymat, Jr., *The Victorian Architecture of Iowa* (Des Moines: Elephant's Eye Inc., 1976), 12.
119. Johnson, *Heritage of Dubuque,* 19–20.
120. Diary of Solon Langworthy, 12 January 1861.
121. David Singal, "Towards a Definition of American Modernism," *American Quarterly* 39 (Spring 1987): 7–25; Bushman, *The Refinement of America,* 406–13, 319–35.
122. John R. Stilgoe, *Borderland: Origins of the American Suburb, 1820–1939* (New Haven: Yale University Press, 1988), 56–64.
123. *Northwest Gazette and Galena Advertiser,* 19 September 1843.
124. Diary of Solon Langworthy, 20 April 1859.
125. Diary of Richard Bonson, 25 July, 3 August 1860, Iowa State Historical Society, Iowa City, Iowa.
126. Johnson, *Heritage of Dubuque,* 18–21.
127. Lincoln Clark to Julia Clark, 17 June 1853, 23, 26, 27 May 1854, Lincoln Clark Papers, The Huntington Library, San Marino, California.
128. Diary of Solon Langworthy, 1 September 1858.
129. Johnson, *Heritage of Dubuque,* 18–19; Mathias Hamm House Museum, Dubuque, Iowa.
130. Mahoney, *River Towns in the Great West,* 257, 261; Timothy R. Mahoney, "Down in Davenport, The Social Response of Antebellum Elites to Regional Urbanization," *The Annals of Iowa* 50, no. 6 (Fall 1990): 604; "Pen Pictures of the Central Part of the City of Quincy as It Was When Douglas and Lincoln Met in Debate," *Journal of the Illinois State Historical Society* 18, no. 2 (July 1925): 396; Dorothy Garesche Holland, "The Planters House," *Bulletin of the Missouri Historical Society* 28, no. 2 (January 1972): 109–17; Lowic, *Architectural Heritage of St. Louis,* 52–53; Katherine C. Grier, *Culture and Comfort: Peoples, Parlors, and Upholstery, 1850–1930* (Amherst: University of Massachusetts Press, 1988), 19–58.
131. Hunt, *Elihu Washburn,* 171.
132. Elihu B. Washburne to Adele G. Washburne, 30 December 1845, EBW, HSW.
133. Susan Hempstead Gratiot to Eliza Gratiot, 28 June 1850, AGW; Beckwith, *The Creoles of St. Louis,* 81.
134. Pease and Randall, eds., *Diary of Orville H. Browning,* 1: 24, 105, 153, 234.
135. "Account book containing inventory of books, furniture, in house of William Glasgow Jr. . . . in St. Louis, 1861," William Carr Lane Collection, Missouri Historical Society, St. Louis.
136. Lincoln Clark to Julia Clark, 16 February 1857, Lincoln Clark Papers; St. Nicholas Hotel Register, no. 18, 18 June 1858, New-York Historical Society, New York, New York; Diary of Solon Langworthy, 8 December 1858, 10 February 1859.
137. Charles Lockwood, *Manhattan Moves Uptown: An Illustrated History* (Boston: Houghton Mifflin Co., 1976), 151–59; "St. Nicholas Hotel, Broadway, New York," colored lithograph, J. H. Bufford's Sons Lithographers, Boston, 1875; Grier, *Culture and Comfort,* 29–36.

Notes

138. Matthias Hamm House Museum, Dubuque, Iowa.
139. Diary of Solon Langworthy, 15 April 1860.
140. Steven M. Stowe, *Intimacy and Power in the Old South* (Baltimore: Johns Hopkins University Press, 1987), 22–23.
141. Grier, *Culture and Comfort*, 38–43, 69; John F. Kasson, *Rudeness and Civility, Manners in Nineteenth-Century Urban America* (New York: Hill and Wang, 1990), 173–81.
142. Cynthia A. Kierner, *Traders and Gentlefolk: The Livingstons of New York. 1675–1790* (Ithaca: Cornell University Press, 1992), 243–51; Tamara Platkins Thornton, *Cultivating Gentlemen: The Meaning of Country Life Among the Boston Elite, 1785–1860* (New Haven: Yale University Press, 1989), 1–20.
143. David Davis to son, 25 January 1863, David Davis Papers, Illinois State Historical Library.
144. Bushman, *The Refinement of America*, 289–98; E. Anthony Rotundo, *American Manhood: Transformations in Masculinity from the Revolution to the Modern Era* (New York: Basic Books, 1993), 76–82.
145. Stock Subscription List, Galena and Chicago Union Railroad, 10 August 1847, Charles S. Hempstead Papers, Chicago Historical Society.
146. Elihu B. Washburne to A. S. Washburn, 4 May 1840; Elihu B. Washburne to Adele G. Washburne, 1 April 1861, EBW.
147. Elihu B. Washburne to A. S. Washburn, 20 May, 27 October 1840, EBW.
148. Susan Hempstead Gratiot to Sarah Beebe, 13 October 1839; Susan Hempstead Gratiot to Eliza Gratiot, 26 February 1850, AGW
149. Elihu B. Washburne to Gratiot Washburne, 9 October 1859; Elihu B. Washburne to Adele G. Washburne, 27 July 1860, 1 April 1861, EBW; Horatio Newhall to Elihu B. Washburne, 13 May 1862, EBW, LOC; Adele G. Washburne to Elihu B. Washburne, 18 January 1846, AGW; Elihu B. Washburne to A. S. Washburn, 20 May 1840, EBW.
150. John Lorraine to Elihu B. Washburne, 8 February 1861, EBW, LOC.
151. George W. Campbell to Elihu B. Washburne, 17 February 1865; Joseph R. Jones to Elihu B. Washburne, 3 April 1862, EBW, LOC.
152. B. H. Campbell to Elihu B. Washburne, 29 February 1856; Charles S. Hempstead to Elihu B. Washburne, 16 August 1855, EBW, LOC.
153. Orrin Smith to Elihu B. Washburne, 30 May 1862, EBW, LOC.
154. A. L. Holmes to Elihu B. Washburne, 5 February 1849, EBW, LOC.
155. S. W. McMaster to Elihu B. Washburne, 28 August 1856, EBW, LOC.
156. Elihu B. Washburne to C. C. Washburn, 14 April 52, EBW; Nathan Corwith to Elihu B. Washburne, 8 January 1855; Charles S. Hempstead to Elihu B. Washburne, 16 August 1855, EBW, LOC.
157. Stock Subscription List, Galena and Chicago Union Railroad, 10 August 1847.
158. Elihu B. Washburne to Adele G. Washburne, 29 May 1860, EBW.
159. Cyrus Aldrich to Elihu B. Washburne, 29 January 1849, EBW, LOC.
160. Joseph R. Jones to Elihu B. Washburne, 26 February, 3, 7, 15 April 1862; Nathan Corwith to Elihu B. Washburne, 20 March 1862, EBW, LOC.
161. Joseph R. Jones to Elihu B. Washburne, 13 April 1862, EBW, LOC.
162. Elihu B. Washburne to A. S. Washburn, 16 November 1840, EBW.
163. Elihu B. Washburne to A. S. Washburn, 23 December 1840, EBW.
164. *Galena Directory*, 1847; Susan Hempstead Gratiot to Mary Lisa, 23 December 1844; Adele G. Washburne to Elihu B. Washburne, 12 January 1848, AGW.
165. Thomas Foster to Mary Campbell, 27 September 1844, William Hempstead Collec-

Notes

tion, Illinois State Historical Library; Susan Hempstead Gratiot to Adele Gratiot, 15 May 1843, AGW.

166. Edward H. Beebe to Elihu B. Washburne, 18 July 1862, EBW, LOC; Joseph Russell Jones to L. S. Jones, 7 April 1842, Joseph Russell Jones Collection, Chicago Historical Society.
167. *Galena Directory* 1847.
168. Adele Gratiot to Sarah Beebe, 7 September 1844, AGW.
169. Thomas Foster to Mary Campbell, 27 September, 10 October, 11 November 1844, William Hempstead Collection.
170. Thomas Foster to Mary Campbell, 13 January 1845, William Hempstead Collection; *History of Jo Daviess County*, 619; Susan Hempstead Gratiot to Sarah Beebe, 15 May 1843, AGW; Bartel, ed., *The Parish Register of Grace Church of Galena, Illinois*, vol. 2.
171. Diary of Mrs. Madison Y. Johnson, 1857–1859, Madison Y. Johnson Papers, Chicago Historical Society; *Constitution, By Laws, Records, and Proceedings of the Galena Lodge* (1845).
172. James E. Wright, *History of the First Presbyterian Church (Galena)* (Galena, Illinois: n.p., 1930); Thomas Foster to Mary Campbell, 27 September 1844, 13 January 1845, William Hempstead Collection; Susan Hempstead Gratiot to Eliza Gratiot, 26 June 1849, AGW.
173. Jo Daviess County Tax List, 1845, Jo Daviess County Courthouse, Galena, Illinois; City of Galena Tax List, 1852, Galena Public Library, Galena, Illinois.
174. Susan Hempstead Gratiot to "dear children," 17 November 1853, AGW; Johnson, *The Building of Galena*, 97, 99; Thomas Foster to Mary Campbell. 27 September 1844, William Hempstead Collection.
175. John L. Brooke, *The Heart of the Commonwealth: Society and Political Culture in Worcester County, Massachusetts, 1713–1861* (New York: Cambridge University Press, 1989), 66.
176. Elihu B. Washburne to Gratiot Washburne, 12 September 1859, mentions "Uncle Edward, Charly," EBW.
177. Adele G. Washburne to Elihu B. Washburne, 7 December 1847, AGW; Adele G. Washburne to Cadwallader Washburn, 7 January 1847, 21 September 1845, 18 April 1846, EBW, HSW.
178. Susan Hempstead Gratiot to Sarah Beebe, 13 October 1839; Susan Hempstead Gratiot to Adele Gratiot, 15 May 1843; Susan Hempstead Gratiot to Mary Lisa, 12 June 1848, AGW.
179. Susan Hempstead Gratiot to Eliza Gratiot, 26 March 1850; Susan Hempstead Gratiot to Adele Gratiot, 15 May 1843; Susan Hempstead Gratiot to daughter, 28 June 1850, AGW; *Biography of Thomas McKnight* (Dubuque: Ballou and Winall, 1866), 6.
180. Susan Hempstead Gratiot to Eliza Gratiot, 26 June 1849, AGW.
181. Susan Hempstead Gratiot to Mary Lisa, 12 June 1848, AGW.
182. Susan Hempstead Gratiot to Sarah Beebe, 13 October 1839, Susan Hempstead Gratiot to Adele Gratiot, 15 May 1843, AGW.
183. Susan Hempstead Gratiot to Eliza Gratiot, 26 February 1850; Susan Hempstead Gratiot to daughter, 28 June 1850, AGW.
184. Susan Hempstead Gratiot to "dear children," 17 November 1853; Susan Hempstead Gratiot to Adele G. Washburne, 5 January 1854, AGW.
185. Susan Hempstead Gratiot to Eliza Gratiot, 26 February 1850; Susan Hempstead Gratiot to children, 26 March 1850; Adele Gratiot to Sarah Beebe, 7 September 1844, AGW.

Notes

186. Susan Hempstead Gratiot to Adele Gratiot, 5 January 1854; Susan Hempstead Gratiot to Elihu B. Washburne, 15 January 1854, AGW.
187. E. A. Small to Elihu B. Washburne, 22 February 1859, EBW, LOC.
188. Johnson, *The Building of Galena,* 27, 97; Susan Hempstead Gratiot to "My dear children," 17 November 1853, AGW.
189. Susan Hempstead Gratiot to Sarah Beebe, 16 February 1827, AGW; Horatio Newhall to Isaac Newhall, 1 March 1828, HN.
190. Hempstead and Stahl, comps., *Stephen Hempstead and His Descendents,* 61.
191. Eliza Hempstead Cook, "Charles Wilt Hempstead," Hempstead Family Papers.
192. Horatio Newhall to Isaac Newhall, 11 December 1840, HN; Elihu B. Washburne to A. S. Washburn, 23 December 1840, 16 January 1841, EBW.
193. Joseph R. Jones to L. S. Jones, 7 April 1842, Joseph Russell Jones Collection.
194. Edward Hempstead to Thomas Edward Beebe, 19 March 1843, Stephen Hempstead Collection, Missouri Historical Society.
195. Thomas Foster to Mary Campbell, 27 December, 27 September 1844, William Hempstead Collection; Elihu B. Washburne to Cadwallader Washburn, 14, 21 December 1844, EBW, HSW; A. L. Norris to Elihu B. Washburne, 27 December 1845, EBW, LOC; Adele G. Washburne to Elihu B. Washburne, 18 January 1846, AGW; Adele Gratiot Washburne to Cadwallader Washburn, 7 January 1847, EBW, HSW.
196. B. F. Felt Diary, Galena Public Library, Historical Collections.
197. Susan Hempstead Gratiot to Elihu B. Washburne, 15 January 1854, AGW.
198. Susan Hempstead Gratiot to Adele G. Washburne, 5 January 1854, AGW.
199. Elihu B. Washburne to Adele G. Washburne, 27 July 1860; Adele G. Washburne to Elihu B. Washburne, 23 June 1862, EBW.
200. Baxter, *Orville H. Browning,* 74–79.
201. Pease and Randall, eds., *The Diary of Orville H. Browning,* vol. 1.
202. Ibid.
203. Ibid.; Grier, *Culture and Comfort,* 69.
204. Mrs. John Sherwood, *Manners and Social Usages* (New York: Harper and Brothers, 1884), 55.
205. Karen Halttunen, *Confidence Men and Painted Women: A Study of Middle-Class Culture in America, 1830–1870* (New Haven: Yale University Press, 1982), 113.
206. Pease and Randall, eds., *Diary of Orville H. Browning,* vol. 1.
207. A. Johnston to Henry Asbury, 22 November 1860, Henry S. Asbury Collection.
208. Pease and Randall, eds., *Diary of Orville H. Browning,* vol. 1.
209. Ibid.
210. Ibid.
211. Lucretia Robinson to Sarah Davis, 7 July 1851, David Davis Papers, Illinois State Historical Library.
212. Pease and Randall, eds., *Diary of Orville H. Browning,* 1: 37.
213. Ibid., 54.
214. Ibid.
215. Ibid.
216. Ibid.
217. Ibid., 143–44.
218. *History of Adams County,* 415; Pease and Randall, eds., *Diary of Orville H. Browning,* 1: 321, 324, 325, 334–36, 340–41.

Notes

219. Pease and Randall, eds., *Diary of Orville H. Browning*, 1: 321; Jackson Grimshaw to Ozias M. Hatch, 5 April 1858, Ozias M. Hatch Papers, Illinois State Historical Library.
220. Jackson Grimshaw to Ozias M. Hatch, 29 May 1858, Ozias Hatch Papers.
221. Pease and Randall, eds., *Diary of Orville H. Browning*, 1: 324; Richard Wade, *The Urban Frontier* (Chicago: University of Chicago Press, 1959), 206–7; Dana O. Jensen, ed., "I at Home . . . 1829–1931," *Bulletin of the Missouri Historical Society* 22 (July 1966): 411.
222. "Laban Fleak," CFD.
223. William Worth Belknap to Clara B. Wolcott, 2 October 1852, William Worth Belknap Papers, Princeton University Libraries, Princeton, New Jersey.
224. Pease and Randall, eds., *Diary of Orville H. Browning*, 1: 324.
225. Jackson Grimshaw to Ozias Hatch, 29 May 1858, Ozias Hatch Papers.
226. Pease and Randall, eds., *Diary of Orville H. Browning*, 1: 334–36, 340–41.
227. Ibid., 345.
228. Jackson Grimshaw to Ozias M. Hatch, 17 December 1858, Ozias Hatch Papers.
229. Pease and Randall, eds., *Diary of Orville H. Browning*, 1: 345.
230. Ibid., 345; Jackson Grimshaw to Ozias M. Hatch, 17 December 1858, Ozias Hatch Papers.
231. Pease and Randall, eds., *Diary of Orville H. Browning*, 1: 133.
232. Ibid., 310, 345, 330.
233. A. J. Williams to Ozias M. Hatch, 18 January 1859, Ozias Hatch Papers.
234. Mary P. Ryan, *Women in Public: Between Banners and Ballots, 1825–1880* (Baltimore: Johns Hopkins University Press, 1990), 29–30; Sherwood, *Manners and Social Usages*, 50–54, 160–68; Grier, *Culture and Comfort,* 69.
235. Elizabeth Blackmar, *Manhattan for Rent, 1785–1850* (Ithaca: Cornell University Press, 1989), 139–40.
236. Eugenie Berthold, *Glimpses of Creole Life in Old St. Louis* (St. Louis: Missouri Historical Society, 1933), 11.
237. Dana O. Jensen, ed., "I At Home . . . 1827–1828," *Bulletin of the Missouri Historical Society* 22, no. 2 (January 1966): 180, 196.
238. Edward Bates, Diary, 1 January 1847, 1 January 1848, Edward Bates Collection, Missouri Historical Society, St. Louis, Missouri.
239. Susan Hempstead Gratiot to Mary Lisa, 1 December 1846, AGW; Adele G. Washburne to Cadwallader Washburn, 7 January 1847, EBW, HSW; Cunningham and Blythe, *The Founding Family of St. Louis*, 311.
240. George W. Berrian to William Berrian, 3 January 1849, Daniel Weed Collection.
241. *Galena Gazette and Advertiser,* 5 January 1851.
242. Pease and Randall, eds., *Diary of Orville H. Browning*, 1: 89, 166, 220, 311, 346.
243. Obituary for Mrs. George Sargent, *Davenport Democrat*, 15 March 1896.
244. The Diary of Solon Langworthy, 1 January 1861; U.S. Census, Manuscript, Dubuque County, Iowa, 1860.
245. A. Williams to Ozias M. Hatch, 18 January 1859, Ozias Hatch Papers.
246. George W. Kilbourne to David W. Kilbourne, 3 January 1860, George W. Kilbourne Papers, Des Moines, State Historical Society of Iowa; Diary of Charles Mason, 1 January 1859, Charles Mason Papers, Iowa State Historical Library, Des Moines.
247. The Diary of Richard Bonson, 1 January 1859, Iowa State Historical Society, Iowa City, Iowa.

Notes

248. Susan Hempstead Gratiot to Adele Gratiot Washburne, 5 January 1854, AGW; Elihu B. Washburne to Adele Gratiot Washburne, 1 January 1856, EBW.
249. Diary of Charles Mason, 1 January 1856, Charles Mason Papers.
250. Howard K. Beale, ed., *The Diary of Edward Bates. 1859–1866* (1933; rpt., New York: Da Capo Press, 1971), 221; Sherwood, *Manners and Social Usages,* 167–68.
251. C. M. Wilkinson to Mrs. John F. Darby, 15 August 1851, John F. Darby Collection, Missouri Historical Society, St. Louis, Missouri; "R. B. Ogden," CFD.
252. Theodore Rodolf, "Pioneering in the Wisconsin Lead Region," *Collections of the State Historical Society of Wisconsin,* vol. 15 (Madison: State Historical Society of Wisconsin, 1900), 338, 357, 374.
253. Elihu B. Washburne to A. S. Washburn, 15 March 1840, EBW.
254. "R. B. Ogden," CFD.
255. Logan U. Reavis, *St. Louis, Future Great City of the World* (St. Louis: Published by Order of the St. Louis County Court, 1870), 723.
256. Hon. Samuel Shaw to Dear Sir, 29 November 1839, Washburn Papers.
257. Reavis, *St. Louis, Future Great City of the World,* 490.
258. Beale, ed. *The Diary of Edward Bates,* 93.
259. Robert W. Johannsen, ed., *The Letters of Stephen A. Douglas* (Urbana: University of Illinois Press, 1961), 60–61; Marvin R. Cain, *Lincoln's Attorney General, Edward Bates of Missouri* (Columbia: University of Missouri, 1965), 59.
260. W. Lemmels to David W. Kilbourne, 21 April 1853, George W. Kilbourne Collection, Iowa State Historical Society, Des Moines.
261. Elihu B Washburne to A. S. Washburn, 16 November 1840, EBW.
262. Henry Austin Diary, 28 December 1837; CFD.
263. Elihu B. Washburne to A. S. Washburn, 30 November 1841, ASW.
264. Richard Wightman Fox, "Intimacy on Trial, Cultural Meanings of the Beecher-Tilton Affair," in Richard Wightman Fox and T. J. Jackson Lears, eds., *The Power of Culture: Critical Essays in American History* (Chicago: University of Chicago Press, 1993), 104–05.
265. A. L. Norris to Elihu B. Washburne, 16 December 1845, EBW, LOC; Elihu B. Washburne to Cadwallader Washburn, 30 December 1845, 4 October 1846, EBW, HSW; Susan Hempstead Gratiot to Mary Lisa, 1 December 1846, AGW; Elihu B. Washburne to Adele G. Washburne, 8 December 1846, EBW.
266. Elihu B. Washburne to Cadwallader Washburn, 15 December 1847, 27 July 1848, EBW, HSW; Elihu B. Washburne to C. C. Washburn, 30 January 1848; Elihu B. Washburne to "Charles," 2 August 1848; Elihu B. Washburne to C. C. Washburn, 12 December 1848, EBW; C. C. Washburn to Elihu B. Washburne, 1 February 1849, EBW, LOC; Elihu B. Washburne to Cadwallader Washburn, 26 November, 9, 29 December 1848, 14 March 1849, EBW, HSW; Adele G. Washburne to Eliza Gratiot, 27 June 1849, AGW; Francis Ladd to Elihu B. Washburne, 23 September 1849, EBW, LOC; Earl Schenck Miers, ed., *Lincoln, Day-by-Day: A Chronology, 1809–1865,* vol. II: *1849–1860* (Washington: Lincoln Sesquicentennial Commission, 1960), 9; Benjamin P. Thomas, ed., *Lincoln, 1847–1853, Being the Day-by-Day Activities of Abraham Lincoln* (Springfield, Illinois: The Abraham Lincoln Association, 1936), 115; Allen Thorndike Rice, ed., *Reminiscences of Abraham Lincoln by Distinguished Men of His Time* (New York: North American Publishing Co., 1886), 19–20.
267. Elihu B. Washburne to Adele G. Washburne, 10 December 1853, 27 April 1854; Elihu

Notes

B. Washburne to Father, 18 February 1855, EBW; Elihu B. Washburne to Cadwallader Washburn, 16 December 1851, 23 June, 14 July 1852, EBW, HSW.
268. Adele G. Washburne to Elihu B. Washburne, 7 December 1847, 12 January 1848, AGW; Adele G. Washburne to Cadwallader Washburn, n.d., 1847, EBW, HSW.
269. Elihu B. Washburne to Cadwallader Washburn, 30 December 1845, EBW, HSW.
270. A. L. Norris to Elihu B. Washburne, 16 December 1845, EBW, LOC; James E. Wright, *Centennial Celebration of the First Presbyterian Church* (Galena: n.p., 1931); Wright, *History of the First Presbyterian Church*.
271. Charles S. Hempstead to Elihu B. Washburne, 26 December 1845; A. L. Norris to Elihu B. Washburne, 27 December 1845, EBW, LOC.
272. Baker, *Mary Todd Lincoln*, 109; Susan Hempstead Gratiot to Sarah Beebe, 18 April 1846, AGW; Elihu B. Washburne to Cadwallader Washburn, 9 April 1846, EBW, HSW; Adele G. Washburne to "My dear lady," 15 January 1846, AGW.
273. Elihu B. Washburne to Cadwallader Washburn, 9 April 1846, EBW, HSW; Susan Hempstead Gratiot to Sarah Beebe, 18 April 1846, AGW.
274. Adele G. Washburne to Cadwallader Washburn, 18 April 1846; Adele G. Washburne to Cadwallader Washburn, 7 January 1847, EBW, HSW; Susan Hempstead Gratiot to Mary Lisa, 1 December 1846, AGW.
275. Elihu B. Washburne to Susan Hempstead Gratiot, 1 January 1844; Elihu B. Washburne to C. C. Washburn, 21 July 1845, EBW; Susan Hempstead Gratiot to Mary Lisa, 23 December 1844; Susan Hempstead Gratiot to "My Dear Sister" 18 April 1846; Susan Hempstead Gratiot to Eliza Gratiot, 28 July 1850; Susan Hempstead Gratiot to Mary Lisa, 1 December 1846, AGW.
276. Susan Hempstead Gratiot to Mary Lisa, 1 December 1846; Adele G. Washburne to Elihu B. Washburne, 12 January 1848; Susan Hempstead Gratiot to Mary Lisa, 12 June 1848; Susan Hempstead Gratiot to Eliza Gratiot, 26 June 1849, AGW.
277. Susan Hempstead Gratiot to Eliza Gratiot, 28 July 1850, AGW.
278. Elihu B. Washburne to Adele G. Washburne, 27 April 1854; Susan Hemsptead Gratiot to Eliza Gratiot, 18 February 1854; Susan Hempstead Gratiot to "Sister," April 1854, AGW; Cunningham and Blythe, *The Founding Family of St. Louis*, 321.
279. Hunt, *Elihu Washburn*, 179; Rose, *Victorian America and the Civil War*, 126–27, 245–55.
280. Hempstead and Stahl, comps., *Stephen Hempstead and His Descendents*, 58–61.
281. *The Sons of Maine, Proceedings at the Banquet of the Sons of Maine in Illinois Held at Palmer House. Chicago. June 16 1881* (Chicago: n.p., 1881).
282. Elihu B. Washburne to C. C. Washburn, 23, 30 December 1842, EBW.
283. Elihu B. Washburne to "Charles," 2 August 1848, EBW; Susan Hempstead Gratiot to Eliza Gratiot, 28 July 1850, AGW; Elihu B. Washburne to Adele G. Washburne, 10 December 1853; Elihu B. Washburne to Adele G. Washburne, 4 February 1855, EBW; Elihu B. Washburne to Cadwallader Washburn, 16 December 1851, EBW, HSW; Edith Wilson Gammon, ed., "Transcripts of Washburn Journal, Volume I, September 24 1866—May 15 1868," Washburn-Norlands Humanities Center, Livermore, Maine.
284. William Hempstead (nephew of Susan) to Lyman Draper, 8 July 1868, Lyman Draper Collection, State Historical Society of Wisconsin; Hempstead and Stahl, comps., *Stephen Hempstead and His Descendents*, 44–45, 42–43; Florence Gratiot Bale, "A Packet of Old Letters," *Wisconsin Magazine of History* 11 (1927–28): 168; Rev. H. J. Coe, *A Sermon Occasioned by the Death of Mrs. Susan Gratiot* (Washington, D.C.: Buell and Blanchard Printers, 1854), AGW.
285. Elihu B. Washburne to Adele G. Washburne, 6 July 1854, EBW.

Notes

286. Hempstead and Stahl, comps., *Stephen Hempstead and His Descendents*, 60.
287. Cunningham and Blythe, *The Founding Family of St. Louis*, 311; Hempstead Family Genealogy, Stephen Hempstead Collection.
288. Elihu B. Washburne to Adele G. Washburne, 31 December 1854, EBW.
289. Elihu B. Washburne to Adele G. Washburne 17 December 1854, 4 February 1855, EBW.
290. Elihu B. Washburne to Adele G. Washburne, 16 May 1855, EBW; Nelson, "The Early Life and Congressional Career of Elihu B. Washburne," 123–25; Hunt, *Elihu Washburn*, 183; Elihu B. Washburne, "The Paris Exposition, Speech in Response to Request Appropriations for 1867 Paris Exposition, March 14 1866" (Washington, D.C., 1866); Elihu B. Washburne to Charles Henry Ray, 13 May [1855], Charles Henry Ray Papers.
291. Elihu B. Washburne to Adele G. Washburne, 27 May, 6, 25, 29 June 1855, EBW.
292. Elihu B. Washburne to Adele G. Washburne, 6 June 1855, 6 January 1856, 31 December 1854, 2 December 1855, EBW.
293. Diary of Solon Langworthy, 1 April 1860.
294. Ibid., 12 October 1858, 9 September, 21 January, 12 February, 18 March, 29 January, 21 January, 5 February 1860.
295. Ibid., 14 July 1860, 11 May 1859.
296. Singal, "Towards a Definition of American Modernism," 8–10.
297. Diary of Solon Langworthy, 23 January 1859, 10 October 1858.
298. Ibid., 3 October 1858, 11 May, 22 June, 21 July, 29 May, 26 April, 21 May 1859; 14, 29 July 1860.
299. Ibid., 9 June, 3, 9 September, 18 August 1860, 26 April 1859.
300. Ibid., 7, 14 July 1860.
301. Ibid., 29 July, 19, 28, 18 August 1860; Diary of Richard Bonson, 11 July–1 August 1860.
302. Diary of Solon Langworthy, 12 February 1860; Diary of Charles Mason, 15 July 1855, Charles Mason Papers.
303. Diary of Solon Langworthy, 14 July, 22 February, 18 August 1860; 29 October 1859, 12 January 1861.
304. Ibid., 16 September, 18 February, 1 January 1860; 23 January 1859; Langworthy, comp., *The Langworthy Family*, 262, 268–69, 271–72.
305. Ibid., 262, 269, 272.
306. Diary of Solon Langworthy, 4 December 1858; "Autobiographical Sketch of Solon M. Langworthy," *Iowa Journal of History and Politics* 8, no. 3 (July 1910): 335–36.
307. Diary of Solon Langworthy, 4 December 1858; "Obituary of Mrs. Orrin Smith," 14 June 1881, Langworthy Family Scrapbook, Solon M. Langworthy Collection, Iowa State Historical Society.
308. Diary of Solon Langworthy, 22 February 1860.
309. "Obituary of Valeria Langworthy," *Davenport Democrat*, 8 May 1899, "Obituary of Pauline Langworthy," *Davenport Democrat*, 1892, Langworthy Scrapbook, Iowa State Historical Society.
310. Diary of Solon Langworthy, 20 April, 29 October 1859, 1 July, 16 September 1860.
311. Ibid., 12 January 1861.

Chapter 5. Regional professional culture

1. Robert H. Wiebe, *The Opening of American Society* (New York: Alfred A. Knopf, 1984), 287–90.

Notes

2. Ibid., 287–90, 299; William Francis English, "The Pioneer Lawyer and Jurist in Missouri," *The University of Missouri Studies* 21, no. 2 (1947): 21–34.
3. Elihu B. Washburne to Algernon S. Washburn, 17 May 1840, Algernon S. Washburn Papers, Minnesota Historical Society (hereafter cited as ASW).
4. Russell K. Nelson, "The Early Life and Congressional Career of Elihu B. Washburne" (Ph.D. dissertation, University of North Dakota, 1953), 14.
5. William Worth Belknap to Clara B. Wolcott, n.d., 1850, William Worth Belknap Collection, Princeton University Libraries (hereafter cited as WWB).
6. J. Y. Scammon to Mother and Father, 18 October 1835, J. Y. Scammon Papers, Chicago Historical Society.
7. Henry Hitchcock to Uncle, 11 November 1850, Hitchcock Collection, Missouri Historical Society, St. Louis, Missouri.
8. "Early Quincy, 1822–1830," in *Transactions of the Illinois State Historical Society for the Year 1915* (Springfield: Illinois State Historical Society, 1916), 154; *The History of Adams County Illinois Containing a History of the County, Its Cities, Towns, etc.* (Chicago, 1879), 416.
9. Edward H. Stiles, *Recollections and Sketches of Notable Lawyers and Public Men of Early Iowa* (Des Moines: Homestead Publishing Company, 1916), 95.
10. Ibid., 124.
11. Elihu B. Washburne to A. S. Washburn, 4 April 1840, Elihu B. Washburne Papers, Washburn-Norlands Humanities Center, Livermore, Maine (hereafter cited as EBW).
12. Elihu B. Washburne to A. S. Washburn, 20 May 1840, EBW.
13. R. H. McClellan, "The Early Bar of Galena," *Proceedings of the Illinois State Bar Association* (Springfield: Illinois State Register Book Publishing House, 1895), 222.
14. Augustus L. Chetlain, *Recollections of Seventy Years* (Galena: The Gazette Publishing Company, 1899), 26; McClellan, "The Early Bar of Galena," 222.
15. Stiles, *Recollections and Sketches*, 92–96, 47; 83–86.
16. Ibid., 56–57; Elihu B. Washburne, *Historical Sketch of Charles Hempstead* (Galena: Gazette Book and Job Printing House, 1875).
17. John Clayton, comp., *The Illinois Fact Book and Historical Almanac. 1673–1968* (Carbondale: Southern Illinois University Press, 1970), 100, 102; McClellan, "The Early Bar of Galena," 221; *History of Adams*, 412.
18. Stiles, *Recollections and Sketches*, 24.
19. Frederic B. Crossley, *Courts and Lawyers of Illinois* (Chicago: The American Historical Society, 1916), 202.
20. *Letter of Charles Mason to Gen. A. C. Dodge in Regard to the Halfbreed Question* (Burlington: Charles I. Baker, 1880), 8, 10; Charles Mason Papers, Iowa State Historical Library, Des Moines, Iowa (hereafter cited as CMP).
21. "David W. Kilbourne," Caleb Forbes Davis Collection, Keokuk Savings Bank and Trust Co., Keokuk, Iowa; "Diary of Henry Austin," ibid.; Theodore Calvin Pease and James G. Randall, eds. *The Diary of Orville Hickman Browning*, vol. 1, *1850–1864*, Collections of the Illinois State Historical Library, vol. 20 (Springfield: Illinois State Historical Library, 1925), 100; Chetlain, *Recollections of Seventy Years*, 39; Gaillard Hunt, *Israel, Elihu, and Cadwallader Washburn: A Chapter in American Biography* (1925; rpt., New York: Da Capo Press, 1969), 315–16.
22. Diary of Charles Mason, 11 July to 8 August 1836, CMP.
23. Stiles, *Recollections and Sketches*, 24; William Salter, *The Life of James W. Grimes* (New York: D. Appleton and Company, 1876), 10.

Notes

24. Stiles, *Recollections and Sketches*, 123.
25. Ibid., 739; Crossley, *Courts and Lawyers of Illinois*, 202.
26. Stiles, *Recollections and Sketches*, 295; Pease and Randall, eds., *Diary of Orville H. Browning*, 1: 4.
27. David F. Wilox, ed., *Quincy and Adams County, Illinois: History and Representative Men*, vol. 1 (Chicago: Lewis Publishing Company, 1919), 158–59.
28. Ibid., 159.
29. Clayton, comp., *The Illinois Fact Book and Historical Almanac*, 109–10.
30. Elihu B. Washburne to Algernon S. Washburn, 2 May 1840, EBW.
31. Charles Gilman to Edward Warren, 6 June 1839, Edward Warren Collection, Chicago Historical Society, Chicago, Illinois; Hunt, *Elihu Washburn*, 306–7.
32. Junius Hall to John Hall, 3 June 1836, Junius Hall Papers, New York Public Library (hereafter cited as JH).
33. Elihu B. Washburne to A. S. Washburn, 4 April 1840, EBW; Hunt, *Elihu Washburn*, 171.
34. Hunt, *Elihu Washburn*, 172; Elihu B. Washburne to A. S. Washburn, 4 April 1840, EBW.
35. William Worth Belknap to Clara Wolcott, n.d., 1850, 6 February 1851, WWB.
36. Lincoln Clark to Julia Clark, 1, 16 June, 5 July 1843, 22, 24 June, 17 August 1846; Joanna Howe to Lincoln Clark, 26 September 1846, Lincoln Clark Papers, The Huntington Library, San Marino, California (hereafter cited as LC).
37. Lincoln Clark to Julia Clark, 5 March 1847.
38. Ibid., 28 March 1847.
39. Ibid., 4, 6 April 1847.
40. Ibid., 5 July 1847.
41. Stiles, *Recollections and Sketches*, 740.
42. Lincoln Clark to Julia Clark, 14 October 1847, LC.
43. Ibid., 18 October 1847.
44. *The History of Adams County*, 413.
45. *The Code of Iowa, Passed at the Session of the General Assembly of 1850–51* (1851; rpt., Des Moines: Emory H. English, 1912), 176–77; Wayne G. Temple, "Lincoln's First Step to Becoming a Lawyer," *Lincoln Herald* 70 (Winter 1968): 207. Also see Ann Fidler, "'Young Limbs of the Law': Law Students, Legal Education, and the Occupational Culture of Attorneys, 1820–1860" (Ph.D. dissertation, University of California at Berkeley, 1996), 66–67.
46. Usher F. Linder, *Reminiscences of the Early Bench and Bar of Illinois* (Chicago: The Chicago Legal News Company, 1879), 74–75; Salter, *The Life of James W. Grimes*, 12.
47. Theodore S. Parvin, *Historical Lectures upon Early Leaders in the Professions in the Territory of Iowa* (Iowa City: Iowa State Historical Society, 1894), 73; Stiles, *Recollections and Sketches*, 561, 826.
48. Crossley, *Courts and Lawyers of Illinois*, 202; Robert A. Sprecher, "Lincoln As a Bar Examiner," *Illinois Bar Journal* 42 (August 1954): 918; *Pioneer Law-makers Association of Iowa, Reunions of 1886 and 1890* (Des Moines: G. H. Ragsdale, 1890), 85; Elizabeth Gaspar Brown, "The Bar on a Frontier: Wayne County, 1796–1836," *The American Journal of Legal History* 14 (1970): 136–56, 136–39, 149–50; Temple, "Lincoln's First Step to Becoming a Lawyer," 207; Gustave Koerner, *The Memoirs of Gustave Koerner, 1809–1896*, vol. 1, Thomas J. McCormack, ed. (Cedar Rapids: The Torch Press, 1909), 371–75.
49. *Pioneer Law-makers Association of Iowa, Reunions of 1886 and 1890*, 85.
50. Horace White, *The Life of Lyman Trumbull* (Boston: Houghton Mifflin, 1913), 6.

Notes

51. Stiles, *Recollections and Sketches*, 819.
52. Ibid., 826; *Report of the First Annual Meeting of the Iowa State Bar Association* (Davenport: Egbert, Fidlar and Chambers, 1895), 37; Parvin, *Historical Lectures upon Early Leaders in the Professions*, 86.
53. Robert W. Johannsen, ed., *The Letters of Stephen A. Douglas* (Urbana: University of Illinois Press, 1961), 60–61.
54. Stiles, *Recollections and Sketches*, 191; *Pioneer Law-makers Association of Iowa, Reunions of 1886 and 1890*, 88.
55. Stiles, *Recollections and Sketches*, 135–36.
56. Gordon Morris Bakken, *Practicing Law in Frontier California* (Lincoln: University of Nebraska Press, 1991), 33–39; Gordon Morris Bakken, "Industrialization and the Nineteenth Century California Bar," in Gerard W. Gawalt, ed., *The New High Priests, Lawyers in Post-Civil War America* (Westport: Greenwood Press, 1984), 125–49; English, "The Pioneer Lawyer and Jurist in Missouri," 94–130; C. Robert Haywood, *Cowtown Lawyers: Dodge City and Its Attorneys, 1876–1886* (Norman: University of Oklahoma Press, 1988); Wayne K. Hobson, "Symbols of the New Profession: Emergence of the Large Law Firm, 1870–1915," in Gerard W. Gawalt, *The New High Priests*, 3–27; Wayne K. Hobson, *The American Legal Profession and the Organizational Society, 1890–1930* (New York: Garland Publishing Co., 1986), 155–208; Mark E. Steiner, "Lawyers and Legal Change in Antebellum America: Learning From Lincoln," *University of Detroit Mercy Law Review* 74, no. 3 (Spring 1997): 427–64, 459–64; Lincoln Clark to Julia Clark, 4 October 1848, LC.
57. Mark M. Krug, *Lyman Trumbull, Conservative Radical* (New York: A. S. Barnes and Company, 1965), 70–71; Morton S. McAtee to Lyman Trumbull, 20 April 1857, Lyman Trumbull Papers, Library of Congress.
58. *Quincy and Adams County, Illinois*, 159.
59. Salter, *The Life of James W. Grimes*, 33; *Pioneer Law-makers Association of Iowa. 1892* (Des Moines: G. H. Ragsdale, 1893), 139; Theodore S. Parvin, *William Williams Chapman* (Des Moines: Iowa Printing Co., c. 1893), 2.
60. John W. Rankin to Charles Mason, 22 September 1850, CMP; *Letter of Charles Mason to A. C. Dodge*, 18–19; Stiles, *Recollections and Sketches*, 28; William Worth Belknap to Anna Mary Belknap, 18 January 1852, WWB.
61. Junius Hall to John Hall, 16 September 1836, JH.
62. Salter, *The Life of James W. Grimes*, 12–13.
63. Stiles, *Recollections and Sketches*, 25; Maurice G. Baxter, *Orville H. Browning: Lincoln's Friend and Critic* (Bloomington: Indiana University Press, 1957), 9–10; *Quincy and Adams County, Illinois*, 159.
64. Junius Hall to John Hall, 16 September 1836, JH.
65. William Worth Belknap to Anna Mary Belknap, 18 January 1852, WWB.
66. Andrew Johnston to Henry Asbury, 22 November 1860; B. M. Prentiss to Henry Asbury, 13 March 1861, Henry Asbury Collection, Chicago Historical Society; *Quincy and Adams County, Illinois*, 165–66, 159; *History of Adams County*, 413, 415.
67. Stiles, *Recollections and Sketches*, 295.
68. John Dean Caton, *The Early Bench and Bar of Illinois* (Chicago: Chicago Legal News Company, 1898), 50–51; English, "The Pioneer Lawyer and Jurist in Missouri," 65–93.
69. *Laws of the State of Illinois* (Springfield: Wm. Walters, 1841), 101–11; *Laws of the State of Illinois* (Springfield: Walters and Weber, 1843), 128–37; *Laws of the State of Illinois* (Springfield: Lanphier and Walker, 1853); *Laws of the State of Illinois* (Springfield:

Notes

Charles H. Lanphier, 1849); Benjamin P. Thomas, "Lincoln and the Courts, 1854–1861," *Abraham Lincoln Association Papers* (Springfield: Abraham Lincoln Association, 1934), 49, 59–60, 63.

70. In Illinois, the state legislature reorganized the state judiciary in 1835, 1841, and 1848 and redistricted the judicial circuits in 1853 and 1857. The Territory of Iowa was divided into three judicial districts. When Iowa became a state the districts were redrawn. They were subsequently revised in 1848, 1853, 1855, and 1858. Up to 1835, the four supreme court judges of Illinois were assigned a circuit to ride in addition to their supreme court duties. In 1835 circuit judges were appointed to cover the circuit courts. In 1841 the legislature reversed itself and went back to the old system, with nine supreme court judges, each of whom were assigned to ride a particular circuit. In 1848 the state constitution was revised and Illinois instituted a system with three rotating elected judges in the supreme court and separate judges, elected to six-year terms, for each of eleven circuits. In both states, the circuit courts were assigned spring and fall sessions at each periodic revision of the court system to be held in a specific counties during specific weeks, thus formally establishing the sequence or "direction" of each circuit. See *Laws of Illinois; Laws of Iowa;* A. T. Andreas, *A. T. Andreas' Illustrated Historical Atlas of the State of Iowa* (Chicago: Andreas Atlas Company, 1875), 414, 416–17.
71. Mark E. Neely, Jr., *The Abraham Lincoln Encyclopedia* (New York: Da Capo Press, Inc., 1982), 96.
72. Stiles, *Recollections and Sketches*, 739.
73. Elihu B. Washburne to A. S. Washburn, 24 June 1840, EBW.
74. Ibid., 12 February 1841, EBW.
75. Cadwallader Washburn to Elihu B. Washburne, 7 August 1842, Cadwallader C. Washburn Papers, Washburn-Norlands Humanities Center, Livermore, Maine (hereafter cited as CW).
76. Junius Hall to John Hall, 20 April 1841, JH; Thomas, "Lincoln and the Courts, 1854–1861," 66; Lincoln Clark to Julia Clark, 19 February 1848, 18 July 1850, 21 May 1849, and 21 October 1850, LC.
77. *History of Adams County*, 415; "Letter of E. B. Washburne to John Dixon," *Journal of the Illinois State Historical Society* 6 (1913): 224–25, 228–29; Caton, *The Bench and Bar of Illinois*, 242; Stiles, *Recollections and Sketches*, 739.
78. Robert W. Johannsen, *Stephen A. Douglas* (New York: Oxford University Press, 1973), 97.
79. Ibid., 106.
80. Pease and Randall, eds., *The Diary of Orville H. Browning*, 1: 15–24, 114–19.
81. Ibid., 1: 123.
82. Ibid., 1: 40–48, 130–38, 144, 153–60; Timothy R. Mahoney, *River Towns in the Great West: The Structure of Provincial Urbanization in the American Midwest. 1820–1870* (New York: Cambridge University Press, 1990), 130–32.
83. "Letter of E. B. Washburne to John Dixon," 227; Elihu B. Washburne to Cadwallader Washburn, 2 October 1845, 4 October 1846, Elihu B. Washburne Papers, Wisconsin Historical Society; Benjamin R. Sheldon to David Davis, 24 January 1851, David Davis Collection, Chicago Historical Society; Ebenezer Peck, ed., *Reports of the Cases Determined in the Supreme Court of the State of Illinois*, vol. 12 (Chicago: Callaghan and Co., 1881); McClellan, "The Early Bar of Galena," 227–28.
84. Leon Herbert Swett, comp. and ed., *A Memorial of Leonard Swett: Lawyer and Advocate of Illinois* (Chicago, 1895), 18, 28; Harry E. Pratt, *Lincoln, 1840–1846: Being the Day-by-*

Notes

Day Activities of Abraham Lincoln (Springfield, Illinois: Abraham Lincoln Association, 1939); Richard Friend Lufkin, "Mr. Lincoln's Light from Under a Bushel – 1850," *Lincoln Herald* 52 (December 1950): 2–20, 7; Lufkin, "Mr. Lincoln's Light from Under a Bushel – 1851," *Lincoln Herald* 53 (Winter 1952): 2–25, 7.

85. Harry E. Pratt, *Lincoln, 1840–1846;* Mark E. Neeley, Jr., qualifies his description of Lincoln traveling the circuit by noting that "he could return to Springfield for weekends when the county seat was nearby." Neely, *The Abraham Lincoln Encyclopedia,* 96; David Davis to Sarah Davis, 31 August 1851, David Davis Collection; Benjamin P. Thomas, ed., *Lincoln, 1847–1853: Being the Day-by-Day Activities of Abraham Lincoln* (Springfield: The Abraham Lincoln Association, 1939).
86. Lincoln Clark to Julia Clark, 19 February, 15 April, 15 May, 4, 19 October, 1848, 17, 21 May, 12 September, 1 October 1849, 14, 18 July, 23 September, 21 October 1850, 12, 21, 22 September 1855, LC.
87. Koerner, *Memoirs of Gustave Koerner,* 1: 389–90, 394–95.
88. McClellan, "The Eary Bar of Galena," 221; "Letter of E. B. Washburne to John Dixon," 226–27.
89. *Quincy and Adams County, Illinois,* 158–59, 161; Henry S. Asbury Papers, Illinois State Historical Library.
90. *History of Adams County,* 413–16; Neely, *The Abraham Lincoln Encyclopedia,* 140.
91. Stiles, *Recollections and Sketches,* 29, 30, 31; *Report of the First Annual Meeting of the Iowa State Bar Association* (Davenport, Iowa: Egbert, Fidlar, and Chambers, 1895), 43–44, 46.
92. Stiles, *Recollections and Sketches,* 568.
93. Ibid., 571.
94. Thomas, "Lincoln and the Courts, 1854–1861," 68–77, details who the local lawyers were in the Eighth Circuit; Swett, comp., *A Memorial of Leonard Swett,* 20– 21.
95. Henry C. Whitney, *Life on the Circuit with Lincoln* (Boston: Estes and Lauriat, 1892), 73.
96. Swett, comp., *Memorial of Leonard Swett,* 19; Lufkin, "Mr. Lincoln's Light from Under a Bushel – 1850," 3–8; Lufkin, "Mr. Lincoln's Light from Under a Bushel – 1851," 4–6.
97. Caton, *The Bench and Bar of Illinois,* 53, 242; Stiles, *Recollections and Sketches,* 56; Lincoln Clark to Julia Clark, 12 September 1849, LC.
98. For lawyers who crossed over in the 1830s, see: "Letter of E. B. Washburne to John Dixon," 224–25, 228–29; Charles S. Hempstead to William Hempstead, 28 September 1835, William Hempstead Collection, Missouri Historical Society; John Reynolds, *My Own Times, Embracing Also the History of My Life* (Belleville, Illinois: B. H. Perryman and H. L. Davison, 1855), 282, 202, 222; Caton, *Bench and Bar of Illinois,* 242, 223, 225; Stiles, *Recollections and Sketches,* 264, 266–67, 24, 734, 56, 191, 24; *Pioneer Law-makers Association of Iowa, Reunions of 1886 and 1890,* 89, 85; Linder, *Reminiscences of the Early Bench and Bar of Illinois,* 215; Thomas C. Scharf, *History of St. Louis City and County* (Philadelphia: McDonough and Company, 1883), 1: 678; John W. Rankin to Charles Mason, 20 September 1850, CMP.
99. For lawyers who crossed over in the 1840s, see: Stiles, *Recollections and Sketches,* 342–43, 124; David W. Kilbourne to Hiram Barney, 10 July 1841, 19 March, 27, 30 April 1842, 25 March, 23 September, 3 October 1843, Hiram Barney Papers, The Huntington Library; "Judge [T.S.] Wilson's Address," *Pioneer Law-Makers Association of Iowa. Reunions of 1886 and 1890,* 85–86; Elihu B. Washburne, *Address of Hon. Elihu B. Washburne and Response of Governor Thomas Chrittenden on the Occasion of the Presentation of Portrait of Hon. Edward Hempstead to the State of Missouri* (Jefferson City: Tribune Publishing Co., 1881), 9; Junius Hall to John Hall, 20 April 1841, JH; Linder, *Reminiscences*

Notes

of the Early Bench and Bar of Illinois, 276, 142, 189, 103, 374, 248, 70, 163, 244, 192, 170, 183, 201; *Report of the First Annual Meeting of the Iowa Bar Association*, 43–44; Lincoln Clark to Julia Clark, 12 September 1849, LC; Pratt, *Lincoln, 1840–46*, 73, 126, 148, 199, 281, 356, 231; Thomas, "Lincoln and the Courts, 1854–1861," 74–75; Orville H. Browning to Isaac N. Arnold, 15 September 1880, Isaac N. Arnold Collection, Chicago Historical Society.

100. *Revised Statutes of the Territory of Iowa* (1843; rpt., Emory H. English, 1911), 99–102; *Laws of a Public or General Nature of the State of Missouri* (Jefferson City: W. Lusk & Son, 1842), 380–82.
101. See Appendix 4.
102. Caton, *Bench and Bar of Illinois*, 51.
103. W. H. Underwood to Joseph Gillespie, 15 January 1851, Joseph Gillespie Collection, Chicago Historical Society.
104. Caton, *Bench and Bar of Illinois*, 53.
105. J. Young Scammon, ed., *Reports of the Cases Argued in the Supreme Court of the State of Illinois*, vols. 1–4 (Chicago: Callaghan and Company, 1879, 1880, 1886); Charles Gilman, ed., *Reports of the Cases Argued and Determined in the Supreme Court of the State of Illinois*, vols. 5–10 (Chicago: E. B. Myers and Company, 1886); Ebenezer Peck, ed., *Reports of Cases Determined in the Supreme Court of the State of Illinois*, vols. 11 and 12 (Chicago: Callaghan and Company, 1881, 1886).
106. David Donald, *Lincoln's Herndon* (New York: Alfred A. Knopf, 1948), 44.
107. John J. Duff, *A. Lincoln, Prairie Lawyer* (New York: Bramhall House, 1960), 247–48.
108. Paul M. Angle, "Abraham Lincoln: Circuit Lawyer," *Lincoln Centennial Association Papers* (Springfield: Lincoln Centennial Association, 1928), 31–32.
109. Roy P. Basler, ed., *The Collected Works of Abraham Lincoln*, vols. 1 and 2 (New Brunswick: Rutgers University Press, 1953), 1: 270, 304, 370, 344, 394, 406; 2: 100–101, 100, 104, 117–18, 120, 331, 315, 191.
110. Clayton, comp., *Illinois Fact Book and Historical Almanac*, 98–106; Charles Manfred Thompson, *The Illinois Whigs Before 1846* (Champaign-Urbana: University of Illinois Graduate School, 1915), 132–50; among the thirty-six lawyers who visited the Illinois Supreme Court when it met once a year in December during the mid-1840s, eighteen (50 percent) held an elective or appointed office at some point in their careers. Three were appointed public officers, eight were elected to the Illinois state legislature, two to the Illinois state senate, six to the United States Congress, four to the United States Senate, two were appointed Foreign Ministers to European countries, and, of course, one was elected sixteenth President of the United States.
111. Neely, *The Abraham Lincoln Encyclopedia*, 32.
112. Caton, *Early Bench and Bar of Illinois*, 228. This group of forty-four lawyers, whose record of cases tried indicates that they all rode the circuit, closely correlates (including all but six lawyers who arrived later than 1845) with John D. Caton's memory, in 1893, of a "few of the other lawyers who traveled the circuit, more or less, forty years ago."
113. Parvin, *Historical Lectures upon Early Leaders in the Professions in the Territory of Iowa*, 89–91.
114. Allen Thorndike Rice, ed., *Reminiscences of Abraham Lincoln by Distinguished Men of His Time* (New York: North American Publishing Company, 1886), 13.
115. Augustus L. Chetlain, *Recollections of Seventy Years*, 31–32; McClellan, "The Early Bar of Galena," 224; Rice, ed., *Reminiscences of Abraham Lincoln*, 14; Elihu B. Washburne to Algernon S. Washburn, 20 May 1840, EBW.

Notes

116. Elihu B. Washburne to Cadwallader Washburn, 4 July 1847, EBW, HSW.
117. J. Young Scammon, ed., *Reports of the Cases Argued and Determined in the Supreme Court of the State of Illinois*, 4: v; James N. Adams, comp., "Index to the Springfield Journal" (typescript, Illinois State Historical Library, Springfield, 1944–46), 306.
118. Neeley, *The Abraham Lincoln Encyclopedia*, 15–16; for Edward D. Baker's California career, see Philip J. Ethington, *The Public City: The Political Construction of Urban Life in San Francisco, 1850–1900* (New York: Cambridge University Press, 1994), 178–83.
119. Linder, *Reminiscences of the Early Bench and Bar of Illinois*, 55–64, 55, 83, 361.
120. Robert H. Wiebe, "Lincoln's Fraternal Democracy," in John L. Thomas, ed., *Abraham Lincoln and the American Political Tradition* (Amherst: University of Massachusetts Press, 1986), 21–22.
121. Michael Grossberg, "Institutionalizing Masculinity: The Law as a Masculine Profession," in Mark C. Carnes and Clyde Griffen, eds., *Meanings for Manhood: Constructions of Masculinity in Victorian America* (Chicago: University of Chicago Press, 1990), 134; Fidler, "Young Limbs of the Law," 192, 29–36, 116–17; Steiner, "Lawyers and Legal Change in Antebellum America: Learning from Lincoln," 432–38.
122. Stephen Hempstead to William Hempstead, 5 September 1835, William Hempstead Papers, Missouri Historical Society, St. Louis, Missouri.
123. "Letter of Elihu B. Washburne to John Dixon," 223; Usher F. Linder, *Reminiscences of the Early Bench and Bar of Illinois*, 12.
124. Elihu B. Washburne to Algernon S. Washburn, 20 May, 27 October 1840, EBW.
125. Elihu B. Washburne to A. S. Washburn, 20 May 1840, EBW.
126. John M. Palmer, ed., *Bench and Bar of Illinois: Historical and Reminiscent* (Chicago: Lewis Publishing Co., 1890), 680.
127. *History of Adams County*, 416; Whitney, *Life on the Circuit with Lincoln*, 62.
128. Rice, ed., *Reminiscences of Abraham Lincoln*, 12–15; Elihu B. Washburne, "Abraham Lincoln in Illinois," *North American Review* 141 (1885): 311–12.
129. Rice, ed., *Reminiscences of Abraham Lincoln*, 15; Elihu B. Washburne, "Abraham Lincoln in Illinois," 312.
130. Koerner, *Memoirs of Gustave Koerner*, 1: 595.
131. Whitney, *Life on the Circuit with Lincoln*, 177–78.
132. Elihu B. Washburne to Adele G. Washburne, 8 December 1846, EBW.
133. Pease and Randall, eds., *Diary of Orville H. Browning*, 1: 30; Koerner, *Memoirs of Gustave Koerner*, 1: 509.
134. McClellan, "The Early Bar of Galena," 221.
135. Isaac N. Arnold, "Reminiscences of the Illinois Bar of Forty Years Ago," in Edward G. Mason, ed., *Early Illinois* (Chicago: Fergus Publishing Company, 1889–1890), 136.
136. Linder, *Reminiscences of the Early Bench and Bar of Illinois*, 87, 386, 378.
137. Palmer, ed., *Bench and Bar of Illinois*, 182.
138. Arnold, "Reminiscences of the Illinois Bar of Forty Years Ago," 133, 136.
139. Palmer, ed., *Bench and Bar of Illinois*, 556.
140. Rice, ed., *Reminiscences of Abraham Lincoln*, 12.
141. Elihu B. Washburne, *Memorial Address on the Life and Character of Hon. Isaac N. Arnold* (Chicago: Fergus Printing Company, 1884), 11.
142. Koerner, *Memoirs of Gustave Koerner*, 1: 509.
143. *History of Adams County*, 415, 417; Palmer, ed., *Bench and Bar of Illinois*, 680; Harry E. Pratt, "A Beginner on the Old Eighth Judicial Circuit," *Journal of the Illinois State His-*

Notes

torical Society 44, no. 2 (Summer 1951): 246; Whitney, *Life on the Circuit with Lincoln*, 61–68, 174–97.

144. See Donald, *Lincoln's Herndon*, 44–46; Isaac N. Arnold, *The Life of Abraham Lincoln* (Lincoln: University of Nebraska Press, 1994), 59; John P. Frank, *Lincoln as a Lawyer* (Urbana: University of Illinois Press, 1961), 20–23; Linder, *Reminiscences of the Early Bench and Bar of Illinois*, 111, 201–2; Neeley, *The Abraham Lincoln Encyclopedia*, 96.
145. Lincoln Clark to Julia Clark, 21 October 1850, 12 September, 21 May 1849, LC; Lincoln Clark disliked shared accommodations intensely.
146. "Letter of E. B. Washburne to John Dixon," 221–22; Rice, ed., *Reminiscences of Abraham Lincoln*, 12.
147. Arnold, "Reminiscences of the Illinois Bar of Forty Years Ago," 136.
148. White, *The Life of Lyman Trumbull*, 12.
149. Pease and Randall, eds., *Diary of Orville H. Browning*, 1: 30, 57–58, 86, 89, 121, 164, 223, 272, 313, 326, 348, 342; Angle, "Here I Have Lived," 87–90; Elihu B. Washburne to Adele G. Washburne, 8 December 1846, EBW.
150. *History of Adams County*, 416; Thomas, "Lincoln and the Courts, 1854–1861," 53–55; "Early Quincy, 1822–1830," 153, 157; William A. Richardson, Jr., "Pen Pictures of the Central Part of the City of Quincy as It Was When Lincoln and Douglas Met in Debate," *Journal of the Illinois State Historical Society* 18, no. 2 (July 1925): 397.
151. Carl H. Johnston, Jr., *The Building of Galena: An Architectural Legacy* (Stevens Point, Wisconsin: Worzalla Publishing Company, 1977), 55–56.
152. Thomas, "Lincoln and the County Courts," 53–54; Whitney, *Life on the Circuit with Lincoln*, 43, 48ff., 56ff.; Paul M. Angle, "Where Lincoln Practiced Law," in *Lincoln Centennial Association Papers* (Springfield: Lincoln Centennial Association, 1927), 20–21.
153. Virginia Wilcox Ivins, *Pen Pictures of Early Western Days* (n.p., 1905), 44.
154. Angle, "Where Lincoln Practiced Law," 20–21, 27–28, 33–42, 40.
155. Elihu B. Washburne to Algernon S. Washburn, 4 April 1840, EBW.
156. Nelson, "The Early Life and Congressional Career of Elihu B. Washburne," 32–33.
157. Henry Asbury, *Reminiscences of Quincy, Illinois* (Quincy, Illinois: D. Wilcox and Sons, 1882), 213; "Early Quincy, 1822–1830," 155.
158. Salter, *The Life of James W. Grimes*, 13–14.
159. Stiles, *Recollections and Sketches*, 246, 573.
160. Angle, "Where Lincoln Practiced Law," 27, 32, 41–42.
161. Nelson, "The Early Life and Congressional Career of Elihu B. Washburne," 33.
162. Donald, *Lincoln's Herndon*, 72.
163. *History of Adams County*, 416; Fidler, "Young Limbs of the Law," 219–26; Stiles, *Recollections and Sketches*, 191.
164. Stiles, *Recollections and Sketches*, 191; Swett, comp., *Memorial of Leonard Swett*, 22; *History of Adams County*, 417; Johannsen, *Stephen A. Douglas*, 65–67, 77–78; Linder, *Reminiscences of the Early Bench and Bar of Illinois*, 12, 14–17.
165. Caton, *Bench and Bar of Illinois*, 240.
166. *History of Adams County, Illinois*, 415.
167. Stiles, *Recollections and Sketches*, 342.
168. Caton, *Bench and Bar of Illinois*, 229–232.
169. Stiles, *Recollections and Sketches*, 191.
170. Caton, *Bench and Bar of Illinois*, 416.
171. Ibid., 242, 51, 223.

Notes

172. Ibid., 241–42.
173. Henry Asbury, "Reminiscence of His Life," 1883, Henry S. Asbury Collection; Henry Asbury, *Advice Concerning the Duties of Justices of the Peace or Constables* (Quincy: C. M. Wools, Newton Flagg, 1850); Henry Asbury, *Illinois Form Book; or, Advice Concerning the Duties of the Justice of the Peace and Constables with Forms Required to Be Used in Discharge of their Respective Duties* (St. Louis: Edwards and Bushnell, 1856).
174. *Report of the First Annual Meetings of the Iowa Bar Association*, 46.
175. Swett, comp., *Memorial of Leonard Swett*, 18.
176. *History of Adams County*, 417; Swett, comp., *Memorial of Leonard Swett*, 18–19.
177. Linder, *Reminiscences of the Early Bench and Bar of Illinois*, 157; Angle, *"Here I Have Lived,"* 106–8.
178. Stiles, *Recollections and Sketches*, 263.
179. Adams, comp., "Index to the Springfield Journal," 480.
180. Pratt, *Lincoln, 1840–46*, 156–58; Henry W. Starr, David Rorer, Johnathan C. Hall, James W. Woods, Lacon D. Stockton, James W. Grimes, F. D. Mill [all locals], and Cyrus Walker [of Illinois] to Charles Mason, 26 November 1846, CMP.
181. Adams, comp., *Index to the Springfield Journal*, 89, 169.
182. "Obituary," in Charles Gilman, ed., *Reports of the Cases Argued and Determined in the Supreme Court of the State of Illinois*, vol. 5 (Chicago: E. B. Meyers and Company, 1886).
183. *Chicago Daily Tribune*, 11 July 1854.
184. Basler, ed., *The Collected Works of Abraham Lincoln*, 2: 310.
185. Stiles, *Recollections and Sketches*, 255.
186. Ibid.
187. Frederick T. Hill, *Lincoln, the Lawyer* (New York: The Century Company, 1913), 176; Caton, *Bench and Bar of Illinois*, 51–52.
188. Stiles, *Recollections and Sketches*, 325.
189. Ibid., 255, 273.
190. Sprecher, "Lincoln as a Bar Examiner," 919–20.
191. Stiles, *Recollections and Sketches*, 17.
192. Ibid., 343.
193. Angle, *"Here I Have Lived,"* 87–88, 98–100.
194. Arnold, "Reminiscences of the Illinois Bar Forty Years Ago," 137–38.
195. Ibid., 137; Pease and Randall, eds., *Diary of Orville H. Browning*, 1: 352, 32, 29–32, 34–36, 85–93, 121–26, 165–71, 223–24, 272–75, 313–15, 348–55, 392–95.
196. Caton, *Bench and Bar of Illinois*, 52.
197. Swett, comp., *Memorial of Leonard Swett*, 18–19; *Report of the First Annual Meeting of the Iowa State Bar Association*, 46.
198. Caton, *Bench and Bar of Illinois*, 52–53, 222; Pratt, *Lincoln, 1840–46*, 264; Lamon, *Recollections of Abraham Lincoln, 1847–1865* (1911; rpt., Lincoln: University of Nebraska Press, 1994), 19. "Moot court" was initiated in the American colonies, drawn from English practice at the Inns of Court, at the College of William and Mary Law School in 1774. By the 1830s it had become a part of law school education. "Moot trials" also took place informally among lawyers in law offices, the local bar, and on the circuit. David Hoffman, *A Lecture Being the Third of a Series of Lectures* (Baltimore: J. D. Toy, 1826), 42–62; David Hoffman, *A Course of Legal Study* (Baltimore: Joseph Neal, 1836), 801–25; Milton M. Klein, "The Rise of the New York Bar: The Legal Career of William Livingston," in David H. Flaherty, ed., *Essays in the History of Early American*

Notes

Law (Chapel Hill: North Carolina University Press, 1969), 392–417; Duff, *A. Lincoln, Prairie Lawyer*, 183–84. Also see Ann Fidler, "Youngs Limbs of the Law," 226–30. For use of the word "roast," see Whitney, *Life on the Circuit with Lincoln*, 181.
199. Hill, *Lincoln, the Lawyer*, 176.
200. Angle, "Abraham Lincoln: Circuit Lawyer," 29; Caton, *Bench and Bar of Illinois*, 52–53, 222; Frank, *Lincoln as a Lawyer*, 23; Whitney, *Life on the Circuit with Lincoln*, 46.
201. There are at least three spellings of this made-up word (Donald, *Lincoln's Herndon*, 44): "Orgmathorial" is in Whitney, *Life on the Circuit with Lincoln*, 46, 50; Frank, *Lincoln as a Lawyer*, 23; Willard L. King, *Lincoln's Manager, David Davis* (Cambridge: Harvard University Press, 1960), 89. But the reference in King is to Lamon, *Recollections of Abraham Lincoln*, 19. Lamon uses the word "ogmathorial" (without the "r"), making it a matter of Whitney's against Lamon's word. Richard Friend Lufkin, in "Mr. Lincoln's Light from Under a Bushel – 1850," 7, confuses matters by calling it the "Orgamathorical Court."
202. Pratt, *Lincoln, 1840–1846*, 264.
203. Caton, *Bench and Bar of Illinois*, 52–53; Swett, ed., *Memorial of Leonard Swett*, 18.
204. King, *Lincoln's Manager, David Davis*, 76; Stiles, *Recollections and Sketches*, 17; Frank, *Lincoln as a Lawyer*, 23; Hill, *Lincoln, the Lawyer*, 173; Fidler, "Young Limbs of the Law," 190; Angle, "Where Lincoln Practiced Law," 36; Stiles, *Recollections and Sketches*, 346; Whitney, *Life on the Circuit with Lincoln*, 45.
205. Frank, *Lincoln as a Lawyer*, 23.
206. Whitney, *Life on the Circuit with Lincoln*, 45, 44.
207. Leonard Swett, *Address Before the Bar Association of the State of Illinois* (Chicago, 188–), 18.
208. Whitney, *Life on the Circuit with Lincoln*, 62.
209. Taylor, "Letters from Absent Members," *Pioneer Law-Makers Association of Iowa. Reunions of 1886 and 1890*, 131.
210. Stiles, *Recollections and Sketches*, 346.
211. Ibid., 333, 746; Caton, *Bench and Bar of Illinois*, 53, 222.
212. King, *Lincoln's Manager, David Davis*, 80.
213. Linder, *Reminiscences of the Early Bench and Bar of Illinois*, 127, 82.
214. James W. Singleton, *The Remarks of Jas. W. Singleton of Quincy or Memorial Address on the Life and Character of Hon. O. H. Browning* (Quincy, Illinois: Quincy Bar, 1881), 3–4.
215. *Quincy and Adams County, Illinois*, 158.
216. Taylor, "Letters from Absent Members," *Pioneer Law-Makers Association, 1886 and 1890*, 131.
217. McClellan, "The Bar of Galena," 228.
218. George Frazier, "The Early Bar of Iowa," in *Report of the First Annual Meeting of the Iowa Bar Association*, 54, 56.
219. *Report of the First Annual Meeting of the Iowa State Bar Association*, 49.
220. Elihu B. Washburne to A. S. Washburn, 20 May 1840, EBW; *History of Adams County*, 416.

Chapter 6. Constructing a regional society

1. William Prescott Smith, *The Book of the Great Railway Celebrations of 1857* (New York: D. Appleton & Co., 1858), 3.
2. Timothy R. Mahoney, *River Towns in the Great West: The Structure of Provincial Urban-*

Notes

ization in the American Midwest, 1820–1870 (New York: Cambridge University Press, 1990), 77–84.
3. Ibid., 166–75.
4. *History of Jo Daviess County* (Chicago: H. F. Kett & Co., 1878).
5. Henry Hitchcock to Uncle, 8 August 1851, Henry Hitchcock Collection, Missouri Historical Society, St. Louis.
6. Theodore C. Pease and James G. Randall, eds., *The Diary of Orville Hickman Browning*, vol. 1, Collections of the Illinois State Historical Library, vol. 20 (Springfield: Illinois State Historical Library, 1925), 85.
7. "Letter of E. B. Washburne to John Dixon," *Journal of the Illinois State Historical Society* 6 (1913): 220–21.
8. Isaac Arnold, "Reminiscences of the Illinois Bar Forty Years Ago," in Edward G. Mason, ed., *Early Illinois* (Chicago: Fergus Historical Series, 1889–90), 137.
9. Edward H. Stiles, *Recollections and Sketches of Notable Lawyers and Public Men of Early Iowa* (Des Moines: Homestead Publishing Company, 1916), 30.
10. Gustave Koerner, *Memoirs of Gustave Koerner. 1809–1896*, vol. 1, Thomas J. McCormack, ed. (Cedar Rapids, Iowa: The Torch Press Publishers, 1909), 592–93; Lincoln Clark to Julia Clark, 19 December 1848, Lincoln Clark Papers, The Huntington Library, San Marino, California (hereafter cited as LC).
11. Stiles, *Recollections and Sketches*, 30.
12. Russell K. Nelson, "The Early Life and Congressional Career of Elihu B. Washburne" (Ph.D. dissertation, University of North Dakota, 1953), 35, 69.
13. Diary of Charles Mason, 14 July 1836, Charles Mason Papers, Iowa State Historical Society, Des Moines, Iowa (hereafter cited as CMP).
14. Charles Hempstead to Stephen Hempstead, Sr., 3 December 1829, William Hempstead Papers, Missouri Historical Society, St. Louis (hereafter cited as WHP).
15. Horatio Newhall to Penelope Newhall, 19 May 1838, Horatio Newhall papers, Illinois State Historical Library, Springfield, Illinois (hereafter cited as HN).
16. Elihu Washburne to Cadwallader Washburn, 23, 30 December 1842, Elihu Washburne Papers, Washburn-Norlands Humanities Foundation, Livermore, Maine (hereafter cited as EBW).
17. Horatio Newhall to Penelope Newhall, 6, 10 May, 22 June 1838; Horatio Newhall to Brother, 11 December 1840; Horatio Newhall to Penelope Newhall, 15 May 1846, HN.
18. Charles Mason to unknown, 9 July 1852, CMP.
19. James N. Adams, "Index to Springfield Journal" (1944–46), typescript, Illinois State Historical Library, Springfield, 488.
20. Robert J. Casey and W. A. S. Douglas, *Pioneer Railroad: The Story of the Chicago and Northwestern System* (New York: McGraw-Hill Book Company, 1948), 32.
21. John Carl Parish, *George Wallace Jones* (Iowa City: State Historical Society of Iowa, 1912), 171.
22. Casey and Douglas, *Pioneer Railroad*, 47–52.
23. Diary of Charles Mason, 20 April 1856, CMP.
24. Ibid., 30 January, 19 July 1858, CMP.
25. Ibid., 28 July, 4 August 1858, CMP; Diary of Richard Bonson, 19, 25 May, 3–5 June, 17, 29 August 1853, Iowa State Historical Society, Iowa City.
26. Charles S. Hempstead to Elihu B. Washburne, 26 December 1845, Elihu B. Washburne Papers, Library of Congress (hereafter cited as EBW, LOC).
27. A. L. Norris to Elihu B. Washburne, 16 December 1845, EBW, LOC.

Notes

28. Charles S. Hempstead to Elihu B. Washburne, 27 December 1845, EBW, LOC.
29. Robert F. Klein, ed., *Dubuque: Frontier River City* (Dubuque: Research Center for Dubuque Area History, 1984), 77–78, 85, 94–95.
30. Ibid., 85; David S. Wilson to George Wallace Jones, 11 January 1849, George Wallace Jones Papers, Iowa State Historical Society, Des Moines (hereafter cited as GWJ).
31. Klein, ed., *Dubuque: Frontier River City*, 111.
32. Mildred Throne, "The Burlington and Missouri River Railroad in Iowa," *The Palimpsest* 33 (January 1952): 2–6, 10–14.
33. Diary of Charles Mason, 6 April 1856, 2, 16 September 1858, CMP.
34. James L. Estes to Charles Mason, 13 June, 2 July, 6, 30 September 1853, 23 November 1854, CMP.
35. H. W. Sample to David Wells Kilbourne, 22 August 1857, George W. Kilbourne Papers, State Historical Society, Des Moines (hereafter cited as GWK).
36. Diary of Charles Mason, 24, 25 July 1855, CMP.
37. James Neal Primm, *Lion of the Valley: St. Louis, Missouri* (Boulder: Pruett Publishing Company, 1990), 211.
38. Carl Abbott, *Boosters and Businessmen: Popular Economic Thought and Urban Growth in the Antebellum Middle West* (Westport, Connecticut: Greenwood Press, 1981), 189.
39. Robin Einhorn, *Property Rules: Political Economy in Chicago, 1833–1872* (Chicago: University of Chicago Press, 1990), 61–68.
40. Don H. Doyle, *The Social Order of a Frontier Community* (Urbana: University of Illinois Press, 1978), 42–47.
41. Casey and Douglas, *Pioneer Railroad*, 32.
42. A. L. Norris to Elihu B. Washburne, 27 December 1845, EBW, LOC; Charles S. Hempstead Papers, Chicago Historical Society.
43. Adams, "Index to Illinois State Journal," 529.
44. Harry E. Pratt, *Lincoln, 1840–46: Being the Day-by-Day Activities of Abraham Lincoln* (Springfield: The Abraham Lincoln Association, 1939), 300; Gustave Koerner, *Memoirs of Gustave Koerner*, 1: 565; Usher F. Linder, *Reminiscences of the Early Bench and Bar of Illinois* (Chicago: Chicago Legal News Company, 1879), 121–22.
45. Pease and Randall, eds., *Diary of Orville H. Browning*, 1: 38; Landry Genosky, ed., *A People's History of Quincy and Adams County: A Sesquicentennial History* (Quincy: n.p., 1974), 634.
46. Thomas J. Brown, "The Age of Ambition in Quincy," *Journal of the Illinois State Historical Society* 75, no. 4 (Winter 1982): 249–50.
47. Primm, *Lion of the Valley*, 214–17, 229; "Speech of Honorable Edward Bates at the Pacific Railroad Celebration 4 July 1851"; Diary of Edward Bates, 2 December 1852, Edward Bates Papers, Missouri Historical Society.
48. Stiles, *Recollections and Sketches*, 744–45; Franc B. Wilkie, *Davenport Past and Present* (Davenport: Luse, Lane and Co., 1858), 109.
49. William H. Thompson, *Transportation in Iowa: A Historical Summary* (Des Moines: Iowa Department of Transportation, 1989), 24; Klein, ed., *Dubuque: Frontier River City*, 111.
50. Stiles, *Recollections and Sketches*, 826; Dubuque and Pacific Railroad Company, Illinois Central Collection, Newberry Library, Chicago.
51. Stiles, *Recollections and Sketches*, 828.
52. Klein, ed., *Dubuque: Frontier River City*, 146; *Receipts and Expenditures of the Dubuque Western Railroad and Its Present Condition* (Dubuque: n.p., 1858).

Notes

53. "Circular Letter," circa December 1851, CMP.
54. Thompson, *Transportation in Iowa*, 24.
55. Charles Ballance to Charles Mason, 27 December 1851; Onslow Peters to Charles Mason, 8 January 1852; Charles Ballance to Charles Mason, 10 February 1852; Onslow Peters to Charles Mason, 7 December 1852; CMP.
56. Diary of Charles Mason, 23, 28 July 1858, CMP.
57. William Salter, *The Life of James W. Grimes* (New York: D. Appleton and Company, 1876), 26–27, 30–31.
58. Throne, "The Burlington and Missouri River Railroad in Iowa," 1–4; James Grimes to Charles Mason, 2, 3, 6, 13 February, 23 March, 12 April 1852, CMP.
59. Stiles, *Recollections and Sketches*, 252; Throne, "The Burlington and Missouri Railroad," 11–12, 17; see David E. Lotz, "Burlington, Iowa, Heart of the C B & Q," *Burlington Bulletin*, no. 23 (May 1991), 7.
60. Diary of Charles Mason, 20, 27 December 1856, 7 January, 6 February 1857, CMP.
61. Stiles, *Recollections and Sketches*, 248.
62. George Kilbourne to David Wells Kilbourne, 11 February 1852, GWK.
63. Hugh T. Reid to David Wells Kilbourne, 21 June, 9 July 1857, GWK; Stiles, *Recollections and Sketches*, 328.
64. Davis Wells Kilbourne to B. Johnson, 27 February 1860, GWK; Diary of Charles Mason, 27 December 1856, CMP.
65. James L. Estes to Charles Mason, 6 September 1853, 9 March 1861, CMP.
66. James Grimes to Charles Mason, 27 January 1851, CMP.
67. Elihu B. Washburne to Cadwallader Washburn, 11 March 1853, Elihu Washburne Papers, Wisconsin State Historical Society (hereafter cited as EBW, HSW).
68. Charles Hempstead Papers, Chicago Historical Society.
69. Timothy R. Mahoney, "Down in Davenport: A Regional Perspective on Antebellum Town Economic Development," *The Annals of Iowa* 50 (Summer 1990): 471.
70. Klein, ed., *Dubuque: Frontier River City*, 111.
71. Primm, *Lion of the Valley*, 215.
72. James L. Estes to Charles Mason, 13 June 1853, CMP.
73. Ibid., 4 February 1860, CMP.
74. Charles Hempstead Papers; Nelson, "The Early Life and Congressional Career of Elihu B. Washburne," 49.
75. Genosky, *A People's History of Quincy and Adams County*, 634.
76. Klein, ed., *Dubuque: Frontier River City*, 94.
77. Genosky, *A People's History of Quincy and Adams County*, 635.
78. Platt Smith to Jesse P. Farley, 31 August 1857, Dubuque and Pacific Railroad Co., Dubuque Office, In-Letters, Illinois Central Collection.
79. Nelson, "The Early Life and Congressional Career of Elihu B. Washburne," 49.
80. Charles Hempstead Papers.
81. Wilkie, *Davenport Past and Present*, 108–9.
82. "List of Preferred Stockholders of the Dubuque and Pacific Railroad Company," Dubuque and Pacific Railroad Company, Out-Letters, 1856–1861, Illinois Central Collection.
83. James L. Estes to Charles Mason, 15 August 1853, CMP.
84. Throne, "The Burlington and Missouri River Railroad in Iowa," 11.
85. Charles Mason to stock subscribers, May 1852, CMP.
86. Richard Friend Lufkin, "Mr. Lincoln's Light from Under a Bushel – 1851," *Lincoln*

Notes

Herald 53 (Winter 1952): 10–13; Roy P. Basler, ed., *The Collected Works of Abraham Lincoln,* vol. 2 (New Brunswick: Rutgers University Press, 1953), 98–102, 105–7, 110; William D. Beard, "'I have labored hard to find the law': Abraham Lincoln and the Alton and Springfield Railroad," *Illinois Historical Journal* 85 (Winter 1992): 209–20.

87. *The Receipts and Expenditures of the Dubuque and Western Railroad and Its Present Condition;* Hobart C. Carr, *Early History of Iowa Railroads* (New York: Arno Press, 1981), 65–71.
88. Thomas Nairn to George Wallace Jones, 9 January 1851, GWJ; Klein, ed., *Dubuque: Frontier River City,* 104, 111, 125, 136, 146, 159.
89. Carr, *Early History of Iowa Railroads,* 71.
90. Wilkie, *Davenport Past and Present,* 129–30.
91. Throne, "The Burlington and Missouri River Railroad in Iowa," 16.
92. Carr, *Early History of Iowa Railroads,* 71.
93. Brown, "The Age of Ambition in Quincy, Illinois," 249–51.
94. *Chicago Daily Tribune,* 4 October 1851.
95. *Report of the Dubuque and Pacific Railroad* (Dubuque: n.p., 1858), 18, 19, 15.
96. Richard P. Morgan, *Engineer's Report, Davenport and Iowa City Railroad* (Davenport: n.p., 1851), 7; *Report of the Engineer of the Iowa Western Railroad* (Muscatine: H. D. LaCassitt, 1851), 6–7; Throne, "The Burlington and Missouri River Railroad," 5.
97. Casey and Douglas, *Pioneer Railroad,* 46.
98. "Resolutions of Davenport, Iowa River Convention, October 1849," CMP.
99. *Chicago Daily Tribune,* 29 October 1851.
100. Pratt, *Lincoln, 1840–1846,* 310.
101. *Proceedings of a Convention of Delegates for the Promotion of Internal Improvements Within the State of Missouri Held at the City of St. Louis on the Twentieth of April 1836* (St. Louis: Charles Keemle, 1836); John F. Darby to Hon. Joseph Gillespie, 3 August 1876, Joseph Gillespie Papers, Chicago Historical Society.
102. Pratt, *Lincoln, 1840–1846,* 307, 310; Adams, "Index to the Springfield Journal," 36, 342, 503, 529.
103. Casey and Douglas, *Pioneer Railroad,* 47–49.
104. Elihu B. Washburne to Cadwallader Washburn, 9 January 1846, EBW, HSW.
105. Mahoney, "Down in Davenport," 470; *Davenport Gazette,* 8 November 1849.
106. *Proceedings of the Rapids Convention Held at Burlington Iowa on the 23rd and 24th of October, 1851* (Burlington: Morgan and McKenney, 1852).
107. Ibid., 22–23; *Chicago Daily Tribune,* 20 October 1851.
108. John C. Rives, ed., *Appendix to the Congressional Globe,* vol. 25 (Washington: John C. Rives, 1852), 679.
109. *The Congressional Globe,* vol. 24 (Washington: John C. Rives, 1852), part I, p. 348.
110. George Kilbourne to David Wells Kilbourne, 11 February 1852, GWK.
111. *Proceedings of North Missouri Railroad Convention at St. Charles* (St. Louis: M. Neidner, 1852).
112. Diary of Charles Mason, 20, 22, 23 July, 21 August 1858, CMP.
113. Ibid., 24, 25 July 1855, CMP.
114. James Grimes to Charles Mason, 27 January 1852; James Knox to Charles Mason, 15 December 1851; Charles Ballance to Charles Mason, 27 December 1851; Onslow Peters to Charles Mason, 8 January 1852, CMP.
115. Abbott, *Boosters and Businessmen,* 135.

Notes

116. Charles William Hunter to Zebina Eastman, 25 May 1850, Zebina Eastman Collection, Chicago Historical Society.
117. Throne, "The Burlington and Missouri River Railroad in Iowa," 4–5.
118. Pease and Randall, eds., *The Diary of Orville H. Browning*, 1: 38–39.
119. Genosky, *A People's History of Quincy and Adams County*, 635.
120. William B. Ogden to Charles S. Hempstead, 31 July 1849; Thomas Drummond to Charles S. Hempstead, 12 December, 24 August 1850, 18 December 1851, Charles Hempstead Papers.
121. Genosky, *A People's History of Quincy and Adams County*, 635.
122. *Davenport Gazette*, 21 February 1850.
123. Thomas Drummond to Charles S. Hempstead, 12 December 1850, Charles Hempstead Papers.
124. Ibid., Petition, 20 December 1850; Thomas Drummond to Charles S. Hempstead, 21 December 1850; D. L. Rother to Charles S. Hempstead, 22 May 1851; William Larabee to Charles S. Hempstead, 5 September 1851; Thomas Drummond to Charles S. Hempstead, 18 December 1851; William Larabee to Charles S. Hempstead, 18 September 1852, Charles Hempstead Papers.
125. Elihu B. Washburne to Cadwallader Washburn, 31 December 1852, EBW, HSW.
126. William Y. Lovell and Lucius H. Langworthy to George Wallace Jones, 15 January 1852, GWJ.
127. Rives, ed., *Appendix to the Congressional Globe*, vol. 25 (1852): 674, 680, 679, 674.
128. C. Quimbly to Charles Mason, 12 February 1852; E. Farnham to Charles Mason, 28 February 1852; Julius Manning to Charles Mason, 21 December 1852; Onslow Peters to Charles Mason, 16 December 1852; James Grimes to Charles Mason, 28 July, 22 October 1852; Henry W. Starr to Charles Mason, 8 January 1853; James Knox to Charles Mason, 7 January 1853, CMP.
129. Onslow Peters to Charles Mason, 1 January 1853, 16 December 1852, CMP.
130. Pease and Randall, eds., *Diary of Orville H. Browning*, 1: 81.
131. Hugh T. Reid to David Wells Kilbourne, 22 June 1857, GWK.
132. Rives, ed. *Appendix to the Congressional Globe*, vol. 25 (1852): 680.
133. Abel Corbin to George Wallace Jones, 15 November 1851, GWJ.
134. Parish, *George Wallace Jones*, 171–72.
135. Klein, ed., *Dubuque: Frontier River City*, 77–78.
136. *The Congressional Globe* (14 May 1856), 1213.
137. Klein, ed., *Dubuque: Frontier River City*, 77–78.
138. Charles Mason to David Rorer, 23 March 1852, David Rorer Papers, Iowa State Historical Library, Des Moines, Iowa; Edward Kilbourne to David Wells Kilbourne, 9 January 1852, GWK.
139. Throne, "The Burlington and Missouri River Railroad in Iowa," 4.
140. Edward Kilbourne to David Wells Kilbourne, 9 January 1852, GWK.
141. James Grimes to Charles Mason, 13 February 1852, CMP; Petition, Burlington Iowa (1852) to George Wallace Jones, GWJ.
142. James Grimes to Charles Mason, 2, 3, 6 February 1852, CMP.
143. Lincoln Clark to Julia Clark, 25 February, 17 April, 12 June 1852, LC.
144. Ibid., 19 March 1852.
145. Lucius H. Langworthy to George Wallace Jones, 7 February 1852, GWJ.
146. James W. Grimes to Charles Mason, 23 March, 12 April 1852, CMP; *The Congressional Globe*, vol. 25 (1852), 669, 709, 723, 761–62, 772.

Notes

147. James M. Grimes to Charles Mason, 23 March 1852, CMP.
148. Charles Mason to David Rorer, 23 March 1852, David Rorer Papers, Iowa State Historical Library, Des Moines; Lincoln Clark to Julia Clark, 10 April 1852, LC; David Dale Owen, *Report of a Geological Exploration of a Part of Iowa, Wisconsin, and Illinois* (Washington, D.C.: Senate of the United States, 1844), 13.
149. James Grimes to Charles Mason, 23 March, 12 April 1852, CMP.
150. Rives, ed., *Appendix to the Congressional Globe*, vol. 25 (1852), 495–98.
151. Augustus C. Dodge to Charles Mason, 4 May 1852, CMP.
152. Rives, ed., *Appendix to the Congressional Globe*, vol. 25 (1852), 672–75, 678–82.
153. George Wallace Jones to Charles Mason, 18 May 1852, CMP.
154. Lincoln Clark to Julia Clark, 6 June, 31 July, 12, 16 August 1852, LC.
155. Mentor L. Williams, "The Background of the Chicago Harbor and River Convention, 1847," *Mid-America* 30, no. 4 (October 1948): 219–32.
156. Adams, "Index to the Springfield Journal," 342, 434, 480, 503.
157. Robert W. Johannsen, *Stephen A. Douglas* (New York: Oxford University Press, 1973), 169–72; *Sangamon Journal*, 12 June 1845; *National Intelligencer*, 28 June 1845.
158. *National Intelligencer*, 17 July 1845.
159. J. D. B. De Bow, *The Commercial Review of the South and West*, vol. 1 (1846), 7–22, 12.
160. Ibid., 12; Clyde N. Wilson, ed., *The Papers of John C. Calhoun*, vol. 22: *1845–1846* (Columbia: University of South Carolina Press, 1995), 275–85, 286, 291–93.
161. De Bow, *The Commercial Review of the South and West*, 12; Williams, "Background of the Chicago River Convention," 219–32.
162. Mentor L. Williams, "The Chicago River and Harbor Convention, 1847," *Mississippi Valley Historical Review* 35, no. 4 (March 1949): 607–8.
163. Einhorn, *Property Rules, Political Economy in Chicago, 1833–1872*, 61, 68–75.
164. Williams, "The Chicago River and Harbor Convention, 1847," 607–26.
165. *The Commerce and Navigation of the Valley of the Mississippi and Also That Pertaining to the City of St. Louis, a Report for the Chicago Convention, July 5 1847* (St. Louis: Chambers and Knapp, 1847).
166. Robert Fergus, comp., *Chicago River-and-Harbor Convention* (Chicago: Fergus Printing Company, 1882), 47–69; Earl Schenck Miers, ed., *Lincoln Day-by-Day, a Chronology, 1809–1865*, vol. 1: *1809–1848* (Washington: Lincoln Sesquicentennial Association, 1960), 290–91.
167. Robert Fergus, comp., *Chicago River-and-Harbor Convention*, 60.
168. Elihu B. Washburne to Cadwallader Washburn, 4 July 1847, EBW, HSW; Allen Thorndike Rice, ed., *Reminiscences of Abraham Lincoln by Distinguished Men of His Time* (New York: North American Publishing Company, 1886), 16; Abraham Lincoln to Orville H. Browning, 24 June 1847, in Basler, ed., *The Collected Works of Abraham Lincoln*, 1: 394–95.
169. Robert Fergus, comp., *Chicago River-and-Harbor Convention*, 51–69; Jesse B. Thomas, *Report of Jesse B. Thomas as Member of the Executive Committee Appointed by the Chicago Harbor and River Convention of the Statistics Concerning the City of Chicago* (Chicago: R. L. Wilson, 1847).
170. Williams, "The Chicago River and Harbor Convention, 1847," 624.
171. Nelson, "The Early Life and Congressional Career of Elihu B. Washburne," 71; Elihu B. Washburne to Cadwallader Washburn, 4 July 1847, EBW, HSW.
172. Diary of Edward Bates, July 1847, Edward Bates Papers.
173. Rice, ed., *Reminiscences of Abraham Lincoln*, 17.

Notes

174. Johannsen, *Stephen A. Douglas*, 210–11.
175. Primm, *Lion of the Valley*, 214.
176. *Proceedings of the National Railroad Convention Which Assembled in the City of St. Louis* (St. Louis: Chambers & Knapp, 1850), 17–27; T. D. Robertson to Charles Hempstead, 8 October 1849, Charles Hempstead Papers.
177. Theodore S. Parvin, *Historical Lectures upon Early Leaders in the Professions in the Territory of Iowa* (Iowa City: State Historical Society, 1894), 81; *National Intelligencer*, 30 October 1849; Primm, *Lion of the Valley*, 214–15; *National Intelligencer*, 31 October, 3 November 1849; *Proceedings of the National Railroad Convention Which Assembled in the City of St. Louis*, 23–27.
178. *National Intelligencer*, 3, 10 November 1849.
179. *Proceedings of the Convention in Favor of a National Rail Road to the Pacific Ocean Through the Territory of the United States* (Philadelphia: Crissy and Markley, 1850), 20–21.
180. J. B. D. De Bow, ed., *De Bow's Review* 15, no. 111 (September 1853): 256–65; *Official Proceedings of the Mississippi Valley Railroad Convention Held at Varieties Theater, in St. Louis, 15–16 November 1852, Together with Memorial to Congress Ordered by Said Convention* (St. Louis: M. Niedner, 1852).
181. Diary of Charles Mason, 6 April 1856, CMP.
182. George Nightengale to George Wallace Jones, 15 May 1856, GWJ.
183. Salter, *The Life of James W. Grimes*, 81-82.
184. Diary of Richard Bonson, Iowa State Historical Society, Iowa City, Iowa; Lincoln Clark to Julia Clark, 28 June 1856, LC.
185. Diary of Richard Bonson, 30 June–12 July 1856.
186. Casey and Douglas, *Pioneer Railroad*, 63–64.
187. Paul Angle, *"Here I Have Lived": A History of Lincoln's Springfield* (Springfield: The Abraham Lincoln Association, 1935), 163.
188. Wilkie, *Davenport Past and Present*, 115, 126–27.
189. Lotz, "Burlington, Iowa, Heart of the C B & Q.," 9–10.
190. "Hon. O. H. Browning and His Relations to the C. B. and Q., and Knox College" (Galesburg, Illinois: n.p., 1933), 5; Genosky, *A People's History of Quincy and Adams County*, 636; Pease and Randall, eds., *Diary of Orville H. Browning*, 1: 242.
191. William Baillache to wife, 4 February 1864, Baillache-Brayman Papers, Illinois State Historical Library.
192. Klein, ed., *Dubuque: Frontier River City*, 132.
193. Ibid., 130.
194. Wilfred M. McClay, *The Masterless: Self and Society in Modern America* (Chapel Hill: University of North Carolina Press, 1994), 11–13; James Gilbert, *Perfect Cities: Chicago's Utopias of 1893* (Chicago: University of Chicago Press, 1991).
195. Angle, *"Here I Have Lived,"* 99–100.
196. Ibid., 163.
197. *Burlington Tri-Weekly Hawk-eye*, 28 May–6 June 1855.
198. *Chicago Daily Tribune*, 17 February 1854.
199. Wilkie, *Davenport Past and Present*, 115; *Chicago Daily Tribune*, 22 February 1854.
200. *Burlington Tri-Weekly Hawk-eye*, 4 June 1855; Angle, *"Here I Have Lived,"* 163; *Chicago Daily Tribune*, 6 June 1854; Diary of John R. Munn, vol. 22, p. 144, John R. Munn Collection, Chicago Historical Society.
201. Smith, *Great Railway Celebrations of 1857*, 217, 224.

Notes

202. *Chicago Daily Tribune*, 21 March 1853.
203. *Burlington Tri-Weekly Hawk-eye*, 28 May 1855.
204. Salter, *The Life of James Grimes*, 71.
205. Klein, ed., *Dubuque: Frontier River City*, 130.
206. Diary of John R. Munn, vol. 22, p. 143, John R. Munn Collection; Smith, *Great Railway Celebrations of 1857*, 224.
207. Wilkie, *Davenport Past and Present*, 115.
208. *Chicago Daily Tribune*, 22 February 1854.
209. Ibid., 6 June 1854.
210. Diary of John R. Munn, vol. 22, p. 143, John R. Munn Collection.
211. *Chicago Daily Tribune*, 22 February 1854.
212. Smith, *Great Railway Celebrations of 1857*, 231, 224; *Burlington Tri-Weekly Hawk-eye*, 2 June 1855.
213. Koerner, *Memoirs of Gustave Koerner*, 1: 608–9.
214. Smith, *Great Railway Celebrations of 1857*, 224–26.
215. *Chicago Daily Tribune*, 14 June 1855.
216. Ibid., 12 March 1853.
217. Salter, *The Life of James Grimes*, 71.
218. Koerner, *Memoirs of Gustave Koerner*, 1: 612.
219. Diary of John R. Munn, vol. 22, pp. 148, 150, John R. Munn Collection.
220. John Kirk to Calvin Kirk, 21 March 1853, vol. 2, John Kirk Letter Book, Chicago Historical Society.
221. Diary of John R. Munn, vol. 22, pp. 150–53, John R. Munn Collection; Richard Yates to L. U. Reavis, 2 May 1875, Logan Uriah Reavis Papers, Chicago Historical Society.
222. Gustave Koerner, *Memoirs of Gustave Koerner*, 1: 609; Angle, *"Here I Have Lived,"* 163; *Chicago Daily Tribune*, 22 February 1854.
223. Klein, ed., *Dubuque: Frontier River City*, 130.
224. *Burlington Tri-Weekly Hawk-eye*, 2, 4, 6 June 1855; *Chicago Daily Tribune*, 15 June 1855.
225. *Burlington Tri-Weekly Hawk-eye*, 2 June 1855; Koerner, *Memoirs of Gustave Koerner*, 1: 611.
226. Diary of John R. Munn, vol. 22, p. 153, John R. Munn Collection.
227. Wilkie, *Davenport Past and Present*, 116.
228. *Burlington Tri-Weekly Hawk-eye*, 30 May 1855; Klein, ed., *Dubuque: Frontier River City*, 130; Smith, *Great Railway Celebrations of 1857*, 249.
229. Ibid., 230–32.
230. Lotz, "Burlington, Iowa, Heart of the C B & Q," 10.
231. Smith, *Great Railway Celebrations of 1857*, 227–28.
232. *Chicago Daily Tribune*, 18 February 1854.
233. *Burlington Tri-Weekly Hawk-eye*, 4 June 1855.
234. *Chicago Daily Tribune*, 18 February 1854.
235. *Burlington Tri-Weekly Hawk-eye*, 4 June 1855; *Chicago Daily Tribune*, 15 June 1855.
236. Ibid., 24 February 1854.
237. Klein, ed., *Dubuque: Frontier River City*, 132–34; *Burlington Tri-Weekly Hawk-eye*, 2, 4 June 1855; Smith, *Great Railway Celebrations of 1857*, 233–34.
238. Richard Friend Lufkin, "Mr. Lincoln's Light from Under a Bushel – 1854," *Lincoln Herald* 56 (Winter 1954): 12–13; Lufkin, "Mr. Lincoln's Light from Under a Bushel –

Notes

1855," *Lincoln Herald* 58 (Spring-Summer 1956): 23; Miers, *Lincoln Day By Day, a Chronology, 1809–1865*, vol. 2: *1849–1860*, 173–74.

239. Florence Gratiot Bale, "A Packet of Old Letters," *Wisconsin Magazine of History* 11 (1927–28): 168; Lincoln Clark to Julia Clark, 23 May 1854, 17 February 1855, LC.
240. Nelson, "The Early Life and Congressional Career of Elihu B. Washburne," 126.
241. Pease and Randall, eds., *The Diary of Orville H. Browning*, 1: 242–44.
242. Ibid., 1: 249.
243. Diary of Charles Mason, 13 July, 6 September 1855, 5 April, 27 October 1856, CMP.
244. John R. Munn Diary, vol. 22, p. 160, John R. Munn Collection.
245. Rice, ed., *Reminiscences of Abraham Lincoln*, 14–15.
246. Benjamin P. Thomas, "Lincoln and the Courts, 1854–1861," *Abraham Lincoln Association Papers* (Springfield: Abraham Lincoln Association, 1934), 59–62.
247. Richard Friend Lufkin, "Mr. Lincoln's Light from Under a Bushel – 1851," *Lincoln Herald* 53 (Winter 1952): 6–7; Lufkin, "Mr. Lincoln's Light from Under a Bushel – 1853," *Lincoln Herald* 55 (Winter 1953): 3, 7, 9; Lufkin, "Mr. Lincoln's Light from Under a Bushel – 1854," 13, 17; Lufkin, "Mr. Lincoln's Light from Under a Bushel – 1855," 19, 23; Thomas, "Lincoln and the Courts," 61–62.
248. Diary of Charles Mason, 28, 29 August 1855, CMP.
249. Lyman Trumbull to Julia Trumbull, 23 October 1860, Lyman Trumbull and Family Papers, Library of Congress.
250. Diary of Charles Mason, 12 August 1855, CMP.
251. William Carr Lane to Ann Lane, 1 March 1854, William Carr Lane Papers, Missouri Historical Society, St. Louis.

Epilogue

1. William L. Barney, *The Passage of the Republic* (Lexington: D. C. Heath, 1987), 182–83.
2. Robert H. Wiebe, *The Opening of American Society* (New York: Alfred A. Knopf, 1984), 287–90; Daniel H. Calhoun, *Professional Lives in America: Structure and Aspiration, 1750–1850* (Cambridge: Harvard University Press, 1965), 62.
3. D. W Meinig, *The Shaping of America: A Geographical Perspective on 500 Years of History*, vol. 2: *Continental America, 1800–1867* (New Haven: Yale University Press, 1993), 273.
4. Harry J. Carman and Reinhard H. Luthin, *Lincoln and the Patronage* (New York: Columbia University Press, 1943).
5. Olivier Zunz, *Making America Corporate, 1870–1920* (Chicago: University of Chicago Press, 1990), 12.
6. Peter Dobkin Hall, *The Organization of American Culture, 1700–1900* (New York: New York University Press, 1982), 200.
7. John R. Stilgoe, *Metropolitan Corridor: Railroads and the American Scene* (New Haven: Yale University Press, 1983).
8. Robert H. Wiebe, *The Search for Order, 1877–1920* (New York: Hill and Wang, 1967), 2, 44.
9. Ibid., 44.

Selected bibliography

The following sources are recommended for further reading.

Abbott, Carl. *Boosters and Businessmen: Popular Economic Thought and Urban Growth in the Antebellum Middle West.* Westport, Connecticut: Greenwood Press, 1981.
Abzug, Robert. *Cosmos Crumbling: American Reform and the Religious Imagination.* New York: Oxford University Press, 1994.
Adler, Jeffrey S. *Yankee Merchants and the Making of the Urban West.* New York: Cambridge University Press, 1991.
Alford, Richard D. *Naming and Identity: A Cross-Cultural Study of Personal Naming Practices.* New Haven: Hraf Press, 1988.
Barney, William L. *The Passage of the Republic: An Interdisciplinary History of Nineteenth-Century America.* Lexington: D. C. Heath, 1987.
Baxter, Maurice G. *Orville H. Browning, Lincoln's Friend and Critic.* Bloomington: Indiana University Press, 1957.
Beckwith, Paul. *The Creoles of St. Louis.* St. Louis: Nixon-Jones, 1893.
Berthold, Eugenie. *Glimpses of Creole Life in Old St. Louis.* St. Louis: Missouri Historical Society, 1933.
Blumin, Stuart M. *The Emergence of the Middle Class.* New York: Cambridge University Press, 1989.
Brown, Richard D. *Knowledge Is Power: The Diffusion of Information in Early America, 1700–1865.* New York: Oxford University Press, 1989.
Bushman, Richard L. *The Refinement of America: Persons, Houses, Cities.* New York: Alfred A. Knopf, 1992.
Calhoun, Daniel H. *Professional Lives in America: Structure and Aspiration, 1750–1850.* Cambridge: Harvard University Press, 1965.
Carnes, Mark C. *Secret Ritual and Manhood in Victorian America.* New Haven: Yale University Press, 1989.
Carnes, Mark C., and Clyde Griffen, eds. *Meanings for Manhood: Constructions of Masculinity in Victorian America.* Chicago: University of Chicago Press, 1990.

Selected bibliography

Carr, Hobart C. *Early History of Iowa Railroads.* New York: Arno Press, 1981.
Carr, Kay J. *Belleville, Ottawa, and Galesburg: Community and Democracy on the Illinois Frontier.* Carbondale: Southern Illinois University Press, 1996.
Casey, Robert J., and W. A. S. Douglas. *Pioneer Railroad: The Story of the Chicago and Northwestern System.* New York: McGraw-Hill, 1948.
Cayton, Andrew R. L., and Peter S. Onuf, eds. *The Midwest and the Nation: Rethinking the History of an American Region.* Bloomington: Indiana University Press, 1990.
Cunningham, Mary B., and Jeanne C. Blythe. *The Founding Family of St. Louis.* St. Louis: Midwest Technical Publications, 1977.
Davis, Susan G. *Parades and Power: Street Theatre in Nineteenth-Century Philadelphia.* Philadelphia: Temple University Press, 1986.
Doyle, Don H. *The Social Order of a Frontier Community: Jacksonville, Illinois, 1825–1870.* Urbana: University of Illinois Press, 1978.
Duff, John J. *A. Lincoln, Prairie Lawyer.* New York: Bramhall House, 1960.
Einhorn, Robin. *Property Rules: Political Economy in Chicago, 1833-1872.* Chicago: University of Chicago Press, 1990.
Erikson, Kai T. *Wayward Puritans: A Study in the Sociology of Deviance.* New York: John Wiley and Sons, 1966.
Faragher, John Mack. *Sugar Creek: Life on the Illinois Prairie.* New Haven: Yale University Press, 1986.
Foley, William E., and C. David Rice. *The First Chouteaus, River Barons of Early St. Louis.* Urbana: University of Illinois Press, 1983.
Frank, John P. *Lincoln as a Lawyer.* Urbana: University of Illinois Press, 1961.
Gawalt, Gerard W. *The New High Priests, Lawyers in Post–Civil War America.* Westport, Connecticut: Greenwood Press, 1984.
Gilbert, James. *Perfect Cities, Chicago's Utopias of 1893.* Chicago: University of Chicago Press, 1991.
Gilekson, John S., Jr. *Middle-Class Providence, 1820–1940.* Princeton: Princeton University Press, 1986.
Gilfoyle, Timothy. *City of Eros: New York City, Prostitution, and the Commercialization of Sex, 1790–1920.* New York: W. W. Norton, 1992.
Gray, Susan E. *The Yankee West: Community Life on the Michigan Frontier.* Chapel Hill: University of North Carolina Press, 1997.
Grier, Katherine C. *Culture and Comfort: Peoples, Parlors, and Upholstery, 1850–1930.* Amherst: University of Massachusetts Press, 1988.
Hall, Peter Dobkin. *The Organization of American Culture, 1700–1900.* New York: New York University Press, 1982.
Halttunen, Karen. *Confidence Men and Painted Women: A Study of Middle-Class Culture in America, 1830–1870.* New Haven: Yale University Press, 1982.
Hobson, Wayne K. *The American Legal Profession and the Organizational Society, 1890–1930.* New York: Garland Publishing, 1986.
Hunt, Gaillard. *Israel, Elihu, and Cadwallader Washburn: A Chapter in American Biography.* 1925. Rpt. New York: Da Capo Press, 1969.
Johnson, Carl H., Jr. *The Building of Galena, an Architectural Legacy.* Stevens Point, Wisconsin: Worzalla Publishing, 1977.
Kasson, John F. *Rudeness and Civility: Manners in Nineteenth-Century Urban America.* New York: Hill and Wang, 1990.

Selected bibliography

Klein, Robert F., ed. *Dubuque: Frontier River City*. Dubuque: Research Center for Dubuque Area History, 1984.

Lystra, Karen. *Searching the Heart: Women, Men, and Romantic Love in Nineteenth-Century America*. New York: Oxford University Press, 1989.

Mahoney, Timothy R. *River Towns in the Great West: The Structure of Provincial Urbanization in the American Midwest, 1820–1870*. New York: Cambridge University Press, 1990.

McClay, Wilfred M. *The Masterless: Self and Society in Modern America*. Chapel Hill: University of North Carolina Press, 1994.

McDermott, John F., ed. *Frenchmen and French Ways in the Mississippi Valley*. Urbana: University of Illinois Press, 1969.

Meinig, D. W. *The Shaping of America: A Geographical Perspective on 500 Years of History*. Vol. 2: *Continental America, 1800–1867*. New Haven: Yale University Press, 1993.

Nardulli, Peter, ed. *Diversity, Conflict, and State Politics: Regionalism in Ilinois*. Urbana: University of Illinois Press, 1989.

Nolan, Patrick B. *Vigilantes on the Middle Border: A Study of Self-Appointed Law Enforcement in the States of the Upper Mississippi from 1840 to 1880*. New York: Garland Publishing, 1987.

Novick, Peter. *That Noble Dream, the "Objectivity Question" and the American Historical Profession*. New York: Cambridge University Press, 1988.

O'Brien, Michael J., ed. *Grassland, Forest, and Historical Settlement: An Analysis of Dynamics in Northeast Missouri*. Lincoln: University of Nebraska Press, 1984.

Pred, Allan. *Making Histories and Constructing Human Geographies*. Boulder: Westview Press, 1990.

Primm, James Neal. *Lion of the Valley: St. Louis, Missouri*. 2d ed. Boulder: Pruett Publishing, 1990.

Rose, Ann C. *Victorian America and the Civil War*. New York: Cambridge University Press, 1992.

Rotundo, E. Anthony. *American Manhood: Transformations in Masculinity from the Revolution to the Modern Era*. New York: Basic Books, 1993.

Ryan, Mary P. *Women in Public: Between Banners and Ballots, 1825–1880*. Baltimore: Johns Hopkins University Press, 1990.

Scanlan, Peter L. *Prairie du Chien: French, British, American*. Menasha, Wisconsin: Banta Publishing, 1937.

Schama, Simon. *Dead Certainties (Unwarranted Speculations)*. New York: Alfred A. Knopf, 1991.

Schieck, William. *The Half Blood: A Cultural Symbol in Nineteenth Century American Fiction*. Lexington: University of Kentucky Press, 1979.

Stiles, Edward H. *Recollections and Sketches of Notable Lawyers and Public Men of Early Iowa*. Des Moines: Homestead Publishing, 1916.

Stilgoe, John R. *Borderland: Origins of the American Suburb, 1820–1939*. New Haven: Yale University Press, 1988.

Stilgoe, John R. *Metropolitan Corridor: Railroads and the American Scene*. New Haven: Yale University Press, 1983.

Taylor, Alan. *William Cooper's Town: Power and Persuasion on the Frontier of the Early American Republic*. New York: Alfred A. Knopf, 1995.

Thompson, William H. *Transportation in Iowa: A Historical Summary*. Des Moines: Iowa Department of Transportation, 1989.

Selected bibliography

Thorne, Tanis C. *The Many Hands of My Relations: French and Indians on the Lower Missouri.* Columbia: University of Missouri Press, 1996.

Wade, Richard. *The Urban Frontier: Pioneer Life in Early Pittsburgh, Lexington, Louisville, and St. Louis.* Chicago: University of Chicago Press, 1959.

Wallace, Anthony F. C. *Rockdale: A History of an American Village.* New York: Alfred A. Knopf, 1978.

White, Richard. *"It's Your Misfortune and None of My Own": A History of the American West.* Norman: University of Oklahoma Press, 1991.

White, Richard. *The Middle Ground: Indians, Empires, and Republics in the Great Lakes Region, 1650–1815.* New York: Cambridge University Press, 1990.

Wiebe, Robert H. *The Opening of American Society.* New York: Alfred A. Knopf, 1984.

Wiebe, Robert H. *The Search for Order, 1877–1920.* New York: Hill and Wang, 1967.

Wilcox, David F., ed. *Quincy and Adams County, History and Representative Men.* 2 vols. Chicago: Lewis Publishing Company, 1919.

Zunz, Olivier. *Making America Corporate, 1870–1920.* Chicago: University of Chicago Press, 1990.

Index

African Americans: population, 28; slaves, 25, 26, 28, 34, 37, 42; vigilante action against, 78
Aiken, Josiah, 172
Ainsworth, S. C., 83
Allen, Thomas, 222, 240, 242
Alton and Springfield Railroad, 222
Alton and Terre Haute Railroad, 231
American Fur Company, 24
Americans: interaction with Native Americans, 14, 15, 16, 17, 18, 20, 25, 28–29; immigration patterns, 16, 26–29, 31, 32–33, 40–42, 54, 61, 64–72, 115–16, 118–19; interaction with French, 18, 35; interaction with mixed-blood people, 21–23, 25; forts and outposts, 19, 20, 23–24; economic development, 26–29
Arnold, Isaac N., 196, 202, 203, 208, 220, 264
Asbury, Henry, 128, 141, 146, 147, 172, 177, 184, 205, 206, 209, 222
Austin, Henry S., 22, 73, 75, 154, 172

Bailey, Gideon, 184
Baker, David J., 240
Baker, Edward D., 184, 193–97 passim, 202, 215, 233, 264
Ballance, Charles, 193, 223, 232
balls and cotillons, 101–2, 138–40, 147, 148

Barney, William J., 223, 253
Bates, Edward, 149, 151, 153; and Pacific Railroad, 222; and Chicago River and Harbor Convention, 241–42, 253
Beebe, Edward, 136
Beebe, Elijah, 40–41
Beebe, Mary, 46
Beebe, Sarah Hempstead, 46, 47, 48, 50, 51, 52, 60, 136
Belknap, William Worth, 85, 86, 147, 170, 173, 176, 177
Benedict, Kirby, 184
Benton, Thomas Hart, 242, 243
Berrian, George, 149
Birdsall, Dr., 77, 83, 101
Bissell, Frederick E., 223
Blackwell, R. S., 194, 204, 209
Bledsoe, Albert T., 194
Blondeau, Maurice, 21, 24
Boilvin, Nicholas, 20, 24
Bond, Benjamin, 209
Bonson, Richard, 132, 151, 226, 244–45
boosterism, 84–85; impact on migration, 82, 83, 84–85; booster ethos, 3, 63, 76, 81, 83–85, 113, 257–58, 260–61; booster network, 81–83; booster system, 134, 217–39
Booth, Caleb, 222, 223
Bouthillier, François, 24, 26

Index

Breese, Sidney, 184, 208
Bridgeman, Arthur, 82, 83, 230
British, trade, 14, 16, 17, 25; in War of 1812, 15, 20, 23
Brooks, John, 83, 89, 93, 95, 99, 101
Brown, A., 82, 83, 85, 89, 90, 91, 93, 96, 101
Browne, Jesse B., 76, 80, 90, 92, 93, 95, 98, 111, 208
Browne, Thomas C., 206
Browning, Eliza, 128, 129; and genteel society, 141–48
Browning, Milton D., 103, 172, 178, 182, 208, 211, 229, 245, 266, 268
Browning, Orville, H.: arrival in Quincy, Ill., 116; early career, 116–17; upbringing, 117; social relations, 127–28, 211; marriage, 128–29; house in Quincy, 129, 135; and genteel society, 140–48, 150; law career, 177, 178, 182, 184, 189, 193, 195, 196, 197, 202, 203, 204, 207, 208, 209, 264; travel, 214, 253, 254; railroad support, 222, 231, 232
Burlington, Iowa, 171, 174; railroads, 218, 219, 220, 223, 228, 229, 233, 234, 252; 1851 convention, 229–30, 233; excursion, 252
Burlington and Missouri Railroad, 219, 227, 230, 231, 236, 244, 245
Burt, James, 244
Bushnell, Nehemiah: arrival in Quincy, Ill., 116; partnership with Orville Browning, 117; house in Quincy, 129; society, 141; law practice, 128, 173, 177, 178, 184, 189, 193, 209, 222, 234, 264
Butterfield, Justin, 189, 193, 202, 264

Calhoun, John C., 243
calls, genteel system of, 134, 141–52
Campbell, Benjamin H., 136, 137, 139
Campbell, David B., 184
Campbell, George, 57, 136
Campbell, Henry J., 76, 78, 82, 83, 93, 99, 103, 230
Campbell, Isaac, 42, 90
Campbell, Mrs. George, 137
Campbell, Thompson, 184; at supreme court law library, 194, 195, 196, 200, 215, 230, 233, 237, 239

Carter, James, 122
Caton, John D., 189, 202, 209, 210, 252
Cedar Rapids and Missouri Railroad, 244
celebrations, *see* excursions; frolics; jollifications
Cerré, Gabriel, 17
Chambers, A. B., 240, 252
Chapman, William W., 177, 268
Chicago, Ill., 15, 16, 17, 20, 60, 148; as place for lawyers to settle, 170, 172, 174–75, 176, 252; roads around, 215, 217; railroads, 217, 218, 220, 229, 233, 243, 253; River and Harbor Convention, 240–42; as metropolis of regional system, 224, 235, 245, 252, 255, 260, 261, 262
Chicago, Alton and St. Louis Railroad, 245; excursion, 247
Chicago, Burlington and Quincy Railroad, 223, 231; excursion, 248
Chicago, Rock Island and Pacific Railroad, 222, 227, 245; excursion, 247, 248
Chittenden, Abraham, 77, 81, 82, 90, 100, 106, 110, 230
Chouteau, Auguste 15, 17, 19, 55
Chouteau, Pierre, Jr., 19, 25
Chouteau, Pierre, Sr., 17, 35
Chouteau–Sarpy Fur Company, 17
circuit court system, 178–81
Claggett, Thomas, 224, 229
Clark, Joseph, 79, 90, 93, 96
Clark, Lincoln, 132, 133; locational decision, 174–75; 181, 183, 215; and railroads, 213, 233, 236, 237, 238, 239, 245, 253
Clark, William, 78–83 passim, 90, 93, 95, 97, 99, 101, 103, 111, 230
Coleman, Nancy, 93
Coleman, William, 83, 88, 89, 90, 93, 95, 99, 100
Collins, James, 202, 207, 220
community: defined, 80, 114, 258; set of relations, 45; "trans-local," 5
Conkling, J. C., 193, 194
conventions, 239–45; Chicago River and Harbor, 240–42; Memphis, 240; St. Louis, 242–43; Philadelphia, 243
Cook, Ebenezer, 176, 222, 266
Cook, John P., 189, 211, 222, 266

326

Index

Coolbaugh, William F., 221, 245
Corbin, Abel, 235
Corbin, Austin, 176, 177, 252
Corwith, Henry, 122, 136, 137
Corwith, Mrs. Henry, 140, 225
Corwith, Nathan, 122, 136
Cosmopolitan Society, 103, 109
Cowles, A., 202
Cox, John, 128, 129, 141, 143, 145
Crawford, James, 134
Cuming, Thomas B., 229

Darby, John F., 242
Daughtery, James, 79
Davenport, George, Sr., 24–25, 42
Davenport, Iowa, 22, 53; society in, 150, 191, railroads, 218, 219, 220, 222, 228; convention, 229, 243; railroad excursion, 252
Davenport and Iowa City Railroad, 228
Davis, A. H., 136
Davis, David, 135
Davis, George T. M., 222
Davis, Levi, 176
Davis, David, 176, 182, 184, 202, 203, 207, 210, 211
Davis, Timothy, 266
Des Moines Valley Railroad, 224
Dickey, T. Lyle, 184
Dierdorff, Dan, 93, 101, 106, 109
Dietz, Edward, 82, 83
Dillon, John F., 176, 177, 205
Dodge, Augustus C., 93, 171, 176, 229, 235, 236–37, 240, 244, 268
Douglas, Stephen A., 153, 176, 182, 195, 196, 197, 211, 233, 237, 243, 250, 253
Dreschler, John, 208
Drummond, Thomas, 119, 121, 136, 138, 153, 184, 195, 197, 199, 202, 209, 220, 226, 229, 232, 253
Dubuque, Julien, 18
Dubuque, Iowa: settlement of, 14, 18, 19, 27, 53, 54, 58, 62, 65, 115–16; society at, 137, 150, 163–67, 171, 174; railroads, 218, 219, 220, 222, 223, 226, 227, 229, 230, 235, 243; terminus of Illinois Central Railroad, 233; excursion, 252
Dubuque and Keokuk Railroad, 219, 230, construction of, 233; resolutions for, 235–36, 237
Dubuque and Pacific Railroad, 222, 226; stockholders, 227; 228, 244, 253
Dubuque and Western Railroad, 223, 226
Dubuque, St. Peter's and St. Paul Railroad, 223
Dyer, John, 222

Eddy, Henry, 264
Edwards, Ninian, 209, 252
Europe, travel to, 162–63
excursions, 246; Lake Michigan, 242; fusion of cultures, 247, Northern Cross, 247; Chicago, Alton and St. Louis Railroad, 247, 249, 251; Chicago and Rock Island Railroad, 247, 249, 251, 252; Great Rail and River Excursion, 248–52 passim; Chicago, Burlington and Quincy Railroad, 248, 250, 251, 252; Great Railway Celebration, 248, 249–50, 252, 253

family: individual roles and functions, 31–32, 35–39, 45–57; system, 32, 35, 40, 45–60, 51, 53, 54; regional support network, 34, 35, 40, 48–49, 51–52, 53; behavior, 36, 38, 155–67; rituals, 37; social patterns, 37–38; culture, 39, 155–56; migration systems, 40, 115–16; subculture, 114; history, 155, 159
Farley, Jesse P., 222, 226
Felt, Benjamin, 140
Felt, Lucius S., 136, 140
Ficklin, Orlando B., 184, 195, 196, 264
Fleak, Laban, 76–83 passim, 88, 89, 90, 92, 93, 95, 100, 101, 138
Ford, E. R., 81, 82, 83, 85, 105
Ford, Thomas, 171
Forsythe, Thomas, 20, 21, 22
Fort Armstrong, 23, 24, 25
Fort Clark (Peoria, Ill.), 24
Fort Clark (Kansas), 40
Fort Crawford, 23
Fort Madison, Iowa, 20, 21, 24, 73, 79, 171; railroads, 219, 220, 229
forts, American, 19, 20, 23, 24, 25; *see also names of specific forts*

327

Index

Foster, Thomas, 136, 137, 139
French: trade with Americans, 13, 27; trade with Indians, 15, 16, 18; intermarriage with Indians, 16; immigration, 16; couriers du bois, 16; endogamy 16, 18; important families in St. Louis, 17–18, 33–34; interaction with Americans, 27, 34–35; intermarriage with Americans, 33–34
French Canadians, 15, 16, 18, 21, 23, 24, 28, 30, 42, 56
frolics, 55, 88, 103, 109, 211, 249, 251; *see also jollifications*
Fulton, Harry, 83, 89, 101, 102
fur trade, 13, 14, 16, 18, 23, 25

Gaines, John, 90
Gaines, Mrs. John, 76, 81, 82, 93, 96
Galena, Ill.: first traders at, 26, 27; early settlement of, 28, 29, 32, 42–43, 45, 54; society at, 50, 65, 75, 85, 118–27, 134–40, 149–50; development of, 58, 59, 60, 62, 65; railroads, 218, 219, 220, 232–33
Galena and Chicago Union Railroad, 136, 219–33 passim, 243, 245, 253
Galesburg, Ill., railroads of, 222, 231, 234
Galland, Isaac, 73, 75, 77, 79, 81, 84, 89, 93, 100, 105, 110–11
Garber, Christian, 90, 111
Gear, H. H., 122
Gear, John, 267
gentility, 5, 113–15, 120–35 passim, 141–42, 151–52, 154, 155, 163–64, 259–60; introduction into the West, 35, 58, 62–63, 75; French, 35, 134; marriage, 125, 129; housekeeping, 129–34; "parlor culture," 132–34, 138–40; in borderlands, 132–33; defined in 1840s, 134, 135; behavior and etiquette, 134, 141–52; circles or sets, 134, 135–40, 141–48; values, 135, 155; and family culture, 155–67; *see also* balls and cotillons; gentlemen; letters of introduction
gentlemen: French, 35, 46, 58; Chesterfield, 98, 106, 110, 111, 117, 135, 163, 267–68; Virginian, 98, 111; defined, 110–11, 118–19, 135; in male subculture, 110–12; "of the old school," 117, 268; Christian, 117; Kentucky, 117, 268; New England, 118,

267; code of behavior, 118–19; *see also* male subcultures
Gillespie, Joseph, 189, 195, 196, 197, 199, 202, 204, 211, 222, 252, 264
Gillock, Baxter, 77
Gilman, Charles, 173, 192, 196, 206
"good society," 3, 32, 33, 43, 55, 62, 75, 86, 113
Goodhue, Josiah, 220
Goodrich, Grant, 202
Graham, John A., 81, 101, 110, 111, 243
Grant, James, 172, 175, 177, 181, 182, 184; and Chicago and Rock Island Railroad, 222, 234, 236, 238, 245
Gratiot, Adele, *see* Washburne, Adele Gratiot
Gratiot, Adele Perdeauville (Mrs. John Gratiot), 38, 43, 44, 46, 47, 48
Gratiot, Charles, 17, 41
Gratiot, Charles (brother of Henry), 59
Gratiot, Charles (Susan's son), 47, 137
Gratiot, Edward Hempstead, 47, 57, 124, 137
Gratiot, Eliza, 47, 137, 160
Gratiot, Henry, 17, 34, 36, 37, 47, 49, 51, 55, 215; settlement at Fever River, 26, 42; relationship with Indians, 27, 57–58; move to Meramac River, 41; founding Gratiot's Grove, 42–43; retirement, 58; death, 59
Gratiot, Henry (Susan's son), 47
Gratiot, John ("Bugnion"), 26, 41, 42, 43, 46, 49, 55
Gratiot, Mary, 47
Gratiot, Paul, 42, 45, 50
Gratiot, Stephen, 47, 137
Gratiot, Susan Hempstead, 47, 125, 126, 137; marriage, 17, 28, 34, 35; interaction with parents, 36, 37, 38, 51; sets of social relations, 38, 45–56 passim, 75, 121, 125, 136, 137–38, 140, 151; arrival at Galena, 42; arrival at Gratiot's Grove, 43, 58, 86; interaction with Native Americans, 44, 57–58; relationship with Henry Gratiot, 45; children of, 47–48, 49; widowhood, 59–60; values and character, 62; religious life, 123–25; relationship with Elihu Washburne, 126, 158; relationship with

Index

Adele Gratiot (Washburne), 157–58; death, 159
Gratiot, William, 47
Gratiot, Victoire Chouteau, 17, 38, 41
Griffith, A. W., 80, 83, 90, 101, 110, 111
Grimes, James M., 153; law career, 172, 177, 205, 208; as railroad man, 221, 223, 229, 231, 234–38 passim, 248, 250, 252–53, 266, 267; governor of Iowa, 244; 245
Grimshaw, Jackson, 128, 146–49, 178, 184, 204

Haines, Artemus M., 130, 140
half-breed, *see* mixed blood
Half Breed Tract, 22, 72, 73, 81
"half-breed war," 73–74, 78, 88
Hall, Jonathan C., 93, 184, 189, 194, 208, 223, 229, 230, 266, 268
Hall, Junius, 86, 177, 181
Hannibal and St. Joseph Railroad, 222
Hardin, John J., 195, 196, 197, 202
Harper, Cyrus, 101
Harris, Daniel Smith, 27, 136
Harris, Meeker, 138
Hastings, Seranus C., 194, 266
Hatch, Ozias, 146, 147, 184
Heaight, Silas, 83, 93, 94, 95, 105–6, 107, 109, 111, 211, 229
Hempstead family: early history, 33–34; migration west, 33, 34; weddings, 34; family system, 36–39, 49, 51; local family system, 36–37; exchange system, 36–39; deaths and funerals, 38, 39; regional family system, 49, 51; *see also names of specific individuals*
Hempstead, Charles S.: at St. Louis, 33, 37, 45, 47; at Galena, 49, 56, 59, 60, 121–26 passim, 137, 139, 140, 151, 162; relationship with Susan Hempstead Gratiot, 52, 125; law career, 184, 199; as railroad man, 215, 216, 219, 220–22, 225, 229, 232
Hempstead, Charles W., 139
Hempstead, Edward (Susan's brother), 21, 23, 33–40 passim
Hempstead, Edward (Susan's nephew), 139
Hempstead, Edward L. (Susan's son), 47

Hempstead, Mary, *see* Lisa, Mary Hempstead Keene
Hempstead, Mary (Mrs. Stephen Hempstead, Sr.), 35, 37, 38, 39
Hempstead, Sarah, *see* Beebe, Sarah Hempstead
Hempstead, Susan, *see* Gratiot, Susan Hempstead
Hempstead, Stephen Jr., 21, 25, 33, 35, 40
Hempstead, Stephen Sr., 32–39 passim, 51, 56, 123, 149, 216
Hempstead, Stephen (Susan's cousin), 99, 171, 245, 266
Hempstead, Thomas, 33, 36, 37, 40, 41
Hempstead, William, 41, 45, 48, 49, 50, 52, 55, 56, 60, 121, 124, 126, 159, 160
Henn, Bernhart, 237, 238, 268
Herndon, William, 193
Hill, Ward Lamon, 193
Hillis, John, 76, 77, 78, 81, 83, 92, 93, 95
Hine, Adam, 80, 82, 83, 90, 92, 93, 94, 96, 101, 109
Hine, Dan, 76, 79, 80, 82, 90, 93, 99, 101, 102, 103, 111, 229, 230
historical methodology: structuralist, 7–8, 10; externalist, 8; internalist, 8; case study method, 8–9; contextualization, 8, 10; network analysis, 8, 10, 45–60, 50, 51, 53, 54, 81–83, 91–98, 135–38, 143–46, 184–89, 191–94, 194–97; systems analysis, 8–9, 45–60, 66–72, 217–39; regional history, 8–9; local history, 9; narrative, analytic, 10; "sedimentation," 64; migration analysis, 66–72
Hitchcock, Henry, 170–71, 214
Hoge, Joseph Pendleton, 130, 136, 184, 200
Holbrook, Rev. John C., 163, 174
Holmes, Artemus L., 121, 122, 136, 199
Houghton, Horace H., 119, 120, 136
Houghton, Liberty Holmes, 243
housekeeping, genteel, 129–34
Hughes, Ross B., 77, 81, 82, 83, 85, 88, 93, 101, 105, 111
Hunter, Charles, 231

Illinois Bar Association, 195
Illinois Central Railroad, 222, 225, 232, 233, 245, 247, 253

329

Index

immigrants: from France, 16, 27; Kentucky, 26, 66, 72–73, 116; New England, 31, 33, 65–66, 72–73, 81–82, 118; Middle Atlantic, 65, 66, 69, 72–73, 81–82; Virginia, 66

Indians: towns and villages 14, 15; treaties, 14, 15; in Illinois, 14; American policy, 16–17, 20, 23–24, 25, 29, 30, 57; War of 1812, 19, 20; in Iowa, 24; American outposts and forts, 25, 26; wives of traders, 25, 26, 42, 56; war at Galena in 1827, 46, 57; *see also names of specific tribes*

Iowa Western Railroad, 228

Iroquois, 14

Irvin, David, 171, 184, 268

Ivins, Charles, 83, 89, 90

Jacksonville, Ill., 115, 176; railroads, 218, 220

Jessup, F. S., 226

Johnson, James, 26

Johnson, John W., 40

Johnson, Lyman E., 78, 83, 90, 93, 96, 99, 101, 110, 223, 224, 230, 243

Johnson, Madison Y., 122, 137, 194

Johnstone, Andrew, 172, 177, 194

Johnstone, Edward, 184, 224, 229

jollifications, 91, 248

Jonas, Abraham, 128, 177, 222

Jones, George Wallace, 133, 171, 172, 173, 176; supports railroads, 219, 222, 235, 236–37, 239, 243, 244; and Illinois Central, 233

Jones, Joseph Russell, 136, 137, 138, 139, 140

Judd, Norman, 148

Kaskaskias, 14

Kennett, Luther M., 242

Kent, Aratus, 123, 124

Keokuk, Iowa, 42, 63, 171; migration to, 66–72, 72–73; early description, 72; history, 72–80; "half-breed war," 73–74; Rat Row, 73, 76, 88, 99, 106; male subculture in, 87–112; railroads, 218, 219–20, 228, 229, 233, 243

Keokuk, Mount Pleasant and Muscatine Railroad, 224, 229–30

Keokuk and Minnesota Railroad, 224

Kickapoo, 24

Kilbourne, David Wells, 73, 74, 75, 78, 90, 93, 154, 172, 224, 234, 243, 253

Kilbourne, Edward, 229, 230, 236, 243

Kilbourne, George W., 150, 229

Kittoe, E. D., 122

Knox, James, 234

Koerner, Gustave, 117, 183, 202, 215, 222, 249, 250

Krum, John M., 202, 242, 264

Langworthy, Edward, 115, 116, 132, 166, 167, 223

Langworthy, Harriet, 131, 166

Langworthy, James: arrival in Lead Region, 115; in Dubuque, 116, 131, 166; and railroads, 223

Langworthy, Lucius Hart, 115, 116; in Dubuque, 131, 132, 166; and railroads, 222, 223, 234, 235, 236, 237, 244

Langworthy, Maria, 115, 166

Langworthy, Mary Ann, 115, 166

Langworthy, Solon, 115; in Dubuque, 116, 131–34, 150; family life, 163–67; religious views, 163; and railroads, 223

Langworthy, Stephen, 115, 116

Lawrence, Charles, B., 175, 204, 207, 222

lawyers: migration to the West, 170–72; locational strategies, 172–75; local bars, 175–76, 197–201, 203, 206–7, 267–69; procedures in the bar, 175–77; local practice, 177–78; partnerships, 177–78; circuit riding, 181–85, 201, 205, 206, 207, 263, 264, 265; state supreme court, 190–97, 201–2, 203, 208–9, 263–66; legal fraternity, 198, 211, 212; and masculinity, 198; offices and courtrooms, 204–05; moot or mock courts, 209–11; booster ethos, 212; as railroad men, 220–39, 224–25

Lead Region, 23; encroachment into, 15; lead trade, 19, 20, 21, 40, 41–43; beginnings of, 19, 25–26; smelting, 26

LeClaire, Antoine Jr., 21, 22, 225

LeClaire, Antoine Sr., 21

Leffler, Shepard, 244–45

Leighton, William, 110

Index

letters of introduction, 116, 119, 152–55, 176
Lewis, Garry, 96
Lincoln, Abraham: friend of Orville H. Browning, 117; law practice, 181, 183, 184, 205, 207, 208, 227; at Illinois supreme court, 192, 193, 194, 195, 196, 197, 202; travel, 215, 253, 254; as railroad supporter, 222, 240
Lincoln, Mary Todd, 117, 129, 208
Linder, Usher F., 184, 189, 197, 199, 202, 211, 222, 252, 264
Lisa, Manuel, 39, 41
Lisa, Mary Hempstead Keene ("Aunt Manuel"), 34, 36, 47, 52, 56, 60, 126, 131, 159, 160
Lockwood, James H., 121
Logan, Stephen T., 184, 192, 195, 202, 207, 222, 264
Loomis, Harvey, 77
Lorimer, Peter, 27, 52, 55, 56, 133
Lorraine, John, 122, 136, 137
Lorraine, Sherwell, 122, 136, 137
Lott, Peter, 144, 207
Love, James, 223, 230
Lovell, William, 245
Lowe, Ralph P., 153, 176, 177, 194, 229, 266, 268
Lucas, James H., 226, 242

MacDougall, James, 184, 189, 193, 195, 196, 202
Mackley, James, 93, 99
male subcultures, 3, 4, 56, 86–112, 113, 122, 199, 200, 201, 208, 250–51, 259–60, 262, 288 n. 2; location of, 55, 87, 120; behavior in, 86–89; defined, 87–89; nicknames, 88, 91–98, 103; verbal jousting, 88, 98–99; practical jokes and pranks, 88, 97, 99–100, 101; oppositional events, 88–89, 103–110; frolics, 88, 103, 109, 251; sarcasm, 89; membership, 91–92; parties and societies, 91, 100–101; gentlemen in, 110–12; friendships, 117; *see also* Cosmopolitan Society; gentlemen
Manning, Julius, 194
Marsh, James, 131
Martin, William, 177, 193, 222, 227, 264

Mason, Charles, 150, 151; legal career, 171, 172, 184, 206; travel, 215–16, 217, 253, 254–55; as railroad man, 219–39 passim, 267
Mayotte, Catharine, 43, 56, 57
McCall, M., 76, 100
McClellan, R. H., 171, 184
McCloskey, H. F., 136
McConnell, Murray, 176, 193, 220, 264
McGavic, Lee, 101, 102, 110
McGavic, William, 77, 81, 82, 83, 90, 100, 101, 110, 243
McMaster, S. W., 136
Meeker, Moses, 27
Menard, Pierre, 17, 18
merchants: migration strategies, 70–71; first rush, 70; activities, 76–77
Merriman, Halsey O., 194
Mesquakies, 19, 26, 28
Michigan Southern Railroad, 238
middle class: development, 4–5, 54, 56, 58, 61, 112, 125; origins, 4–5, 13, 45, 56; social strategies, 45, 62–63, 87, 102, 110, 113–14; professional culture, 63, 122, 127–28, 168–71
migration, 31–32, 63, 65–66; systems, 32, 65, 66–69; entrepreneurial, 32, 68; family, 32; patrimonial, 32, 68; proletariat, 32; and local social development, 64; strategies, 71
Millard, Dr. Justin, 79, 83, 99, 100
Miller, Daniel F., 93, 172, 219, 224, 229
Mills, Benjamin, 184, 202
Minshall, William A., 197, 264
Mississippi and Missouri Railroad, 222, 225, 244
Missouri Border War, 95
Missouri Compromise, 66
Missouri tribe, 14
Mitchell, J. P., 77, 83, 93, 97, 101
mixed-blood people, 16, 18, 56, 57; employed by Americans, 16, 24; American attitudes toward, 17, 22–23; in Peoria, 21–22; at Fever River, 28
Moore, Charles, 77, 78, 79, 80, 81, 82, 83, 90, 99, 101
Moore, Clifton H., 187
Morehouse, D. B., 121

Index

Morgan, Richard P., 231, 234, 237, 238
Mormons, 78, 80, 95
Morris, Buckner S., 193
Morris, Isaac N., 222
Morrison, William, 17
Muir, Samuel, 26, 42
Munn, John, 248, 250, 251

Native Americans, *see* Indians; *names of specific tribes*
"near frontier," 31, 54, 58
New England Land Company, 172
New York Land Company, 73, 77, 78, 93
Newhall, Horatio, 85, 86, 120, 121, 123, 124, 136, 137, 138, 139, 157, 216–17
nicknames, 88, 91–98, 103
Nightengale, George N., 230, 244
Norris, A. L., 140, 220
Northern Cross Railroad, 220, 222, 226, 231, 245; excursion, 247

O'Fallon, John, 226
Ogden, R. B., 152
Ogden, William B., 174, 231, 241, 243
Ohio and Mississippi Railroad, 228; excursion, 248, 249
Omaha tribe, 15
Osages, 14, 20
Otoes, 15

Pacific Railroad Company, 223, 226
Page, Daniel, 226
Palmer, John M., 202
Parvin, Theodore, 176, 184, 194, 243, 268
Patterson, Julia (Mrs. Solon Langworthy), 132, 133, 134
Patterson, William, 81, 101
Pawnees, 14
"pays d'en haut," 14, 15
Pekin and Wabash Railroad, 227
Peoria, Ill., 15, 16, 17, 21–22, 53, railroads, 223, 234
Peoria and Oquawka Railroad, 223, 227, 231, 234, 236, 237, 245
Peters, Onslow, 193, 194, 223, 232, 234, 264
Phelps, William, 42, 95
Pike, Zebulon, 19

Pope, William, 209
Potawatomis, 20, 22, 24
Powell, Elihu N., 193, 194
practical jokes, *see under* male subculture
Prairie du Chien, Wisc., 15, 17, 19, 20; British at, 23, 24; U.S. arrival at, 25, 26, 27, 40, 41; conference at, 45
Price, Hiram, 222
Price, William, 77, 78, 92, 93
provincialization, 13–14
Purple, Norman, 194, 195, 196, 264

Quincy, Ill., 98, 115, 116–18; society at, 127–29, 129–30, 140–48, 171, 174; railroads, 218, 219, 222, 226, 228
Quincy and Toledo Railroad, 222

railroads, 224–26; "mania" or fever, 218–19, 220–21; meetings, 218–20, 229; circular letters, 221, 223, 231, 242; subscriptions, 225–228; construction, 228, 245; railroad letters, 232; and eastern capital, 234–35; railroad society, 246; excursions and jubilees, 246–53; impact on business and social interactions, 253–56; *see also names of specific railroads*
Ralston, J. H., 128, 177, 184
Rankin, John, 177, 243
Rebman, William, 223
Reed, John P., 82, 83, 110, 111
Reeves, Lewis R., 79, 92, 96, 229, 243, 266
Reid, Hugh T., 93, 110, 223, 224, 229, 230, 234, 240, 244, 266
Reid, J. M., 92, 93, 97, 99, 105
religious revivals, 123–25, 163
Reynolds, John, 176, 215, 252
Rich, Alfred, 208
Richardson, William, 237
Rindisbacher, Peter, 55
Rock Island and LaSalle Railroad, 222
Rockford, Ill., 173; railroad meeting, 219, 220; convention, 229
Rodolf, Theodore, 45, 54, 152
Rogers, Thomas, 176
Rorer, David, 194, 205, 215, 221, 223, 229, 230, 236, 266, 268
Rotundo, E. Anthony, 87
ruffians, 63, 75, 77, 78, 85, 97

Index

St. Louis, Mo.: early trade, 13, 15, 16; French families at, 17–18, 19, 20, 21–22, 26, 27, 28; Hempstead family at, 32–41, 47–54 passim, 60; immigration to, 65; 115, 135; railroads, 222, 226, 228, 229; excursion, 251, 252
Sample, Hugh W., 93, 103, 234, 236
Samuels, Ben, 230, 244, 245, 253
Sanford, H. W., 226
Sangamon and Alton Railroad, 227
Sargent, George B., 241, 244
Sauk and Fox tribes, 14–15, 19, 20, 21, 24, 26, 28
Savage, Charles, 172
Scammon, J. Young, 170, 189, 192, 196, 202, 220, 229, 231, 232, 264
Scates, Walter B., 264
Semple, James, 208
Sheldon, Benjamin, R., 183
Sherman, T., 95, 101
Shields, James, 195, 196, 197, 208, 264
Shull, Jesse, 24, 26, 43
Singleton, James, 128, 129, 184, 211, 222, 234
Sioux, 14, 15, 24
Skinner, Onias, C., 222
Smith, Davis, 204, 264
Smith, Joseph, 79
Smith, Orrin, 115, 136
Smith, Platt, 196, 222–23, 226, 228, 234, 245
Smith, Theophilus C., 220
Smith, William, 184
Smythe, George, 111
Snyder, William, 252
Spann, Solomon, 106, 109
Spring, Giles, 189, 202, 264
Springfield, Ill.: state legislature at, 116, 195–97; supreme court at, 191, 192, 193, 194, 195, 196, 197, 202, 203, 204; hotels at, 204, 208; railroads, 218, 222, 229; convention, 240
Stahl, Frederick, 122, 130, 136
Stahl, Mrs. Frederick, 138, 154
Stahl, Mrs. Nicholas, 139, 140
Stahl, Nicholas, 138
Starr, Henry W., 153, 177, 208, 221, 223, 229, 230, 241, 243, 252, 266, 267

Starr, William H., 244, 266
state supreme court: schedules, 191–92; lawyers at, 191, 192, 194; cases at, 191, 192; law library, 194–97; visiting at, 202, 208–9
steamboats: on the upper Mississippi, 41–42; impact of, 213; diminishing returns, 213, 214; system, 213–14
Stillman, Mrs. Nelson, 139
Stillman, Nelson, 137, 139
Stockton, Lacon D., 229, 230, 268
Stone, Judge Dan, 139
Strode, James, M., 184
Stuart, John T., 184, 194, 207, 208
Swanick, Thomas, 102
Swett, Leonard, 183, 184, 206, 209, 211

Taylor, Hawkins, 77, 81, 90, 91, 93, 106, 109, 208, 211, 229
Thomas, Jesse B., 241, 264
Thomas, William, 264
Thorington, James, 244
Thurman, T. B., 95
Tillson, John, 204
Treat, Samuel, 222
Trumbull, Lyman, 176, 177, 193, 196, 197, 202, 203, 255, 264
Turney, John, 122, 139, 184, 200

Van Antwerp, Verplanck, 111, 224, 230, 243, 267
Van Fossen, Squire Samuel, 106
VanDever, Charles, 245
Vanmeter, A. P., 24, 26, 27, 42, 43
Vanorsdal, Valencourt, 76, 77, 78, 82, 83, 93, 97, 100, 101, 111
Veile, Phillip, 184
vigilantism, 73, 77–81 passim, 84, 85, 95; and social development, 80, 84

Walker, Cyrus, 184, 266
Wann, Daniel, 124
War of 1812, 20, 23; and American Indian policy, 20
Warren, Calvin, 128, 172, 177, 178, 184, 214, 222, 231
Warsaw and Lafayette Railroad, 226
Washburne, Adele Gratiot: birth, 44, 45, 47;

relations with Winnebagoes, 58; move to Galena, Ill., 60; meets Elihu B. Washburne, 125–26; education, 126; courtship and marriage, 127, 130–31; domestic activities, 131–32; social relations in Galena, 135, 137–40, 149, 150, 250–51, 253; married life, 155–63

Washburn, Cadwallader, 119, 137, 151, 181

Washburne, Elihu Benjamin: migration west, 118–19; arrival in Galena, Ill., 119–20; law practice, 119–22, 171, 181, 182, 183, 184, 193, 194, 196, 197, 199, 200–204 passim, 211, 241, 254; early social activity, 121–26; courtship and marriage, 126–27; house in Galena, 130–31, 133; social relations in Galena, 135–39, 139, 152, 154; married life, 155–63; trip to Europe, 162; at Illinois supreme court, 194–97; travel, 214–15, 216, 253; and railroads, 219, 220, 225, 233, 234

Weldon, Lawrence, 184

Wells, Guy, 230, 243

Wentworth, John, 202

Wheat, Almeron, 128, 184, 222

Wichler, Stephen, 184, 189, 194, 266, 267

Wiebe, Robert, 112, 262

Williams, Archibald, 116, 127, 146, 147–48, 150, 172, 177, 178, 182, 184, 189, 193, 196, 202, 204, 264

Williams, George H., 241

Wilson, R. S., 252

Wilson, Thomas, S., 171, 223, 230, 253, 266

Wiltse, Henry, 223

Winnebagoes, 19, 20, 24, 26, 28, 56, 57–58, 60

Wise, James H., 89, 93

Wood, John, 115, 116, 204, 209

Woodman, Cyrus, 172

Woods, James, 94, 184, 206, 208, 223, 267

Woodward, W. G., 189, 266

Wyeth, D. C., 136

Yates, Richard, 251

yellow handbill meetings, 84, 105–10

Young, Richard M., 191, 211